LIBERAL EDUCATION AND CITIZENSHIP IN A FREE SOCIETY

LIBERAL EDUCATION AND CITIZENSHIP IN A FREE SOCIETY

EDITED BY
JUSTIN BUCKLEY DYER AND
CONSTANTINE CHRISTOS VASSILIOU

UNIVERSITY OF MISSOURI PRESS
COLUMBIA

Publication of this volume made possible with the generous support
of the Kinder Institute on Constitutional Democracy

Copyright © 2023 by
The Curators of the University of Missouri
University of Missouri Press, Columbia, Missouri 65211
Printed and bound in the United States of America
All rights reserved. First printing, 2023.

Library of Congress Cataloging-in-Publication Data

Names: Dyer, Justin Buckley, 1983- editor. | Vassiliou, Constantine
  Christos, editor.
Title: Liberal education and citizenship in a free society / edited by
  Justin Buckley Dyer and Constantine Christos Vassiliou.
Description: Columbia : University of Missouri Press, 2023. | Series:
  Studies in constitutional democracy | Includes bibliographical
  references and index.
Identifiers: LCCN 2022048790 (print) | LCCN 2022048791 (ebook) | ISBN
  9780826222831 (hardcover) | ISBN 9780826274885 (ebook)
Subjects: LCSH: Education, Humanistic. | Democracy and education. |
  Citizenship--United States. | Professional education--Moral and ethical
  aspects.
Classification: LCC LC1011 .L4577 2023 (print) | LCC LC1011 (ebook) | DDC
  370.11/2--dc23/eng/20221220
LC record available at https://lccn.loc.gov/2022048790
LC ebook record available at https://lccn.loc.gov/2022048791

⊚™ This paper meets the requirements of the
American National Standard for Permanence of Paper
for Printed Library Materials, Z39.48, 1984.

Typefaces: Gravesend Sans and Garamond

STUDIES IN CONSTITUTIONAL DEMOCRACY

Jeffrey L. Pasley and Jay K. Dow, Series Editors

In partnership with the Kinder Institute on Constitutional Democracy, this series explores the history and development of American constitutional ideas and democratic practices both in the United States and as they have reverberated throughout the world. The volumes in this series showcase interdisciplinary scholarship that helps readers gain insight into both new and traditional themes in American politics, law, society, and culture, with an eye to both practical and theoretical applications.

PREVIOUS TITLES IN STUDIES IN CONSTITUTIONAL DEMOCRACY

A Fire Bell in the Past: The Missouri Crisis at 200, Volume I
Western Slavery, National Impasse
Edited by Jeffrey L. Pasley and John Craig Hammond

A Fire Bell in the Past: The Missouri Crisis at 200, Volume II
"The Missouri Question" and Its Answers
Edited by Jeffrey L. Pasley and John Craig Hammond

Contesting the Constitution: Congress Debates the Missouri Crisis, 1819–1821
Edited by William S. Belko

The Panic of 1819: The First Great Depression
Andrew H. Browning

The Pursuit of Happiness in the Founding Era: An Intellectual History
Carli N. Conklin

Lloyd Gaines and the Fight to End Segregation
James W. Endersby and William T. Horner

Disestablishment and Religious Dissent:
Church-State Relations in the New American States, 1776–1833
Edited by Carl H. Esbeck and Jonathan J. Den Hartog

Aristocracy in America: From the Sketch-Book of a German Nobleman
Francis J. Grund
Edited and with an Introduction by Armin Mattes

The Federalist Frontier: Settler Politics in the Old Northwest, 1783–1840
Kristopher Maulden

From Oligarchy to Republicanism: The Great Task of Reconstruction
Forrest A. Nabors

Bureaucracy in America:
The Administrative State's Challenge to Constitutional Government
Joseph Postell

The Myth of Coequal Branches: Restoring the Constitution's Separation of Functions
David J. Siemers

Contents

LIST OF CONTRIBUTORS ... ix

CHAPTER ABSTRACTS ... xvii

INTRODUCTION ... 3
Justin Buckley Dyer and Constantine Christos Vassiliou

PART ONE: LIBERAL ARTS AS A CLASSROOM OF CHARACTER AND JUDGMENT

1. THE MODERN ACADEMY AND THE ANCIENT VIRTUE OF *Phronesis* ... 11
   Lorraine Smith Pangle

2. TWO CHEERS FOR DEPAROCHIALIZATION ... 31
   Clifford Orwin

3. THE CONTOURS OF THE CANON:
   LIBERAL EDUCATION, UNIVERSALISM, AND REPRESENTATION ... 51
   Lindsay Mahon Rathnam and Lincoln E. F. Rathnam

4. AN OUTSIDER LOOKING IN:
   CHRISTINE DE PIZAN ON CLASSICAL LEARNING ... 71
   Anna Marisa Schön

5. SHAME AND THE LIBERAL EDUCATION OF THE DEMOCRATIC SELF ... 87
   Alin Fumurescu

6. LIBERAL EDUCATION AS CIVIC EDUCATION:
   THE PHILOSOPHER'S CURRICULUM IN PLATO'S *Republic* ... 103
   Dustin Gish

PART TWO: LIBERAL ARTS AS A CLASSROOM OF CITIZENSHIP

7. THE GARDEN OF CITIZENSHIP:
   LIBERAL EDUCATION AS THE CULTIVATION OF JUST SENTIMENTS ... 151
   Constantine Christos Vassiliou

8. LIBERAL EDUCATION AS "SPIRITUAL EXERCISE":
   ON THE LIFE OF THE MIND IN THE AGE OF SOCIAL MEDIA 173
   Aurelian Craiutu

9. LIBERAL EDUCATION AND THE LIMITS OF SCIENCE AND TECHNOLOGY:
   LESSONS FROM THE COVID-19 PANDEMIC 197
   Carson Holloway

10. LIBERAL EDUCATION IS ANTITECHNOLOGICAL 213
    Steven McGuire

11. TRANSFERENCE AND THE FUTURE OF TEACHER-STUDENT INTIMACY 223
    Sarah Rich-Zendel

12. FROM IMPATIENCE TO COMPASSION:
    EDUCATING FROM RESTLESSNESS TO RESPONSIBILITY 239
    Sarah Beth V. Kitch

13. THE COSMOPOLITAN EDUCATION OF HOBBITS: FRIENDSHIP AND
    POLITICAL DELIBERATION IN TOLKIEN'S *The Fellowship of the Ring* 257
    William E. DeMars

PART THREE: LIBERAL ARTS AND THE FUTURE OF THE CLASSROOM

14. ACADEMIC FREEDOM AND THE FUTURE OF THE LIBERAL ARTS 289
    Lee Ward

15. LEO STRAUSS AND THE HUMANITY OF LIBERAL EDUCATION 307
    José Daniel Parra

16. LIBERAL EDUCATION AND AMERICAN DEMOCRACY 327
    George Thomas

17. HOW BUSINESS SCHOOLS CAN PREPARE STUDENTS FOR TWENTY-
    FIRST-CENTURY SUCCESS BY RENEWING THEIR LIBERAL ARTS ROOTS 347
    Donald Drakeman and Kendall Hack

18. THE ROLE OF LIBERAL EDUCATION IN PROFESSIONAL STUDIES 373
    Steven Frankel

19. THE PARADOX OF LIBERAL EDUCATION AND MODERNITY 393
    Gregory A. McBrayer

INDEX 421

Contributors

Aurelian Craiutu is professor of political science at Indiana University, Bloomington. Since 2018, he has been Senior Fellow at the Niskanen Center in Washington, D.C. Craiutu is the author and editor of several books in modern political thought, most recently *A Virtue for Courageous Minds: Moderation in French Political Thought, 1748–1830* (Princeton, 2012) and *Faces of Moderation: The Art of Balance in an Age of Extremes* (University of Pennsylvania Press, 2017). He has received awards and grants from many institutions, including the Institute for Advanced Study (Princeton), the National Endowment for Humanities, and the American Council of Learned Societies. Craiutu's new book, *Why Not Moderation? Letters to Young Radicals* will be released by Cambridge University Press in September 2023.

William DeMars is professor of government and international affairs at Wofford College. He received his PhD from the University of Notre Dame in 1993. His primary research focus is on NGOs, with publications appearing in the *World Policy Journal* and the *International Journal of Intelligence and Counterintelligence*, and he has published multiple books and contributed to several collections as well.

Donald Drakeman is a Distinguished Research Professor at the Center for Citizenship and Constitutional Government at the University of Notre Dame. He has written extensively about the intersection of law, religion, and constitutional interpretation. His seven books include *The Hollow Core of Constitutional Theory: Why We Need the Framers*, and *Church, State, and Original Intent*, which was named a CHOICE Outstanding Academic Title. He received a BA. from Dartmouth College, a JD from Columbia University and a PhD in religion from Princeton University. He is a Fellow of the Royal Historical Society, the Royal Society of Biology, and the Burgon Society. He has served as a trustee of Drew University, the University of Charleston, and the Woodrow Wilson National Fellowship Foundation.

Justin Buckley Dyer is executive director of the Civitas Institute, professor of government, and Jack G. Taylor Regents Professor at The University of Texas at Austin. He also is professor (by courtesy) of business, government, and society in the McCombs School of Business. Dyer writes and teaches in the fields of American political thought, jurisprudence and constitutionalism, with an emphasis on the perennial philosophical tradition of natural law. He is the author or editor of eight books and numerous articles, essays and book reviews. Previously, he was professor of political science at the University of Missouri, where he served as the founding director of the Kinder Institute on Constitutional Democracy, a signature academic center for the study of American political thought and history.

Steven Frankel received his PhD from the Committee on Social Thought at the University of Chicago in 1997. His scholarly work, which focuses on the relationship between philosophy and religion, has appeared in over a dozen journals including the *Review of Metaphysics, Interpretation, Archiv fur Geshichte der Philosophie, The Review of Politics, International Philosophical Quarterly, Teaching Philosophy*, and the *Journal of Jewish Thought and Philosophy*. His book with Martin Yaffe, *Civil Religion in Modern Political Philosophy*, appeared in 2020 (Penn State UP), and his most recent book with John Ray is *Equality and Excellence in Ancient and Modern Political Philosophy* (SUNY Press, 2023).

Alin Fumurescu received his PhD from Indiana University, Bloomington. His dissertation, "Compromise and Representation—A Split History of Early Modernity," received the 2013 American Political Science Association's Leo Strauss Award for the best doctoral dissertation in the field of political philosophy. Currently, he is associate professor of political science at the University of Houston. In addition to articles and book chapters, he has published *Compromise: A Political and Philosophical History* (Cambridge UP, 2013), *Compromise and the American Founding: The Quest for the People's Two Bodies* (Cambridge

UP, 2019, and, with Anna Marisa Schön, *Foundations of American Political Thought: Readings and Commentary* (Cambridge UP, 2021).

Dustin Gish is associate professor of political science in the Honors College at the University of Houston.. He is also the associate director of Phronêsis, an Honors minor and program in politics and ethics. Gish received his doctorate in politics from the Institute of Philosophic Studies at the University of Dallas. He taught previously at The American University of Rome (1999–2006) and College of the Holy Cross (2007–2012) and held a residential fellowship at the International Center for Jefferson Studies and Jefferson Foundation Library at Monticello (2013). His most recent book is *Thomas Jefferson and the Science of Republican Government: A Political Biography of "Notes on the State of Virginia"* (Cambridge UP, 2017). His research on Homer, Xenophon, Plato, Shakespeare, Jefferson, and the history of political thought has been published in numerous journal articles, book chapters, and review essays.

Kendall Hack is a director at a nationwide career mobility and education company with the mission of unlocking opportunity for America's workforce through education, skills, support, and career pathways. Previously, Kendall consulted for an innovation and growth strategy firm, where she focused on education, healthcare, and transformation strategy. She has served as a Fulbright Fellow in Malaysia and as an education policy fellow in the South Caroline governor's office. Kendall holds a BA from Wake Forest University, an MBA from the Wharton School at the University of Pennsylvania, and an MPA from the Kennedy School of Government at Harvard University.

Carson Holloway is professor and chair of the political science department at the University of Nebraska Omaha, having taught there since 2002. He received his PhD from Northern Illinois University in 1998 and his research primarily focuses on the American founding, and modern problems in democracy. He has published numerous books, his most recent being *Hamilton versus Jefferson in the Washington Administration: Completing the Founding or Betraying the Founding?* (Cambridge UP, 2015). He has written numerous articles and has been published in the *Review of Politics*, *Interpretations: A Journal of Political Philosophy*, and *Perspective on Political Science*.

Sarah Beth Kitch is associate director for the Civitas Institute at the University of Texas at Austin. Her scholarship is in political theory and American political thought, with articles in the *American Journal of Political Science* and the *Journal of Church and State*. Dr. Kitch's research focuses on agency and resources for action. At present, her research examines Martin Luther King, Jr.'s political theology and how King's participation in the prophetic tradition shapes his politics. She was the 2016-2017 Thomas W. Smith Postdoctoral Research Associate in the Department of Politics at Princeton University. She won the Northeastern Political Science Association's 2016 Award for Best Paper by a Female Political Scientist.

Gregory A. McBrayer is an associate professor of political science and the director for the Citizens Programs and University Core Curriculum at Ashland University. He received his PhD from the University of Maryland and has published articles in *Interpretation: A Journal of Political Philosophy*, *Kentron: Revue Pluridisciplinaire du Monde Antique*, *Interpretation*, *The Journal for Hellenic Studies*, *The American Journal of Islamic Social Science*, and *Political Science Quarterly*. He was formerly an assistant professor at Morehead State University and a postdoctoral fellow at Emory. He has also published on classical Greek thought, namely Plato and Xenophon.

Steven McGuire is currently the Paul & Karen Levy Fellow in Campus Freedom and was previously the director of the Matthew J. Ryan Center for the Study of Free Institutions and the Public Good and associate teaching professor in the Augustine and Culture Seminar Program at Villanova University. He is the co-editor of *Eric Voegelin and the Continental Tradition*, *Subjectivity: Ancient and Modern*, and *Nature: Ancient and Modern*. His writing has also appeared in the *Philadelphia Inquirer*, *Broad and Liberty*, *RealClearPolitics*, *Inside Higher Ed*, *The Public Discourse*, *Church Life Journal*, *Modern Age*, *Perspectives on Political Science*, and the *Political Science Reviewer*.

Clifford Orwin is a professor at the University of Toronto with the political science department who specializes in the problem of compassion and its relation to justice, as explored through the writings of the greatest thinkers who have addressed the subject. This has included Rousseau among the modern writers and Thucydides among the ancient ones. Dr. Orwin also specializes in Jewish political thought, and his main current project is a book on the Hellenistic Jewish thinker Flavius Josephus. He has written and translated articles on Herodotus, Thucydides, Plato, Machiavelli, Montesquieu, Churchill, Charles Taylor, American religion, and humanitarian military intervention. His books are *The Humanity of Thucydides* (1994), and *The Legacy of Rousseau* (1997) (co-editor and co-author).

Lorraine Smith Pangle studies and teaches ancient, early modern, and American political philosophy, with special interests in ethics, the philosophy of education, and problems of justice and moral responsibility. She has held fellowships from the National Endowment for the Humanities, the Social Sciences and Humanities Research Council of Canada, and the Earhart Foundation. She is Professor of Government and Co-Director of the Thomas Jefferson Center for the Study of Core Texts and Ideas at the University of Texas at Austin. Her prior publications include *Reason and Character: The Moral Foundations of Aristotelian Political Philosophy* (2020), *Virtue is Knowledge: The Moral Foundations of Socratic Political Philosophy* (2014), *The Political Philosophy of Benjamin Franklin* (2007), and *Aristotle and the Philosophy of Friendship* (2003), alongside numerous academic articles on related topics.

José Daniel Parra received his PhD in political philosophy from the University of Toronto. His research topics address classical, modern, and contemporary European thought with special emphasis on German thought, Socratic education, the liberal arts, and the history of political philosophy. He is currently a professor of the government and international relations program and of the doctorate in political studies at the Universidad Externado de Colombia.

Lincoln E.F. Rathnam is an assistant professor of political science and the associate chair for the division of social sciences at Duke Kunshan University. He received his PhD from the university of Toronto in 2018. His research interests are in political theory and comparative politics. He is currently completing a manuscript on freedom and toleration, as understood in ancient China and early modern Europe. Future projects include a re-examination of the "Asian values" debate and a comparative study of the concept of justice. In addition, he is engaged in research into the history of American political thought, with a particular focus on issues concerning disagreement, diversity, and the reception of non-Western thought within the U.S.

Lindsay Mahon Rathnam is an assistant professor of political science at Duke Kunshan University. Her research areas are ancient political thought, the history of political thought, and comparative political theory. She is currently at work on a book exploring how emotion suffuses cross-cultural encounters in the work of Herodotus, as well as a project on freedom of speech in the ancient world and its implications for contemporary liberalism. She received her PhD from the University of Toronto in 2018 and has been published in the *American Political Science Review* for her work on the marketplace of ideas and Herodotus.

Sarah Rich-Zendel is a Social Sciences and Humanities Research Council Postdoctoral Fellow at Osgoode Hall Law School at York University, specializing in international relations with her work primarily focusing on Nepal and Nepali institutions. She has been published in both academic journals and the popular press. She received her PhD from the University of Toronto.

Anna Marisa Schön is a post-doctoral associate of political science at the Trinity College of Arts and Sciences at Duke University. She has published on a range of topics, with her most recent works being a coauthored book with Alin Fumurescu, *The Foundations of American Political Thought*, and a translation of J. G. Fichte's *Contribution to the Correction of the Public's Judgments on the French Revolution*.

George Thomas is Wohlford Professor of American Political Institutions and Director of the Salvatori Center for the Study of Individual Freedom at Claremont McKenna College. He is the author of *The Madisonian Constitution* and *The Founders and the Idea of a National University: Constituting the American Mind*, and coauthor of the two-volume *American Constitutional Law: Essays, Cases, and Comparative Notes*. He has published numerous scholarly articles on Constitutional Law and American Constitutionalism, and his essays have appeared in *The Atlantic* and *The Washington Post*. He has received fellowships from the National Endowment for the Humanities and the Huntington

Library and is the recipient of the Alexander George Award from the American Political Science Association.

Constantine Christos Vassiliou received his PhD in Political Science at the University of Toronto. He is Visiting Research Fellow of the Civitas Institute at the University of Texas at Austin. Vassiliou is a political theorist and historian of ideas and teaches courses in ancient, modern, and American political thought. His book, *Moderate Liberalism and the Scottish Enlightenment: Montesquieu, Hume, Smith, and Ferguson* (Edinburgh University Press 2023), examines how the foundational liberal theories of key Enlightenment thinkers responded to the moral and civic challenges of early capitalism. Vassiliou contributed to and co-edited *The Spirit of Montesquieu's Persian Letters* (Lexington Press 2023), and he co-edited *Emotions, Community, and Citizenship: Cross-Disciplinary Perspectives* (University of Toronto Press 2017).

Lee Ward is a professor of political science at Baylor University. He has published widely in the areas of political theory and American political thought. His books include *The Politics of Liberty in England and Revolutionary America* (Cambridge UP, 2004), *John Locke and Modern Life* (Cambridge UP, 2010), *Modern Democracy and the Theological-Political Problem in Spinoza, Rousseau, and Jefferson* (Palgrave McMillan, 2014) and *Recovering Classical Liberal Political Economy: Natural Rights and the Harmony of Interests* (Edinburgh UP, 2022). He is editor of John Locke's *Two Treatises of Government* (Hackett Publishing, 2016). He has also published articles on John Locke, Thomas Hobbes, Aristotle, Montesquieu, Algernon Sidney, Plato, Baruch Spinoza, Jean-Jacques Rousseau, Tom Paine, Irish republicanism, John Rawls, and Jürgen Habermas that have appeared in several leading academic journals.

Chapter Abstracts

Chapter 1: The Modern Academy and the Ancient Virtue of *Phronesis*
By Lorraine Smith Pangle

This essay argues that in times of national division and social turmoil, the task of scholars in the academy is to be more helpfully relevant precisely by stepping back and being more deeply reflective. By asking better questions, often questions no one is asking, by bringing divergent views into fruitful dialogue, and by modeling rigorous, searching, and fair-minded inquiry, we can best equip the citizens who are our students to address our nation's ills constructively. A central part of our task, especially in troubled times, is to model through our scholarship and teaching the ancient virtue of *phronesis* or active wisdom. Tracing Aristotle's elucidation of this virtue in book 6 of the *Nicomachean Ethics*, the essay explores active wisdom's delicate twin tasks of supporting the best commonsense moral judgments of one's own society while also encouraging critical questioning. It ends with a reflection on how Aristotelian active wisdom might give guidance for thinking about one fraught question in the modern academy, free speech on college campuses.

Chapter 2: Two Cheers for Deparochialization
By Clifford Orwin

A burgeoning new field in political science is "Comparative Political Theory," which seeks to "deparochialize the curriculum" by introducing more "non-Western" content to it. Having myself participated in this tendency within my modest capacities to do so, I recognize the advantages to students and teachers alike of thus broadening the scope of their reflections. At the same time, we must recognize the doubtful aspects of this project. If we require students to read too many books, too hastily, and without sufficient cultural background to understand them, we will end up not deparochializing the curriculum but merely diluting it. We must question whether most of our colleagues (including our teaching assistants) are even minimally qualified to teach these works, lacking non-Western languages as they do. Lastly, in an era of ever diminishing student awareness of the political and cultural legacy of the West itself, we must ask whether its revitalization is not where the greater urgency lies.

Chapter 3: The Contours of the Canon: Liberal Education, Universalism, and Representation
By Lindsay Mahon Rathnam and Lincoln E. F. Rathnam

We suggest that the most plausible critique of the canon is that sources relevant to a sincere investigation into human life are being neglected when we accept a curriculum almost exclusively devoted to Western texts, and that the very enterprise of liberal education as it has traditionally been construed urges that this be remedied. We should seek wisdom in the works of Confucius or Al-Farabi for the same reasons that we do so in those of Plato or Shakespeare. We then explore the prospects for an agreement between universalists who value the existing canon and those who seek to expand it. We argue that some of the most influential thinkers of both Europe and Asia endorsed the universalist view, and sought to learn more about other communities and cultures precisely in order to make credible their claims to knowledge of human affairs. This, we contend, allows us to understand liberal education as a global project aimed at responding to a genuine human need for self-knowledge by seeking a more empirically informed awareness of the varied forms that human lives have taken.

Chapter 4: An Outsider Looking In: Christine de Pizan on Classical Learning
By Anna Marisa Schön

The traditional portrayal of Christine de Pizan as a "proto-feminist" is overly simplistic and distracts from a more profound observation she makes about her own identity: through her reflections on and dialogues with these classical texts, Christine comes to know herself not merely as a woman, but as a human being and she learns to perceive the multiple dimensions of her identity. Her study of philosophy enables Christine to transcend the narrow perspective afforded by her gender and to acquire a broader view of her person as a rational human being, capable of virtue. I suggest that the self-knowledge obtained through the study of philosophy allowed her to rise above her hardships and to master the conditions of her life, encouraging other women to do the same. I argue that the inclusion of Christine's writings in our teaching curricula would offer students a vivid illustration of how engagement with the Great Books enables us to step out of our particular circumstances and to transcend the relevant but narrow viewpoints furnished by our "lived experiences."

Chapter 5: Shame and the Liberal Education of the Democratic Self
By Alin Fumurescu

Is shaming an outdated practice of which one should be ashamed? Not anymore, or, at any rate, the claim is not made as forcefully as before, since, by and large, the ethical high grounds have changed hands, and the change began in colleges. Among the means available for "reforming" society, shaming has lately become the weapon of choice of the weak against the powers-that-be and the status-quo. Thanks primarily to the new media, public shaming is costless and extremely efficient in the form of cancel culture, boycotting, or internet-shaming in and outside of academia. Yet the same efficiency has also amplified to alarming levels older forms of shaming, from bullying to slut-shaming, fat-shaming, age-shaming, and the like, with devastating consequences, ranging from loss of self-esteem to suicide. The chapter argues that by contrasting the use of shame by Socrates with its employment by Diogenes the Cynic one can differentiate not only between the inner and the outer shame, but also between the 'pedagogical' shaming, meant to educate democratic souls, and the 'pernicious' type, meant to reinforce the tyrannical tendencies of the postmodern selves. Being thirsty for public attention means to voluntary enslave oneself to the tyranny of numbers.

Chapter 6: Liberal Education as Civic Education: The Philosopher's Curriculum in Plato's *Republic*
By Dustin Gish

The tradition of liberal education as civic education entered modernity through the writings of Renaissance humanists, beginning with Francesco Petrarca. But the origin of that tradition can be traced back to antiquity in the work and career of Marcus Tullius Cicero, and even further back to Plato's *Republic*. Cicero reoriented Socrates' argument, or account, of the studies that constitute the philosophic life (in *Republic* VII) around the demands of Roman republican politics, making what Socrates considered liberal, or liberating, education into the foundation for civic education. Cicero's humanistic studies (*studia humanitatis*), which Petrarca in the modern era revived and perpetuated as civic humanism, thus derives its origin from the Socratic argument about Justice in the *Republic*. The main thread running throughout this tradition is the idea that quieting the turmoil in the soul through the proper pursuit of wisdom prepares the way for engaging virtuously in politics. Studying closely the origin of this tradition in the account of the education of the philosopher-ruler, which is to say, the Philosopher's Curriculum, reveals that true liberal education establishes the foundation for civic education and serves as the keystone in the arch of Justice.

Chapter 7: The Garden of Citizenship: Liberal Arts as the Cultivation of Just Sentiments
By Constantine Christos Vassiliou

This chapter defends both the traditional curricular content and the institutional experience of a classic liberal education. It demonstrates why the latter is a fundamentally more important battleline if universities are to succeed at 1) nourishing students' capacity for sound civic and moral judgment, and 2) promoting liberty and equality. The first section draws from Plato's *Republic* to highlight how one's intellectual and civic education can go awry, shorn of an institutional experience that fosters a spirit of comradery, liberality, and a deep sense for the public good. It emphasizes the need to create structures that provide students with the cognitive leisure that is necessary for the study of transformative texts. The second section illuminates the intangible qualities of a classic liberal arts experience that make it a more egalitarian conveyor of independent student learning. It examines how universities may teach socially responsible citizenship without inadvertently reproducing the social inequality embodied by the liberal arts institutions of yesteryear. A careful treatment of this question will dovetail with a meditation on the classic American film, *It's a Wonderful Life*—a metaphor for liberal education that provides us with a framework for teaching citizenship in the modern research university.

Chapter 8: Liberal Education as "Spiritual Exercise": On the Life of the Mind in the Age of Social Media
By Aurelian Craiutu

This chapter is based on a final lecture that I occasionally give in the courses I teach in political theory at Indiana University, Bloomington. By drawing on a wide array of authors from Seneca and Cicero to Machiavelli and Montaigne,

I make the case for liberal education as a form of "spiritual exercise" as defined by French philosopher Pierre Hadot (1922–2010). I begin by examining the present crisis of humanities and the intense spirit of competition that dominates our students' lives. Next, I turn to the mission of teachers and the nature of classroom education. Finally, I examine an unorthodox type of liberal education that I had in communist Romania under the private mentorship of a philosopher, Mihai Șora (b. 1916–2023). I show how my unconventional liberal education and the reading of philosophical texts helped discipline my attention and free myself from the banality and vulgarity of everyday life under communism.

Chapter 9: Liberal Education and the Limits of Science and Technology: Lessons from the COVID-19 Pandemic
By Carson Holloway

A reconsideration of these fundamental lessons—about both the importance and limits of science and technology—has been forced upon us by the COVID-19 pandemic of 2020–2021. The usefulness of science and technology in addressing the pandemic has been rather evident, as it has been trumpeted by governments and the mass media. The limits of science and technology, on the other hand, have been somewhat overlooked. This chapter seeks to advance the aims of liberal education by meditating on what the response to the pandemic teaches us about the limits of science and technology. Reflecting critically on the scientific and technological responses to the pandemic sharpens our capacity for intelligent deliberation about the common good by bringing to light the kinds of goods that science and technology can and cannot supply.

Chapter 10: Liberal Education Is Antitechnological
By Steven McGuire

As the need for an immediate response to the COVID-19 crisis fades, we should step back and ask what this experience might mean for the future of liberal education in America. Now more people than ever have had a taste of online education, and, as social-distancing requirements dragged on, more and more of us became better prepared to undertake it; many of us grew accustomed to it, and some of us even learned to like it. The most important objection, however, is not that we lack the requisite technology to pursue liberal education online, which would leave open the possibility that online education could eventually replace or even surpass in-person liberal education. This chapter contends that online education, and the arguments in favor of it, exhibit a technological way of thinking that is directly at odds with the nature and purpose of liberal education.

Chapter 11: Transference and the Future of Student-Teacher Intimacy
By Sarah Rich-Zendel

Feminists have long recognized a tension in women's lives between sexual danger and sexual pleasure. In 1982, Barnard College hosted a feminist conference entitled "Towards a Politics of Sexuality," which highlighted this deep divide in feminist thinking about sex. Feminists either focus on pleasure and dismiss the patriarchal structure in which women act or they focus on danger and violence, denying women's sexual agency and "unwittingly increas[ing] the sexual terror and despair in which women live." This chapter explores this tension as it plays out on college campuses through the administration of sexual misconduct. Bringing together work by Jennifer Doyle and Laura Kipnis, two women professors who published books on their own Title IX cases, with feminist work on desire and pleasure, I argue that the litigious and paranoid sex culture on today's campus is limiting women's freedom of sexual expression, and foreclosing on opportunities for women to enjoy explorations of pleasure and desire that facilitate a liberal arts education.

Chapter 12: From Impatience to Compassion: Educating from Restlessness to Responsibility
By Sarah Beth V. Kitch

For all the things they study, do American students gain a moral education that prepares them to deal with the impact of human suffering on civic life? A pedagogy of suffering can contribute to a moral literacy that sustains democratic practices such as listening, serving, and deliberating. It is easy, however, to view topics like love and suffering as sentimental or merely private. But in order to understand American politics, students need adequate ways to talk about the political meaning of pain. Perhaps more fundamentally, the skills to engage suffering—one's own and others'—are key to an adequate civic education. To approach this problem, I reflect with Abraham Joshua Heschel, James Baldwin, Aristotle, and Aeschylus. I draw on virtue ethics to propose a pedagogy of suffering that fosters democratic citizenship.

Chapter 13: The Cosmopolitan Education of Hobbits: Friendship and Political Deliberation in Tolkien's *The Fellowship of the Ring*
By William E. DeMars

Today we face a novel conflict between provincialism and cosmopolitanism, concurrent with a profound crisis in liberal education. J.R.R. Tolkien's pedagogical proposal of liberal, cosmopolitan education is deeply relevant for these interwoven challenges. The critical literature on Tolkien's epic, *The Lord of the Rings*, has only recently begun to explore politics. This chapter is the first analysis of political deliberation in the trilogy, focusing on the first volume, *The Fellowship of the Ring*. The story is situated in contemporary debates with insights from Kwame Anthony Appiah on the ethical demands of the current challenge of cosmopolitanism, and from Hannah Arendt on links between friendship, politics, deliberation, and education. Tolkien sets the Hobbits on a pedagogical journey. Before they can play their appointed roles in the War of the Ring, Frodo and his friends must undertake a cosmopolitan, liberal education for freedom and leadership in a larger, more morally and culturally complex world. With this insight, it is clearer how several puzzling strands not only advance the story, but also contribute to our understanding of cosmopolitan political deliberation, including the Hobbit genius for friendship, the anomaly of Tom Bombadil, the power of weakness at the Council of Elrond, and the link between knowledge and suffering.

Chapter 14: Academic Freedom and the Future of the Liberal Arts
By Lee Ward

The intention of this chapter is not to provide the case for liberal education in the modern world. My task is more specific and perhaps more mundane. I seek to identify the major challenges confronting liberal education as institutions of higher learning across the United States undergo a massive process of structural reorganization, which endangers the continued survival of the liberal arts in their natural habitat, namely, the modern comprehensive university and liberal arts college. I wish to suggest that the idea of academic freedom must play a central role in preserving, and even renewing, the spirit of liberal education in the contemporary academic milieu. However, my approach is different from most discussions of academic freedom today that tend to focus on the issues of faculty freedom with respect to control over teaching, research and both intramural and extramural speech.

Chapter 15: Leo Strauss and the Humanity of Liberal Education
By José Daniel Parra

Leo Strauss is recognized by students and critics alike as one of the rediscoverers of classical political rationalism in the contemporary academia. The return to classical thought, in Strauss' understanding, is a "necessary and tentative or experimental" attempt to put again to the fore some of the fundamental questions at the core of the examined life. Such questions, in his view, are not abstract theorems, but are reflected in an ongoing relation between the themes of the "city and man." It is in this philosophical context that Strauss brings together the history of political philosophy and liberal education. This chapter offers a reading of Strauss' remarks on the rationale for liberal education in late modernity. Although it focuses on the essays devoted to this theme in *Liberalism Ancient and Modern* (Chapters 1–2) the text draws from a variety of sources in Strauss' oeuvre. Is the study of the great books "the one thing needful" in the modern research university? Is it possible to somehow reconcile the emphasis Strauss puts on the notion of logographic necessity essential to classical thought and the contingency inherent to the liberal worldview? Can liberal studies enhance the tone of our modern self-understanding? The text addresses these and some other key questions as it makes the case for the importance of the study of classical literature.

Chapter 16: Liberal Education and American Democracy
By George Thomas

This chapter examines the teaching of history as a powerful way to bring out American political principles. It looks to the history around the founding generation who saw education as an essential complement to republican government, with leading founders advocating for the development of educational institutions to complement and complete the newly established constitutional order—including the establishment of a national university. It then considers how our contemporary institutions of higher education seek to pass on and engage civic knowledge and understandings. Finally, it seeks to illustrate how American history can be taught in a manner that embraces the conflicts and controversies at the center of the American experiment in self-government. In doing so, I consider how constitutional law, which is inevitably built around constitutional disputes, might offer a particularly promising way to both teach American history and the civic attitudes necessary to sustain American democracy.

Chapter 17: How Business Schools Can Prepare Students for Twenty-First-Century Success by Renewing Their Liberal Arts Roots
By Donald Drakeman and Kendall Hack

MBA programs promise to provide students with the tools and methods "critical to success" in their business careers. For the last fifty years, that success has primarily been measured by corporate profitability, which was business's only "social responsibility," according to a highly influential essay by economist Milton Friedman in 1970. But times have changed. Today, large numbers of students, customers, and business leaders see businesses as just one part of a broader community, and they believe that those businesses have important civic and moral responsibilities. We argue that adding greater attention to the liberal arts will help MBAs better understand the nature of their employers' place within the broader community. It will also provide valuable insights into the political and social environment in which their businesses will operate, and it can even contribute to their own career success. In this chapter, we make a series of specific recommendations for reviving the original ideals of business education, enhancing the MBA curriculum, and revising the influential ranking systems.

Chapter 18: The Role of Liberal Education in Professional Studies
By Steven Frankel

My goal is to explain and justify the creation of liberal arts programs and centers inside professional schools, as we have done with the Stephen S. Smith Center in the Williams College of Business at Xavier University. I want to respond to some of the most serious criticisms of such projects, beginning with Allan Bloom's critique of professional schools—especially business majors and the MBA degree—in *The Closing of the American Mind*. *The Closing* has a strong rhetorical element, aimed at undergraduates; however, if you look at his other essays on liberal education such as "Commerce and Culture" and the "Crisis of Liberal Education," a different picture emerges. In fact, Bloom helps make the case for such programs in the liberal arts and it is useful to revisit his analysis. In addition, the acceleration of certain trends in the university, which Bloom had already identified, such as historicism and hostility to liberal education within the humanities, also contribute to understanding the value of liberal arts outposts in professional schools.

Chapter 19: The Paradox of Liberal Education and Modernity
By Gregory A. McBrayer

This chapter seeks to understand the preconditions for liberal education in the modern world. The modern world is distinctive, especially as it relates to science and technology. Modernity offers opportunities for liberal education unknown to the premodern world—one need only reflect on the abundant availability of books—but it also poses unique challenges to it. Accordingly, the preconditions for and requirements of liberal education may be different in the modern world than they were in the premodern. The trivium and quadrivium are relics of an age gone by. In the first part of the chapter, I address the preconditions and obstacles one encounters in the pursuit of liberal education. Then, in the second part of the paper, I turn to the requirements or content of liberal education itself. What are the things that ought to be studied? What, in modernity, is truly liberating? Can the study of science liberate us, or does its service in pursuit of the relief of man's estate render it illiberal in serious ways? Is the old admonition to study Great Books outmoded, or is it even more important in modernity?

LIBERAL EDUCATION AND CITIZENSHIP IN A FREE SOCIETY

Introduction

Justin Buckley Dyer and Constantine Christos Vassiliou

Liber, THE LATIN WORD MEANING *free*, is the etymological root of *liberal*, and a liberal education was, in its original conception, an education befitting a free man. In the Middle Ages, such an education in and for freedom entailed mastery of the seven liberal arts, composed of the Trivium (grammar, logic, and rhetoric) and the Quadrivium (arithmetic, geometry, astronomy, and music). The first three were not so many subjects to be mastered as they were foundational intellectual skills. Dorothy Sayers memorably called these first three liberal arts "the lost tools of learning" in her eponymously titled essay lamenting the state of education in midcentury England.[1] Today, we might simply call these critical thinking skills, to the extent that we think critically about what critical thinking entails.

At a small liberal arts university in Ashland, Ohio, one will find banners around campus that proclaim the school's mission is to teach students "how to think, not what to think." Sayers would have approved: her essay concludes that "the sole and true end of education is simply this: to teach men how to learn for themselves."[2] Well and good as that aim is, the schoolmen also thought students should take their acquired tools and put them to use studying the specific subjects of the Quadrivium.

We have largely moved in higher education from the seven liberal arts to a general education, but this remains closely connected to the idea of freedom. Harvard University's 1945 report *General Education in a Free Society* noted that "if one cling[s] to the root meaning of liberal as that which befits or helps to make free men, then general and liberal education have identical goals." The crucial difference is that general education is to be generally available, the province of every citizen rather than the few whose leisure is made possible by other men's labor. "The task of modern democracy," the Harvard report proclaimed, "is to preserve the ancient ideal of liberal education and to extend it as far as possible to all the members of the community."[3]

At its best, general education in a modern democratic society aims to make citizens free from prejudice, parochialism, and superstition; free to form and exercise reasoned judgment, to acquire new knowledge, and to master new subjects; and, finally, free to engage in society and in government as one who can, as Aristotle put it, rule and be ruled in turn. Like liberal education, general education thus aims to be a liberating education.

In a free society, education in and for freedom is closely connected to education in and for citizenship. Many involved in higher education today have thus renewed the call for a fusion of liberal and general education with a distinctively American civic education focused on US history, institutions, and culture. As George Thomas writes in his essay in this volume, "Knowing the history and principles of the American polity is a first step in thinking about and applying political principles to contemporary issues."[4]

Abraham Lincoln, toward the end of the war, lamented that "the world has never had a good definition of the word liberty, and the American people, just now, are much in want of one."[5] There was no neutral ground between the liberty of the master and slave, just as there is no neutral ground between the liberty of the wolf and the sheep.

As Burke insisted that liberty, rather than being considered abstractly, must "inhere in some sensible object,"[6] so too did Lincoln point to the particulars of the American political tradition when advocating for the extension and perpetuation of liberty in the United States. Lincoln saw the Civil War as an epic struggle testing whether any nation conceived in liberty could long endure, and the new birth of freedom for which he labored was midwifed through the culture, institutions, and events that defined the American people.

Liberty and liberal education are intertwined. Liberal education requires open inquiry, reasoned debate, civil discussion, and freedom of thought and speech, but these commitments do not stem from a position of neutrality. One cannot be neutral on these core questions of what freedom is and what it entails. If the very idea of liberal education is to be coherent, we must hold as foundational axioms at least that the mind is free and not determined by an inevitable chain of material cause and effect, that the mind is able to gain knowledge of objective reality, and that reason yields insight into both what exists and how we should live. Without that, education is propaganda, reason is power, liberty is tyranny.

Only a worldview that can account for the freedom of a mind gathering knowledge about objective reality and reasoning about what is and what ought to be can provide the necessary intellectual scaffolding to support liberal education. These foundational axioms stand in contrast to any conception of education that denies the freedom of the mind, reduces knowledge to social construction, and relegates universal moral claims to the realm of mere subjective values.

In a prescient essay, Harry Jaffa claimed that the freedom of the mind is the freedom to discover, know, and be guided by "the truth about man, God, and the universe." But, he argued, modern education is built on, or at least has implicitly adopted, the thesis "that there is no objective knowledge of, or rational ground for distinguishing good and bad, right and wrong, just and unjust."[7] The constellation of ideas that led to a denial of the objectivity of value leads to a conception of freedom indistinguishable from tyranny. *Sic volo, sic jubeo; stat pro ratione voluntas.*[8] Yet if will is not to stand for a reason—if might is not to be confused with right—then there must be a shared wisdom about the use of man's freedom. Liberal education is at once a liberating education and a quest for wisdom about how to live freely.

The quest for that wisdom is properly undertaken both through exposure to the best that has been thought and said *and* through an intimate engagement with the sensible objects in which the abstraction of liberty has inhered in our culture, institutions, and history. Only from that dual vantage point may one provide an informed, loving, and constructive critique of one's own.

As freedom is relevant to liberal democratic politics, liberal education is relevant to politics in a free society. Yet it is perhaps best to see liberal education in a free society as properly *pre*political. Liberal education is prepolitical in the sense that it is concerned with preserving through education the habits and virtues necessary to live freely and to exercise that freedom responsibly, with others, by sharing in the project of self-government.

Jaffa wrote of the "necessity of the scholarship of the politics of freedom," but the essays in this volume are concerned with something slightly different that is captured by a reordering of words: the necessity of the politics of the scholarship of freedom, that is, of the prudential judgments and trade-offs we must make to preserve liberal and civic education—education in and for freedom—in light of the unique market, technological, and intellectual challenges faced by advocates of liberal education in the first quarter of the twenty-first century.

The chapters in part 1, "Liberal Arts as the Classroom of Character and Judgment," are primarily oriented toward discussing the philosophical rigors of a classic liberal education. They demonstrate how the purpose of learning the great books is not just to understand these texts as works of iconoclastic thought but to internalize their wisdom as structures of discipline that favor the habits and virtues necessary for living freely. In short, the chapters in this section subvert the view that liberal education and civic education are mutually exclusive forms of pedagogy.

The chapters in part 2, "Liberal Arts as the Classroom of Citizenship," share the view that a traditional liberal arts *experience* is indispensable to learning those habits and virtues of freedom. They respond to the various features of modern-day academic life that frustrate educators' efforts to reproduce a salutary community of learning for students. Each of the chapters stress how students need the scaffolding of the physical campus community—a space where lifelong mentorship bonds and friendships will organically develop, nourishing the resilience necessary to meaningfully engage with the great books.

The chapters in part 3, "Liberal Arts and the Future of the Classroom," consider the viability of "the classroom" moving forward. In so doing, they enumerate the intellectual and practical challenges educators encounter in their pedagogy, and then offer unique perspectives on how to promote and protect a classical liberal education within the modern research university. Many scholars will look askance at those who primarily defend classic liberal education for its practical benefits (civic, commercial, professional). So long as we accept generous patronage from the academic institutions that employ us, however, we must be responsive to practical considerations. The democratized university offers us the opportunity to recompense those who have afforded us the privilege of learning and teaching the art of living freely.

Our broader aim with this project is to help build a market for contemplation and leisure in academic life—an indispensable feature of a liberal education that permits students to reflect upon what it means to live nobly before assuming their place as custodians of a free society.

NOTES

Many thanks to our research assistants, Ms. Kirsten Ehlers and Mr. Jonah McCoy, for their excellent work during multiple stages of this project. We are also grateful to The Elizabeth D. Rockwell Center on Ethics and Leadership at the University of Houston's Hobby School of Public Affairs for generously supporting our book project.

We both enjoyed the blessings of a classic liberal education thanks to the generous mentorship we received from a community of scholars throughout our undergraduate years. Justin Dyer: I would like to dedicate this book to Allen Hertzke, whose class on the foundations of American politics derailed my plans to get a business degree and led me to the Political Science Department, where I met George Thomas, whose class on constitutional law derailed my plans to go to law school and sent me off to the University of Texas instead. Constantine Vassiliou: I would like to dedicate this book to my professors at Concordia University, with special thanks to James Moore and Horst Hutter. Jim's course, Political Thought in the Era of the Reformation and the Enlightenment, drew me away from the stimulating world of banking to become a scholar of eighteenth-century political thought. Horst's seminar course on Nietzsche's *Thus Spoke Zarathustra* prepared me intellectually for the resilience that I would need as I pursue my calling in the academy.

1. Dorothy Sayers, "The Lost Tools of Learning."
2. Sayers, "Lost Tools of Learning," 13.
3. *General Education in a Free Society: Report of the Harvard Committee*, 52, 53.
4. See chapter 15 in this volume.
5. Roy P. Basler, ed., *Collected Works of Abraham Lincoln*, 301.
6. Edmund Burke, "On Conciliation with the Colonies" (March 22, 1775).
7. Harry V. Jaffa, "The Reichstag Is Still Burning," 101.
8. "Thus I will, thus I command. My will stands for a reason."

BIBLIOGRAPHY

Basler, Roy P., ed. *Collected Works of Abraham Lincoln*. Vol. 7. Brunswick, NJ: Rutgers University Press, 1953.

Burke, Edmund. "On Conciliation with the Colonies." March 22, 1775. https://teachingamericanhistory.org/document/on-conciliation-with-the-colonies/.

General Education in a Free Society: Report of the Harvard Committee. Cambridge, MA: Harvard University Press, 1945.

Jaffa, Harry V. "The Reichstag Is Still Burning." In *The Rediscovery of America: Essays by Harry V. Jaffa on the New Birth of Politics*, edited by Edward J. Erler and Ken Masugi. Lanham, MD: Rowman & Littlefield, 2019.

Sayers, Dorothy. "The Lost Tools of Learning." *Hibbert Journal: A Quarterly Review of Religion, Theology, and Philosophy* 46 (October 1947–July 1948): 1–13.

PART ONE

LIBERAL ARTS AS A CLASSROOM OF CHARACTER AND JUDGMENT

1. The Modern Academy and the Ancient Virtue of *Phronesis*

Lorraine Smith Pangle

IN THIS TIME OF NATIONAL turmoil, bitter partisanship, deepening social divisions, and distrust in our leaders and institutions, many of us in the academy are questioning what our response should be to the problems that beset our country. Two clusters of issues have come to the fore especially in the academy, with controversy over the proposed remedies in both cases. On one hand, in response to renewed concerns about inequality and especially racial disparities in America, we see calls for redoubled efforts to promote diversity, to advance the careers of minority scholars and revise curriculums to highlight their work, and otherwise to direct university policies to the support of social justice. These initiatives have generated disputes about what kind of equality, what kind of diversity, and what kind of justice, if any, the university should be dedicating itself to fostering. On the other hand, we see concerns about political correctness, encroachments on academic freedom, and the emergence of "cancel culture," leading to calls for the robust defense of individual rights in education and disagreements about the right principles governing campus discourse. All of these issues are important to discuss, but deeper reflection is needed if we are to get to the heart of what has gone wrong in the modern academy and what is needed to set it right again.

What is needed, above all, is a renewed commitment to a core task of the university, a task that schools and colleges of liberal arts are, of all institutions, best equipped to carry out. First, we need a rededication to our central task of serving as centers of deep, searching, and courageous inquiry about our society, its challenges, and the ideas about human nature and human thriving and justice that it rests on. Second, in support of this crucial task we need to work more deliberately to foster the moral and especially the intellectual virtues that a successful community of inquiry requires. This essay describes the type of inquiry that belongs at the center of our work in the liberal arts, taking the problem of racial justice as an example of the kind of questions that need to be asked. It then offers a suggestion about the intellectual virtue that our pedagogy at its best can model or teach, the ancient virtue of *phronesis* or active or practical wisdom, and explores its rich exposition in Aristotle's *Nicomachean Ethics*. Finally, it offers some thoughts on what Aristotelian *phronesis* might look like in practice, applied to the problem of campus free speech.

THE TASK OF THE LIBERAL ARTS

Our task includes putting problems in context. The context for the recent turmoil around race in America, for example, is a broader crisis in American civil life. Not only is income inequality high and rising, but deepening cultural divisions are accompanying it. Political polarization is sharp and increasing. Americans of both parties increasingly see members of the other party as irredeemably bad. Bipartisanship in Congress is moribund, and public trust in Congress is at an all-time low. Trust in science is eroding. Belief in democracy itself is waning among young Americans. We can mitigate but cannot solve the problem of race in America without addressing the problem of inequality more generally; we cannot do that without systemic reforms to many of our public policies and institutions, especially our schools, and we cannot do that without bipartisan support, which is to say without addressing the crisis of political polarization and distrust in our country.

How can we in the academy make a difference with any of this? As citizens we contribute and can contribute more by voting and serving our communities as mentors, commentators, volunteers, donors, and advocates for the candidates and policies and organizations that we judge best. But as scholars the most important contributions we can make to a nation in distress lie not in the actions or even the stances that we take but in slowing down and asking the right questions, often the questions that no one else is asking, listening to our first thoughts and our second thoughts, listening especially to the voices that the prevailing opinion within our own social bubble is inclined to scorn and to exclude, and creating constructive dialogue between diverse and even clashing perspectives. Our task is to be more helpfully relevant precisely by stepping back and being more deeply reflective.

Our task centers around asking good questions. For example, moments of impassioned demands for change such as the recent demonstrations over race and policing in America sometimes result in lasting reforms but often do not. Do we know enough about what makes the difference, and about the pitfalls to be avoided? What do historical examples, from the French and Russian Revolutions to the American labor and civil rights movements, have to teach us about successful and unsuccessful reform movements and their leaders? Often we discuss our problems in America as if no other nation were confronting the same ones. Are we learning all that we can from international comparisons? Many of us study pressing social problems, but how good are we at asking unfashionable questions and studying unfashionable topics? For example, have we been giving enough attention to studying the culture of armies and police departments, the character of those attracted to serving in the military and law enforcement, the problems of public sector unions, and the successes and failures of policing and criminal justice systems around the world?

On the topic of race, we recognize the dangers of prejudice and overgeneralizations, but do we know enough about the diversity of the black experience in our own country? Do we understand well enough not only why many are suffering and some are failing but why many others are succeeding and how their successes can be replicated? What do we understand about healthy and unhealthy communities and how the latter can be improved? About schools that succeed in these communities and those that fail? About psychological resilience and how it is best cultivated? Are we looking hard enough at all possible causes and all possible remedies for the troubles that concern us? To be sure, there are good reasons for our discomfort with certain questions: ill-meaning participants in public debates often raise questions and use data for self-serving or partisan purposes, a trend that is perniciously amplified by social media. But the misuse of information is not a reason for us in the academy to avoid hard discussions; it is a reason why precisely we, precisely here, precisely now have a duty to pursue them in a way that is searching, dispassionate, and fair-minded. There is no other institution in our society that is as well equipped to lead in this delicate but crucial work.

Our task as scholars and instructors includes listening to a diversity of voices and letting them challenge our own and our students' thinking. How good are we at searching for wisdom among representatives of diverse schools of thought and bringing these views into constructive dialogue?

How well are we doing in our writing and in our classrooms at helping Left and Right in America listen to one another with goodwill and with openness to finding, behind one another's shrill rhetoric, experiences that we need to understand, grains of truth that we need to meditate on, and ideas that we need to challenge ourselves with? How open are we to the thought of other times and places with which we reflexively disagree?

Finally, our task includes pursuing our research and teaching in such a way that our work is practical in the highest sense, which is to say informed by and conducive to the ancient virtue of *phronesis*. This task lies in between and connects a university's other essential tasks of pursuing basic research and offering practical solutions to immediate problems. While both of these are important, perhaps most valuable of all is the critical work of modeling a way of asking questions thoughtfully and courageously and connecting them both to immediate issues and to deeper insights into human nature. In cultivating the virtue of *phronesis*, we cultivate thoughtfulness about what makes life worth living, in all its varieties and commonalities; we cultivate clarity about the forces in human nature that make constructive change difficult; we foster the ability to negotiate these challenges with patient determination and without harsh vindictiveness.

Many of us already try to do this in our research and teaching, but it is hard to do it well. It is all too easy to get lost in arcane studies that advance our careers without shedding light on the most important of human problems; it is all too easy to take shortcuts to relevance by connecting our research to contemporary causes that we join without demanding of ourselves the hard, unpopular work of challenging them where they need challenging; it is all too easy to teach critical thinking in a way that merely unmasks hypocrisy and makes cynics of our students; it is all too easy to content ourselves with attacking the evils that are clear to us and never get around to the harder work of understanding the complex ways in which good and bad are inextricably mixed in every human being, human institution, and human society.

ARISTOTLE ON PRACTICAL WISDOM

The kind of questioning outlined above can be pursued in any field of the liberal arts, but especially fruitful as a locus of deep inquiry into fundamental questions is the study of the great books that provide the lodestone for each of our disciplines. With a view to reflecting more deeply on this virtue of *phronesis*, what it entails, and what makes it challenging, we can do no better than to turn to one of the great books that first elucidated this crucial virtue as a distinct quality of soul and that also embodies it, Aristotle's *Nicomachean Ethics*.[1]

In Aristotle's account, *phronesis* is a high virtue with a unique importance and dignity. It is an intellectual virtue but not merely a virtue of thought; it is closely connected with character and with the proper cultivation of taste as well as judgment. It does not exist apart from the moral virtues, nor they apart from it. *Phronesis* gives guidance for all of life and every choice, including the choice to practice philosophy, but it especially governs the dignified sphere of life that the Greeks called *praxis* or action. This sphere consists neither in detached contemplation nor in manual labor but in the serious activities judged most appropriate for flourishing, well-brought-up citizens of free republics: managing independent estates, engaging in political and military leadership, promoting the arts, and otherwise exercising virtue, not primarily for the sake of any mundane result but just because it is noble. It is this spirit, embodied by the gentlemen who set the tone for the best classical republics, that Aristotle evokes, defends, queries, and refines throughout the *Ethics*.

The unique recognition Aristotle confers on the realm of *praxis* is reflected in his recognition of moral virtue and *phronesis* as the perfections of distinct parts of the soul. Moral virtue is the perfection of the passions through habituation, passions that are not themselves rational or irrational but that constitute a part of the soul capable of listening to reason. The *phronesis* that guides the realm of *praxis* is likewise the perfection of its own deliberative part of the soul, quite distinct from the contemplative part that is the seat of *sophia*, or theoretical wisdom. Before Aristotle *sophia* and *phronesis* had different shades of meaning, but he was the first to thematically separate them, assigning to *sophia* the contemplation of the highest things and a sphere of eternal, unchanging truths and to *phronesis* the realm of human affairs. Thus *phronesis* operates independently, in its own sphere, neither subservient to the needs of the body nor dependent on philosophy. This at least is the official presentation of the *Ethics*, although even as he first introduces the idea of separate parts of the soul in 1.13 Aristotle says that this account is good for all practical purposes yet may ultimately be misleading. His demarcation of the spheres of *sophia* and *phronesis* in book 6 may also be less clean than it first appears. His formulation suggests a complete separation: as he puts it, *sophia* contemplates "those beings whose principles do not admit of being otherwise," and *phronesis* "those that do admit of being otherwise" (1139a5–8). In fact, however, it is not quite clear which it is that comprehends things that move and change but that have consistent, knowable natures, including all living beings and especially human beings. Is it neither, or one of them, or might it after all be both?

What Aristotle does make explicit is that *phronesis* comes into its own in deliberations that involve the human good as a whole and in serious matters that are not governed by an art or reducible to rules (1140a25–30). *Phronesis* is thus closely connected to the understanding or good judgment that we see in excellent historians, who bring a capacious understanding of human nature and its possibilities and limitations to bear in assessing the characters of statesmen and the choices they make under pressure and with incomplete information. It is likewise closely connected to the equitable spirit of a good judge, who recognizes the exceptional cases when strict application of the laws would be a miscarriage of justice, and the difference between crimes committed voluntarily that call for punishment and those done under pressure that no one could bear and therefore call for forgiveness.

At the highest level, as a form of wisdom that is both comprehensive and adaptable, *phronesis* bears a special connection to the highest form of justice, natural right, which Aristotle says has the same power everywhere and yet is all changeable. Somehow in both *phronesis* and natural right there are universal principles at work that provide solid guidance, yet ones that cannot be reduced to fixed rules. Both *phronesis* and natural right recognize the importance of law and at the same time its limitations. In assigning a comprehensive scope to *phronesis* and likewise in giving the highest place in his book on justice to changeable natural right, Aristotle supports the thought that although there are no universally valid rules, there is always a best thing to do, which is therefore the right thing to do. Although the right course may be hard to find and even harder to follow, it is not the case that a good man need ever do what is unjust.

The complex and shifting character of natural right is closely connected to the complex character of the common good that is the core meaning of justice. This spans the most basic needs of material well-being; the often urgent needs of security and civil peace, which demand in turn fair dealings and retribution for crime; the higher needs of the spirit that are fulfilled through freedom, the cultivation of virtue, the arts, religion, and education; and the demands of humanity. Pursuing the common good wisely requires understanding the nature of each good and the tensions that can arise between them, keeping the higher ones clearly in view, and yet recognizing the moments in which the lower ones must be given precedence in order to maintain the conditions under which a people is able to pursue the higher ones at all. It hence requires both a keen sense of the difference between the high and low that is fostered by a serious education of the taste and judgment, and the realism that comes from extensive experience of human affairs of every kind.

In particular, understanding natural right requires understanding the crucial role played by the regime in shaping every people, a consideration that Aristotle brings into his explication of natural right with the statement that "the just things that are not natural but human are not everywhere the same, since the regimes are not either; but everywhere there is only one regime that is in accord with nature, the best regime" (1135a3–5). Now the very best regime appears in the *Politics* to be the unfettered rule of wisdom. But since this is in fact never available for human beings, the best regime for each time and place is the closest approximation to the rule of wisdom possible under existing circumstances, which may be a very distant approximation. It is not the difference between actual regimes but the difference in peoples' capacities over time to approach the unfettered rule of reason that more than anything makes natural right changeable, for whatever approximation to it is possible, as the best possible, is in fact just. It is no more just to try to impose a regime that cannot succeed than it is to enforce a law when doing so will do more harm than good. The wise statesman who follows this thought will attend to making his country the best version of itself that it can be. He will content himself with small steps in the right direction when larger ones are unavailable and will eschew dogmatism, partisan fervor, and moral and religious fanaticism, as well as the cynicism that too often results from hard encounters with human limitations. His will be the true spirit of humanity.

Phronesis as an individual virtue must attend to the same diversity of ends that natural right must take into account, and in a certain way is even more complex. For if being a good statesman means setting aside all partiality for oneself and one's own, being a wise individual still requires judging well about one's own good as well as that of one's family, friends, countrymen, and country. This complexity in *phronesis* emerges as Aristotle articulates on one hand the intuition that *phronesis* belongs especially to men like Pericles "because they are able to contemplate what is good for themselves and for human beings" (1140b9–10), and on the other hand the intuition that a wise person attends to his own good and regards politicians as "busybodies" who have an unreasonable desire to lord it over others and do not understand the true limits of what is good for them (1142a1–2).

But ultimately the understanding needed to find and apply natural right and the understanding at the heart of *phronesis* are one and the same: the wise conduct of an individual life requires, just as much as wise political leadership does, an understanding of human thriving simply, beginning with an ability to sort out the tangle just mentioned. It is the task of *phronesis* to guide every virtue, including justice, through a clear grasp of the relevant end and through applying general principles to each particular case to finds the right mean between improper extremes. Aristotle's cryptic chapter on natural right in book 5 points to the need for complex balancing at the pinnacle of political judgment, but it is not until the start of book 6 on the intellectual virtues that he takes up thematically the all-important question of the target that reason looks to in identifying the mean.

But the astonishing and disappointing thing about book 6 is that no sooner has Aristotle raised the critical, long-deferred question of what the target (*skopos*) is that reason looks to in defining the measure (*horos*) of the mean than he allows it to drop. Pointing out that while it is true to say it is "neither too much nor too little," this is as inadequate in virtue as it is in medicine, he turns instead to defining the measure (*horos*) of reason itself, focusing on distinguishing the different intellectual capacities and virtues (1138b22–34). The failure of the standard to appear more clearly in Aristotle's careful, phenomenological account of moral judgment suggests that while something about this standard is intuitively clear, something about it is especially elusive, and perhaps even that moral judgment itself resists being pinned down on its standard. The problem is certainly connected to the complexity of the good that reason must always consider in guiding human life well and the consequent need for experience that we have discussed. It is even more connected to the importance of having a sense of high and low, which in turn requires the right cultivation of passions and tastes. To one who cannot "see" the beauty or nobility of a generous deed, it is not possible to demonstrate it through cold reason. But it is also connected further to a curious feature of the moral virtues that emerges in books 2–5, that they are defined more clearly by what they are not than by what they are. Many of the virtues embody in different ways a spirit of freedom: courage is a freedom from excessive fear, for example, moderation from excessive attachment to pleasure, and liberality from greed, each showing an ability to rise above basic passions and even fundamental biological needs that control less impressive human beings. This love of freedom resists being pinned down on what consideration would compel compliance beyond "the noble itself." That is to say, the standard is elusive because at the core of virtue is an insistence on doing the right thing simply for its own sake. To take as a standard by which to measure the virtuous act any mundane need or lower purpose or indeed any other purpose at all extrinsic to the act would seem to violate the intuition that the highest thing is just virtue itself. Yet the result is the famous cul-de-sac that moral reasoning falls into at the end of book 6. Having long argued that virtue means doing the right thing, in the right way, at the right time, and for the right purpose under the guidance of reason, and finally returning at the end of book 6 to the question of reason's goal or target, Aristotle now says that "virtue makes the target correct, and practical wisdom finds the things conducive to this" (1144a7–10). *Phronesis* and moral virtue form a circle, each somehow taking its guidance from the other.

Reflecting on this circle, we notice another curious feature of the *Ethics*: the whole book took off from the thought, in 1.7, that perhaps we can understand the human good by considering what the work of a human being is. That work was never identified. Instead, Aristotle only got as far as saying that our work must be some activity of the soul in accordance with reason, and that since fulfilling one's function and fulfilling it well or excellently are the same, it is an activity also in accordance with excellence or virtue. From there he instigated a long quest to define that excellence—that is, to define what doing whatever-it-is well might mean, without ever identifying our proper work. Little wonder, then, that we are still adrift. If we have never identified with precision the work that practical wisdom governs and the aim it pursues, if morality somehow wants to insist that its activity really is for its own sake and bows to no standard beyond itself, then there is no way we can say with clarity what the standard is that governs it. We are left with moral virtue claiming to follow reason, even though the reason that is supposed to lead has no better guide than moral virtue itself. And so we meet the pair of them wandering arm in arm through a forest, as it were, and each cheerfully proclaiming, "I'm just following him."

Now one of the many fascinating things about the *Ethics* is that even with this major lacuna, the primary story the book tells about virtue provides remarkably sound guidance for life. There is something powerful in the intuition that the best things in life should be just for themselves, something compelling in the thought that we should do what is right for its own sake, and something transformative in taking even a mundane task and allowing the "doing it well" to become one's end. This insight is taken to irrational extremes by the Stoics but presented with sublime sobriety by Aristotle. It is in fact an excellent principle of living to focus on meeting as well as one can whatever challenge life gives one to tackle, with whatever resources one has, like the shoemaker who can make the best shoes out of whatever leather is available or the general who can make the most of the army he has (1.10), and very many challenges are worthwhile. By making one's own good performance of the task one's goal, one gains independence of spirit and considerable freedom from the vicissitudes of fortune. It may not be in one's power to win the war, coach the team to a win, land the contract, or cure the patient, but whatever one's work is, by attending to doing one's part as wisely, bravely, effectively, and gracefully as possible and letting the results be what they may, one has the basis for a life free from tumultuous passions, dignified in its independence, and in all likelihood happy. This is already a great deal. If supported by the proper habituation of a good upbringing and deference to traditional wisdom, or as Aristotle puts it, to "the undemonstrated opinions of experienced and older people," who through the lens of an experienced eye "see correctly" (1143b13–14), might it not still be enough? In many times and places for very many individuals, surely it is.

Yet there are problems with conceiving of practical wisdom as taking its guidance from moral virtue in this way. On this account practical wisdom turns out not to be a single unified source of guidance but a lucky combination of cleverness or shrewdness with virtue, virtue that, if not grounded directly in reason, is grounded in habituation and the received wisdom of one's own time and place. Received wisdom always contains the distilled experience of one's forebears; as such it can be capacious and balanced and more sober than ideologies inspired by abstract and simplistic theory. At its best it also takes guidance from faith in the divine sources of one's tradition and the profound works of poets or other sacred scriptures. But received wisdom also invariably contains prejudice. How is *phronesis* to transcend prejudice if it does not have its own access to truth? If *phronesis* is a distinct virtue at all, it seems on this account to be the perfection not of a part that knows but only of an opining part, as Aristotle ultimately concedes (1140b27)—or perhaps better, if we do not in fact opine and reach truth with separate parts of the soul, the perfection of sub-philosophic opinion. Moreover, while received opinion and experienced judgment both have the advantage of recognizing the complexity of the human good and of the principles that deserve respect, they lack an articulation of how to weigh different considerations. Conventional moral opinion teaches that one should consider one's own highest good, that one should put others first, and that one should do what is right for its own sake regardless of its effect on anyone. It teaches that virtue should be rewarded and vice punished, and that virtue is its own reward while vice reflects an unhealthy and unenviable soul. How do these thoughts fit together? Finally, conventional moral opinion, being less than perfectly clear on its principles, is especially prone to the changeability that Aristotle discusses in book 7, *akrasia*, or the lapse of self-control. There he describes the way an incomplete understanding leaves people without a solid hold on what they think they know is best, so that frequently they do what they think they know is not best and their lives are spent tossing between self-control and lapses of control.

But if we are unsatisfied with this official account of *phronesis* in the *Ethics*, in which it purportedly guides the virtuous life yet ultimately is guided by it, Aristotle in fact gives us signposts throughout the *Ethics* to a second and perhaps ultimately better way of conceiving of *phronesis*. One such signpost is his suggestion that the soul may not in fact have separate parts, so that passions and judgments about good and bad are just two sides of the same movements of the soul toward perceived goods and away from perceived evils. According to this thought there would be no separate parts of the rational part either, and the art, science, *phronesis*, intelligence, and theoretical wisdom that he discusses in book 6 would be not separate entities but different aspects or characteristic activities of a single human intellect. This thought fits with a number of suggestions that *phronesis* is in fact closely related to both art and theoretical wisdom. Often Aristotle uses the medical art's study of bodily health as an analogy to his own investigation into the soul. The soul's healthy thriving according to nature would on this model be the goal of practical wisdom. Likewise, although he says that *phronesis* governs matters for which there is no art, he in fact begins the *Ethics* with the proposition that there is an art of arts, the political art, that pursues the human good simply. If the goal of this art is nothing other than human happiness according to nature, and it is theoretical wisdom whose task it is to understand the natures of all beings, theoretical wisdom would in fact not have a separate sphere from practical wisdom but an overlapping or even the same sphere. For all of philosophy's most serious questions are relevant to the human good and to our understanding of the nature of the cosmos in which we find ourselves, what it demands of us, where we stand in it, what our own natures and natural needs are, and what is possible for us. That would mean that *phronesis* is simply applied wisdom or wisdom in action or active wisdom, which is perhaps its best English translation. On this understanding, *phronesis* is in a sense higher than first appears, being an aspect of wisdom simply, but in another sense humbler than Aristotle's gentlemanly primary audience is inclined to think. Its realm is not after all quite action for its own sake, but rather action with a view to meeting the needs and desires nature gives us, including the desire to know, and finding such happiness as their satisfaction allows.

Thus the *Ethics* in fact adumbrates two forms of *phronesis*. The first, presented in the foreground or official account, is allegedly the perfection of an opining part of the soul and actually the distillation of conventional wisdom, often offering good guidance but ultimately resting only on opinion or trust. The second and higher form of *phronesis* is simply wisdom in action, the work of a profound philosophical investigation into human nature, theoretically more adequate yet dangerous in its habits of critical questioning that can easily become destructive. By foregrounding the former teaching, Aristotle shows his judgment that philosophy can make its most constructive contribution to a people's collective life by supporting and clarifying the most serious and noblest strands of its conventional wisdom, and especially its judgment that virtuous activity lies at the center of a good life. By making this project the introduction to the human good also for his young philosophic students, Aristotle indicates moreover that even for those aspiring to go furthest in philosophy and most inclined to engage in critical questioning, the best starting point for their study is to listen as quietly and receptively as possible to just this dialogue between the philosopher and their most respected elders, as the philosopher gently interrogates their outlook while also powerfully evoking these elders' and the young students' own deepest moral attachments and highest aspirations. To move too quickly through this investigation, to attempt too radical a liberation from conventional opinion, is to risk becoming a skeptic or even a cynic alienated from both one's own community and the deepest yearnings of one's own heart.

PHRONESIS AND THE PROBLEM OF FREE SPEECH

Let us consider, then, how Aristotelian *phronesis* might inform our thinking on one fraught question of our time especially relevant to the academy: the issue of freedom of speech. This issue is important for America because it is a basic principle of our regime that speech and the press, religious thought and thought of all kind should be free, and that leaders should be chosen and public policy determined on the basis of good information and reasoned deliberation. It is likewise a bedrock principle of the university that it should welcome the unfettered study of every question that presents itself as important, and we have seen how even the most controversial problems benefit from an open exploration of all possible solutions. Yet today, with our republic beset by polarization and a proliferation of conspiracy theories, with an openly partisan press, with social media actively pushing disinformation and stoking animosities, with heightened concerns about subtle racism and microaggressions, with calls for the disinvitation or canceling of allegedly pernicious speech and speakers, and with the erosion of trust in science and indeed in truth altogether, it is not clear how to find common ground on the issue our common discourse. In this impasse, what might the spirit and example of Aristotelian *phronesis* have to offer us?

Following Aristotle's indications about the importance of the regime and the example of his own procedure in writing the *Ethics*, we might begin with thought that it is an essential task of political theory to make the case for the best version of what we are. For classical Greece this was the regime that balanced democracy with aristocracy and the ethos of the gentleman that sets the tone for a moderate mixed regime. For us it is constitutional democracy and the spirit of the self-reliant, freedom-loving, civically engaged patriot. Now the commitments to freedom of the mind and reasoned inquiry are foundational virtues of our regime. At all times in America but especially in times of turmoil and national soul-searching, young citizens need to revisit their nation's basic principles and think deeply about the fundamental human questions to which they offer one compelling set of answers. Yet *phronesis* teaches that this task is a delicate one, that we must be mindful of the dangers of endeavoring to question everything and the deep need humans have for a sense of belonging, unquestioned attachment, and reverence. Thus, at the heart of our commitment to the freedoms that include freedom of speech and press is this paradox and challenge: to thrive as one people we may need to share certain common principles and beliefs, yet the commitment to free speech is a commitment to allowing the open questioning of all principles and beliefs.

In light of all this, Aristotelian *phronesis* requires that we reflect more deeply on the principle of freedom of speech itself and its ends. Now our founders were well aware that they were embarking on a new, untried experiment as they set out to enshrine this and other enlightenment principles in the Constitution. They were aware, for example, of the arguments of Montesquieu, their brightest guiding light, that the principle of republics is virtue, that the virtuous and free Roman republic rightly made terrific demands on its people, keeping the citizens poor and the city rich, and that the time when Rome could reasonably allow greatest freedom for the people to say and believe whatever they wanted was after the republic became corrupt and had fallen under the rule of an emperor. The republic depended on the character and dedication of its citizens; the empire did not. But our founders argued that with the right constitutional structure and the right republican education, it was possible to make room for more individual liberty and more genuine openness than republics in the past had managed to afford their citizens, and that this individual liberty could be put together with collective political liberty or self-government better than proponents of classical republicanism had supposed. This was a noble and daring experiment, one that we are still trying to demonstrate can work.

In the founders' understanding, our First Amendment freedoms were not absolute rights or ends in themselves but fundamental principles of government, grounded in arguments about the ends they could serve: freeing people from unnecessary and hence unjustified governmental interference with their religion, promoting the benefits of scientific discovery, and above all enabling the thorough vetting and review of policies and leaders that democracy requires. Thus the freedoms of speech and press were directly tied to their end of promoting rational self-government for the people collectively and the intelligent conduct of personal affairs for each individually. In keeping with this end, it is fitting and significant that what the founders affirmed as worthy of constitutional protection was the freedom to speak and write and print—the free exchange of knowledge and ideas—and not what has become the more common idiom of recent decades, the freedom of expression. They were not affirming an inalienable right of individuals to vent their feelings in any way they might wish, but a precious sphere for reasoned inquiry, persuasion, and common deliberation, precious because of the good life that it helps to constitute. Unlike conversation, self-expression is a one-way street. It becomes a right with no accompanying responsibility to listen and engage rationally with one another. Even if in practice we cannot safely protect good arguments without also protecting bad ones (which we cannot), or protect calm reasoning without also protecting impassioned rants (which we cannot), it matters that we stay clear on what we are intent on protecting and why.

These ideas were part of a new science of politics that the founders thought had brought the most important political truths to light for all time. So they opened the country up to free debates about politics on the basis of a confidently affirmed common civic faith. As Thomas Jefferson said in his first inaugural address, "If there be any among us who would wish to dissolve this Union, or to change its republican form, let them stand undisturbed as monuments of the safety with which error of opinion may be tolerated, where reason is left free to combat it." But as all of the founders also saw, and none more keenly than Jefferson, the project would work only with an education designed to teach our republican principles and to instill the democratic virtues a free society needs.

In the latter part of the twentieth century we witnessed a creeping expansion of relativism that undermined confidence in the tenets of Jefferson's civic faith, and free speech itself came to be most often defended on relativistic grounds. This defense was incoherent, for if there is no truth, democracy is no better than totalitarianism and free speech no better than forcibly silencing those with whom we disagree. Little wonder then that the Left's defense of free speech, once so uncompromising, has frayed. But in a fascinating development that offers confirmation to Aristotle's own observations about human nature, this relativism is already giving way to new forms of moral fervor, spawning new forms of intolerance on campus and in public discourse. It seems that we are, just as Aristotle taught, deeply social and political beings who need to draw sustenance from belonging to a community with shared moral commitments. As we witness the resurgence of crude tribalism and illiberalism on the Right and the eruption of simplistic thinking about social justice and vengefulness on the Left, we also see confirmation of Aristotle's recognition that the human moral and political instincts need long and careful education if we are to wrest and keep ourselves out of barbarism. Hence a crucial task of the university is to elicit students' yearning for a just cause to which to dedicate themselves and to educate this yearning, teaching them how to think carefully about the difficult problem that justice is and to listen to arguments that challenge their unexamined assumptions.

Yet the depths of our divisions again provoke the question of whether a successful nation does not require a shared national faith—if not a religious faith, at any rate a common identity built on a set of unquestioned principles to which we all adhere. But if every people does indeed need this, how is this need realizable for us today, and how is it compatible with our adherence to the ideal of intellectual freedom, including precisely the freedom to raise radical questions?

Again taking guidance from Aristotle's example of articulating for a people the best version of itself to which it might aspire, we may provisionally say this: Americans do not need an orthodoxy that is beyond question. We do not need to believe in Locke's state of nature or Jefferson's God. Certainly we do not need an established religion. But we do need shared aspirations and hopes; we need to be dedicated to a common project. And, both as citizens and as members of our own university, we need to consider seriously that this project may demand more of each of us than we have been inclined to think.

As a nation, what we need is a rededication simply to our noble and still unproved experiment of trying to make liberty work for a whole people over the long run, including in our new, more complicated, and more diverse world. This is the experiment Lincoln spoke of in the Gettysburg Address when he called American democracy the last best hope on earth. As Lincoln also reflected, for example in his address "The Perpetuation of Our Political Institutions," the glue we need to hold us together must be more than merely a shared commitment to cold ideas and bare procedures such as majority rule and checks and balances. Rather, we need to find it in us to love our country—for its promise, if not for its record so far in achieving it. We need to find a way to celebrate our national heroes for their good ideals and the steps they took toward them, even if they left us work to do in finishing what they began. We need to find better ways to talk about justice, better ways to listen to one another, better ways to take seriously the hunger for meaning that we share, and to make respectful room for each other's ways of seeking it, even while continuing to engage one another. One important part of this project is developing a national narrative that is both inspiring and honest. An excellent example is Wilfred McClay's American history text *Land of Hope: An Invitation to the Great American Story*.

As a university, we need a renewed dedication to a common project of pursuing truth, with a working faith that truth can be found and that more open discussions can yield richer understandings, with a willingness to bravely if carefully question anything, and with a shared sense of the importance of this project and the difficulty of getting it right. If Aristotle is right about the close connection between the intellectual and moral virtues, our task involves envisioning together the kind of community of thoughtful discourse we want to create and the virtues and habits we might need to cultivate to make robust free speech work well for us. With a view to advancing that discussion, I would like to suggest a few more virtues and habits to supplement *phronesis* itself.

Perhaps most fundamentally, a university needs a spirit of inquiry, curiosity, and intellectual openness. This means actively welcoming diversity, especially viewpoint diversity, and ensuring that diverse perspectives, including views that we ourselves oppose, are heard and taken seriously in our classrooms. It includes respecting others' rights to speak and publish their thoughts, whatever they are; to hear any speakers they wish to invite to address them; and to debate any question they wish to raise. Most of all, it means a commitment to depth of inquiry, to asking hard questions, connecting them to more fundamental questions, and helping one another to articulate and test different answers to them.

The second virtue a university needs is intellectual honesty. This virtue, rooted in the love of truthfulness and even more the love of truth, is the essential source of all genuine fair-mindedness. Intellectual honesty begins with the determination to discover and question one's own prejudices and unexamined assumptions. It continues with the process of continually striving to frame one's ideas in ways that recognize the merits of alternative views, that invite testing and correction, and that show a willingness to learn from discussion.

Third, we need civility. Civility means not just politeness or tact; civility constitutes the habits of discourse necessary to sustain a free, self-governing community. We often think of civility as primarily a quality of speech, but true civility begins with the way we listen to others before we speak. Civility means hearing the other out, seriously trying to understand the other's experience and thoughts, looking for common ground, and making certain and evident that one has understood the other before voicing disagreement. Civility means presenting one's own arguments in such a way as to maximize the chances of their being fairly considered and to minimize the chances of deepening divisions. It means avoiding sweeping generalizations. It means responding to arguments with counterarguments and not by impugning others' motives. Civility means respect. It means refraining from vilifying, demeaning, or spreading rumors about any individual or group. It means never assuming that another is unable to learn or improve, and never assuming that someone who does not share our experiences or background is incapable of understanding us or of joining in any intellectual inquiry. When problems arise, civility means confronting them honestly and directly, in ways designed to build or restore mutual trust. The American Association of University Professors, in its statement on academic freedom, makes a good case that it is best not to try to legislate civility. The lines between civility and incivility are hard to draw with the blunt instrument of the law, especially when we get so close to vital rights that involve us in passionate disagreements. Except in extreme cases formal sanctions are not well suited to instill the behavior we need on campuses, for at heart civility is a matter not of following rules but of intention, judgment, and good taste. But if civility cannot be legislated, that is all the more reason why it is incumbent on each of us to practice it and to gently, civilly push our friends to practice it too.

Finally, we need to cultivate resilience. It takes resilience to tolerate the rough-and-tumble of free debate. Ideas are powerful and can be powerfully disturbing, and diverse communities can be uncomfortable. But resilience can be learned. It is possible to learn to take pride in being open to learning and in being able to acknowledge what we do not know. Socrates claims it is in fact better to lose an argument than to win it: when we lose, he says, we learn more. Resilience means realizing that someone else's rudeness or insensitivity is something about them—or indeed merely about their momentary state of mind—and not something about us. Resilience means knowing that we have options: we can get angry if we want to, but we do not have to. Resilience means taking pride in finding the resources we need to solve our own problems and to create the kind of life we want for ourselves and our community.

No citizen can think every important question through independently to the bottom, and most of us can at most hope to find good guides to trust and imitate. But we can all do a better job of listening, suspending judgment, and cultivating open-mindedness and fair-mindedness. We can learn to take pride in becoming more rational and more curious versions of the beings that we are. If we do, we may succeed in bequeathing to the next generation an American academy that can be a blessing to all of us.

NOTES

1. This essay is adapted in part from my essay "The Task of the Liberal Arts in Troubled Times," *Heterodox Academy Blog*, September 9, 2020, and is based in part on my book *Reason and Character: The Moral Foundations of Aristotelian Political Philosophy*.

All quotations from Aristotle in this essay are taken from the *Nicomachean Ethics* and are cited in the text by Stephanus number. Translations are my own.

BIBLIOGRAPHY

Aristotle. *Ethica Nicomachea*. Edited by I. Bywater. Oxford: Clarendon Press, 1894.
Lincoln, Abraham. "The Perpetuation of Our Political Institutions." Speech presented at the Young Men's Lyceum of Springfield, Illinois, January 27, 1838.

McClay, Wilfred. *Land of Hope: An Invitation to the Great American Story*. New York: Encounter Books, 2020.

Pangle, Lorraine. *Reason and Character: The Moral Foundations of Aristotelian Political Philosophy*. Chicago: University of Chicago Press, 2020.

———. "The Task of the Liberal Arts in Troubled Times." *Heterodox Academy Blog*, September 9, 2020.

2. Two Cheers for Deparochialization
Clifford Orwin

AS YOU MAY HAVE RECOGNIZED, the "Two Cheers" of my title is an indication of its genre. The inventor of that genre was likely the British novelist and critic E. M. Forster, who mustered *Two Cheers for Democracy* in 1951. Another celebrated cheer miser was Irving Kristol, who raised just *Two Cheers for Capitalism* in 1978. Forster could not be thought hostile to democracy, or Kristol to capitalism. Rather, each sought to benefit his subject, but to do so as only a friend of unusual candor could. It is in the same spirit that I offer this far more modest discussion of "deparochialization" and its potential contribution to liberal education.

What is deparochialization? It is roughly coextensive with the practice of comparative political theory, which seeks to broaden the scope of the latter by giving "non-Western" (including aboriginal) perspectives their due. Comparative political theorists seek to foster genuine dialogue among the world's vast variety of outlooks on political life, most of which have until recently received short shrift.

Should you be unfamiliar with the discourse of comparative political theory, you might begin with the excellent recent collection edited by my colleague Melissa S. Williams.[1] Several years in the making, the volume brings together numerous luminaries in this newish field. It includes both general discussions of comparative political theory as a practice and applications of it to particular regions and issues. Professor Williams also provides an excellent introduction to the current state of the enterprise. Of special interest to readers of this volume will be the two contributions that explicitly consider comparative political thought as an aspect of liberal education: those of Stephen G. Salkever and Terry Nardin.[2]

As for what I mean by liberal education, I was pleased to see that is not fundamentally different from what Salkever and Nardin mean by it. Here I can do no better than to cite some excellent recent statements by Jonathan Marks. "Liberally educated people will . . . know what it's like to put the question of what one is and of how one should live at the center of their concerns, and be familiar with the pleasure, usefulness, and freedom of reflecting on these questions. . . . [They will share] an experience of and a taste for reflecting on fundamental questions, for following arguments where they lead, and for shaping their thoughts and actions in accordance with what they can learn from those activities."[3]

So yes, liberal education so understood (and as I suppose that most readers of this volume understand it) presumes the existence of fundamental questions. (Which is not to say that it depends on a claim to have provided satisfactory [that is, dogmatic] answers to these.) It is in the context of liberal education so conceived that we will consider "deparochialization."

OF CANONS AND OTHER READING LISTS

By identifying itself as a process, deparochialization implies the existence of an object in need of processing. The most frequently designated such object is "the canon." Hardly anything on campus wears a blacker hat than it these days. It has become proverbial for narrowness (to say nothing of phallocentrism, white privilege, and any number of other offenses). You can hardly position yourself less advantageously in the current campus culture wars than as a defender of the canon. Yet that is the position generally ascribed to defenders of liberal education by their adversaries and all too often by themselves.

There is, however, nothing particularly "deparochializing" about such an ideologically motivated critique of the "canon." Indeed, it is merely an expression of the latest (and therefore, temporally speaking, the very most parochial) Western prejudice, which is therefore not to be confused with "deparochialization" in the serious sense. Salkever puts this with admirable conciseness.

> Confucius and Xunzi and Plato and Aristotle are not our contemporaries and must not be read as if they were. They do not share our endoxa, or our imaginaries, or our immediate pasts and futures. On

the other hand, they also must not be read as if they either confirmed "our" sense of our own moral and intellectual superiority (as good democratic opponents of various forms of dogmatic despotism) or, at the opposite extreme of the student expectations I have encountered, "our" sense of the moral and intellectual bankruptcy of modern Western materialism and individualism.[4]

It is a mistake to cast liberal education (including the teaching of "canonical" thinkers) as implying either presumed support of the status quo or presumed opposition to it. Liberal education is in bed with no party, and to present it as being so is to subvert its goals at the outset.

At the same time, precisely as defenders of liberal education we must concede something to critics of the canon. There is in fact no necessary connection between liberal education and deference to anything like a canon. Canons originated in religion, and there the term should have remained. A canon for Episcopalians makes perfect sense. Liberal education not being a church, it can and should dispense with the notion.

But aren't some books more worth reading than others, for undergraduates as for the rest of us? Yes. Are there books that every student should read to become an educated human being? Yes again. It's a long and diverse list, however, too long for a course or even a four-year curriculum. (Too long even for the curriculum at an institution like St. John's College, which devotes the whole of its program to teaching great books, yet always and inevitably comes up short.)

Nor could we fall back on a noncontroversial shorter "canon." You would expect some overlap among good-faith versions of such a list but nothing close to agreement. No two courses are alike: each is inevitably specific to its place, time, and institution, as well as to its function in the program of that institution. Inevitably, reasonable colleagues will disagree as to the curriculum appropriate to that course.

But this, in my view, is precisely the appropriate disagreement, not over the canon (which is a red herring) but over curriculum. Works from someone's version of a canon may well belong in many or most introductory undergraduate courses, not because of their authority as canonical, but because of their appropriateness to the course in question. By the same token, works not previously recognized as canonical, or that may belong to some canon other than the alleged Western one, or to that of some discipline but not to the supposed one of political theory, may be appropriate to a course. I knew a great teacher who slipped *Gulliver's Travels* and *Madame Bovary* into his introductory political theory course. No one would include either of these in any version of a political theory canon, yet they worked brilliantly in that particular course.

For this reason, I have never resented others exercising their discretion in course design and have never hesitated to do so myself. Did a colleague offering a version of our large introductory course in the history of political thought devote several lectures to Christine de Pizan (1382–1433) while slighting Machiavelli? Did I in my section of the course stick with my long-ingrained practice of a lengthy and intensive reading of *The Prince*, while continuing to ignore Ms. de Pizan? Machiavelli was a titan of thought; Christine was not. On the other hand, she did provide a woman's point of view, not to mention a female role model. For my purpose of challenging my students' views on justice by presenting them with the most radical critique of it available, Machiavelli remained the man for the job. My colleague's priorities were different.

So too for the rest of my version of our large introductory course. As justice is the fundamental question of political philosophy, so it supplies the focus of the course. Yes, we honor the tradition that this particular course covers Western political thought from Plato through Locke. (A sequel picks up where it leaves off.) And yes, we read only famous names and works: Plato's *Republic*, Aristotle's *Politics*, *The Prince*, Hobbes's *Leviathan*, and Locke's *Second Treatise* and *Letter on Toleration*. Yet I have chosen just these works, six to be read over the entire year, to sharpen the focus on justice. And I present them in an eccentric order (Machiavelli, Hobbes, and Locke in the first semester, Plato and Aristotle in the second) and with an emphasis on *The Prince* (to whom we devote six of our twelve weeks in the fall) and the *Republic* (nine of our twelve weeks in the spring). As a result, the course reaches its climax with my discussion of Plato's cave.

In introducing students to political philosophy, it is my firm conviction that less is more. Only by wrestling through close reading with the arguments of these first-rate thinkers can the students make them their own and reflect on the implications for their own lives. Yes, this carries an opportunity cost: I omit medieval thought altogether, as well as the works of the chosen thinkers other than the handful just listed. If there was enough and time, I would include additional thinkers and works, but given the painstaking reading I practice, there isn't.

This then is one reason I would not introduce non-Western thinkers into the course: our hands are full as it is. Additional works, whether familiar or novel, would dilute the course more than they would enrich it. Nor is there anything parochial about an understanding of justice based on the study of these writings, as among them they make the cases for it and against it (as well as exploring different understandings of it) as well as can be done for the purposes of introductory teaching. So it appears to me, anyway. By requiring students to wrestle with fewer works over a longer period of time, we can foster a deeper appreciation not only of the works but crucially of the problems posed by them. It makes an awfully big difference for the students' grasp of the problem of justice whether they have spent just four weeks on Plato's *Republic* (the better to leave room for Augustine or the Bhaghavad Gita) or nine.

Most of my colleagues, even those keenest on deparochialization, seem to agree that the usual Western suspects must occupy most of the room at least in an introductory course. For them the question is how much you can abbreviate your treatment of these works in order to make room for non-Western ones. That question is perfectly sensible. It may be merely my quirk and my students' misfortune that my answer to it is not at all, given my intensely textual approach. For me the relevant query is how to lobby Ontario's provincial legislature to expand our much too short academic year (just twenty-four weeks of instruction) to give me more time to cover the works that I treat already.

Constraints of time weigh heavily in considering a further drawback to presenting the literature of non-Western traditions. A fling with Buddhism (of which more below) taught me that Indian, Tibetan, and Chinese works are bashful. They require extensive introduction before they consent even to begin to disclose themselves to Western readers. How much time must we spend to instill in our students that considerable understanding of Indian society required to make sense of Indian works? Having done so will we then have adequate time for the works themselves? Can we at least leverage the time spent explaining Indian society to them by continuing to focus on Indian books as our examples of non-Western approaches? Or would that be unfair to the Chinese (just to begin a list that could be extended at length)?

DEPAROCHIALIZATION IN AN AGE OF IGNORANCE

No, we can't presume that many of our students know much about non-Western thought. The "deparochializers" have that right. Unfortunately, however, neither can we presume those students "parochial" in any positive sense, that is, knowledgeable about "Western" thought. In fact, they know little (if anything) more of Western history or thought than of its non-Western counterparts. Plato and Moses are as foreign to most of them as Lao Tzu. I've had students acquainted with neither the Renaissance nor the Reformation, neither Michelangelo nor Martin Luther.

Under these circumstances we must not neglect the continuing civic function of a liberal education. My own university claims to educate citizens of the world. Either it counts on their high schools to have educated them as citizens of Canada, or it sees no distinction between these two tasks. Yes, this era of globalization calls for us to cultivate a certain global awareness in our students. Even so, there is no such thing as global citizenship, so the task of educating for it is specious. The necessity of preparing students to be citizens of their own countries remains. So I see little justification for an introductory course devoted to "decentering" a body of thought that has already lost whatever centrality it formerly enjoyed, while remaining crucial to informed citizenship. What my Canadian students need most from me is enrichment of the thin gruel that passes for their understanding of the Western tradition.

To which I must add that not all my students at Toronto are Canadians, or "Westerners" of any description. Among our undergraduates, as most likely among yours, there is a growing presence of foreign students, many the children of illiberal societies. They know even less about the basics of liberal democracy than our North American students. To these students, then, the paradigm of "deparochialization" is irrelevant. At the same time, at least some of them are deeply eager to learn "Western" ways. As a Chinese student recently insisted to me (in private, of course), it was not to learn about Marxism that he decided to study in Canada instead of China. (Nor was it to learn about Confucianism.)

Indeed, a majority even of Canadian undergraduates at Toronto hail from homes in which English is not the first language spoken. Most are immigrants or the children of immigrants from non-Western societies, the first generation of their families to attend university. They look to higher education not for deparochialization but for a further progress in their Canadianization. Paradoxically, as increased globalization generates unparalleled levels of immigration, so it underlines the increasing centrality to liberal education of transmitting the tradition of Western thought to students unfamiliar with it. So yes, I favor not decentering the neglected foundations of liberal democratic thought but recentering and renewing them.

This is not to say that the task of liberal education is ever one of indoctrination into the status quo. Indoctrination of whatever sort, into whatsoever, is incompatible with the fundamental goal of liberal education: to foster students qualified to think for themselves. In teaching my introductory course, whether in considering liberal or protoliberal thinkers (Hobbes and Locke) or preliberal ones (Plato, Aristotle, and Machiavelli), I return constantly to liberal democracy and its problems. Even if one's intention is to problematize liberalism, however, one has to begin by clarifying it. To this end, Western works are for obvious reasons more useful than non-Western ones. These importantly include the preliberal Western works to which foundational liberal thinkers were responding and who provide the necessary background to their emergence.

None of which is to impugn introducing comparative political theory into the undergraduate curriculum. I would suggest, however, delaying that introduction until an intermediate or advanced stage of it. First things first, and that means a basic knowledge that is no less lacking to most of our students because both they and it are Western.

DEPAROCHIALIZATION AND ME: TWO EXPERIMENTS

I myself have undertaken two experiments in comparative political theory, one at least a modest success, the other mostly a failure. To end this section on a high note, I will relate the failure before the success.

In 1996, with the main scholarly achievement of my life, my book on Thucydides, already in hand, I decided on something completely different. I resolved to devote six months of my life to the study of Buddhist texts. I had recently lectured in South Korea and visited the most important Buddhist shrines there, which had piqued my interest in the subject. Not that I was a Buddhist in the making. This wasn't a matter of personal attraction. It was that I had heard—as perhaps have you—that Buddhism was the world's most compassionate religion. Compassion was one of my scholarly beats, and had been for the longest time—since my first essay as an undergraduate. It had furnished the subject for my dissertation—on the place of compassion in the thought of Rousseau—and for many essays and articles since. It therefore seemed just the right place to begin my adventure in Eastern thought.

There was also the happy coincidence that I had received an invitation to return to Korea to participate in the 1997 meeting of the International Political Science Association. The invitation came from the Korean Political Science Association, which by IPSA tradition was allotted a panel of its own. They proposed a panel in comparative political theory, featuring two Korean scholars and Fred R. Dallmayr of Notre Dame, distinguished scholar of twentieth-century Western thought and a pioneer in the then emergent field of comparative political theory. It was, so far as anyone knew, the first such panel ever held at IPSA. Professor Dallmayr would speak on a comparative topic in Confucianism and Western thought, and I was invited to do the same for Buddhism. Our Korean colleagues would speak on comparative topics as well. This invitation was not only an honor but an opportunity too good to decline.

I did not regret my participation in this panel, nor any other aspect of my six months' foray into Buddhism. In the end, however, I was less enlightened than perplexed. It wasn't just that I still found myself bound to the wheel of *Samsara*, as far from nirvana as ever. I had expected that. As mentioned, I hadn't been looking to become a Buddhist. Nor was it that the scholars of Buddhism whom I consulted in person had been less than welcoming. In fact, they had proved unfailingly helpful. Last, the problem wasn't that the six months I had allotted to my task proved too little, for that too I had anticipated. Rather, it was my inability to see a way forward to accomplishing my original intention: to establish my understanding of Buddhism on a firm-enough footing to introduce it into my teaching.

The difficulty here was twofold. On the one hand, Buddhist literature was endlessly voluminous. Over the millennia since the Buddha, so many Buddhist sects had flourished, each claiming to possess the true understanding of his teachings, each generating its own corpus of scriptures. Buddhism had successfully adapted over these millennia to a remarkable diversity of societies—India, Ceylon, Tibet, those of Southeast Asia, China, Korea, and

Japan—and, lacking any central doctrinal authority, the abundance of sects had rung every change imaginable on the Buddha's core teachings. (In this respect the history of Buddhism is not so different from that of Christianity, just even longer.)

The obverse of the variety and voluminosity of these materials was their inaccessibility. It didn't help that they had been composed in so many different and often unrelated languages—Pali, Sanskrit, Tibetan, Chinese, and Japanese, for starters. Few even of the most eminent scholars of Buddhism could lay claim to all of these. To an interloper this Babel posed an insuperable obstacle. It left me entirely reliant on translations the accuracy of which I was unable to gauge. Given, moreover, the proliferation of Buddhist texts, anthologies of Buddhist thought were the rule, condemning the reader to the bane of the serious scholar, a diet of preselected snippets.

Where a text had been translated in its entirety, that was a step in the right direction, but I remained the helpless victim of the translator. Because in my teaching of Western works I had confined myself almost entirely to works accessible to me in their original languages, I was painfully conscious that I confronted Buddhism as a blind man incapable of knowing whether my guides were so much as one-eyed. With all respect for scholars and translators of Buddhism, I simply wasn't used to being so abjectly dependent on the decisions of others.

That these texts were in need of interpretation in order to be intelligible to an outsider like myself posed yet a further barrier. Were the thinkers of the Madhyamaka school and their master Nāgārjuna (ca. 150–250 CE?) really precursors of postmodernism?[5] Who was I to say, without access to the original texts? Consider also that the thinkers of the Mahayāna school (which would emerge as predominant and of which Madhyamaka was a subgroup) openly avowed their practice of esoteric reading and writing. They read the older scriptures esoterically in deciphering the true teachings of the Buddha and wrote their own esoterically in presenting these to a world still not entirely ready for them. Just how deep did this esotericism go? Deep enough to imply a challenge of the very teachings they presented to the wider public as authoritative, as would prove the case with certain leading writers of the Middle Ages, whether Islamic, Jewish, or Christian? Without access to the texts in their entirety and their original languages, I was simply in no position to experiment with any such reading.

I can't deny that I learned from my six-month immersion in Buddhist texts. Certainly, on the issue of compassion (my motive for turning to Buddhism in the first place), I came to see Western humanitarianism in a new light. It now seemed superficial in comparison with the *Mahākaruṇā* (ultimate compassion) of the Bodhisattva. Buddhism addressed the problem of the all-pervasiveness of suffering in life with a rigor that humanitarianism lacked. (At the same time, *Mahākaruṇā* had problems of its own, not least its political quietism.)

Yet, as already stated, when the six months had elapsed, for all the reading I had done I did not judge myself competent to introduce Buddhist materials into my teaching. Nor, I foresaw, was I likely ever to judge myself to be so. Was I asking too much of myself here? Was it excessive to apply the same standards to which I submitted in teaching Western thinkers, namely, access to the works in their original languages? After all, if I was not to make an exception for works written in an Eastern language, I could have predicted from the outset that no Buddhist work would find its way into my syllabus.

Yet in the end this reservation was only reinforced by the others I have mentioned. Condemned as I was by my ignorance of the languages and cultures to remain a dilettante, and with no reasonable prospect of repairing these deficiencies, the gulf between my understanding of these works and of the Western ones I taught seemed too great to bridge. It seemed downright unfair to Buddhism to approach it with so much less care than I made a point of according Western thought. So not only Buddhism but Taoism, Confucianism, and so on, I similarly left to go their own ways.

Yet that I was the wrong person to take this step (or that it was too late in my career for me to do it) surely does not imply that no one could. There is none of my students of whom I'm prouder than one who has moved in a comparative direction. That is Lincoln Rathnam, who currently teaches at Duke Kunshan University in the city of that name just outside Shanghai. Having resolved at an early age to master Mandarin, he spent the requisite years to do so, including many months of studies in China. He proceeded to write a dissertation on a highly demanding topic in comparative political theory, comparing the political thought of Montaigne with that of another reputed skeptic, the Taoist thinker Zhuangzi of the Warring States period.[6] This project required him to master not only the two difficult languages and different epochs but the large and entirely distinct literatures on his two subjects. His achievement would have been impossible without the enthusiastic collaboration of the late professor Vincent Shen of Toronto's East Asian Studies Department, a renowned scholar of ancient Chinese thought. Vincent cosupervised and on the completion of the dissertation hosted a celebratory formal Chinese dinner. A revised version is forthcoming from Oxford University Press in its Comparative Political Theory series. It represents the most ambitious project in the comparative history of political thought to emerge from our department.

I am also proud of the fact that not just Rathnam but two other political theorists at Duke Kunshan wrote their dissertations under my direction. One of these is Lindsay Mahon Rathnam, who wrote hers on Herodotus as the founder of comparative political theory. William B. Parsons, the senior of the three and a specialist in Machiavelli, enjoys not just tenurability but tenure. A joint venture of Duke University, the Chinese government, and the municipality of Kunshan, Duke Kunshan aims to provide a genuinely multicultural liberal education, equally featuring Chinese works and Western ones, to a student body drawn in equal parts from China, the Chinese diaspora, and non-Chinese communities. I'm honored that the founders of Duke Kunshan entrusted so much of its political theory program to these students of mine.

Last, I'm delighted that my son Alexander has pursued a comparative path, in his case bringing Islamic thinkers into dialogue with both classical thinkers and modern Western ones, and introducing such comparison into his teaching at both the graduate and the undergraduate levels. For that of course he has been required to learn classical Arabic and several other relevant languages, and to learn them well. Surely a necessary if not sufficient test of the seriousness of one's engagement with comparative political thought must be proficiency in at least one non-Western culture and therefore with the language of that culture. All the rest is just jousting with phantoms (as in my foray into Buddhism), and perpetual dependence on scholars whose expertise exceeds your own.

If my venture into Buddhism proved no more than a mixed blessing, there was another more fortunate experiment, this one a graduate seminar. It requires more explanation, being a less obvious instance of "deparochialization." Here my project has been not so much to reshape what others would describe as the canon, but to "decanonize" and thereby to liberate and, yes, deparochialize it.

The format of the course is simple. It is a combined graduate/undergraduate seminar, it runs for the full year, and we meet three and a half hours per week to allow for ample discussion. We read three texts, one from the Hebrew Bible, one classical, and one modern, that address a common theme. In one version of the course, for example, that theme was the origins of society and their implications for understanding political life. We read the book of Genesis, Lucretius's *On the Nature of Things*, and Rousseau's *Discourse on the Origins of Inequality*. In another, the theme of which was leadership, we read Exodus, Leviticus, and Numbers (taken as a single unbroken narrative of the career of Moses); Xenophon's *Anabasis*; and Rousseau's *Political Economy*. This format has permitted me to deepen my understanding of the Hebraic tradition without disappointing my graduate students, most of whom have come to Toronto to study the Hellenic and modern ones. So far none have complained about all the time we spend on the Bible.

All the readings for this course thus fall within the purview of what most people would call Western civilization—except that, in fact, as I have already suggested, neither the Hebrews nor the Hellenes belonged to "Western civilization." Their works were later co-opted or (as the saying goes today, appropriated) by Western civilization and reinterpreted accordingly as its predecessors. This isn't to deny that Western civilization, emerging as it did from the ashes of the Roman Empire after the latter's Christianization, was from the outset both Christian and the heir to classical civilization, albeit at first in its Roman rather than Hellenic version. There followed a complicated history that included a rediscovery of Hellenic thought at first through the mediation of Islamic and Jewish philosophy and then through the westward migration of Greek scholars and manuscripts following the fall of Constantinople. Theological, hermeneutic, and subsequently academic traditions coalesced around both sets of writings. Beginning in the nineteenth century both science (in the form of modern philology) and historicism (the classic form of modern philosophy) have further enriched and complicated the study of these works—while also further distancing us from them.

The aspiration of my seminar has been to rescue Hebraic and Hellenic texts from their pigeonholing as "Western." We have sought to liberate them from the received wisdom that views them as foundational for the Western understanding but for that very reason as superseded by it. This requires reading them with new eyes provisionally freed from the blinders of traditions of exegesis that have perforce been only too Western traditions. Our aim in the course has been to permit these texts to speak with their own distinctive (and distinctly non-Western) voices. So read (and only so read) can these books be enlisted in the urgent task of the self-understanding and self-criticism of the West.

On this last point there is then no disagreement between me and others who promote deparochialization. We both seek to broaden the discussion by introducing non-Western perspectives. The only difference is that the non-Western perspectives of which I suppose myself the most useful interpreter are these "pre-Western" ones. They are the ones whose texts are accessible to me in their entirety and in the original languages, as any intensive study of them requires. They are the ones to which I may devote myself without excuse or embarrassment. They are the ones to which I may apply my modest gifts as an interpreter without the vast reservations imposed by ignorance of the original languages.

You don't need to tell me that my chosen task of navigating among three such different outlooks as the Hellenic, Hellenic, and Western is already a hard one. Indeed, many today would proclaim it impossible. They would deny that the minds of those long dead and separated from us by such deep chasms of every kind can disclose themselves to us. Yet by this point in the history of the West, must we not regard such historicism as itself another Western convention as subject to question as all the rest? (An uncomfortable question for those partisans of "deparochialization" who understand their case for it to rest on just such historicism, thus offering a parochial Western justification of their project.) I should stress that as a questioner of historicism, it is not my claim that the Buddhist tradition was closed to me (or any ancient non-Western tradition closed to any scholar) because I or that scholar is modern and Western. Were there but world enough and time (to master the requisite languages and the necessary cultural baggage), I might have continued my Buddhist journey.

As for Hebraic and Hellenic texts, it can't be denied that they pose problems for their interpreters comparable to any other such rich and ancient traditions including those of South and East Asia. Even if understanding them is possible in principle, it proves exceedingly difficult in practice. Of this I forever remind my students and try to remember to remind myself. I intend this not as a counsel of despair, but as an injunction to try harder, returning to the texts again and again with the determination to get them right this time.

In interpreting the pre-Western legs of my tripod, I have sought inspiration from an earlier generation of scholars far superior to myself. These include Umberto Cassuto[7] and those who have followed his lead in interpreting the Bible afresh, rejecting the reductionism of the higher criticism and respectful of rabbinic readings but not always deferring to them. They also include Leo Strauss,[8] Pierre Vidal-Naquet, Arnaldo Momigliano, and Sergei Averintsev.[9] All have in their very different ways renewed our appreciation not only of the Hebraic and Hellenic traditions but of the complex relations between them. All have served me as models for the version of deparochialization described above, that of making the old and familiar new, strange and challenging again.

Among my many purposes in mounting this course is to demonstrate the following truth. The so-called Western tradition (even the so-called Western canon) is so far from being monolithic that it is an ongoing contest between incompatible alternatives of reason and revelation. These difficulties present themselves already in the clash of biblicism and Hellenism beginning from Alexander's conquest onward (in the thought of Philo and Josephus, for example, as in that of the church fathers culminating in Augustine), as well in the great medieval projects of philosophy undertaken in all three Abrahamic communities. Modern thought has proved unable to escape this difficulty despite its manifest ambition to do so. (Nietzsche and Heidegger, after all, in their rejection of modern Western rationalism, can be said to return to respective idiosyncratic versions of reliance on something more akin to revelation than reason.) For all these reasons, the supposed "Western" enterprise has been defined primarily by its tensions rather than by the agreement or homogeneity sometimes presumed by its critics. On the level of those thinkers worthy of consideration for purposes of liberal education, there is no Western "outlook"; there is only a web of problems discerned by Western thinkers (which is not to say that these problems have occurred only to Western thinkers). "Western tradition" is a misnomer.[10]

A BROADER SOCRATISM?

If a Chinese notable had appeared in Athens, proficient in Greek and ready to rumble, who can doubt that Socrates would have betaken himself to him? One way of viewing comparative political theory is in just this Socratic sense. Plato presents no Egyptian characters, but he himself had traveled to Egypt, as had Herodotus before him. Herodotus is a favorite author of mine and for just this reason: that he was the Hellene most concerned to discover what his countrymen could learn from foreigners. Without wishing to diminish the differences between Herodotus and the Socratics, there is a proto-Socratic aspect to his project. Self-knowledge, which is to say knowledge of what it means to be human, required knowledge of modes of human being other than the one in which you happen to have been raised. As Norma Thompson has argued, Herodotus prefigured postmodernism in his focus on rival narratives.[11] He differed from it in viewing these as ladders to a more adequate and authoritative narrative. So considered, comparative political theory or "deparochialization" implies no rejection of "Western" (actually, here, pre-Western) models, but the promotion of the one of those models most central to the notion of a liberal education.

True, it has been the fate of comparative political theory to be practiced primarily by postmodernists. There is, however, as I have just argued, no necessary connection between the two. One can confront "Western" (and pre-Western thought) with its non-Western counterparts in the nonhistoricist spirit just suggested. For some years now, Stephen G. Salkever, a noted scholar of Aristotle[12] who teaches at Bryn Mawr College, has expounded Chinese philosophy in his courses. He began by doing so in concert with Michael Nylan, a leading authority on Chinese thought.[13] Since Nylan's departure from Bryn Mawr, however, Salkever has continued teaching these courses without her. He nowhere claims to know Mandarin (although he must have amassed a significant glossary in his years of teaching with Nylan). That this has not deterred him merely confirms that he is not as particular on this subject as I am. In keeping with the credo endorsed earlier, it's his course and his call. At Bryn Mawr he teaches only undergraduates: Would he foist his Chinese-thought-in-translation on graduate students?

There is much in Salkever's and Nylan's account of their teaching that I found exemplary of what liberal education should be, not least that "each [of their] courses begins from a particular problem that seems to be shared by Chinese and European thinkers, and the principal activity in all of them is a close reading of a relatively small number of works."[14]

Salkever and Nylan obligingly include their course syllabi in their article. From these we learn that they included many authors both Hellenic and Chinese who spanned the whole range of genres. As emerges also from

Salkever's chapter in the Williams volume, he rejects any narrow or excessively disciplinary notion of what constitutes political philosophy as inimical to the spirit of a liberal education. As the world knows him primarily as a scholar of Aristotle, so Aristotle has played an important role in his comparative teaching. As he has stressed in his account of this experiment, Aristotle and the corresponding Chinese thinkers do not simply talk past each other. On the contrary they have much in common, sometimes over and against modern Western thinkers. Certainly, dialogue between them (and, consequently, among the students) is possible, and Salkever does his best to stage it.[15]

À chacun sa chacune. Some colleagues may conclude with Salkever that the advantages of a broader curriculum outweigh the drawbacks of one's lack of facility in the relevant languages. If only I had had the wit to solicit the collaboration of Vincent Shen in my teaching as in the Rathnam dissertation, I might have taken this road myself. My career is approaching its end, so what better time to indulge my proclivity for the avuncular? Here then are my final pronouncements. Best for younger scholars bent on the *via comparativa* would be to emulate Rathnam or my son by cultivating a non-Western language. Yet those for whom this is impossible may yet embrace Salkever's option as a mean. He is an Aristotelian, after all.

NOTES

1. Melissa S. Williams, ed., *Deparochializing Political Theory*.
2. Stephen G. Salkever, "Teaching Comparative Political Thought: Joys, Pitfall, Strategies, Significance"; Terry Nardin, "Teaching Philosophy and Political Thought in Southeast Asia." Note also the contributions of James Tully, "Deparochializing Political Theory and Beyond: A Dialogue Approach to Comparative Political Thought"; and Duncan Ivison, "Why Globalize the Curriculum?"
3. Jonathan Marks, *Let's Be Reasonable: A Conservative Argument for Liberal Education*, 11, 15. The book as a whole is not to be missed, as a powerful reply to all who trash liberal education whether from the Right or the Left.
4. Salkever, "Teaching Comparative Political Thought," 238.
5. As claimed by, for example, Kennard Lipman, "The *Cittamatra* and Its Madhyamika Critique: Some Phenomenological Reflections," 305; Joseph Magliola, *Derrida on the Mend*, 283–84; and Kenneth Liberman, "The Grammatology of Emptiness: Postmodernism, the Madhyamaka Dialectic, and the Limits of the Text." Liberman also likens the Madhyamaka position to that of Maurice Merleau-Ponty, *The Visible and the Invisible, Followed by Working Notes*.
6. Lincoln F. E. Rathnam, "The Politics of Skepticism: Montaigne and Zhuangzi on Freedom, Toleration, and the Limits of Government." See now also Rathnam, "Wandering in the Ruler's Cage: Zhuangzi as a Political Philosopher."

7. Umberto Cassuto, *The Documentary Hypothesis and the Composition of the Pentateuch; Eight Lectures*. Cassuto also authored magisterial commentaries on Exodus and Genesis (the latter of which remained unfinished at his death).

8. Much has been written about Strauss's project of recovering the classical writers in their pristine splendor and opening a dialogue between them and both the biblical and the modern traditions. A good place to begin is Arthur M. Melzer, "Esotericism and the Critique of Historicism," republished in revised form as chap. 10 of Melzer, *Philosophy between the Lines: The Lost History of Esoteric Writing*. For a thoughtful critique of Strauss's presentation of the ancient thinkers, see Victor Gourevitch, "Philosophy and Politics."

9. Pierre Vidal-Naquet, "Du bon usage de la trahison" and *Flavius Josèphe et la guerre des juifs*; Arnaldo Momigliano, *Alien Wisdom: The Limits of Hellenization* and *Essays on Ancient and Modern Judaism*; Sergei Averintsev, "Ancient Greek 'Literature' and Near Eastern 'Writings': The Opposition and Encounter of Two Creative Principles."

10. See the following comment of Nardin: "One might also object that the identity of the West is itself problematic because of its vast geographical, temporal, and cultural scope (especially if we include the ancient Mediterranean world) as well as the many changes it has undergone." Nardin, "Teaching Philosophy and Political Thought in Southeast Asia," 258. So too Salkever: "The term 'modern West' is a pleonasm. The West has no existence prior to its construction in Western Europe starting in the sixteenth and seventeenth centuries. It is a conceptual phenomenon that displaces Christendom just as Christendom once displaced the ancient Hellenic and Roman worlds. There is nothing, contra Hegel, Marx, and various liberal forms of Western progressivism, necessary or fated about these successive displacements. . . . Calling Plato and Aristotle 'Western' philosophers is thus profoundly misleading, though they are plausibly 'pre-Western'—that is, they are identified by the constructors of the modern West as members of a culture out of which the West necessarily emerged, an assertion that is, absent historicist assumptions, surely open to question." Salkever, "Teaching Comparative Political Thought," 244n37.

11. Norma Thompson, *Herodotus and the Origins of Political Community: Arion's Leap*. As already mentioned, Lindsay Mahon Rathnam has developed this side of Herodotus's thought in her dissertation: "Herodotean Journeys: Diversity and Political Judgment in Herodotus' *Histories*." See also her "The Madness of Cambyses: Herodotus and the Problem of Inquiry." For a prolonged reflection on the relation of Herodotus to Socratic thought, see Seth Benardete, *Herodotean Inquiries*.

12. See Stephen G. Salkever, *Finding the Mean: Theory and Practice in Aristotelian Political Philosophy*.

13. See Salkever and Nylan's joint account of their first years of teaching these courses, "Comparative Political Philosophy and Liberal Education: 'Looking for a Friend in History.'" Salkever recounts his subsequent experience as a sole practitioner in "Teaching Comparative Political Thought,"

14. Salkever and Nylan, "Comparative Political Philosophy and Liberal Education," 239.

15. For a thoughtful exposition of the obstacles to comparative political thought and an ambitious presentation of its possibilities, see Tully, "Deparochializing Political

Theory and Beyond." I differ with Tully inasmuch as he reads Socratism as an obstacle to genuine comparativism, while I read it as an invitation to it. Briefly, Tully understands Socratic/Platonic rationalism metaphysically and therefore as limiting the dialogic character of their thought, while I see dialogue as primary for them and their never-the-same-twice utterances about Being as merely provisional spin-offs from it.

BIBLIOGRAPHY

Averintsev, Sergei. "Ancient Greek 'Literature' and Near Eastern 'Writings': The Opposition and Encounter of Two Creative Principles." Pts. 1–2. *Arion* 7, no. 1 (1999): 1–39; no. 2 (1999): 1–26.

Benardete, Seth. *Herodotean Inquiries*. The Hague: Martinus Nijhoff, 1969.

Cassuto, Umberto. *The Documentary Hypothesis and the Composition of the Pentateuch: Eight Lectures*. Translated from the Hebrew by Israel Abrahams. Jerusalem: Magnes Press, Hebrew University, 1961.

Forster, E. M. *Two Cheers for Democracy*. London: Edward Arnold, 1951.

Gourevitch, Victor. "Philosophy and Politics." Pts. 1–2. *Review of Metaphysics* 22, no. 1 (1968): 58–84; no. 2 (1968): 281–328.

Ivison, Duncan. "Why Globalize the Curriculum?" In *Deparochializing Political Theory*, edited by Melissa S. Williams, 273–90. Cambridge: Cambridge University Press, 2020.

Kristol, Irving. *Two Cheers for Capitalism*. New York: Basic Books, 1978.

Liberman, Kenneth. "The Grammatology of Emptiness: Postmodernism, the Madhyamaka Dialectic, and the Limits of the Text." *International Philosophical Quarterly* 31, no. 4 (1991): 435–48.

Lipman, Kennard. "The Cittamatra and Its Madhyamika Critique: Some Phenomenological Reflections." *Philosophy East and West* 32 (1982): 295–308.

Magliola, Joseph. *Derrida on the Mend*. West Lafayette, IN: Purdue University Press, 1984.

Marks, Jonathan. *Let's Be Reasonable: A Conservative Case for Liberal Education*. Princeton, NJ: Princeton University Press, 2021.

Melzer, Arthur M. "Esotericism and the Critique of Historicism." *American Political Science Review* 100, no. 2 (2006): 279–95.

———. *Philosophy between the Lines: The Lost History of Esoteric Writing*. Chicago: University of Chicago Press, 2014.

Merleau-Ponty, Maurice. *The Visible and the Invisible, Followed by Working Notes*. Edited by Claude Lefort. Translated by Alphonse Lingis, with marginalia by Northrop Fry. Evanston, IN: Northwestern University Press, 1968.

Momigliano, Arnaldo. *Alien Wisdom: The Limits of Hellenization*. Cambridge: Cambridge University Press, 1975.

———. *Essays on Ancient and Modern Judaism*. Edited by Silvia Berti. Translated by Maura Masella-Gayley. Chicago: University of Chicago Press, 1994.

Nardin, Terry. "Teaching Philosophy and Political Thought in Southeast Asia." In *Deparochializing Political Theory*, edited by Melissa S. Williams, 254–72. Cambridge: Cambridge University Press, 2020.

Rathnam, Lincoln E. F. "The Politics of Skepticism: Montaigne and Zhuangzi on Freedom, Toleration, and the Limits of Government." PhD diss., University of Toronto, 2018.

———. "Wandering in the Ruler's Cage: Zhuangzi as a Political Philosopher." *Philosophy East and West* 69, no. 4 (2019): 1076–97.

Rathnam, Lindsay Mahon. "Herodotean Journeys: Diversity and Political Judgment in Herodotus' *Histories*." PhD diss., University of Toronto, 2018.

———. "The Madness of Cambyses: Herodotus and the Problem of Inquiry." *Polis* 35, no. 1 (2018): 61–82.

Salkever, Stephen G. *Finding the Mean: Theory and Practice in Aristotelian Political Philosophy*. Princeton, NJ: Princeton University Press, 1990.

———. "Teaching Comparative Political Thought: Joys, Pitfall, Strategies, Significance." In *Deparochializing Political Theory*, edited by Melissa S. Williams, 230–53. Cambridge: Cambridge University Press, 2020.

Salkever, Stephen G., and Michael Nylan. "Comparative Political Philosophy and Liberal Education: 'Looking for a Friend in History.'" *PS: Politics and Political Science* 27, no. 2 (1994): 238–47.

Thompson, Norma. *Herodotus and the Origins of the Political Community: Arion's Leap*. New Haven, CT: Yale University Press, 1996.

Tully, James. "Deparochializing Political Theory and Beyond: A Dialogue Approach to Comparative Political Thought." In *Deparochializing Political Theory*, edited by Melissa S. Williams, 25–59. Cambridge: Cambridge University Press, 2020.

Vidal-Naquet, Pierre. "Du bon usage de la trahison." In *La Guerre des Juifs*, edited by Flavius Josèphe and translated by Pierre Savinel. Paris: Éditions de Minuit, 1977.

———. *Flavius Josèphe et la guerre des juifs*. Paris: Bayard, 2005.

Williams, Melissa S., ed. *Deparochializing Political Theory*. Cambridge: Cambridge University Press, 2020.

3. The Contours of the Canon:
Liberal Education, Universalism, and Representation

Lindsay Mahon Rathnam and Lincoln E. F. Rathnam

ONE OF THE PRINCIPAL AIMS of liberal education is to allow students to understand and appraise the assumptions into which they have been enculturated through the cultivation of critical judgment.[1] Traditionally, a key component of this approach has been the careful study of books—especially those "masterpieces" that challenge, provoke, and teach all at once. The centrality of these to traditional liberal education has given rise to the concept of the "canon," a core set of "great books" that are of special pedagogical value. At present, this view of liberal education confronts a variety of challenges, both theoretical and practical. Some attack it as a relic, contending that it inadequately prepares students for professional life and thus hinders their economic prospects. In recent years, however, an even more profound difficulty has emerged. Students and scholars have argued, with greater frequency and power, that the "great books" are merely a parochial cultural inheritance, rather than a genuinely emancipatory source of critical insight.

In the fall of 2016, a group of Reed College students began a prolonged protest outside of the meetings of the college's mandatory humanities course, Hum 110. That course, the roots of which extend to the 1940s, covered a variety of sources—largely but not entirely European—from the *Code of Hammurabi* to Herodotus's *Histories* and the dialogues of Plato.[2] The protesters argued that the course contents perpetuated racist views that valorize European "great books" and therefore denigrate non-Western cultures. As a result, the syllabus was expanded to include precolonial Mexican works and those of the Harlem Renaissance.[3] Concerns about diversity also seem to have motivated curricular changes at Yale University's Department of Art History.[4] Yet in such cases, both proponents of the existing curriculum and those who sought to reform it often seem dissatisfied by the outcome.

Charges of Eurocentrism present a profound challenge to liberal education because they purport to expose an inconsistency in its own self-understanding. While the economic argument against liberal education can be met with a plethora of persuasive rebuttals—its advocates can make an economic case for such education or defend its intrinsic value—charges of parochialism cut to the heart of liberal education itself. After all, one of its central aims is to allow one to think independently, to evaluate in an evenhanded manner both the tradition and culture in which one lives and other such traditions and cultures. If liberal education is just another form of enculturation into an arbitrary set of conventions, then it falls radically short of the ambitions that its most thoughtful practitioners have set for themselves. The fundamental question is whether these criticisms are true.

Defenders of the canon might point out some of the questionable assumptions undergirding this line of criticism. Many works that are now regarded as components of the canon would not have been understood by their own authors as constituting, or even aspiring to constitute, such a canon. Indeed, even their "Western" character is often a reflection of our contemporary categories rather than inherent features of the work themselves. As it has been repeatedly argued, boundaries between West and East are porous, ever shifting, and constantly renegotiated—who is to say where Saint Augustine of Hippo, to take one example, is to be placed on this continually revised map. More germane, however, is the common (and persuasive) argument that thinkers such as Plato and Shakespeare can speak to human beings wherever (or whenever) they are. Their works spur reflection on the fundamental questions of human life, and will continue to do so as long as they are read. Yet as persuasive as this argument is, it neglects the most vital element of the critique of Eurocentrism.

We suggest that the most plausible critique of the canon is that sources relevant to a sincere investigation into human life are being neglected when we accept a curriculum almost exclusively devoted to Western texts and that the very enterprise of liberal education as it has traditionally been construed urges that this be remedied. We should seek wisdom in the works of Confucius or Al-Farabi for the same reasons that we do so in those of Plato or Shakespeare. If grappling with the ideas and arguments of the greatest minds is essential to our intellectual liberation, then we are only hurting ourselves by arbitrarily ignoring some such minds. If there are in fact general human concerns that transcend time and place, then it would be surprising if they were not addressed thoughtfully in many different times and places. Moreover, this is not a novel methodological insight. As Susan McWilliams has argued, theory has always been comparative; its purview has always been potentially global.[5] "Western" thinkers, from the Greeks onward, have sought to engage with radically unfamiliar ideas and customs. They believed that they could make universally valid claims about human life only if they engaged seriously with ideas arising out of communities very different from their own.

We begin by arguing that, in spite of the deep disagreements dividing the canon's advocates from its critics, there are points of significant agreement that unite scholars and students across these divides. Both groups have universalists, who defend their preferred curriculum on the basis of its ability to speak to general human concerns, and particularists, who are concerned with capturing the experience of particular communities or cultures. We then explore the prospects for an agreement between universalists who value the existing canon and those who seek to expand it. We argue that some of the most influential thinkers of both Europe and Asia endorsed the universalist view and sought to learn more about other communities and cultures precisely in order to make credible their claims to knowledge of human affairs. This, we contend, allows us to understand liberal education as a global project aimed at responding to a genuine human need for self-knowledge by seeking a more empirically informed awareness of the varied forms that human lives have taken.

To illustrate the way in which such an inquiry might proceed, we then examine how influential texts from two different contexts—classical Greece and ancient China—have grappled with funeral rituals and death. Examining this subject clarifies how a more globally minded perspective might illuminate our shared human condition. Because of the inescapable fact of human mortality, all cultures must attend to death in some way. Yet given the absolute finitude of death, no cultural response can ever perfectly meet the challenge it poses; no *way* of life can grasp completely the *end* of life. The necessity of a cultural response to death, combined with the inadequacy of any particular such response, renders funeral ritual a particularly fecund object of philosophic reflection on the intersection of the particular and the universal. We then conclude by drawing upon our experiences putting a cross-cultural approach to the liberal arts into practice. We teach at Duke Kunshan University, an English-language liberal arts institution located in China and a joint venture between American and Chinese partners. The particular experience of teaching at such an institution has made us more aware of the virtues—and challenges—of teaching across traditions and the necessity as well as the value of expanding the canon.

UNIVERSALISM, PARTICULARISM, AND THE CLAIMS OF GREAT BOOKS

We cannot reconcile the opposing attitudes towards the "Western canon" without establishing some shared sense of the ends of liberal education and the way in which particular texts achieve them. While advocates and critics of a classic liberal arts education are deeply divided in their practical stances toward pedagogy, both camps are crosscut by similar philosophical divisions. Both sides have their universalists, who stake the claim to their preferred curriculum on its capacity to generate insights that can travel outside of the context in which they were articulated, and their particularists, who emphasize the customs, ideas, or experiences of particular communities. At first glance, this may appear to introduce more complexity into an already vexed debate. As we shall see, however, these crosscurrents also open up new opportunities for dialogue that promises to generate progress on what seem to be intractable issues in contemporary liberal education.

Objections to the canon are often framed in a particularistic manner. These critiques begin from an observed mismatch between the diversity of contemporary students and the alleged homogeneity of the traditional canon. The fundamental concern is that many students will not see their own experiences reflected in the texts that they read. This line of criticism is often conjoined with criticisms of the concepts of the "Western canon" and the "great books." The Western canon, some contend, was created in order to distinguish a supposedly higher civilization from other ones. This argument sometimes emphasizes the moral problems with the texts themselves and sometimes emphasizes the questionable intentions that motivated their selection and elevation.[6] This argument holds that the canon therefore has the effect of marginalizing students who do not identify with the European or Western tradition. The proposed solution is to study a more representative set of authors. To be representative, in this sense, is to match particular demographic characteristics of the student body or the national population as a whole.

While such arguments are often associated with criticisms of the great books coming from the Left, there are also particularists among conservative partisans of the canon. They argue that we must study a set of classical texts chosen for their influence on subsequent European and American philosophical and political traditions. They note, for example, that the American founding fathers were inspired by classical models, while also adapting those models on the basis of the ideas of John Locke and other modern philosophers. Given this, the argument goes, American citizens would do well to attend to the great books of European political philosophy in order to realize the highest ambitions implicit in their own institutions. Both kinds of particularists make reasonable points, so far as they go. Different communities have distinctive histories and experiences that are worthy of consideration within liberal education, whether those communities are defined along ethnic, racial, religious, or national lines.

At the same time, there are limits to the particularist approach. Surely, we should not care about the works of John Adams or W. E. B. Du Bois *only* because of their significance for a particular community. They have something to say to human beings more generally. Considering such works from this point of view is especially important when we confront decisions about which texts to include within the curriculum and about how to present them to students. While including texts that speak to particular groups of students is indeed desirable, it may often be impossible to adequately represent all groups in their particularity, given the diversity of contemporary universities. For this reason, we must hope that the texts we select will be able to speak to students who do not have any particularistic connection to them. We must look to the way in which they address the human condition and therefore speak across contexts.

To defend a given set of texts in a universalistic manner is to claim that it speaks to people across temporal and geographic boundaries. This has been perhaps the most common argument in defense of the canon-centered view of liberal education. Contemporary advocates of such an approach emphasize the liberating potential of studying a small group of great texts, often largely or exclusively Western. Consider, for example, a characteristic statement summarizing the mission of the great books program at St. John's College: "Through close engagement with the works of some of the world's greatest writers and thinkers—from Homer, Plato, and Euclid to Nietzsche, Einstein, and Woolf—undergraduate and graduate students at

St. John's College grapple with fundamental questions that confront us as human beings."[7] What should be noted here is that the "Western" thinkers in question are not being studied for the sake of learning about, say, ancient Greece or twentieth-century Britain. The assumption is that there are some issues that are of concern to all human beings and that they are addressed in a compelling way by texts such as those enumerated. This is surely a substantive philosophical view, and it is one that requires some defense. Moreover, even if one grants its truth, the nature of the curriculum that best speaks to these fundamental questions may remain in dispute. Nonetheless, this statement of the universalistic view is modest in an important respect. It does not claim that any specific text or tradition has all the answers, but rather that many of them speak to a shared set of questions. It thus seems to invite students to consider a range of ways of looking at the world and is in that respect pluralistic at its foundations.

There are universalists among critics of the traditional curriculum as well. These scholars raise the question of how an education can be truly liberating if it neglects some of the world's most powerful works of thought. Bryan Van Norden's *Taking Back Philosophy* is exemplary in this regard. On Van Norden's view, Euro-American academic philosophy has arbitrarily excluded not only philosophical traditions originating outside of the West, but also various marginalized traditions within the West. While he suggests that a more expansive conception of philosophy is likely to attract students of non-European backgrounds, his central justification for studying non-Western texts is simply that they contain compelling accounts of the human condition. Philosophy as a human pursuit, he argues, will be enriched by grappling with the most serious such arguments. If we neglect those works, our intellectual resources will be impoverished. Van Norden suggests, for example, that the great Confucian thinker Mencius provides an account of virtue and ethical development that is distinct from, and on his view superior in some respects to, Aristotelian virtue ethics. Similarly, Owen Flanagan has contended that Buddhist texts articulate views on anger that are both philosophically compelling and unavailable within Western texts.[8]

Some scholars may find the arguments in question implausible. That, however, should not stop them from approaching the relevant texts with a genuine openness to learning from them. After all, the works of Herodotus, Plato, Montaigne, and Hobbes are not vital components of a liberal education because, taken together, they teach the correct set of doctrines. Indeed, the views of one are often incompatible with those of another. Nonetheless, they all offer compelling perspectives on important dimensions of human life that force us to call into question our own views. We do not have to affirm their teachings in order to learn from them. In the same way, we can appreciate Confucian or Buddhist thought even if we do not become Confucians or Buddhists ourselves.

The plausibility of this kind of modest universalism should not lead us to neglect the importance of particularity and context. We must be attentive to the way in which each thinker articulates his or her project, as well as the social and intellectual conditions within which it is articulated. We may also have to consider the distinctive methods by which thinkers have sought to develop their insights.[9] All of these considerations, however, can be understood as ways of accessing insights of general human significance, rather than as obstacles to genuine dialogue. Indeed, many texts that were articulated outside of the West make universalistic claims that seem to call for such engagement across temporal and geographic boundaries.

The case of Confucius and Confucianism may help to clarify this point. Confucius might seem like an arch-particularist, insofar as he looks backward to the supposed golden age of his own community, the early days of the Zhou dynasty, as a way of determining how society should be organized. As he is said to have remarked, he transmits and does not innovate. On the other hand, he finds the rituals of Zhou valuable precisely because they are of general human significance. He contends that they could be used to govern even the nomadic tribes outside of the Chinese cultural sphere. The great twentieth-century New Confucian philosopher Mou Zongsan, who developed his own view after deep engagement with the work of Immanuel Kant and other European philosophers, once made the following remark in a lecture series on the history of Chinese philosophy: "All philosophical truth is universal; when philosophy establishes a concept, a principle, it normally has universality. For example, consider Confucius talking about ren 仁 [humanity; humaneness]. Confucius was a man of the Spring and Autumn period [722–481 BCE], he was a Chinese man, but when he talked about *ren* he was not only talking to Chinese people. Confucius was a native of Shandong, but when he talked about *ren* he was not only talking to the people of Shandong. He was talking to all men."[10] Like, say,

Herodotus or Aristotle, Confucius aspired to speak to human beings across temporal and geographic boundaries. The rituals of Zhou are not valuable, for Confucius, because they are Chinese, but instead because they are good. We are, of course, under no obligation to accept his claims if they cannot be substantiated. In order to determine whether that is the case, however, we must engage with them.

THE WESTERN CANON GOES ABROAD

While engaging seriously with ideas, practices, and texts arising far from Europe or North America is sometimes presented, both by its advocates and by its critics, as an innovation, it is in fact true to the spirit of the thinkers who are taken to constitute the "Western canon." Many of the now canonical European thinkers recognized that, if their insights were to have the universal validity to which they aspired, they had to investigate the broadest possible range of human communities. Plato, Xenophon, and Aristotle, for example, give us some of our most trenchant critiques of Athenian democracy. Their awareness of the strengths and weaknesses of that regime, however, was no doubt nourished by their knowledge not only of other Greek city-states but also of another, very different, regime— that of the Persian Empire. Moreover, it is difficult to imagine Aristotle developing his political science in general, and his classification of regimes in particular, without his awareness of the variety of ways in which human communities were actually organized in the world familiar to him. His assiduous efforts to collect the constitutions of different communities are, of course, well known. Aristotle approaches the variety of constitutions of his day not in the spirit of the collector of eccentricities and novelties, but because they shed light on the different possible permutations of human flourishing and political life.

If thinkers such as Aristotle are taken to represent what is best in liberal education, then we ought to follow their model by being open, and indeed eager, to find wisdom by engaging with ideas and communities far different from our own. We will try to provide a model of what such engagement might look like by thinking through the issues raised by death and mourning in the work of Homer and Herodotus, before turning to the investigations of these themes in the works of the Confucian and Mohist schools of ancient China. Our claim is that while there is no generally shared view of how exactly we should respond to our mortality, some of the problems created by that condition have been recognized in both Greece and China.

The problem that the brute fact of human mortality poses for the living was evident to the ancient Greeks since the time of Homer: the crux of the *Iliad*, after all, is Achilles's unhinged response to the death of Patroclus, his consequent desecration of the body of his slain foe Hector, and his eventual recognition that enmity ends at death. The grief of Hector's aged father, Priam, sparks this recognition; confronted with the old man's tearful supplication, Achilles's rage gives way to pity, and he and Priam together lament their losses. The dramatic culmination of the *Iliad* then, lies in the affirmation of the shared humanity of combatants and the sacred character of funerary rituals; enemies in life will alike one day meet their death, will one day leave behind others to grieve—and corpses to be attended to. That the foundational text of ancient Greece is, at its core, a meditation on mortality suggests the seriousness with which this particular people grappled with the ultimate shared human condition. The brevity of life and the finitude of death, that all mortal lives, whether Trojan or Greek, Eastern or Western, will come to an end: "such is the way the gods spun life for unfortunate mortals".[11]

If the *Iliad* clarifies how death can remind us of our shared humanity, Herodotus investigates how differences in our response to death threaten to obscure what we share. His treatment of death thus fits his method and subject; in the proem to the work, he promises to uncover both the universal and the particular. The opening lines of the *History* declare that Herodotus is "here setting forth my history, that time may not draw the colour from what man has brought into being, nor those great and wonderful deeds, manifested by both Greeks and barbarians, fail of their report, and, together with all this, the reason why they fought one another."[12] The purpose of the work makes plain his global perspective; he will save from the ravages of time what man (all of humanity) has brought into being, and the exemplary and worthy deeds of Greek and barbarian (particular peoples) alike. Yet that his subject is also war makes plain how the particularity of peoples can obscure and even threaten "what man has brought into being." Our differences can lead to warfare, with its attendant great deeds and outrageous destruction.

Herodotus's most explicit commentary on the ways in which custom can limit thought occurs through the story he tells about the Persian king

Darius's experiment with funeral rituals. In this story, Darius calls both Greeks and Indians of the Kallatian tribe to his court. He asks the Greeks, who traditionally burn the dead, whether they would eat the bodies of their fathers, and they respond that "no price in the world would make them do so." When he asks the latter, who were accustomed to eating the dead, if they would be willing to burn their dead, they scream, "Don't mention such horrors!" From this, Herodotus declares, "Custom is king of all."[13]

Custom affects all three peoples in this story differently—Greeks, Kallatian, and Persians. Darius's attitude toward his subjects suggests that he takes himself to be free of custom—he perceives himself as something like an objective inquiring scientist conducting an experiment. But he too is enmeshed in custom—all the more so for denying its power over himself. Persian customs are left unchallenged here, for the Persians neither eat nor burn their dead. Darius's experiment, meant to instruct Greeks and Kallatians alike in the irrationality of their custom, instead shows to Herodotus's reader the dangers of taking one's own perspective for granted. Darius assumes his own rationality, that he is free from convention—and is thus all the more deeply ensnared within it. No one is entirely free from custom's rule, least of all those who refuse to see it.

If custom is king of all—if it shapes our most profound experiences, such as those associated with the death of loved ones, we might wonder whether we can ever truly liberate ourselves from it. Yet different customs affect us differently. The Kallatians shout, Darius ignores his own bias—and the Greeks, who similarly cannot come to embrace the ways of others, at least can bear listening to them. This difference is important. We should note here the significance of Herodotus's dictum: he declares that custom is king (*basileus*)—not tyrant (*tyrannos*). All regimes involve power and compulsion—but differences in how these are enacted matter. If custom is not a tyrant, its rule can be nudged—if only we can become aware of the way in which we dwell within its rule. If we can recognize its power, we can better negotiate with it. This then undercuts the temptation to read this story as Herodotus's endorsement of some form of relativism.

Herodotus suggests, then, that to liberate ourselves from custom, we have to first see how deeply enmeshed within it we are—how particular is our particularity. The goal, however, is not to totally escape particularity or custom, but rather to come to an awareness of it. This awareness allows us to choose what to keep and what to discard, what to nudge or transform, and what to maintain. That is, Herodotus's narrative suggests that we can understand liberal education as aiming not for the false liberation of a facile relativism, nor for the fantasy of an escape from the world into a position of perfect neutrality, but instead for the ability to live mindfully within our cultures rather than to reject them wholesale or cling to them fearfully. That is, his narrative can equip us to live, judge, and act well within the human context of pluralism and uncertainty without ceding either to relativism or parochialism. Contra those who argue that we can only appreciate difference if we practice deep immersion within it—that is, exchange one tyranny of custom for another—encounters with difference promise to up our potential horizons by making us aware of the situated quality of our perspective—and thus the way forward to enlarging it.

Because of this, Herodotus's complex treatment of the relationship between death and custom both unsettles our own cultural assumptions and prepares us to become better judges about such assumptions. As we seek to cultivate our judgment of custom, however, there is no reason to stop at the particular set of customs of which Herodotus was aware. Given the distances that Herodotus traveled in order to learn about the customs of others, there is every reason to suppose that he would willingly engage with the texts from various times and places of which we can now avail ourselves. Indeed, as we shall see, the reflections on death found in the *Histories* raise questions with which most of the major schools of thought in ancient China also grappled. The tension between the universality of human mortality and mourning and the particularity of every cultural response to the phenomena is also evident in that context.

Like all societies, China during the Spring and Autumn and Warring States periods had a complex set of practices concerning death, the dead, and mourning. These practices were part of a broader network of rituals that, from the Confucian point of view, constituted the normative backbone of society. According to Confucius and his followers, the best rituals were those practiced during the early days of the Zhou dynasty. Those rituals protected social order, established correct relations among people, and allowed individuals to perform beautiful actions. One such ritual demanded that the death of a parent should lead to a three-year period of mourning. Confucius defends this ritual by observing that "a child is completely dependent on the care of his parents for the first three years of his life—this is why the three-year mourning period is the common practice throughout the world."[14]

Confucius was surely aware that his preferred mourning practices were not literally shared by all human beings. Even among the Chinese states, he knew, the rituals of Zhou no longer commanded universal assent. What he seems to have meant is that properly educated people can recognize the reasons that the mourning rituals of Zhou are appropriate responses to the deaths of loved ones. Confucius's endorsement of those rituals does not depend on their antiquity. Instead, he notes that they correspond to the three years in which a child is most vulnerable and therefore most in need of parenting, which makes the ritual richly appropriate to the relationship that it commemorates. Confucius, in this way, emphasizes the universal dimension in human mourning. While he celebrates a particular set of rituals, developed in a particular time and place, their justification can be readily understood by people in other contexts.

The value of studying ancient Chinese thought is not derived from the Confucian tradition alone. It is the complexity of the debates over ritual and mourning, and the variety of positions articulated and defended, that makes it so valuable for liberal education. Mozi and his eponymous Mohist school attacked Confucian rituals on the basis of their expense. He claimed that long periods of mourning discouraged work and thus impoverished the community and made good government impossible.[15] In making this case, of course, he opened himself up to being attacked as an enemy of long-established practices. While he responded in part by arguing that his recommendations were consistent with those of the ancient sage kings, he also argued that customs differed so much that they could not be taken as unquestionable guides to what is right.[16]

When an opponent of Mozi defended the extended mourning periods favored by Confucius, claiming that the sage kings must have promulgated such practices given that "the noble men of the central states practice them and don't stop them, implement them and don't abandon them?" Mozi responds that those who make such arguments make the error of "[considering] one's habits convenient and one's customs *yi* [right and proper]." In other words, they confuse the mores of their people with what is right. It is not enough, for Mozi, simply to accept long-established custom. In order to demonstrate that custom is not authoritative, he adduces three cases of customary burial practices from different communities. In Kaimu, when an eldest son was born, they cut him up and ate him, a practice that they called "fitting for the younger brother." The same community abandoned grandmothers after the death of grandfathers because they did not want to "live with the wife of a ghost." Among the Yan people, Mozi claimed, the flesh of deceased parents was allowed to rot and then thrown away, before the bones were buried. In Yiqu the children burned the bodies of their deceased parents.[17] Custom points in different directions, depending on the community in which one finds oneself. This suggests that custom cannot provide reliable guidance for our conduct.

Mozi is no relativist. While he attacks cultural chauvinism, he remains confident that his preferred arrangements can be supported by argument. He suggests that an impartial calculation of benefits and harms can give us correct answers about what sort of practices we ought to endorse. On the basis of such considerations, he suggests burial in an inexpensive box without lavish funerals or lengthy morning periods.[18] These practices, he thinks, conserve resources that are needed elsewhere. Whatever one thinks of this argument, Mozi's reasons for endorsing it are accessible to a contemporary reader. Indeed, some contemporary interpreters regard him as a kind of utilitarian, akin in certain respects to thinkers like Jeremy Bentham, John Stuart Mill, or Peter Singer. Students who might be attracted to the quasi-utilitarian and seemingly "modern" aspects of his thought may be surprised, however, to find him arguing that a healthy society requires a belief in ghosts. He attributes the disorder of his own time to the fact that people no longer "clearly understand that ghosts and spirits are able to reward the worthy and punish the wicked."[19] As we have argued, it is this combination of the familiar and the unfamiliar that makes a text particularly useful for cultivating the mode of critical reflection that is central to liberal education.

Xunzi, the third most eminent ancient Confucian after Confucius and Mencius, sought to defend the traditional rituals against the attacks of Mozi and others. His account of ritual begins from the idea that human beings have unruly desires and that these desires will lead them into conflict with one another if they are not channeled in a harmonious direction. Ritual allows people to achieve satisfaction without generating violent conflict and other social ills.[20] Mourning rituals respond to our need to express both respect for the deceased and our own sorrow. Xunzi's account is quite detailed. He argues, for example, that the body needs to be adorned so that, during the prolonged mourning period during which it is visible, it does not cause disgust.[21] Disgust, he suggests, would diminish the sorrow that it is the purpose of mourning to express. At its best, mourning "makes use of weeping and sorrow" in a way that does not "lead to dejection or self-harm."[22] It is not difficult for a student of Western literature to adduce examples of the harms brought about by dangerous mourning. One need only consider Homer's portrayal of Achilles's response to the death of Patroclus.

The possibility of a conversation informed by a multitude of distinct traditions, on the basis of shared problems and concerns, thus emerges. Moreover, this conversation need not be confined entirely to the classroom. How to deal with mourning is a pressing question, both for individuals and for society more generally, simply because human beings remain mortal. Engaging with these texts does not dictate any particular answer to our contemporary problems. Doing so can, however, help us to confront them in a more serious manner.

THE PRACTICE OF LIBERAL EDUCATION IN A GLOBAL CONTEXT

Even teachers who find the idea of teaching non-Western texts attractive may wonder how best to do this. There is no single strategy that must be adopted by all. Different scholars may reasonably choose to expand the range of their own teaching in a number of different ways. Nonetheless, in order to clarify the practical dimension of the issues raised, it may be useful to reflect on our own experiences teaching at Duke Kunshan University, a liberal arts institution in China. Duke Kunshan University is a joint venture between Duke University in the United States and Wuhan University in China, hosted by the city of Kunshan in Jiangsu Province. The institution resembles a traditional liberal arts college in terms of both its size and its structure. Part of its distinctive mission, however, is to encourage a cross-cultural approach to liberal education across all dimensions of the curriculum.

Along with several colleagues, we teach Foundational Questions in Social Science, a course required for students across all of the social sciences. The aim of this course is to help students to connect the social scientific tools and methods that they are in the process of developing to basic questions about human life. We consider issues such as the role of religion in society, whether the family is a human universal, what causes societies to become wealthy, and why war occurs. In trying to address these questions, we avail ourselves of the work of contemporary economists, political scientists, sociologists, and anthropologists.

In addition to this, however, we try to remind students that the social sciences were developed in order to address vital questions that predated them. To clarify those foundational questions, we look at influential early social scientists such as Max Weber, Emile Durkheim, and Bronisław Malinowski. We also engage with philosophers and social thinkers from across the globe, such as Hobbes, Thucydides, Ibn Khaldun, and Xunzi. Students are exposed to a variety of disciplines, traditions, and concerns; this beginning, this taste, aims to make them aware of the multiple approaches to the shared concerns animating both philosophy and social sciences. No one discipline or tradition holds the key to all knowledge.

Moreover, we want to suggest that the technical tools of the social sciences, as valuable as they are, can be adequately utilized only if we can ask the proper questions. This, in turn, forces us to ask which questions are really enduring. There is no way to answer this without investigating what sorts of things people have actually found significant in their lives, across many different contexts. Taking this perspective encourages students to think of their education as responding to something more than just the demands of the twenty-first-century academy. We seek to make clear that the social sciences address urgent questions that have puzzled thoughtful human beings around the world, and across several millennia.

In addition to this, one of us teaches Conceptions of Democracy and Meritocracy, which considers competing claims to justice, legitimacy, and efficacy made by adherents of popular sovereignty against those who argue for a right to rule based on considerations of virtue, wisdom, or technical expertise. In this class, students read Aristotle, Mill, and Tocqueville, alongside Mencius and Xunzi. Our international student body renders this class both particularly challenging and especially fruitful. Students have grown up under a variety of regime types and possess a wide spectrum of ideological commitments; some of them encounter ideas that they have never been previously exposed to and are asked to discuss topics or themes that had perhaps been deemed off-limits. This can make these discussions especially fraught. Yet this diversity of background encourages all students to consider other ways of life and ask new questions about their own.

The goal here is not to make Chinese students become Millian liberals or Tocquevillian democrats or Western students staunch Confucians in the mode of contemporary political theorist Daniel Bell (a Canadian-born Confucian). Rather, it is to render each tradition legible to the other, and in the process make one's own strange. This makes possible mutual understanding—but more than that, it better equips students to live informed, reflective lives, by helping them to judge better—and for themselves. The aim is not indoctrination, but thoughtfulness, and this is better accomplished through deep yet near-simultaneous immersion in these competing traditions and through meaningful and lively conversations with one another. Conversation, thought, and friendship: they support each other, and all contribute to a human life that is recognizably good and flourishing, whether in ancient Greece, early America, or modern China. By its nature, the canon is capacious; in expanding it, we contribute to its end—a flourishing and full human life.

Yet as we know, our efforts to teach a diverse range of texts will be constrained not only by the circumstances of the classroom, but also by our own expertise, knowledge, and interests. Yet we do not consider this to be a particularly daunting obstacle. Any effort to expand the range of texts in a given course will rightly be influenced by the expertise of particular teachers and the thematic concerns of the course itself. Scholars of ancient Greek thought may find classical Confucian accounts of virtue and the flourishing community to be fruitful ways of deepening their reflections on such matters, despite their lack of familiarity with ancient China. Scholars studying twentieth-century or contemporary thought may find Gandhi or Tagore more relevant to the concerns emphasized in their courses. For anyone whose own education was primarily focused on Western texts and methods, such teaching will no doubt require an investment of time and effort. For this reason, scholars may reasonably opt to emphasize a small number of texts at first, as they develop the historical, linguistic, and philosophical skills required to do them justice.

We would do well to admit, at times, that we too struggle to adequately understand great works, particularly those arising out of traditions to which we have limited exposure. Indeed, recognizing their complexity is a precondition for truly learning from them. Approaching a limited number of texts with a serious awareness of both the challenges that inhibit us from grasping their meaning and the rewards that come from doing so demonstrates a more sincere commitment to broadening one's horizons than a cursory look at a multitude of texts from disparate times and places. While such efforts may not always satisfy the demands of those who seek a curriculum that looks like the contemporary student body, they may at least indicate to students that their professors are engaged in an ongoing effort to cultivate their own understanding rather than resting content with the training that they received when they were students themselves.

By seeking to learn from the insights of great thinkers wherever they have arisen, scholars can model the love of wisdom and the desire to transcend the confines of our parochial perspectives that is central to the very idea of liberal arts education. We do not have to grasp perfectly and totally a text in order to teach it; in fact, to think that we can ever do so is to miss the point. As Plato's *Symposium* suggests, love is a pursuit—a fleeting vision of the beautiful that urges us onward. We might be surprised by the vast differences we can be impelled to traverse by a promise only briefly glimpsed. A chance encounter with Mencius might open up whole new vistas of possibility; or, more modestly, it can briefly decenter us from our parochial satisfactions. Both responses are important aspects of a liberal education. Our students are not all the same; neither should be their responses, their loves, their questions. Our goal is to enable these beginnings, to stir these longings, not perfectly and forever satisfy them. Diversifying the canon promises to help us spark the wonder of our students; as Aristotle knows, this is the beginning (not the end) of wisdom.

NOTES

1. We do not wish to claim that liberal education always entails the rejection of one's community or culture, nor to deny that the works of one's community may play a special role in achieving the self-understanding at which liberal education aims. For an account of the emancipatory dimension of liberal education that also gives significant weight to the inheritance of particular communities, see the essays collected in Michael Oakeshott, *The Voice of Liberal Learning*.

2. Chris Lydgate, "Taking a Fresh Look at Hum 110."

3. Katie Pelletier, "Hum 110 Turns Its Lens on Mexico City"; Katie Pelletier, "Hum 110 Moves to Harlem."

4. Bendor Grosvenor, "Is Art History Becoming Too Woke?"
5. Susan McWilliams, *Traveling Back: Toward a Global Political Theory*.
6. The classic statement of the former objection is Edward Said, *Orientalism*. For a recent statement of the latter objection, see Johanna Hanink, "A New Path for Classics."
7. St. John's College, "About St. John's," https://www.sjc.edu/about.
8. Bryan Van Norden, *Taking Back Philosophy: A Multicultural Manifesto*, 67–70; Owen Flanagan, *The Geography of Morals: Varieties of Moral Possibility*, 159–67.
9. Leigh K. Jenco, "What Does Heaven Ever Say?," 753.
10. Mou Zongsan, "Lecture 1: The Special Character of Chinese Philosophy," 2.
11. *The Iliad*, 24.525, 511.
12. *The History*, 1.1, 33.
13. *The History* 3.38, 228. For more on this narrative and its consequences for Herodotus's *History*, see Lindsay Mahon Rathnam, "The Madness of Cambyses: Herodotus and the Problem of Inquiry."
14. Confucius, *The Analects*, 17.21, 209.
15. Mozi, *The Book of Master Mo*, 25.5, 116–17.
16. On Mozi's view of the sage kings, see Mozi, *The Book of Master Mo*, 25.10, 120–21.
17. Mozi, *The Book of Master Mo*, 25.15, 123.
18. Mozi, *The Book of Master Mo*, 25.16, 124.
19. Mozi, *The Book of Master Mo*, 31.1, 150.
20. *Xunzi*, 201.
21. *Xunzi*, 208.
22. *Xunzi*, 209.

BIBLIOGRAPHY

Confucius. *The Analects of Confucius*. Translated by Edward Slingerland. Indianapolis: Hackett, 2003.

Flanagan, Owen. *The Geography of Morals: Varieties of Moral Possibility*. New York: Oxford University Press, 2017.

Grosvenor, Bendor. "Is Art History Becoming Too Woke?" *Art Newspaper*, March 6, 2020. https://www.theartnewspaper.com/news/art-history-has-never-been-morally-appropriate-nor-should-it-be.

Hanink, Johanna. "A New Path for Classics." *Chronicle of Higher Education* (February 11, 2021). https://www.chronicle.com/article/if-classics-doesnt-change-let-it-burn.

Herodotus. *The History*. Translated by David Grene. Chicago: University of Chicago Press, 1988.

Homer. *The Iliad of Homer*. Translated by Richmond Lattimore. Chicago: University of Chicago Press, 2011.

Jenco, Leigh K. "What Does Heaven Ever Say?" *American Political Science Review* 101, no. 4 (2007): 741–55.

Lydgate, Chris. "Taking a Fresh Look at Hum 110." *Reed Magazine*, April 20, 2017. https://www.reed.edu/reed-magazine/articles/2017/hum-110-fresh-look.html/.

McWilliams, Susan. *Traveling Back: Toward a Global Political Theory*. New York: Oxford University Press, 2014.

Mou Zongsan. "Lecture 1: The Special Character of Chinese Philosophy." In *Nineteen Lectures on Chinese Philosophy*. Accessed August 5, 2021. https://nineteenlects.org/Lect1.pdf.

Mozi. *The Book of Master Mo*. Translated by Ian Johnston. London: Penguin, 2013.

Pelletier, Katie. "Hum 110 Moves to Harlem." *Reed Magazine*, April 5, 2019. https://www.reed.edu/reed-magazine/articles/2019/hum-110-harlem.html.

———. "Hum 110 Turns its Lens on Mexico City." *Reed Magazine*, March 12, 2019. https://www.reed.edu/reed-magazine/articles/2019/humanities-110-mexico-city.html.

Rathnam, Lindsay Mahon. "The Madness of Cambyses: Herodotus and the Problem of Inquiry." *Polis: The Journal for Ancient Greek and Roman Political Thought* 35, no. 1 (2018): 61–82.

Said, Edward. *Orientalism*. New York: Vintage Books, 2014.

St. John's College. "About St. John's." Accessed August 5, 2021. https://www.sjc.edu/about.

Van Norden, Bryan. *Taking Back Philosophy: A Multicultural Manifesto*. New York: Columbia University Press, 2017.

Xunzi. *Xunzi*. Translated by Eric Hutton. Princeton, NJ: Princeton University Press, 2014.

4. An Outsider Looking In
Christine de Pizan on Classical Learning
Anna Marisa Schön

WOMAN AUTHORS CONTINUE TO MAKE rare appearances on political theory syllabi, especially pre-nineteenth-century writers. Sure enough, the pool of female political thinkers is much smaller than that of their male counterparts—for much of history, women simply did not have the same access to education or the same opportunities to engage in scholarship and writing—yet a few possible candidates have not received the consideration they deserve. Focusing on Christine de Pizan (1364–ca. 1430), I argue in this essay that her position as an outsider—a woman, an immigrant, and a person of non-noble birth—awarded her a unique perspective on the Western philosophical tradition. Weaving back and forth between her biography and her allegorical writings, I aim to show how Christine's classical education allowed her to rise above the particularities of her situation and connect her own experiences and sorrows to a rich tradition of inquiry into the human condition, making her, in turn, a great contender for inclusion in the teaching canon.

Christine de Pizan would have been a remarkable woman in any century. Born in Venice as the daughter of a court physician and astrologer from Pizzano, she moved to France with her family at the age of four when her father entered the service of King Charles V. Throughout her life, she would maintain close ties with the Valois court. We know more about Christine's life than that of most medieval persons thanks to the abundance of autobiographical references in her works. In 1379, she married Etienne du Castel, a notary and royal secretary. The marriage appears to have been "a singular happy one."[1] Tenderly, she confides, "A sweet thing is marriage / I can well prove it by my own experience."[2] Etienne died young, however, and, widowed at the age of twenty-five, Christine was left to support her three children, her mother, and a niece. Commenting on the weight of her responsibilities, she notes, "I was six times myself."[3] Faced with serious financial difficulties, she turned to writing to make a living.[4] Her love ballades caught the attention of wealthy patrons within the court, and Christine became the first professional woman of letters in Europe. Later in her career, she transitioned from court poet to social and political commentator, producing no fewer than nine treatises broadly concerned with political life.[5]

Thanks to her pioneering role as a woman in the literary world, there is a tendency among scholars of Christine to examine her work through a feminist lens and to describe her as a "proto-feminist" and a "forerunner of all subsequent movements on behalf of women's rights."[6] Early in her career as a poet, Christine was involved in the "Quarrel of the Rose," a literary debate about the merit of Jean de Meun's part in *The Romance of the Rose*.[7] Charity Willard observes that Christine was willing to acknowledge the literary merit of the poem, but deplored the author's disparaging portrayal of women. "It was this feminist aspect of the debate that caught popular attention, since to find a woman rising to the defense of her sex against the sort of attack that was traditional through the Middle Ages was quite unheard of."[8] Christine's ensuing moral defense of women, as well as the trials of widowhood and the dangers of courtly love for young women, remained prominent themes in her writings throughout her life.

Yet I want to suggest here that what makes her works most remarkable is not simply the vindication of her gender, but her engagement with canonical texts and the way in which her perspective as a woman was transformed and elevated through her study of classical sources. Although familiar with the world of scholarship through her father, Christine was, in a very true sense, self-educated. It was only after her widowhood, seeking to escape her grief and loneliness, that she "turned to the path to which my own nature and the stars incline me, that is, the love of learning." She recounts "Rather, like the child one first puts to his ABCs, I began with the ancient histories from the beginning of the world . . . proceeding from one to the other, descending from the Romans to the French to the Britons . . . and thereafter to the deductions of the sciences, according to what I could understand at the time I studied them."[9] Her writings reveal familiarity with Aristotle's *Ethics* and *Politics* as well as his *Rhetoric* and *Metaphysics*, Cicero, Seneca,

Livy, Boethius, John of Salisbury, Giles of Rome, and other classical and Christian authors.[10]

The traditional portrayal of Christine as a " protofeminist" is overly simplistic and distracts from a more profound observation she makes about her own identity: through her reflections on and dialogues with these classical texts, Christine comes to know herself not merely as a woman but as a human being, and she learns to perceive the multiple dimensions of her identity.[11] Her study of philosophy enables Christine to transcend the narrow perspective afforded by her gender and to acquire a broader view of her person as a rational human being, capable of virtue. I focus on two works, *The Book of the City of Ladies* (1404–1405) and *The Vision of Christine* (1405), to trace her path from despair over the slanderous representations of her gender—a commonplace in medieval literature—to a more sophisticated self-understanding.

In turn, I suggest that the self-knowledge obtained through the study of philosophy allowed her to rise above her hardships and to master the conditions of her life, encouraging other women to do the same.

In turn, the inclusion of Christine's writings in our teaching curricula would offer students a vivid illustration of how engagement with the great books enables us to step out of our particular circumstances and to transcend the relevant but narrow viewpoints furnished by our "lived experiences." Christine was quite unique in her realization that our search for a virtuous and happy life—as well as the quest for a just and harmonious political society—is necessarily and rightly informed by our subjective experiences, which are often shaped by gender, race, ethnicity, sexuality, or socioeconomic background. Yet in pursuit of the good life, we cannot dwell there, but must rise above our particularities.

A CITY OF LADIES

Arguably Christine's most ostensibly feminist work, *The Book of the City of Ladies*, offers an ideal starting point for examining Christine's thoughts on the situation of her gender. At the outset of the work, Christine describes herself as one evening perusing a little book on women's education by Matheolus.[12] Leafing through the pages, she is repulsed by the invectives against women and the portrayal of the female sex as intrinsically sinful and immoral. Even so, the reading prompts in her "an extraordinary thought:

why is it that so many men . . . have always been so ready to say and write such abominable and hateful things about women and their nature?" Against her better judgment, she becomes engulfed by these thoughts. She considers how she could find "no truth in [men's] condemnation of women's nature and moral character," yet the sheer number of such assertions and the authors' repute make it "hard to ignore their opinion." Entrenched in her female identity, she is unable to dissociate herself from descriptions of her gender and compelled to conclude that "God created a vile creature when he fashioned woman." The thought of "despising myself and the entire feminine sex as an aberration of nature" makes her "deeply unhappy," and she laments that "God has put me into this world in a female body."[13]

As Margaret Brabant and Michael Brint note, Christine's resignation and her acceptance of the slanderous representations of her gender reveal "the loss of her self-identity. . . . A stranger to herself, she has forgotten who she really is."[14] Consequently, the remainder of the book may be best understood as an account of Christine's journey to self-knowledge through the recollection of the virtues and achievements of women in the past. She describes this journey in terms of her encounter with three supernatural ladies—Dame Reason, Dame Rectitude, and Dame Justice—who invite her to build a City of Ladies. "We have come," Reason explains in a kind of dream vision, "to tell you about a certain building project in the shape of a strong, well-constructed city that you are destined to erect with our help and guidance."[15] The three dames then take turns leading Christine in the construction of the city by retrieving copious examples of highly accomplished and virtuous women of the past and present.[16]

The image of the city, of course, evokes Augustine's City of God, "the classic symbol of the ideal community held together by its common pursuit of virtue."[17] But for Christine the City of Ladies refers not only to this impersonal sisterhood, but also to the defensive fortress she constructs in speech. Christine assumes her task so that "all other worthy women will have a refuge and a place where they can defend themselves from assailants. These ladies have been defenseless for too long now," and Christine is chosen as the "champion to take up their cause."[18] Thus, through the survey of exemplary women, which she takes from ancient and medieval literature as well as the Bible, Christine mounts a moral defense of women against misogynist slander and, at the same time, returns from estrangement back to certainty of her own identity.

Dame Reason leads the way, calling on Christine to "go to the Field of Letters. There we will found the City of Ladies. . . . Take the spade of your mind and dig a deep trench along the lines I have traced."[19] The building of the city proceeds in three stages, roughly corresponding to the three parts of the book. First, Christine commences by removing the soil—prejudices and false claims about women—for the city's foundation. Next, she erects the walls of the city by rewriting the true image of women's nature and their contributions to society. Finally, she adorns the structure with examples of the most divinely favored women. The *exempla* of virtuous women include strong warriors, powerful and respected queens, philosophers and poets, inventors, prudent and resourceful housewives, loving daughters, and faithful wives. Many of the examples have been adapted and embellished from the sources, but historical accuracy is secondary to the main purpose, that is, the enumeration of a variety of praiseworthy qualities. There are the Amazonian queens, who represent strength and political acumen; Pallas, the creator of the Latin alphabet, and Minerva, inventor of smithery, who demonstrate intelligence and ingenuity of mind; Queen Dido, who shows perseverance, courage, and prudence; Claudine, who represents filial love; and Sarah, Rebecca, and Ruth, who stand for chastity. Altogether, the discussion includes more than 150 examples, covering a wide range of virtues from wisdom and justice to constancy and devotion.

Guided through the historical sources by Reason, Rectitude, and Justice, Christine is able to refute a number of contemporary prejudices against women and expose the falsity of traditional depictions of her gender. She shows that women are not categorically gluttonous, infantile, captious, perfidious, unfaithful, fickle, or inconstant. In place of these traditional opinions, she constructs an image of women's excellence and achievements. However, what is most remarkable about the City of Ladies is that Christine does not merely show what women are good at in comparison to men. Rather, she emphasizes women's and men's common human qualities.

Upon completion of the city, Christine exclaims, "I understand that all things that can be done and known, whether they involve the body or the mind or any other faculty, can all be managed by women with ease."[20] The reason that women are seen less often engaged in certain activities, especially scholarship, is simply that they lack opportunity, not potential. Women are handicapped in the pursuit of science and philosophy because they are generally expected to attend to their families and households. Christine observes that women appear to know less "without a doubt . . . because women do not get involved in as many things. . . . There is nothing more instructive to a rational creature than practice and concrete experience of many different things." Yet society does not consider it necessary or appropriate for women to get involved in occupations left to men. "And it is based on that experience [alone] . . . that one arrives at the conclusion that they have less intelligence." If little girls were sent to school, as it is customary for boys, their understanding would flourish just as well.[21]

Ultimately, Christine's moral defense of women amounts to an argument about their equal human nature as creations in God's image. She points out how "when some people hear that God created man in His image, they are foolish enough to believe that this refers to His material body. . . . In fact, it refers to the soul, the intellectual spirit that will last to eternity in God's image. God created this soul and put equally good and noble souls in the bodies of men and women." Consequently, "People's superiority or baseness does not depend on their gender but on the perfection of their morals and virtues."[22] That is, woman, like man, is a rational creature imbued with the ability for moral and intellectual self-improvement through reflection and study. Thus, through the conversation with the three allegorical figures, Christine comes to see herself not merely as a woman but as a human being, and she is able to perceive the multiple layers of her identity. She is no longer confined by disparaging descriptions of her gender but able to transcend and challenge them. In turn, her female readers can become part of the city by emulating the qualities, if not the deeds, shown by the exceptional women. Christine invites her audience to "rejoice and be jubilant about our new City. . . . All of you who love glory, virtue, and respect may reside here in great honor."[23]

Pointing to Christine's advice for aspiring residents of the city, some authors have suggested that her defensive building project is undermined by her adherence to gender-specific roles and a gendered division of labor. In the last chapter, upon inviting women from all walks of life to enter the city through virtuous actions, Christine indeed offers a number of rather conventional recommendations: married women ought "not [to] be indignant about having to submit to [their] husbands, because it is not always in a person's interest to be free," virgins should be "pure, sober, and tranquil" and "listen rather than speak," and widows "modest in [their] dress, conduct, and speech."[24] In light of these prescriptions, Sheila Delany has called Christine "the voice of the patriarchy" and "at best a contradictory figure" who "ignores the independent woman of her time."[25] Somewhat more benevolently, Rosalind Brown-Grant observes that "rather than to propose the reform of society so as to grant women equal access to all social roles," Christine "encourage[s] women to pursue personal virtue within their existing social conditions."[26] Whereas men act in public, women's place appears to confined to domestic roles.

This characterization, however, is exaggerated and unfair. The examples Christine offers throughout the three books of the *City of Ladies* demonstrate that women have excelled in the full range of human virtues, not merely in traditionally female occupations. *Exempla* of virtuous daughters and wives sit side by side with political leaders, warriors, inventors, and discoverers—hardly what one calls "feminine roles." What is more, by representing those diverse occupations on equal footing, Christine is able to valorize the roles that are traditionally ascribed to women. The common quality of all of Christine's exemplary ladies is that they rise to the challenges that come along with their situations and master them virtuously, regardless whether of they are managing a household or fighting a war. Christine probably took a pragmatic approach in her educational efforts, understanding that most women would not be willing to give up family and worldly desires to follow the path of learning. Even so, she sought to encourage them "to stand on their own feet, to make some sort of contribution to society, to dominate the conditions of their lives that make or break them."[27] In short, Christine wanted women to come into their own as rational beings.

THE COMFORT OF PHILOSOPHY

In *The Vision of Christine*, the author returns to the question of her own identity in a more direct and—as the title suggests—personal tone. *The Vision* recounts her dreamlike visits with Dame Libera, Dame Opinion, and Dame Philosophy in the halls of the University of Paris. Part 3, in particular, constitutes a personal *consolatio* in the Boethian tradition, in which Christine laments the many hardships of her life and receives advice from Dame Philosophy.[28] Many scholars have interpreted the third part as an explicitly feminine defense of her place in society,[29] but I argue here that her *Vision*, in fact, illustrates how Christine learned to transcend her particular situation—the hardships she ascribes to her gender—and to achieve a broader perspective on her condition through dialogue with Philosophy.

Following conversations with Dames Libera and Dame Opinion, respectively, Christine encounters Dame Philosophy in a beautifully adorned room at the top of the university's highest tower. She is overwhelmed with awe at first, but Philosophy's compassionate welcome leads Christine to tell her about the many misfortunes of her life: "And as the weight of my troubles is kept hidden and secret by me, not revealed to the worldly . . . therefore to you, celestial knowledge . . . the just and true physician, I will release the complaints of my meditations, confident that your kindness will not scorn the humble voice of your servant, and that you will oversee the reparation of my ruined hopes laid low by the blasts of Fortune."

Seeking consolation and guidance, she begs Philosophy "to extend the assistance of your counsel to aid the feebleness of my thoughts."[30] Over the course of twelve chapters, Christine proceeds to tell the radiant dame of the series of misfortunes that have befallen her throughout her life: first, the death of King Charles V, which tossed the family into the first bout of financial insecurity, and then the death of her father followed soon by the loss of her beloved husband. Etienne's early death, in turn, brought on great financial hardship for his widow as well as years of lawsuits and legal actions in the effort to retrieve some of the money owed to him. Christine recalls the condescension she faced in the courts as a woman, the loss of patrons, the fear of not being able to provide for her children and relatives, and her grief and loneliness. Most of all, however, she laments "the obstacles [Fortune] erects to my studies through these occupations . . . many times they trouble my fantasy so that the understanding cannot wander to the good that pleases it—so troubled is it by the bitter stings."[31]

Dame Philosophy's response to Christine is consoling yet forceful and admonishing. "Certainly friend," she says, "from your speech I perceive how foolish partiality deceives you in the judgment of your condition." Emphasizing again the importance of self-knowledge, she calls Christine a "woman who little knows herself."[32] Philosophy offers comfort to her devout protégé by exhorting her to reflect on two related points. In the first place, she prompts Christine to reconsider the role of Fortune and to acknowledge her own agency in the events of her life. Rather than blindly attributing her situation to Fortune, Christine must recognize the power of her response to ill-fate. Second, Philosophy urges Christine to take a larger view of her life and, rather than focus on the sorrows of widowhood, to value her moral and intellectual accomplishments.

The role of Fortune in human affairs is first broached in the second part of the *Vision*, where Christine converses with Dame Opinion about the source of differences and disagreements between human beings. Against Christine's conviction that Fortune determines the course of human lives, Dame Opinion explains that what actually propels human beings are their *beliefs about* the incidents in their lives. Opinion is "the first cause of human undertakings" and if she "were not the origin, no work in humans would have any effect." She tells Christine that "you were quite mistaken . . . when you authorized the power of Dame Fortune so much that you said [in *The Mutation of Fortune*] that she was the sole directress of the deeds prevalent among men, and my sovereign power over all mutual influences in common deeds . . . you forgot."

While Fortune has the power to guide individual events, good and bad, she "can operate only in matters already designated by me to receive her influence, in matters exterior and external." Yet "in the bastions of thought where I am hidden, she has no power."[33] As Brown-Grant observes, this shift in emphasis from Fortune to Opinion is of primary significance to Christine and her readers. "By effectively throwing out the 'alibi' of the influence of Fortune, the *Vision* underlines the importance of self-knowledge and free will which are needed to combat the ill-effects of Opinion."[34] This argument is not to deny the effects of Fortune—which would be foolish, too—but to take account of our ability to navigate the impact of that which Fortune hands us through our responses.[35]

Dame Philosophy adds to these considerations by pointing out to Christine that her misfortunes have also given rise to great fulfillment and true happiness through Christine's own enterprise. It was out of grave necessity, after all, that she turned to the path of learning that ultimately brought her such profound contentment. Philosophy reminds her that "This benefit of study I know you will admit that not for all Fortune's favors would you have missed being occupied there . . . and without the pleasures that suit you so well. Then you should not consider yourself wretched when you have among other blessings one of the worldly things that it most delights and pleases you to have, namely, the sweet taste of knowledge." Losing the love of one's life may strike the modern reader as an unbearable price to pay, but the tragic nature precisely underscores Christine's most important realization: "There is no greater good in the world . . . than that which comes from understanding and which perfects in knowledge."[36]

The second stage of Philosophy's consolation to Christine is then "to encourage her to re-think her own fortunes for their general significance in the light of Christian eschatology,"[37] leading Christine to shift her gaze from the hardships she faces as a widowed woman to her moral and intellectual constitution, that is, her human essence. Christine had lamented the many difficulties of widowhood—poverty, lack of social connections, powerlessness in court, and the gossip and insults of neighbors. Yet none of these troubles affect humans' pursuit of their ultimate end. On the contrary, wealth, honor, power, and fame are often not conducive to eternal beatitude because "worldly pleasures are harder to use for the good of the soul than tribulations." Whereas "trouble opens the ear of the heart many times . . . worldly prosperity closes it."[38] Thus, Christine may consider herself unfortunate in material terms, but she is, in fact, immensely fortunate in spiritual terms, having been able to devote herself to improving her moral understanding through study.

Guided by Philosophy, Christine at last recognizes that in order to know true happiness, she must focus not on her material condition, defined to a large extent by her gender, but on her human mind and soul. When Philosophy proposes—for didactic purposes—that Christine imagine she could change her "simple condition and way of life . . . and even [her] feminine and feeble body . . . to a man's," she declines forthrightly. Having come to see herself not merely as a woman facing difficulties, but as a human being in pursuit of moral goodness, she rejects the suggestion that swapping places with a powerful prince, and thus her troubled female form for that of a man, might make her happier. She exclaims that "for all of Fortune's favors I would not have willingly exchanged my life for another's," and Philosophy confirms that, indeed, this must mean her womanhood can be viewed separately from her human happiness.[39]

Consistent with Christine's other writings in defense of women, Brown-Grant has observed that the *Vision* "treats gender as a feature of human identity which, in Aristotelian terms, is 'accidental' rather than 'essential.'"[40] For Aristotle, "the essence of something consists of those of its characteristics on which all its other characteristics in some fashion depend," whereas an accidental characteristic may be present or not without changing the essence.[41] On this view, the essence of human beings is that they are self-reflective, rational bipeds, whereas, say, sex or skin color are accidents. Christine first illustrates this view in part 1 of the *Vision*, where she offers an allegorical account of her birth. In this allegory, she describes how she first existed as a spirit, was then "cooked" in a mold "until a small human shape was made for me," and finally given the feminine sex at the end of the process, stressing that she became a woman because nature "wished it to be so rather than because of the mold."[42] Christine emphasizes here that men and women have in common both the spiritual essence of their soul and the physical essence of their human body, differing materially only in respect of the accidental attribute that is their sex.[43] In rejecting the proposition that a change of sex would help her improve her moral and spiritual lot, Christine once again reinforces this point. She demonstrates that her gender ceases to be a defining factor with regard to her happiness and suggests that one must assume a more complex sense of self to properly account for one's different pursuits and roles in life.

Importantly, even as Christine learns to recognize the importance of her human essence, she does not discount her womanhood. There are aspects of her life that are shaped, possibly defined, by her female gender (the hardships of widowhood, but also the joys of motherhood),[44] and there are pursuits in her life that transcend her gender (her scholarship and writing as well as the state of her soul), and they are both constitutive of her sense of self. Rather than the feminist defense of her gender, this is arguably Christine's most valuable and timeless insight: we are complex persons, and any account of ourselves that singles out one particular identity gives an inadequate picture of who we are.

CONCLUSIONS

Thanks to her literary defense of women and her own trailblazing activity as the first professional penwoman in Europe, Christine has gained a place—albeit contested—among the ranks of feminist writers. Yet as this essay suggests, the focus on her feminist efforts—and their shortcomings—does not do justice to her philosophical contributions. Through her reading of classical texts, represented in her allegorical conversations with Dame

Reason and Dame Philosophy, she comes to a more universal realization about human beings: we are multifaceted creatures whose common human essence goes beyond gender (or race or sexuality). Thus, along her path to self-knowledge, Christine's particular task is to reconcile the conflict between universalism and particular categories of identity and alterity. In *The Book of the City of Ladies*, Christine "show[s] that the male exploitation of women depended on the manipulation of dialectically arranged categories of essential differences between men and women."[45] Against this line of argument, she proposes a universalist ideal in the *Vision*. However, as Brabant and Brint point out, rather than focusing exclusively on otherness or sameness, "Christine offers a different path, one that reaches for a politics predicated on the mutual respect for our difference not in terms of gender or class but in terms of our complex character as human beings."[46]

In turn, Christine's writings illustrate why particularistic identities—be they based on gender, race, sexuality, ethnicity, or other—can sometimes furnish very narrow perspectives on ourselves and our situation, how they can indeed be confining and oppressive. As Avigail Eisenberg has argued, a plurality of contexts is important for a robust self-image because "each group provides for the individual a different vantage from which she can critically assess her attachment to other groups." In particular, by offering different perspectives, "some communities can mediate the confusion or challenge the oppressions found in other communities."[47] Through the guidance offered by Reason, Christine was able to distance herself from her female identity, to look at herself, as it were, from the point of view of her human nature, and thus to discerningly evaluate and refute the slanderous representations of her gender. When we think of ourselves exclusively as women—or as members of a given race or ethnicity—we are more likely to embrace stereotypes or conventions associated with these identities. We need to be able to step back and see ourselves from a different, wider angle. Often, the differences that give rise to particular identities appear to be more decisive in shaping our lives, making it all the more important to cultivate a shared perspective.

As political discourse is focusing increasingly on group-based identities, and college campuses and lecture halls are becoming more diverse, it is more important than ever to provide a common intellectual context in which to converse with one another. Classical education can provide one such framework for accommodating and enriching a variety of particularistic perspectives. A classic liberal arts education often has the reputation of being an "aristocratic" privilege, but Christine's example demonstrates that it is also an important equalizer. The inclusion of authors like Christine on political theory syllabi may illustrate to students how literature mediates between their particular situations and a shared human experience.

NOTES

1. Kate Langdon Forhan, *The Political Theory of Christine de Pizan*, 13.
2. Christine de Pizan, "Ballade XXVI," 51.
3. Christine de Pizan, *The Vision of Christine*, 98.
4. Charity C. Willard surmises that Christine may have copied manuscripts or run a workshop otherwise related to book production in the decade between her husband's death and her first literary successes.
5. The most thorough account of Christine's life can be found in Charity C. Willard, *Christine de Pizan: Her Life and Works*.
6. Margarete Zimmerman, "Vox Femina, Vox Politica," 114; Willard, *Christine de Pizan*, 73.
7. See Joseph Baird, *The Quarrel of the Rose: Letters and Documents*; Rosalind Brown-Grant, *Christine de Pizan and the Moral Defense of Women*, 7–51; and Jillian Hill, *The Medieval Debate on Jen de Meung's "Roman de la rose": Morality versus Art*.
8. Willard, *Christine de Pizan*, 73. For other feminist approaches to Christine, see Joan Kelly-Gadol, "Early Feminist Theory and the *Querelle des femmes*, 1400–1789"; John V. Fleming, "Hoccleve's 'Letter to Cupid' and the 'Quarrel' over the *Roman de la rose*"; Eleanor Glendinning, "Reinventing Lucretia: Rape, Suicide and Redemption from Classical Antiquity to the Medieval Era"; and Alexandra Verini, "Medieval Models of Female Friendship in Christine de Pizan's *The Book of the City of Ladies* and Margery Kempe's *The Book of Margery Kempe*."
9. Pizan, *The Vision of Christine*, 104.
10. Kate Langdon Forhan notes that some of the sources probably stem from *florilegia*, collections of excerpts from classical authors that were popular source books among many medieval writers, especially Valerius Maximus, *Memorable Deeds and Sayings: One Thousand Tales from Ancient Rome*; and Christine de Pizan, *The Book of the Body Politic*, xxi.
11. See Alin Fumurescu, *Compromise: A Political and Philosophical History*, 95. The word "identity" was, of course, not known to medieval persons in the modern sense—in medieval Latin, *identitas* referred to the shared features of the three persons of the Holy Trinity—but we must assume that medieval individuals were aware of the different roles they occupied and the different communities, such as religion or nationality, that they were part of.
12. Mathieu de Boulogne, *Lamentations* (ca. 1295–1300).
13. Christine de Pizan, *The Book of the City of Ladies*, 21–23.

14. Margaret Brabant and Michael Brint, "Identity and Difference in Christine de Pizan's *Cité des Dames*," 207–8.
15. Pizan, *City of Ladies*, 27.
16. On Christine's place in the catalog genre vis-à-vis Boccaccio and Petrarch, see Brown-Grant, *Moral Defense of Women*, 132–40.
17. Brown-Grant, *Moral Defense of Women*, 134.
18. Pizan, *City of Ladies*, 26.
19. Pizan, *City of Ladies*, 31.
20. Pizan, *City of Ladies*, 112.
21. Pizan, *City of Ladies*, 68–69.
22. Pizan, *City of Ladies*, 37.
23. Pizan, *City of Ladies*, 188, 219.
24. Pizan, *City of Ladies*, 220.
25. Sheila Delany, "History, Politics, and Christine Studies: A Polemical Reply," 197; Sheila Delany, "Mothers to Think Back Through: Who Are They?," 189.
26. Brown-Grant, *Moral Defense of Women*, 152.
27. Willard, *Christine de Pizan*, 146.
28. Boethius, *The Consolation of Philosophy*.
29. For example, Sylvia Huot has argued that "[Christine's] use of the analogy between poetic creation and child-bearing serves to valorize feminine creativity and to authorize her own literary activity." Huot, "Seduction and Sublimation: Christine de Pizan, Jean de Meun, and Dante," 372. Similarly, Kevin Brownlee suggests that Christine "officially establishes her authority as woman author by distancing herself from any possible sexual identity as historically specific woman." Her "autobiographical self-representation," he claims, rests on the "combination of three gendered subject positions—virtuous widow, caring mother, and female author." Brownlee, "Widowhood, Sexuality, and Gender in Christine de Pizan," 339–40.
30. Pizan, *The Vision of Christine*, 91.
31. Pizan, *The Vision of Christine*, 110.
32. Pizan, *The Vision of Christine*, 110, 112.
33. Pizan, *The Vision of Christine*, 74–75.
34. Brown-Grant, *Moral Defense of Women*, 109–10.
35. Readers may note how Christine anticipates Machiavelli's discussion of *virtù* and *fortuna* in Niccolò Machiavelli, *Selected Political Writings*, 18–21, 74–77.
36. Pizan, *The Vision of Christine*, 116–17.
37. Brown-Grant, *Moral Defense of Women*, 117.
38. Pizan, *The Vision of Christine*, 119–20, 124–25.
39. Pizan, *The Vision of Christine*, 121–22.
40. Brown-Grant, *Moral Defense of Women*, 119.
41. Jonathan Barnes, "Metaphysics," in *The Cambridge Companion to Aristotle*, 99.
42. Pizan, *The Vision of Christine*, 20.
43. See Brown-Grant, *Moral Defense of Women*, 120. Christine emphasizes men and women's shared human essence partially in response to those misogynists who asserted that the differences between men and women *were* essential, not accidental, such as the

thirteenth-century author of the *Contenance de fame* who claimed that only men, not women, were created in God's image. It was also not uncommon to cite the "vileness" of women's reproductive organs as evidence of their essential physical otherness.

44. This is not to suggested that motherhood is inherent to being a woman, but for Christine certainly the two were intertwined.

45. Earl Jeffrey Richards, "French Cultural Nationalism and Christian Universalism in the Writings of Christine de Pizan," 90.

46. Brabant and Brint, "Identity and Difference in Pizan's *Cité des Dames*," 219.

47. Avigail Eisenberg, *Reconstructing Political Pluralism*, 4–5.

BIBLIOGRAPHY

Baird, Joseph. *The Quarrel of the Rose: Letters and Documents*. Chapel Hill: University of North Carolina Press, 1978.

Barnes, Jonathan. "Metaphysics." In *The Cambridge Companion to Aristotle*. Cambridge: Cambridge University Press, 1995.

Boethius. *The Consolation of Philosophy*. Translated by Victor Watts. London: Penguin, 1999.

Brabant, Margaret, and Michael Brint. "Identity and Difference in Christine de Pizan's *Cité des dames*." In *Politics, Gender, and Genre: The Political Thought of Christine de Pizan*, edited by Margaret Brabant, 207–22. Boulder, CO: Westview Press, 1992.

Brown-Grant, Rosalind. *Christine de Pizan and the Moral Defense of Women*. Cambridge: Cambridge University Press, 1999.

Brownlee, Kevin. "Widowhood, Sexuality, and Gender in Christine de Pizan." *Romanic Review* 86 (1995): 339–53.

Delany, Sheila. "History, Politics, and Christine Studies: A Polemical Reply." In *Politics, Gender, and Genre: The Political Thought of Christine de Pizan*, edited by Margaret Brabant, 193–206. Boulder, CO: Westview Press, 1992.

———. "Mothers to Think Back Through: Who Are They?" In *Medieval Texts and Contemporary Readers*, edited by Laurie A. Finke and Martin B. Shichtman. Ithaca, NY: Cornell University Press, 1987.

Eisenberg, Avigail. *Reconstructing Political Pluralism*. New York: State University of New York Press, 1995.

Fleming, John V. "Hoccleve's 'Letter to Cupid' and the 'Quarrel' over the *Roman de la rose*." *Medium Ævum* 40 (1971): 21–40.

Forhan, Kate Langdon. *The Political Theory of Christine de Pizan*. Aldershot: Ashgate, 2002.

Fumurescu, Alin. *Compromise: A Political and Philosophical History*. Cambridge: Cambridge University Press, 2013.

Glendinning, Eleanor. "Reinventing Lucretia: Rape, Suicide and Redemption from Classical Antiquity to the Medieval Era." *International Journal of the Classical Tradition* 20 (2013): 61–82.

Hill, Jillian. *The Medieval Debate on Jean de Meung's "Roman de la rose": Morality versus Art*. Studies in Medieval Literature, 4. Lewiston, NY: Edwin Mellen Press, 1991.

Huot, Sylvia. "Seduction and Sublimation: Christine de Pizan, Jean de Meun, and Dante." *Romance Notes* 25 (1985): 361–73.

Kelly-Gadol, Joan. "Early Feminist Theory and the *Querelle des Femmes*, 1400–1789." *Signs* 8, no. 1 (1982): 4–28.

Machiavelli, Niccolò. *Selected Political Writings*. Edited and translated by David Wootton. Indianapolis: Hackett, 1994.

Maximus, Valerius. *Memorable Deeds and Sayings: One Thousand Tales from Ancient Rome*. Translated by Henry John Walker. London: Hackett, 2004.

Pizan, Christine de. "Ballade XXVI." In *The Writings of Christine de Pizan*, translated by Charity C. Willard. New York: Persea Books, 1994.

———. *The Book of the Body Politic*. Edited by Kate Langdon Forhan. Cambridge: Cambridge University Press, 1994.

———. *The Book of the City of Ladies*. Translated by Ineke Hardy. Indianapolis: Hackett, 2018.

———. *The Vision of Christine*. Translated by Glenda McLeod. Cambridge: D. S. Brewer, 2005.

Richards, Earl Jeffrey. "French Cultural Nationalism and Christian Universalism in the Writings of Christine de Pizan." In *Politics, Gender, and Genre: The Political Thought of Christine de Pizan*, edited by Margaret Brabant, 75–94. Boulder, CO: Westview Press, 1992.

Verini, Alexandra. "Medieval Models of Female Friendship in Christine de Pizan's *The Book of the City of Ladies* and Margery Kempe's *The Book of Margery Kempe*." *Feminist Studies* 42, no. 2 (2016): 365–91.

Willard, Charity C. *Christine de Pizan: Her Life and Works*. New York: Persea Books, 1984.

Zimmerman, Margarete. "Vox Femina, Vox Politica." In *Politics, Gender, and Genre: The Political Thought of Christine de Pizan*, edited by Margaret Brabank, 113–27. Boulder, CO: Westview Press, 1992.

5. Shame and the Liberal Education of the Democratic Self
Alin Fumurescu

AFTER RUTH BENEDICT PUBLISHED IN 1946 her seminal book *The Chrysanthemum and the Sword*, dozens of monographs and countless studies accepted and reinforced a theoretical framework that distinguished between cultures of shame and cultures of guilt, to the benefit of the latter at the expense of the first. Shame was deemed a characteristic of traditional and inherently oppressive societies, replaced in modern ones by a guilt culture. Shame, went the argument, impairs the whole self, generating a feeling of worthlessness. "I feel ashamed for *being* this or that." Thus, shaming would be employed by majorities to abusively control minorities' behaviors. Guilt, on the other hand, involves just "a self-critical reaction to certain actions: I feel guilty for *having done* this or that."[1] According to this orthodoxy, unlike shame, guilt would be a subjective and punctual feeling, easier to address and to redress. It does not involve the whole self, but only a particular action at a particular moment in time.

It goes almost without saying that a liberal education meant by default to question the status quo enthusiastically embraced this approach. In its footsteps, ideologies of empowerment took aim at shame and criticized it as a weapon of an intolerant society, deployed to ostracize otherness, "the painful embodiment of a social order premised on the subjection and exclusion" of minorities.[2] In most colleges and psychotherapy offices, shame came to be considered an "ugly emotion."[3] "In contemporary democratic societies shame is often construed as one of the negative emotions that we need to avoid in our deliberations, institutions, and practices. . . . Gays and lesbians, women, the disabled, and members of different races have all been shamed and stigmatized."[4] As a result, it was claimed that "much modern sensibility feels that it is a shame that shame exists,"[5] and that public shaming has lost its power over the powerless. According to their own assessment and rhetoric, former victims of shaming have become not only shameless but also proud of it. Jill Locke, for example, praises what she labels "unashamed citizenship" as "the work of courageous and unapologetic people" who "interrogate and denaturalize the terms of shame and shaming, . . . claim space for themselves in the world *by whatever means available*, and fight for a reconstituted social order that gives *real* meaning to democratic commitments."[6]

Since shame presupposes a vertical dimension—one *fails* to reach some ethical high ground, or one *falls* from it—it was to be considered implicitly antidemocratic. Its inherent antiegalitarian remnants were to be eradicated. To be unashamed, went the argument, is to be truly democratic, fighting the systemic inequality promoted by shame culture. "Democratic citizens . . . orient themselves in the world in direct opposition to what they perceive to be the requirements of shame. . . . We can still say *with confidence* that part of the power of the democratic commitment to popular rule is the turn away from aristocratic deference to claims of religion, identity, and traditions."[7] "Do not be ashamed!" became the rallying cry for several generations of college students. In a different context, it would have been a shame that so few spoke French to appreciate Édith Piaf's song "Non, je ne regrette rien."

Is shaming, then, an outdated practice of which one should be ashamed? Not anymore, or, at any rate, the claim is not made as forcefully as before, since, by and large, the tables have turned. The ethical high grounds have changed hands, and once again the change began in colleges. Among the "means available" for reforming society, shaming has lately become the "weapon of choice of the weak"[8] against the powers that be and the status quo, and critical race theory success is but one example of shaming at a historical level. Thanks primarily to the new media, public shaming is costless and extremely efficient in the form of cancel culture, boycotting, or internet shaming in and outside of academia. According to Anne Charity Hudley, "'Canceling is a way to acknowledge that you don't have to have the power to change structural inequality. . . . But as an individual, you can still have power beyond measure.' The internet heightens that power by collectively amplifying the voices of marginalized people who may be a minority—and otherwise silenced—in their physical communities."[9] Yet the same efficiency has also amplified to alarming levels older forms of shaming, from bullying to slut-shaming, fat-shaming, age-shaming, and the like, with devastating consequences, ranging from loss of self-esteem to suicide. The varieties of contemporary shaming are legion, but one thing is certain: despite former claims to the contrary, shame is very much alive and well, and the COVID-19 pandemic has served as a magnifying glass for assessing the amplitude of the phenomenon.

This is not a new development to be overlooked, especially when it comes to the liberal education of democratic citizens. Is shaming beneficial or detrimental for democracy? And if one should distinguish between a "good" and a "bad" shame, what would be the criteria to differentiate the two? As has been evidenced time and time again, metamorphoses in the meanings and the usages of a word signal deeper changes in the Weltanschauung that are either prompted or amplified by other significant historical developments.[10] And if one accepts that shame or the lack thereof affect somehow the whole self, one also has to accept that such rapid transformation signals a deeper change in the apprehension of the self prompted by a historical shift.

Apparently, we are facing a double paradox. In traditional societies, we are told, shaming was a powerful weapon for *maintaining* the status quo, yet nowadays, in the hands of the weak, it has become a powerful weapon for *challenging* it. At the same time, not only do the powerful fall prey to the new forms of shaming, but also, or even more so, do innocent victims. It looks like there is an Achilles' heel for the arrows of shaming in both the powerful and the weak, the guilty and the innocent.

The key for understanding these new developments might be hiding in plain view. Inside the ongoing debates about the proper way to understand and cope with shame, there are at least two major points of agreement. First, that shame is intimately related with the self.[11] Second, that shame has a dual nature, described alternatively as "objective and subjective," "cognitive and affective," "external and internal," "private and public," and so forth, a dualism that seems reflected in the fact that most languages have at least two different words for shame.[12] Both aspects speak directly to the largely forgotten dialectic that for centuries has informed the understanding of the self—or of the soul, as it used to be called.

Most of the time, we are thinking about the self as either (neo)liberal and highly individualistic or as communitarian and embedded, but one-dimensional nevertheless. It has been argued, for example, that shaming penalties are commended from a communitarian perspective, and condemned from a liberal one.[13] But according to the classical understanding, the self is bidimensional, being composed of two fora, distinct yet constituting each other.[14] *Forum internum*—the inner self—was the forum of authenticity, uniqueness, and complete freedom. No one could regulate or control the *forum internum*, not even the church. On the other hand, in *forum externum*—the outer self—one was an "I" insofar as one shared in the membership of various communities/*universitates* and one played by the rules and the hierarchies of the community: it was the forum of sameness and conformity. In other words, one was an "I" because one was at once unique and the same as everyone else. One had an *identity* insofar as one was *identical* to everyone else, and one was identical to everyone else because one had a unique identity. The common etymological root of the two words is no accident.

Yet during the sixteenth century, the rapid spread of the printing press prompted a revolution of information that, coupled with other factors, rushed the beginning of early modernity. As argued elsewhere, it was also the time when we are witnessing a change in the understanding of the self.[15] The dialectic of the self between the two fora split across the Channel between a French centripetal individualism, for which *forum internum* represented the only true self, while *forum externum* was relegated to the status of a mere costume, and a British centrifugal individualism—focused almost exclusively on *forum externum* as the visible, trusted self. The result were two distinct forms of understanding political representation, with long-lasting consequences.

It comes at little surprise if the digital revolution affected the representation of the self once again with a huge political impact. This relationship between the understanding of the self/soul and politics is not to be ignored, since for millennia the connection between the soul-type and the constitution of the polity was considered of the highest importance.[16] Nowadays, this relationship has been replaced and mirrored by the explosion of identity politics. But if one agrees that shame illuminates the bridge between the inner and the outer self, and between an individual's and society's value systems, it is a hypothesis still worth exploring. Some value system ought to inform both fora—the inner self as private morality, and the outer one as ethical conduct,[17] and one cannot ignore the relationship between the two, especially nowadays, when the gulf between them seems uncrossable.

Hence, if liberal education is not satisfied with merely transmitting information, it should aim to educate the soul, and for this purpose the lessons of the past prove invaluable. They provide not only diagnoses of contemporary democratic malaises connected with the new media, but also useful solutions for redressing the balance between the inner and outer self, and implicitly between one's inner morality and the outer ethical system. From this perspective, the story of Genesis can serve as a good starting point to better understand the various usages of shame, and implicitly the classic dialectic of the self.

In the most influential text for all three major monotheistic religions, Adam and Eve were naked in Eden, but they were *unashamed* (*yiṯ·bō·šā·šū*), not having yet tasted from the tree of knowledge of good and evil (Gen. 2:25). Only after they bit from its fruit and *knew* the distinction between the two ("the eyes of both of them were opened and they *knew* they were naked") did they cover themselves, presumably because now they were *ashamed* (Gen. 3:7). Being naked was wrong *for themselves*, regardless of any external standard, since God was not yet in the picture. Their knowledge, however, remained partial, thus somehow *doubtful*, for according with the narrative they never got to finish the fruit.

When "they heard the voice of the Lord God," Adam and Eve realized that by covering their "shameful parts" they had revealed yet another, presumably more important, shortcoming, so now they hid *entirely* from the presence of God. "The shame before God seems to be different from the shame before each other. Before each other man and woman hide only their genitalia. Before God, they seek to hide themselves completely."[18] Why? Because, as Adam confessed, they were afraid of being naked. But this could not have been, the attentive reader will notice, for they were already covered with aprons made from fig leaves.[19] Hence, the explanation for their fear remains that both were afraid of being *shamed* for being *seen* as disobedient. What are the consequences of this fear, besides the urge to hide? Adam passes the responsibility onto Eve, and Eve onto the serpent, and they are punished by God in the reverse order—first the serpent, then Eve, and, in the end, Adam (Gen. 3:11–19).

This short story captures well the distinction between being *ashamed* and feeling *shamed*. On the one hand, being *ashamed* presupposes the *knowledge* of what is morally wrong *for oneself*. (God does not tell Adam and Eve that it is wrong to be naked—they come to *know*.) It is a feeling *internalized*, and it implies *accepting the responsibility*, followed by the attempt to redress the perceived wrong (in this case, cover oneself, if only with fig leaves). On the other hand, feeling *shamed* is the result of an *external* act, performed by someone else (God, in this instance), for failing to act according to an *external* value system, and comes *au pair* with the feeling of fear, the impulse to hide, *to get out of sight*, and the attempt to *pass the responsibility*. In other words, being ashamed is an *active* feeling, while feeling shamed is a *passive* one, unless the recipient of shaming also feels ashamed as a result, as presumably Adam and Eve did.

Considering the classic dialectic between the inner and the outer self, one can see how being ashamed involves the former, while being shamed, the latter. One is *ashamed* in one's inner self, when one fails the value system one believes in, and one is *shamed* in one's outer self, when one fails to comply with an external value system. Since the two fora are interrelated and constitutive of each other, and since they are both parts of one's self, it goes without saying that the distinction between *being ashamed* and *feeling shamed* is not an easy one. In traditional societies, the confusion is further amplified by the fact that the external and the internal value systems largely coincide, so one usually feels ashamed for being shamed, which makes shaming such a powerful motivator. Nevertheless, the forgotten dialectic of the self can bring some order in this apparent linguistic, conceptual, and emotional chaos.

Throughout the Old Testament, there are two different words for *shame*—in Hebrew, *bō·šə·nū* (being ashamed) and *kə·lim·māh*. The latter stands for feeling shamed and is paired with helplessness, fear, or despair (or a combination). It makes one blush, hide, or cover, much like Adam and Eve did. Consider Psalm 69. King David too feels hopeless. There is nothing he can do by himself. Only God can help him. But the Psalmist's sins, which he is the first to acknowledge, are not the reason his enemies hate him—they hate him (Ps. 69:4) because of his faith: "For I endured scorn for your sake, and shame (*kə·lim·māh*) *has covered my face*." The Psalmist feels that he has been undeservedly *shamed* (*kə·lim·māh*), but he supplicates God not to let others "that seek thee" to be *ashamed* (*yê·ḇō·šū*) (Ps. 69:6) only because he, the king, was shamed for it.

Here, unlike in the case of Adam and Eve, one witnesses a gap between the outer shaming and the inner feeling of being ashamed. It is also a warning about confounding the two. God is asked by King David to make the Hebrews understand this distinction: for this type of *wrongful* shaming, there is no need to be ashamed. "People can be ashamed of being admired by the wrong audience in the wrong way. Equally, they need not be ashamed of being poorly viewed, if the view is that of an observer for whom they feel contempt."[20] The ancient Greeks understood this very well.

The Greek difference between *aidōs* and *aisckhunē*, so heavily disputed among scholars, can be clarified in a similar way. In the *Nicomachean Ethics*, Aristotle explains *aidōs* as a kind of fear [*phobos*] of disgrace [*adoxia*].[21] In other words, *aidōs* stands for feeling *shamed* in one's outer self, rightfully or not. *Aisckhunē* (sometimes transliterated *aischunē* or *aischyne*), on the other hand, is usually translated as "to be *ashamed*," that is, in one's inner self. If Socrates was unashamed (*anaiskhuntia*), it was because his concitizens' attempts to shame him was done for the wrong reasons, by the wrong people.

During his trial, Socrates repeatedly pointed out that his accusers were unashamed, (*anaiskhuntia*),[22] caring to acquire wealth, reputation, and honor, while failing to care for the improvement of their souls. They were unashamed because they cared only for the appearance of shamelessness (*anaides*), not for their true selves.[23] At the same time, he acknowledged that he himself was unashamed of telling the truth that needed to be told,[24] namely, that people who have the reputation of wisdom are not wise, or for engaging in an occupation that puts him at risk of death.[25] So what is the difference? The difference is one between believing one knows and knowing one does not know, between unquestionable convictions and reasonable doubt. Paradoxically, at first sight, the allegedly democratic Athenians acted tyrannically against Socrates, convinced of their ethical high ground, while the accused one tried to preserve open the necessary space for doubt, and thus for democratic debates. "It is he, not they, who is the true patriot and true Athenian."[26]

If the worrisome polarization of our public life starts inside of the soul, the education of the soul becomes crucially important, and who else but the all-questioning Socrates can serve as an example? Obviously, a self-confident soul, the soul who "knows" beyond any doubt and works with moral and/or ethical certitudes, cannot be ashamed. The main characteristic of the tyrannical soul is precisely the absence of doubt. In book 1 of *Republic*, Thrasymachus spells it out: "I do not think it, by Zeus, I know it!"[27] But there is hope. One cannot shame someone who "knows," but one can shake the fake beliefs (*doxa*) of one's interlocutor, like Socrates proceeded with Thrasymachus. Naturally, Socrates's cross-examination (*elenkhos*) implies shaming—the famous Socratic irony, of which Thrasymachus complained.[28] But as the dialogue progresses, the famous Sophist began to reluctantly agree with Socrates's arguments and started sweating. "And then," confesses Socrates, "I saw something I had never seen before—Thrasymachus *blushing*."[29] After being shamed, the formerly unashamed and confident interlocutor stopped roaring "like a wild beast,"[30] and became gentle, ceasing to be difficult, and graciously accepted the defeat.[31] The beast was tamed through respectful shaming.[32]

There is hope, then, that given enough time and the right form of education, even the tyrannical soul can be made to doubt its certitudes. In other words, it can (re)become democratic. According to book 8 of *Republic*, the tyrannical soul is surprisingly close to the democratic one, and Socrates's concern is that the smooth transition from democracy to tyranny both in the souls and in the *poleis* is facilitated precisely by the similarities between the two. The democratic individual who is about to become tyrannical is not only devoted to *isonomia*, equal political rights, but it is also "a multifarious man and full of all sorts of characters, beautiful and complex, like the democratic city. Many men and women would envy his life because of the great number of examples of constitutions and characters it contains within it."[33] Among the warning signs of this seamless transition from democracy to tyranny, Socrates mentions labeling shame (*aidōs*) as "cowardliness"[34] and shamelessness (*anaides*) in following one's unfiltered passions as "courage,"[35] all signaling a turning upside down of the *outer* ethical value system.

From antiquity all the way through modernity, the idea that a republic cannot survive absent a shared *ethos*, which in turn demands a certain education of the souls, went largely undisputed. But today it becomes increasingly difficult to even define such a common *ethos*, considering the widening gap between different camps with radically different ethical certitudes. Many contemporary political theorists have argued, and rightfully so, that democratic states ought to educate the youth in critical thinking in such a way that they will become independent-minded citizens prepared to engage and challenge any form of authority, much like Socrates did in Athens.[36] But even if we leave aside the question of how many Socrateses are among us, before we start educating future generations, we better make sure we actually understand *what* Socrates did in Athens.

In order to do that, a comparison with "another Socrates" who, allegedly according to Plato, went mad—Diogenes the Cynic—might be useful.[37] Here, the difference between being ashamed in one's inner self (*aisckhunē*) and feeling shamed in one's outer self (*aidōs*) proves crucial for disentangling Diogenes from Socrates. Both used shaming (*aidōs*) to make their interlocutors feel ashamed (*aisckhunē*) for not taking proper care of their souls. Socrates tried to persuade his fellow Athenians that "the unexamined life is not worth living" (*Apology* 38a). As for Diogenes, "to someone who claimed to be inept at Philosophy, he said, 'Then why do you live, if it's not your concern to live well?'"[38] One can see why Diogenes continues to exercise not only fascination but also admiration or, at the very least, sympathy.[39] The similarities between Socrates and Diogenes, however, stop here.

True, like Diogenes, Socrates could not be shamed by his fellow Athenians, since their opinions and priorities were patently wrong in his eyes, but this doesn't mean that he was not a respectful human being and a respectful citizen. Precisely because he knew he was not the keeper of any ultimate truth, he performed all his citizen duties faithfully, from going to war, to serving as an *epistates*, to showing up in court for trial, to accepting the verdict, and more. He did not want to "stand out" for the sake of shocking his audience. He did not masturbate in public, when invited to parties he did not spit in the host's face, he did not live in a barrel, and so forth. He went even further, saying, "I have the *utmost respect and affection* for you, men of Athens," even though he would "obey the god" rather than his fellow citizens in cases of disagreement.[40] As demonstrated in *Crito*, such a declaration was neither irony nor window-dressing for the sake of convenience. Socrates respected his concitizens, despite their shortcomings, because he respected his self in both fora—the inner and the outer. He acknowledged that his outer self at least was the "product" of Athens. It would have been a shame to respond to injustice with injustice, endangering the city by disrespecting its laws.[41] Yet, in equal measure, he was also faithful to his inner self and to the god that informed it, so he followed his inner calling with the risk of his life.[42]

Diogenes stands at the other side of the spectrum, and not only because he chose a life in exile to avoid a few years of imprisonment for an accusation he was the first to acknowledge was correct, while claiming that since then he had become a better person.[43] The reason Diogenes stands opposite to Socrates has mainly to do with his self, which he considered fully *auto-nomos*. As a self-declared "citizen of the world (*cosmopolites*),"[44] he recognized no roots and no dues. Since he did not consider himself part of any society, he also refused to accept that society was part of him. In other words, he denied his outer self. As a result, his gaze was always directed top-down, never the other way around. As a scholium on Aristotle's *Rhetoric* notices, like the dogs from which they got their name, the Cynics "make a cult of shamelessness, not as being beneath *aidōs*, but as superior to it."[45]

His "looking down" on people and "heaping scorn on others"[46] spared no one. He indiscriminately mocked Plato and the demagogues, the wealthy and the poor, the old and the young, the slaves and the slave masters, and others. Unlike Socrates, the notion of *respect* for others or for oneself seemed foreign to Diogenes. No historical account, no matter its accuracy, has recorded any moment of doubt in his life or in the judgments he passed onto others. Diogenes could neither be ashamed nor feel shamed because he did not acknowledge any outer value system, and his inner one had no ideal from which to fall or fail to reach. He was *eccentric* (ex-centric) both literally and figuratively, for he lacked a "center." He had nothing to look up to, but only down on. Diogenes could not be disappointed by himself; only the world could disappoint him—and it did by not taking him seriously. But it was the respectful Socrates who was put to death in a democracy, not the outrageous Diogenes.

Does this mean that liberal democracies are doomed, as many scholars of late have argued? I dare hope not. The reason for my hope rests on democracy's own weakness, its own Achilles' heel. In contemporary liberal democracies, people might not believe in (or even despise) society's *ethos*—as did Diogenes. They might act shamelessly while also trying to shame others—like Diogenes proudly acted. They might cherish their independence of mind and their free spirits, while accusing others of hypocrisy—much like Diogenes did. But Diogenes, too, had his weakness: despite appearances, he had an unquenchable thirst for fame.

Most favorable accounts have it that he misunderstood the Oracle of Delphi when it told that he could "change the civic currency." Being young, goes the excuse, he thought god gave him permission to alter the actual coinage, while the real meaning was to alter the *political* currency, by challenging the status quo. The other version, more plausible, of the same event is rather conveniently ignored. According to the second account, he "went to Delphi to inquire not whether he should restamp the coinage, but what he should do to become *surpassingly famous*."[47]

While most people thought Diogenes's actions proved that he was the least interested in public opinion, Plato saw in his outrageous behavior nothing but a vanity turned upside down. "How much vanity you expose, Diogenes, by not appearing to be vain!"[48] He was willing to do what it took in order to remain the focus of attention, from copulating in public to babbling if serious talk did not attract the expected audience.[49] It worked. He was admired by many Athenians who presented him with a new tub when the one he lived in was broken by a boy. The boy, on the other hand, was severely punished.[50] It seems, therefore, that despite his appearance, or precisely because of it, Diogenes did care, after all, about his outer self quite a lot and knew how to attract attention.

One may go as far as to say that Diogenes was the precursor of social media's new stars. One does not get to be a media darling by "minding one's business," like Socrates did. And while some of these acclaimed media stars may use their fame to draw attention to some of society's failures, most want to be in the spotlight for the sake of being in the spotlight. The new media is undoubtedly amplifying this hunting for attention, by making it easier. Such wannabe media stars are on the lookout to increase the number of "followers" and "likes" by all means necessary, and some of their exploits would probably make Diogenes look like a boring petit bourgeois. Yet the same "virtual shamelessness" goes hand in hand with the devastating effects of internet shaming, varying from loss of self-esteem to medical depression and suicide.

This conundrum becomes easier to solve once one considers that the capacity to be ashamed signals the presence of a consistent inner value system. If one has a reliable moral compass, like Socrates, one is impervious to outside shaming or emotional bullying, for either the accusations are correct, in which case one should also be ashamed and try to redress the mistake, like Adam and Eve, or they are not, like the Psalmist, in which case one should not be affected. If one does not have such a consistent inner value system, or if it fluctuates based on circumstances and whims, like in the case of Diogenes, one can never be ashamed, for there is no ideal from which to fall or fail to reach. But by the same token, one becomes increasingly vulnerable in the outer self, for the weakening of the inner self makes the outer one more dependable on other people's recognition.

It might be tempting to blame many of the contemporary challenges on these outer, empty selves, "shell-selves" unable to find a stable identity except on the outside, be this a fickle public opinion or characteristics over which one has no choice and thus no merit. But this would be to miss the opportunity created precisely by the weakness present in the penchant for public admiration. One has to remember that the only way of reaching someone's inner self, over which no one else has control, is via the outer. By using external shaming (*aidōs*), Socrates manages to make Thrasymachus ashamed (*aisckhunē*) of his previous certitudes. The increased influenceability of the contemporary outer self can be used to strengthen the inner one.

This is not a revolutionary idea. Since people will always want public admiration, educators who know about the soul should redirect these energies by changing the object of popular admiration, which is usually, but not necessarily, money. From Jean-Jacques Rousseau and David Hume to the American founders praising what they called "the natural aristocracy" or "the aristocracy of merit," it has been said that the "love of fame" can be "the ruling passion of the noblest minds"[51] and that "the object of public admiration will invariably be the object of wishes of individuals, and if one has to be rich in order to shine then being rich will always be the dominant passion."[52] Therefore, the challenge of education is to redirect public respect and admiration to the right objects. In Benjamin Rush's words, "Private virtue requires a collective effort to cultivate."[53]

It seems, therefore, that by using the right methods, the weakness of the outer self can be employed to strengthen the inner one, by redirecting its aspirations upwards. Yet this is exactly what the cultivation of respect and, implicitly, of the ability to be ashamed does. If there are any worries that by moving on a vertical, upward-downward dimension, shame and respect are inherently antiegalitarian and therefore antidemocratic, one of Alexis de Tocqueville's observations should put them to rest: "There is in fact a manly and legitimate *passion for equality* that spurs all men to wish to be strong and *esteemed*. This passion tends to elevate the lesser to the rank of the greater. But one also finds in the human heart a *depraved taste for equality*, which impels the weak to want to bring the strong down to their level, and which reduces men to preferring equality in servitude to inequality in freedom."[54]

If so, the question becomes: What equality do we want to cultivate in the youth? One that looks respectfully upward or one that looks disdainfully downward on anyone who refuses to share one's moral certitudes? The very possibility of shaming in an allegedly shameless society may turn out to be a blessing in disguise if the classical liberal arts education rises to the challenge of educating democratic selves—selves with a reliable inner moral compass, yet mindful to the fact that we have never finished the fruit of knowledge of good and evil.

NOTES

1. Peter N. Stearns, "Shame, and a Challenge for Emotions History," 199.
2. Natalie Kwok, "Shame and the Embodiment of Boundaries."
3. June P. Tangney, "Moral Affect: The Good, the Bad, and the Ugly."
4. Christina H. Tarnopolsky, *Prudes, Perverts, and Tyrants: Plato's "Gorgias" and the Politics of Shame*, 1.
5. John Hollander, "Honor Dishonorable: Shameful Shame," 1068.
6. Jill Locke, *Democracy and the Death of Shame: Political Equality and Social Disturbance*, 12 (emphasis added).
7. Locke, *Democracy and the Death of Shame*, 10 (emphasis added).
8. I borrow this expression from the classic book by James C. Scott, *Weapons of the Weak: Everyday Forms of Peasant Resistance*. See also 1 Cor. 1:27: "God chose the weak of the world to shame (*kataischynē*) the strong."
9. Nicole Dudenhoefer, "Is Cancel Culture Effective?"
10. See, for example, Quentin Skinner, "Language and Political Change."
11. See, for example, Mark R. Leary and June Price Tangney, *Self and Identity*.
12. In Hebrew, kə·lim·māh and bō·šə·nū; in Greek, *aidṓs* and *aisckhunē*; in Latin, *pudor, verecundia*, etc.; in French, *pudeur* and *honte*; in Italian, *vergogna* and *onta*, in Spanish *pudor* and *vergüenza*, in German, *Scham* and *Schand*; and so on. See further.
13. Martha C. Nussbaum, *Hiding from Humanity: Disgust, Shame, and the Law*.
14. See Alin Fumurescu, *Compromise: A Political and Philosophical History*.
15. See Fumurescu, *Compromise* and his *Compromise and the American Founding: The Quest for the People's Two Bodies*.
16. See, for example, Plato, *The Republic*, bk. 8; St. Augustine, *City of God*, bk. 19, chap. 21; or Al Farabi, *The Political Regime*, pt. 2.
17. I am using here the Hegelian distinction between "morality" and "ethics" as discussed in the introduction to his *Philosophy of Right*.
18. Leon R. Kass, *The Beginning of Wisdom: Reading Genesis*, 91n40. Kass goes on making the parallel between this episode and the two Greek words for shame. See further.

19. One could also consider the theological explanation according to which Adam and Eve acquired physical bodies only after God clothes them with "garments of skin" (Gen. 3:21). Thus, in the first instance, it was their souls that were naked for God to see their sin. Both interpretations point in the same direction.

20. Bernard Williams, *Shame and Necessity*, 82.

21. Aristotle, *Nicomachean Ethics*, 1128b12–13.

22. For example, Plato, *Apology*, 17b, 31b, 38b.

23. Plato, *Apology*, 29d.

24. Plato, *Apology*, 22b.

25. Plato, *Apology*, 28b.

26. J. Peter Euben, *Corrupting Youth: Political Education, Democratic Culture, and Political Theory*, 33.

27. Plato, *Republic*, 345d.

28. Plato, *Republic*, 337a.

29. Plato, *Republic*, 350d.

30. Plato, *Republic*, 336b.

31. Plato, *Republic*, 354a.

32. I borrow this expression from Tarnopolsky, *Prudes, Perverts, and Tyrants*. See further.

33. Plato, *Republic*, 561e.

34. Plato, *Republic*, 560d.

35. Plato, *Republic*, 560e.

36. See, for example, Amy Gutmann, *Democratic Education*; Dana Richard Villa, *Socratic Citizenship*.

37. Diogenes Laertius, *Lives of the Eminent Philosophers*.

38. Laertius, *Lives of the Eminent Philosophers*, 6:65.

39. For example, see Donald R. Dudley, *A History of Cynicism from Diogenes to the 6th Century A.D.*; Martha Nussbaum, "Patriotism and Cosmopolitanism"; David Mazella, *The Making of Modern Cynicism*; and Locke, *Democracy and the Death of Shame*.

40. Plato, *Apology*, 29d (emphasis added).

41. *Crito*, 50b.

42. Twice, during the dialogue (49b, 52c), when Socrates argues that replying with injustice to injustice would be shameful and threatening for the city, he uses derivatives of *aisckhunē*.

43. Laertius, *Lives of the Eminent Philosophers*, 6: 56.

44. Laertius, *Lives of the Eminent Philosophers*, 6:63.

45. Aristotle, *Rhetoric,* iii 10.7. Quoted in Dudley, *A History of Cynicism*, 5.

46. Laertius, *Lives of the Eminent Philosophers*, 6:24.

47. Laertius, *Lives of the Eminent Philosophers*, 6:21 (emphasis added).

48. Laertius, *Lives of the Eminent Philosophers*, 6:26.

49. Laertius, *Lives of the Eminent Philosophers*, 6:27.

50. Laertius, *Lives of the Eminent Philosophers*, 6:43.

51. Alexander Hamilton, "Federalist 72," 375.

52. Jean-Jacques Rousseau, "Considerations on the Government of Poland," 188.

53. Quoted in Benjamin T. Lynerd, *Republican Theology: The Civil Religion of American Evangelicals*, 90.

54. Alexis de Tocqueville, *Democracy in America* (I, 1:3), 52 (emphases added).

BIBLIOGRAPHY

Aristotle. *Nicomachean Ethics*. Translated by H. Rackham. Cambridge, MA: Harvard University Press, 1999.

Benedict, Ruth. *The Chrysanthemum and the Sword: Patterns of Japanese Culture*. 1945. Reprint, Boston: Mariner Books, 2005.

Dudenhoefer, Nicole. "Is Cancel Culture Effective?" *Pegasus, the Magazine of the University of Central Florida* (Fall 2020). https://www.ucf.edu/pegasus/is-cancel-culture-effective/.

Dudley, Donald R. *A History of Cynicism from Diogenes to the 6th Century A.D.* Cambridge: Cambridge University Press, 1937.

Euben, J. Peter. *Corrupting Youth: Political Education, Democratic Culture, and Political Theory*. Princeton, NJ: Princeton University Press, 1997.

Fumurescu, Alin. *Compromise: A Political and Philosophical History*. Cambridge: Cambridge University Press, 2013.

———. *Compromise and the American Founding: The Quest for the People's Two Bodies*. Cambridge: Cambridge University Press, 2019.

Gutmann, Amy. *Democratic Education*. Princeton, NJ: Princeton University Press, 1999.

Hamilton, Alexander. "Federalist 72." In *The Federalist*, edited by George E. Carey and James McClellan. Indianapolis: Liberty Fund. 2002.

Hollander, John. "Honor Dishonorable: Shameful Shame." *Social Research* 70, no. 4 (2003): 1061–74.

Kass, Leon R. *The Beginning of Wisdom: Reading Genesis*. Chicago: University of Chicago Press, 2003.

Kwok, Natalie. "Shame and the Embodiment of Boundaries." *Oceania* 82, no. 1 (2012): 28–44.

Laertius, Diogenes. *Lives of the Eminent Philosophers*. Edited by James Miller. Translated by Pamela Mensch. New York: Oxford University Press, 2020.

Leary, Mark R., and June Price Tangney. *Self and Identity*. New York: Guilford Press, 2012.

Locke, Jill. *Democracy and the Death of Shame: Political Equality and Social Disturbance*. Cambridge: Cambridge University Press, 2016.

Lynerd, Benjamin T. *Republican Theology: The Civil Religion of American Evangelicals*. Oxford: Oxford University Press, 2014.

Mazella, David. *The Making of Modern Cynicism*. Charlottesville: University of Virginia Press, 2007.

Nussbaum, Martha. *Hiding from Humanity: Disgust, Shame, and the Law*. Princeton, NJ: Princeton University Press, 2004.

———. "Patriotism and Cosmopolitanism." In *For Love of Country?*, edited by Joshua Cohen, 3–20. Boston: Beacon Press, 2002.

Plato. *The Republic*. Translated by Allan Bloom. New York: Basic Books, 1987.
Rousseau, Jean Jacques. "Considerations on the Government of Poland." In '*The Social Contract' and Other Later Political Writings*, edited by Victor Gourevitch. Cambridge: Cambridge University Press, 1997.
Scott, James C. *Weapons of the Weak: Everyday Forms of Peasant Resistance*. New Haven, CT: Yale University Press, 1985.
Skinner, Quentin. "Language and Political Change." In *Political Innovation and Conceptual Change*, edited by Terence Ball, James Farr, and Russel L. Hanson, 6–23. Cambridge: Cambridge University Press, 1998.
Stearns, Peter N. "Shame, and a Challenge for Emotions History." *Emotion Review* 8, no. 3 (2016): 197–206.
Tangney, June P. "Moral Affect: The Good, the Bad, and the Ugly." *Journal of Personality and Social Psychology* 64, no. 4 (1991): 598–607.
Tarnopolsky, Christina H. *Prudes, Perverts, and Tyrants: Plato's "Gorgias" and the Politics of Shame*. Princeton, NJ: Princeton University Press, 2010.
Tocqueville, Alexis de. *Democracy in America*. Edited and translated by Harvey C. Mansfield and Debla Winthrop. Chicago: University of Chicago Press, 2002.
Villa, Dana Richard. *Socratic Citizenship*. Princeton, NJ: Princeton University Press, 2001.
Williams, Bernard. *Shame and Necessity*. Berkley: University of California Press, 1993.
Wolack, Jennifer. *Compromise in an Age of Party Polarization*. Oxford: Oxford University Press, 2020.

6. Liberal Education as Civic Education
The Philosopher's Curriculum in Plato's *Republic*
Dustin Gish

THE PHRASE "LIBERAL ARTS EDUCATION" elides intellectual traditions that have distinct etymological histories and have inspired diverse pedagogic aims. In our own contemporary educational milieu, phrases such as "the liberal arts," "liberal education," "liberal arts education," or "the humanities" can conjure radically different meanings and associations. In returning to the ancient origination of the idea of liberal education, which is to say that transformation of the human being through learning which makes us free, we discover a bond that is still vital today between the pursuit of knowledge and wisdom (*philosophia*), the desire for justice, and the purpose of civic education. This tradition of liberal education as civic education entered modernity through the writings of the Renaissance humanists who, following in the footsteps of Petrarca, the founder of that movement, articulated a course of studies for youth in ancient history, literature, and moral philosophy as the best preparation for living a good life, and being in a position to rule over others, if called upon to assume positions of leadership, with virtue and wisdom. For his part, Petrarca understood humanist studies to be focused on primarily Roman and to a lesser extent Greek texts. On this path back to the ancients taken by Petrarca and his fellow Renaissance humanists, Cicero was the guiding light (as Vergil had been for Dante). His speeches and writings modeled for Petrarca the way of life that he hoped to revive in his own times. Cicero, in turn, had reoriented the traditional understanding of liberal education, which he had inherited from Socrates and Plato's *Republic*, around the needs of Roman political life, thus making liberal education the foundation for civic education. The main thread that runs through this tradition is the idea that quieting the turmoil in our own souls through the pursuit of wisdom prepares the way for us to engage virtuously in politics.[1]

CICERO'S *PRO ARCHIA* AND THE *STUDIA HUMANITATIS*

Marcus Tullius Cicero, in a judicial oration delivered in the year immediately after his Consulate, proposed a radical refounding of Roman republican politics. This refounding would be based on an idea of liberal education conceived in response to his recent experiences as consul with radical republican strife and informed by his study of Platonic political philosophy—an education that, reinforced with rhetorical training and guided by Roman law and history, Cicero celebrated as the source of his own extraordinary success as an orator and statesman.[2] In this speech (*Pro Archia*), rediscovered by Francesco Petrarca in 1333, Cicero defends the Roman citizenship of his Greek friend and mentor, Archias, a sublime poet and beloved teacher, in terms that directly associate Archias' case for Roman citizenship with his contribution to liberal education.

Cicero opens his defense of Archias by asking the indulgence of his Roman audience for proceeding with a new kind of argument, one that his fellow Romans would no doubt find novel, but one that would, upon reflection, compel the jurors (at least those among them with ears to hear) to consider the crucial role that liberal education plays as the basis of Roman—or, more precisely, human—virtue. Cicero refers to this education, and in particular the studies that comprise it, as the *studia humanitatis*, which is to say the "studies of humanity" (II.3), the collective study of what it means to be human. Cicero's phrase, and the idea of liberal education (*artes liberales*) to which he refers, descended to him from (what would later be called by Quintilian) the Greek concept of *enkuklios paideia*, literally the "encircling" or "well-rounded" education, an educational concept revived by the civic humanists of Renaissance Italy and the origin of our own modern concept of the humanities. The first recorded uses of the phrases *artes liberal* (and its synonyms) and *studia humanitatis* appear in Cicero's writings.[3]

In the context of his speech in defense of Archias, Cicero argues that liberal education, which he here refers to as the "humanistic studies," should not be narrowly conceived in relation to his defense of Archias' particular talent as a poet, or his own (not unremarkable) talent as an orator-statesman. Liberal education, rather, must be viewed in light of a certain "common bond" (*commune vinclum*) of kinship that binds together—as one—all of the studies most befitting free human beings. Thus, as he proclaims to the Roman citizen-jurors, "Know that I myself have never been wholly devoted to only one discipline. Indeed, all the arts which pertain to humanity have a kind of common bond (*omnes artes quae ad humanitatem pertinent habent quoddam commune vinclum*) and are joined together among themselves as if by a certain familial relation" (I.2). Calling himself as witness, Cicero testifies to his own lifelong devotion to humanistic studies and to the example set by Archias, a teacher whose contribution to the studies are beyond question, he argues. More important than his defense of a friend, however, is Cicero's lucid articulation of the "cultivation of soul" and "restoration of mind" that the studies themselves produced in him through learning.[4] In a world beset by disorder and violence,[5] his ears ringing with the noise and tumult down in the forum, Cicero's studies restore a profound sense of tranquility in his soul, preparing him to return with renewed vigor to the active life of Roman republican politics that, even in exile, he never forsakes (VI.12–13; see *De Officiis* III.1). These humanistic studies, then, are in the view of Cicero the source of order and harmony.[6]

Given his explicit devotion to Plato and the Academy, there is good reason to think that Cicero's therapeutic vision of the *studia humanitatis* takes its bearings from the care-taking art of the human soul, which is the hallmark of Socratic philosophy and the Platonic dialogues.[7] Indeed, as we shall see, even the idea of a familial bond unifying all the best studies—the ones appropriate for "free" human beings—finds its first formulation in Plato's *Republic*. Cicero's account of soul-healing reveals a psychology familiar to readers of the Platonic dialogue, for it too reflects upon the kind of education or formation of the soul that is best able to restore concord to the soul by setting each part or aspect of the soul in order, in relation to both the other parts as well as the whole. This restoration of harmony in the soul through study is arguably *the* principal philosophic task of Plato's *Republic*. Dissonance of soul comes to light in Socrates' arguments as *the* obstacle to human happiness, while liberal education, which sets us upon a path or "dialectical journey" toward our proper end and ultimate good, supplies the remedy.

Though the words we use today to refer to this kind of education are derived from Cicero, transmitted through the medieval liberal arts tradition (studies in the Trivium and Quadrivium) and then transformed by the alterative studies proposed by the Renaissance civic humanists, we find in the text of Plato's *Republic* the most profound and influential account of liberal education in western civilization.[8] This liberal or liberating education, outlined by Socrates through images and vivid figures of speech in Books 6 and 7 of the *Republic*, culminates in the non-poetic presentation of the philosopher's curriculum.[9]

PLATO'S *REPUBLIC* AND THE ART OF SOUL-LEADING AS CIVIC EDUCATION
The first extant explicit description of liberal education belongs to Aristotle, who describes in his *Politics* the education of the young not in "all the useful arts" that provide practical skills or lead to narrow mechanical vocations, but in those "free pursuits" appropriate to free human beings, pursuits aimed not at merely making a living but living well. The kind of learning that is undertaken to satisfy the human desire to know; that is, the kind of learning that takes place for its own sake and not as a means to some other end besides knowing. This learning is liberal, according to Aristotle, because it distinguishes those who are free from those who are not. This disinterested intellectual delight in coming to know and in knowing accords with our nature as human beings. But the content of that knowledge also matters. Aristotle speaks broadly of gymnastic and musical education for young citizens, but it is Plato who first laid out a course of studies, or curriculum.

More precisely than Cicero's *studia humanitatis*, Plato's Socrates outlines in the *Republic* a veritable *cursus honorum* of studies in his account of the decades-long intellectual training of Guardian-Rulers. This philosopher's curriculum stands as the first and fullest ancient expression of liberal education. This prospective course of studies constitutes the core of the dialogue as the educational path to be traveled by the would-be philosopher-kings conceived by Socrates as the gold-souled rulers of the just *polis*-in-*logos*. In scope and trajectory, as we shall see, this education follows the pattern laid down in the preceding images (of the Ship of State, Sun, Divided Line, and Cave) that assist the intellect in being led out of darkness toward the light, that is, the journey of the human soul toward contemplation of the Idea of the Good. By means of these provocative representations of enlightenment within the context of the dramatic argument, Socrates seeks to moderate the erotic desire of Glaucon, one of his two main interlocutors in the dialogue, persuading him through speeches that the virtue of justice is inherently good for human souls.

The completion of the radical liberal education in the *Republic* is meant to lead a select few among the Guardians of the city-in-speech out of the cave-darkness, which encloses the Craftsmen and Auxiliaries, and up to the light. But this liberal education becomes, in effect, a civic education. At the end of the liberal education, these Guardians are prepared by virtue of their philosophical Enlightenment to go back down into the dark environs of the city-in-speech and rule it with wisdom and moderation, thereby satisfying the ultimate condition for the establishment of political justice, according to Socrates:[10] "Unless philosophers rule as kings or those now called kings and chiefs genuinely and adequately philosophize, and political power and philosophy coincide in the same place, while the many natures now making their way to either apart from the other are by necessity excluded, there is no rest from ills for the cities, my dear Glaucon, nor I think for human kind; nor will the regime we have now described in speech ever come forth from nature, insofar as possible, and see the light of the sun" (473c–e; see 499b–c, 539e–540b). This condition is admittedly "very paradoxical" and requires defense, an apologia without which Socrates runs the risk of having to "pay the penalty" in scorn, not to mention having to confront an angry mob armed and stripped for battle against him (473e–474a). In response to tumults arising from the paradoxical character, or problem, of this "third wave"—the mere statement of which prompts an attack from his interlocutors—Socrates points to education as the solution. What makes possible this coincidence of political power and philosophy, apart from some divine intervention, he argues, is whether a soul with a philosophic nature "chances upon a suitable course of learning" so that "it will necessarily grow and come into every kind of virtue" (492a; cf. 496a–e). If indeed a philosophically-inclined soul does discover and undertake such a curriculum, the reorientation made possible by liberal education becomes civic in its outward manifestation and the only proper foundation for Justice in the *polis*.

At an earlier stage in the dialogue, with the assent of his interlocutors/ fellow founders,[11] Socrates had charged the Guardians with the task of preserving and protecting "the one great—or rather than great, the one sufficient—thing," namely, their own "education and rearing" within the city-in-speech. For "sound rearing and education" when preserved bring into being harmonic and well-ordered souls, and the Guardians in particular are the citizens of the city-in-speech who "must cleave to [their education]" above all else, "not letting it become corrupted unawares, but guarding it" from degradations or innovations that run contrary to the established regime, that is, the order of the *politeia* (423e–424b). If we are persuaded by the argument, it is clear that what is most in need of being guarded and kept safe by the Guardians (also called Overseers: 412a–b, 424b, 506b) is their education—and not simply the musical and gymnastic education that they share with the Auxiliaries, but more "precisely"[12] that education which resides in their souls as philosophers and remains as rulers and is brought to fruition through the studies in Book 7. This curriculum of studies is liberal education insofar as it sets human beings free in the fullest sense of the word (Gr. *eleutherios*, L. *liberos*); it is the path to the finest education that, in turn, is said to be the greatest safeguard and bulwark of the city-in-speech (416b). These studies reside in the *akropolis* of the soul and preserve the order as "watchmen and guardians" ruling over the whole (cf. 560a–561e).

To speak more broadly for a moment, liberal education is that training and study which renders a human being "free" from ignorance and self-neglect through examination and inquiry, thus distinguishing a free human being from an enslaved one, with all the attendant connotations for living generously and spiritedly in a manner befitting a true citizen. While even a slave may be trained and skilled in an art (*technê*) or a trade, managing tasks well, and even expertly so, those who are fully free must also be capable of exercising and preserving those skills, or arts, that are most necessary to the order of the regime. In the just city-in-speech of the *Republic*, each citizen through his or her practice of a particular art—in other words, by minding his or her business as a citizen—contributes to the justice and happiness of the *polis* as a whole. But only the Guardians must learn to philosophize in order to perform their task in the most precise way.[13]

These Ruling-Guardians with philosophical natures are anticipated from the very beginning of Socrates' argument (375a–376c) as rare souls distinguished by their "love of [all] learning" and, hence, "love of wisdom" (376b). These philosophic souls must prove their mettle, however, by first engaging in extensive gymnastic and musical training (described in Books 2 and 3), then followed by a rigorous course of studies that sharpens their senses, hones their keen minds, and draws them toward the truth they desire but do not yet know. In striving intensely for "every kind of truth," or the whole of truth, the ones who are "by nature" lovers of wisdom desire only knowledge, and thus reject all opinion (*doxa*) as misleading and false; they cherish the truth and what truly *is*, but never what *seems* to be (474c–480a, 484a–487a). They are concerned only with the pleasures appropriate to the soul, not those of the body, and they completely shun "illiberality" (*aneleutherias*) (485d–486a). These philosophic souls must rule if Kallipolis is to be just.

This assertion rouses Socrates' interlocutors, who now assault him armed with objections. Responding to Socrates' extended description of these philosophic souls who must rule in just city-in-speech, Adeimantus[14] contends that this cannot happen because these philosophers of necessity will *appear* either vicious or useless to the un-philosophic, unwise multitude dwelling contentedly within the realm of opinion (487b–d, 494a). In his defense of philosopher-kings, Socrates employs first an "image" and then a "sensible apology" (487e5, 490a8; see 488a5) to answer accusations raised by anyone who might wish to challenge Socrates' claim that philosophers are worthy of ruling—and there are many who do (see 473e–474a). The image of the Ship of State introduced by Socrates explains the apparent uselessness of philosophers in the cities, or at least in a democracy like Athens (488a–489d), whereas the *apologia* defends true philosophers from slander created by the confusion of philosophy with sophistry and by the corruption of the young men with potentially philosophic souls (489d–497a, 500b; cf. Alcibiades' portrait in Plato's *Alcibiades I*, *Alcibiades II*, and *Symposium*, as well as Xenophon's *Memorabilia* I.2).

The unarmed Socrates, in this manner, intends to kill two birds with one stone, so to speak, by "soothing" his potential enemies with persuasive speeches, *both* the serious gentlemen inclined to oppose the rule of philosophers with violence (476d–e; cf. 498c–d, 499d, 501c–e) *and* the many easily misled by false speeches who are more likely to despise philosophers out of ignorance and confusion, or who mistakenly believe a philosophic nature such as Socrates describes cannot exist, let alone flourish (498b–502c).[15] Before turning attention to "the greatest studies" (503e–504a), or rather "the greatest and most fitting study" (504d–505a), as a result of which "the saviors [that is, the philosopher-kings] will take their place within our regime," according to Socrates (502d), let us pause to consider the method

Socrates has chosen—and will continue to employ—in order to "soothe" the factious and unruly tempers that inevitably disrupt and overthrow the finely tuned order of the just city-in-speech (545a ff.).

SOCRATIC RHETORIC AND LIBERAL EDUCATION: PHILOSOPHICAL FIGURES-IN-SPEECH

Having been compelled by Polemarchus (328a–b) to remain 'down' in the Peiraieus-Cave longer than expected, and then at the insistence of Adeimantus (449b, 487b) to prolong his stay with lengthy speeches, Socrates is now 'forced' to "go through the good" in argument in order to gratify the desire of Glaucon (506d; see 368c). Using devices borrowed from the rhetorical art, Socrates employs metaphors, analogies, parables, and paradoxes to move his interlocutors from the familiar to the unfamiliar, the known to the unknown, by way of relations and proportions,[16] persuading them to follow the *logos*.[17] Put simply, Socrates practices rhetoric.[18] With only a few notable exceptions, Socratic poetry and rhetoric are most dominant in the section of the dialogue immediately preceding the philosopher's curriculum.

When Adeimantus voices his objection to the rule of philosophers on behalf of the many who utterly fail to see how philosophic natures are useful and not harmful, Socrates sees that the question itself "needs an answer given through an image" (487e). The word *eikōn* in Greek has connotations that refer to any likeness, such as a painting or a reflection of an object in still water or a polished mirror. Socrates suggests with a *logos* of this sort that the faculty of imagination must be used to demonstrate to the un-philosophic multitude the usefulness of philosophers, not to mention their distinctive virtue. Fortunately, as Adeimantus playfully points out, Socrates is no stranger to fashioning images in speech; however, this particular method (*meth-odos*) for moving through *logoi* will prove insufficient to the task—if, that is, precision is what is in fact required (cf. the provocative ellipsis about the soul, at 435c–d). But if the aim of his speech is persuasion, philosophical poetry—in other words, Socratic rhetoric—must suffice to lead the way (cf. 388e). Socrates admits to Adeimantus "how greedy" (and how adept) he is at speaking through images, especially when it comes to making such difficult arguments (487e–488a).[19]

This reference to images and the faculty of imagination anticipates the categories within the Image of the Divided Line that will be introduced by

Socrates near the end of Book 6. For the moment, it prepares the way for a sequence of passages that rely heavily on Socrates' creation of rhetorical figures in speech, despite (or because of) the necessity to speak here with "the greatest precision" about "the greatest things."[20] Though not always precise, his figures are so vivid as to be unforgettable, beginning with the Image of the Ship of State. Since this image is a familiar one—as Socrates says to Adeimantus—there is no need "to scrutinize the image to see that it resembles the cities in their disposition toward the true philosophers" (489a). What must be done, then, is to "teach the image" (*didaske tên eikona*) to whoever "wonders" at dishonor heaped on philosophers in the cities such as they are and "persuade" them to marvel instead at how it could be otherwise. Images, when well-constructed and carefully scrutinized, are useful rhetorical tools for defending the role of philosophy within the *polis*.[21] This lesson proponents of liberal education in our times often fail to understand by assuming the self-evident worth of what they study and teach.

Socrates here scrutinizes his own Ship of State image only to the point of revealing its most direct application to the problem posed by the (not entirely false) perception of the philosophers as useless. The stargazer aboard the ship does not appear to perform a task that is obviously useful, and so he seems useless to the rest. Because he does not seek to compete with the ambitious sailors for the pilot's job, the knowledge of the art that he has acquired as a result of his studies will not be put to good use. In other words, because the wise do not desire rule over the Ship of State, their precise knowledge of how to rule will be useful only *if* they are sought out by the unwise. The image explicitly, therefore, offers an account of why philosophers are perceived as useless; it also points implicitly to the more serious problem raised by the third wave, namely, that philosophers must be *compelled* to return to the Cave and rule.

This form of Socratic rhetoric, with its appeals to mathematical precision and reflection, has little in common with the art or 'knack' of cookery-in-speech ridiculed by Socrates in the first part of Plato's *Gorgias* (464b ff.), but rather resembles the true art of rhetoric and politics, practiced by Socrates, which is grounded in a dialectical understanding of the soul (*psychê*). In other words, Socratic rhetoric is guided by and in tune with a philosophic psychology that is truly therapeutic and concerned with taking care of the soul. This dialectical understanding requires, in turn, as we learn in Plato's *Phaedrus* (269c ff.), knowing how each of the discrete parts (as those of an animal, a human being, or a *logos*) relate to each other and the whole. Such understanding requires an exploration of the soul, both in its parts or aspects and as a whole, of the sort that is undertaken by the *Republic* itself.[22] While precision is not always a virtue of rhetoric, dialectic requires it.[23]

PRELUDE TO THE PHILOSOPHER'S CURRICULUM:
IMAGES OF THE SUN AND OF THE DIVIDED LINE

Adeimantus finally requests of Socrates that, despite his objections, he proceed to explain "in what way and as a result of what studies" the Guardian-Rulers will take up their place within "our regime" and become "saviors" of the city-in-speech (502c–d). Socrates hesitates, since only "the greatest studies" (503e–504a) give rise to the "most precise education" (503d) and therewith to "the most precise guardians" (503b). And we know "the greatest things [are] worth the greatest precision" (504e). As it turns out, the study of Justice itself—the search for which has preoccupied them for some time—is not what Socrates understands to be "the end of the greatest and most fitting study" (504d). Hence, it appears that the argument of the dialogue thus far about Justice is to be transcended by the pursuit of the True and the Good. When pressed by Adeimantus to say what "the greatest study [is] and what it concerns," and not to think he will escape from their grasp (503e; cf. 327c–328b, 357a, 449a–451b), Socrates concedes:

> At all events, it is not a few times already you have heard it; but now, either you are not thinking, or you have it in mind to take hold of me again and make trouble for me. I suppose it is rather the latter, since you have many times heard that the *idea* of the Good is the greatest study, and that—concerning the just things and all the rest—it is by availing oneself of [the idea of the Good, or the study thereof] that those things themselves become useful and beneficial. (504e–505a)

What is more, Socrates continues, "you know very well that this is what I would say, and besides this, that we don't have sufficient knowledge of it" (505a). Without knowledge of that which confers advantage and benefit (or profit), which is to say in the absence of complete knowledge of the Good, we cannot know that the use we make of anything else—including Justice—will be either prudent or profitable.

When it comes to what we pursue as good, argues Socrates, "no one is satisfied with what is opined to be [good] but each seeks the things that really *are* [*ta onta*], and despises from here on out the opinion" (505d). Although the soul is "at a loss" about what it most desires and pursues, "and for the sake of which it does everything" (cf. *Cleitophon* 410d6–e1), nonetheless, it "divines" that [the Idea of] the Good really exists, even though it is "unable to get a sufficient grasp of just what it is" (505e). It is the articulation of this divination that Adeimantus requires and that Glaucon (who at 505d replaces his brother as Socrates' interlocutor) eagerly takes to be "the end" toward which their conversation has been tending all along. Not unlike the cunning sea god Proteus in the hero's tale from Homer (*Odyssey* IV), Socrates cannot be released by the spirited young men who have now seized him until he says what he thinks the Good, or the idea of the Good, is.

Resorting to his rhetoric once more, Socrates agrees to say not what the Good itself is, but what resembles or looks to him like "a child" of the Good, namely, the Sun. This Image of the Sun in turn generates the Image of the Divided Line with its proportional relations between especially the Light cast by the Good itself by which Ideas or Thoughts are grasped with clarity, and the light of the Sun by which we see all that is visible. In other words, while the Good itself is the first principle and cause (*archê*) of the Intelligible realm, it also—by virtue of bringing into being the Sun, which is its *analogos*—is the *archê* of the Visible realm (507b–c, 517b–c).[24]

Once the Image of Sun issues in speech from the Good itself, Socrates prompts Glaucon to "consider" further or scrutinize the meaning of the Image of the Sun. The power of the light of the Sun, which stimulates the natural capacity for sight in human beings by illuminating that which is seen, explains by analogy how the Good itself is the source of knowledge and truth in the realm of the Intellect, and thus is also "beyond them in beauty" (509a). Moreover, while sunlight also causes generation, growth, and nourishment (at least for natural things) in the visible realm, it is not the source of coming-into-being for such things; that power belongs to the Good (509b): "Say then that not only being known is present in things that are known as a consequence of the Good, but also existence and being are in them besides because of it, although the Good itself is not Being but still is beyond Being, exceeding it in both dignity and power." With a certain "daemonic excess," it seems that Socrates here has reached the peak of philosophy, understood as epistemology or metaphysics, through a figure-of-speech. Upon hearing in speech this sublime divination of an ineffable Good, which Socrates forewarned his young companions would be beyond their grasp (cf. 506d8–e1), even if they are "blessed men" (506d7), Glaucon feels compelled to invoke Apollo, god of the sun and light—and "quite ridiculously" so, says Socrates, because even the pronouncements of Apollo, as the god of the Delphic Oracle, must be scrutinized (see *Apology* 21a–23b).[25] Although he speaks under compulsion (of one sort or another) and claims he must omit "a throng of things," Glaucon insists that Socrates continue and leave nothing out.[26] The non-political image of the Divided Line thus becomes a crucial means of interpreting both the political Image of the Cave and the philosopher's curriculum that immediately follow.[27]

Socrates, submitting, orders Glaucon to conceive that the Good and the Sun rule over two realms or Forms (*eidê*), the Intelligible and the Visible. He then commands Glaucon to consider the realms on a line that is cut or divided in two unequal segments, each of which is further cut or divided according to the same proportion (whatever it may be) as the line itself. The resulting four segments along the Divided Line, geometrically speaking (*Gorgias* 465b–c), now stand in relation or in proportion to one another in such a way that each of the pairs reflects precisely and internally (that is, with respect to its own parts) the same *logos* or ratio that defines the line as a whole or taken all together (that is, with respect to the two parts, or pairs, which belong to it). Glaucon, in a passage that illuminates the virtue of his soul,[28] understands that Socrates is fashioning this Image of a (thrice) Divided Line in order to make clear that the Intelligible realm in particular is also divided, not one. In one segment or part, various "arts" (*technai*) compel thought to begin from hypotheses and proceed through arguments to conclusions using Rhetoric (510b–511b), while, in the other, intellection begins from fundamental "first principles" (*archai*) without hypotheses because grasped immediately with Dialectic (511b–c).[29] The relation of thought to intellection in the Intelligible realm is proportionally the same as the relation between imagination and trust in the Visible realm. Four corresponding affections, or conditions, of the soul are also ranged along the line in relation to each other according to the degree to which each participates in truth and clarity with respect to what each uniquely grasps.

Once this arrangement of the soul's faculties has been made clear through the Image of the Divided Line, Socrates has prepared the way to offer his most memorable[30] image of all—in order to display "the condition of our nature in its education and want of education" (514a). The Image of the Cave thus thrusts upon us a powerful, even overwhelming means of visualizing our natural condition with respect to knowledge of the soul, both in its enlightenment and in its lack thereof, or darkness. The "rough, steep, upward way" out of the Cave and into the light of the Sun becomes the path of education for human beings, from the familiar and fleeting, 'up' toward the unfamiliar yet Eternal (or at least perennial) truths or Forms, from blissful ignorance to genuine knowledge. Though the ascent is a hard one, and our natural inclinations to ascend are weakened and obstructed by our attachments to opinions, the image shows beyond doubt that the "soul's journey up to the Intelligible realm" is most desirable for human beings (517b).

However, we must remind ourselves of the discussion that closed Book 6 (as Socrates' interlocutors were forewarned) that Socrates' method for rendering this account of (the Idea of) the Good itself as the object of contemplation in "the greatest study" is rhetorical, not dialectical. Insofar as thought falls short of grasping sufficiently what *is*, and is exceeded by intellection (to the same degree by analogy that trust in perception apprehends what can be seen with more clarity than the imagination thereof), Socrates' representation of the Good must be questioned and scrutinized. The degree to which the images or figures-in-speech are philosophical should be carefully examined, in light of their rhetorical or shall we say propaedeutic and protreptic purpose, which is to prepare his interlocutors for the philosopher's curriculum—the Socratic articulation of which will *not* itself partake of images.[31]

THE ART OF LEADING SOULS TO THE LIGHT: THE IMAGE OF THE CAVE AS EDUCATION

At the beginning of Book 7, Glaucon immediately begins to scrutinize the image and he rightly intuits that there is something "strange" about Socrates' Image of the Cave—not the image per se as much as the 'prisoners' within it, who are bound legs and neck, immobile, living out their life in a miserable dream of falsehood, deceived by shadows and images of reality (514a–515a; cf. 510d–e). It *is* strange, indeed. Insofar as it is intended to open a window into the human soul, the image reveals in harsh terms a psychological dilemma of enslavement of the sort that has been haunting the entire dialogue, namely, that we are not really as *free* as we want to believe we are. What is perhaps worse, we tend to resist and even struggle against our own liberation from the chains of ignorance that bind us[32] in the darkness. Socrates explains (515c):

> Consider what their release and healing from bonds and folly would be like, if *something of this sort* were *by nature* to happen to them. Take a person who is released [from bonds] and compelled suddenly to stand up, both to turn his neck around and to walk and look upward the light; all this, moreover, being done in pain both on account of being dazzled and unable to make out those things whose shadows he saw before—what do you suppose he would say if someone were to tell him that, before, he saw silly nothings, whereas now, because he is much nearer to *what is* and more turned toward *the things that are*, he sees more correctly; but . . . showing him each of the things passing by, what if someone were to compel him to answer questions about what they are? Do you not suppose he would be at a loss, and believe what was seen before is 'more true' than what he is now being shown?

To be dragged out of the Cave "by force" and compelled to ascend up into the Light must intensely distress and annoy, as well as disorient, whoever is being dragged, to such a degree that one who strives "to release and lead up" the prisoners likely will be resisted with violence, perhaps even killed (515e, 517a). Having considered this fate, perhaps it would be better for the one who might assist in the liberation of others to heed Socrates' warning earlier in the dialogue, that it is best for the one who sees the truth to "keep quiet and mind his own business" (496d–e)—seeking shelter, as a calculating man does when in the midst of a storm, and huddling "beside a little wall" (514b)—when the violent anger of recalcitrant Cave-dwellers is aroused.[33]

Plato's readers, if not his young interlocutors in the *Republic*, would hear Socrates' words here as ironically prophetic, in light of his trial and execution at the hands of his fellow Athenians. His death resulted from an inability to persuade his jurors that his way of life—openly questioning unexamined opinions and not believing he knows what he does not know—was liberating, insofar as the condition for searching for knowledge is first realizing that what you think know is not really knowledge. To seek wisdom we must first break the invisible chains of our own ignorance. So too, contemporary teachers and professors can hear in Socrates' words an ironic foreshadowing of the paradox created in higher education by compelling students to take required courses. A liberating, or liberal, education ought to be embraced and desired voluntarily (and not only in retrospect—as former students frequently point out to former teachers), but it seems inevitable that such education will be perceived by most of those who lack it as compulsory, and perhaps even opposed on those very grounds. This paradoxical and potentially dangerous aspect of teaching and learning Socrates now addresses by scrutinizing the Image of the Cave.

Socrates proposes, considering this dilemma, that there must be an art of "turning around" such imprisoned souls—away from what is *passing-in-and-out-of-being* (in the Cave), and toward that which truly *is* (beyond the Cave), and then finally toward "the brightest part of that which *is*" (the Light of the Sun and the Good itself). This art of turning-around souls and leading them to the light is education: the "release and healing" of a soul from the bonds that otherwise bind it to the shadow-images in the Cave. Yet this liberal education differs from what is usually professed by "certain men" who declare that they can educate others by pouring knowledge into their minds, "as though they were putting sight into blind eyes" (518b). Such men, says Socrates, claim to teach what the soul lacks by nature, rather than educating a soul to make use of what properly speaking belongs to it. Education rightly understood is the turning-around of "the whole soul" by somehow compelling "the power in each soul" that is its means of apprehending what *is*—its natural gaze, as it were,[34] to awaken and to look 'up' toward the Light (518c; 518b–519b). Thus awakened, the turning-around of souls "from a day that is like night to the true day" constitutes the very beginning of "that ascent to what truly *is*" that Socrates proclaims we can "truly affirm to be philosophy" (521c–d). The activity of philosophy, therefore, is a liberal education, which is to say the liberation of our soul from chains of ignorance binding us in and to the darkness.

How does Socrates' ode to liberal education evade the strange aspect of compulsion that dominates the Image of the Cave? How can we be 'forced' to be free? By what means is this liberal education administered? In what way is the release of the soul from its shackles by force to be viewed as "healing" and therapeutic care of the soul? Must the soul be compelled, or led, toward its own freedom? Does a philosophic soul somehow suffer injustice on account of being compelled against its will (at least initially) to abandon the Cave and go up toward the light, despite Socratic assurances[35] to the contrary? Or, perhaps, is the path of enlightenment inherently compelling, which is to say attractive and appealing to human beings—at least once the notion of a natural light beyond the darkness of the cave has been adequately conceived or imagined?

On the grounds that their pursuit of justice requires it, and that it would be impossible for the city-in-speech that is just to exist unless those with "education and experience of truth" are made to rule, Socrates asserts that "our job as founders" is "to compel the best natures to go to the study which before we were saying is the greatest," which is to say "to see the good and to go up that ascent" (519c–d). The argument now turns to the philosophic education of the ones who indeed have the best nature and will become the true guardians of the just city (521c): "Do you want us to consider in what way such men will come into being and how one will lead them up to the light, just as some are said to have gone from Hades up to the gods?" In answer to his own question, Socrates embarks on a lengthy and detailed account of the "studies" that have the power to lead and "draw the soul" upward "from Becoming to Being" (521d).

The studies in the philosopher's curriculum, to which Socrates now turns, are liberating, in that they effect a forceful *"haul upward"* on the soul, working on the soul like a winch, and raising it up from the darkness to the light.[36] But it must be noted that, while the studies serve as a kind of hoist for the soul, the motion upward is not irreversible. These studies do not guarantee only an upward motion in the same way that a mechanical ratchet and pawl prevent backsliding, or a downward motion, under the influence of a strong gravitational pull.[37] Progress on this ascent is not assured. When undertaken in the right way, the ultimate effect of this philosophic education—which is consistent with the earlier treatment of the guardians' education in gymnastic and music,[38] but goes beyond and thus completes it—is to haul up those souls with the best natures beyond the confines of the city-in-speech. For those who manage to break the chains of ignorance, ascend the Visible segments of the Divided Line, and escape the Cave, their liberal education is only partially complete. The liberating studies beyond the Cave that comprise the philosopher's curriculum and correspond to the pursuit of knowledge in the Intelligible realm prepare these souls to return to the Cave and rule, precisely by virtue of the fact that they have transcended the *polis* in the direction of the Good on account of their love of wisdom (520e4–521a2)—their inherent and inward desire for which has 'compelled' them to make the ascent.

Let us turn, therefore, to the sequence of liberating studies in the philosopher's curriculum, bearing in mind that Socrates no longer speaks through figures of speech and images throughout this section. He does not, however, cease speaking both rhetorically and dialectically.

THE PHILOSOPHER'S CURRICULUM
Numbers and Calculation

What must be learned first, as a foundational study, is something in which all the arts and all kinds of knowledge participate, and which, in Glaucon's view, makes us distinctively human: the "lowly business" (*to phaulon*) of separating "One, Two, and Three"—or, to put it "succinctly, Number and Calculation" (522c–e). The study of arithmetic leads souls to the Intelligible realm by summoning the intellect to examine and judge the intolerable impression of contradictions embedded in the things we perceive, especially when viewed in relation to each other. In order to explain to Glaucon what he means, Socrates calls his attention to the fact that "some objects of sensation do not summon the intellect (*tên noêsin*) to the activity of inquiry, because they seem to be adequately judged by the senses, while others bid [the intellect] in every way to make an inquiry, because sense seems to produce nothing healthy" (523b). What follows is the first in a series of revealing errors by the otherwise keen Glaucon, for he takes Socrates to be referring here to the unreliability of sense perception—for example, when it comes to seeing things clearly and distinctly across great distances as opposed to seeing up close (cf. 368c–369b). According to Socrates, Glaucon has entirely missed the point of what was said. In clarifying, Socrates leads Glaucon through a *logos* that turns him around toward the truth.[39]

Socrates explains in a lengthy digression how the intellect is summoned to 'make sense' of the "strange interpretations" to which a soul is led by sensations without thought (523c–524c). Socrates wants Glaucon to understand that when the senses are perplexed and "at a loss" (*aporeô*), due to apparent contradictions in what is perceived, intellect is aroused to inquire and adjudicate (524e). When sensations appear to conflict—as when something seems both larger and smaller, or one and many—then the soul is "compelled" (523d, 524) to call upon the intellect to distinguish with clarity what attributes of a sensory object really are. Summoning or "setting in motion" the intellect through inquiry inevitably causes the intellect to raise the 'What is . . . ?' question that is the beginning of Socratic philosophy. This motion of the soul turning around toward truth and being, with respect to what is perceived by the senses, is the beginning of the philosophic ascent.

Socrates and Glaucon now agree the study of Numbers and their attributes (*arithmētikē*) as well as the related art of Calculation (*logistikē*), which involves using numbers in operations such as subtraction, addition, or multiplication, are particularly "apt to lead and turn around [the soul] toward the contemplation of what *is*" and the whole truth (524e–526c). It seems, however, that for Glaucon their agreement that the contemplation of Number and the study of Calculation should be set down in law as the basis of the philosopher's curriculum is partly contingent on the inference that mathematics is a subtle skill especially useful for the Guardian who must be both warrior and philosopher. Knowledge of Numbers and Calculation is directly related to the tactics of generalship.[40] But this inference is Glaucon's second error.

While it is true that such knowledge is useful in war, among other practical activities, Socrates says that the study of Calculation is really useful for "turning the soul itself around" particularly on account of the way "it leads the soul powerfully upward and compels it to discuss numbers themselves" (525c–d). This activity stimulates intellection to do that work in the soul that it alone and by nature[41] is best suited to perform; hence, "this study is really compulsory for us, since it evidently compels the soul to use the intellect itself on the truth itself" (526b). But how is the theoretical study of Numbers and Calculation, this "lowly business" useful to anyone, necessary for philosophy? The word *arithmos* in Greek refers both to the numbers counted and to the act of counting itself; that the ordered plurality of numbers or countable parts attached to—but not inseparable from—the things themselves suggests a close affinity between countability and knowability; and that, consequently, there seems to be a definite "epistemic reliability" with regard to Numbers and Calculation.[42] To calculate well (*phronimōs logizomenon*) is to know (*eidota*; see *Laches* 193a). Paradigmatic of all kinds of *technê*, the method as well as the result of counting and calculating produces clarity and authority, by supplying the necessary condition for apprehension and intelligibility. Mathematics, as the Pythagoreans argued, is *the* model of determinacy, in which every *technê* and *epistêmê* "is compelled to participate" (522c).

When the intellect is "summoned" to stabilize the contradictions of sensation, the work of thinking (*dianoia*) accomplished through the study of Numbers and Calculation in relation to perceived objects, permits us to rely or 'count on' counting as a legitimate and certain means of discriminating and collecting, of putting in order and thus making harmonious the (apparently) dissonant multiplicity of things that confronts and perplexes our senses. Mathematical knowing and apprehension overcomes perceived confusion. But in the very act of counting, the soul is also turned around from the objects being counted toward the intangible Numbers—or the Idea of Number itself—invoked by the intellect to perform the act of counting, but is separable from the objects themselves.[43] By the "trivial" or elementary act of counting, we gain access to the realm of pure, intelligible, and stable entities, which, when studied conceptually, lead the soul "powerfully upward," turning us away from vague perceptions through the ordinary process of counting toward substances worth thinking about.[44] Put simply, the determinate status of Numbers that awakens the intellect through Calculation sets the soul in motion on a course of studies in the philosopher's curriculum that is the educational equivalent for Guardian-Rulers of the "Thrasymachean" principle of precision that emerged in Book 1, and then culminated in Book 4 with a *polis*-in-*logos* built around the perfection and use of *technai*.[45]

With this as the beginning of their studies, philosophic natures start to conceive "an ideal and inkling of formal perfection" through a mode of thinking whose precision and exactness[46] renders life among the erratic and confused shadow-images of the Cave deeply unsatisfying and profoundly disturbing. We are thereby drawn upward from opinion to knowledge, and toward a more satisfying life—not just one of greater stability and clarity, but of profound beauty as well; the symmetry, order, and elegant complexity of mathematical knowledge appeals to the intellect, for reasons far beyond the practical application and use of such knowledge to the visible realm that had momentarily tempted Glaucon. The precariousness of an uncertain existence, which is riddled with contradictions and leads potentially to violent disputes, is being left behind as the soul ascends through the sections of the Divided Line and enters the realm of thought, turning itself around away from riotous images and objects toward a world of intelligibility and harmony grasped only by the 'eyes' and 'ears' of the soul.

Geometry and Astronomy
Once contradictory perceptions have been surveyed and smoothed by an aroused intellect, the activity of distinguishing, counting, and clarifying relations yields to an "adjoining study" (526c), which is to say, the act of 'sizing up' and measuring by comparison and with precision. This next study, like the first one, is said to be useful in "the business of war"; Glaucon launches into a description of the martial tasks that knowledge of Geometry helps the generals to perform. As with Calculation, Socrates does not disagree but points to the usefulness of Geometry in some higher sense. For utilitarian purposes only, "a small portion of geometry—as of calculation—would suffice"; but Socrates suggests that the whole of geometry must include a "greater and more advanced part" that "tends to make it easier to make out the *Idea* of the Good" insofar as the study itself "compels the soul to turn around" in the direction of that realm "inhabited by the happiest part of what *is*" (526c–e).[47] Socrates cannot proceed unless Glaucon sees precisely what kind of studies are (and are not) "suitable" for the philosopher's curriculum.

Just as images seen *as images* are seen *through*, and the more 'trustworthy' objects that the images represent and on which they depend are themselves beheld, so too the properties of visible objects seen by the eyes lead the intellect to grasp at the "objects of thought" (*ta noēta*) upon which, by analogy, those things we happen to trust themselves depend. But evidence of the resemblance between visible and invisible objects materializes in the way geometricians often use diagrams or models written in sand (or chalkboards). Such "artful images" of symbolic importance elucidate essentially intellectual or abstract demonstrations; strictly speaking, the demonstrations appeal only and directly to the mind.[48] This fact is a point that geometricians and other practitioners of the arts who seek to "apply" technical knowledge to the physical world around us (for whatever purpose or reasons) all-too-often forget (527a–b): "For they surely speak in a way that is as ridiculous as it is necessary. They speak as though they were men of action and were making all the arguments for the sake of action, uttering sounds like 'squaring,' 'applying,' 'adding,' and everything of the sort, whereas the whole study is surely for the sake of knowing . . . what is always, and not at all for what is at any time coming into being and then passing away." The principles of geometry (and arithmetic) thus transcend images (in speech or otherwise) that might be manufactured to transmit or teach those principles in the same way or proportion that the visible objects upon which imagination depends convey to us a sense of trust and security that the mere shadow-images of those objects cannot (510b–e). Access to knowledge and truth increases as we move 'up' the levels of the Divided Line in the direction of the Good; to descend is the equivalent of sliding back down into relative darkness and obscurity, as we seek to travel along the very path that leads us out of the Cave and into the Light of the Sun.

The temptation to apply learning, in fact, subverts the upward haul of the liberal studies. Just as those who are charmed by poetry may be tempted into a forgetfulness of sensible objects by the power of images, so too those who 'practice' the mathematical arts may be tempted by the utilitarian charms of arithmetic and geometry in the application of their knowledge in a way that seeks to govern the realm of objects. Rather than ascending through—that is, into and beyond—mathematical studies, the soul would be drawn back down again. (This temptation to descend is all the more striking in light of the one crucial visual and geometrical feature of the Divided Line drawn by Socrates: the realm of mathematical knowledge and the realm of sensible things have been constructed in a way that renders the two realms exactly equal in extent. The profitability of such knowledge in its applications to the 'real world' obscures the intermediary character of that same knowledge as a useful stepping-stone in the ascent along the Divided Line.)[49]

The point is not lost on Glaucon, who now boldly asserts that "geometrical knowing" is, properly speaking, concerned above all with the study of "what *is* always" (527b). His emphatic agreement elicits from Socrates an unusual familiar address, followed by an important revelation regarding the city-in-speech constructed in Books 2–5 (527b–c):

"Then, you noble man,[50] [the study of geometry] would draw the soul toward truth and be productive of philosophical thinking (*dianoias*) in directing upward what now improperly we direct downward."

"To the greatest extent possible," [Glaucon] said.

"Then to the greatest extent possible," [Socrates] said, "the men in your Beautiful-Polis (*kallipolis*) must be enjoined in no way to abstain from geometry, for even its by-products are not insignificant.'"

Unlike the recalcitrant Callicles in Plato's *Gorgias* who disregards geometry and so neglects that community, friendship, orderliness, moderation, and justness that wise men say bind together human beings and gods in one unified *kosmos* (*Gorgias* 508a),[51] there is indeed something noble about the erotic nature of Glaucon's soul. He swears by the difference between one who is devoted to the philosophic study of Geometry and one who is not (527c). His original longing for precise knowledge of Justice itself has been subsumed within a devotion to the pursuit of the Good itself through the studies outlined by Socrates in the philosopher's curriculum. And it is in this context of geometrical precision that Socrates names their city-in-speech for the first and only time in the course of the dialogue. (We will return to the significance of this observation later.)

Yet despite (or because of) his evidently noble and erotic soul, Glaucon is still impetuous. When asked by Socrates whether he would agree to set down Astronomy, after Geometry, as the third study in the philosopher's curriculum, he leaps too quickly ahead. In one breath, he affirms the study and declares the utility of Astronomy (albeit more for its use in farming and navigation than in generalship). Amused by this silliness, Socrates reins-in Glaucon by revealing to him that he has made not only a mistake with respect to what is truly useful about Astronomy, but also an error with respect to what comes next in the sequence of studies (527d–e). The latter as much as the former is indicative of Glaucon's soul, for he overlooks or neglects the study of Stereometry or solid (as opposed to plane) Geometry.[52] In its attention to the "dimension of depth" this study in particular marks a crucial turning point in the studies, for it directs the intellect toward interior spaces and volumes that, because confined within the boundary of surface, are not visible, which is to say are not as readily or immediately perceived and grasped by the senses. Such an inward-looking gaze is essential to the Socratic task of acquiring self-knowledge (which is the purpose of the examined life as described in the *Apology* and *Phaedo*).[53] In losing 'sight' of this study during his haste to 'ascend' Glaucon may be neglecting himself— or that part of himself that opens up within his bodily form and fills it out so to speak with animating substance, namely, the invisible expanse of soul. In his neglect of the whole human being, as with his overlooking of the "greater and more advanced part" of each study, Glaucon runs the risk of being trapped in the Cave with the other non-philosophic prisoners.[54]

"Retreat a way," orders Socrates (528a6; cf. 528d6). This regression in the articulation of the studies is prompted by Socrates' awareness that, in their long "dialectical march" (*dialektikē poreia*: 532b4) toward the Idea of the Good and the rest that awaits them at the heights of the Intelligible realm (532d–e), he may be leaving behind the well-intentioned Glaucon, eager though he is to advance forward in the dialectical journey. Socrates' rebuke amounts to a questioning of Glaucon's tendency not "to command"[55] studies that would seem 'useless' to the Many who fail to see what is good for its own sake (or for the soul: 527e6–528a5, 530b; cf. 357a–d). To put this in the terms of the study at hand, the lover of wisdom cannot be 'taken in' by appearances or fall victim to honoring the studies that charm the Many with their demonstrations of usefulness, and especially the profit gained from using them (528c–d). What *seems* three-dimensional but is really two-dimensional (plane geometry) cannot be allowed to create an utter disregard for the study of what is truly three-dimensional (solid geometry), without which it is impossible to move up to the study of Astronomy and "the motion of what has depth" (528a–e).[56]

The commission of errors reaches a climax in the discussion of the fourth and final study, prior to Dialectic itself. Socrates forgives Glaucon's previous errors, on the grounds that Socrates himself in his "haste to go through everything quickly" was the cause of their [he says, "my"] being slowed down. (Socrates also laments the "ridiculous state" of their effort to articulate the course of studies in the philosopher's curriculum.) Having learned his lesson, it seems, Glaucon now attempts to praise the study of Astronomy without reference to the vulgar who may desire it strictly for the sake of utility and profit. He explains that "it is plain to everyone that Astronomy compels the soul to see what's above [our heads] and [therefore] leads it [up] there away from the things [down] here" (529a; these bracketed words supply what Glaucon mistakenly believes, as we learn from what he says subsequently, although the words he actually uses would suffice if spoken by someone who understands what Socrates is trying to make clear). While the language echoes that of Socrates, and in particular recalls the imagery of the Cave in relation to education and the art of soul-turning, a subtle preoccupation with the physical and visible realm persists.

Socrates playfully reproaches Glaucon for his hyper-literal interpretation of how a study of Astronomy assists in the liberation and ascent of the philosophic soul from the darkness and distractions of the Cave. To be precise, he rebukes Glaucon for believing that, by tilting our head and eyes 'upward' away from the visible objects around us in order to contemplate objects in the heavens "above," we are therewith accomplishing the turning-around of the soul. In other words, Socrates chides Glaucon for confusing (parts of the) body with (parts of the) soul (529b–c): "I, for my part, am unable to hold that any study makes a soul look upward other than the one that concerns both what *is* and is invisible. If a man, gaping up or squinting down, attempts to learn something of sensible things, I would deny that he ever learns—for there is no knowledge (*epistêmê*) of such things—or that his soul looks up, rather than down, even if he learns while laying on his back either on land or sea." Like the diagrams and models of geometricians, "these decorations in the heaven embroidered on a visible ceiling" fall short of the truth about the kinetic motion and energy of solid bodies that is "grasped by argument (*logos*) and thought (*dianoia*), not sight" (529c–d). As with Calculation and (the two forms of) Geometry, there is a philosophic approach to the study of Astronomy (perhaps more correctly termed Kinematics). Even the most precise images used in this study, such as the complex and intricate astronomical models designed by the Pythagoreans and (later) by Ptolemy, are to be conceived as nothing more than "patterns" (*paradeigma*; cf. esp. 592b)—"most beautiful in execution," yet "ridiculous to examine seriously as though one were able to grasp truth . . . *in* them" (529d–e).

Instead, Socrates argues that "by the use of problems (*problêmasin*), as in geometry, we shall also pursue astronomy; and we shall let the things in the heaven go, if by partaking in astronomy we are going to convert the prudence that is by nature in the soul from uselessness to usefulness" (530b). Contrary to "the Many" (*hoi polloi*) who see no benefit or profit worth mentioning from this kind of study, Socrates sees each of the studies, and this one especially, as crucial for the conversion or turning-around of the soul, for he claims the curriculum accomplishes a purification and rekindling of the soul's perceptive faculty, or organ (*organon*)—which is "more important to save than ten thousand eyes"—and is beneficial beyond words (527d–e): "For it is with this alone that the truth is seen." Glaucon accepts the "just penalty" for his error—namely, Socrates' reproach—and now realizes that the tasks or studies being prescribed by Socrates are quite far from and "many times greater than what is now done" by those who profess to teach and learn these same studies (529c, 530c).[57] Having now glimpsed the radical means and ends of the studies in the philosopher's curriculum, Glaucon is beginning to understand that the usefulness of each study derives from nothing other than its contribution to the soul's turning-around and ascent toward the Good. This is the only benefit or gain for those who love wisdom; the practical application of knowledge is "labor without profit" (531a).

Harmonics and the Song of Dialectic
This education and conversion of (the power of) the soul from uselessness to usefulness, properly understood, also marks the turning point in the philosopher's curriculum from directing the gaze of "the mind's eye" (*tēn tēs psuchēs opsin*) upwards toward the Light, to the cultivation of 'the mind's ear' and the faculty of hearing.[58] In so doing, Socrates turns Glaucon's attention, away from vision (*thean*, 525c2), conceived as seeing (*katidein / idein*, 526e2–5) with the mind, not the eyes (*noēsei all' ouk ommasi theōrein*, 529b2), toward the contemplation of harmony, again with the mind, not the ears. The rough-hewn instruments of bodily perception are all being surpassed and transcended by the use and perfection of faculties associated with the whole soul. The next study in the curriculum, Harmonics, grasps concordance through argument and thought, not hearing. Just as the eyes (*ommata*) are fastened on astral sights (*astronomian*), as it were, so the ears (*ōta*) are fastened on harmonic sounds (*enarmonion*) (530d). Harmonics is introduced as the "antistrophe" of Astronomy (530d4). It is therefore analogous to the second phase of the Guardians' education which paired training in gymnastic with music (522a3, 539e; see Aristotle, *Rhetoric* I.1). These two kinds of knowledge, Socrates and Glaucon agree, are "akin"

(*adelphai*) to each another, like siblings born of the same parents (530d7) who resemble one another.

With the study of Harmonics, the philosopher's curriculum also comes around full circle, returning once more to a consideration of Numbers, which ones are "concordant and which not," and the reasons why (531c). Glaucon exclaims that Socrates' proposal is "daemonic" because he demands that the studies be conceived in terms of abstract proofs or "problems" (*problēmata*) in the realm of the Intelligible, and not the Visible realm, as before with Geometry and Astronomy; the sounds of taut strings beings plucked are as irrelevant to the philosopher as the figures drawn to represent geometrical shapes or astronomical motions. Only when the studies transcend things associated with sense perceptions, insists Socrates, will their "striving after what is both noble and good" become useful to them (531c). Glaucon, tentatively, agrees. Socrates pushes the point about the radical nature of this philosopher's curriculum even further by stating, for the first time, that in fact their "work" (*to ergon*) of inquiring into all the studies that they have gone through thus far must, in addition, gather all their studies and conclusions together and discover their "commonwealth and kinship," that is, if the whole process (*methodos*) is to avoid being "a labor without profit" (531c9–d5; see 531a). Glaucon, too, somehow "divines" that this is true, and that the "task," or deed, is indeed a great one.

Socrates, amazingly undeterred by the magnitude of the task, acts surprised that Glaucon has not noticed that the serious business of philosophy has not yet even begun. Everything they have just agreed must be done is only the "prelude" (*prooimion*; cf. 357a2) to the serious work that itself is made possible as a result of the final study, Dialectic. Only now, when his young friend has glimpsed how great is the task of liberal education, does Socrates now tempt him with the "song" (*nomos*) of Dialectic itself (531d). For, he says, they will be unable to make use of all the other studies at all, unless they learn how "to render a true account (*logos*) and receive one" in turn, which is the task and performance of Dialectic itself. This is the completion and end of their "dialectical journey" through the intelligible realm of thought and intellection. Only by means of a dialectical—as opposed to poetic or rhetorical—account of their path through the philosopher's curriculum will their own souls accomplish a "release" from the bonds of the Cave, and a genuine turning-around: away from the shadow-images and phantoms of visible objects glimpsed darkly, and toward grasping the truth by intellection in the light of the Sun and, ultimately, in the Light of the Good itself (532b–c).

Urged on by the beautiful image of completion disclosed here, Glaucon eagerly desires that Socrates proceed directly to the song of Dialectic, and bring their long night's journey to its finale, the resting place and "haven" at the end of the path of their *logos*:

> It seems to me, [Glaucon] said, extremely hard to accept [what you propose], however, in another way it is hard not to accept. All the same—since not only now must these things be heard, but also they must be returned to many times in the future—taking for granted that all this is as has now been said, let's proceed to the song itself and go through it just as we went through the prelude (*prooimion*). Say, therefore, what exactly is the character (*tropos*) of Dialectic's power, and, then, into exactly what forms (*eidē*) it is divided; and finally what are its ways (*hodoi*). (534e, 532d–e)

Of course, we know that Socrates cannot—or at least will not—sing the song of Dialectic for the sake of his friend, despite, or rather because of, Glaucon's passionate desire to hear it. He no doubt perceives rightly that Glaucon's spirited desire to hear from Socrates the song of Dialectic exhibits the extent to which the arousal of his *erōs* by the discussion of the studies themselves—the very motion of the soul from which the city-in-speech and dialogue as a whole abstracts[59]—has become at this point almost inseparable from his *thumos*. At the risk of upsetting the eager young man, Socrates refuses, on the grounds that, despite Socrates' own eagerness (*prothumias*) to gratify Glaucon,[60] Glaucon himself would be unable to follow him to the end of the argument and *logos* by listening to Socrates—since, if they were to arrive at the end, Glaucon would no longer be perceiving what his soul desires as an image (*eikona*) in speech conjured by Socrates and his rhetoric, but "the truth itself" (*auto to alêthes*), "at least as it looks" to Socrates (533a), who has sought to represent it in speech. If, indeed, Glaucon were able to proceed dialectically, Socrates could cease speaking rhetorically altogether. But such a path or "road" (*hodos*) would of necessity have to include arguments that are "many times longer" than the ones they have already gone through (534a). Whatever this "longer" road may be and wherever it might lead remains one of the enduring mysteries of the *Republic*.

But returning to the road traveled in the dialogue, we must note that the rhetorical means by which Socrates has aroused Glaucon's erotic desire, first for Justice itself and now for the Good itself, partakes of a certain erotic imagery[61] that has driven their discussion of and journey through the philosopher's curriculum. Ironically, this imagery participates as much in a downward motion and "descent" (*katabasis*, cf. the first word of the text), as it does in an upward motion or "ascent" (*anabasis*, cf. 519c–d), along the Divided Line and its categorical divisions.[62] In the absence of the "song" of Dialectic, which must be placed "at the top of all the studies like a coping-stone" (534e), Socrates says that Glaucon must insist upon at least this much—that the power of Dialectic alone is sufficient to render an account to one who has had experience of all the studies (533a). Dialectic, unlike Rhetoric or Poetry, refuses to proceed on the basis of any unquestioned hypotheses, but is fully "awake" to the realm of the Intelligible, and therefore to what each thing really *is*: "Only the dialectical way of inquiry [*hē dialektikē methodos*] proceeds this way, destroying the hypotheses," by examining and sifting through them, rather than leaving them unexamined, in order to arrive at and understand "the beginning itself," and thus, in light of "the Idea of the Good itself"—which has been separated out and distinguished from all the other Forms—to weave together knowledge of "the being of each thing" (*tēs ousias ekastou*) in one unified and complete account, with reasons that are truly certain and secure (533b–534b). Such an account would surely transcend, Socrates implies, the account he himself has given.

Taken altogether, then, the interwoven Images of the Sun, the Divided Line, and the Cave (not to mention the Story of Gyges' Ring, Noble Lie of Three Metals, Paradox of Three Waves, Ship of State, Hybrid Soul, and Myth of Er) represent for us as Readers, upon careful reflection, not a dialectical failure, but precisely the kind of therapeutic soul-caring, or psychological art of soul-leading, which is the distinctive trait of Platonic dialogues in general, and Socratic rhetoric in particular. In the shifting verbal forms (of *eikōn, analogos, parabolē, paradoxos, logos, analogia, apologia, allēgoria*, or *muthos*), we must confront a Socratic argument replete with philosophical poetry that has descended out of necessity along the path of reasoning, from Dialectic to Rhetoric—only in the hope of leading us back up again. By perplexing us with 'strange' images and figures-in-speech, Socrates unsettles our rigid acceptance of our own opinion, stimulates and awakens our intellect, and so provokes us to consider (and then re-consider) what it is we think we know in such a way that we may begin to apprehend our lack of knowledge, and come to grasp with clarity and firmness the truth—or at least the way to the truth—to which our mind and our soul our being summoned.[63] Thus, we are inclined to say that reading (and re-reading) as well as discussing (and re-examining) the dialogue is the best kind of liberal education.[64] Hence it is that Plato's *Republic* stands at the origin of the ancient tradition of liberal education as civic education, which Aristotle seconded, Cicero redefined as the *studia humanitatis*, and Petrarca and the Renaissance humanists revived and transmitted to modernity.

LIBERAL EDUCATION AS THE CAPSTONE TO JUSTICE

At the conclusion of the philosopher's curriculum, Socrates pauses before turning to the assignment of the sequence of liberal studies to appropriate age groups (537aa–540b), and makes two final observations worth noting. The first reveals the embedded status of compulsion in the Image of the Cave and in the philosopher's ascent out of it by means of study. This aspect of compulsion is of particular interest in relation to the Socratic work (*ergon*) of liberating Glaucon from his 'chains,' the task that has preoccupied Socrates throughout the articulation of the philosopher's curriculum. The second speaks to the effect of liberal education on the soul. It should go without saying that both observations also address contemporary concerns with the relevance and significance of genuine liberal education in our own times.

First: Socrates argues, at the end of the philosopher's curriculum, that the spirited youth or war-lovers of the city-in-speech—who are all initially to be trained as Guardian-Auxiliaries and some of whom possess natural qualities that will render them "conducive to this education" that produces Guardian-Rulers (535a–b)—must not be set upon the ascent toward philosophy by compulsion. Their "instruction must not be given the aspect of a compulsion to learn" (536d). In fact, because the one who is going to be "free" in the full sense of the word "ought not to learn any study slavishly," it must follow then, according to Socrates, that force or coercion must not be used "in training the children in the studies—but rather play" (536e).

The best young men and young women by nature, the ones who most show themselves to be worthy of the highest studies, must be led through each stage of the curriculum by their own desire. For it is not under the aspect of compulsion that liberal education ever comes to dwell in the soul.

Contrary to the impression left behind by "the steep and rocky ascent" out of the Cave accomplished by a series of 'turns' under compulsion on the road to enlightenment, the dialogue between Glaucon and Socrates suggests that liberal education is a matter not of compulsory studies but really of desire—erotic desire, a longing for that which we lack and which, we suspect, will be the source of our becoming whole and complete. The end of the road that Glaucon eagerly desired is reached in the dialogue through friendly conversation. Dramatic aspects of the dialogue suggest that an affection for his interlocutors is at the very heart of Socrates' willingness to spend a very long evening (into the early morning) in discourse with (and replying to the challenges posed by) his spirited young companions.

Thus, at the end of his *logos* about the philosopher's curriculum and the liberal education of the Guardian-Rulers—an education uncomfortably wrought at many 'turns' by compulsion, Socrates surprisingly declares that, unlike the body itself that benefits from forced training and compulsory habituation, "no forced study abides in the soul" (536e). Intelligence, the natural end of a mind, and Prudence, the natural virtue of an embodied soul, can be cultivated only by desire, which is to say freely. In other words: "Liberal education has as its end the free mind, and the free mind must be its own teacher."[65] When properly pursued, these studies are desired as ends in and of themselves. Thus, the liberal education whose pattern is laid down by Socrates for the sake of Glaucon must be understood not only as instructive, liberating, and psychologically healing, but also as attractive—perhaps even 'compelling' in the sense that the Beautiful commands assent in the soul. (The powerful sway which the Beautiful holds over human beings, however, on account of *Erōs*, is *not* the central concern of *this* dialogue.)[66]

Glaucon has demonstrated he possesses the prerequisites for becoming a philosopher: like Socrates, he is both erotic (474d–475a)[67] and musical (398e). The liberal education of Glaucon at the center of the *Republic* corresponds to the founding of another (that is, fourth) *polis*, this time not just in speech (*logos*), but also in deed (*ergon*)—and this deed of Socrates is central to the argument about Justice in the *Republic* as a whole: the pattern for a just city is founded within Glaucon.⁶⁸ Thus, in the *Republic*, an ascent out of the Piraeus-Hades-Cave has been accomplished, insofar as Glaucon is concerned, if he 'guards' and preserves the order in his soul brought about by his liberal education (591d–e). The ascent came about because Socrates properly used rhetoric, understood as being subordinate to philosophy and the true art of politics.⁶⁹

Second, whatever the order in which the studies happen to be pursued, since they are to be taken up according to the inclination of each student, there must be a time when the studies are gathered together in a synopsis, and bound to one another in their likeness as separate disciplines in terms of the nature of things, or the whole of which they are all part:

> The various studies acquired without any order by the children in their education must be integrated into an over-view [*sun-opsin*] which reveals the profound kinship of these studies with one another and with the nature of that which *is* [*kai tēs tou ontos phuseōs*].
>   At least only such a study, Glaucon said, remains fast in those who receive it.
>   And it is the greatest test of the dialectical nature, and the one that is not; for he who is capable of an overview [*sun-optikos*] is dialectical, the other isn't. (537b–c)

But this need for a *synopsis*, or comprehensive surveying, in the *Republic* brings us here full circle, back to the question which Cicero had posed to his audience regarding the *studia humanitatis*: How are we to understand the apparent 'separateness' and isolation of the arts and disciplines in light of the fact that—as "liberal" education—they are woven into a cohesive and comprehensive unity? In what sense are the liberal studies truly bound, in the words of Cicero, with a *commune vinclum* as familial parts of a unified whole (*Pro Archia* I.2; cf. *De oratore* 3.19–22)?

The synoptic character of the liberal arts is a reflection of their common end, or rather aim, as a sequence of disciplines that test and refine the powers of a keen mind in order to prepare the intellect for its highest and most comprehensive activity, the contemplation of [the Idea of] the Good itself, "the greatest study" of all and the one which makes all the other studies both "useful and beneficial" (504c–505a). The one who has intelligence, therefore, must strain with all of his or her power to preserve the *politeia* within—which is to say that regime and way of life which, once its pattern is established in the soul, sets a human being free, and therefore must constantly be guarded—by "honoring the studies" that brought such a soul and its harmony into being in the first place. In honoring the liberal studies, we guard that education which best cultivates and exercises the virtues of the soul, pursuing with the eyes and ears of the soul that precision and elusive Beauty that only the intellect can fully enjoy, because it is capable of catching a glimpse of an order that transcends the fragmented and disjointed realm of "academics" and binds all the arts and disciplines—at least those that "do lay hold of something of *what is*" (533b)—into an intelligible and harmonious whole.

But a question arises: Must we honor the studies by engaging in them in the order Socrates represents them in the dialogue? To judge from Socrates' rhetorical education of Glaucon, which does not depend upon *his* having followed precisely the course of liberal studies enshrined in the city-in-speech, the answer must be no. Even if a strict adherence to the sequence of studies in the philosopher's curriculum eludes us, as it has for Glaucon, as well as Socrates, the articulation and discussion of the studies themselves constitute a kind of education that is similar to gymnastic and especially music for the soul. This heavenly music is understood as the harmony that quiets the turbulent 'uproar' and 'din' of the Cave. Socrates speaks of the "noise" and "echoes" therein as the "democratic education" supplied by the *hoi polloi*, who are the 'educators' of the city and its "greatest sophists" (492a–c, cf. 515b).[70] It is for this reason—which is to say on account of its therapeutic power to restore tranquillity to the mind and harmony to the soul—but not only for this reason,[71] that the Roman philosopher-orator-statesman Cicero admires the "liberal studies," which, he argues, includes Poetry and Rhetoric, the means by which Plato's Socrates has set Glaucon free. It is also for this reason that we, the readers of the *Republic*, in working through its arguments with care can discover the means by which to liberate ourselves from the din and commotion that creates turmoil in the Cave of our own souls.

Glaucon's demand in Book 2 for a defense of justice itself as inherently good, without any consideration of goods that follow from being just (including the good of the individual soul), prompts Socrates to a defense of the perfect harmony of *polis* and soul that is literally compelling in its precision. The beautiful order that is the end of the philosophic education ushers the soul to an end far beyond the *polis* that is inherently desirable, and it is this very glimpse of a life beyond all politics, a better life most worth living, that renders the philosophers alone most knowledgeable about what must be done in the *polis* from the perspective of ruling in the precise sense, as well as most trustworthy with the possession of political power. At the heart of the Guardians' education, so to speak, is the philosopher's curriculum, the capstone to the argument that has established a perfectly just regime for a *polis* and, by analogy, for the soul. The education of the Guardian-Rulers is analogous to the liberal education of the rational part of the human soul, an education that frees us from opinions to search for knowledge, begins with a desire to separate appearances from reality, and culminates with a vision of the principles of natural right—illuminated by the Good—that guide the way for our pursuit of Justice in political life through their prudential application.

But within the limiting confines of the perfectly just city-in-speech imposed upon Socrates' argument by Glaucon's desire, we—the readers of the *Republic*—are made aware of the dangers posed by an immoderate or excessive (not to say tyrannical) insistence upon perfect Justice among human beings. This insistence may be moderated if one sees, as any reasonable interlocutor must, that when the analogy ceases to be understood as an image of the liberal education of human souls and instead is taken as a blueprint for establishing an actual *polis*, the means to achieve that perfect Justice would require the institution of extreme political and educational measures too rigid and severe for embodied human beings to accept. To desire justice as adamantly as Glaucon does may be the starting point of liberal education, but it is not the end. Socrates, through the philosopher's curriculum, gradually turns his young friend toward the Good itself as the true end of the human desire to know. The philosopher's curriculum thus accomplishes two aims, one rhetorical, the other pedagogic: it is the rhetorical capstone to the Socratic argument for Justice itself being good and the cause of happiness for human beings, based on the city-soul analogy, and it is Socrates' way of liberating of Glaucon from the sublimation of his *erôs* through *thumos*, and hence also from an excessive desire for Justice rather than the Good, which is the true end of liberal education.

Plato's *Republic* teaches us that those who follow their philosophic nature, break the chains of ignorance, and ascend beyond the cave of politics into the light will have their liberal education embedded within their souls, and thereby become genuine rulers of themselves by establishing and preserving a just and well-ordered way of life (*politeia*, the ancient Greek word traditionally given to this dialogue as its title). Then and only then, according to Socrates, does the arduous task of founding a just *polis*-in-*logos* come to its proper end (*telos*). For only those souls are truly "free" who adhere to the education completed by the philosopher's curriculum, and only those the rightful guardians and rulers not only of themselves but of the *polis*; only to "them" (and not to others),[72] Socrates argues, can the founders of Kallipolis prudently turn over political power (590e–591a): "Having cared for the best part in them with the like in ourselves—we establish a similar guardian and ruler, in them, to take our place; only then, do we set them free." The establishment of civic justice, therefore, ultimately depends upon the liberal education of rulers who are worthy of ruling precisely because they have come to know what justice truly is in light of the good. In a republican form of government, such as ours was intended to be, even the rulers must be held accountable by the people, but the people themselves must be properly educated so as to render them "the safe, as the ultimate, guardians of their own liberty."[73] Thus, their liberal education must also be their civic education and the keystone that both secures and guarantees the arch of republican justice.

NOTES

1. The views of liberal education expressed in his chapter have been shaped by reading the writings of Eva Brann, Jacob Klein, and Leo Strauss, as well as more recent efforts to understand how the tradition of the humanities can reform and advance higher education by Robert Proctor, Eric Adler, and Roosevelt Montás.

2. On Cicero's education, see Cicero, *Brutus* 304–16; and Henri Marrou, *A History of Education in Antiquity*, 247, 258–60. Cicero exemplified the refounding of Roman virtue that he envisioned for the late Republic: Cicero, *De oratore* I, 158–59, 201; *Orator* 120. He insisted on a foundation for statesmen in Greek philosophy and rhetoric, to which must be added the study of Roman history and law: Marrou, *History of Education in Antiquity*, 285.

3. On the origin of these phrases, see Bruce A. Kimball, *Orators and Philosophers: A History of the Idea of Liberal Education*; and Robert E. Proctor, *Defining the Humanities: How Rediscovering a Tradition Can Improve Our Schools*.

4. On "refreshing" the mind with studies or philosophy, see Shakespeare, *Taming of the Shrew* I.i.294–330, III.i.1276ff. This is the only play of Shakespeare that mentions Socrates by name, and although it does so indirectly (see I.ii.70), it is ironically in tune with Cicero's remarks.

5. On the "noise" in the forum, see Plato's *Republic* 492b. Cicero here refers to the recent turmoil created by the conspiracy of Catalina, as well as the social strife and relentless civil wars of the preceding decades. On the relation between the impending collapse of the Roman Republic and Cicero's efforts to restore the Republic through his philosophical and educational writings, see Proctor, *Defining the Humanities*; and Ingo Gildenhard, *Paideia Romana: Cicero's "Tusculan Disputations."*

6. Cicero was not the only proponent of the *artes liberales* as the basis for an architectonic science. Vitruvius makes the case too, but for architecture. See Frank E. Brown, "Vitruvius and the Liberal Art of Architecture," 99, who argues that the most perceptive among the Romans sought "a synthesis of both the Greek and the Roman past . . . inculcated by education" and "found the model of its curriculum in the *enkuklios paideia*, or Liberal Arts, of the Hellenistic world." See Vitruvius, *De architectura* I.1. See also Marrou, *History of Education in Antiquity*, 281. Seneca, too, appropriated the phrase.

7. On care of the soul in the Platonic dialogues, see *Gorgias* 464a and 521d; *Phaedrus* 276a; and *Seventh Letter* 341c–d. See also Zdravko Planinc, ed., *Politics, Philosophy, Writing: Plato's Art of Caring for Souls*.

8. On the status of Plato's *Republic* as the first extant account of liberal education and foundational discourse in the tradition of humanistic studies, see Andrea Nightingale, "Liberal Education in Plato's *Republic* and Aristotle's *Politics*," 133. See also L. M. de Rijk, "'Enkylios paideia': A Study of Its Original Meaning."

9. The phrase "philosopher's curriculum" refers to the sequence of studies detailed by Socrates in the *Republic* VII.521c–537a3. Highet translates Jaegar's *Paideia* chapter title "Die Formenlehre des Staates als Pathologie der menschlichen Seele" as "The Philosopher's Curriculum," although a more precise rendering would be something like "The Doctrine of the Regimes as a Pathology of Human Souls." See Werner Jaeger, *Paideia: The Ideals of Greek Culture*, 312–20. Otherwise, the phrase is rarely used. See Eva T. H. Brann, *The Music of the Republic: Essays on Socrates' Conversations and Plato's Writings*, 268.

10. Quotations are taken, with slight emendations, from Bloom's translation of Plato's *Republic*.

11. See *Republic* 374e, 497d, 519c–d, 525b, 527c, and 530c.

12. On the verge of the philosopher's curriculum, Socrates begins to stress that the education itself and the Guardian-Rulers who partake of it must be considered in "the most precise" sense (*akribestata*: 503b3, 503d7, and 504e1–2; cf. 341b8 and context).

13. See 495d; see also the dialogue's center, 474b–c: "It is by nature fitting for them to engage in philosophy and to lead a city, and for the rest not to engage in philosophy and to follow the one who leads."

14. Adeimantus re-enters the dialogue (487b), after a lengthy absence (cf. 449a–e), to voice his concerns; the objection is reminiscent of Callicles' attack on philosophy in the *Gorgias*.

15. Socrates appears purposefully to conflate the two groups who must be soothed, alternating his reply first to one group and then the other, thereby concealing or temporarily ignoring a crucial difference between the two specific threats to philosophic rule perceived by Glaucon and Adeimantus (respectively, the spirited and armed men, and the confused and untutored many). The rhetorical success of Socrates' apology, as Adeimantus makes clear, depends not only upon the willingness of disputants to listen (327c12) but also on their capacity to apprehend arguments (501a1), and the possession of a virtue not usually attributed to them (moderation: 501d1). Conflating the two groups may be warranted. The prospects for taming the passions that lead to anti-philosophic sentiments in more than one person at a time, whether spirited few or untutored many, even with the art of rhetoric, seem bleak (see *Gorgias*); misperceptions on the part of either group, however, can lead to violence (see *Apology*).

16. On the rhetorical use of *analogia* as a persuasive and pedagogical device—a metaphorical 'carrying' or transference of borrowed meaning from one *logos* to another *logos*—which is also pleasant for the crowd, see Aristotle, *Rhetoric* III 2.8–9, 10.2, 11.6; cf. *Metaphysics* I 1, with Gorgias' *Encomium of Helen* 5 and Plato's *Gorgias* 464b–465d.

17. See 394d. The metaphor for *logos* is later altered (504b, cf. 506d), poetically reminding us of 'the road not taken' in the dialogue (see 435c–d, cf. 608d–612b, with 354a–c).

18. On the rhetorical nature of Socrates' arguments, see Kathy Eden, "Get on Down: Plato's Rhetoric of Education in the *Republic*."

19. On the greediness or desire of Socrates for images, see John Sallis, *Being and Logos: Reading the Platonic Dialogues*, 399.

20. See 529c (regarding the studies of "the fairest and most precise of such things") and esp. 534d (". . . these children of yours whom you are rearing and educating in speech, if you should ever rear them in deed, I don't suppose that while they are as irrational as lines you would let them rule in the city and be sovereign of the greatest things")—namely, the studies that lead them to what *is*, and enable them to dialectically 'give an account of' themselves, as well as the whole and their place within it.

21. But in making their apology "sensibly" or "in a measured way" (*metriōs apologēsometha*), Socrates is assuming that Adeimantus will be teaching some 'one' who is tolerant (if not moderate) enough to listen to him, rather than the un-philosophic multitude—and moreover, 'one' capable of understanding the likenesses embedded in the proportionality of this figure-in-speech (490a). Adeimantus claims that, for him, Socrates' apology is "the most sensible" (*metriōtata*: 490b).

22. See Eden, "Get on Down," 238–39.

23. As a whole, of course, the argument of the *Republic* is rhetorically based on the over-arching analogy or proportionality of the city (*polis*) and the soul (*psuchē*), an analogy—and method—the appropriateness of which may be dialectically debatable or simply "evidently questionable and untenable" (see 368c–369b; see also Leo Strauss, *The City and Man*, 138).

24. Thus, the inquiry into the Good itself and the contemplation of its *idea* serves also as an inquiry into the first causes or causality itself, which Aristotle defines as the true knowledge sought by the philosopher (as opposed to the sophist)—that is, knowledge of causes (*Posterior Analytics* 71b9–13); see Eden, "Get on Down," 240.

25. This is the seventh and central use in the *Republic* of a Greek word related to *daimonion*. Consider also Socrates' use of the word, just before and after this: 496c and 540c, the latter points toward the just rewards of philosophic souls in the after-life (cf. *Apology* 31d, 27d–e). It is thought that *daimones* are divine beings that travel between gods and humans. See Allan Bloom, trans., *The Republic of Plato*, Book II, note 55.

26. Socrates promises that, insofar as possible at the present, he will omit nothing "willingly" (509c), but the dialogue as a whole—and the argument of its action—unfolds under the influence of Necessity, *Anagkē*.

27. Allan Bloom, *The Republic of Plato*, 403: "Only by constant reference back to the divided line can one understand the cave." See James Carey, "The Theoretical Presuppositions of Liberal Education," 74–75n32.

28. Glaucon's grasp of the Divided Line image, displayed in his summary at 511c–d, is praised by Socrates as "very sufficiently" (*'ikanōtata*) demonstrated (from *apodeiknumi*, not *epideiknumi*; cf. *Gorgias* 447a5).

29. See Xenophon, *Memorabilia* IV 6.13–15.

30. Brann argues, in several works, that the Divided Line is the most "suggestive mathematical analogy for guiding a philosophical speculation." On the segments of the Divided Line, see Jacob Klein, *A Commentary on Plato's "Meno,"* 112–15. Klein stresses in this section of his work that we are most 'at home' amid the unfathomable familiarity of the visible realm, where an unshakeable sense of "unquestionable trust" settles within us. For we trust that "the familiar features of the visible world are here to stay, that things are as we see them."

31. See Eden, "Get on Down," 246: "In the *Republic* . . . Plato arguably has Socrates use these rhetorical devices to philosophical ends, that is, to turn us toward a deeper understanding of our own capacity to turn around; he has Socrates use them to educate us about how we become educated. To this end—the philosophical end of self-reflection—the Socrates of the *Republic* challenges the rhetorician with his own weapons."

32. See Bloom, *The Republic of Plato*, 405: "To break [these bonds which tie us to the cave and its images] requires rare passion and courage." See also Rousseau, *Du Contrat Social* I.i: "*L'homme est né libre, et partout il est dans les fers*." As will become evident, there are two types of bonds that we forge for ourselves on account of two temptations of the mind: false piety, and the charms of scientific knowledge. "These two temptations are aided by two of man's most noble arts: poetry and mathematics." See Bloom, *The Republic of Plato*, 406.

33. See Allan Bloom, "The Ladder of Love," 150: "Socrates tells us in the *Republic* that the philosopher is the only truly just man, but his justice is practiced all alone without a community that one could live in, which offers such satisfaction to most men." See also *Republic* 486b, 496d, 517b–d, 591–92, 629b–d, 620c.

34. Socrates later states that this power (*dunamis*) in the soul of each is the natural virtue of the soul to "exercise prudence" (*phronêsai*), a virtue "more divine" (*mallon theioterou*) than all of the others, one which is not cultivated by habit or practice, and never loses strength or fades, but which by means of liberal education is converted from uselessness to usefulness (518d–e; 530c: *to phusei phronimon en tê psychê*). Socrates speaks immediately thereafter of the soul's "vision" (*tên opsin*), which may be translated

as 'the mind's eye' (519a5, 519b3; see *Symposium* 219a; *Sophist* 254a; Aristotle, *NE* 1144a30; cf. *Phaedo* 99e). However, this instrument of knowledge in the soul may not be limited to an analogy with sight, for Socrates later speaks of the purification and rekindling of the soul's "organ" (*organon ti psychês*) through the liberal studies—something more important to preserve than "ten thousand eyes" (*muriôn ommatôn*) (527d–e). In the passage at hand, Socrates compares this power in the soul to the eye (*omma*); however, the power itself is called an "organ" (*to organon*) (518c5). In light of the progress in the philosopher's curriculum from the geometry and astronomy to harmonics and dialectic, the generic word "organ" may be usefully thought of as both 'the mind's eye' and 'the mind's ear'—the strangeness of the latter in English as well as Greek would be consistent with Socrates' purpose throughout this section of the dialogue in breaking the familiar chains that unwittingly bind his listeners to the Cave. In the final reference to this power at the end of the philosopher's curriculum, however, Socrates refers to this power as "the eye of the soul" (*to tês psychês omma*), which dialectic—using the studies (*technai*) as its "assistants and helpers"—gently draws forth out of the "barbaric bog" in which it has been sunk, and leads it up above to the first principle and starting-point (*autên tên archên*) of all true knowledge (*epistêmê*) (533c4–e2). Socrates, of course, has already stated, in speaking of the Idea of the Good itself (and its Light) as analogous to the Sun (and its light) that the eye is the "most sun-like of all the organs of perception" (*êlioeidestaton tôn peri tas aisthêseis organôn*) and the "power" it possesses comes from an overflow of the sun's own richness (508b1–4).

35. Consider the main difficulty of the founders' task at 519b–520d, in light of Glaucon's claim at 520e; consider also the thrust of Adeimantus' objection at 419a–421c.

36. See Brann, *Music of the Republic*, 102, 115, 216–37.

37. On the "intellectual gravity" (or the temptation to 'apply' technical mathematical knowledge to the realm of objects) that must be defied during the ascent through the curriculum, in order to continue the upward flight of the soul, see David Roochnik, *The Beautiful City: The Dialectical Character of Plato's "Republic,"* 35–37, 54–55, 68. The erotic soul partakes of the "unique energy" that supplies the necessary internal compulsion or urge to ascend against this downward gravitational pull.

38. As opposed to the training of the Craftsmen in the banausic or illiberal arts (495d–e and 590c; cf. *Gorgias* 512c; and Aristotle, *Politics* 1258b20–26 and 1278a6–11).

39. Even if he does so by means of Images, it must be recalled that the imagination is also a distinctively human faculty; the capacity to see an image *as an image* and thus to see *through* it: see Klein, *Commentary on Plato's "Meno,"* 114–15; see also Eden, "Get on Down," 241: "Socrates descends the divided line, which, as *eikōn* or image, is the product of the lowest portion [of the line], in order to teach his interlocutors about its uppermost portion."

40. See Xenophon, *Memorabilia* III 1–2; but cf. *Cyropaedia* I 5.4–5 and II 1.1–10, with Book II, note 3, in the translation of Wayne Ambler: ". . . good statesmanship may require bad math."

41. See, analogously, Socrates' intriguing remark at 530a. In the passage at hand, Socrates makes frequent reference to *phusis*; for example, at 526c4–5: "For all these reasons then, this study should not be neglected and the best natures must be educated

in it." On "nature" in the *Republic*, see 496a–c; and on the best natures, see Xenophon, *Memorabilia* IV 1.

42. See David Roochnik, "Counting on Number: Plato on the Goodness of *Arithmos*," 543–47, esp. 547: "Plato understood that the authoritative precision of mathematics results in extraordinary reliability: not only can we count with *arithmos*, we can also count on it," and 554: "Arithmos is the principle of determinacy; it is clear, stable, and epistemically reliable. We can count on it, and it represents a realm in which agreement is prior to hostility." Questions of morality or politics lack any comparable degree of certitude and clarity. See Klein, *Commentary on Plato's "Meno"*; and Jacob Klein, *Greek Mathematical Thought and the Origin of Algebra*.

43. See Roochnik, "Counting on Number," 558–62; see also Klein, *Commentary on Plato's "Meno,"* 115–25, esp. 117.

44. Roochnik, "Counting on Number," 559: "Simply to count . . . is fundamentally informative: it tells us that noetic stability can and does intervene into human experience, that there is something, even amidst the 'barbaric bog' (*Rep.* 533d1) of human life, on which we can count. In this sense, *arithmos* can turn the soul around, away from becoming to being, for it can become a compelling invitation to shift one's sights, away from the sensible toward the noetic."

45. Thrasymachus insists that his definition of justice as the advantage of the stronger must be construed in "the most precise sense" (340c–341c) and that he himself is speaking precisely in his arguments. This precision, however, works to Socrates' advantage (see 341c–342e). On the partially 'Thrasymachean' basis of the *Republic* as a whole, see Seth Benardete, *Socrates' Second Sailing: On Plato's "Republic,"* 169–70, 178, 182; and Seth Benardete, *Encounters and Reflections*, 129. On the precise and technical character of Kallipolis, the *polis*-in-*logos*, see Strauss, *The City and Man*; and Roochnik, *Beautiful City*.

46. Klein, *Commentary on Plato's "Meno,"* 117: "Continued reflection on that act of counting leads to the establishment of *technai* which supply us with a *precise* knowledge of all things numerable insofar as they are numerable and of their properties as well as their mutual relations which are rooted in their numerability."

47. See Plato, *Symposium* (Diotima's ladder of love and the ascent of the soul toward what *is*).

48. See Edna St. Vincent Millay, "Euclid Alone Has Looked on Beauty Bare." Jacob Klein (*Commentary on Plato's "Meno,"* 118–20) considers geometric imagination in thinking as a kind of *dianoetic eikasia* Klein.

49. See Roochnik, *Beautiful City*, 35–36: "In an astonishing prefigurement of modern physics and the technology to which it gave birth, the divided line depicts technical knowledge as applied mathematics. Because the sensible world and the mathematicals fit together so well, the former is manipulable through the knowledge available in the latter." "Because [the two realms] fit so well, because mathematical knowledge is so amazingly useful in the sensible world, it is always tempting to submit to the force of 'intellectual gravity', to apply mathematical knowledge to the sensible realm—that is, to engage in the *technai*."

50. The only use of *gennaie* as a familiar address in the *Republic*; cf. 375a, 409c, and esp. 414c.

51. See Roochnik, "Counting on Number," 557: "Socrates attempts to reform Callicles by offering him a vision of an orderly and knowable whole. In other words, Socrates follows the advice that Aristotle later will give: the only effective cure for the man of tyrannical desires is philosophy (*Pol.* 1267a10–16)."

52. See Brann, *Music of the Republic*, 230: "Solid geometry, the study that comes between earth measurements and the motion of the skies [i.e., in the heavens], aiming at the objects that lie between heaven and earth, is . . . in some special way the city's business; it is a political affair, which ought to be carefully supervised." Stereometry concerns the intellect with measuring the volumes of various solid figures and surfaces that exist in three-dimensional Euclidean space; the human body is one of the most complex, or irregular, such surface. Taking the measure of our interior volume refers not only to the study physical matter but also to all that is somehow taken to be situated 'within' us (or confined within our bodies) as human beings—including the soul.

53. See Klein, *Commentary on Plato's "Meno,"* 191–92, esp. 192: "The assigning of stereometry, instead of astronomy, to the third place in the sequence of required studies necessitates a *regress* in the enumeration of those studies. Is not this regress comparable to the *reflexive* motion of the soul looking into itself?" In other words, though he is eager to proceed, Glaucon may be neglecting the study of his "whole" soul in a crucial way, an oversight to which Socrates calls his attention at this point.

54. The mathematicians, geometers, astronomers, and dialecticians of the usual sort are no less "prisoners" of the Cave insofar as their visible "constructions and theorems" replicate the Cave and fail to transcend it: Benardete, *Socrates' Second Sailing*, 172, 176. A great effort is needed to break free of this pull of *dianoia* toward the familiar, visible world in order to resume "the *initial* impulse of the *dianoia* to which we owe our admittance to the domain of the intelligible" and this effort could not be undertaken without "an intense desire to embark upon, and to stay on, the new path" of philosophy: Klein, *Commentary on Plato's "Meno,"* 124–25.

55. Socrates frequently makes use of military terminology when speaking to Glaucon in the *Republic*: see Klein, *Commentary on Plato's "Meno,"* 123n42, 192n1; Bloom, *The Republic of Plato*, 465n14. See also Benardete, *Socrates' Second Sailing*, 182: "The coupling of the warrior and the philosopher through the knowledge of number represents as dramatically as possible the monstrous character of political philosophy [in the *Republic*]."

56. Socrates blames himself for this error, not Glaucon: "My haste to go through everything quickly is the cause of my being slowed down." But this is partly "due to the ridiculous state of the search" (cf. 354a–c). On the place of laughter in the studies, a distinctively human if un-mathematical trait, see Leon H. Craig, *The War-Lover: A Study of Plato's "Republic,"* 287: "notice especially the role of various kinds of *mistakes* in [Socrates'] and Glaucon's arriving at a correct understanding of this curriculum (cf. 523b, 524d–e, 526d–e, 527d–528b, 528e–529c). Perhaps more puzzling are the repeated references to laughing and what is laughable ("ridiculous": 525d, 527a, 528d, 529e–530a, 531a; cf. 388e–389a, 451a–b, 452d, 604b–c, 606c)." See also Benardete, *Socrates' Second Sailing*, 181–82: "These corrections [to the sequence of studies] illustrate dialectics and bear to mathematical education the same relation that the dialogic

city does to the city in speech. . . . It is, then, in the arguments for mathematics rather than in mathematics itself that the ascent of dialectics is to be found."

57. Cicero says Plato devoted himself to certain Pythagoreans and their studies, spending time with at least one man, Archytas, whose brilliant contributions to Greek geometry did not distract him in the least from engaging in the true art of politics and ruling: *Academics* 1.10.16; cf. Plato, *Seventh Epistle* 350a–b.

58. On the soul's move from the active life of performance to the contemplative life of spectacle-gazing, see Nightingale, "Liberal Education," 143–54.

59. See Strauss, *The City and Man*, 128: "The abstraction from *eros* . . . characteristic of the *Republic* [is] an abstraction which is also effective in the simile of the Cave in so far as that simile presents the ascent from the cave to the light of the sun as entirely compulsory (515c5–516a1)."

60. Socrates later admits that he has already gone too far on account of his *thumos*, and perhaps spoken "too seriously" in defense of philosophy: see 536b–c and 498c.

61. See Craig, *War-Lover*, 271: Still, one should not "overlook what can be learned about one's own soul in the course of its laboring to understand whatever the images themselves convey. But presuming the suitability of the erotic language [Socrates] uses to introduce and discuss the images (506d–507a, 508b, 509a), the more precise understanding of the soul must also require an expanded conception of *eros*."

62. The argument and the action of the dialogue would seem to demonstrate, in the words of Heraclitus, that the way up and the way down are one and the same. See Craig, *War-Lover*, 284. See also Sallis, *Being and Logos*, 450–51; Benardete, *Socrates' Second Sailing*, 177–81.

63. See Craig, *War-Lover*, 270: "The Sun-Good Analogy, the Divided Line, and the Allegory of the Cave are among the most famous images—not merely of this dialogue, or of the Platonic corpus—but of our entire philosophical tradition." See also Eden, "Get on Down," 242: "As careful readers, we learn from the analogy as well as the story. We also recognize the analogy between analogical argument and storytelling." To understand most clearly the power of such Images or serious philosophical protreptic, one must consider why a Socratic student and writer like Xenophon rejected them.

64. See Brann, *Music of the Republic*, 258: Socrates' "sketch of these philosophers' curriculum" is "the outline of a liberal arts curriculum" such as is brought into being by the New Program at St. John's College.

65. See "The Last Don Rag" by Scott Buchanan, one of the principal founders of the New Program at St. John's College (accessible online at the St. John's College website).

66. See Leo Strauss, *Leo Strauss on Plato's "Symposium,"* 244: "The *Republic* presents philosophy as transcending [or ascent from] the polis and descent to the polis. The two aspects are inseparable. In the *Symposium* this is absent. What Socrates says in the end about generating true virtue [in the *Symposium*] has nothing to do with the polis. . . . The love of the beautiful triumphs completely over the love of one's own in the *Symposium*. It does not triumph in the *Republic*. You see also how difficult it is to find Plato's true teaching, because it is divided into many dialogues and must be put together."

67. See Strauss, *The City and Man*, 110–11, 124–25: Those with a philosophic nature are "dominated by the desire, the *eros*, for knowledge as the one thing needful," and without concern for the political affairs of human beings.

68. See Eva T. H. Brann, "The Music of the *Republic*," 21–25; and Craig, *War-Lover*, 288–89. See Sallis, *Being and Logos*, 400–401, 440, 446, 453–54, esp. 396–97: "Socrates' descent into Hades—a descent which, in the order of the Socratic recollection in which the entire *Republic* is enclosed—was followed almost immediately by the beginning of Socrates' ascent out of Hades. But the ascent was interrupted, and then the issue became that of Socrates' winning his release from Hades by means of persuasion." This effort at liberation requires that Socrates become a founder of cities: a healthy city, a feverish city, an un-erotic city of geometrical necessity, and a city ruled by philosopher-kings in which Socrates overcomes the paradoxical exclusion of *erōs*, incorporates it into the city through the education of a philosophic soul. Perhaps the "paradox rooted in the city's exclusion of *eros* could be surpassed if the very activity of founding the city were, at the same time, an activity of love—if, for instance, the founding of the city were Socrates' way of bestowing his love on Glaucon."

69. See *Gorgias* 510d.

70. The "democratic education" in Athens is thus inseparable from that supplied by the "wage-earning" sophists themselves (493a; cf. the 'wages' earned by those who, because they practice the 'illiberal' arts, the mercantile and servile banausic arts, lack leisure and hence virtue, have not developed good habits and character, are unable to rule over the inclinations of the irrational parts of their souls, and are unfit to rule: see 395c–d [those who are to rule must never imitate what is not fitting for them, things that are "illiberal"; cf. Xenophon, *Oikonomikos* 4.2–3; Aristotle, *Politics* 1278a6–11]) as well as by the conniving poets and scurrilous politicians (493c–d)—all of whom are "illiberal" pretenders to the wisdom of the philosophers (495c–496a; cf. *Apology*). See Nightingale, "Liberal Education," 140, 134–36, 139.

71. Cicero, *Pro Archia* VII.15–17: "Though even if no such great advantage were to be reaped from them, and if pleasure by itself were sought from these studies, nevertheless, I believe, you would judge this recreation of the soul to be the most human and most befitting a free human being. For nothing else befits all times, all seasons, or all places; whereas these studies are really the sustenance of youth and the delight of old age; the ornament of prosperity, the refuge and solace against adversity; a joy at home, no hindrance abroad; our companions by night, during our travels, and in our home outside the city. And if we ourselves were for some reason not able to arrive at these advantages, nor even taste them with our own senses, still we ought to admire these studies, especially when we see them in others."

72. On whether cave-dwellers must be appeased or avoided, see Benardete, *Socrates' Second Sailing*, 178: "No philosopher as such, Socrates implies, should ever risk his life in attempting to free and lead the Cavemen up, for, should they ever get their hands on the perfectly wise, they would kill him (517a5–6). The Cavemen are the prisoners of the wise; only if their hands were tied would [the wise man] venture to return [to the Cave]." On the seeming necessity of doing harm in establishing any political regime, and the consequences of that particular realization for action, see Xenophon, *Anabasis* IV.6.1–4; cf. Machiavelli, *Prince*.

73. Thomas Jefferson, *Notes on the State of Virginia* (first published, London and Philadelphia, 1787), Query XIV—"The Administration of Justice and Description of the Laws."

BIBLIOGRAPHY

Adler, Eric. "Allan Bloom on the Value of the Ancients; or, The Closing of the American Classics Department." *Arion: A Journal of Humanities and Classics* 24, no. 1 (2016): 151–60.

———. *The Battle of the Classics: How a Nineteenth-Century Debate Can Save the Humanities Today*. New York: Oxford University Press, 2020.

———. "The Battle of the Classics: The Humanities without Humanism." *Antigone* (2021). https://antigonejournal.com/2021/09/humanities-without-humanism/.

Benardete, Seth. *Encounters and Reflections*. Chicago: University of Chicago Press, 2002.

———. *Plato's "Symposium."* Translated by Seth Benardete. Chicago: University of Chicago Press, 2001.

———. *Socrates' Second Sailing: On Plato's "Republic."* Chicago: University of Chicago Press, 1989.

Bloom, Allan. "The Ladder of Love." In *Plato's "Symposium,"* translated by Seth Benardete. Chicago: University of Chicago Press, 2001.

———, trans. *The Republic of Plato*. 1968. Reprint, New York: Basic Books, 1991.

Brann, Eva T. H. "The American College as *the* Place for Liberal Learning." *Daedalus* 128, no. 1 (1999): 151–71.

———. "The Music of the *Republic*." *Agon: Journal of Classical Studies* 1, no. 1 (1967): 1–117. Substantially revised and published in *St. John's Review* 39, nos. 1–2 (1989–90), and reprinted in *The Music of the Republic: Essays on Socrates' Conversations and Plato's Writings*, by Eva T. H. Brann. Philadelphia: Paul Dry Books, 2004.

———. *The Music of the Republic: Essays on Socrates' Conversations and Plato's Writings*. Philadelphia: Paul Dry Books, 2004.

———. *Paradoxes of Education in a Republic*. Chicago: University of Chicago Press, 1979.

Brown, Frank E. "Vitruvius and the Liberal Art of Architecture." *Bucknell Review* 11, no. 4 (1963): 99–107.

Carey, James. "The Theoretical Presuppositions of Liberal Education." In *The Envisioned Life: Essays in Honor of Eva Brann*, edited by Peter Kalkavage and Eric Salem, 50–77. Philadelphia: Paul Dry Books, 2007.

Craig, Leon H. *The War-Lover: A Study of Plato's "Republic."* Toronto: University of Toronto Press, 1994.

Eden, Kathy. "Get on Down: Plato's Rhetoric of Education in the *Republic*." In *A Companion to Rhetoric and Rhetorical Criticism*, edited by Walter Jost and Wendy Olmsted, 238–47. Blackwell Companions in Literature and Culture. Malden, MA: Blackwell, 2004.

Gildenhard, Ingo. *Paideia Romana: Cicero's "Tusculan Disputations."* Cambridge Classical Journal. Proceedings of the Cambridge Philological Society, supplementary vol. 30. Cambridge: Cambridge Philological Society, 2007.

Howland, Jacob. *The Republic: The Odyssey of Philosophy.* 1993. Reprint, Philadelphia: Paul Dry Books, 2004.

Jaeger, Werner. *Paideia: The Ideals of Greek Culture.* Vol. 2, *In Search of the Divine Center.* Translated by Gilbert Highet. Oxford: Oxford University Press, 1943.

Kalkavage, Peter, and Eric Salem, eds. *The Envisioned Life: Essays in Honor of Eva Brann.* Philadelphia: Paul Dry Books, 2007.

Kimball, Bruce A. *Orators and Philosophers: A History of the Idea of Liberal Education.* New York: College Entrance Examination Board, 1995.

Klein, Jacob. *A Commentary on Plato's "Meno."* Chapel Hill: University of North Carolina Press, 1965.

———. *Greek Mathematical Thought and the Origin of Algebra.* Translated by Eva Brann. Cambridge, MA: MIT Press, 1968.

———. "The Idea of Liberal Education." In *The Goals of Higher Education,* edited by Willis D. Weatherford. Cambridge, MA: Harvard University Press, 1960. Reprinted in *Lectures and Essays,* edited by Robert B. Williamson and Elliott Zuckerman, 157–70. Annapolis, MD: St. John's College Press, 1985.

———. *Lectures and Essays.* Edited by Robert B. Williamson and Elliott Zuckerman. Annapolis, MD: St. John's College Press, 1985.

———. "On Liberal Education" (public lecture). *Bulletin of the Association of American Colleges* 52, no. 2 (1966). Reprinted in *Lectures and Essays,* edited by Robert B. Williamson and Elliott Zuckerman, 261–68. Annapolis, MD: St. John's College Press, 1985.

Marrou, Henri. *A History of Education in Antiquity.* Translated by George Lamb. Madison: University of Wisconsin Press, 1982.

Montás, Roosevelt. *Rescuing Socrates: How the Great Books Changed My Life and Why They Matter for a New Generation.* Princeton, NJ: Princeton University Press, 2021.

Newell, Waller. *Ruling Passion: The Erotics of Statecraft in Platonic Political Philosophy.* Lanham, MD: Rowman & Littlefield, 2000.

Nightingale, Andrea. "Liberal Education in Plato's *Republic* and Aristotle's *Politics.*" In *Education in Greek and Roman Antiquity,* edited by Yun Lee Too, 133–73. Boston: Brill, 2001.

Planinc, Zdravko, ed. *Politics, Philosophy, Writing: Plato's Art of Caring for Souls.* Columbia: University of Missouri Press, 2001.

Proctor, Robert E. *Defining the Humanities: How Rediscovering a Tradition Can Improve Our Schools.* 2nd ed. Bloomington: Indiana University Press, 1998. Originally published in 1991, as *Education's Great Amnesia.*

———. "The Studia Humanitatis: Contemporary Scholarship and Renaissance Ideals." *Renaissance Quarterly* 43, no. 4 (1990): 813–24.

Rijk, L. M. de. "'Enkylios paideia': A Study of Its Original Meaning." *Vivarium* 3, no. 1 (1965): 24–93.

Roochnik, David. *The Beautiful City: The Dialectical Character of Plato's "Republic."* Ithaca, NY: Cornell University Press, 2003.

———. "Counting on Number: Plato on the Goodness of *Arithmos.*" *American Journal of Philology* 115, no. 4 (1994): 543–63.

Sallis, John. *Being and Logos: Reading the Platonic Dialogues.* 3rd ed. Bloomington: Indiana University Press, 1996.

Strauss, Leo. *The City and Man.* Chicago: Rand McNally, 1964.

———. *Leo Strauss on Plato's "Symposium."* Edited by Seth Benardete (transcript of 1959 University of Chicago course). Chicago: University of Chicago Press, 2001.

———. "What Is Liberal Education?" Commencement address for the Basic Program of Liberal Education for Adults at the University of Chicago, 1959. Reprinted in *The College*, published by St. John's College, 1974.

PART TWO

LIBERAL ARTS AS A CLASSROOM OF CITIZENSHIP

7. The Garden of Citizenship
Liberal Education as the Cultivation of Just Sentiments
Constantine Christos Vassiliou

> The task of the modern educator is not to cut down jungles but to irrigate deserts. The right defense against false sentiments is to inculcate just sentiments.
>
> —C. S. Lewis, *The Abolition of Man*

THIS CHAPTER EXAMINES THE RELATIONSHIP between traditional higher learning and America's constitutional ideals. I draw from my training in political theory and my institutional experience as both a student and a teacher to demonstrate how the study of transformative texts, namely, the "great books," is an important adjunct to teaching citizenship in the United States. A student who decides to major in political science will learn from day one that our discipline is principally concerned with the question, "How does power work?" Political theory is the subdiscipline of political science that preoccupies itself with the question, "To what end should this power be wielded?" Traditionally, students and teachers worked with a compendium of great books that have examined and come to terms with the human soul as a conflicted space. They would discursively reflect upon enduring philosophical and ethical questions that concern the human condition: What is a just action? What does it mean to live a happy, meaningful life? What are the conditions that make an ethical life possible in an increasingly cosmopolitan and automated world?"

In recent years, a Puritan orthodoxy has permeated humanities and social science departments, with a growing number of scholars flagging the great books of the Western tradition for being avatars of systemic oppression. In a recent essay, Mark Edmundson observed how this fashionable labeling of our philosophical inheritances has produced a pedagogy that encourages students to examine classic texts through an unmitigated cynical lens.[1] Academic cynicism has shaped the direction of my own field of study, political theory. As political science departments across the United States are deparochializing (de-Westernizing) political theory at an unrelenting pace,[2] important theoretical and normative questions have fallen secondary to the empirical question, "Who is it that wields power?" leaving many students with the impression that premodern iterations of justice could be understood by simply working out power differentials that existed in the author's immediate context. To be sure, the Western tradition entails a vast degree of atrocities that need to be reckoned with, but it also entails an enduring intellectual struggle to develop better dispensations of justice. In book 1 of Plato's *Republic*, we learn through the characters of Cephalus and Polemarchus, who unreflectively trust the wisdom of their cultural inheritances, that justice is something people claim to know but only partially understand. Yet we also learn from Socrates that we can approximate the nature of our positions through reason and critical reflection. The great books contain myriad philosophical and well-reasoned accounts of what constitutes a just society. A rigorous engagement with these works will enable students to purposefully take part in present-day intellectual battles over questions concerning justice.

In his classic commentary, C. S. Lewis deemed the study of old books critical to one's emotional education. He explains how our predecessors were not wiser nor more virtuous, but they did not "make the same mistakes as us. They will not flatter us in the errors we are already committing; and their own errors, being now open and palpable, will not endanger us."[3] Our past transmits wisdom that has no interest or impulse to satisfy current-day prejudices, norms, and values. The great books are depositories of profound reflection over the most important questions concerning the human condition that help us put the "controversies of the moment in their proper perspective." Conversely, Lewis warns us that "an exclusive contemporary diet" of literature will yield a penchant for fashionable ideas and concepts, shrouding the caveats and signposts previous thinkers erected to help us navigate the vicissitudes of the human condition.[4]

Despite Lewis's reverence for the great books, his anxieties about modern education point to how the texts themselves are not guarantors of moral virtue and sound citizenship. Intellectual growth does not simply constitute an unmitigated retention of *theoria* in the abstract. In *Abolition of Man*, Lewis states that our reasoning over questions concerning justice and morality requires the aid of emotion. The great books would become lifeless abstractions and sources of manipulation, shorn of an institutional experience that tends to our frailties. If we stand outside the concrete reality of our circumstances, "judgments of value cannot have any ground except the emotional strength of the impulse." We will develop the false sense that our ideals are endowed with the strength of dispassionate reason, when in reality, such an approach to learning, conditions "man. . . to treat himself as a mere 'natural object' and his own judgements of value as raw material for scientific manipulation to alter at will." When we approach philosophical questions in such a clinical manner, our judgments will be nothing more than the affirmation of a momentary emotional affect. As Lewis writes, "The little human animal will not at first have the right responses. It must be trained to feel pleasure, liking, disgust, and hatred at those things which really are pleasant, likeable, disgusting and hateful." There is a natural ebb and flow in the way ideas percolate through our minds. Yet Lewis warns us how we can become so volatile and acidic without a proper channeling of the emotions to protect us against our own destructive impulses. As he famously writes, "the task of the modern educator is not to cut down jungles but to irrigate deserts. The right defense against false sentiments is to inculcate just sentiments."[5]

The physical classroom itself is a conveyor of just sentiments. It is an ideal space for deft educators to develop a sense of their students, to channel the emotions at play during lectures or seminars towards a spirit of empathy and common humanity, the preconditions for prudent moral and political reflection.[6] But a wholesale liberal arts experience extends beyond the classroom. It takes place in a learning environment where local communities organically develop—a place where students could comfortably go to a pub after class to discuss with others what they learned from the great books, economics, physics, or whatever field of human interest they gravitated toward to gain a more coherent understanding of the world. It is during those critical moments following an illuminating seminar when adrenaline levels are still high that spirited discussions concerning first principles conduce toward enduring, life-enriching friendships; this is when one another's humanity becomes most apparent, with all the foibles and frailty that entails. The physical environment of a traditional liberal arts college best approximates these circumstances.

This chapter defends both the traditional curricular content and the institutional experience of a classic liberal education. It demonstrates why the latter is a fundamentally more important battle line if universities are to succeed at both nourishing students' capacity for sound civic and moral judgment, while cultivating a healthy spirit of iconoclasm, and promoting liberty and equality: the most noble ideals of a self-governing republic. In the first section, I draw from Plato's *Republic*—a powerful metaphor for traditional higher learning—to highlight how one's intellectual and civic education can go awry, shorn of an institutional experience that fosters a spirit of camaraderie, liberality, and a deep sense for the public good. I emphasize the need to create structures that provide students with the cognitive leisure that is necessary for the study of transformative texts. In the second section, I illuminate the intangible qualities of a classic liberal arts experience that make it a more egalitarian conveyor of independent student learning. It is well known that for more than two centuries, liberal education was reserved for privileged students who distinctly had the leisure to reflect upon the most enduring questions that concern the human condition. Allan Bloom observed as much in *The Closing of the American Mind* and held that we may as well teach them the art of being people of great soul and character during their proverbial paths to nobility.[7] Fortunately, liberal education is more widely accessible today, and large state institutions are ideally positioned for providing an elite education to a student body that is more representative of America's current-day demographics. To their credit, some flagship institutions have moved in that direction. However, as Dr. Roosevelt Montás correctly warns, "liberal education threatens to retreat to these bastions of privilege, with technical, vocational, and professional education, much of it online for everyone else."[8] How then, do universities teach socially responsible citizenship without inadvertently reproducing the social inequality embodied by the classic liberal arts institutions of yesteryear? How do universities approximate a nonelitist philosophy of social duties in the face of inescapable socioeconomic disparities that exist in the democratized university?[9] A careful treatment of this question will dovetail with a meditation on the classic American film *It's a Wonderful Life*: a metaphor for liberal education that provides us with a framework for teaching citizenship in the modern research university.

CUTTING DOWN THE JUNGLE: THE INTRODUCTION TO LIBERAL EDUCATION

As a student, I had the good fortune to read Plato's *Republic* in a first-year philosophy class at a quintessential liberal arts college in the bucolic town of Sackville, New Brunswick. The course was a life-changer. Today, I enjoy the privilege of witnessing students undergo a similar transformative experience when reading *Republic*. I recall recently encountering a student who was enamored with Plato's ideas concerning education but disturbed that his own education might have robbed him of the possibility to live a happy, rigorous, and philosophical life. Questions such as "Oh God . . . am I in the cave? What is Good? What is valuable? Do I really want to be a lawyer or a stockbroker?" gnawed at him. Plato similarly induced my first panic attack in university—a rite of passage supported by an organic intellectual community of friends in the natural sciences, social sciences, and humanities. Our discussions were mediated by professors who took part in our weekly drinking sessions, entitled "beer materialism." Such rituals gave professors the opportunity to know their students, and to offer helpful interjections, assuring them for instance that clinical psychology has disproven many of Plato's assumptions concerning the human psyche!

The great books are vehicles for profound reflection that both speak to and bring out one's inner voice. It is critical to students' intellectual formation that they engage with primary materials independently, but we should not suppose that student engagement with the classics could effectively take place anywhere, under any circumstances. In *Republic*, Plato anticipates the hazards of philosophical learning, offering readers clues about the obstacles that stand in the way of a just, happy life: the blinding effects of the sun, the dragging out of the Cave, the character of Thrasymachus who possesses all the "techniques" of philosophy (to list a few) each present a warning of how it could all go awry.

Plato's *Republic* itself exemplifies the perils of reading the great books in physical isolation. The dialogical style of writing urges us to ponder what is good, but in a way where we encounter characters who accord with people we know. That is how personalized the style is. We all know the person whose sense of self-worth is derived from their wealth, or the person who has a Thrasymachean penchant for weaponizing philosophy and likes to own you in argumentation for sport. Such an intimate identification with the characters might compel readers to conclude that everything around them is pathological once they put the book down. On the one hand, we get a seductive account of what the just, happy, flourishing soul is while in the company of Socrates in Kallipolis, but on the other, when we return to our world, we might look around and say, "Oh my God . . . everything around me is so rotten!"

The starting point for thinkers such as Plato, Rousseau, and Nietzsche, among others, is that "culture around us *itself* is a sick pathology." The dramatic style of writing may amplify such a feeling among readers. We need to be aware the disgust that even Plato's critique can incite may lead readers down dangerous avenues,[10] *when* in combination with a political vision that accords privilege to reason and philosophy for establishing good politics. The more one finds oneself looking for pathologies of liberalism and combines that feeling of disgust with an uncompromising impulse for truth (objective in the case of Plato, or self-generated in the case of Nietzsche and his disciples), one's solution to the problems of modernity is in real danger of matching the magnitude of disgust against the current order of things.

The great books encourage us to think critically about our norms and question beliefs we take for granted. However, they should do so in a manner that does not constantly disenchant us with the superficiality of life. As educators we have a responsibility to preserve an environment that mitigates against disenchantment. We must play an active role in the rituals, institutions, and intellectual traditions that constitute a wholesome university life. Many universities will throw the material at students in large class sizes. Some of the students may immediately grasp the profundity of these works by reading carefully on their own, but possibly in an environment that forces them to process the material in the company of whichever deranged puppeteer they find lurking in whatever dark, unsavory corner of the internet. Such intellectual engagement is unnatural. Important philosophical and normative questions need to be worked through in the form of a dynamic dialogue within the physical setting of a university community.

I cannot see how students (and professors, for that matter) can develop a healthy sense of humility within an increasingly professionalized university that blunts students' and professors' capacity to forge important touchstones that keep them grounded throughout their scholarly journeys and beyond. Left to their own devices, shorn of a community of friends and mentors, students will never gain as lucid an understanding of the strengths or weaknesses that shape their civic, moral, and intellectual identities. Classic canonical texts such as *Antigone, Republic,* and *Othello* contain character archetypes that serve as some of the most powerful heuristic devices available for deepening our understanding of the human condition, and ourselves. But if we apply such archetypes in the abstract, in isolation, they will more likely yield a cynical, life-denying outlook that mirrors the academic cynicism many defenders of a classic liberal education bemoan.

Zena Hitz's *Lost in Thought: The Hidden Pleasures of an Intellectual Life* provides a compelling defense of liberal education for its intrinsic worth, something sorely needed given the extent to which scholarly life has become mired in a spirit of careerism. In one of the book's more polemical passages she writes:

> Our vision of the love of learning is distorted by notions of economic and civic usefulness. I can be more blunt. We do not see intellectual life clearly, because of our devotion to lifestyles rich in material comfort or social superiority. We want the splendor of Socratic thinking without his poverty. We want the thrill of his speaking truth to power without the full absorption in the life of the mind that made it possible. . . . We want Einstein's brilliant insights without the humiliation of joblessness followed by years of obscurity working in a patent office. . . . So we lie to ourselves that what we really care about is the realm of the intellect, when in reality we would sacrifice it in a second to our idols—comfort, wealth, and status.[11]

Hitz suggests that the intellectual life, which is "so often denied or diminished by social life and social circumstances,"[12] ". . . is a refuge from distress; a reminder of one's dignity," available to anyone willing to temporarily withdraw from worldly concerns related to comfort, wealth, and status. Her own example of growing up in a suburban San Francisco home, choosing a life of poverty, and then discovering the hidden pleasures of the life of the mind, as she recounts in her introduction, is inspiring. But there is a distinction between inherited poverty and poverty that is determinant, shorn of the psychological burdens that constitute *actual* poverty. An overburdened and financially stressed student who has grown sensitized to human beings' differentiated capacities for enjoying leisure spaces and thinking uselessly may contend that Hitz's fealty to the untainted life of the mind inadvertently masquerades as radical. It presupposes anyone can choose this path, that one's pecuniary circumstances do not excuse one's failure to pick up Tolstoy. If one chooses to transmute poverty by voluntarily living a monastic life, one may be left with a false sense of the actual effort it took to enjoy "the inner pleasures" our liberal education may unlock. A person may be preoccupied with the cheap joys of social media and the bread and circuses of the twenty-first century because he or she is too exhausted, afflicted by a psychological sense of precarity. By contrast, a person who is *voluntarily* poor is privileged with greater cognitive capacity to choose a "nobler" path, untainted by careerism. In a world mediated by technologies whose algorithms are designed to hijack our attention, under material circumstances that produce psychological exhaustion and dis-ease even among middle-class income earners, we will be hard-pressed to find many people with the capacity to seamlessly replace four hours of *Monday Night Football* with *The Death of Ivan Ilyich*. Indeed, we can find magnificent souls throughout our history, such as Albert Einstein, Christine de Pizan, or Simone Weil, who were living examples of this ethos, proving its possibility.[13] But we cannot ground education on the scant evidence of larger-than-life, historical figures who transcended their unfortunate circumstances.

A monastic life of the mind may foster a quietist disposition—an Augustinian dissatisfaction with the corrupt world around us. One needs to be mindful of how easy it is to destroy a civic culture if one succeeds at persuading fellow citizens that the world's material and reputational rewards are so debased. Such an outlook can accommodate the most brutal types of political regimes. Augustinian quietism perhaps offers the most straightforward avenue toward a spiritually fulfilling life, but it does not speak for the entirety. We need to refrain from being so purist in our orientation, with the assumption that faith in the inner life alone can elevate the poor.

To be sure, liberal democracies need to preserve the undisturbed, untainted calling of the life of the mind. But liberal education cannot renounce politics, the world of things, or we will be denying most human beings the opportunity to discover transcendent meaning in their lives. Yes, our role as scholars is to step out of politics and observe the machine from the outside. We need people questioning the prevailing *doxa* and critiquing the machinery of state, but that does not mean the machine does not need to be run. In a republic, the garden needs to be tended and held up by people of sound moral character. If we construct a dichotomy between the untainted life and the fallen world to serve as the guiding principle of academic life, we will fail to understand what is ennobling and what is dangerous about the life of action. Abraham Lincoln illustrates how worldly concerns, free of ideology, can sometimes shed a more viable path toward philosophical and political greatness. Having grown up in deplorable conditions in Kentucky with a brutal father, Lincoln recognized his own intelligence, deeming it worthy of esteem. Yet we see that his naked ambition for material and reputational awards underwent an alchemy of sorts. It did not impede his capacity to ground the republic in nobler principles.

To return to *Republic*, Socrates of course provides a defense of the life of the mind for its intrinsic value. He nonetheless appreciates the necessary tension between the contemplative and active life. He is under no illusions about turning Glaucon to the philosophical life, but instead wants to infuse the life of action in democratic Athens with philosophy—to produce benevolent leaders without denying the honor that incites their sense of nobility. Socrates acknowledges that societies will have people of noble character who prefer the life of action over the contemplative life. If we hold the naive view that everyone has the capacity for contemplative prayer and looking at the stars, regardless of the concrete circumstances, then the temper, disposition, and outlook of our popular culture will fall prey to the direction of zealots and demagogues. We need to exercise humility vis-à-vis those who could simply be leavened through the exercise of our compassion.

IRRIGATING THE DESERT:
THE CULTIVATION OF A LIBERAL EDUCATION

Many of our contributors in this volume emphasize how critically important it is to provide students the leisure to meaningfully reflect upon the big questions during their brief time in college. While canceling debt and developing practical utilities such as Zoom may yield short-term conveniences, inequalities will reconstitute themselves unless "leisure" becomes a valued currency in our universities. However, with the unrelenting pressure to achieve gainful employment preoccupying most students, the current pathway to achieving worldly success will continue to foster a profound disconnect between what it takes to be a socially responsible citizen, on the one hand, and the exercise of economic and political power, on the other. At a bare minimum, liberal arts universities could admit students who, like Glaucon, are poised for a life of action and give them the tools to stand back and reflect on the *doxa* of their age; otherwise, they will merely become instruments rather than shapers of *doxa*.

A traditional liberal arts experience affords students the leisure to think "uselessly," to develop a sense of social responsibility as they pursue "nobility." Such intangibles are a tough sell when a spirit of careerism and market rationality have permeated the academy, afflicting both scholars who well understand the demands of a buyer's—publish or perish—academic job market, and students for whom university is about acing standardized tests and curating the best possible resume, with the grandeur of working in Big Law, Big Tech, or finance serving as the only lodestar for guidance during their four years. The fortunate ones will punch through and realize their ambitions but without having ever been afforded the luxury to reflect on what it means to live purposefully. If we are serious about increasing accessibility and the opportunity for self-made scholarship, large universities need to recognize the intrinsic value of a classic liberal arts education without forcing students to choose between a job in the STEM (science, technology, engineering, and math) fields that could be secured through online learning, and the privilege to develop one's character.

Universities that are congenial to the traditional university experience risk deepening social inequality if the education they offer is mostly accessible to the limited demographic that can afford it. The best way to optimize their return on investment is through ensuring wider accessibility. It is not simply a question of fairness. The quality of the institution is at stake. Consider the student from a struggling rural community that converges around the pulpit every Sunday to help keep it all together, the African American student who witnesses a parent's humiliation after getting carded by a police officer, an Israeli-born student raised in a kibbutz with a unique vantage point for weighing in on discussions concerning the relationship between the communal family and citizenship. Such experiences shape students' emotional development long before entering the academy. Such experiences might foster a greater emotional receptivity to some of the underappreciated insights contained within the great books. With the proper scaffolding of a physical liberal arts environment, their perspectives will amplify the intellectual and civic dynamism of a university culture. In failing to give them standing in a manner that fosters critical self-reflection, resilience, and personal overcoming, universities will fuel a culture of resentment, further poisoning America's civic well. In short, fairness is a windfall gain for a liberal arts college that creates opportunities for underrepresented demographics and offers a physical space congenial to a diversity of perspectives clashing in a civil and respectful manner. Yet we need to be mindful that many of our struggling students are cognitively incapable of leisure, even when we make it logistically possible for them. The choice many students face when entering the academy is to either follow the careerist playbook for success, which yields no time for quiet reflection, or to live in precarity: to achieve power without capacity to empathize, or to learn to empathize without any capacity to wield power.

In a recent essay, Daniel Markovits laments how the frenetic pace of achievement within the modern academy has eclipsed education even at our most elite institutions. He takes aim at Ivy League universities that purport to undergird the principles of equal opportunity, intimating that they are neither promoting equality nor producing real education. Universities are grappling with a new postwar myth, an instinct for meritocracy that transcends all ideologies, leaving one unaware of their privileged status as elites. Markovits warns that as universities approximate meritocracy in the crass commercial sense, our future leaders will fail to recognize their privilege, attributing their success to the potency of their agency, the force of their Promethean will—an outlook that will reproduce the inequalities many of our elite universities purport to be remedying.[14]

The relationship between leisure and nobility of character is something Plato himself presents in Socrates's discussion with Cephalus at the beginning of book 1 in *Republic*. Prima facie, the exchange seems like a throwaway part of the dialogue to illustrate how flimsy and impressionable a character Cephalus is compared to Socrates's other interlocutors, adumbrating the value of dialectic in a democracy, notwithstanding the weird conclusions it leads us to in later books. It is easy to dismiss Cephalus as a simple placeholder for *doxa*. But Socrates's challenge to Cephalus's account of justice forces the latter to make an admission that should give readers pause. We discover that Cephalus *kind of* likes money because it enables him to be just.[15] However, Socrates gets him to admit that his ability to be just with his money is related to the psychological equanimity he enjoys with his secure and comfortable lifestyle.[16] There is no intrinsic value to his wealth; rather, it is the fact that he inherited his wealth that enables him to be just.

Plato is attuning readers to the relationship between money, reflection, and justice in this early part of the dialogue. Citizens such as Cephalus may not need to be as reflective as the "self-made" man. One's inherited wealth makes it easier to develop a sense of noblesse oblige, which is why Cephalus exits the dialogue without any controversy or contention. He shows readers how a comfortable prepolitical *oikos* enabled him to accrue a partial understanding of justice. In short, Cephalus's relationship with others exists in proportion to his empathy, made possible by his perceived security.

Cephalus's role is germane because the discussion provokes readers to reflect upon the perils associated with a modern ethos of achievement that glorifies the notion that "life is what one makes of it." However, merit-based achievement is an insufficient condition of justice. Justice requires that we do not associate one's sense of agency with one's ability to achieve economic security by the dint of one's efforts. Socrates and Cephalus agree such people will make bad company because they constantly need to draw attention to their self-made wealth. Such people are less likely to accrue a sense of "indebtedness" or responsibility toward others since that would undermine the greatness of their own achievement: the principal source of their sense of self-worth.

In a recent article, George Thomas observes that university today entails little more than "resume building and piling up dizzying credentials that have little if anything to do with genuine leadership, particularly of the civic variety."[17] A person who achieves current-day nobility by ticking the checkboxes that make one's CV employable is unlikely to develop a deep sense of paterfamilias. The removal of leisure from the campus experience leaves no time for future leaders to reflect and forge profound friendships. Such circumstances will produce the opposite of humility and responsibility, blinding us to actual categories of privilege that exist, including our own.

Paradoxically, to approximate socially responsible citizenship we need to acknowledge the limits of meritocracy and recognize the role fortune or benevolence may have played to support our meritorious efforts along the way. To be sure, it is not practical or desirable to re-create a disposition of say, the Roosevelts, whose greatness stemmed from an education designed to accommodate America's Gilded Age scions. How, then, will a sense of responsibility become more widespread when it is such a time-intensive and delicate process that was previously grounded in a subjective sense of nonprecarity?

THE JUSTICE OF JUST SENTIMENTS:
THE COMMUNITY OF LIBERAL EDUCATION

In this volume, George Thomas compellingly argues that constitutional studies should be a mandatory component of liberal arts curricula.[18] Civic literacy is especially important for a Promethean political society whose constitution is so foundationally grounded in its written documents. If we do not engage in a careful study of the constitutive factors that endow greater intelligibility to the words on our foundational documents, we are more likely to interpret history as a litany of sins with America's Constitution being nothing more than a stalking horse for oppression. The importance of including classic texts in constitutional studies is self-evident, but it extends even beyond their practical utility. To be sure, we are cultivating a better sense of constitutional self-understanding when we examine how the great books informed the founders' notions of liberty and equality. However, it is when we engage with past philosophers on their own terms that they most effectively incite us to reflect upon the deeper questions. My most rewarding seminars on Locke, Hume, and Montesquieu took place when we temporarily parked discussions concerning their legacies in America. We gave due consideration to their rich philosophical accounts of what constitutes human happiness, while the course's mission kept us tethered to the most pressing moral and civic challenges that concerned our particular circumstances. Such discussions, which later reverberate in informal interactions, cultivate an instinct to reflect upon the "purpose" of whatever activities students engage in as they climb the meritocratic latter.

Patrick Deneen is among the few current-day defenders of a classic liberal education who recognizes that commercial meritocracy alone is an insufficient condition for justice.[19] His writings on liberal education reveal a genuine concern about the university's declining capacity in producing socially responsible citizens through civic education. He intimates how a subjective feeling of nonprecarity is no longer sufficient for teaching citizenship when universities are no longer undergirded with a common culture that enables students "to share something thicker" with their fellow citizens. To support his position, Deneen juxtaposes "two competing ideals of liberty" that coexisted throughout America's history: the one undergirded by its classical and Christian inheritances, and the other by the science and technology that has gradually liberated us from nature's constraints.[20] These competing notions of liberty correspond with the premodern "humble books" that attune us to our devotions and our cultural inheritances, and the "great [modern] books that advance a version of Promethean greatness."[21] Deneen contends that our classic ideal of liberty has been eclipsed by the modern ideal in recent decades, resulting in "an approximately century-long process of disaffiliation of the nation's colleges and universities from their various religious foundations, identities, and commitments."[22] He follows that a common culture may be reproduced only if colleges recapture the religious identities that gave students of yesteryear their moral bearings.

Deneen's argument is compelling if we agree that higher education should be widely accessible; we agree that the university experience should provide students with a sense of purpose, resilience, and noblesse oblige; and, finally, we agree that it is impossible for a promising STEM student to develop one's character by simply enrolling in a course on Aristotle's *Nicomachean Ethics* at some point during the tenure of his or her undergraduate career. Some may find Deneen's call for restoring the university's (and America's, for that matter) Christian foundations seductive because any person can easily differentiate religion from the material life, whereas with civics we will be hard-pressed to reach consensus over its meaning, given the disagreement even among sympathetic contributors to this volume! However, it is impractical to suppose that we could inspire a widespread sense of "thou art thy brother's keeper" through religion in the present day. How, then, do we welcome upwardly mobile souls to the academy and infuse them with a sense of social responsibility in the absence of religious faith? Is constitutional studies really a viable alternative within a technomediated academic environment that teaches students who arrive to university and begin to develop political consciousness that civics is the area of human activity where people call each other villains?

This dilemma is presciently captured in the classic Christmas film *It's a Wonderful Life*, which responds to a perennial question over the morality of capitalism in American democracy: Where do free societies derive their axiology of value in an age of declining Christian faith? If seen from a certain vantage point, the film serves as an illuminating metaphor for the destructive impact a cosmopolitan liberal education may have on a town such as Bedford Falls—a fictional idyllic American community, not shorn of the ambition and greed one will find in larger commercially dynamic cities, except that its pernicious figures are bounded by the small town's institutional confines. It tells the story of George Bailey, a young dreamy-eyed man who is poised to attend college, but whose worldly ambitions become shattered when his father unexpectedly dies. George inherits the family mortgage-lending business, "Bailey Brothers Building & Loans," which kept him tethered to Bedford Falls. Throughout the film, the villainous real-estate mogul, Mr. Potter, who has a near-wholesale monopoly over Bedford Falls, relentlessly attempts to buy out George. George refuses Mr. Potter's multiple lucrative offers, knowing that he would be betraying his fellow townspeople if he freed himself from the cumbersome family business. His personal freedom would have delivered a final death blow to his fellow citizens' pursuit of the quintessential American dream of owning a home. George's personal sacrifices keep Bedford Falls on even keel. His personal magnanimity is what makes him such a revered and nostalgic figure in American film.

Deneen's analysis of the film aptly recognizes its germaneness for highlighting the limits of meritocracy in an age of spiritual decline. His primary criticism of George Bailey's character in the film dovetails with a core claim in his best-selling book, *Why Liberalism Failed*, where he responds to the toxic, hyperindividualistic culture our liberal ideology has produced—the practical result of a monolithic liberal political philosophy rooted in the thought of Machiavelli and Hobbes. Deneen's analysis is infused with a revivalist impulse for the Christian institutions and manners that previously gave liberalism its guardrails, and, moreover, gave ontological grounding to our principles of toleration, moral equality, and equal dignity, principles that our technomediated commercial order has been dismantling at an accelerated pace. As Deneen writes, "The modern scientific project of human liberation from the tyranny of nature has been framed as an effort to 'master' or 'control' nature, or as a 'war' against nature in which its study would provide the tools for its subjugation at the hands of humans."[23]

Deneen does not offer a flattering account of George Bailey, presenting the film's hero as a well-intentioned Hobbesian avatar who lacks reverence for America's long-standing institutions. Yes, Bailey's commercially innovative designs successfully thwarted Mr. Potter's selfish attempts to establish a monopoly, but Deneen notes that he had no regard for the institutions that made the ethical life possible in Bedford Falls.[24] Bailey "re-engineer(s) life for mobility and swiftness, one unencumbered by permanence, one no longer limited to a moderate and comprehensible human scale." Bailey's dreams may have been shattered, but he never "abandon(s) the dream of transforming America."[25]

Deneen's critique of liberalism is baked into his analysis of George Bailey's character, leaving little room for an internal response to modernity's spiritual challenges. However, his study conspicuously ignores foundational strands of liberal thought—which profoundly shaped America's founding—that took for granted that human beings are social, relational beings[26] and that liberal nations have a capacity for self-correction under modern commercial circumstances. Scholars have taken aim at Deneen for providing a strawman account of modern liberalism. Yet it is precisely this narrow treatment of modern liberalism that resonated with so many readers. His best-selling book articulates a sense of anxiety felt across the ideological spectrum, over the vaporousness of our increasingly atomistic world. Deneen's version of liberalism seems poised to become our reality as the current generation of technology has taken firm hold, casting doubt over the alternative strands. Indeed, George Bailey embodies the spirit of liberal modernity, but as we shall see, his community-level patriotism instructs us in how to transcend its pathologies from *within* liberalism's ecosystem.

George's heroism is most apparent when we juxtapose his life trajectory with that of his brother, Harry, whose insidious role has recently been noted by Brad Schaeffer in an excellent article that portrays him as the film's symbolic villain.[27] It reminds viewers that when the brothers lost their father, George gave his college money to Harry with the expectation that he will go to university in four years, once his brother returns to take over the family business. Harry fails to honor his end of the bargain. He instead decides to work at his father-in-law's company, keeping George tethered to Bedford Falls. A few years later, Harry receives a hero's welcome when he returns home with a Medal of Honor for fighting in World War II. Meanwhile, George had been declared unfit to fight due to a burst eardrum he suffered during his youth, after jumping into freezing-cold water to save Harry from drowning. Funnily, Harry was the symbolic cause of George's mental breakdown and attempt to commit suicide after his bank's $8,000 went missing. Schaeffer reminds us that it was only when their foolish uncle bragged about *Harry's* achievements to Mr. Potter that the money fell on the latter's lap. Despite achieving all the rewards that one would expect from one's 'liberal education' in the modern academy, Harry failed to develop the sense of responsibility and citizenship Bedford Falls depended on for its survival. Had George not been saved by his guardian angel, Clarence, Harry's education would have been the principal cause of Bedford Falls' downfall.

George needed to overcome his own flaws that would have surely led to Bedford Falls' destruction. Yes, he lives in a dream world throughout the film, obsessed with abstractions. The movie is replete with musings of fantastic journeys and abstract imaginings of living his brother's life. George's life is a chaotic, modernist stream flowing onward with no purpose, obscuring his connection with the immediate that is hiding in plain sight—a reality he arrives at only through God's saving love after ruminating the most fundamental existential question: "Would it not be better for everyone if I never existed at all?" George gains insight into the reality he is a part of only when Clarence shows him what would have happened to the people of Bedford Falls without the bonds of love that George forged with them over the years.

Yes, George's education is contingent upon supernatural grace, which seems to affirm Deneen's penchant for a return to America's Christian past. But Christianity really played only a vestigial role throughout the movie. God made a couple of brief cameos as an amorphous figure hovering in the stars, and Clarence was a bumbling angel. If we compare Harry's glories with George's quiet heroism, the latter did not result so much from George being a good Christian but simply a community leader with remnant Christian impulses. A sense of patriotism is the centripetal force that will keep everything together, a microcosm of which we find in Bedford Falls. Consider when word got around that the $8,000 went missing, the townspeople raised the money among themselves. Their individual sacrifices were not divinely inspired. Rather, it was George's community-level patriotism that enlivened their just sentiments. He is a model that fellow citizens could stand on and reincarnate—a vestigial character of virtue in a public sphere that becomes a substitute for the church. As for George, we witness how his happiness is restored when he discovers the meaning and purpose of his local citizenship. Christianity saved him from committing suicide, sparing Bedford Falls. Yet George's patriotic sacrifices would have redounded to his benefit anyway with the townspeople having already pooled their resources to spare him from disgrace. In short, the theodicy unfolded through George's benevolent, civic-minded actions.

We see in *It's a Wonderful Life* that the battle line for confronting America's existential challenges and maintaining its liberal foundations at the localized level is as important as the ones drawn on the global stage. George cares about fighting the battles of Bedford Falls, Harry about fighting the Nazis; both share a virtue, but George's patriotism is about tending the garden within. As their uncle tells Mr. Potter, "Not all the heels were in Germany; some people had to stay home." Even though my entire upbringing and professional life has been as cosmopolitan as it gets, I have found it interesting how as a second-generation Montrealer, I related so much with students from the rural Midwest during my tenure at the Kinder Institute on Constitutional Democracy. It is quite empowering to overcome the meekness one feels when first arriving at college, having previously been naive to the subtleties of the cosmopolitan world's fashionable norms and practices that were so alluring from the outside—a healthy experience, but one that could foster resentment rather than a sense of responsibility, as we see in *both* the Bailey brothers throughout the film. Our liberal education gives voice to and a deeper understanding of our frustrations toward the provincialism of the communities we grew up in. Yet Harry symbolizes the hazards of liberal education shorn of a proper civic education that affords students the leisure to nourish their just sentiments.

The Bailey brothers' tension points to a perennial civic challenge in the United States, harking back to the famous Hamilton-Jefferson debates: a commercial instinct to innovate and boost industry, reflected in the thought of Alexander Hamilton versus an organic sense of community reflected in the thought of Thomas Jefferson. Their tension mirrors the urban-rural tensions fueling America's polarization today: a prevailing cosmopolitan mentality that lionizes innovation and social progress versus an instinct to preserve enduring American values of patriotism and civic community in more rural parts of the country. Many universities today are at the heart of it, with our book's authors demonstrating how a classic liberal education can aid in alchemizing a tension that we have been attempting to reconcile since the creation of the republic.

Indeed, the cosmopolitan sophistication we develop might confound the actual pedagogical ends of a traditional liberal arts education. It was already hard enough to foster a civic sense of noblesse oblige when "Harry Bailey" attended college in the mid-twentieth century; it is even harder in the absence of a traditional learning space that enables us to re-create local communities to keep us grounded throughout our cosmopolitan journey. The "publish or perish" realities in the academy yields a spirit of careerism among scholars, concealing for many the profundity of what will be lost should we fail to preserve the classic liberal arts experience.

University gives us the cultural, ideational, and eventually the economic capital to afford a more privileged life, but students and professors are cognizant that a $100,000 degree will not guarantee that the latter will ever materialize. It, therefore, should not surprise us that reasonable personal security considerations are crowding out the time and space (in the literal sense) to reflect upon the purposeful ends we strive for as we pursue our ambitions. That being said, we have greater agency to shape the direction of liberal education within the universities that currently employ us,[28] as opposed to the fleeting sense of empowerment we enjoy when signing the most recent petition circulating on social media to save the classic liberal arts from being gutted at some renowned institution. There are equally important battles to fight in Bedford Falls.

It takes a lot of courage not to be Harry Bailey in current-day academic life.

NOTES

I am grateful to William DeMars and Donald Drakeman for the wonderful discussions. Special thanks to Justin Buckley Dyer, whose balancing of conviction and ecumenical generosity exemplifies the sympathetic citizen, a model that I do my best to teach others.

1. Mark Edmundson, "Teach What you Want: A Modest Proposal for Professors in Literature."

2. See Clifford Orwin's chapter for his judicious treatment of this subject.
3. C. S. Lewis, "On the Reading of Old Books," 598.
4. Lewis, "On the Reading of Old Books," 597.
5. C. S. Lewis, *Abolition of Man*, 5, 33, 36, 6.
6. See Carson Holloway's chapter in this volume, "Liberal Education and the Limits of Science and Technology: Lessons from the COVID-19 Pandemic."
7. Allan Bloom, *The Closing of the American Mind: How Higher Education Has Failed Democracy and Impoverished the Souls of Students*.
8. Roosevelt Montás, "Why the Core Matters for a New Generation: Required Classes Bring Campuses Together and Are a Boon to the Humanities—If Done Right."
9. I am deeply grateful to Donald Drakeman for our private and public interchanges, which helped clarify my thinking about this question. Donald Drakeman and Constantine Vassiliou, "Liberal Education and Citizenship in a Self-Governing Republic."
10. See Michael P. Zuckert and Catherine Zuckert, *Leo Strauss and the Problem of Political Philosophy*.
11. Zena Hitz, *Lost in Thought: The Hidden Pleasures of an Intellectual Life*, 116.
12. Hitz, *Lost in Thought*, 57.
13. Hitz, *Lost in Thought*, 116.
14. Daniel Markovits, "How College Became a Ruthless Competition Divorced from Learning."
15. Plato, *Republic*, 329e.
16. Plato, *Republic*, 330a.
17. George Thomas, "Liberal Education and American Democracy."
18. See George Thomas's chapter in this volume, "Liberal Education and American Democracy."
19. For an excellent instantiation of this argument, see Patrick J. Deneen, "The Ignoble Lie: How the New Aristocracy Masks Its Privilege." See also Roosevelt Montás, *Rescuing Socrates: How the Great Books Changed My Life and Why They Matter for a New Generation*.
20. Patrick J. Deneen, "After the Interregnum."
21. Patrick J. Deneen, "Against Great Books: Questioning Our Approach to the Western Canon."
22. Deneen, "After the Interregnum."
23. Patrick J. Deneen, *Why Liberalism Failed*, 23, 14.
24. "George Bailey's vision of a modern America eliminates his links with his forbears, covers up the evidence of death, supplies people instead with private retreats of secluded isolation, and all at the expense of an intimate community, in life and in death." Patrick J. Deneen, "It's a Destructive Life," *First Things*, Dec. 12, 2012.
25. Deneen, "It's a Destructive Life."
26. Dennis C. Rasmussen, *The Pragmatic Enlightenment: Recovering the Liberalism of Hume, Smith, Montesquieu, and Voltaire*; Constantine Vassiliou, *Moderate Liberalism and the Scottish Enlightenment: Montesquieu, Hume, Smith, and Ferguson*.
27. See Brad Schaeffer, "It's a Wonderful Life . . . If You're Harry Bailey."
28. Lee Ward, "Academic Freedom and the Future of the Liberal Arts" (in this volume).

BIBLIOGRAPHY

Bloom, Allan. *The Closing of the American Mind: How Higher Education Has Failed Demcracy and Impoverished the Souls of Students.* New York: Simon and Schuster, 1987.

Deneen, Patrick J. "After the Interregnum." *Academic Questions* 27 (Winter 2014): 368–75.

———. "Against Great Books: Questioning Our Approach to the Western Canon." *First Things* (January 2013). https://www.firstthings.com/article/2013/01/against-great-books.

———. "The Ignoble Lie: How the New Aristocracy Masks Its Privilege." *First Things* (April 2018). https://www.firstthings.com/article/2018/04/the-ignoble-lie.

———. "It's a Destructive Life." *First Things* (December 27, 2012). https://www.firstthings.com/web-exclusives/2012/12/its-a-destructive-life.

———. *Why Liberalism Failed.* New Haven, CT: Yale University Press, 2018.

Drakeman, Donald, and Constantine Vassiliou. "Liberal Education and Citizenship in a Self-Governing Republic." *Starting Points* (October 1, 2021).

Edmundson, Mark. "Teach What You Want: A Modest Proposal for Professors in Literature." *American Scholar* (September 11, 2020).

Hitz, Zena. *Lost in Thought: The Hidden Pleasures of an Intellectual Life.* Princeton, NJ: Princeton University Press, 2020.

Lewis, C. S. *The Abolition of Man.* Quebec: Samizdat University Press, 1943.

———. "On the Reading of Old Books." In *The Great Tradition: Classic Readings on What It Meant to Be an Eudcated Human Being*, edited by Richard M. Gamble. Wilmington, DE: ISI Books, 2018.

Markovits, Daniel. "How College Became a Ruthless Competition Divorced from Learning." *Atlantic*, May 6, 2021.

Montás, Roosevelt. *Rescuing Socrates: How the Great Books Changed My Life and Why They Matter for a New Generation.* Princeton, NJ: Princeton University Press, 2021.

———. "Why the Core Matters for a New Generation: Required Classes Bring Campuses Together and Are a Boon to the Humanities—If Done Right." *Chronicle of Higher Education* (November 16, 2021).

Rasmussen, Dennis C. *The Pragmatic Enlightenment: Recovering the Liberalism of Hume, Smith, Montesquieu, and Voltaire.* Cambridge: Cambridge University Press, 2014.

Schaeffer, Brad. "It's a Wonderful Life . . . If You're Harry Bailey." *Patch* (December 19, 2012).

Thomas, George. "Liberal Education and American Democracy." *American Interest* (August 24, 2015).

Vassiliou, Constantine. *Moderate Liberalism and the Scottish Enlightenment: Montesquieu, Hume, Smith, and Ferguson.* Edinburgh: Edinburgh University Press, forthcoming.

Zuckert, Michael P., and Catherine H. Zuckert. *Leo Strauss and the Problem of Political Philosophy.* Chicago: University of Chicago Press, 2014.

8. Liberal Education as "Spiritual Exercise"
On the Life of the Mind in the Age of Social Media
Aurelian Craiutu

> It is not that we have a short time to live, but that we waste a lot of it.... We are not given a short life, but we make it short, and we are not ill-supplied but wasteful of it.... Our lifetime extends amply if you manage it properly.
> —Seneca, "On the Shortness of Life"

MACHIAVELLI'S LESSON

EVERY YEAR, I TEACH AN introductory course in political theory in which we read and comment on several foundational texts in the history of political thought. We read representative selections from major works such as Thucydides's *History of the Peloponnesian War*, Cicero's *On Duties*, Machiavelli's *The Prince*, Tocqueville's *Democracy in America*, and Mill's *On Liberty*. The course offers a broad framework for discussing topics that are central to our lives: political power, laws and constitutions, morality and politics, democracy, justice, freedom, and equality.

I encourage my students to also reflect on a few other important questions: What is the purpose of their reading these texts, and what might they gain from them? Are they worth their money, energy, and time, apart from the grade that would allow them to fulfill yet another requirement toward graduation? I would consider my task fulfilled as long as students have had a chance to exert their minds and improve their ability to think at a more nuanced level. At the same time, I also warn them that at the end of the course, they might have as many open-ended questions as at the outset, or perhaps even more.

In order to inspire in them the conviction that the intellectual life still matters in our age of Twitter, Instagram, and Facebook, I like to choose a memorable fragment from a letter Niccolò Machiavelli sent to his friend Francesco Vettori on December 10, 1513. "When evening comes," Machiavelli wrote,

> I return home and enter my study; before I go in, I remove my everyday clothes, which are very muddy and soiled, and put on cloths that are fit for a royal court. Being thus properly clad, I enter the ancient courts of the men of old, in which I am received affectionately by them and partake of the food that properly belongs to me, and for which I was born. There I do not hesitate to converse with them and ask them why they acted as they did; and out of kindness they respond. For four hours I experience no boredom, I forget all my troubles and my fear of poverty, and death holds no more terrors for me: I am completely absorbed in them.[1]

It would be difficult to find a more inspiring plea for intellectual life than Machiavelli's words. He reminds us not only that we stand on the shoulders of real giants who help us see further and better than we could otherwise, but also that these towering figures are present for us, day and night, ready to converse with us about the most important matters. They invite us to join them in a fascinating dialogue on what is perhaps the crucial topic: How ought we to live?

THE CRISIS OF HUMANITIES AND THE DECLINE OF LEISURE

But how can we answer such a daunting question? I propose we start with a more mundane question: How do our students live today, here and now? Let's consider a few concrete details. At America's top private universities, parents pay today approximately $75,000 a year to put their children through college, or close to $300,000 for a bachelor's degree. The figure is, of course, smaller at public universities, but the high level of debt incurred by students and their parents still imposes a big burden upon their shoulders. The average debt for students attending public and nonprofit colleges was $28,800 in 2019, and the most recent numbers show that the US student loan is $1.71 trillion, spread out among about 44.7 million borrowers.[2] These numbers are deeply concerning, and they show that universities in the United States suffer from administrative bloat and have become far too expensive and partly unaccountable, with tuition rates rising faster than parents' salaries.³

The situation is equally worrisome if we consider the packed schedules that fill the daily lives of our students. Most of them are encouraged to choose only classes that allow them to get quickly into professional schools, not knowing that many of those classes prepare them only for what a recent commentator cynically dubbed "bullshit jobs."⁴ Some students schedule appointments just to chat with their friends. Many regret that they do not have the time to put into real human relationships. Very few students can afford spending some time in a coffee shop just chatting about philosophical issues or reading literature for pleasure.

It is true that our students address philosophical, social, and political questions in a much different way compared to previous generations. Six decades ago, the young struggled with something that was directly threatening and affecting their lives: the danger of communism, the specter of nuclear war, or the prevalence of overt racial discrimination. The current generation lives in an entirely different world, dominated by constant technological innovation, short-attention-span activities, self-help therapies, and YouTube or TikTok. Many students ask for safe spaces, safe speech, and trigger warnings. They obsess over microaggressions and want to be coddled. While they believe in the virtues of meritocracy, many want to achieve quick success with little intellectual effort.⁵

Whether this interpretation is entirely accurate or not, I think it may be possible to agree on a few undisputed facts. First, most of our students tend to be pragmatic spirits who learn early on that the main forces that dominate their lives are the market and the bureaucracy that have taken over our schools and universities. They are taught how to navigate the free market by seeing themselves as customers seeking as many credentials as possible rather than students searching for genuine education. They are encouraged to choose disciplines and techniques that are useful to life: law, business, medicine, information technology, nursing, health care, and marketing.

Not surprisingly, the humanities and liberal arts are in crisis, a trend confirmed by the National Center for Education Statistics. In 2015 the share of humanities diplomas among all bachelor's degrees dropped to 6.1 percent, the lowest level since record keeping began in 1948.⁶ The number keeps going down for degrees in disciplines such as English, philosophy religious studies, and foreign languages. At the same time, the demand for new degrees is on the rise in subfields such as nursing and health management, parks and recreation, homeland security and law enforcement, or public administration and social services. This trend is impossible to ignore. According to Vicki Baker, a professor of economics at Albion College, a high percentage of small colleges that once called themselves liberal arts three decades ago can no longer be described as such.[7] They have significantly changed their curriculum under the pressure of the market and student demand by combining humanities disciplines with nursing, data science programs, accounting, and statistics. If these colleges didn't do that, they might have been obliged to eliminate the humanities disciplines altogether.

Some administrators express concern about the decline of liberal arts, but the situation will not improve as long as they expect faculty to produce "revenue," the new mantra, and as long as success is measured only by the teachers' ability to generate "credit hours" and revenue. The decline of interest in the humanities and liberal arts might also be linked to the fact that we seem to have little or no leisure anymore. Everyone seems overworked, one way or another. The titles of two books (by Juliet Schor) I teach in a class on happiness speak for themselves: *The Overworked American* and *The Overspent American*.

To better understand the situation, let us consider a few numbers. In 2020 Harvard accepted 4.92 percent of applicants to the class of 2024, representing a total 1,980 students out of a pool of 40,248 applicants. A year before, in 2019, the admission rate was even lower, around 4.5 percent.[8] How can you win the rat race if you are not doing something all the time? Some parents start coaching their kids early on to be among the very few chosen to attend top universities. Not surprisingly, students enrolled in both elite universities and small liberal arts colleges are overbooked and overcharged, and they feel under the pressure of being somewhere and doing something every minute. They feel like they are little more than tools for processing information and sources of revenue for universities.

In 1985, only 18 percent of college freshmen told a University of California at Los Angeles national freshman survey that they felt overwhelmed; financial concerns existed back then, but they were not overwhelming. Now, the numbers are significantly higher. As indicated in the 2019 issue of the *National Freshman* edited by a team of experts at the UCLA's Higher Education Research Institute, in 2015, 18.4 percent of incoming first-year students came from households with an income in the $100,000–$149,999 range and of those, no less than 61.7 percent of them had some/major financial concerns. Such worries concerns along with anxieties about the job market continued to increase between 2015 and 2019 across all income levels. Their impact on the emotional health of students may not be ignored. As the same survey points out, "From 1985 to the present, incoming college students' self-reported physical and emotional health have continued to decline. . . . Possible reasons for this consistent decline include: an increasingly competitive market in accessing and persisting in college, the influx of technology and social media, etc."[9] What students learn early on and what their college experience confirms is that the meritocratic race begins at birth and never ends, with busy parents and well-paid coaches constantly standing by children's side.

But do we really find real unhappiness with this situation? The surprising thing is that very few students would seriously consider living in any other way. Almost nobody remembers that leisure and contemplation, as Josef Pieper once pointed out, are of a higher order than the *vita activa*.[10] What are students doing with their lives, you might ask? Their daily routines involve endless multitasking between schoolwork, hourly paid jobs, athletics, scheduled socializing, internships, and, if time allows, community work. They are also active on Facebook, Twitter, Instagram, and TikTok.[11]

Not surprisingly, many students do not perceive a great discrepancy between what they study and the types of life they live. They no longer expect their studies to change their tastes, preferences, and priorities in life; to form their character; or to teach them the art of attention. Most of them do not expect to find in their teachers models worth following, nor do they envisage being inspired by them. Sadly, many do not come to college with the expectation of learning the meaning of friendship or being guided to discover what is true and beautiful, the meaning of the good life, and what it takes to become a flourishing human being. The surprising thing is to discover that many students like and want to be that busy; as a result, their activities are rarely ends in themselves. They are rather means of résumé building, and college has become just one step on the stairway of advancement.

CAN THE STUDENTS SURVIVE THE RACE?

What is there to be done, one might ask? How can students resist the powerful impersonal forces that dominate their lives? Each of us, I am sure, has a particular answer to this question. My preferred one was given by the Spanish philosopher Ortega y Gasset in *What Is Philosophy?*—an inspiring book based on a series of lectures addressed to a general public, initially in Buenos Aires in 1928 and repeated a year later in Madrid. "Rather than abandoning ourselves to that fate which would imprison ourselves within a generation," Ortega wrote, "we must work against it."[12] He believed that we can and must always push back against the impersonal forces in our lives by trying to constantly renew ourselves. He considered this exercise to be a vital hygiene of the soul. We must do our best to avoid becoming dry, soulless, and decrepit in the midst of our lives. We must seek to preserve a youthful enthusiasm for everything and avoid becoming prisoners of our own age or generation.

To this effect, we can become "contemporaries" with the great minds of mankind by being part of a larger conversation, the best that liberal education has to offer. Contrary to the common view, we are not fatally limited to belonging to one single generation, conceived of as the aggregate of individuals who are more or less of the same age. A generation may not be reduced to a particular age or date; it comprises, to use Ortega y Gasset's phrase, a "zone of dates"[13] and multiple possibilities that give access to a larger epistemic community. Thus defined, as a set of "spiritual exercises,"[14] liberal education allows us to expand the time horizon to include people who lived before us and belonged to previous generations that pursued different goals. In our back room, as it were, far from the sound and fury of the outer world, we can engage them in conversations that transcend the limits of time and space. These conversations are similar to the dialogues that Machiavelli had every evening with the ancients who lovingly received him in their courts of yesteryear and allowed him to forget his worldly worries for a while.

This is exactly what I invite my students to do. They are given an opportunity to study authors who sought to answer a fundamental question for all of us: How should we live? Plato, Aristotle, Cicero, Saint Augustine, and Saint Thomas Aquinas along with Machiavelli, Hobbes, Rousseau, Tocqueville, and Mill reflected on the human condition, set sail for the unknown, and returned with their own imperfect answers. In studying their writings, we witness the continual reappearance of certain topics: power, authority, freedom, justice, and equality. We realize that they disagreed with each other, but at the same time, we learn the importance of (civil) disagreement in politics and society. We also note that almost all the major works in political philosophy were written during times of crises. Thucydides wrote during a prolonged war that threatened to destroy his beautiful Athens. Saint Augustine wrote *The City of God* after the barbarians' invasion of Rome. Hobbes wrote *The Leviathan* during the bloody English Civil War. They all sought to reconstruct a new political cosmos out of the political chaos in which they lived. They give us hope that we, too, may be able to do the same one day, if we ever face similar challenges.

The question that most students struggle with today is how to read these books written centuries ago and how to interpret their messages intended for past audiences. One way would be to read them without trying to really appropriate what these authors tried to convey. This is what I would like to call "horizontal reading." This style of reading is the simple mental skating down the page without paying close attention to details. Learning for quizzes achieves this lower goal. But there should be a better way of reading these texts, one that starts from recognizing that we are incomplete and ignorant and in need of perfection in some way or another.

And this is precisely the point from which college education should start. A moment must come when, after learning what others wrote a long time ago, we are called to reformulate their old questions on our own and answer them in our own voice. This is the time of "vertical reading," which requires deep immersion into the world of the great minds with whom we become contemporaries by the mere fact that we think with them about similar issues—freedom, equality, justice, good government, and so on. The answers cannot be found immediately; they may be arrived at only after long detours. The main goals of these texts are not to impart information; they seek to form us in the proper sense of the word. Not surprisingly, this type of vertical reading requires from us three types of exercises: the discipline of desires, the discipline of judgment, and the discipline of action.[15]

As any reader of Descartes's *Meditations* knows—a book that offers a set of exercises meant to make one's thoughts, actions, and judgments conform to reason—this is when the young start looking for the harmonious whole that will complete the tiny and imperfect fragment they already are. They sense that something is missing and realize that each of us is only an essay or sketch of what of we might be. In everything and everyone they encounter in the world, the young find a "fracture line" and perceive "the stump of something absent," and "the scar of its ontological mutilation." They resonate with the cry of this stump and share its nostalgia for the whole that is lacking.[16] Operating under the imperative of autonomy, the young minds begin by doubting and purging their spirit of received ideas and natural opinions, while searching for a firm foundation for their beliefs. This is not an easy task, because they must create a new order out of the existing chaos. They must read serious books, attend classes in person, take notes, listen to others, and sit in classrooms and crowded amphitheaters that are not always comfortable.

We must not forget that a classroom is a highly unusual place, especially in our internet age. Here you can find teachers addressing complex ideas, interpreting challenging books, and attempting to make them meaningful to a contemporary audience that has a particular set of experiences and expectations. They try to engage students so that they can join important conversations with each other and with the authors who lived long ago. Yet classrooms are often uncomfortable spaces because they require physical presence as well as sustained attention, a rare commodity in the age of social media.

This is something that few teachers can do well no matter how hard they try. One of the reasons is that what they offer is mostly instruction, mere information, which is rarely exciting. To get their students' full attention, those who teach liberal arts courses should offer them more than simple instruction. This is hardly a new lesson; Cardinal Newman, among others, knew it well. More than a century and a half ago, he pointed out that education is a higher and nobler goal because it implies the formation of character and the exercise of our highest faculties, some of which risk to remain dormant unless we bring them to life by constant exertion.[17]

A good university, Newman reminds us, should be an *alma mater*, a nourishing mother, who knows her children well, cares deeply about them, and gives them the opportunity to exercise their highest faculties. This is not possible in a university that sees itself as a knowledge factory where everyone is expected to get at least a B with minimal effort; the internet and the (in)famous "University of Phoenix" would be enough for that.

The courses students take in a real university are supposed to give them a genuine education whose aim is not only to impart knowledge, but also to offer an opportunity to engage their minds in dialogue with the best that mankind has to offer.

This cannot be properly done online: lecturing and interacting in a classroom are essential. A good lecture is supposed to promote true learning by keeping students' minds active, whetting their intellectual appetite, and opening new vistas. The art of attention is a key prerequisite that should help students control their habits and prejudices. PowerPoint presentations can go only so far, and they often turn students into passive receivers of ready-made materials. As some of them already know (even if they have not read Lord Acton), power corrupts and PowerPoint corrupts . . . absolutely. A good lecture should be much more than that; it cannot be a mere rehearsal of information culled from internet sources. It requires a genuine exchange of ideas and discussion and puts a premium on highlighting the connections between disparate facts. All this can usually be done only, or mostly, through face-to-face dialogue, close reading, and serious reflection and debate allowing for different viewpoints.

That is why a good lecturer should also teach students how to engage in a conversation: how to craft an argument, how to present their thoughts clearly and elegantly, how to dissect and engage with others' ideas, how to say a lot in a few well-chosen words, and with as few "likes" in a phrase as possible. Finally, a skilled lecturer needs to teach students the art of listening to help them clear their minds and be able to concentrate on what is really important for them. A good lecture is therefore an exercise in attention building, a mental workout that counteracts the junk food of social media and offers a welcome break from the students' busy, multitasking lives. Inspiring lecturers also teach note taking, a skill that is rarely cultivated today. Students should be able to synthesize, reach the essence of an argument, detect any form of sophistry, and be able to separate what is relevant from what is ultimately irrelevant.

"LIBERAL" EDUCATION

This brings me to the essence of *liberal* education. In the proper sense of the word, "liberal" means liberating, freeing individuals from the constraints of utility, monetary profit, and the narrow pursuit of self-interest poorly understood. In the original sense of the term, "liberal" is opposed to "servile," the mechanical employment of our faculties in which our mind has little or no part to play.[18] A truly liberal education is not utilitarian in the sense that it does not "minister" to another end. It seeks to cultivate critical sense, sound habits of thought, and good taste and sympathy for what is good, beautiful, and true. In so doing, it helps us overcome our self-incurred immaturity and come out of the darkness in which we had previously lived.

As already mentioned, discipline is essential to anyone engaged in intellectual work. The enemies of learning are many, and they include stupidity, sloth, excessive sensuality, pride, envy, and irritation.[19] The life of the mind at the heart of liberal education follows a certain method and discipline that fight against these temptations. It combines simplicity, attention, and openness to the world around us with moderation, humility, and patience. As such, it is the opposite of sloth, vainglory, and shallow curiosity and cultivates the capacity to admire and discern what is noble.[20] This is precisely how those who established universities in the Middle Ages, perhaps in the footsteps of Plato, thought of education: the term comes from *educere*, to lead forth, to bring out, to lead out of the dark cave of immaturity into the splendor of light.[21]

At the same time, liberal education seeks to give students a cultivated intellect, an elegant vocabulary, attentiveness to nuances of style and thought, a rich imagination, and a judicious taste that can make the difference between junk and gold. We should also teach our students courtesy, propriety, and polish of word and action that make possible a noble and courteous bearing in the conduct of life and outward appearance. As Eton master William Cory once said:

> You go to a great school not so much for the knowledge as for arts and habits: for the habit of attention, for the art of expression, for the art of assuming at a moment's notice, a new intellectual position, for the art of entering into another person's thoughts, for the habit of submitting to censure and refutation, for the art of indicating assent or dissent in graduated terms, for the habit of regarding minute points of accuracy, for the art of working out what is possible in a given time, for taste, discrimination, for mental courage, and mental soberness. And above all you go to a great school for self-knowledge.[22]

As such, liberal education seeks to bring students' minds into proper form since their minds, much like their bodies, tend to get out of shape. If not properly cultivated, they remain ignorant about what they can bear and how to manage the surfeit of information that floods our lives. Our minds tend to become immoderate and vulnerable to falling sick when they have no solid principles as a foundation for the intellect to build upon. This may happen when students have no discriminating convictions and believe that truth is relative; they never really "wonder" at anything since they are told that everything is relative, and therefore, not worth admiring. Their sad slogan is "Whatever!"

Yet being unable to discriminate between things of different worth is the state of children who still have a long way to grow up. Those who remain in this state of immaturity tend to squander their lives by wasting time through "groundless sorrow, foolish joy, greedy desire, the seductions of society."[23] They do not live fully, but let life flow impersonally through them. Liberal education can save them by giving them the power of viewing many things at once, by teaching them their respective values, and by helping them determine their proper place in a larger hierarchy of values. To see this unity in plurality, as Plato suggested, is perhaps the highest state to which human beings may aspire. And even today, it is the "university" rather than a fragmented "multiversity" that can offer students a path to becoming "free."

We should recognize that the liberating work which is the true mission of liberal education is quite difficult; it takes a lot of work to become "free" from utilitarian concerns. No one can do this for our students, in their stead, yet they still need our guidance along the way. In order for us to be able to do our job properly, our students must be "teachable" to begin with, that is, to some extent, open, curious, intellectually hungry, and thirsty. A good education is more like "a guide for the perplexed," but there is a deep irony at the end of this process. If our students are to benefit from it, they must remain together with us, as it were, perplexed to the very end. That is why their encounter with the great minds of mankind should help them make the painful transition from being unlearned, and perhaps unperplexed, to a higher form of *docta ignorantia*,[24] a learned type of "ignorance" based on a great deal of good reading, writing, listening, and thinking.

Since we are talking about what good education is, we should also try to say a few words about its opposite. A little learning, someone once said, is a dangerous thing because it leads to a hazy view of many things. This is the outcome of a poor education that gives us a semblance of knowledge, many bits of knowledge unrelated to one other, and a hanging cloud of information or ideologies that distract and enfeeble the mind. Such an education can often cause lasting mental harm by requiring students to act mechanically and remain passive, without exertion and discipline. This type of education does not cultivate the intellect and does not open our intellectual eyes.

WHAT ABOUT THE TEACHERS?

We should also talk a little about teachers. The truth is that we, too, face increasing challenges today. We are subject to major pressures from many quarters and also have among us the good, the bad, and the ugly. Our task is as difficult as our students'. Some of us teach because we love the life of learning and believe that it has its intrinsic attractions, sometimes combined with sabbaticals. Even if scholars no longer have the moral authority of the sages of yesteryear, those who pursue the life of learning still believe that by studying books, manuscripts, and forgotten pages or writing commentaries and histories, they resist the annihilation of what has been created in the past.

To use the title of a great movie by Canadian director Denys Arcand, we are doing our part to stave off the new "barbarian invasions" that threaten to destroy our civilization, much like the barbarian tribes put an end to the Roman Empire sixteen centuries ago. The books we read and engage with are gateways to the "royal courts" where we and our students are received by the great minds ready to communicate and share with us the ambrosia reserved for gods. As Seneca memorably put it, "None of these will be too busy to see you, none of these will not send his visitor away happier and more devoted to himself, none of these will allow anyone to depart empty-handed. They are at home to all mortals by night and day."[25]

If we choose the right books and read them well, they strip our minds of empty thinking and lay down a firm foundation for sound judgment.[26] They also give us a sense of community with those with whom we can become "contemporaries" in thought. As such, the life of the mind helps us achieve detachment and serenity by escaping the ephemeral worries associated with ordinary life. Reading and discussing books can be a form of "spiritual exercise" that implies disciplining one's attention, improving one's memory, enlarging one's imagination, and developing genuine appreciation for what is good, beautiful, and true, the permanent things of enduring worth.[27] Those who pursue the life of the mind in this manner can rise to a universal viewpoint where they may be able to see all things from a larger perspective. It is then that, to use Cicero's words, "the walls of the world fly apart," and we receive the rare gift of the panoramic view from above.[28]

Yet attempting to achieve this bird's-eye view only through reading is not without risks and may not be enough. The Talmud is quite clear on this point: "Warm yourself before the fire of the wise, but beware of being singed by their glowing coals, for their bite is the bite of a fox, and their sting is the sting of a scorpion, and their hiss is the hiss of a serpent, and all their words are like coals of fire."[29] Virtue is essential to intellectual work and passions, and vices may deter our attention. That is why, as a wise Dominican thinker (A.-D. Sertillanges) put it, "the purity of thought requires the purity of soul."[30] Sertillanges followed in the footsteps of Saint Thomas Aquinas who recommended a moderating temperance in the pursuit of knowledge. "*Altiora te ne quaesieris,*" do not seek what is beyond your reach. Instead, we must practice balance and proceed by small steps; to get to the ocean, we should not try the shortest route, but need to go by tributaries first.[31] According to this view, to be properly educated requires two things. First, one must be aware of how much it is healthy and possible to know. Second, one should also have the courage not to be tempted, or tempt others, to go beyond this limit.[32]

Hence, we may not ignore Montaigne's warning against the danger of reading too many books in a haphazard manner; the pursuit of knowledge can sometimes become a form of vanity.[33] Because we can develop an indigestion from reading, we should proceed with due caution. Some books can enlighten us; others may poison us. Perhaps one way to avoid this danger would be to realize that the life of the mind that we seek to share with our students may take place not only in lecture halls and seminar rooms, but also in other more open spaces such as book clubs or private residences where people gather to discuss ideas, watch movies, or listen to music. These are also manifestations of the same love of learning that led some of us to become teachers in the first place, and we should encourage our students to engage in these activities as well.[34]

This may be easier said than done. It is true that the constraints posed by academic life tend to stifle curiosity and engender conformity. Professional academics may be the natural stewards of intellectual life, but their marriage to the life of the mind is not without trials and sometimes grows stale and lifeless. To avoid that, the life of the mind must be sheltered from the pressure to produce immediate tangible economic, social, or political outcomes. It cannot flourish without leisure, which is a rare commodity. As such, liberal education is a good in itself and its value lies in its apparent uselessness.

Whenever our universities focus on what is narrow, superficial, and divisive, we should be concerned about the degradation of intellectual life, a complex phenomenon that might be attributed in part to the rise of professional schools (including the schools of education!).[35] More important, we should be worried when politics invades liberal education since the latter is often at odds with the narrow categories and priorities of political life. Politics fosters division and faction and remains at the surface of things, feeding on apparent victories and temporary setbacks. Since politics involves a certain degree of mental vulgarity, oversimplification, and crass opportunism, our obsession with politics may be seen as the surest sign of a general decay in a society. In this regard it is hard to disagree with Michael Oakeshott who believed that "a universal preoccupation with rights, interests, affairs of government, political questions in general is fatal to the public peace & individual happiness."[36]

We have the opportunity to test the veracity of Oakeshott's claim today in our new world dominated by the obsession with "social justice" and "cancel culture," left and right. We are currently facing calls to reform or "decolonize" the curriculum and replace the "sage on the stage" with student-led discussions or inverted classrooms.[37] Some texts and authors are silently removed from curricula because they tend to offend our postmodern sensibilities. These calls are not always unreasonable, although they must be taken with a grain of salt. Who can deny that there is always room for improvement? Yet these demands for radical reforms coincide with a broader crisis of confidence in liberal arts education and other calls to abolish entire departments in humanities and even to end tenure. Furthermore, the temptation to turn our universities into for-profit institutions is strong and can be felt in more and more quarters.[38]

Nonetheless, the truth is that universities are not for-profit organizations. We should never forget this, but we may not live in the past either. Universities have always been precious fragile institutions that allow for the study of obscure and odd subjects of little immediate utility. They have been, and still are, places where we can study peculiar subjects such as Plato, hieroglyphics, Zen philosophy, and Coptic as well as string theory, the theory of relativity, and the habits of lemmings. As Abraham Flexner, the founding director of the Institute for Advanced Study in Princeton, once wrote, "The pursuit of these useless satisfactions proves unexpectedly the source from which undreamed-of utility is derived."[39] Paradoxically, one can speak then of "the usefulness of useless knowledge" as demonstrated by the successful example of the Princeton-based institute. The remarkable scholars associated with it remind us that efforts aimed at the immediately practical will always fail unless they are based upon a long succession of experiments and theoretical endeavors that initially had no practical use.

AN UNORTHODOX TYPE OF LIBERAL EDUCATION AND ITS UNEXPECTED BENEFITS

Thus far, I have made a plea for liberal education as a form of "spiritual exercise" in the footsteps of an old tradition of thought made popular these days by the writings of French philosopher Pierre Hadot (1922–2010). I am prepared to admit that this view of liberal education might not gain many converts, and it may appear as too conservative or eclectic in the eyes of some. But eclecticism properly practiced can also be a virtue, I am ready to embrace it *cum grano salis*. As Emerson once put it, "A foolish consistency is the hobgoblin of little minds, adored by little statesmen and philosophers and divines."[40]

My arguably eclectic perspective has deeper roots in an unforgettable paideic experience I was privileged to have behind the Iron Curtain.[41] Deprived of the possibility of being active in the political realm, the life of the mind became for those of us living under a totalitarian regime a form of spiritual oxygen that gave us a chance to choose whose disciples we wanted to be. Some took refuge in culture as a way of maintaining their own dignity. Others focused on the pursuit of scientific truths, which, in

Descartes's own words, are "clear and distinct and verifiable at every step" and can hardly be distorted by ideology.

In the 1980s, while enrolled in college in Bucharest (Romania) and pursuing a major in economics that I did not really care about, I had the privilege of meeting and being mentored privately by a true philosopher, Mihai Șora (1916–2023). He guided me through the labyrinth of culture and gave me the best liberal education a young mind can dream of. A former student of Mircea Eliade[42] at the University of Bucharest in the mid-1930s, Șora spent ten years in France where he published his first book, *Du dialogue intérieur: Fragments d'une anthropologie métaphysique*. Written in French during the summer of 1944, it appeared at the prestigious Gallimard Publishing House in early 1947 in the collection "Jeune philosophie." The book offered an original synthesis of neo-Thomism, phenomenology, Christian existentialism, personalism, and Marxism and elicited the admiration and enthusiasm of prominent philosophers and theologians such as Étienne Gilson and Jacques Maritain.

A year later, Șora returned to Romania to visit his family and was not allowed to go back to France. In Bucharest he became a highly respected editor but was never part of the official educational system. Șora directed a popular collection, "Biblioteca pentru toți" (Everyman's Library), which published the most representative works from Romanian and world literature and culture. Its breadth was truly extraordinary. It included classical works such as the speeches of Greek orators and Persian stories, historical gems like Jacob Burckhardt's *The Culture of the Renaissance in Italy*, and literary works such as Rousseau's *The Reveries of a Solitary Walker* (translated by Șora himself) and Proust's monumental *In Search of Lost Time*.

Șora's second book, *The Salt of the Earth* (*Sarea pământului*) was published three decades later in 1978 in Romanian and was followed by "*To Be, to Do, and to Have*" (*A fi, a face, a avea* [1985]). After the fall of communism in 1989, he served for six months as the country's first postcommunist minister of education and became one of the country's most respected civic leaders. As minister of education, Șora campaigned for increasing the autonomy of the existing universities and reforming the legislation to allow for the creation of private colleges and universities in Romania. He promoted social dialogue and tolerance and gave ethnic minorities more opportunities for pursuing education in their mother tongue.

Starting in the mid-1980s, I visited Șora weekly for several years, usually on Tuesday mornings, for several years. He discreetly took over my general education and encouraged me to read widely, not only philosophy, but also literature, history, theology, and economics. His fabulous private library in several languages (Greek, Latin, French, German, Italian, Spanish, and English) was a lifeline in a country with poor public libraries and proved to be an inexhaustible source of discoveries for the young student that I was then in search of an indispensable compass. I remember that one of the first books he encouraged me to read was Ernst von Aster's *Geschichte der Philosophie*, a classic and solid introduction to philosophy in the best German academic tradition (the copy he lent me used the old Gothic script, which I came to like a lot!). Under Șora's gentle guidance, I learned to argue with Socrates, struggled with Aristotle's *Metaphysics*, delved into Plotinus's mystical philosophy (without ever finishing his *Enneads*), and "relaxed" with Saint Augustine's *Confessions*, Pascal's *Pensées* (one of Șora's favorite authors!), and Kierkegaard's journals. It was Mihai Șora who introduced me to Martin Buber's dialogical and Hassidic writings, Meister Eckhart's sermons, and Simone Weil's reflections on gravity and grace. He also encouraged me to read history (including history of economic thought) and literature (Goethe, Hölderlin, Novalis, Paul Claudel, and Charles Péguy, among others), and improve my knowledge of foreign languages, especially French and German. Under his supervision, I was able to closely study dense philosophical texts in the original, from Descartes to Husserl, whose *Cartesianische Meditationen* Șora encouraged me to translate and publish in Romanian. We also descended into the agora and took long walks in the city, often commenting on the sad condition of our country. In 1987 and 1988, we spent two memorable sojourns at a famous sixteenth-century monastery, Sucevița, in northern Romania. We took long walks and talked philosophy and politics. Above all, we admired the divine beauty of the old church's frescoes, with the glorious Ladder of Virtues of Saint John Climacus, painted on the northern wall.

With the benefit of hindsight, I realize today that my conversations with Mihai Șora over all those years were also spiritual exercises, even if that might not have been our original intention. What I initially thought of as pure theory turned out to have important practical implications that taught me where to look for treasures and how to unlock them. The books that Mihai Șora encouraged me to read trained me to see the world with new eyes, to be attentive to the universe around us. He used to remind me that ideas emerge not only from books, but also from chance conversations and events as well as from casual strolls in the city or the countryside. If we are attentive to the spectacle of the world—a point also made by Father Sertillanges in his splendid book on the life of the mind—we will see that "everything holds treasures, because everything is in everything . . . and every light striking on an object may lead up to the sun; every open road is a corridor to God."[43] Everything can be an oracle. Thus, the dialogue with Șora allowed the novice in me to recognize a superior norm and set of values to which I felt compelled to elevate myself in order to be able to enter the conversation with the great minds of mankind. I was a neophyte, but I was also a *dilettante* in the best sense of the term:[44] I was privileged to experience the pure delights of the life of the mind.

My unconventional liberal education and the reading of philosophical texts, including Șora's own books, brought about a profound transformation of my self. Trying to understand difficult or obscure philosophical texts disciplined my attention and diverted my focus from lower to higher goals. It filled major gaps in my education and helped free myself from banality and vulgarity. Above all, I learned how to avoid wasting time and was taught how to manage it properly. I may not have achieved the tranquillity of the soul that the ancient philosophers preached, but I gained something equally important. The life of the mind allowed us to maintain our dignity and reminded us of our common heritage. Thus, I learned how to face with stoicism the daunting specter of scarcity, failure, and oppression around us. The books I read from Șora's library gave me access to a sanctuary in time, through which I could roam freely, undisturbed by the constraints of daily life under communism.

Hence, the benefits of philosophy were real even—or perhaps especially—under a totalitarian regime that exercised a tight control over the life of the mind. Who would have thought that liberal education could provide such a precious shelter in dark times? Nobody described these benefits better than Seneca. He remarked that "by the toil of others we are led into the presence of things which have been brought from darkness into light. We are excluded from no age, but we have access to them all. . . . Since nature allow us to enter into a partnership with every age, why not turn from this brief and transient spell of time and give ourselves wholeheartedly to the past, which is limitless and eternal and can be shared with better men than we?" While it is not in our power to choose our parents, Seneca went on, "we can choose whose children we would like to be. There are households of the noblest intellects: choose the one into which you wish to be adopted, and you will inherit not only their name, but their property too." And here lies the great paradox of liberal education: the more this common heritage is shared, the greater it will become. And time will not reduce its significance. On the contrary! "Honours, monuments, whatever the ambitious have ordered by decrees or raised in public buildings are soon destroyed: there is nothing that the passage of time does not demolish and remove. But it cannot damage the works which philosophy has consecrated: no age will wipe them out, no age diminish them."[45]

It would be difficult to overestimate the significance of Seneca's memorable words. What he describes as the benefits of philosophy applies perfectly to liberal education as well. Its treasures allow us to resist all forms of vulgarity and barbarism around us. Our world may become a better place if we learn a little German, Greek, Latin, French, Italian, or Spanish, and if we are able to read forgotten or obscure authors and texts in their original languages. That is exactly what we tried to do behind the Iron Curtain. Were we wrong to think that by reading books we could make the world around us a little more bearable? I don't think so. Today, looking back at our experience, our lofty retreat into culture may seem quixotic to some. Yet we were happy speaking our *lingua sacra* and cultivating our little garden, reminiscent of Castalia, that imaginary realm devoted to the life of the mind described by Hermann Hesse in *The Glass Bead Game*. We, too, looked at the life of the world as one of disorder and coarseness. And we, too, sought to escape from it through the life of the mind, like Joseph Knecht, the *Magister ludi*, and his spiritual brothers, in Hesse's novel.

Younger readers today may find it difficult to comprehend how for all its obvious limitations, our "Castalian order" could have been an island of freedom in a closed and oppressive world. Nonetheless, those who received the gifts of liberal education will easily understand why we felt lovingly received in the courts of the great minds whose books we read and commented upon. Like Machiavelli, we forgot our worries for a while and tasted the ambrosia reserved only for gods. Although we could not select the society or age in which we wanted to live, we were able to choose whose disciples we wanted to be. *That* freedom we never lost. The "view from above" we acquired by reading books was, in many ways, the beginning of our "salvation." It gave us the necessary detachment and distance that allowed us to survive in a hostile universe.

Our students today live in a much better world, but they, too, need to discover on their own the real "Good" and acquire the salutary distance from society's conventions and judgments. If the cures for the spirit have already been discovered by the ancients and our predecessors "have worked much improvement," they have not worked out all the problems. Our task, as Seneca reminds us, is to find the appropriate method and apply the correct treatment at the right time.[46] With our students, we can try to do precisely that. By sharing with them the jewels of liberal education, we give them a precious "ticket to another world"[47] and help them choose wisely whose "children" they want to be.

NOTES

I would like to thank Constantine Vassiliou, Kirsten Ehlers, Binyan Li, Costica Bradatan, and Zach Goldsmith for their useful comments on previous drafts of this chapter. This chapter develops some arguments originally presented in Aurelian Craiutu, "The Beginning of Our Salvation."

1. Niccolò Machiavelli, *The Prince*, 93.

2. For more information, see the recent student loan debt statistics here: https://studentloanhero.com/student-loan-debt-statistics/. According to this source, "Among the Class of 2019, 69% of college students took out student loans, and they graduated with an average debt of $29,900, including both private (https://studentloanhero.com/featured/best-private-student-loans/) and federal (https://studentloanhero.com/featured/federal-student-loans-guide/) debt. Meanwhile, 14% of their parents took out an average of $37,200 in federal parent PLUS loans."

3. See, *inter alia*, Derek Bok, *Our Underachieving Colleges: A Candid Look at How Much Students Learn and Why They Should Be Learning More*.

4. David Graeber, "On the Phenomenon of Bullshit Jobs."

5. Blake Smith, "The Woke Meritocracy," *Tablet Magazine*, April 5, 2021, https://www.tabletmag.com/sections/arts-letters/articles/merit-blake-smith?fbclid=IwAR05U-sYyfTEvW0s-d6F9ebjF8RoAFfxwfhGkafdb2-89jd-WqKg-UQZD6Q.

6. Douglas Belkin, "Liberal Arts Lose Luster," *Wall Street Journal*, April 25, 2017.

7. As quoted in Belkin, "Liberal Arts Lose Luster." See also Michael T. Nietzel, "Whither the Humanities: The Ten-Year Trend in College Majors."

8. Benjamin L. Fu and Dohyun Kim, "Harvard College Admits 4.92 Percent of Applicants to Class of 2024," *Harvard Crimson*, March 27, 2020, https://www.thecrimson.com/article/2020/3/27/harvard-admissions-2024/.

9. *The American Freshman: National Norms, Fall 1985*, https://www.heri.ucla.edu/PDFs/pubs/TFS/Norms/Monographs/TheAmericanFreshman1985.pdf; *The American Freshman: National Norms, Fall 2019*, https://www.heri.ucla.edu/monographs/TheAmericanFreshman2019-Expanded.pdf.

10. See Josef Pieper, *Leisure: The Basis of Culture*, 31.

11. For more on the lives of students today and extracurricular activities, see George Thomas's chapter in this volume.

12. José Ortega y Gasset, *What Is Philosophy?*, 36.

13. José Ortega y Gasset, "The Idea of the Generation," 47.

14. On this issue, see Pierre Hadot, *Philosophy as a Way of Life*, esp. pt. 2 (79–144).

15. See Pierre Hadot, *The Present Alone Is Our Happiness: Conversations with Jeannie Carlier and Arnold I. Davidson*, 63.

16. See Ortega y Gasset, *What Is Philosophy?*, 94.

17. For a classical statement on this issue, see John Henry Cardinal Newman, *The Idea of the University*.

18. See Newman, *The Idea of the University*, 133.

19. See A.-D. Sertillanges, *La vie intellectuelle: Son esprit, ses conditions, ses méthodes*, 22–23. For an English translation, see *The Intellectual Life: Its Spirit, Conditions, Methods*. All quotations in this chapter are from the 1965 French edition of Sertillanges's book.

20. See Sertillanges, *La vie intellectuelle*, 29–32.

21. See Eva T. H. Brann, *Paradoxes of Education in a Republic*, 14–20.

22. As quoted by Michael Oakeshott in "The Voice of Poetry in the Conversation of Mankind," 491–92.

23. Seneca, "On the Shortness of Life," in *Dialogues and Letters*, 62.

24. I borrow here the title of one of Nicolas of Cusa's most famous books, *De docta ignorantia*.

25. Seneca, "On the Shortness of Life," in *Dialogues and Letters*, 76–77.

26. For more discussion on this issue, see Lorraine Smith Pangle's chapter in this volume; see also Sertillanges, *La vie intellectuelle*, 78–81. I am reminded of the following inscription on one of the historic buildings located on the beautiful campus of Indiana University, Bloomington: "A good book is the lifeblood of a sensitive soul."

27. On philosophy as "spiritual exercise," see Hadot, *Philosophy as a Way of Life*, 79–144, and Pierre Hadot, *What Is Ancient Philosophy?* For more discussion on how the traditional liberal arts experience can mitigate the hazards of spiritual indigestion, see William DeMars's chapter in the present volume.

28. Cicero's phrase appears in his book *On the Nature of Gods* and is quoted in Hadot, *What Is Ancient Philosophy?*, 203.

29. *Talmud*, Pirkei Avot 2:10, https://www.sefaria.org/Pirkei_Avot.2.10?lang=bi&with=all&lang2=en.

30. Sertillanges, *La vie intellectuelle*, 23.

31. Sertillanges, *La vie intellectuelle*, 26–29.

32. This is exactly the position advocated by Michael Oakeshott in *Notebooks, 1922–1986*, 147. Also: "The intellectual life of the majority of men & women is cankered by a passion for indiscriminate knowledge. . . . And the result has been the vast body of disconnected nonsense which is poured like an avalanche from our printing presses on every conceivable subject" (147).

33. Here is Montaigne's warning: "Like the rest of men's goods, knowledge is one which . . . has much inherent vanity and natural feebleness. And it costs us dear. To acquire such pabulum [nourishment] is more hazardous than the acquiring of other food or drink; for in other cases whatever food we have bought we can carry home in containers, which gives us time to decide on its worth, and on how much of it we shall take and when. But from the outset all kinds of learning can be put into no container but our soul: as we buy them, we ingest them, leaving the market-place either already contaminated or else improved. Some of them, instead of nourishing us, burden us and hamper us; others still, under pretense of curing us, poison us." Montaigne, *The Complete Essays*, 1175.

34. This view is defended by Zena Hitz in *Lost in Thought: The Hidden Pleasures of an Intellectual Life*. I have reviewed the book in "The Beginning of Our Salvation."

35. For more discussion on the issue of how some professional institutions are becoming more congenial to classics rather than social science or humanities departments, see Drakeman and Hack as well as Steven Frankel's chapters in this volume.

36. Oakeshott, *Notebooks, 1922–1986*, 315.

37. On this issue, see Clifford Orwin's chapter in this volume.

38. For a response to this problem, see Lee Ward's and Steven Frankel's chapters in this volume.

39. See Abraham Flexner, *The Usefulness of Useless Knowledge*, 52.

40. Ralph Waldo Emerson, "Self-Reliance," 265.

41. Also see Aurelian Craiutu, "Mihai Șora: A Philosopher of Dialogue and Hope." For another fascinating intellectual experience under a different mentor (and friend of Șora), Constantin Noica (1909–87), see Gabriel Liiceanu, *The Păltiniș Diary*, xxxi. See also Sorin Antohi, "Commuting to Castalia: Noica's 'School,' Culture, and Power in Communist Romania," published as a foreword to the English translation of *The Păltiniș Diary*, vii–xxiv.

42. In his *Autobiography*, Mircea Eliade (1907–86), who taught in the Divinity School at the University of Chicago, fondly remembered Mihai Șora and his wife, Mariana Șora (1917–2011), whom he met again in Paris soon after the war. It was Șora who partly translated from Romanian into French Eliade's *Le mythe de l'éternel retour* (*The Myth of Eternal Return*) in 1946. See Mircea Eliade, *Autobiography*, 1:292–93, 2:4, 113, 121.

43. Sertillanges, *La vie intellectuelle*, 72–73.

44. *Diletto* means "pleasure" in Italian.

45. Seneca, "On the Shortness of Life," in *Dialogues and Letters*, 76, 77.

46. Seneca, *Epistles 1–65*, 443.

47. See Sertillanges, *La vie intellectuelle*, 96.

BIBLIOGRAPHY

Antohi, Sorin. "Commuting to Castalia: Noica's 'School,' Culture, and Power in Communist Romania." In *The Păltiniș Diary*, translated by James Christian Brown. Budapest and New York: Central European University Press, 2000.

Astin, Alexander W., Kenneth C. Green, William S. Korn, and Marilynn Schalit. *The American Freshman: National Norms for Fall 1985*. Los Angeles: Higher Education Research Institute Graduate School of Education, University of California. https://www.heri.ucla.edu/PDFs/pubs/TFS/Norms/Monographs/TheAmericanFreshman1985.pdf.

Bok, Derek. *Our Underachieving Colleges: A Candid Look at How Much Students Learn and Why They Should Be Learning More*. Princeton, NJ: Princeton University Press, 2006.

Brann, Eva T. H. *Paradoxes of Education in a Republic*. Chicago: University of Chicago Press, 1979.

Craiutu, Aurelian. "The Beginning of Our Salvation." *Los Angeles Review of Books*, December 20, 2020. https://lareviewofbooks.org/article/the-beginning-of-our-salvation/?fbclid=IwAR1WWKBCqBu1kFAfESsgyV4huP0GF7-asFFIzqo2n2bZG_XKQF0fGJ1Jy58.

———. "Mihai Șora: A Philosopher of Dialogue and Hope." In *In Marx's Shadow: Knowledge, Power, and Intellectuals in Eastern Europe and Russia*, edited by Costica Bradatan and Serguei Oushakine, 261–85. Lanham, MD: Lexington Books, Rowman & Littlefield, 2010.

Eliade, Mircea. *Autobiography*. Vol. 1, *1907–1937: Journey East, Journey West*. Translated by Mac Linscott Ricketts. San Francisco: Harper & Row, 1981.

———. *Autobiography*. Vol. 2, *1937–1960: Exile's Odyssey*. Translated by Mac Linscott Ricketts. Chicago: University of Chicago Press, 1988.

Emerson, Ralph Waldo. "Self-Reliance." In *Essays and Lectures*, edited by Joel Porte, 257–82. New York: Literary Classics of the US, 1983.

Flexner, Abraham. *The Usefulness of Useless Knowledge*. Princeton, NJ: Princeton University Press, 2017.

Graeber, David. "On the Phenomenon of Bullshit Jobs." *Strike! Magazine*, August 2013. https://www.strike.coop/bullshit-jobs/.

Hadot, Pierre. *Philosophy as a Way of Life*. Edited by Arnold I. Davidson. Translated by Michael Chase. Oxford: Blackwell, 1995.

———. *The Present Alone Is Our Happiness: Conversations with Jeannie Carlier and Arnold I. Davidson*. Translated by Marc Djaballah. Stanford, CA: Stanford University Press, 2009.

———. *What Is Ancient Philosophy?* Translated by Michael Chase. Cambridge: Belknap Press of Harvard University Press, 2002.

Hesse, Hermann. *The Glass Bead Game*. Translated by Richard and Clara Winston. Harmondsworth: Penguin, 1972.

Hitz, Zena. *Lost in Thought: The Hidden Pleasures of an Intellectual Life*. Princeton, NJ: Princeton University Press, 2020.

Liiceanu, Gabriel. *The Păltiniş Diary*. Translated by James Christian Brown. Budapest and New York: Central European University Press, 2000.

Machiavelli, Niccolò. *The Prince*. Edited by Quentin Skinner and Russell Price. Cambridge: Cambridge University Press, 1988.

Montaigne. *The Complete Essays*. Translated by M. A. Screech. London: Penguin, 1991.

Newman, Cardinal John Henry. *The Idea of the University*. New York: Doubleday, Image Books, 1959.

Nietzel, Michael T. "Whither the Humanities: The Ten-Year Trend in College Majors." *Forbes*, January 7, 2019. https://www.forbes.com/sites/michaeltnietzel/2019/01/07/whither-the-humanities-the-ten-year-trend-in-college-majors/?sh=791ecbbd64ad.

Oakeshott, Michael. *Notebooks, 1922–1986*. Edited by Luke O'Sullivan. Exeter: Imprint Academic, 2014.

———. "The Voice of Poetry in the Conversation of Mankind." In *Rationalism in Politics, and Other Essays*, edited by Timothy Fuller, 488–542. Indianapolis: Liberty Fund, 1991.

Ortega y Gasset, José. "The Idea of the Generation." In *Man and Crisis*, translated by Mildred Adams. New York: W. W. Norton, 1958.

———. *What Is Philosophy*. Translated by Mildred Adams. New York: W. W. Norton, 1960.

Pieper, Josef. *Leisure: The Basis of Culture*. Translated by Alexander Dru. Indianapolis: Liberty Fund, 2000.

Seneca. *Epistles 1–65*. Translated by Richard M. Gummere. 1917. Reprint, Cambridge, MA: Harvard University Press, 2002.

———. "On the Shortness of Life." In *Dialogues and Letters*, edited and translated by C. D. N. Costa. London: Penguin, 1997.

Sertillanges, A.-D. *The Intellectual Life: Its Spirit, Conditions, Methods*. Translated by Mary Ryan. Westminster, MD: Newman Press, 1960.

———. *La vie intellectuelle: Son esprit, ses conditions, ses méthodes*. Paris: Les Éditions du Cerf, 1965.

Smith, Blake. "The Woke Meritocracy." *Tablet Magazine*, April 5, 2021. https://www.tabletmag.com/sections/arts-letters/articles/merit-blake-smith?fbclid=IwAR05U-sYyfTEvW0s-d6F9ebjF8RoAFfxwfhGkafdb2-89jd-WqKg-UQZD6Q.

9. Liberal Education and the Limits of Science and Technology
Lessons from the COVID-19 Pandemic
Carson Holloway

THE MODERN UNIVERSITY IS PARTICULARLY interested in the promotion of science and technology. This is altogether fitting and proper. Universities are dedicated to the pursuit of knowledge, and science and its technological applications are admittedly a valuable department of human understanding. Moreover, the modern university is supported by modern democracy. Public universities are directly subsidized by the taxpayers, and even private universities receive considerable indirect public support in the form of financial aid to their students. As the beneficiaries of such support, universities owe a debt to the community that sustains them. They pay that debt in part by fostering the scientific knowledge and technological know-how that offer so many benefits to the community.

The university, however, owes the community something more than just the promotion of science and technology. It also, in fact, owes the community instruction in the *limits* of science and technology. Again, the modern university is sustained by modern democracy. Accordingly, it owes to our democracy not just the knowledge and skills that democracy finds materially useful but also the knowledge and skills that are necessary to perpetuating democracy itself. As Aristotle reminds us in the *Politics*, a truly democratic education is not so much an education in the things that democracies "enjoy" as in the things that are necessary "to have a regime that is run democratically."[1] Democracies certainly enjoy the ease and comfort that come from the power over nature that science and technology can provide. Such power and ease, however, will not alone cause a democracy to flourish over time. Accordingly, we would hardly think that the university had done its duty if it only served as the tip of the spear of scientific and technological innovation while neglecting to inculcate the ideas and habits that are necessary for a people to govern themselves thoughtfully, responsibly, and successfully.

Put another way, the success of our democracy requires that our citizens learn to deliberate well about the common good. Intelligent deliberation about the common good in turn requires that we discern the difference between the things that are merely tools and the things that are good in themselves, or that we can distinguish between the ends we ultimately seek and the things that are merely means to those ends. Intelligent deliberation also requires that we see that even the things that are good in themselves are often only partial goods, that there are others that also have claims on our attention and allegiance. In other words, successful democratic deliberation requires us to see that the common good of our society is complex, and that it therefore cannot be achieved by the fanatical pursuit of one good but only by the prudent balancing of various goods. With such considerations in mind, we recall that the university's mission is not only to advance science and technology, but also to offer a traditional liberal education, the education that is necessary to train the minds of free human beings who are capable of governing themselves.

A reconsideration of these fundamental lessons—about both the importance and limits of science and technology—has been forced upon us by the COVID-19 pandemic of 2020–21. The usefulness of science and technology in addressing the pandemic has been rather evident, as it has been trumpeted by governments and the mass media. The limits of science and technology, on the other hand, have been somewhat overlooked. This chapter seeks to advance the aims of liberal education by meditating on what the response to the pandemic teaches us about the limits of science and technology. Reflecting critically on the scientific and technological responses to the pandemic sharpens our capacity for intelligent deliberation about the common good by bringing to light the kinds of goods that science and technology can and cannot supply.

THE LIMITS OF SCIENCE

We need not dwell at length on the importance of science in addressing the pandemic. Science identified the new virus and the novel public health threat that it posed. Science identified ways to mitigate the spread of the virus. Science discovered ways to treat the virus, or at least to control its symptoms, and science has most recently devised a vaccine that can help promote immunity to the virus.

In the face of all these benefits, science has paradoxically become a matter of controversy in the context of the COVID-19 pandemic. The controversy, though paradoxical, is also understandable. Some of the safety measures promoted by the scientists are costly—costly to society in general and painfully costly to some members of society in particular. To take an obvious example, efforts to ensure "social distancing" have cost society at large the pleasure and convenience of public entertainment and restaurant dining, and have cost those who work in those industries a great deal more, in some cases depriving them of the ability to make a living. Unsurprisingly, such measures have been met with a good deal of criticism. The critics have questioned the efficacy of some of the steps that have been taken to slow the spread of the virus. This has in turn led others to condemn the critics as being opposed to science or rejecting the findings of science. Thus, we have been admonished to "trust science" or to "believe in science."

Trust or belief in science has thus become a national catchphrase. It can be found on bumper stickers and yard signs. It has become a refrain of elected officials, who assure voters that they will be guided by science in addressing the pandemic.

What are we to make of such claims? Should liberally educated people trust science? On the one hand, there is an obvious sense in which the liberally educated will do so. It is certainly not the part of the liberally educated to reject science or to promote superstition or irrationalism. On the other hand, as I have already suggested, this is not the whole story. Liberal education will teach us to respect science while also respecting its limits.

In the first place, the liberally educated person will recall that *science* is not exactly the same thing as *scientists*. Science is a body of knowledge built up on the basis of observation and experiment. To the extent that it has been rationally verified, it commands our assent. Scientists, however, are the people who practice science. And, like all other human beings, they are fallible. The liberally educated person will know something of the history of science, and will therefore know that the scientific consensus on various issues has changed over time—which is another way of saying that later scientists came to the conclusion that earlier scientists had been mistaken. Indeed, scientists have been known to disagree not only over time but also at the same time, when a question has not yet been definitively settled.[2]

Such disagreements among scientists have been evident during the course of the pandemic. Over a period of months, mainstream scientific opinion changed on how best to approach the problem. Perhaps most famously, some authorities held early on that widespread wearing of masks by ordinary citizens would be of little help in mitigating the spread of the virus, but later came to the conclusion that such a measure would in fact be helpful and even necessary to public health.[3] In addition, there have been scientific differences not only across time but also across space. Different jurisdictions—various nations around the world, various states and municipalities within the United States—have pursued somewhat different policies precisely because the local scientists advising them have offered somewhat different recommendations.

None of these observations should be used to take cheap shots at science, holding that scientists are inconsistent or confused. It is entirely proper, for example, for scientists to change their minds as *new* evidence comes to light about how best to control the spread of a disease. And local conditions may actually influence how communicable a disease is, so local scientists can be right to tailor their recommendations accordingly. These facts about the variability of scientific opinion, however, do justify us in concluding that there is no absolute, unqualified sense in which properly educated citizens can be commanded to simply "trust" or "believe" science.

There is another point relevant to the distinction between science and scientists. Many of the scientists that we have been told to trust during the pandemic are in fact not just theoretical scientists but public health authorities. Their job is not merely to study things and report what they have learned but to make rules about how we must act, or to advise those who are to make such rules. Bearing this in mind, simply saying that we must "trust science" is like saying that we must trust credentialed people who hold public authority. This, however, is hardly advice that can be given without qualification to a free people, the citizens of a democracy. Democracy means self-government, which in turn means that citizens will not simply be ruled by scientists. Here the liberally educated person might recall with profit Thomas Jefferson's observation that the "degree of talent" of human beings "is no measure of their rights," and that just "because Sir Isaac Newton was superior to others in understanding he was not therefore Lord of the person or property of others."[4] Free citizens, then, are under no obligation to "trust science" in the sense of simply submitting to the opinions of scientists, although prudence will certainly demand that citizens listen respectfully to what the scientists have to say.

This mention of prudence brings us, in the second place, to another limitation of science brought to light by the COVID-19 pandemic. As has already been admitted, modern science is a legitimate form of knowledge without which we could not hope to navigate the pandemic successfully. Nevertheless, science is not the only kind of knowledge required for such navigation. We also need prudence. Prudence, we learn from Aristotle, is the intellectual virtue—that is, the kind of knowledge or wisdom—by which we act rightly not only in light of permanent principles, but also in light of particular facts, which are variable.[5] By prudence we make the most of a given set of circumstances, or achieve as much of the good as we can despite the limitations that continually press upon us. Prudence, thus understood, implies a gap between what is absolutely best, or what is perfect in principle, and what is actually possible given the imperfect or bad necessities that we always face. Put another way, prudence implies that there are various goods that human beings seek and that they are sometimes in competition with each other. In the face of this situation, we need some knowledge that can balance the various goods that we seek, so that some are not completely sacrificed to others.

These imperfections, limitations, and necessities, these conflicts among competing goods, have been evident in the pandemic. As noted earlier, the public health measures recommended by scientists carry certain costs—which is another way of saying that the results of those measures are not purely good. Whether and to what extent to pursue them depends on some weighing of the various goods at stake. Science, however, is utterly incompetent when it comes to this unavoidable weighing of competing goods. Science can *inform* the decision, but it cannot *make* it. Health science may tell us that a given mitigation regimen—say, the closure of all restaurants—will likely save a certain number of lives. The social science known as economics may tell us how much such a regimen will damage the economy. There is no science, however, that can tell us how many lives must be saved to justify shuttering a certain number of businesses and thus hampering or destroying a certain number of livelihoods.

This problem exists even when, as in the example above, both of the competing goods are quantifiable by some kind of scientific measurement. More difficult problems arise, however, when nonquantifiable goods come into play. Besides the economic costs of mitigation, there are what we might call moral, cultural, or political costs. Some have complained that efforts to slow the spread of the virus impinge on civil liberties: in order to protect public health, for instance, the right to travel, or even to leave one's home, has been curtailed. There is a real cost encountered here. Presumably, we wish to maintain, for the long run, a society that is democratic and safe and that also allows ample room for individual freedom. Our efforts to protect human life from communicable disease, however, carry the unavoidable consequence of habituating our citizens to ongoing restrictions on their traditional rights and liberties. This will be worrisome to any citizen who cherishes freedom as well as life. Prudence will seek a path that involves not a complete suffice of one good to the other, but some kind of balance appropriate to the circumstances. That balance, again, cannot be provided by science—although it certainly requires listening to scientists about the consequences of such balancing for the goods that science can in fact measure.

This brings us, in the third place, to the final and most fundamental limitation of modern science: it is empirical and not normative. It is concerned with what tends to happen and not what ought to happen. The scientists themselves admit that this is the proper scope of their inquiry. Accordingly, while science can tell us the consequences of various courses of action for the things we hold to be good, it cannot tell us what is good.

Consider the good with which we have been most concerned during the pandemic: human life. Science can tell us much about *how* human life may be preserved, but it cannot tell us that human life is good and *ought* to be preserved. As far as science qua science is concerned, it is just part of the ordinary course of nature that disease will strike some human beings and that some of those who are thus struck will succumb to it and die. That human life is to be protected is not a scientific conclusion but a moral principle. Without that principle, all of science's wisdom will be irrelevant to us, because we will not even know whether we should *want* to protect vulnerable human lives.

The successful navigation of the pandemic, then, requires a kind of knowledge—knowledge of fundamental moral principles—that science cannot provide. Where, then, do we get such knowledge? It is available to us in the content of a traditional liberal education. We might turn to philosophic elaborations of the natural law. We might look, for example, to John Locke, who instructs us that moral reason can perceive a "law of nature" that commands that each man "ought," to the extent that he is able, "preserve the rest of mankind."[6] Or we might seek guidance from the great religious traditions that have shaped our civilization, such as the biblical understanding of human beings as created in the image and likeness of God, which supports a duty to love one's neighbor as oneself (Gen. 1:26; Lev. 18:19). This is not to say that these particular claims—derived from natural law, or divine revelation—will necessarily be convincing to every liberally educated person. It is to say, however, that a liberally educated person will see that some principle of moral knowledge, which modern science cannot provide, is necessary, and that therefore neither the COVID-19 pandemic nor any other public emergency can be successfully addressed merely by "trusting science."

LIBERAL LEARNING AND THE LIMITS OF TECHNOLOGY

Liberal education instructs us not only in the uses and limits of science, but also in the uses and limits of modern science's practical offspring, technology.[7] Here again the COVID-19 pandemic offers a helpful case study. Technology has been used to continue university instruction under pandemic conditions: we can easily achieve social distancing, and thereby protect public health, when students and teachers are "meeting" only virtually, in online classes. Thus can modern technology advance the cause of liberal education. Liberal education also, however, provides us the intellectual tools to question whether online instruction can wholly succeed, whether technology can entirely supplant more natural or traditional approaches to education.

In the spring of 2020, as it became clear that the coronavirus called for nationwide efforts at mitigation, most American universities and colleges shifted entirely to online instruction for the remainder of the spring semester. As the pandemic persisted, so too did this new approach to higher education. Most institutions remained primarily online in the summer and fall terms of 2020, and also continued the practice into the spring semester of 2021.

Although American higher education already had considerable experience with online instruction, the change was still wrenching for many, both among faculty and students. Many of our colleges and universities have been offering more and more online classes over the past decade. Nevertheless, online classes were not the predominant method of instruction. A sizable number of teachers[8] and students[9] were thrown into an environment to which they were not accustomed and with which they struggled. As with other steps taken to slow the spread of the virus, online instruction turned out to be less than an unmitigated good. It, too, carried costs that were felt with particular force by some members of our society.

The experience of these costs raises the following question: For the purposes of higher education, which is *generally* better, online or in-person teaching? This question is made more pressing by the fact that some will use the present crisis as an occasion to urge the nation to move more decisively and permanently in the direction of online higher education—not because the virus will never go away, but because online instruction is somehow more efficient, more modern, or more innovative.

There are admittedly certain advantages to online instruction. It eliminates the need for classrooms in buildings that are expensive to maintain. It saves time for teachers and students who no longer have to travel to the place where the class meets. You can't transmit a virus through online instruction (at least not the kind that infects humans instead of computers), and so online instruction cannot pose a risk to anybody's health (unless you count the metaphorical possibility of boring someone to death).

These advantages, however, are obviously extrinsic rather than intrinsic. They do not relate to the quality of the educational experience itself. We are forced to ask, then, whether higher education would be better *as education*, and not just whether it would be more convenient or safer, if it were conducted exclusively online.

Here it is especially important not to be deceived by the terminology that tends to develop around technological innovations. Universities often speak of "internet-mediated" instruction. Similarly, it is common to refer to a distinction between the classroom and the internet as the "mode of delivery" of a course. Such language obscures what is at stake by implying that the fundamental good at issue is unaffected by the tools adopted to supply it. "Education," it seems, is the good to be achieved, and the means by which it is "mediated" or "delivered" is a secondary consideration, and indeed a neutral factor having no bearing on the good itself.

What is implied by such language is obviously sometimes true. If I want to eat a pizza or read a book at home, I can go to the store and buy the item or have it delivered to me. Here the way in which the good is delivered has no direct bearing on my experience of it.

A moment's reflection, however, reveals that the "mode of delivery" is not always a neutral consideration. I might wish hear a performance of Beethoven's *Ninth Symphony*. I may have a choice of "modes of delivery," or of "mediation" between the performers and me. I can buy a CD and listen to it, or I can attend a public performance by a live symphony orchestra. Any lover of music will inform us, however, that these are not at all the same thing. When the good to be enjoyed is an experience and not a physical artifact, the mode of delivery may not be just a neutral consideration. Indeed, the difference in the mode of delivery may make the experience itself qualitatively different. Listening to music is both an intellectual and a physical experience. If you listen to a CD, your mind is in some sense receiving the same "information" as if you were in the symphony hall. But the physical sensations, and therefore the human experiences, are different and more vivid if you are actually in the presence of the performing orchestra.

Liberal education is obviously not just a physical artifact. It is much more like an experience, or a set of experiences, that are changed depending on the way in which it is "delivered"—in the classroom or through the internet. These considerations caution against a wholesale replacement of in-person instruction with online instruction.

I hasten to add that I do not intend a blanket criticism of online college classes. They have a place and often serve a real need. Some students have family or work obligations that prevent them from attending classes on campus. For them, online courses are justified by necessity, by being the only practical way they can learn the subject matter they want to study. And, as we have learned during the pandemic, online teaching is better than wholesale cancellation of classes when a widespread illness makes it unsafe for teachers and students to assemble in the traditional classroom. But using online instruction where necessity requires it does not justify us in replacing in-person teaching with online teaching where no necessity compels such a move.

Why should we think that the experience of in-person instruction is necessary to the aims of liberal education? We might begin with the following preliminary consideration. In-person education is the traditional method that has proved its efficacy for a long period of time. Our civilization is the source of many blessings, and it has been developed and transmitted in part through the encounter that happens when teacher and students meet together in person. If some part of our way of life has proven itself presumptively beneficial, why jettison it permanently in response to a temporary crisis?

While this argument has real force, liberal education itself reveals that it is, on its own, insufficient for us. We learn from Alexis de Tocqueville's seminal study, *Democracy in America*, that the denizens of a democracy are usually deaf to appeals to traditional ways of doing things. Because of their experience of and commitment to equality, democratic citizens tend to be individualistic rationalists. Since they take every human mind to be equal, they expect that each individual has equal access to the truth. They judge everything for themselves, and accordingly do not acknowledge the authority of tradition—which is, after all, nothing more than the ways developed by earlier people who were no better than we are. Indeed, Tocqueville observes that democratic peoples tend to be positively attracted to the idea of progress and change. In contrast to the stability of an aristocracy, everything is on the move in a modern democracy, and new ways of doing things are constantly proposed. The nature of a democracy, Tocqueville teaches us, is to want to embrace innovation rather than to defer to tradition.[10]

And, in any case, the nature of higher education itself is to be oriented not so much toward tradition as to truth. As Aristotle observes in the opening sentence of his *Metaphysics*, "All men naturally desire knowledge."[11] For all of its increasing sophistication and complexity, the university seems addressed above all to this elementary human desire. And, as Aristotle observes in the *Politics*, we generally seek what is good and not merely what is customary.[12] We must ask, then, whether the traditional approach to higher education—that is, in-person instruction—can be defended on some other, deeper ground than its mere status as tradition.

That deeper ground is indicated by Aristotle's attention to the "nature" of human beings as such. We must seek not the mode of higher education that is most innovative and therefore most flattering to our democratic prejudices, nor the mode that is most traditional and therefore apparently hallowed by time and the approval of our venerated ancestors. We must seek the mode of higher education that is most consistent with human nature.

We learn from Aristotle that man is by nature a sociable and political animal, and indeed the most political of animals. The evidence for this conclusion, he contends, can be found in our natural capacity for speech, as opposed to mere voice. By means of voice nonhuman animals can communicate the painful and the pleasant. But human beings alone, by means of speech, can deliberate together about the advantageous and disadvantageous, the just and the unjust, the good and the bad. In addition, Aristotle contends, human being have an impulse toward the political association in which they can exercise their capacity for speech.[13] That is, human beings just *want* to associate and speak with people beyond their family and tribe.

Armed with this permanent insight into human nature, we see that there is something bad about forcibly isolating members of the same political community from each other, even if an emergency makes such isolation necessary to protect human life. Human beings are made to interact with each other—to debate, think, and inquire together—outside their immediate families. Without such activities, their natures are stunted, their flourishing impaired, their happiness marred. There is something questionable about online education's isolation of teachers from students, students from teachers, and students from each other.

Here one might respond in defense of online education that it is, in fact, compatible with our sociable nature. It is, after all, an exaggeration to say that the participants in online education are simply isolated from each other. Rather, they exercise their natural sociability by interacting through modern technology. That is why we call it internet *mediated* instruction. In an online class the instructor can communicate with students by posting video lectures, for example, and the students can interact with each other, and with the teacher, by writing comments on a discussion board. They may even be able to simulate the experience of being together in real time by participating in a video conference.

There is some truth in these claims, but they do not quite meet the issue. Let us return to Aristotle and pay careful attention to his language. He does not merely say that humans are by nature political beings but says they are by nature political *animals*.[14] As animals we are *embodied* beings. This means that our sociable and political nature is most completely or perfectly in play—this aspect of our nature is most fully realized—when we are in each other's physical presence.

This general argument based on human nature is confirmed by thinking through some of the specific advantages that result when students and teachers are physically present to each other in the traditional classroom. In the first place, we should not overlook the role of perplexity in education. Perplexity is the feeling we get when we sense that something is intelligible but we have not yet been able to understand it. Obviously, higher education tends to provoke considerable perplexity in students, who are mostly young and have just begun to inquire into complex intellectual problems. The point at which they experience perplexity is a crucial one; it is the point at which the teacher needs to try to explain again, but perhaps somewhat differently, using different examples or analogies.

It is, however, far easier to detect and respond to another's perplexity in person. Often a teacher can tell by the students' facial expressions that they are confused, and that moment of confusion may be the critical point at which clarity can be achieved and education advanced. The necessary awareness of the inner life of another person, as reflected in the face, is impossible in an asynchronous online class in which the teacher is posting videos and reading comments submitted later. Of course, some students might admit openly in an online discussion forum that they are puzzled by the material. Then again, they might instead choose to conceal their confusion. For the teacher, and for the educational mission, the advantage of being together in person is that the students' perplexity may manifest itself involuntarily on their faces, so that the teacher knows it is necessary to help them understand, without them having to face the embarrassment of admitting their lack of understanding. This advantage of in-person teaching, moreover, cannot be replicated in video conferences. It is very difficult to "read" another person in a video conference, much less to "read" a group of people, on a video conference—if for no other reason than that their faces are smaller and much less distinct on a monitor than when seen in person.

In addition, it is valuable for the students to experience the *teacher's* occasional perplexity, as when a question arises that the teacher had not before considered. A wise colleague once advised me not to conceal my perplexity from the students. It shows them that the subject matter is vast and difficult to master completely even after years or decades of study, and therefore demands the students' utmost sustained exertion to try to understand it. This experience is valuable for the teacher, too, who may need to be disabused of pretensions of self-sufficiency, to a complete mastery of the material. Perplexity is an aid to humility, which is the proper disposition toward subject matter that may not be perfectly grasped even in a lifetime of study. But, again, we are much more likely to encounter this humane experience of seeing a teacher temporarily at a loss when we meet together in person to discuss complicated issues.

Perplexity, then, is an essential experience of the student's mind, the teacher's awareness of which is necessarily impeded by online education. Teaching, however, is not just a matter of the mind but also of the heart. It is a sentimental cliché—but none the less true for all that—that good teachers care about their students. Everyone understands, for example, that a good teacher's care will show itself in a sympathetic response to whatever hardships a student may confide that are impeding his or her education. More central to the educational mission, however, is the teacher's caring about the students' actual learning. Teachers have a certain intrinsic superiority over their students; they understand things that the students are struggling to learn. The teacher's job is thus to help people who are in a position of relative weakness, and that undertaking depends to a considerable extent on the teacher's care for the students' learning. This in turn depends on the teacher's sympathy for the students as human beings. Surely this solicitude, so essential to education, is easier to experience for people with whom one meets in person on a regular basis. A conscientious teacher conducting an online class will derive satisfaction from seeing the progress the students are making. But how much more satisfaction is experienced by the teacher who has an opportunity to see the progress and to see, be with, and know the people who are making the progress?

This solicitude that flourishes most fully when we are bodily present to each other is also an important motivation for the students. Students learn more readily when they care about their teacher. The best teachers want students to be animated by a love of learning, which is not a pure, bloodless mental activity. Students are moved to learn to some extent by their sympathetic experience of the teacher's joy in knowledge. Seeing that the teacher loves the subject matter, they are moved to love it, too (although rarely as much as the teacher would wish). Some students may be moved to learn through a sympathetic desire not to disappoint the teacher. And some are energized by an ambitious desire to impress the teacher.

These various forms of care are also an important motivator *among* the students. A successful student may make time to meet with a struggling student to discuss the material outside of class because the former has seen and sympathized with the latter's difficulties. Again, ambitious students may exert themselves to perform well in class in order to impress other students. These are, to be sure, not the highest motives to education, but they are very human motives, and their force is increased when the participants in the educational venture meet together in person.

One might object that these considerations introduce an element of emotion that should rather be excluded from the training of our highest intellectual faculties. But such emotions will inevitably play a part in even the intellectual education of embodied sociable beings such as ourselves. From the beginning, the greatest teachers have understood this. In Plato's *Gorgias*, Socrates claims that the best philosophic interlocutor is someone who possesses not only knowledge and candor but also goodwill—one who cares about those he is seeking to instruct.[15] And Socrates, we recall, conducted *his* education exclusively in-person. Technology may permit us to supplement, but it should not lead us to discard, the personal Socratic education that does full justice to human nature and has contributed so much to the development of our civilization.

CONCLUSION

The modern university tends to understand itself as dedicated to the discovery of *new* insights and the development of *new* powers. This is the scientific and technological impulse. According to an earlier understanding, the university was dedicated to the preservation and transmission of the *old*—ancient and venerable wisdom about the human condition, imparted according to time-honored practices, such as Socratic education. This was the impulse behind liberal education as it was traditionally understood.

Our experience of COVID-19 reminds us that both of these impulses have an important contribution to make to our society. Navigating the dangers of a pandemic requires not only the most up to date scientific knowledge, but also timeless virtues, such as prudence and knowledge of elementary moral principles, that were first grasped and explained ages ago, when human beings first began to reflect on their condition. And while technology can help us to overcome or adapt to new challenges, there are some elementary human experiences that it cannot replace—such as the experience of teachers and students being together and inquiring together, and thus learning both to love the quest for knowledge and to care about each other. To fulfill its mission, the university must embrace and nurture both scientific inquiry and traditional liberal education, because both are essential to the flourishing of our democracy.

NOTES

1. Aristotle, *Politics*, 167.
2. See Thomas Kuhn, *The Structure of Scientific Revolutions*, a classic popular exposition of the disagreements among scientists, and one often used for purposes of liberal education in the university.
3. Ali Swenson, "CDC Now Recommends That Even Healthy People Wear Masks," Associated Press, May 27, 2020, https://apnews.com/article/8937511824.
4. Thomas Jefferson, *Thomas Jefferson: Writings*, 1202.
5. Aristotle, *Nicomachean Ethics*, 345–47, 349–51.
6. John Locke, *Second Treatise of Government*, 9.
7. This section of the chapter is an expanded version of an essay published online. See Carson Holloway, "Social, Political Animals: Embodied Learning and the Limits of Online Education," *Public Discourse*, May 17, 2020, https://www.thepublicdiscourse.com/2020/05/63449/.
8. Zia Sampson, "Professors Struggle through Online Teaching," *Maroon* (Loyola University), September 25, 2020, https://loyolamaroon.com/10029405/news/professors-struggle-through-online-teaching/.
9. Lilah Burke, "Moving into the Long Term."
10. Alexis de Tocqueville, *Democracy in America*, 403–7, 426–28.
11. Aristotle, *Metaphysics*, 3.
12. Aristotle, *Politics*, 73.
13. Aristotle, *Politics*, 37.
14. Aristotle, *Politics*, 37.
15. Plato, *Gorgias*, 395.

BIBLIOGRAPHY

Aristotle. *Metaphysics*. Translated by Hugh Tredennick. Cambridge, MA: Harvard University Press, 1989.

———. *Nicomachean Ethics*. Translated by H. Rackham. Cambridge, MA: Harvard University Press, 1999.

———. *Politics*. Translated by Carnes Lord. Chicago: University of Chicago Press, 1984.

Burke, Lilah. "Moving into the Long Term." *Inside Higher Ed* (October 27, 2020). https://www.insidehighered.com/digital-learning/article/2020/10/27/long-term-online-learning-pandemic-may-impact-students-well.

Holloway, Carson. "Social, Political Animals: Embodied Learning and the Limits of Online Education." *Public Discourse* (May 17, 2020). https://www.thepublicdiscourse.com/2020/05/63449/.

Jefferson, Thomas. *Thomas Jefferson: Writings*. Edited by Merrill D. Peterson. New York: Library of America, 1984.

Kuhn, Thomas. *The Structure of Scientific Revolutions*. Chicago: University of Chicago Press, 2012.

Locke, John. *Second Treatise of Government*. Indianapolis: Hackett, 1980.

Plato. *Gorgias*. Translated by W. R. M. Lamb. Cambridge, MA: Harvard University Press, 1991.

Tocqueville, Alexis de. *Democracy in America*. Edited and translated by Harvey Mansfield and Delba Winthrop. Chicago: University of Chicago Press, 2000.

10. Liberal Education Is Antitechnological

Steven McGuire

THE MASS MIGRATION FROM IN-PERSON to online education during the COVID-19 pandemic highlighted the need for reflection on the relationship between technology and liberal education. As campuses shut down in the spring of 2020, faculty, students, and administrators had to consider as a practical matter how to use digital technology to accomplish their purposes while scrambling to complete the semester online. Those who continued to work and teach online that summer and during the 2020–21 academic year might have found time for more intentional reflection and preparation, but, on the whole, most of us simply adopted Zoom and other digital technologies and did the best we could.

As the need for an immediate response to the crisis fades, we should step back and ask what this experience might mean for the future of liberal education in America. One possibility is that it will advance the growth of online education. Proponents of this course jumped at the opportunity to argue that we should exploit this crisis to do just that. To some extent, they already had inertia on their side, as many institutions have been adding online options for years. The pandemic was an unexpected accelerant. Now more people than ever have had a taste of online education, and, as social-distancing requirements dragged on, more and more of us became better prepared to undertake it; many of us grew accustomed to it, and some of us even learned to like it (although many faculty and students acknowledge that the educational experience was not as good as in-person instruction). As administrators and others continue to push for more online education in response to the dire economic and demographic situations their institutions face, will students and faculty be more willing to participate?

The arguments in favor of online education sound compelling, and to some extent they are. The most important one is that it is cheaper in a time when the cost of higher education is growing beyond reach for many Americans. It is also potentially more convenient: students do not have to move or commute, they can take their classes at times that work for them, and they might even be able to finish their degrees more quickly. Finally, online education might advance democracy and social justice by making education more accessible.

But the counterarguments are also compelling. First, each of these arguments is questionable on its own terms: first-rate online education is expensive to provide, especially up front, and tuition costs are often similar; studying at home, away from a community of learners, is likely to be distracting, less motivating, and therefore inconvenient and ineffective; online education might still be inaccessible to many Americans for a variety of reasons, and the difference between the quality and reputation of online and in-person degrees exacerbates inequality.

Second, even though some students, faculty, and especially administrators have learned to like online education, most seem to find that it is simply not as good as in-person education. Certainly, those who experienced online education for the first time during the pandemic found it to be a mixed bag. But most faculty and students know that even well-designed online education is inferior from an educational perspective. The technology does not always work like it is supposed to, and even when it does cannot facilitate the range or depth of a liberal education grounded in personal relationships and a common life of inquiring together.

The most important objection, however, is not that we lack the requisite technology to pursue liberal education online, which would leave open the possibility that online education could eventually replace or even surpass in-person liberal education. Rather, the third and most fundamental objection is that online education, and the arguments in favor of it, exhibit a technological way of thinking that is directly at odds with the nature and purpose of liberal education.

Modern technology is not just a series of inventions; rather, it is an ideology—a way of thinking about the world and our place within it. As George Grant writes, "Modern technology is not simply an extension of human making through the power of a perfected science, but is a new account of what it is to know and to make in which both activities are changed by their co-penetration."[1] This new account, which forms the horizon of our thinking in modernity, subordinates knowing to making and expansively reconceives what can be accomplished by human making. It is expressed in the idea that our primary goal should be to manipulate and master nature for the sake of material well-being or the "relief of man's estate," as Francis Bacon puts it.[2] Karl Marx encapsulates this view well when he claims that "philosophers have only *interpreted* the world, in various ways; the point, however, is to *change* it."[3]

The spirit of modern technology fundamentally contradicts the traditional understanding and practice of liberal education because it "exalts the possible above what is,"[4] rather than aiming to understand reality as it is. Viewed through its lens, nature is not something beautiful to behold or good in itself, but, rather, as a resource to be used. Scientific knowledge is not pursued above all for the sake of truth, but because it can be applied. In other words, modern technology is anticontemplative. Liberal education as traditionally conceived is, by contrast, inherently contemplative. It involves reflecting on the nature of things, including ourselves, and thinking about how we ought to live our lives. Rather than manipulating or redefining reality, liberal education aims to understand it, recognizing that our ultimate purpose is to know the true, the good, and the beautiful for their own sake. The aim is to allow the truth of reality to present itself to us and to conform our minds to it.

At the same time, liberal education is an inexhaustible human activity because it takes place within a horizon of mystery that cannot be overtaken. The questions of liberal education must be asked anew by every human being because they can never be answered fully and with absolute certainty. Modern technology doesn't look at the world this way. From its perspective, mysteries are just problems that have yet to be solved, and every problem is capable of a solution. For this reason, technology is also inherently progressive; once a problem is solved, we can move on to the next one—which is why teachers of technological subjects tend to use textbooks that summarize the state of their disciplines. Liberal educators and their students, by contrast, dwell in an eternal present, asking the same questions as those who came before them and reading the old masters over and over again. Individuals and communities can deepen their understanding of these questions, but they never solve them and leave them behind.

Furthermore, modern technology, once applied to liberal education, has an almost ineluctable tendency to remake it in its own image. Ostensibly operating solely within the sphere of instrumental reason, technology appears to be concerned only with how we do things. If this were the case, we could happily consider how various technologies might be used to enhance liberal education without concern. However, it actually advances an already determined account of the human good. Modern technology assumes an answer to the question of the purpose of human life—material comfort and security—and then figures out how to achieve it. Thus, it is closed to the liberating practice of asking perennial questions such as what we should do and why we should do it. The technological perspective obscures and suppresses the questions that constitute liberal education because it has already solved them.

In sum, modern technology is antithetical to the spirit and practice of liberal education and seeks to replace it. For a quick demonstration of how successful it has been in this regard, one could simply ask almost any group of American students why they want to go to college. Very few, if any, will mention the idea of knowledge for its own sake. Instead, the most common answers will be to get a better job and make more money, which makes sense, given how much education costs. This is what we've all been taught our entire lives. Even many liberal educators themselves think of what they do as valuable because they are teaching skills or contributing to society (both of which are good but represent an incomplete understanding of liberal education on their own). The technological understanding of education obscures the view of liberal education as an intrinsic end—an activity worth doing for its own sake. Long before the COVID-19 pandemic, we were all taught to think of education solely as a means to an end.

But education is like other things we do for their own sake, such as sport, for example. There are many reasons to play a sport: honor and glory, physical health, camaraderie, remuneration. But, at the end of the day, none of these potential benefits explains the existence of sport, since all of them could be reaped without it. Thus, sport is an irreducible activity: its existence, the fact that we do it, cannot be fully explained in terms of some other cause or purpose. Sometimes we just play for the love of the game.

There are many other human activities of this sort: art, friendship, family, politics, religion—and liberal education. Michael Oakeshott captured this well in his characterization of the university as the site of an ongoing conversation.[5] The conversation might have many ancillary benefits, such as the development of skills, but part of the purpose of participating in a conversation—like playing a sport or going for coffee with a friend—is the conversation itself. From this perspective we can see how alien the technological way of thinking is to liberal education.

For example, just as it would be odd to talk about making our friendships more efficient, so too is it odd to suggest that liberal education should become more efficient. Beyond the fact that it is an activity we should enjoy and want to prolong (like a great novel, for instance), liberal education is, in a sense, the opposite of efficient. It requires cultivating a capacity, as well as time and space, for receptivity because, as Josef Pieper wrote, "the highest form of knowledge comes to man like a gift—the sudden illumination, a stroke of genius, true contemplation."[6] Surely, we have all had the experience of struggling to learn something and then suddenly "getting it." Insight cannot be rushed. It cannot even be guaranteed. The consequence of applying efficiency to liberal education is superficiality. Liberal education is simply not susceptible to the technological imperative of efficiency. Similar points could be made with respect to demands for innovation and progress.

Liberal education is a kind of "serious play," to use a phrase coined by Plato. It is something we do when our work is done, yet it is even more important than our work. This points to the sense in which liberal education is liberating: it is one of the things we do when we are free from necessity—a necessity that characterizes technology. Technology also aims to liberate us (from need and want), but we end up subject to its logic of endless progress instead. We ourselves become part of the nature we attempt to master. Thus, we have human *resource* departments and talk about social *capital*. These might seem like harmless turns of phrase, but they indicate a way of thinking that is fundamentally inhumane. Human beings are not just resources or a form of capital. We need to defend liberal education against the advances of modern technology because doing so is essential to preserving our humanity.

As detrimental as the theory behind modern technology might be to our intellectual, moral, and spiritual lives, we must acknowledge that it has compelling arguments in its favor. The most obvious one is that it has led to a previously unimaginable explosion of material prosperity that has raised billions of people out of poverty. Another is that it makes possible the relative comfort in which many of us live. Who would want to give up electricity, running water, or modern medicine, to give just a few examples? It even supports and arguably makes possible our modern ideals such as liberty, equality, dignity, human rights, and social justice. How plausible would any of these really be without the wealth afforded us by modern technology? Thus, quite rightly, the idea that we should reject modern technology outright is simply unpersuasive, not to mention impossible.

Even liberal education, while at odds with the ideology of modern technology, arguably depends on a certain level of technological advancement itself. Even the most happily retrograde teachers of the liberal arts today gladly make use of certain forms of technology: books, paper, pens and pencils, chalk and chalkboards, desks and tables, chairs, buildings, electricity, laptops, printers. We could perhaps do without these things, and there might be advantages to doing so, but, on balance, most of us would agree that the benefits outweigh the costs. More important, some level of technological civilization is needed to afford people the time and space required to pursue liberal education. While all people in all times have probably engaged in some form of contemplation, it is likely that a figure like Socrates could appear only in a somewhat technologically advanced (although not modern) society. It is certainly true that the democratization of liberal education in modernity depends on technological innovation. As our work has become more efficient and productive, an increasing number of people have a sufficient amount of free time and other resources to pursue liberal education.

It would seem that our choice is not between a pure, technology-free liberal education and illiberal technological education. We live in between these possibilities. If modern technology and liberal education are irreconcilable in theory, they continue to coexist in practice. It follows that, instead of rejecting modern technological society, our goal should be to encourage liberal education within the context of our current historical circumstances. This is in fact what many of us in the academy tried to do during the recent crisis. We accepted our situation, took the technological resources available to us, and tried to make it work. We didn't have to do that, but it seemed prudent to do so, or we at least went along with it.

The key to ensuring that this experience does not have inhumane long-term consequences is acknowledging that both technology and liberal education are goods, but that liberal education is the higher good. In order to do this, we need to attend constantly to the nature and purpose of liberal education and employ the technologies available to us in ways that are consistent with it, if we employ them at all (and our general inclination should be not to use them). Thus, we might use online technologies when necessary or advantageous to do so, but we should strive to maintain the time-intensive, tutorial model of liberal education, rather than embracing the technological goals of efficiency, innovation, and scale that have informed various fads such as MOOCs (massive open online course). This means small classes that focus on depth rather than breadth and that reward thoughtfulness rather than productivity.

We should also draw attention to how the technologies themselves impact the practice of liberal education, as Plato did when he cautioned against the art of writing in his *Phaedrus*:

> it will introduce forgetfulness into the soul of those who learn it: they will not practice using their memory because they will put their trust in writing, which is external and depends on signs that belong to others, instead of trying to remember from the inside, completely on their own. You have not discovered a potion for remembering, but for reminding; you provide your students with the appearance of wisdom, not with its reality. Your invention will enable them to hear many things without being properly taught, and they will imagine that they have come to know much while for the most part they will know nothing. And they will be difficult to get along with, since they will merely appear to be wise instead of really being so.[7]

Plato nevertheless chose to write, but he did so in a way that left open the possibility of true liberal education by calling attention to the problems inherent to the enterprise. He made the use of technology an occasion for liberal education.

Like Plato, when we use technology to pursue liberal education, we should question the ideology behind it. This will be difficult to do and require constant vigilance because of the tendency of modern technology to replace everything with itself. Indeed, even before the pandemic, we faced an uphill battle because the technological paradigm has already so thoroughly infected our understanding and practice of liberal education.

Even before we were all compelled to go online in the spring of 2020, we were already subject to various technological encroachments: outcome-based learning and assessment, hypercredentialization, syllabi as contracts, demands for "relevance," increasing administrative work, calls to involve undergraduates in research and internships, the idea that scholarship needs to be innovative, and more. These are all superficial distractions from the depth and delight of a true search for wisdom.

This is a particularly precarious moment in the history of liberal education in America. Our institutions of higher education are in a state of crisis, economically, as most people know, but also intellectually and spiritually. The spirit of technology has been infiltrating the liberal arts for years. Now its proponents stand at the ready to help us in our time of need. But we need to recognize that the technology that made it possible to continue teaching during the pandemic has the potential to be a Trojan horse. Now that we have accepted it, those who believe in it and benefit from it are ready to advance its cause. There is a good chance they will succeed, but we could also see this moment as a wake-up call. As our experiences highlight the inadequacy of technology and online liberal education, let us reflect on how far down the road of technologization we have allowed our colleges and universities to go and why this is problematic. Rather than simply accepting that inertia is pushing us further and further toward virtual education, we should use this opportunity to awaken ourselves to the troubling trajectory we are already on and think about how we can correct course before it is too late. Liberal education is one of the great joys of human existence; we should be finding ways to share it with our students instead of distracting them from it.

NOTES

1. George Grant, *Technology and Justice*, 13. Grant's reflections on technology are indebted to Martin Heidegger, "the thinker who has most deeply pondered our technological destiny." 17. See Martin Heidegger, "The Question Concerning Technology."
2. Francis Bacon, *The Oxford Francis Bacon*, vol. 4, *The Advancement of Learning*, 32 (quotation modernized).
3. Karl Marx, "Theses on Feuerbach," 145.
4. Grant, *Technology and Justice*, 34.
5. Michael Oakeshott, "The Voice of Poetry in the Conversation of Mankind."
6. Josef Pieper, *Leisure: The Basis of Culture*, 16.
7. Plato, *Phaedrus*, 551–52.

BIBLIOGRAPHY

Bacon, Francis. *The Oxford Francis Bacon.* Vol. 4, *The Advancement of Learning.* Edited by Michael Kiernan. Oxford: Oxford University Press, 2000.

Grant, George. *Technology and Justice.* Concord, Ontario: House of Anansi Press, 1986.

Heidegger, Martin. "The Question Concerning Technology." In *The Question Concerning Technology, and Other Essays*, translated by William Lovitt. New York: Harper & Row, 1977.

Marx, Karl. "Theses on Feuerbach." In *The Marx-Engels Reader*, edited by Robert C. Tucker. New York: W. W. Norton, 1978.

Oakeshott, Michael. "The Voice of Poetry in the Conversation of Mankind." In *Rationalism in Politics, and Other Essays*, edited by Timothy Fuller, 488–542. Indianapolis: Liberty Fund, 1991.

Pieper, Josef. *Leisure: The Basis of Culture.* Translated by Alexander Dru. Indianapolis: Liberty Fund, 2000.

Plato. "Phaedrus." In *Plato: Complete Works.* Edited by John M. Cooper. Translated by Alexander Nehamas and Paul Woodruff. Indianapolis: Hackett, 1997.

11. Transference and the Future of Teacher-Student Intimacy

Sarah Rich-Zendel

THE LIBERAL ARTS COLLEGE IS an environment where education, work, and private life commingle. The blurring of the personal and professional in the context of learning creates a unique environment where intimacy, particularly between teacher and student, can be both a generative and a harmful force. In the ideal case, the student-teacher relationship sparks a desire to learn and arouses within a student the thrill and passion of knowledge and understanding.[1] When students and teachers project these feelings of desire onto each other, rather than the proper object of learning, it creates a conflict of interest, but also a failed pedagogical relationship. When teachers act on erotic feelings for a student, they eliminate the opportunity to channel the student's passion toward learning. And this phenomenon disproportionately affects women. Women are socialized to interpret the feelings aroused in them by their professors as feelings *for* their professors, whereas male students are socialized to interpret these feelings as a desire to *be* their professors.[2]

There is a long history of women's and student group lobbying the university to address this type of sexual misconduct and many other forms of discrimination and gender-based violence that occur on campus. The response from universities has been the creation of a dense administrative infrastructure that includes total bans on student-teacher sexual relationships, regardless of whether those adults are in a direct pedagogical relationship, compliance offices, and committees with the power to investigate and punish misconduct. The litigious and punitive nature of this infrastructure may suppress teacher-student romances. However, it fails to provide guidance necessary for teachers to navigate the reality of complex and amorphous social and intimate relationships with their students in a way that is both ethical and recognizes the pedagogical benefits of this sociality.

This chapter explores the concept of transference as a way to guide teachers on how to cultivate intimacy and sociality in the student-teacher relationship toward the purpose of classroom engagement and learning. Transference is a psychotherapeutic phenomenon that refers to situations when a patient redirects feelings, unresolved emotions, or conflicts within themselves onto their therapist.[3] Psychotherapists have developed ethical standards to engage with the transference that recognizes its inevitability as well as its value for producing positive therapeutic results. Like the therapeutic space, the intimate nature of the liberal arts classroom can leave student and teachers vulnerable to projecting emotions and desire onto each other instead of the proper object of learning. A teacher can easily exploit this situation without an understanding of how to navigate this transferential aspect of the pedagogical relationship. I hope that using the language of transference can enhance this understanding as well as destigmatize the topic of classroom erotics, a topic that is increasingly taboo under a university infrastructure that treats intimacy and sociality in the student-teacher relationships as high risk.

I begin the chapter by describing the pedagogical benefits of classroom intimacy and sociality between teachers and students. These benefits highlight why it is worth finding a framework to guide teachers on how to cultivate and channel these emotions and encourage the creativity and innovation that emerge from them. Then I argue that existing bans against student-teacher sexual relationships may suppress this intimacy and sociality, as teachers and students become more vigilant about crossing lines, but it can never fully eliminate them. Finally, I discuss the concept of transference and explore the possibilities for using it as an ethical guide for helping teachers create a learning environment that fosters deeper connections and engagement with course material.

SOCIALITY AND THE DESIRE TO LEARN

Audre Lorde and other scholars of friendship, love, and desire recognize the power of eros, intimacy, and deep friendship in cultivating the caring relationships necessary to achieve a range of political goals from the emancipation of women[4] to the provision of liberal arts education.[5] Lorde defines the erotic as "the power which comes from sharing deeply any pursuit with another person."[6] The very act of learning renders the classroom an intimate space because students enter as people vulnerable to anxieties over what is yet unknown and the accidents of desire that come with the pleasure of its discovery. Teachers and students also enter the classroom as embodied people with conflictual emotions, experiences, and sexualities that shape their response to each other and the material being taught. Teachers need to develop the capacity to navigate these emotions and experiences with their students and channel them toward learning.[7] This section explores the benefits of this capacity and why we should protect the intimate sociality necessitated by it from either being exploited by teachers or suppressed by institutions.

Sociality describes our tendency to associate with others in a group and the depth of these associations. The foundations of sociality are the spontaneous acts of creative joint activity and prosocial behavior that bring us into communion with each other.[8] In the liberal arts classroom, the alchemy of the student-teacher relationship is made of these immediate forms of innovation. Teachers expose their students to new ideas, and students respond in unpredictable ways as they play with ideas and integrate them into their worldview.

The ideal scenario is when spontaneous sociality, friendship, and even the occasional crush on a professor motivate students toward understanding the material and engaging with it.[9] Attraction to a professor's charisma and intellect should turn students on to new ideas and instill within them a desire to know what the professor knows.[10] In their essay "On the Path of Friendship," Mary Adkins-Cartee and Karni Pal Bhati provide a glimpse into the power of this ideal. In the essay, the two dialogue on forming an intimate intellectual friendship when Adkins-Cartee was a student in two of Bhati's seminar courses in literature at Furman University. The essay begins by explaining why their friendship feels transgressive in a university context that increasingly incentivizes formalized and hierarchical relationships between teachers and students. In Adkins-Cartee's words, her friendship with Bhati fell outside the sanctioning of the "white supremacist capitalist imperialist patriarchy."[11] When Bhati describes the issue of respecting and transgressing relational boundaries, he references Adkins-Cartee's subjectivity as a student:

> You brought such passion and sense of engagement to the things we talked about on our walks around the Furman Lake that I could no longer recall that you were once a student in my class. I see you as a colleague, a fellow traveller in search of a meaningful life—not a life of isolated academic concerns, which is a risk for many at the university level, but one of engagement with the issues of the day at the local, national, and global levels. As our sense of mutual trust grew we were, I think, able to see how our friendship was enriching rather than fraught with a transgressive potential.[12]

While both authors speak of a friendship mediated by a deep intellectual connection, Bhati recognizes the role of attraction in this connection: "While some are incapable of even conceiving alternative ways of being, others are capable of taking the risk to be led by their hearts."[13] His statement speaks directly to the unpredictability and spontaneity of classroom relations but also on the role of *capacity* in being able to navigate the unpredictability, or, as Bhati puts it, "risk," of being led by one's heart in connections across difference, in this case the asymmetrical pedagogical relationship.

This dialogue goes on to paint a powerful description of a common pedagogical experience: the development of an erotic and passionate relationship between a male professor and a female student that inspires intellectual pursuits without being sexualized or exploitative. This representation is crowded out by mainstream media's obsession with the stereotypical lecherous professor and the naive young female student who confuses her passion for learning with her passion for a professor. In this case, Adkins-Cartee was moved by Bhati's interest in her intellect, and the affirmation of a friendship with a professor she respected gave her the confidence to pursue an intellectual life.[14] I do not say this to diminish the harm done by professors who exploit classroom erotics to gain sexual access to their students and, thus, violate their pedagogical responsibilities, nor deny the gendered nature of this exploitation. But I want to highlight that intimate sociality in the pedagogical relationship is usually banal and, in many cases, of profound value to the student.

Even in the cases where intimacy between teachers and students does become romantic, which is an exception rather than a rule, it is not usually experienced by students as more or less harmful than sexual and intimate partnerships in general. Whether adult students can consent to a sexual relationship with a professor or not, particularly one whom they have a pedagogical relationship with, is not a question I explore here. However, given the outsize role the stereotype of the lecherous professor plays in our culture, I want to provide a counterpoint from a 2001 study of sexual relationships between university teachers and adult students. In this study, all the students reported entering freely into the relationship, satisfaction with their involvement in the relationship, and that they would become involved in this type of relationship again. The most commonly reported downside was the stigma they experienced by institutional norms that made the relationship more difficult.[15] This kind of research suggests that adult students are capable of navigating spontaneous and intimate relationships across asymmetries of age and professional status and to form bonds of trust on their own terms using their own judgment.

INFRASTRUCTURE OF SEXUAL VIGILANCE ON CAMPUS

My main concern with the university's infrastructure for policing the sexual exploitation of the student-teacher relationship and banning sex between adult students and teachers is the effect it has on pedagogy. The university is becoming an increasingly industrialized space with custodial surroundings where an ever-powerful administration incentivizes a precarious, adjunctified, and, as such, risk-averse faculty to engage in increasingly uniform instruction and interaction with their students. This environment creates a disjunction between the institution and the student—whose embodied subjectivity defies uniformity and contributes to a campus culture that is atomized and hypervigilant.

Harvard became the first university to institute a total ban on sexual relationships between teachers and students in 1984,[16] and now 84 percent of American universities have them.[17] To enforce these bans and investigate sexual misconduct complaints, universities have set up a quasi-legal infrastructure that includes formal committees, tribunals, and offices with investigative and punitive power. While this infrastructure has been effective at producing complaints,[18] there is little evidence it has improved the culture of sexual harassment on campus or the protection of students from abuse.[19]

What is clear is that the formal separation it creates between teacher and student produces a culture of vigilance and suspicion.[20] An example of this culture was captured in Jennifer Doyle's book *Campus Sex, Campus Security*, where she describes the "administrative trauma" she suffered as a result of a Title IX complaint she filed at the behest of her university's administration when she asked for help regarding a student who was harassing her. As a result of her complaint, Doyle was caught in this web of administrators, investigators, compliance officers, and risk-management consultants whose suggestions included the actual construction of a walled compound around her home. The situation became so strange that she filed a secondary complaint about how the university handled the initial complaint. During the adjudication of the second complaint, the Title IX committee used her scholarship on sexual politics as evidence of her own sexual impropriety to argue that she, in fact, was never being harassed at all.[21]

In another mind-bending example, a woman faculty member at Arizona State University was accused of a Title IX violation through an anonymous reporting system right after her partner, also a woman academic, was offered a job in Michigan, which would include a spousal hire for her.[22] The accuser claimed to be a graduate student in the accused faculty's department and recorded that the accused offered students help with their grades in exchange for sexual favors. The accused faculty was confident of her innocence but knew the claim had to be false because the so-called graduate student referred to her by a name she did not commonly use at work. When she asked the Title IX investigator if they would drop the allegation if it was proven false, she was told that the office had to investigate every complaint to make sure a policy had not been violated, regardless of its veracity. The investigation went on for months and deeply affected the faculty's reputation. The *New York Times* and *Chronicle of Higher Education* were set to publish articles about the alleged abuse. Luckily, right before, the couple was able to prove that another candidate competing for the job her partner applied for had made the false allegations to undermine her credibility so the offer would be rescinded. These cases raise a clear concern about the capacity for university administrations to competently adjudicate quasi-legal claims, but they also highlight how gender justice laws are often mobilized to unfairly target women, faculty, and students of color; LGBTQ+ students and faculty; and undocumented students—groups that also happen to be more likely to face retaliation if they try to use these laws when they face abuse.[23]

My concern here though is the effect that this litigious approach is having on the student-teacher relationships in the classroom. Again, I want to be clear that from an ethical and pedagogical standpoint, I do not think teachers should have sex with students they are currently teaching or supervising. I also do not think that prohibitions address the problem. In fact, as the cases above suggest, the infrastructure to enforce them may even harm the groups they claim to be protecting. And the problem of adjunctification and precarity among the professoriate only exacerbates this problem. Without any job security, teachers have to be hypervigilant so as to not engage in any behavior that could subject them to an investigation and undermine their already precarious position. As a result, teachers are less likely to engage in pedagogical practices that involve informal sociality and could elicit passion and excitement within their students.

It is no surprise that my junior faculty peers, many of whom are adjuncts, seem tacitly afraid of their students. In conversations, we talk about feeling ill-equipped to navigate intense feelings that come up in the classroom, fear of how socializing with our students will be interpreted by other colleagues or the administration, even confusion about how to respond when students share personal information with us or want to have informal or private conversations. In other words, my colleagues are confused about if and how we can treat our students with empathy and humanity without potentially breaching a policy. One colleague described that even the most banal interactions feel like they require consultation with the faculty handbook or a specialized administrative office.

Can we mitigate the harm of sexual misconduct without relying on such a punitive and custodial infrastructure that exploits our precarity? In the current cultural climate, universities may be too risk averse to consider the value of maintaining some space for ambiguous sociality within the asymmetrical teacher-student relationship. However, the pedagogical benefits make it worth exploring forms of ethical guidelines to help teachers feel more comfortable and capable to navigate unstructured and sometimes erotic relations in their classroom and with their students.

TRANSFERENCE AND CHANNELING EMOTIONS IN THE CLASSROOM

In the recent newspaper article "Is It Time for Canadian Universities to Ban Student Professor Relationships?" a professor from the University of Toronto references the transferential nature of learning as a possible alternative lens for regulating teacher and student relationships: "Learning is an intensely romantic endeavor.... There isn't a part of you, when you're really into it, that isn't really alive. . . . [T]here's a vulnerability and an excitement. . . . It can be easy for a student to *mistakenly conflate how they feel about what they're learning with who's teaching them*. . . . [C]ulturally, *what if we asked professors not to take advantage of that?*"[24] Teachers are rarely encouraged by the university to reflect on the affective dynamics of the classroom. Nor are they encouraged to explore how accidents of desire and attraction shape the pedagogical experience for better or worse. In other words, what, other than the curriculum, do teachers communicate to students in the classroom relationship? What happens between people in the exchange of knowledge? How is this exchange experienced emotionally and shaped by love, desire, and fantasies of power and authority?[25]

When Sigmund Freud explored these questions in the context of psychotherapy, he developed the concept of transference: "In every analytic treatment there arises, without the physician's agency, an intense emotional relationship between the patient and the analyst which is not to be accounted for by the actual situation. It can be of a positive or of a negative character and can vary between the extremes of a passionate, completely sensual love and the unbridled expression of an embittered defiance and hatred."[26] In other words, transference is the ways in which we project unresolved emotions within ourselves and with others onto new interactions and relationships.[27] Freud sees transference as an essential component of the therapeutic relationship. Where there is no transference of emotion, there is no possibility of influencing the patient therapeutically. High levels of transference mean high levels of engagement in the therapeutic relationship, and low levels of transference can lead to resistance, and barriers. As such, one cannot evade or "ban" transference; one can only be more or less aware of how it is influencing the process and direct it to enhance or undermine therapeutic goals.

Anna Freud, Sigmund Freud's daughter and a fellow psychoanalyst, expanded the application of transference as a condition that structures many forms of relations, including the pedagogical one. Like a therapist and their patients, teachers and students are also in a relational dynamic where it is difficult to anticipate how they might affect each other. For example, teachers find themselves in a transferential relationship when their own inner anxieties about learning shape how they respond to their students.[28] A teacher may recognize themselves in a particular student's struggle with learning and consciously or unconsciously give the student more or less guidance, attention, or empathy. I was told by a professor who spoke English as a second language that he could not stand when his ESL students expected leniency when it came to writing errors because when he was a student he was never given special treatment and had to work extra hard to meet the basic requirements. This professor's frustration from his own past learning experience led to animosity toward his ESL students who needed some extra help. The framework of transference can provide teachers with the tools to become more aware of this projection and channel it toward enhancing the learning experience. Another way this professor could channel his experience would be to empathize with the extra burden ESL students face in an Anglo-centric institution and that a focus on marking the substance and argumentation of all students' writing rather than focusing on writing errors could make grading fairer for everyone—ESL or otherwise. In this way, transference can be both positive and negative. Positive forms facilitate a high levels of engagement in the working relationship—whether pedagogical or therapeutic—while negative forms lead to antagonism and resistance to the work.[29]

In *Observations on Love in Transference*, Freud discusses the most frequent and significant form of transference: the erotic. Contrary to representations in popular culture, erotic forms of transference are not always negative. When both parties recognize the erotic transference—or, in more colloquial terms, the crush—as unrealistic, it does not need to disrupt the relationship. In fact, the attraction at the heart of erotic transference can encourage more intense participation and openness to the work at hand. However, erotic transference becomes disruptive when one party develops an irrational preoccupation or fantasy of the other, like a persistent hope that the therapist or teacher will reciprocate erotic feelings.[30]

Freud was especially concerned with how to navigate eroticized transference ethically. He thought that therapists should avoid typical outcomes such as creating the circumstances for a legitimate relationship, completely parting ways, or engaging in an illicit love affair because each one pivots the focus away from therapeutic goals. Even the doctor who parts ways with the patient, the ostensibly most ethical outcome, is actually abandoning a patient in need. If transferential feelings emerge with one therapist, they are likely to manifest in future therapeutic relationships if they go unaddressed.

Instead, Freud encourages the therapist to channel transference toward the patient's therapeutic benefit.

The first step toward this goal is to reframe an infatuation as one induced by the therapeutic situation instead of a personal attraction, as one would commonly view it outside the therapeutic context. The second step is to recognize that infatuation and expressions of love in the therapeutic relationship can be a form of resistance to treatment. Thus, evading it or stoking it may harm the patient further. Once these steps are taken, Freud recommends maintaining a stance of complete immunity to temptation while also acknowledging that these feelings are occurring. Thus, the therapist's task is to identify the transference and *not* avoid its existence.[31]

Once the therapist and patient identify the love transference, the therapist should help the patient become more conscious of the source of their feelings and bring them under the patient's control. Naturally, it is a challenge to get a patient to talk about these types of feelings. One strategy is to focus on what they can learn from analyzing their relationships with others and how these relationships shape their feelings about the therapist or the therapeutic process. In these difficult conversations, it is important for the therapist to project comfort with addressing the feelings and minimize the potential for patients to feel embarrassed, rejected, or negatively judged.[32]

Now that I have outlined the approach to transference in psychotherapy, I want to think more directly about how to apply it to the pedagogical relationship. There are two key differences between the therapeutic and pedagogical relationship that require some adaptation when it comes to working through transferential experiences: temporality and scale. The pedagogical relationship is temporally fixed and determined by academic timetables, while the therapeutic relationship is less determinate. Once a course is over, a student may need a professor to write a recommendation letter or to take a course the professor teaches in the future. However, these possibilities are relatively predictable and within the capacity of both student and teacher to consider when deciding whether they want to explore an "ordinary" relationship when pedagogy is no longer the principal goal.

Another difference is the scale of the classroom versus the psychoanalyst's couch. In a classroom, the teacher manages multiple pedagogical relationships simultaneously. As a result, transference occurs in the presence of numerous others. That means the teacher must address transferential emotions as a general condition. For instance, if transference emerges within a student as anger or passion, a teacher can help that student articulate why the material or subject at hand affects them in such a way. A teacher can guide an emotional interaction, prompting the student to think about the specific aspect of the material brings these emotions to the forefront. Does the content evoke an aspect of the student's lived experience and why? This way of addressing transference has pedagogical benefits for all the students by modeling how to connect material to their own lives rather than engagement that is more rote. Teachers can also channel their own transferential feelings through their own self-disclosure of vulnerability or personal experience. When teachers self-disclose the way material shapes their own thinking or lives, they cultivate an intimacy with students that improves engagement while modeling how to navigate and interpret material that excites strong emotion within them. When the classroom is purely content driven and focused on self-mastery, students are abstracted from their experiences and identities, and teachers cannot resolve critical social and emotional dynamics that emerge across relationships of difference such as race, gender, class, and sex that can lead one to resist learning. In short, by engaging with transference directly, teachers can cultivate intimacy and sociality to enhance the pedagogical experience and make it more inclusive.

The first step for teachers toward engaging with transference is recognize it for what it is. The vulnerability, passion, and desire students project onto them as teachers, and vice versa, are not ordinary emotions they are transferential ones. The question of whether a teacher or a therapist can have ordinary love for their student or patient misses the ethical point entirely. As long as one is engaged in a direct therapeutic or pedagogical relationship, reciprocating love is antithetical to the larger goal. As Freud puts it, "Love in transference has slightly less freedom than the love that occurs ordinarily in life and is called normal."[33]

CONCLUDING THOUGHTS

As I think through the benefits of cultivating the capacity to manage classroom erotics through the guidelines of transference, I worry about time and resources. The expectations this places on underpaid and undervalued teachers in the neoliberal university is too high. Rising adjunctification and insecurity leave an increasingly larger proportion of teachers overworked, underpaid, and generally averse to practices that could put their precarious positions at risk. At the same time, rising tuition costs and instrumentalization of university degrees leave students less open to exposing their vulnerability in class and engaging deeply with the material. Instead, getting the piece of paper and moving on to gainful employment is their top priority. In other words, perhaps this whole endeavor is based on an overly romantic picture of university life. Nevertheless, I remain hopeful that forces both outside and inside the university will fight to improve the structural conditions within which we teach and learn.

In *Uses of the Erotic*, Audre Lorde argues that there is a "false belief that only by the suppression of the erotic within our lives and consciousness can women be truly strong."[34] The same logic that Lorde applies to the role of the erotic for the emancipation of women applies to education as well. Denial-based rules will not address the challenging emotions and relationships that arise inside and outside the classroom or on campus. By applying transference to educational relationships, teachers can think more expansively about how to have relationships that are both ethical and intimate.

NOTES

1. For example, T. J. Geiger II, "An Intimate Discipline? Writing Studies, Undergraduate Majors, and Relational Labor"; Alexander W. Astin, "How the Liberal Arts College Affects Students."

2. Amia Srinivasan, "What's Wrong with Sex between Professors and Students? It's Not What You Think," *New York Times*, September 3, 2021, https://www.nytimes.com/2021/09/03/opinion/metoo-teachers-students-consent.html.

3. Deborah P. Britzman and Alice J. Pitt, "Pedagogy and Transference: Casting the Past of Learning into the Presence of Teaching."

4. Niharika Banerjea et al., eds., *Friendship as Social Justice Activism: Critical Solidarities in a Global Perspective*.

5. Kathleen Hull, "Eros and Education: The Role of Desire in Teaching and Learning"; Alison Pryer, "'What Spring Does with the Cherry Trees': The Eros of Teaching and Learning."

6. Banerjea et al., *Friendship as Social Justice Activism*.

7. Hilary N. Tackie, "(Dis)Connected: Establishing Social Presence and Intimacy in Teacher-Student Relationships during Emergency Remote Learning."

8. G. Gurvitch, *Sociology of Law*, 160.

9. Hull, "Eros and Education," 14.

10. Angela Trethewey, "Sexuality, Eros, and Pedagogy: Desiring Laughter in the Classroom."

11. Mary Adkins-Cartee and Karni Bal Bhati, "On the Path of Friendship," 219.

12. Adkins-Cartee and Bhati, "On the Path of Friendship," 227–28.
13. Adkins-Cartee and Bhati, "On the Path of Friendship," 218.
14. Adkins-Cartee and Bhati, "On the Path of Friendship," 220.
15. Marcia L. Bellas and Jennifer L. Gossett, "Love or the 'Lecherous Professor': Consensual Sexual Relationships between Professors and Students."
16. Daniel Luzer, "The End of Relationships between College Professors and Students?"
17. Srinivasan, "What's Wrong with Sex between Professors and Students?"
18. Sarah Viren, "The Accusations Were Lies. But Could We Prove It?," *New York Times*, March 18, 2020, https://www.nytimes.com/2020/03/18/magazine/title-ix-sexual-harassment-accusations.html.
19. Jennifer Doyle, *Campus Sex, Campus Security*; Laura Kipnis, *Unwanted Advances: Sexual Paranoia Comes to Campus*.
20. For example, Doyle, *Campus Sex, Campus Security*; Kipnis, *Unwanted Advances*; and Viren, "Accusations Were Lies."
21. Doyle, *Campus Sex, Campus Security*.
22. Viren, "Accusations Were Lies."
23. Srinivasan, "What's Wrong with Sex between Professors and Students?"; Janet Halley, "Trading the Megaphone for the Gavel in Title IX Enforcement."
24. Jane Gerster, "Is It Time for Canadian Universities to Ban Student-Professor Relationships?"
25. Deborah P. Britzman, *A Psychoanalyst in the Classroom: On the Human Condition in Education*.
26. Sigmund Freud, *An Autobiographical Study*, 42.
27. Britzman and Pitt, "Pedagogy and Transference."
28. Britzman and Pitt, "Pedagogy and Transference," 118.
29. Fatima Noorani and Allen R. Dyer, "How Should Clinicians Respond to Transference Reactions with Cancer Patients?"
30. Noorani and Dyer, "How Should Clinicians Respond?"
31. Noorani and Dyer, "How Should Clinicians Respond?"
32. Noorani and Dyer, "How Should Clinicians Respond?"
33. Sigmund Freud, *The Penguin Freud Reader*, 349.
34. Adrienne Maree Brown, *Pleasure Activism: The Politics of Feeling Good*, 28.

BIBLIOGRAPHY

Adkins-Cartee, Mary, and Karni Bal Bharti. "On the Path of Friendship." In *Friendship as Social Justice Activism*, edited by Banerjea et al. New York: Seagull Books, 2018.

Angel, Katherine. *Tomorrow Sex Will Be Good Again: Women and Desire in the Age of Consent*. New York: Verso Books, 2021.

Astin, Alexander W. "How the Liberal Arts College Affects Students." *Daedalus* 128, no. 1 (1999): 77–100.

Banerjea, Niharika, Debanuj Dasgupta, Rohit K. Dasgupta, and Jaime M. Grant, eds. *Friendship as Social Justice Activism: Critical Solidarities in a Global Perspective*. New York: Seagull Books, 2018.

Bellas, Marcia L., and Jennifer L. Gossett. "Love or the 'Lecherous Professor': Consensual Sexual Relationships between Professors and Students." *Sociological Quarterly* 42, no. 4 (2001): 529–58.

Britzman, Deborah P. *A Psychoanalyst in the Classroom: On the Human Condition in Education.* Albany: State University of New York Press, 2015.

Britzman, Deborah P., and Alice J. Pitt. "Pedagogy and Transference: Casting the Past of Learning into the Presence of Teaching." *Theory into Practice* 35, no. 2 (1996): 117–23. https://doi.org/10.1080/00405849609543711.

Brown, Adrienne Maree. *Pleasure Activism: The Politics of Feeling Good.* Chico, CA: AK Press, 2019.

Doyle, Jennifer. *Campus Sex, Campus Security.* South Pasadena, CA: Semiotext, 2015.

Dziech, Billie Wright, and Linda Weiner. *The Lecherous Professor: Sexual Harassment on Campus.* Urbana: University of Illinois Press, 1990.

Freud, Sigmund. *An Autobiographical Study.* Mansfield Center, CT: Martino, 2010.

———. *The Penguin Freud Reader.* Edited by Adam Phillips. London: Penguin UK, 2006.

Gallop, Jane. "Resisting Reasonableness." *Critical Inquiry* 25, no. 3 (1999): 559–609.

Geiger, T. J., II. "An Intimate Discipline? Writing Studies, Undergraduate Majors, and Relational Labor." *Composition Studies* 43, no. 2 (2015): 92–112.

Gerster, Jane. "Is It Time for Canadian Universities to Ban Student-Professor Relationships?" *Global News*, September 3, 2018. https://globalnews.ca/news/4421521/student-professor-relationship-ban/.

Gurvitch, G. *Sociology of Law.* London: Routledge and Kegan Paul, 1953.

Halley, Janet. "Trading the Megaphone for the Gavel in Title IX Enforcement." *Harvard Law Review* 128, no. 4 (2015). https://harvardlawreview.org/2015/02/trading-the-megaphone-for-the-gavel-in-title-ix-enforcement-2/.

Hirsch, Jennifer S., and Shamus Khan. *Sexual Citizens: A Landmark Study of Sex, Power, and Assault on Campus.* New York: W. W. Norton, 2020.

Hull, Kathleen. "Eros and Education: The Role of Desire in Teaching and Learning." *NEA Higher Education Journal* (2002).

Kipnis, Laura. *Unwanted Advances: Sexual Paranoia Comes to Campus.* New York: HarperCollins, 2017.

Luzer, Daniel. "The End of Relationships between College Professors and Students?" *Pacific Standard* (2017). https://psmag.com/education/the-end-of-hot-for-teacher-professor-student-relationships-64412.

Noorani, Fatima, and Allen R. Dyer. "How Should Clinicians Respond to Transference Reactions with Cancer Patients?" *AMA Journal of Ethics* 19, no. 5 (2017): 436–43. https://doi.org/10.1001/journalofethics.2017.19.5.ecas3-1705.

Pryer, Alison. "'What Spring Does with the Cherry Trees': The Eros of Teaching and Learning." *Teachers and Teaching: Theory and Practice* 7, no. 1 (2001): 14.

Svlurga, Susan. "Harvard Formally Bans Sexual Relationships between Professors and Undergrads." *Washington Post*, February 5, 2015. https://www.washingtonpost.com/news/grade-point/wp/2015/02/05/harvard-formally-bans-sexual-relationships-between-professors-and-undergrads/.

Tackie, Hilary N. "(Dis)Connected: Establishing Social Presence and Intimacy in Teacher-Student Relationships During Emergency Remote Learning." *AERA Open* 8 (January 2022).

Trethewey, Angela. "Sexuality, Eros, and Pedagogy: Desiring Laughter in the Classroom." *Women and Language* 27, no. 1 (2004): 34–39.

12. From Impatience to Compassion
Educating from Restlessness to Responsibility
Sarah Beth V. Kitch

> Education is an art, and an especially difficult one. Yet it belongs by its nature to the sphere of ethics and practical wisdom. Education is an *ethical* art.
> —Jacques Maritain, *Education at the Crossroads*

> Charity, being personally involved in relieving the sufferings of man, is as important to education as the acquisition of technical skills.
> —Abraham Joshua Heschel, *The Insecurity of Freedom*

DEMOCRACY NEEDS PEDAGOGY THAT ENGAGES AGONY

Throughout my experience as a teacher, I have been interested in how students encounter suffering. Do their educations prepare them to bear the suffering they will face? An ability to respond to the harm one encounters is important to becoming a mature human. Do students have ways to approach the pain that appears in their personal lives and in shared political life? This question becomes urgent for me as I watch students graduate with an uneven skill set. For all the things they study, do American students gain a moral education that prepares them to deal with the personal and political consequences of human suffering? Can they identify suffering? Can they attend to it? Can they trace its effects? A pedagogy of suffering can contribute to a moral literacy that sustains democratic practices such as listening, serving, and deliberating.

When students study history or politics, suffering appears frequently—whether we're talking about Fannie Lou Hamer's attempts to register to vote in 1962 Mississippi or the Holocaust or policy trade-offs for undocumented children today. As I work with students in the humanities, I notice they need guidance on how to discern the moral meaning of the suffering they encounter. To develop the ethical skills to recognize suffering is a first step. Beyond that, students need an education that enables them to reflect on and respond to suffering.

In a 2020 *Journal of Politics* article, Alexander Livingston observes, "Love is a source of some anxiety for political theorists." In his diagnosis, political theorists "often denigrate [love] as a private feeling either too sentimental or too otherworldly to confront the tragic conflicts of politics."[1] I think talking about suffering also gives political theorists some anxiety. While it's possible to interpret love as a private experience, suffering *is* a private experience. It is true that communities can share a response to suffering, as New York City did in the wake of 9/11. But a distinctive trait of suffering is that people bear it personally. Suffering is hard to bear, and hard to discuss.

At the same time, suffering features significantly in our common life. Well before the COVID-19 pandemic, the opioid epidemic had captured millions of Americans in search of a remedy.[2] The COVID pandemic has exacerbated the suffering that Americans already face. Even before the pandemic, in the midst of rising contention, Americans wanted to know how to talk about suffering.[3] In a way, our elections are proxies for our pain—ways to protest what hurts. Meanwhile, we have roaring debates that are, at some level, over whose pain counts.

It is easy to view topics like love and suffering as emotional or merely a matter of a person's interiority. But in order to understand American politics, students need adequate ways to talk about the political meaning of pain. As central themes in human life, love and suffering run through our attempt to live well together, to borrow Aristotle's language. Consequently, love and suffering demand attention as central themes in the humanities. The skills to engage suffering—one's own and others'—are key to an adequate civic education. Teachers shape civic education and can cultivate in students skills for approaching human suffering.

To approach this task, I propose a pedagogy of suffering that fosters democratic citizenship. In what follows, I first introduce a pedagogy of suffering as part of a holistic pedagogy. Next, I explore the relationship between democracy and suffering. Finally, I sketch a pedagogy of suffering. There I outline six practices that students can develop through teaching that attends to suffering.

A PEDAGOGY OF SUFFERING:
AN ESSENTIAL DIMENSION OF A WHOLE PEDAGOGY

In order to think about what education is for, we need to think about *who* education is for. In Holocaust survivor and scholar Abraham Joshua Heschel's formulation, the key task of human being is being human.[4] Education is for human beings, who need to learn how to be human. This insight opens us to big questions: What does it mean to be human? Who are my exemplars—who have I encountered in my life or in history or art who strikes me as being good at being a person?

The primary aim of education is to humanize a person—to nurture the loves and virtues that awaken us to truth, beauty, and goodness. The utilitarian aim of education is to enable students to hold a job.[5] A tradition of education that starts with Socrates finds that education is most intensely concerned with forming character. The formation of the person comes before the training of the employee. As he advances the tradition, Aristotle says, "There is a certain sort of education, therefore, in which children are to be educated, not [because it is] useful or necessary," but because it is "liberal and noble"—that is, this kind of education is suitable for a free person and fosters good character.[6] Yet the kind of education that many institutions offer—whether they are known as elite or mediocre institutions—is effectively "childhood as test prep" in the well-meaning but detrimental "resume arms race."[7]

Every day I witness students at an elite institution perform instrumental tasks offered with no rationale of intrinsic value. They stress: if I don't do well on this test, I won't get into the right college, and if I don't get into the right college—well, they're not sure what will happen, but the grown-ups have implied that they best not find out. In their world, the purpose of high school is college, and the purpose of college is a job, and the purpose of a job is a certain standard of living. My students live in a world that is relentlessly about the next social success.[8] There is very little that my students do for *its own sake*—for *their* own sakes. Almost everything they do is for a future goal that someone else has told them they should care about.[9]

Students will need jobs and the training to do those jobs. But they need, more deeply, an education that prepares them for life. Their hunger for a sense of meaning deserves at least as much attention as their college application strategy. The condition of their souls is a concern that belongs within—not beyond—conversations about their educational needs.

Students need, for example, help articulating their questions: What's the purpose of my life? What's friendship? How do I make friends? Why do I suffer? What is my life about? What do I hope for? What do I fear? How do I find love? Is love real? What is mine to care for? Does beauty matter? Do I owe anything to anyone? What is good? What makes a life worth living?[10] Students need to learn to read carefully and write thoughtfully—and to learn that these are skills one can develop even after senior year. Teachers can help prepare students for jobs. They can also help provide, as Elizabeth Corey puts it, "an education that does justice to the full humanity of our students."[11]

Teachers and administrators face astounding challenges. Daily they strive to meet standards, maintain enrollments, balance budgets, attend to student well-being, ensure student success, satisfy parents, secure school safety, and navigate political discontent. Beyond these pressures, many teachers and administrators lack their own experiences of transformative education. In this context, the humanities are unwieldy topics. The easier path by far is to reduce history or politics or art to points to memorize.

But Ariel Burger warns that simply providing students with information is an inadequate education. He writes, "It is a cliché that ignoring history can lead to its repetition. But we also know that the purely technical transmission of information has never been enough to prevent the next tragedy. If memory is to make a moral difference, we need to locate ourselves within it."[12] How can we locate ourselves within memory?[13] One of the ways we can locate ourselves within memory is to follow Burger's teacher Elie Wiesel, who urges: "Listening to a witness makes you a witness."

It is standard in history curricula, for example, to present events without any connection to students' lives. But students want more than facts to memorize for quizzes. After a semester in which I connected the moral questions of a particular moment in history with the questions of our moment, one student commented that the approach "has enabled me to learn about the people in history as real people with real stories rather than information the school wants me to learn."

What can teachers offer to students? Teachers in the classroom confront the task of helping students to develop meaningful moral commitments. But, as Margarita A. Mooney Suarez points out in *The Love of Learning*, "many teachers lack their own moral commitments."[14]

At the 1960 White House Conference on Children and Youth, Abraham Joshua Heschel addresses an audience that expects him to talk about the trouble with young people. A Holocaust survivor, Heschel thinks civilization depends on our ability to practice tenderness and compassion. Consequently, he argues, teachers' chief responsibility is to evoke in students the foundation of tenderness and compassion. Heschel tells his audience, "The mainspring of tenderness and compassion lies in reverence. It is our supreme educational duty to enable the child to revere."[15]

The trouble, for Heschel, is how to inspire reverence. "The problem we face, the problem I as a father face, is why my child should revere me. Unless my child will sense in my personal existence acts and attitudes that evoke reverence—the ability to delay satisfactions, to overcome prejudices, to sense the holy, to strive for the noble—why should she revere me?" He concludes, "Only a person who lives in a way which is compatible with the mystery of human existence is capable of evoking reverence in the child. The problem is the parent, not the child."[16] Here Heschel asks his audience to consider the adults who shape students' experiences. Teachers who develop meaningful visions for their lives have something to offer their students.[17]

Heschel suggests that the ability to revere prepares students to practice compassion and tenderness. Teachers also benefit from cultivating reverence. Roosevelt Montás argues that education begins with a teacher's reverence for students. Education begins in care. Montás contends that what distinguishes education from instruction is care for students. In his account, "education is cultivation into a particular community"—and that begins with human connection. "The first thing that matters is whether teachers care about students. That's step one. If the students do not get a sense that you care about them as individuals, it's game over."[18]

Similarly, Jacques Maritain proposes that reverence is the prerequisite of education. He writes, "Thus what is of most importance in educators themselves is a respect for the soul as well as for the body of the child, the sense of his innermost essence and his internal resources, a sort of sacred and loving attention to his mysterious identity, which is a hidden thing that no techniques can reach."[19] A sound approach to teaching begins with reverence—a sense of the sacredness of persons.

Education is an ethical art, as Maritain suggests, because it aims to form persons toward an awakening of conscience and care.[20] Engagement with suffering is essential to a coherent moral formation. In the first place, an education should help a person know how to meet suffering and how to suffer with others. As Heschel affirms, "Being a person involves the ability to suffer himself, to suffer for others; to know *passio*, passion, as well as compassion."[21] Second, becoming educated involves learning that you are not alone in your suffering. In James Baldwin's insight: "You think your pain and your heartbreak are unprecedented in the history of the world, but then you read."

Third, a coherent education enables students to replace ethical callousness with care. To an American educational system oriented toward material success, Heschel suggests a better aim: "Our greatest threat is not the atomic bomb. Our greatest threat is the callousness to the suffering of man. The most urgent task faced by American education is to destroy the myth that accumulation of wealth and the achievement of comfort are the chief vocations of man."[22] To understand how American civic education might address agony, I next examine the intersection of democracy and suffering.

DEMOCRACY AND SUFFERING

An account of politics that fails to search out and address suffering is blind to important political realities. These realities include suffering as a powerful motivation for acting politically and suffering as a politically combustible reality.[23] These realities also include fear of suffering as a powerful motive for action—and as a factor in passing judgment on whose lives are worth living or protecting. Abraham Joshua Heschel observes democracy in America. He offers an account sensitive to the plight of humans. In his telling, it is difficult for humans to be forthright about the fragility of life. He writes: "Outwardly, Homo sapiens may pretend to be satisfied and strong; inwardly he is poor, needy, vulnerable, always on the verge of misery, prone to suffer mentally and physically. Scratch his skin and you come upon bereavement, affliction, uncertainty, fear, and pain."[24] Heschel concludes that people—and democratic citizens especially—deny their suffering in order to fit into society. "Disparity between his appearance and reality is a condition of social integration. Suppressions are the price he pays for being accepted in society. Adjustment involves assenting to odd auspices, concessions of conscience, inevitable hypocrisies. It is, indeed, often 'a life of quiet desperation.'"[25]

As a Jew who loses sisters and mother and home and culture during the Holocaust, Heschel experiences some of the greatest evils of human action. When he arrives as a refugee in America, he witnesses the ways in which Americans suffer. Some suffer racial injustice.[26] Some suffer from a lack of meaning.[27] Heschel watches Americans in desperate pursuit of satisfaction.

To suffer is part of the human condition. One finds enduring questions in ancient sources as well as in conversations with friends: Why do bad things happen to the people I love? Why do bad things happen to me? Why do people commit harm? Why do floods sweep away houses and children? It belongs to the human condition to suffer—and to question our suffering.

At the same time, democracy exacerbates certain kinds of suffering. What democracy does to suffering is, first, to render it politically relevant. Tocqueville recognizes the connection between political stability and suffering in democracy. He observes, "When the people govern, it is necessary that they be happy in order for them not to overturn the state. Misery produces in them what ambition does in kings."[28] Second, democracy intensifies democratic citizens' search for meaning as it spurs a limitless pursuit of material well-being. In the process, the spread of equality fuels comparison and, consequently, renders one's own suffering more intolerable.[29] Finally, democracy promotes individualism—a temptation to withdraw from public life on liberalism's assumption that I don't need others, owe anything to others, or deserve anything from others.[30] One antidote to that individualism is compassion—an ability to get beyond the rhetoric of liberalism to act to admit my need or address my neighbor's need.[31]

What suffering does to democracy is to reinforce a sense of isolation. The spread of democracy abolishes hierarchies—and in the process renders citizens equally strong, or equally impotent. As Harvey Mansfield and Delba Winthrop write, "The suffering of others, in fact, can add to one's own sense of impotence, thus to the deepest ill of democratic equality, which Tocqueville calls 'individualism,' the self-isolation induced by the belief that an individual by himself can do nothing within a mass of people ruled by vast social forces."[32] Democracy can undermine agency and leave the people feeling helpless in the face of misery.[33]

Suffering is what humans share but want to hide. This state of being has personal as well as political implications. How do we craft an approach to politics that takes in the reality of our plight? A habit of searching out, rather than ignoring or denying, suffering can better inform political understanding.[34]

An immediate counterpoint might be that American education neither ignores nor denies suffering. Instead, one might object, American parents, teachers, and education administrators highlight suffering and treat it with kid gloves. But hypersensitivity to what discomforts students is not the same thing as offering resources to engage suffering. In their 2018 book, *The Coddling of the American Mind*, Greg Lukianoff and Jonathan Haidt argue that in recent years parents, teachers, and administrators have overprotected American students from encounters with difficulty that enable growth.[35] This hypersensitivity to discomfort erodes the skills that enable students to meaningfully approach suffering.

A key place where American high school and college education hides or ignores suffering is in the curriculum. Conventional curricula often address events abstractly; they gloss over human agency and pain. They reflect a habit of thinking in terms of general forces—a failure to notice the persons who live and create events.

Moreover, to expose students to suffering is not the same thing as guiding them through a meaningful encounter with a person or experience or dilemma.[36] Some of the obvious places where we might encounter suffering include events of overwhelming terror or horror. Take, for example, the practice of American slavery or the Holocaust. Richard Rubenstein argues, in his analysis of the causes of the Holocaust, that terror prevents Americans from thinking about the Holocaust. Terror overwhelms thought. Suffering has the capacity to "obscure comprehension."[37] A pedagogy of suffering provides practices that enable teachers to guide students through profoundly difficult stories.

PEDAGOGY OF SUFFERING BUILDS CIVIC EDUCATION

Ethical literacy is a significant dimension of discovering who we are as human beings. A competent ethical literacy is especially important for democratic citizens. Here I consider a pedagogy of suffering as a means to build ethical literacy. The skills to engage suffering—one's own and others'—are key to an adequate civic education. A pedagogy of suffering develops practices that enable democratic citizens to respond to the political significance of pathos. What virtues enable students to approach suffering? I outline six practices that students can develop through a pedagogy that attends to agony.

Develop Courage

First, a pedagogy that attends to agony cultivates courage. Courage enables students to approach suffering. But modern democracy does not, on its own, foster courage. In Tocqueville's account, democratic citizens seek equality over freedom because equality is immediately pleasant, while freedom, as James Baldwin later puts it, "is hard to bear."[38] Democratic citizens seek what is more immediately pleasant. Courage, meanwhile, is a virtue one develops through experiences of not giving up in the face of discomfort or danger.

Democracy encourages citizens to feel helpless, impotent. To counter this tendency, competent civic education should help citizens develop maturity and resilience through courage. James Baldwin makes the connection between courage and maturity in *The Fire Next Time*. He observes America's commercial decadence.[39] He argues that white Americans distract themselves from suffering or celebrating.[40] Their distractions disorient them, and they lose depth of communion with themselves and others.[41]

In Baldwin's account, keeping one another from slipping into this "spiritual and social ease" is "probably, hard and odd as it may sound, the most important thing a human being can do for another—it is certainly *one* of the most important things; hence the torment and necessity of love." Baldwin upholds the value of helping each other resist "spiritual and social ease" because, he insists, "It is the responsibility of free men to trust and celebrate what is constant—birth, struggle, and death are constant, and so is love, though we may not always think so."[42]

As he recognizes what is constant, Baldwin also sees what is tragic: "Life is tragic." He continues, "Life is tragic simply because the earth turns and the sun inexorably rises and sets, and one day, for each of us, the sun will go down for the last, last time." In the face of mortality, Baldwin urges, "One is responsible to life: It is the small beacon in that terrifying darkness from which we come and to which we shall return. One must negotiate this passage as nobly as possible, for the sake of those who are coming after us." The problem, in Baldwin's account, is that "white Americans do not believe in death."[43] That is, in Baldwin's evaluation, white Americans commit to commercial decadence as a means of distracting themselves from suffering and celebrating in the face of mortality.

Baldwin finds resolution in the possibilities of love. He diagnoses a resistance to suffering and celebrating—rooted in a fear of being known by one's fellow citizens. Recall Heschel: "Disparity between his appearance and reality is a condition of social integration."[44] Baldwin considers that love makes it possible to remedy this disparity. "Love takes off the masks that we fear we cannot live without and know we cannot live within." To a society—perhaps even more now than then—fixated on sentimental views of love, Baldwin clarifies his meaning: "I use the word 'love' here not merely in the personal sense but as a state of being, or a state of grace—not in the infantile American sense of being made happy but in the tough and universal sense of quest and daring and growth."[45] Baldwin holds that courage that enables quest and daring and growth will answer a "sore need" for "new standards." These new standards include practices in which persons learn to suffer and celebrate.[46]

Finally, the courage to love—and therefore to suffer and to celebrate—brings maturity. Baldwin finds in a past of horror and suffering "something very beautiful." He clarifies: "I do not mean to be sentimental about suffering—enough is certainly as good as a feast—but people who cannot suffer can never grow up, can never discover who they are."[47] Baldwin's primary hope for Americans is that they will achieve maturity. And the key to maturing is to develop the courage to suffer and celebrate.

Compare a related point on courage. Recall Richard Rubenstein's observation that terror overwhelms thought.[48] Courage, on the other hand, enables students to approach suffering. Courage can repair the rupture with thought in the face of terror to enable students to reflect on who did what to commit mass murder, for example. Following Socrates, Hannah Arendt holds this kind of dialogue with oneself to be critical to moral action.[49]

Recognize Tragic Conflict
A second practice that a pedagogy of suffering facilitates is the work of recognizing tragic conflict. Students who are not attuned to suffering tend to miss the possibility of conflict between legitimate, competing claims. Whether you're reading Aeschylus's *Oresteia* or *Masterpiece Cakeshop v. Colorado* (2018), students benefit when they can see and struggle with tragic conflict.

Current debates in America include, for example, whether to limit access to firearms and whether to end legal abortion. In both debates, citizens need intellectual humility to listen to others' experiences, fortitude to stay in difficult conversations with one another, and an openness to persuasion. A practice of attending to the possibility of conflict between legitimate, irreconcilable claims nurtures these virtues. In turn, these virtues prepare citizens for deliberation in the face of difficult conflicts.

Prepare for Sacrifice
A pedagogy of suffering can, third, incline students to see opportunities for noble sacrifice. In a Hobbesian world that warns against risk, students tend to be unfamiliar with stories or discourse that holds that some things—and people—are worth living and dying for. How can students do the great things a functioning democracy requires if they lack exemplars who are willing to risk safety for noble causes? A pedagogy that attends to agony makes room for those exemplars.

Through encounters with the stories of people who sacrifice for others, students can develop the virtues of love, generosity, and openness to life. Liberal democracy amplifies a native human aversion to suffering. By contrast, the lives of exemplars such as Harriet Jacobs, Fannie Lou Hamer, Malcolm X, Roberto Clemente, Dorothy Day, and Arnaud Beltrame give students admirable models of sacrifice.[50]

To raise one significant example, a readiness to sacrifice for others is also vital in creating a political community that treats persons with physical or mental disabilities with dignity. Many democratic citizens assume that suffering should be "secret or a source of shame."[51] In a political society modeled on the idea of the self-sufficient individual, it is easy for our conceptions of a life worth living to exclude lives that contain suffering. As we extend our technologies, such as selective prenatal screening, ordinary persons find themselves in positions to decide who should live.[52] Exemplars who help us to give ourselves for others prepare us to accompany each other in seasons, or lifetimes, of fragility or disability.

Exercise Empathy
Empathy is a fourth practice that a pedagogy of suffering fosters. "Empathy," writes Martin Luther King Jr., "is fellow feeling for the person in need—his pain, agony and burdens."[53] For King, the possibility of returning from "the far country of racism" to the home of democracy ("soundly grounded on the insights of our Judeo-Christian heritage") depends on empathy. King

concludes, "I doubt if the problems of our teeming ghettos will have a great chance to be solved until the white majority, through genuine empathy, comes to feel the ache and anguish of the Negroes' daily life." The practice of empathy develops the virtue of compassion. Democracy depends on citizens' ability exercise compassion—to imagine or enter others' experiences and act accordingly.

Find Alternatives to Vengeance
Fifth, a pedagogy attentive to suffering can approach the desire for vengeance that grows out of intense pain. From my hometown's exploding homicide rate to my students' insistence that the best justification for the atomic bombs at Hiroshima and Nagasaki is "revenge," I'm convinced that democratic citizens need an education that understands the desire to retaliate—and offers a better path. Ancient Greek poets and contemporary headlines alike confirm that injury breeds a desire to retaliate. The same sources also show that one retaliation provokes another. It is difficult to end the cycle of bloodlust. To address the desire for revenge, we need to notice the agony that feeds it and find an alternative path of action.

Once we get that far, we might turn to Aeschylus or James Cone for suggestions on alternatives to vengeance.[54] We might turn to Hannah Arendt or Elizabeth Bruenig or Rabbi Jonathan Sacks or the Mother Emanuel AME Church community, who offer a way to end the cycle of vengeance.[55] These persons propose forgiveness as a politically significant act. Without forgiveness, we are bound to what others have done. Forgiveness allows for anger and reckoning, while releasing the one who forgives and the one forgiven from the cycle of vengeance. Forgiveness does not erase injury. Instead, it frees us from the irreversibility of action; it allows us to begin again.

Engage the Task of Being Human—and the Humanities
Last, a pedagogy that attends to agony enables students to connect with what Heschel calls *the task of being human*. "It is a fatal illusion to assume that to be human is a fact given with human being rather than a goal and an achievement." He continues, "To be human we must know what humanity means and how to acquire it. Our being human is always on trial, full of risk, precarious. Being human is an opportunity as well as a fact."[56]

Heschel measures a person's response to the task of being human by that person's sensitivity to suffering: "The degree to which one is sensitive to other people's suffering, to other men's humanity, is the index of one's own humanity. It is the root not only for social living but also of the study of the humanities. The vital presupposition of the philosopher's question about man is his care for man." In fact, Heschel holds that human agency and suffering have created new criteria for philosophy itself: "Philosophy cannot be the same after Auschwitz and Hiroshima. . . . Philosophy, to be relevant, must offer us a wisdom to live by—relevant not only in the isolation of our study rooms but also in moments of facing staggering cruelty and the threat of disaster."[57]

Engaging the humanities opens opportunities to act with care. The way a teacher approaches something as simple as showing a documentary on the Holocaust can either leave students feeling helpless or empower students to reflect and act. Simply pressing play on the documentary brings students face-to-face with staggering thoughtlessness and evil. But taking time to talk with students about what kinds of choices people made, and why, enables students to reflect on how they deal with weakness, prejudice, or fear.

For example, I recently showed *The Last Days*, a documentary on the Holocaust of Hungarian Jews.[58] The documentary had been recently rereleased and became part of the curriculum on short notice. I realized I needed to frame the film for my students. I share my approach to the documentary as an example of a classroom practice rooted in a pedagogy of suffering: Before I press play, I talk with my students about why we might watch such a documentary. Elie Wiesel says, "Listening to a witness makes you a witness." We talk about what that means—and what it means for us as we are about to witness painful stories in history class.

Before we watch, I provide questions for reflection, printed with room for students' responses. The first question is, "What do you know about the Holocaust, or Shoah?" They write in silence for two minutes. Then we watch. If I cry in the class period, I do not hide my tears.

After we watch, the students spend a few minutes responding to the next two questions: "What do you want to know now?" and "What did you learn that you did not know before?" We talk through what the students have written. I ask whoever is willing to share their new questions. We take a few minutes to discuss these questions. It is not necessary to try to answer all the questions. The goal is to invite students to share their responses to what they have witnessed.

To close, I describe Hannah Arendt's insight that most people who commit harm do so, initially, not out of malice, but out of *thoughtlessness*. (On another showing, I might talk about Abraham Joshua Heschel's insight on the *evil of indifference*—the evil of not caring what happens to others.) We talk about what thoughtlessness means, and what it looks like in the context of the stories we just witnessed. Finally, we talk about examples of our own thoughtlessness (or indifference), and how we might resist moral callousness in the face of injustices that seem normal in our society.

This kind of framing doesn't take away the sting of wickedness. It is instead designed to help students realize that they do not have to be overcome by evil but can, in ordinary ways, overcome evil with good.

The goal of approaching suffering is not to leave students stunned, but to introduce them to the possibilities of ethical action in response to callousness. A pedagogy that attends to agony justifies the humanities as a reflection on the task of being human.

CONCLUSION

As part of an adequate civic education, teachers can find ways to talk about suffering that move students from impatience to compassion. Heschel writes, "One cannot study the condition of man without being touched by the plight of man."[59] The aim of developing a moral sensitivity to suffering is to respond to the human condition in a way that heals. Students who have the skills to engage suffering can help sustain democracy through practices such as the ability to listen, deliberate, persuade, care about other's well-being, and serve. With practice, this approach fosters virtues that connect students with the "condition and plight of man." When teachers prepare students to attend to suffering, they meet human and democratic restlessness with a summons to respond with care.

NOTES

I am grateful for conversations with Cecil Eubanks, John Kitch, Amanda Achtman, Constantine Vassiliou, Stephanie Aherns, an anonymous reviewer, and my university and high school students.

1. Alexander Livingston, "Power for the Powerless: Martin Luther King, Jr.'s Late Theory of Civil Disobedience," 701.

2. The AMA's opioid epidemic task force tracks data from 2010 to the present at https://end-overdose-epidemic.org/data-dashboard/.

3. As evidence: By May 2022, Bessel van der Kolk's 2014 written-for-specialists study of trauma, *The Body Keeps the Score*, had been on the *New York Times*' best-seller list for 185 weeks—dating back to October 2018. See https://www.nytimes.com/books/best-sellers/.

4. Abraham Joshua Heschel, *Who Is Man?*, 16, 29. Similarly, in his study of education, philosopher Jacques Maritain quotes the Greek poet Pindar on the key task of human beings: our chief duty is *becoming who we are*. Maritain, *Education at the Crossroads*, 1.

5. See Maritain, *Education at the Crossroads*, 10.

6. Aristotle, *Politics*, bk. 8.3, 1338a30–35, 226.

7. Greg Lukianoff and Jonathan Haidt, *The Coddling of the American Mind*, 186, 189.

8. Consider: "Success as the object of supreme and exclusive concern is both pernicious and demonic. Such passion knows no limit." Abraham Joshua Heschel, "The Patient as a Person," in *The Insecurity of Freedom*, 34.

9. I'm concerned here about students chasing their counselors' or parents' markers of social success. I don't dispute the good of having others encourage a person toward good they cannot themselves fully appreciate. See Zena Hitz: "[The objects of our desires] pull us along in a particular direction, opening up possibilities to us that we did not choose or expect. This simple psychological fact is the reason why there is such a thing as education—why using our minds, or learning to paint, or losing weight requires not only discipline and social incentives but also the guidance of wise elders who know what lies along certain pathways, and who are willing to expose their own ignorance and uncertainty when guiding the young." Hitz, *Lost in Thought: The Hidden Pleasures of an Intellectual Life*, 31.

10. Robert P. George and Margarita A. Mooney, "Does Human Nature Matter for Education?," in *The Love of Learning: Seven Dialogues on the Liberal Arts*, ed. Margarita A. Mooney, 6. Robert P. George observes that these kinds of questions are supremely practical questions.

11. Elizabeth Corey and Margarita A. Mooney, "Learning in Love: Authentic Friendships and Liberal Learning," in *Love of Learning*, ed. Mooney, 53.

12. Ariel Burger, *Witness: Lessons from the Classroom of Elie Wiesel*, 23.

13. Thanks to Cecil Eubanks for this conversation.

14. Mooney, *Love of Learning*, 162.

15. Abraham Joshua Heschel, "Children and Youth," in *The Insecurity of Freedom*, 39.

16. Heschel, "Children and Youth," in *The Insecurity of Freedom*, 39–40.

17. Parker Palmer, *The Courage to Teach* and *Let Your Life Speak*.

18. Roosevelt Montás and Margarita A. Mooney, "Is a Liberal Arts Education Elitist?," in *Love of Learning*, ed. Mooney, 158.

19. Maritain, *Education at the Crossroads*, 9–10.

20. Maritain, *Education at the Crossroads*, 2–3.

21. Heschel, "Patient as a Person," in *The Insecurity of Freedom*, 24.

22. Heschel, "Children and Youth," in *The Insecurity of Freedom*, 51.

23. See Martin Luther King Jr., "Letter from Birmingham Jail" and *Where Do We Go from Here?* See also Matthew S. Berry, "The Alt Right and the Religious Impulse: A Tocquevillian Analysis."

24. Heschel, *Who Is Man?*, 15. Also: "Scratch the skin of any person and you come upon sorrow, frustration, unhappiness. People are pretentious. Everybody looks proud; inside he is heartbroken." Abraham Joshua Heschel, *Moral Grandeur and Spiritual Audacity*, 146.

25. Heschel, *Who Is Man?*, 15, quoting Thoreau.

26. Abraham Joshua Heschel, "Religion and Race" and "The White Man on Trial," in *The Insecurity of Freedom*.

27. Abraham Joshua Heschel, *The Sabbath*.

28. Alexis de Tocqueville, *Democracy in America*, I.2.9, 267.

29. Tocqueville, *Democracy in America*, II.2.13, 511–54. See also Benjamin Storey and Jenna Silber Storey, *Why We Are Restless*.

30. Tocqueville, *Democracy in America*, II.2.2, 482–84.

31. Tocqueville, *Democracy in America*, II.2.4–5, 489–92, II.3.4, 545.

32. Tocqueville, introduction to *Democracy in America*, xxxviii.

33. Tocqueville, *Democracy in America*, II.1.20, 471–72.

34. For example, Wendell Berry corrects reductive accounts of American politics with attention to the suffering of rural America in Hope Reese, "Wendell Berry Is Still Ahead of Us."

35. Lukianoff and Haidt, *Coddling of the American Mind*.

36. When we teach students about these events, a statement of fact concerning suffering is not enough. To say who suffered and when and where is insufficient. Instead, it is essential to guide students as they discover the moral meaning of those facts. Thanks to Amanda Achtman for sharing this insight.

37. Richard Rubenstein, *The Cunning of History*, 3.

38. James Baldwin, *The Fire Next Time* (New York: Vintage, 1992 [1963]), 88.

39. Baldwin, *The Fire Next Time*.

40. The significance of celebrating is another important theme for democratic citizens. In his last major interview, Heschel says that, in order to resist despair, young people need to "remember that life is a celebration" and learn how to celebrate. Interview with Carl Stern in *Moral Grandeur and Spiritual Audacity* and at 33:46 in https://www.youtube.com/watch?v=FEXK9xcRCho.

41. Baldwin, *The Fire Next Time*, 43.

42. Baldwin, *The Fire Next Time*, 85–86, 92.

43. Baldwin, *The Fire Next Time*, 91, 92.

44. Heschel, *Who Is Man?*, 15.

45. Baldwin, *The Fire Next Time*, 95.

46. Baldwin, *The Fire Next Time*, 97, 96.

47. Baldwin, *The Fire Next Time*, 98.

48. Rubenstein, *The Cunning of History*, 3; see above.

49. Hannah Arendt, "Thinking and Moral Considerations," in *Responsibility and Judgment*.

50. Harriet Jacobs, author of one of America's most important slave narratives, sacrifices her freedom to rescue her children from abuse. Fannie Lou Hamer endures physical and emotional violence to secure the right to vote in her community. Malcolm X risks his life to articulate injustices he observed. Dorothy Day embraces a life of poverty to serve impoverished Americans. Even as he deals personally with unjust treatment, baseball player Roberto Clemente lives a life of service to others—and eventually dies in the effort. Arnaud Beltrame trades his life to liberate a woman held by ISIS. There are many more examples—often hidden in the topics students are already studying.

51. JD Flynn, "I Have Two Kids with Down Syndrome. Here's What I Wish Those Considering Abortion Knew about Life with Them."

52. Sarah Zhang, "The Last Children of Down Syndrome: Prenatal Testing and the Future of Down Syndrome."

53. King, *Where Do We Go from Here?*, 107.

54. Aeschylus, *Oresteia*; James Cone, *The Cross and the Lynching Tree*.

55. Hannah Arendt, *The Human Condition*, 236–43; Sean Illing, "Why Is It So Hard to Forgive? Elizabeth Bruenig on Forgiveness and the Performative Cruelty of the Digital Age"; Rabbi Jonathan Sacks, "An Unforgiving Age"; Mark Berman, "'I Forgive You': Relatives of Charleston Church Shooting Victims Address Dylann Roof," *Washington Post*, June 19, 2015, https://www.washingtonpost.com/news/post-nation/wp/2015/06/19/i-forgive-you-relatives-of-charleston-church-victims-address-dylann-roof/.

56. Heschel, *Who Is Man?*, 41, 42.

57. Heschel, *Who Is Man?*, 46–47, 13.

58. *The Last Days*, directed by James Moll, produced by Stephen Spielberg, June Beallor, and Kenneth Lipper (1998; Los Angeles: USC Shoah Foundation, remastered 2021).

59. Heschel, *Who Is Man?*, 15.

BIBLIOGRAPHY

Aeschylus. *Oresteia*. Translated by Richmond Lattimore. Chicago: University of Chicago Press, 1953.

American Medical Association. Opioid Epidemic Task Force Data, 2010–2022. https://end-overdose-epidemic.org/data-dashboard/.

Arendt, Hannah. *The Human Condition*. 1958. Reprint, Chicago: University of Chicago Press, 1996.

———. *Responsibility and Judgment*. New York: Schocken, 2003.

Aristotle. *Politics*. Edited and translated by Carnes Lord. 2nd ed. Chicago: University of Chicago Press, 2013.

Baldwin, James. *The Fire Next Time*. 1963. Reprint, New York: Vintage, 1992.

Berry, Matthew S. "The Alt Right and the Religious Impulse: A Tocquevillian Analysis." *American Political Thought* 8, no. 1 (2019): 1–24.

Burger, Ariel. *Witness: Lessons from the Classroom of Elie Wiesel*. Boston: Mariner Books, 2018.

Cone, James. *The Cross and the Lynching Tree*. Maryknoll, NY: Orbis Books, 2013.

Flynn, JD. "I Have Two Kids with Down Syndrome. Here's What I Wish Those Considering Abortion Knew about Life with Them." *America Magazine*, November 19, 2020. https://www.americamagazine.org/faith/2020/11/19/catholic-down-syndrome-adoption-abortion.

Heschel, Abraham Joshua. *The Insecurity of Freedom*. Philadelphia: Jewish Publication Society, 1966.

———. *Moral Grandeur and Spiritual Audacity*. Edited by Susannah Heschel. New York: Farrar, Straus & Giroux, 1996.

———. *The Sabbath*. 1951. Reprint, New York: Farrar, Straus & Giroux, 2005.

———. *Who Is Man?* Stanford, CA: Stanford University Press, 1965.

Hitz, Zena. *Lost in Thought: The Hidden Pleasures of an Intellectual Life*. Princeton, NJ: Princeton University Press, 2020.

Illing, Sean. "Why Is It So Hard to Forgive? Elizabeth Bruenig on Forgiveness and the Performative Cruelty of the Digital Age." *Vox*, July 12, 2021. https://www.vox.com/vox-conversations-podcast/2021/7/12/22379647/vox-conversations-elizabeth-bruenig-forgiveness-social-media.

King, Martin Luther, Jr. "Letter from Birmingham Jail." In *A Testament of Hope*, edited by James M. Washington. New York: HarperCollins, 1963.

———. *Where Do We Go from Here?* 1968. Reprint, Boston: Beacon Press, 2010.

Livingston, Alexander. "Power for the Powerless: Martin Luther King, Jr.'s Late Theory of Civil Disobedience." *Journal of Politics* 82, no. 2 (2020): 700–713.

Lukianoff, Greg, and Jonathan Haidt. *The Coddling of the American Mind*. New York: Penguin, 2019.

Maritain, Jacques. *Education at the Crossroads*. New Haven, CT: Yale University Press, 1943.

Mooney, Margarita A., ed. *The Love of Learning: Seven Dialogues on the Liberal Arts*. Providence, RI: CLUNY Media, 2021.

Palmer, Palmer. *The Courage to Teach*. San Francisco: Jossey-Bass, 1998.

———. *Let Your Life Speak*. San Francisco: Jossey-Bass, 2000.

Reese, Hope. "Wendell Berry Is Still Ahead of Us." *Vox*, October 9, 2019. https://www.vox.com/the-highlight/2019/10/2/20862854/wendell-berry-climate-change-port-royal-michael-pollan.

Rubenstein, Richard. *The Cunning of History*. New York: Harper Perennial, 1975.

Sacks, Jonathan. "An Unforgiving Age." Rabbi Sacks Legacy Trust, September 21, 2019. https://www.youtube.com/watch?v=0MaU0kfkK-k.

Storey, Benjamin, and Jenna Silber Storey. *Why We Are Restless*. Princeton, NJ: Princeton University Press, 2021.

Tocqueville, Alexis de. *Democracy in America*. Edited and translated by Harvey Mansfield and Delba Winthrop. Chicago: University of Chicago Press, 2000.

Van der Kolk, Bessel. *The Body Keeps the Score*. New York: Penguin, 2015.

Zhang, Sarah. "The Last Children of Down Syndrome: Prenatal Testing and the Future of Down Syndrome." *Atlantic*, December 15, 2020. https://www.theatlantic.com/magazine/archive/2020/12/the-last-children-of-down-syndrome/616928/.

13. The Cosmopolitan Education of Hobbits
Friendship and Political Deliberation in Tolkien's *The Fellowship of the Ring*
William E. DeMars

COSMOPOLITANISM AND LIBERAL EDUCATION

In the twenty-first century, we are increasingly thrown together in a tangle of global encounters and mutual influences with more people, some of whom we think we could very well live without. The problem of cosmopolitanism versus provincialism presses urgently once again, not only in American culture and politics, but also in the world.[1] Interdependence often feels more menacing than mellowing. Indeed, we are united by global trade, social media, novel pandemics, the uncertain US dollar, resurgent risks of nuclear crisis or catastrophe, and escalating threats from the gases we emit and exhale. Yet we are divided by all the same things, increasingly withdrawing, with reciprocal outrage, into both tribal nationalism and sometimes equally tribal cosmopolitanism. How can we listen to and learn from each other today, without the psychological armor of a guarantee to a sustainable, or even recognizable, future?

Our crises of cosmopolitanism versus provincialism coincide dangerously with another crisis, in liberal education. American liberal arts colleges (and also American research universities that still harbor an undergraduate liberal arts college) build on traditions of educating free citizens for self-rule that began with the Greeks and Romans twenty-five hundred years ago. Athens and Rome, in their own times, were groundbreaking democracies at the core of extensive international empires, with all the soaring aspirations, prodigious but incomplete achievements, and vicious contradictions implied therein. In these ways they were much like America today. The availability and quality of liberal education—education for liberty—were then and remain profoundly incomplete in their extension to all citizens (picture the young Alexander the Great and friends learning philosophy, politics, ethics, logic, medicine, and art at Aristotle's knee). Despite the enormous historical gaps and changes, however, American liberal arts colleges claim today, with Aristotle's Lyceum then, to be privileged places for the education of free, cosmopolitan citizens.[2]

Today our colleges are hammered by demographic, pandemic, and economic recessions. Many of our students are hobbled by debt, competing fiercely for a place in a shrinking middle class, and anguished by the responsibility to solve the growing catalog of global problems that we elders and teachers have bequeathed to them. As I drafted this chapter, my own students and I were sequestered in our homes or dorm rooms by the unseen threat of coronavirus, struggling to reconnect online, waiting to be saved by science.

At a broader institutional level, college faculties and student bodies are wracked by the same forces as our larger society: cultural insurgencies and counterinsurgencies, clashes between seemingly incommensurable ideologies and experiences, and alternate sets of facts. But the stakes are different on college campuses. If even we—for whom so much time, money, and care are invested to cultivate a space for our free inquiry and dialogue—fail to overcome the obstacles to civil and illumining conversation on the toughest questions, then what hope is there for our peoples and nations? This is why the crises of cosmopolitanism and of liberal education are so tightly intertwined. In short, our colleges are called, against all odds to be sure, to host the vital encounters in which our larger challenges of living together freely and well may be faced, or not. Such encounters and conversations are the stuff of the cosmopolitanism that we need.

The four Hobbits who are the chief protagonists in J. R. R. Tolkien's trilogy *The Lord of the Rings* (regardless of whether one finds them captivating or maddening) can help us navigate these challenges today. Their adventures can expand the imaginative landscape of our thinking about education, cosmopolitanism, friendship, and political deliberation. But first, some philosophical rockhounding is necessary to grasp a few touchstones to make the stories philosophically intelligible.

WITH A LITTLE HELP FROM OUR FRIENDS

Cosmopolitanism is not a single philosophy, religion, educational program, or political position. There have been many cosmopolitanisms in human history, and there are many cosmopolitan proposals today, far beyond the scope of this chapter to survey.³ Nevertheless, Kwame Anthony Appiah and Hannah Arendt may help us understand how some kinds of conversations are central to the cultivation of cosmopolitanism and political deliberation, and also how some capacity for friendship is necessary for those conversations.

Appiah's point of departure is the insight that cosmopolitanism "is the name not of the solution but of the challenge." Recognizing that he possesses no made-to-order formula or philosophy, he sets out at least to map the shape of the challenge, now in the early twenty-first century. The challenge of cosmopolitanism emerges first, from the astonishing power and ease with which we—individually and also collectively through our governments—can send things worth having and also things that harm to "any other of our six billion conspecifics" in the world.⁴ The second part of the current challenge of cosmopolitanism is our capacity through modern communications to learn about the lives of people anywhere.

Our moral challenge of cosmopolitanism, therefore, appears in consequence of our pervasive powers to transport and communicate. For Appiah, the quantitative increase of these powers has created a qualitatively new challenge for our collective humanity: "Each person you know about and can affect is someone to whom you have responsibilities: to say this is just to affirm the very idea of morality. The challenge, then, is to take minds and hearts formed over the long millennia of living in local troops and equip them with ideas and institutions that will allow us to live together as the global tribe we have become." From these contemporary realities two intertwining ethical implications emerge: the first is "the idea that we have obligations to others," including strangers and foreigners, and the second is "that we take seriously the value not just of human life but of particular human lives, which means taking interest in the practices and beliefs that lend them significance."⁵

This second ethical implication—to take interest in the practices and beliefs of others—presupposes that we think we may be able to learn something from them, even those whose beliefs we do not share, disagree with, or abhor. This is the point where Appiah's challenge of cosmopolitanism begins to demand something more than a casual commitment. Appiah's core proposal "begins with the simple idea that in the human community, as in national communities, we need to develop habits of coexistence: conversation in its older meaning, of living together, association."⁶

To develop ingrained habits of coexistence and conversation, especially "conversation between people of different ways of life," could impinge on our lifestyles.[7] In such conversations, Appiah proposes, we would learn what others believe and value, and then, in a much more challenging step, endeavor to identify along with them which values ought to be universal and which others may remain local. Although Appiah does not often discuss friendship, we might infer that conducting such significant and serious conversations presupposes cultivating some degree of trust, or even friendship, between the interlocutors.

Appiah argues that conversations across such borders can be pleasurable. He supports this with captivating tales of his own childhood moving gracefully between nations, social classes, religious faiths, and political struggles, with his English mother (art historian Peggy Cripps Appiah) and his Ghanaian father (lawyer, independence politician, and diplomat Joe Appiah).

However, from a standpoint in 2022, we may need a somewhat stronger response to the question *Why bother?* At a personal level, why would I undergo voluntarily the sheer trouble, cognitive dissonance, and emotional wear-and-tear of listening to, and really taking in, the views and experiences of people I have already decided are probably crazy, certainly dangerous, and possibly traitors to constitutive institutions and norms of civilized life? Why would I take up that secular cross of multicultural dialogue when I can comfortably numb myself in a cocoon of ideological monoculture?

Hannah Arendt may be able to help us here. She also takes seriously, and can help us synthesize, the seemingly disparate realities of civic conversation, friendship, deliberation, and education. However, we cannot ignore the elusive and paradoxical features of Arendt's thought. She strongly admonished her students against abstract theorizing and in favor of thinking and rethinking particular realities of past and present. At the same time, she resolutely read and reinterpreted the entire body of Western political thought from Socrates through Nietzsche. But the best argument against giving up the quest for understanding is her example—she never gave up learning and judging. Therefore, much like for Appiah, the hermeneutical key to Hannah Arendt's thought is her own life story.

Hannah Arendt was born in Germany in 1906 to a family of educated and assimilated Jews and spent most of her youth in Königsberg (now Kaliningrad, the discontinuous Russian enclave on the Baltic Sea). She undertook a harrowing personal and political journey, which paralleled her intellectual itinerary, including romance, betrayal, narrow escapes, flight as a refugee across land and sea, a productive and controversial exile in America, and many intense, transformational friendships.[8] Arendt talked her way out of Gestapo detention in Berlin in 1933 (for the crime of Zionist library research) and escaped a Nazi internment camp again in occupied France in 1940, before landing in New York City in 1941. Along the way, she made a series of judgments, not only practical judgments of what to do, but also piercing recognitions—factual judgments—of events from the past and of realities in front of her in the world. Elisabeth Young-Bruehl testifies to the significance of particular friendships in her life: "Hannah Arendt had, as Hans Jonas remarked at her funeral, a 'genius for friendship.' In her own words, what moved her was the *Eros der Freundshaft*; and she considered her friendships the center of her life."[9]

Arendt's central intellectual preoccupations were how the West had lost the capacity for deliberative speech, judgment, and self-direction and how to reconstitute it in some form without recourse to any of our inherited, and failed, cultural, philosophical, or religious frameworks for assessment and judgment. This concern began to emerge very early in her life. She had read Kierkegaard and Kant before she was sixteen years old.[10] In Marburg she studied with Martin Heidegger, and the two had a secret affair for four years. Even Heidegger's later collaboration with the Nazis to purge Jewish professors from universities did not cause Arendt to denounce him, nor to renounce her gratitude for his intellectual inspiration to "passionate thinking" and many other influences. She earned her doctorate at the University of Heidelberg in 1929, writing her thesis, "The Concept of Love in Saint Augustine," under the direction of the leading existentialist Karl Jaspers.

A minority interpretation of Arendt, led by some of her last group of graduate students, insists that Augustine's influence is the key to understanding all of her later writings.[11] Throughout the rest of her life, Arendt frequently quoted two lines from Augustine that she had emphasized in her 1929 doctoral dissertation. The first is "That there be a beginning, man was created before whom there was nobody." Arendt calls this the concept of natality. The second phrase is *amor mundi*, meaning "love of the world."

Jerome Kohn, Arendt's last research assistant in New York before her death in 1975, wrote in 2003, "Arendt was deeply indebted to Augustine for his experience of thinking as an activity guided by love of the goodness of what exists. Because thinking cannot be guided by evil, since evil destroys what exists, she came to believe that the activity of thinking conditions whoever engages in it against evil-doing."[12] In other words, *amor mundi* (love of the goodness of what exists) guides authentic thinking, which flows into sound judgment of good and evil, which makes it possible to avoid active participation in doing evil. More concisely, love of the world is the link between thinking and judgment. This influence was already embedded in her thinking by the completion of her dissertation on Augustine in 1929, shaping her later responses to the rise of the Nazis, her direct encounters with the Gestapo, their massive aggression and genocide during World War II, and the 1961 Adolf Eichmann trial.

During Eichmann's trial in Israel, which Arendt observed, she wrote that he had carefully avoided thinking about his contribution to the deportation of millions of Jews to Nazi death camps, and had therefore failed to judge and avoid this evil action.[13] Would it be fair for us to conclude that his failure to think and judge can be traced to his lack of love of the world?[14] Are the courage and hope needed to face and judge our own reality, and to do the right thing, part of love for the world, or are they needed in addition to it? How and where and with whom can we develop and cultivate such love of the world in ourselves and each other? Arendt's thinking on friendship and education provides part of an answer.

Arendt agreed with Aristotle that *friendship* between unequal citizens is the glue that holds together political communities: "Aristotle concludes that it is friendship not justice (as Plato maintained in the Republic, that great dialogue about justice) that appears to be the bond of communities. For Aristotle, friendship is higher than justice, because justice is no longer necessary between friends."[15] Frederick Dolan comments on this argument by Arendt: "Justice requires subordination to a universal principle that overrides any relationship between individuals. Talking things through in order to arrive at the truth of an opinion, on the other hand, yields no fixed result, involves give and take, and implies that friendship matters more than any particular assertion that friends might dispute."[16] More connections: love of the world is cultivated by talking things through in discourse between friends in the political community, which generates the habit of thinking things through, which conditions against doing evil actions. Appiah's cosmopolitan conversations and Arendt's talking things through in civic friendship are similar proposals pointing to a common end of living well together.

In addition to friendship (or perhaps as a form of friendship), *education* provides opportunities for cultivating *amor mundi* and talking things through. Both love of the world and also natality are at play in teaching and learning. In a speech in Hamburg, Germany, in 1959, Arendt professed:

> Education is the point at which we decide whether we love the world enough to assume responsibility for it and by the same token save it from that ruin which, except for renewal, except for the coming of the new and young, would be inevitable. And education, too, is where we decide whether we love our children enough not to expel them from our world and leave them to their own devices, nor to strike from their hands their chance of undertaking something new, something unforeseen by us, but to prepare them in advance for the task of renewing the world.[17]

Whether we love the world enough, and whether we love our children enough, are two forms of ardor that may move us to form unlikely friendships and to engage in difficult conversations across different ways of life. They are two answers to the question of *why bother* to do the work of conversation across different ways of life.

There are more forms of love discussed in Arendt's larger body of works than many of her readers knew. Arendt's intellectual diary, her *Denktagebuch*, handwritten on notebook pages mostly during the 1950s and 1960s, has recently been excerpted and analyzed thematically in English. The notebooks address a wide range of ideas on forms of love, including these excerpts by Tatjana Noemi Tömmel: "Arendt was not indifferent toward the 'heart.' Against Marx, for example, she claimed that the 'elementary relation between humans' was not based on coercion but on need (*dem Bedürfen*), that it was, hence, essentially 'Eros': 'Men get together as persons because they need each other (love).'"[18] More people are reading Appiah (who now writes "The Ethicist" column in the *New York Times*), and also Arendt, who is attracting many new and young scholars and readers.[19] What are they looking for if not ways to live and love constructively in this world, and for someone to point the way?

In another era of tortured globalization a century ago, J. R. R. Tolkien received an unconventional, cosmopolitan liberal education, at once completely unique and also not unlike Appiah's cosmopolitan family history or Arendt's harrowing journey as wandering refugee and searcher for love of the world.

Ronald's early life was a mix of hardship and wonder. Born in South Africa in 1892, his father, Arthur, died three years later. His mother, Mabel, moved back to England with Ronald and younger son Hilary. There she converted to Catholicism and lost her Baptist family support. She managed to homeschool her two sons, emphasizing botany and Latin, exploring local bogs and hills, drawing landscapes, and broad reading. This idyllic interlude ended when Mabel died of acute diabetes in 1904, when Ronald was twelve. Mabel left the two boys to the guardianship of her friend Father Francis Xavier Morgan. Ronald formed intense friendships with a group of boys at King Edward's School in Birmingham, who called themselves the Tea Club Barrovian Society, or TCBS. They exchanged letters and shared poetry and essays through college, forming a literary band of brothers and reciprocal mentors. From 1914 on, they all enlisted or were drafted into the Great War. Tolkien conceived the first mythologies of Middle-earth in the deadly trenches of the Battle of the Somme.[20]

All but one of his friends in the TCBS were cut down by the war. Tolkien, choosing against despair, carried on their common mission to light a spark of wonder in the world. He started writing tales of Middle Earth after the war. Two decades after World War I, he wrote much of *The Lord of the Rings* as his own sons left home to fight fascism in World War II. For his cosmopolitan education in courage and resilience, wonder and hope, Tolkien incurred a heavy personal cost—in loss, dislocation, risk, and danger.

The Hobbit, published in 1937, was essentially a children's story. But buried within it was a much darker tale that Tolkien himself only discovered later in writing *The Lord of the Rings*.[21] Is it so farfetched for some of us today to turn to what Tolkien called "fairy-stories" for guidance, courage, and education while deliberating in the age of Trump, coronavirus, climate change, and Russia's invasion of Ukraine?[22]

Hannah Arendt took storytelling seriously as a form of expressing and proposing political judgments. She extolled the value of the *vita activa* in public political space and the parallel importance of recounting as stories such exemplary political action in history, poetry, and literature (including fiction). In her first major work in 1951, Arendt argued that totalitarian thought renders men superfluous by first abolishing the meaning of all human lives.[23] In response to this abolition of human meaning, she proposed in 1958 two powerful forms of opposition and remedy: "the revelatory character of action as well as the ability to produce stories and become historical, which together form the very source from which meaningfulness springs into and illuminates human existence."[24]

The Lord of the Rings portrays the exemplary political action of Hobbits and their friends, and many readers testify that it infuses their lives with human meaning. But is it serious literature, worthy of careful, scholarly attention? In 1965 J. R. R. Tolkien expressed his dislike of allegory and his preference for "history, true or feigned."[25] Many readers and scholars have discovered for decades that Tolkien's epic, *The Lord of the Rings*, and the companion stories about the three ages of Middle Earth are *history so well feigned*, with such depth, density, and consistency of detail, that they can withstand the most intensive and fine-grained analytical gaze.[26] Nevertheless, the massive critical literature on Tolkien has only recently turned to politics, leaving many lacunae.[27] In addition, the long scenes of political deliberation in *The Lord of the Rings* have been neglected by both scholars and the Peter Jackson films. This essay is the first sustained analysis of political deliberation in *The Lord of the Rings*, focusing here on the first volume of the "trilogy," *The Fellowship of the Ring*, and on the role of the four Hobbits in the Fellowship.

THE CALL OF THE HOBBITS, AND THE PROBLEM OF THEIR EDUCATION

Well into its Third Age, Middle Earth is populated by the "free peoples of the world"—Elves, Dwarves and Men, and largely unknown Hobbits—as well as arboriform Ents and Huorns, semimanufactured warrior Orcs, a handful of wizards, and other eccentric characters and monsters. The international society of Middle Earth is highly decentralized, with travel on foot or horseback, little trade, and sporadic wars and predation.

The rising power pursuing a totalitarian, centralizing mission is Mordor, led by Sauron, the shadow of whose malign hegemony is growing as he intimidates and co-opts neighboring peoples. Widely considered the power of the future, Sauron lacks only one weapon to complete his arsenal and seal his domination. The One Ring of Power, which had been lost for centuries, has recently reemerged—in the unsuspecting hands of the Hobbit Frodo Baggins. The pristine, if petty, isolation of the Hobbits' Shire is shattered as Sauron's agents—Ringwraiths or Black Riders—close in to hunt for Frodo and the Ring. With the help of the Wizard Gandalf, Frodo and three friends must flee with the Ring to the Elven enclave of Rivendell, where the Council of Elrond must decide what to do with the Ring.

The above could be the opening scroll for *Fellowship of the Ring* as an international relations action movie. However, Tolkien begins the story well before this moment of Frodo's dramatic departure from the Shire. What is the narrative purpose of seventy-six pages of slow opening ramble? Part of the reason, of course, is the need to recount and recast the events of *The Hobbit* as a prequel. However, there is something else going on that is more central to the entire epic.

Tolkien's narrative logic for this protracted opening, I argue, is that the four Hobbits have never left the provincial Shire, and that they need a cosmopolitan, liberal education, an education for freedom and leadership in a larger, more morally and culturally complex world. Their educational itinerary would bear broad similarities to Tolkien's own, mixing large doses of hardship and wonder with real risk, moral uncertainty, marvelous and painful cross-cultural encounters, and terrifying evil.

Therefore, well before the flight to Rivendell of Frodo and friends begins, *Fellowship of the Ring* opens with two chapters that first illuminate the provincialism of the Shire, and then sharply initiate the education of Frodo to the wonders and dangers of the larger world.

As portrayed by Tolkien, a cosmopolitan liberal education—an education for liberty—also entails an education for citizenship and leadership in a particular community that seeks to survive and thrive in a larger, more complex and dangerous world. It is an education toward political deliberation and action, which must address both the particular community and the universal, cosmopolitan world.

HOBBITS: THE GENIUS OF FRIENDSHIP

Frodo and three friends set off from the Shire with the Ring, and with Sauron's Black Riders hot on their tails. But this was a desperate escape, and not the original plan. Gandalf—the wizard who had drawn Frodo's uncle Bilbo into the adventure that netted the Ring seventy-seven years before—had promised to go with them as a guide.

After a long absence, Gandalf returned to the Shire with ominous news for Frodo. Bilbo had bequeathed to his nephew his Hobbit Hole and all his possessions, including the ring that had appeared to be no more than a trophy and toy. Now, however, Gandalf revealed grimly that he had recently confirmed that this bauble was in fact the great Ring of Power that had disappeared centuries before. More menacingly, Sauron already knew that the Ring was in the Shire and was actively pursuing a Hobbit named Baggins.

Following a long conversation to impart this baleful news to Frodo, Gandalf departed again. He promised to return about five months later, before Frodo's fiftieth birthday, to lead Frodo and his loyal gardener Sam to Rivendell with the Ring. However, Gandalf failed to show up.[28] Frodo decided to set out without Gandalf the day after his birthday. He would have absconded alone to protect his friends from the Black Riders and Sauron, even after Gildor the Elf had advised him, "Do not go alone. Take such friends as are trusty and willing."[29]

Frodo's instinct to depart alone to protect his friends was heroic, but foolhardy. The Hobbits were heroes, but not archetypal mythic heroes who achieve great deeds single-handedly. Among them, the pooled intelligence of at least two friends was a prerequisite for sound decisions. Frodo was willing to take Sam because Gandalf had drafted him. However, Frodo did not know that Sam had been conspiring for years with Meriadoc Brandybuck (Merry), and Peregrin Took (Pippin) to prepare to help Frodo when the Ring became a burden or a threat. Indeed, they had long known something of the Ring; Merry had stolen a glance at Bilbo's book manuscript, and Sam had been secretly collecting information for them. When the three Hobbits finally revealed their conspiracy, Frodo responded that it seemed he could not trust anyone. Merry corrected Frodo's misconception of Hobbit heroism when he explained, "You can trust us to stick to you through thick and thin—to the bitter end. And you can trust us to keep any secret of yours—closer than you keep it yourself. But you cannot trust us to let you face trouble alone, and go off without a word. . . . We know most of what Gandalf has told you. We know a good deal about the Ring. We are horribly afraid—but we are coming with you; or following you like hounds."[30] This moment exemplifies the collective intelligence of friendship, trust, and resolute loyalty that guided the four Hobbits' deliberation and judgments.

The genius of the four Hobbits, Tolkien suggests, sprang from their gifts of trust and friendship, which carried no political agenda, but generated profound political consequences. For the Hobbits, trust was an intelligence for knowing who to depend on and who to be wary of, and friendship was a charism for complete loyalty to those they knew to trust.[31] These genii were the relational resources that guided their deliberation, judgment, and decision making. The genius for friendship was not primarily a fruit of their later cosmopolitan education; instead, it was something they had already received from their earthy upbringing in the Shire. That homely education became a resource for resisting world hegemonic corruption, enriched and uplifted by a liberal education to citizenship in a larger, cosmopolitan world. Tolkien's pedagogical proposal is cosmopolitan education in the service of the local, not in transcendent abdication of it.

As the four Hobbits set forth, they knew to trust Gildor and the Elves whom they encountered in the Shire, and to accept Farmer Maggot's help. Frodo's perception was enhanced by carrying the Ring, so that he could intuit the evil presence of the Black Riders. When Old Man Willow was anesthetizing and swallowing the Hobbits, it was Sam who resisted sleep and cried, "I don't like this great big tree. I don't trust it," and pulled Frodo out from the molesting roots.[32]

For the Hobbits traveling blind without Gandalf, strong friendship did not close them off from the world. Instead, personal friendship became civic friendship, which gave them the courage and intelligence to plunge deeper into the world, and thereby to advance their liberal, cosmopolitan education.

During six days on their own, both within the Shire and beyond it, the four Hobbits made numerous decisions in unfamiliar circumstances. Frodo decided when to leave, what direction to go, whom to trust, when and where to hide, how secretly or openly to move. Some of these decisions spawned evil or mixed results. Merry, Pippin, and Sam also made decisions, most important to all go with Frodo, imposing themselves on him.

On a social-structural stage much larger than the Shire, all four Hobbits tested and increased their capacities to exercise responsibility, deliberation, resilience, forgiveness, and judging their experience. In a word, they expanded their agency. These choices turned out to be political in two senses: first, in the political education of the Hobbits, and, second, in their larger consequences for Middle Earth in the unfolding War of the Ring.

The four Hobbits encountered a marvelous range of characters on the edges of the social structure of Middle Earth: sinister Black Riders, feasting Elves, Farmer Maggot, Old Man Willow, Barrow-wights, Tom Bombadil, and Goldberry. These episodes (told in seven chapters over one hundred pages) are often misunderstood as merely a series of random, inconsequential escapades, designed as episodic entertainment for the young reader in a children's story. However, Tolkien had in mind a deeper level of entertainment. With each encounter, the four Hobbits experienced a cumulative process of multifaceted educational experiences and transformational moments. They became entangled with wide extremes of the amplitude of good and evil, the range of old and new, the depths and limits of their Hobbit luck, and revelations of their true characters. They learned to think through and talk through the particular realities they met. In a word, they received a liberal education, an education for liberty.

Back home in the Shire, nothing was very good or very bad, very old, or very far above or below. The amplitude of extremes was narrow; the standard deviation was small. The strength of the Hobbits was also their weakness: a preoccupation with the intimate, proximate, and carnal, like growing and eating food, drinking ale, smoking pipe weed, enjoying families, and throwing parties. The Shire was an insular monoculture. Provincialism made the Hobbits not only charming but also dangerously naive about the evil actors who sought to dominate them. The Hobbits as a people were young, inexperienced, and unknown among other peoples. How could they step up to undertake a much larger role in the history of Middle Earth?

TOM BOMBADIL:
A LIBERAL EDUCATION TO FREEDOM AND DELIBERATION

Of all the characters encountered by Frodo and his friends through their entire adventure, Tom Bombadil is the biggest puzzle, anomaly, and problem for readers. He does not advance the plot in any obvious way.[33] Not only did Peter Jackson leave Tom out of his films, but many Tolkien scholars seem at a loss with what to make of him.[34] The unstated, but inescapable, conclusion seems to be that leaving Tom in the story was both an act of authorial self-indulgence and an editorial error.

In opposition to this exasperated, tacit consensus, I argue that Tom Bombadil does indeed advance the story in a decisive way, but his role in the plot is discernible only if we understand that the cosmopolitan, liberal education of the four Hobbits is intrinsic and central to the epic.

What happened to the Hobbits by meeting Tom Bombadil? One aspect of the encounter was an explosion of song. In Middle Earth, song is even more important than in our world as a repository of history, culture, and meaning, and a means to convey and renew them. Song plays different roles in the lives of each of the peoples of Middle Earth, and the contrasts are instructive. The Hobbits have their own songs, both traditional songs committed to memory and new songs that they compose or make up on the spot. For the Elves, in contrast, songs run deeper in their culture and in their bones. According to Bilbo in Rivendell, concerning Elves and songs, "They seem to like them as much as food, or more."[35] On the other end of the spectrum, the Orcs possess language, but are bereft of song, which is a telling indicator of both the weakness of their social structure and also the deficiency of their free personal agency.[36]

Tom Bombadil, however, is in a class by himself concerning song, even beyond the Elves. As the "Eldest," his relationship to song says something about all the younger peoples and creatures in Middle Earth. Tom speaks and acts entirely in verse and song. His life and world are a spontaneous operetta. Toward the end of their first day with Tom, the Hobbits too "became suddenly aware that they were singing merrily, as if it was easier and more natural than talking."[37] This echoes the lore of the original creation of Middle Earth by the songs of Eru Ilúvatar.[38] Tom Bombadil, as both eldest and fearless, was closest to those origins, and he reflected the "original position" of all creatures in Middle Earth that language is meant to be like song, to signify something else in a beautiful and compelling way—coherent and beautiful, reflecting, illuminating, and amplifying reality. One could almost say that for Tom, the cosmos of Middle Earth and the free peoples of Middle Earth were mysteriously tuned to each other.

Late at night, after the feast, Tom sang "uncomfortable lore" about the Old Forest and Old Man Willow. "Tom's words laid bare the hearts of trees and their thoughts, which were often hard and strange, and filled with a hatred of things that go free upon the earth, gnawing, biting, breaking, hacking, turning: destroyers and usurpers."[39] The Hobbits took this in, each to the extent that he could, slowly realizing the much wider amplitude of evil and good that existed in the world beyond the Shire.

Tom Bombadil, apparently irrelevant to and disinterested in the future of Middle Earth, served as an essential tutor and witness for the liberal education of the four chosen Hobbits. Even if they did not understand details and context of Tom's songs, they had to realize that Middle Earth was much older, larger, and more morally complex than they had suspected growing up in the Shire. Like children at a family reunion, they caught glimpses of the larger social reality to which they already belonged. Before they would arrive in Rivendell, before they would participate in the Council of Elrond, and before they would take their places as almost half of the *Fellowship of the Ring*, the Hobbits needed a rapid education in agency and social structure, an education of encounter, with life and death at stake. They needed an education for freedom, a liberal education.

FRODO'S AND SAM'S DIVERGENT CURRICULA

In Middle Earth, seeking and gaining more knowledge did not always produce good fruit, as shown by the corruption through lust for knowledge of Sméagol, Saruman, and Denethor.[40] For the four Hobbits, in contrast, the cosmopolitan trajectory of their education was not a deracinated detachment that forgot their roots and ended in pride or despair. In the cases of Frodo and Sam, although they were almost inseparable, they followed divergent paths in coming of age from narrow provincialism to rooted cosmopolitanism.

Samwise Gamgee was a professional gardener and son of a gardener (Ham Gamgee, a.k.a. "The Gaffer"). He lived up to his origins by remaining grounded, rooted, and earthy throughout the journey. Readers may be tempted to see him as simple, or even simple-minded. That would be a mistake. When he met something new (especially Elves), he would reflect upon it and render a judgment in understated, homespun terms, yet often profound. For example, after meeting the Elves in the Shire at the beginning of their flight, Frodo asked Sam if he still liked them. Sam responded, "They seem a bit above my likes and dislikes, so to speak. . . . They are quite different from what I expected—so old and young, and so gay and sad as it were." Much later, after being led into Lothlórien across a river by a tenuous bridge of Elven ropes, Sam exulted, "Live and learn! As my gaffer used to say. . . . Not even my uncle Andy ever did a trick like that!" Inside Lothlórien with the High Elves, the company was brought to

Cerin Amroth, the heart of the ancient realm, where "ever bloom the winter flowers." Sam tried to convey his astonishment to Frodo: "Its sunlight and bright day, right enough. I thought that Elves were all for moon and stars: but this is more elvish than anything I ever heard tell of. I feel I was *inside* a song, if you take my meaning."[41]

Building on reference points from everyday life in the Shire, Sam used several figures of speech to express in familiar and simple language his judgments of new and complex realities. He used understatement ("Not even my uncle Andy"), to indicate that he was trying to say more; dialectic paradox ("so old and young"), to suggest that here was something new beyond the two opposites; and the subjunctive ("as it were"), to point to an additional layer of meaning that he could not articulate directly. Crucially, the movement of Sam's meaning was usually upward, indicating that the new reality he pointed to transcended in some way the ordinary experience of life. He used irony to raise up and enlarge what he encountered, rather than diminish and deflate it. While Sam had his flaws, particularly in his contempt for Gollum later in the story, his greatness lay in the clarity of his recognition of what and who were above him and his faithfulness in serving them.

In his language as well as action, therefore, Sam undertook his cosmopolitan journey in a way that both confirmed his identity as a Hobbit and his roots in the Shire and also elevated and transcended the limitations of his background.

Frodo's education for freedom followed a different itinerary, due to his responsibility to carry the Ring of Power. He appeared to be "chosen" to carry the Ring, not only because it was bequeathed to him by his uncle Bilbo, but also because Frodo possessed the rare quality, shared only with the now elderly Bilbo, to be able to bear the ring without being rapidly corrupted and possessed by its power. None of the great and wise in Rivendell were willing to try (except the brave, but less wise, Boromir, who overestimated his resistance to the Ring's corruption). Of the best Hobbits, neither Merry nor Pippin nor Sam sought the Ring, tacitly recognizing something greater in Frodo (although Sam did pick it up briefly and at great need much later in Shelob's lair). The story never reveals why only Bilbo and Frodo, but no other Hobbit, could carry the Ring.

Gandalf reasoned that the Ring had the same effects on Bilbo and Frodo as on others, only much more slowly. By the time of the Hobbits' flight to

Rivendell, Frodo had already possessed the Ring in his house for seventeen years, as had Bilbo for sixty years before that. In some ways, the effects were similar on them both—a steadily but slowly growing attachment to the Ring and a lengthening and "thinning" of life (much more advanced with Bilbo's longer possession). However, a subtle difference between their responses began to appear during Frodo's journey. Bilbo was more lighthearted, while Frodo was more troubled—in fact progressively more wounded—by possessing and carrying the Ring.

As soon as the four Hobbits commenced their flight from the Shire, Frodo began to exhibit qualities that were not evident at home in the Shire. Twice they heard a horse coming, but only Frodo intuited hostile pursuit. In these encounters, Frodo also experienced a powerful desire to put on the Ring. Something was getting inside of Frodo, under his skin, both warning and luring him. When they lodged for the night with Gildor and the Elves, Pippin and Sam fell asleep, while "Frodo remained long awake, talking with Gildor."[42] These signs showed that Frodo carried a greatly heightened sensitivity to the presence of both evil and good—indeed, a form of judgment, coming from the heart.

This hypervigilance showed that he was more deeply penetrated and moved, more deeply *wounded*, by both ugliness and beauty. At several points in the journey Frodo, and no one else, heard or glimpsed or felt something pursuing them that was not a Black Rider.[43] It turned out to be Gollum, which was confirmed when Sam spotted him floating like a log behind them on the Great River, Anduin. On the other side of the spectrum of ugliness to beauty, both Sam and Frodo meet with the Elf queen Galadriel in Lothlórien to gaze into her Mirror. However, only Frodo could see on her finger Nenya, the Ring of Adamant, one of the three Elven Rings. Galadriel explained: "It is not permitted to speak of it, and Elrond could not do so. But it cannot be hidden from the Ring-bearer, and one who has seen the Eye."[44] Frodo perceived not only Galadriel's ring, but also her heart, in that she divulged vividly to him the regret of the Elves for their ongoing decline and the powerful lure and temptation that the one Ring worked on her.

Tolkien's profound "fairy-story" on the nature of knowledge and the path of education to freedom proposes that while suffering may bring wisdom, so too does knowledge bring suffering. Deep knowledge of things and persons, beautiful or ugly or both, may also be received into our minds and hearts as suffering. To "suffer" also means to undergo, sustain, or receive. Contrary to our contemporary epistemologies, Tolkien suggests, knowledge is more received than constructed. Whatever we learn does not leave us unscathed. When Frodo was physically stabbed on Weathertop by one of the Ringwraiths (Black Riders) with an evil blade, a shard of which remained in his body, the lingering wound echoed and represented his woundedness of knowledge. Aragorn's medicine could only stop the wound from spreading, and Elrond could remove the shard and restore Frodo's strength, but the wound remained with him and deepened as he carried the Ring into Mordor.

In contrast with Sam, Frodo's education for freedom was ultimately too much for him to bear. Yet he bore it. By the end of the saga, Frodo had seen too much, to the point that he could not go home again to the Shire.

There is a cost incurred for the liberation of a cosmopolitan liberal education. For those of us who are educators, are we aware of how our teaching wounds as well as liberates both ourselves and our students? Rather than avoiding both the suffering and the education that comes with it, how can we help our students and each other to bear this knowledge and to suffer this liberation and empowerment?

THE COUNCIL OF ELROND: THE POWER OF WEAKNESS

Having arrived at Rivendell in the nick of time, with wounds and close calls, Frodo and his three Hobbit companions were all included —incongruously—in the political deliberations of the high Council of Elrond, either in the Council itself, or in the decisions made around it.

Three aspects of the Council were striking in the larger history of Middle Earth: its inclusiveness, spontaneity, and urgency.

For the previous five centuries, such matters as going to war and the protection of the free peoples of Middle Earth had been taken up by the elite, "aristocratic" White Council (a.k.a. the Council of the Wise), consisting exclusively of the top Elves (Elrond, Galadriel, and Cirdan the Shipwright) and wizards (Saruman, Gandalf, and Radagast). Men, Dwarves, and Hobbits were all excluded. The Council of Elrond, in contrast, was astonishingly broad, including three Hobbits (Bilbo and Frodo, and also Sam uninvited sitting in the corner), two men (Boromir and Aragorn), two Dwarves (Gloin and his son Gimli), one Sindarin Elf (Legolas), one wizard (Gandalf), one half-elf (Elrond) and various other High Elves of Elrond's household. Also, Saruman was excluded (his secret collusion with Sauron now exposed), Radagast had fled, and Galadriel was prevented from attending by the spreading power of Sauron. This inclusiveness was a radical departure from elite tradition. The Council of Elrond was a crucial step in the evolution of Middle Earth from a divided and corrupt aristocracy, toward a reformed and increasingly republican monarchy. The circle of political deliberation was expanding.

In addition, the Council was called spontaneously, in response to specific, sudden events. It did not escape Elrond's attention that representatives of all the free peoples of Middle Earth (Elves, Dwarves, Men, and Hobbits) had happened to converge on Rivendell all at once, all seeking aid or answers concerning the aggression of Sauron and his allies.

Finally, the Council was convened in a context of high emergency, of great and present danger. The four Hobbits, Aragorn, and Gandalf had arrived only by passing through great peril and surviving nearly fatal attacks. In addition, while Sauron had been building his strength for decades, his enemies were coming together very belatedly, after a catastrophic intelligence failure. Although Sauron's Ringwraiths were scattered, they now knew exactly where the Ring of Power was being held and exactly who was carrying it. Sauron himself would soon know.

The Council began with an extended sharing of intelligence from all present, in the form of telling (for the first time) the entire story of the Ring. Intelligence was collected from broad sources and on a wide range of topics. They consulted the direct experience of young and old (Elrond and Gandalf were each thousands of years old). They recounted the enhanced interrogation of Gollum by both Gandalf and Sauron, the recent rescue of Gandalf from Saruman's detention, the recent escape of Gollum from the Wood Elves' detention, Boromir's dreams, counterintelligence efforts against "spies of many sorts, even beasts and birds,"[45] and lore from inscriptions and scrolls in almost forgotten languages.

This unprecedentedly broad and transparent intelligence sharing was followed by a remarkably clear-eyed political analysis, weighing the relative balance—or rather perilous imbalance—of power resources between Sauron's forces and those of his enemies. Clearly, the advantage of Sauron's forces was so overwhelming that all-out war would strongly favor him, even if his enemies could manage to begin to work together. Therefore, the major alternatives considered were all strategies of the weak: hiding the Ring, throwing it away, or bracing for a siege. The judgment was quickly made that none of the elven strongholds—Rivendell, the Wood-elves' home in Mirkwood, or Lothlórien—could hold out long against Sauron's forces. Tom Bombadil, it was decided, would not be attentive or determined enough to hide the Ring securely, and while the Ring had no power over him, he could not reduce or influence the power it had over others. Casting it into the sea would not be a permanent solution, and heading that direction would be untenable because Sauron would expect them to go that way. Using the three Elven rings against Sauron would be unsound because they were not designed as weapons of war and were tied in an unknown way to the fate of the One Ring itself.[46] These were judgments of particular goods and evils made in conversations across different ways of life in relationships of developing civic friendship; this was collective, cosmopolitan deliberation.

Boromir of Gondor argued that the Ring was a gift that had fallen to them and that should be wielded as a weapon against Sauron. He was willing to use the Ring himself, or give it to one of the more capable Elves or wizards. By our world's standards and history, this was clearly the winning argument: someone would be designated to apply the force of the Ring, while the Council would install and institutionalize certain safeguards and precautions. However, the more capable and wiser among the Council members were entirely unwilling to take up the Ring because they understood too well its power to corrupt them.

In the event, both Boromir's maximalist strategy of all-out war using every available weapon and minimalist options of hiding or hoarding the Ring were recognized as equally false hopes and illusions. With these judgments, the discussion in the Council turned toward a creative but desperate strategy tailored to the specific circumstances and enemy that they faced: the option to destroy the Ring in the volcanic fire of Mordor at the center of Sauron's power. When Erestor objected that this was a path of folly or despair, Gandalf and Elrond responded:

> "Despair, or folly?" said Gandalf. "It is not despair, for despair is only for those who see the end beyond all doubt. We do not. It is wisdom to recognize necessity, when all other courses have been weighed, though as folly it may appear to those who cling to false hope. Well, let folly be our cloak, a veil before the eyes of the Enemy! For he is very wise, and weighs all things to a nicety in the scales of his malice. But the only measure that he knows is desire, desire for power; and so he judges all

hearts. Into his heart the thought will not enter that any will refuse it, that having the Ring we may seek to destroy it. If we seek thus, we shall put him out of reckoning."

"At least for a while," said Elrond. "The road must be trod, but it will be very hard. And neither strength nor wisdom will carry us very far upon it. This quest may be attempted by the weak with at least as much hope as the strong. Yet such is oft the course of deeds that move the wheels of the world: small hands do them because they must, while the eyes of the great are elsewhere."[47]

By knowing the enemy better than he knew either them or himself, and by using the power of weakness that he could not fathom, the Fellowship would turn Sauron's blindness against him. Embracing a realism of humility, Gandalf and Elrond envisioned a strategy of deception and misdirection. But these elder statesmen had to rely on "small hands" to carry out the deception at a tactical level. This collective deliberation required the assent of the weakest and newest people, the Hobbits. For the free peoples of Middle Earth to "let folly be our cloak," Frodo would have to recognize and accept his chosen role in the drama. "I will take the Ring," he finally said, "though I do not know the way," thus bringing the Council to a close.[48]

Frodo's choice to accept the call to carry the Ring thus determined the strategy of the highest council in Middle Earth. His decision was based on the friendship of his Hobbit companions and their loyalty to the Shire, as well as some degree of trust in Gandalf and his Elf friends. But it was also the consequence of a form of political deliberation.

A full two months after the Council, when scouts had fanned out from and returned to Rivendell, Elrond took it upon himself to form the unit that would accompany Frodo. Addressing Frodo, Elrond decided, "The Company of the Ring shall be Nine; and the Nine Walkers shall be set against the Nine Riders that are evil."[49] The nine would include Frodo and his "faithful servant" Sam, who had crashed the Council meeting out of stubborn loyalty. In addition, Elrond announced, "Gandalf will go; for this shall be his great task, and maybe the end of his labours," alluding to his nebulous grand strategic role as a wizard. Legolas, Gimli, and Aragorn would go as well, to "represent the other Free Peoples of the World: Elves, Dwarves, and Men." Aragorn brought in Boromir, since the two of them planned to travel together to Gondor, for a total of seven.

For the two remaining vacancies, Elrond could think of no obvious candidates, so he resorted to reviewing members of his own household. At this, Pippin strenuously and recklessly protested, "But that will leave no place for us!" Elrond was willing to allow Merry, but his heart was against including Pippin. Surprisingly, Gandalf took Pippin's side, suggesting, "I think, Elrond, that in this matter it would be well to trust rather to their friendship than to great wisdom."[50] Elrond relented, relying on Gandalf's closer understanding of the Hobbits' genius for friendship.[51]

In this way, the Hobbits formed almost half of the Fellowship—four out of nine. Each member would undertake a dramatic journey of agency within the social structure of their own particular people, and that of Middle Earth as a whole, which would change each of them and profoundly shape their societies going forward. Sam would almost never leave Frodo's side, but would make crucial contributions to the journey nevertheless. While Merry and Pippin were almost undifferentiated in *Fellowship of the Ring*, each would find his own critical part to play.[52]

A KING'S VISION

With the insights that the journey of the Hobbits is an educational itinerary, and that through the journey Tolkien proposes a liberal, cosmopolitan education entailing political deliberation, several elements of the story of *Fellowship of the Ring* quicken with deeper drama: Frodo's predicament as one called to a dangerous journey with an unreliable guide; the Hobbit genius of friendship as a source of intelligence and courage; the crucial role of Tom Bombadil in elevating the Hobbits into a larger world; the cost of Frodo's growing knowledge in suffering, trauma, and exile; and the power of weakness as a winning political-military strategy.

Reversing the analytical lens, could Tolkien's pedagogical proposal still be relevant for our challenges of provincialism versus cosmopolitanism today? An authentic liberal education—an education for freedom and leadership involving practical, political deliberation and choice—would serve both local communities and peoples, and also the larger cosmopolitan world, in a creative fusion rather than a false dichotomy. The particular and the universal may well be reconciled, but never permanently, always at a price, and with success never guaranteed. The fusion of local and global, and particular and universal, must not only be relearned but also markedly recast for each generation. There is no permanent program to return to.

For those of us who are teachers or students, Tolkien would ennoble our callings, but also raise the bar and raise the stakes on our aspirations. And he would expand the spatial arena and time frame of our educational journey far beyond the classroom, beyond our school years, and beyond the spoken and written word.

The final scene of *Fellowship of the Ring*, "The Breaking of the Fellowship," stamps a tragic but encouraging coda on these themes. To escape Boromir's desperate attack, Frodo resorts to wearing the Ring to become invisible. He then climbs up to the summit of Amon Hen and sits on the great chair amid the ruins. Aragorn had told Frodo that this was the Seat of Seeing, built by great kings of Númenor in the ancient past. Still wearing the Ring, Frodo can see for hundreds of miles. He beholds a panorama of "Signs of War" in many lands, revealing Sauron's overwhelming and invincible power.[53] He is given a king's vision in range, detail, and perspective. The response of almost any king in the face of such overwhelming odds would be somehow to bandwagon with or placate the stronger power. Frodo, however, does not cower or panic. He loyally follows the strategy of the Fellowship, even as the Fellowship fractures.

Then Frodo feels and sees the Eye of Sauron, becoming aware of Sauron's gaze searching for him, almost finding him. (The Eye of Sauron in the book is not flamingly visible to all for hundreds of miles as portrayed in the Peter Jackson films.) He throws himself down, still wearing the Ring. Tolkien explains, "Two powers strove in him." The Eye, beguiling him, "Verily I come to you." And the Voice, commanding, "Fool, take it off! Take off the Ring!" Finally, there is only Frodo, "neither the Voice nor the Eye: free to choose, and with one remaining instant in which to do so. He took the Ring off his finger."[54]

Meanwhile, the rest of the Fellowship realizes that Frodo has been gone too long and is in some kind of trouble with Boromir. Aragorn and Sam run up Amon Hen to look for him, but Sam cannot keep up. Then Sam—alone among all the Fellowship—realizes that Frodo would try to go alone and would take a boat. Sam heads for the shore and sees a boat moving by itself (because Frodo is wearing the Ring). Sam jumps in the water and forces Frodo to save him from being "drownded." Frodo pleads, "But I am going to Mordor," to which Sam replies, "I know that well enough, Mr. Frodo. Of course you are. And I am coming with you."[55] Frodo is relieved, and Frodo and Sam set off together across the river toward Mordor.

In the end, Frodo was not overwhelmed or intimidated by the forces of Sauron that he saw at the summit of Amon Hen, or by Sauron's searching Eye that almost caught him. He had a king's vision on Amon Hen, but he did not become a king or imagine himself as one. Frodo had made the decision to go alone to Mordor on the basis of micro-relational considerations. Of the remaining members of the Fellowship he had thought, "Some I cannot trust. And those I can trust are too dear to me."[56] His deliberation was guided by the criteria of trust and love, but it was guided falsely to the wrong decision to depart the Fellowship alone, as the rest of the story shows. The error was corrected by Sam's deeper understanding of Frodo and loyalty to him. Frodo's political judgment was corrected by the love, knowledge, and judgment of a friend.

Tolkien's epic *The Lord of the Rings* means different things to different people. For many, it is simply a parable of the courage of a small group of friends from an unknown place to face reality, to judge the good and evil in it, and to stand up against the evil things. In my mind's eyes and ears it is also something else: the four Hobbit friends enjoy an ongoing colloquy of storytelling with a growing cast of characters fictional and real, living and dead, including Arendt, Appiah, Tolkien too, and drawing in myself, my colleagues, and my students. Together, they call us to summon the courage for the cosmopolitan conversations of our day across different ways of living. They offer to guide us, if we will allow it, to reimagine and reenchant our own liberal educational itineraries toward more free and sane deliberation, among friends, in our own increasingly dangerous, maddening, and morally and politically complex world.

NOTES

1. I am grateful to J. David Alvis, Constantine Vassiliou, Anthony F. Lang Jr., and an anonymous reviewer for challenging conversation and counsel that helped to shape my argument.

2. Bruce Kimball, *Orators & Philosophers: A History of the Idea of Liberal Education*; Fareed Zakaria, *In Defense of a Liberal Education*; Martha Nussbaum, *Not for Profit: Why Democracy Needs the Humanities*; Allan Bloom, *The Closing of the American Mind: How Higher Education Has Failed Democracy and Impoverished the Souls of Today's Students*; S. Georgia Nugent, *The Liberal Arts in Action: Past, Present, and Future*.

3. For a small sample, see Shuchen Xiang, *Chinese Cosmopolitanism: The History and Philosophy of an Idea*; Martha Nussbaum, *The Cosmopolitan Tradition: A Noble but Flawed Ideal*; Bruce Robbins and Paulo Lemos Horta, eds, *Cosmopolitanisms*; and

Myles Lavan, Richard E. Payne, and John Weisweiler, eds, *Cosmopolitanism and Empire: Universal Rulers, Local Elites, and Cultural Integration in the Ancient Near East and Mediterranean*.

4. Kwame Anthony Appiah, *Cosmopolitanism: Ethics in a World of Strangers*, vii.

5. Appiah, *Cosmopolitanism*, xiii, xv.

6. Appiah, *Cosmopolitanism*, xix.

7. Appiah, *Cosmopolitanism*, xxi.

8. See Elisabeth Young-Bruehl, *Hannah Arendt: For Love of the World*; and a graphic-novel biography, Ken Krimstein, *The Three Escapes of Hannah Arendt*.

9. Young-Bruehl, *Hannah Arendt*, xii.

10. Young-Bruehl, *Hannah Arendt*, 36.

11. The main line of Arendt interpretation is led by Dana Villa, editor of *The Cambridge Companion to Hannah Arendt* and author of *Arendt*. These are essential readings. However, I am not addressing here the mostly implicit debate in Arendt studies between those who view Arendt's 1929 dissertation on love and Saint Augustine as the key to understanding all of her later work, and those, including Dana Villa, who begin their substantive interpretation of Arendt's political thought with her first book, published in 1951, in English and in America, *The Origins of Totalitarianism*.

12. Jerome Kohn, introduction to *Responsibility and Judgment*, by Hannah Arendt, xxv.

13. Arendt published "Eichmann in Jerusalem" as a series of articles in the *New Yorker* starting February 16, 1963 (https://www.newyorker.com/magazine/1963/02/16/eichmann-in-jerusalem-i). It was published as a book the same year by Viking Press in New York.

14. Hannah Arendt never wrote the third volume on "judgment" of her intended trilogy on *The Life of the Mind*. The book was published posthumously with only volume 1, *Thinking*, and volume 2, *Willing*, edited by her friend Mary McCarthy (New York: Harcourt Brace, 1977). When she died in 1975 at age sixty-nine, the first blank page of the third volume on "judgment" was found on her typewriter. This was, in a way, her "last word" before her death. It stands as an invitation and a challenge to us to think and judge for ourselves.

15. Hannah Arendt, "Philosophy and Politics," 83.

16. Frederick M. Dolan, "Arendt on Philosophy and Politics," in *Cambridge Companion to Arendt*, ed. Villa, 267.

17. Hannah Arendt, "The Crisis in Education," in *Between Past and Future*, 193.

18. Tatjana Noemi Tömmel, "*Vita Passiva*: Love in Arendt's *Denktagebuch*," 107 (citing *Denktagebuch*, IX.3.203.

19. See Samantha Rose Hill, *Hannah Arendt*; Regan Penaluna and Samantha Rose Hill, "Hannah Arendt: 'You See the Politics on Her Face'"; and the ardent undergraduate interactions through the Hannah Arendt Center for Politics and Humanities at Bard College, and their "Amor Mundi Newsletter" (https://hac.bard.edu/amor-mundi/).

20. John Garth, *Tolkien and the Great War: The Threshold of Middle-Earth*.

21. J. R. R. Tolkien, *The Hobbit; or, There and Back Again*; J. R. R. Tolkien, *The Lord of the Rings*, vol. 3.

22. J. R. R. Tolkien, "On Fairy-Stories."
23. Arendt, *The Origins of Totalitarianism*, 459.
24. Hannah Arendt, *The Human Condition*, 324.
25. J. R. R. Tolkien, foreword to *The Fellowship of the Ring*, x. This chapter cites the 1966 Del Rey Books, paperback 2nd edition of the trilogy, because it is the most widely read version.
26. For a small sampling, see Tom Shippey, *J. R. R. Tolkien: Author of the Century*; J. E. A. Tyler, *The Complete Tolkien Companion*; Humphrey Carpenter, *J. R. R. Tolkien: A Biography*; Rose A. Zimbardo and Neil D. Isaacs, eds., *Understanding "The Lord of the Rings": The Best of Tolkien Criticism*; and Jane Chance, ed., *Tolkien and the Invention of Myth: A Reader*.
27. On politics in *The Lord of the Rings*, see Abigail E. Ruane and Patrick James, *The International Relations of Middle Earth*; Jane Chance, *"The Lord of the Rings": The Mythology of Power*; Matthew T. Dickerson and Jonathan Evans, *Ents, Elves, and Eriador: The Environmental Vision of J. R. R. Tolkien*; Nancy Enright, "Tolkien's Females and the Defining of Power"; Garth, *Tolkien and the Great War*; Joshua Hren, *Middle-Earth and the Return of the Common Good: J. R. R. Tolkien and Political Philosophy*; and Dimitra Fimi, *Tolkien, Race and Cultural History: From Fairies to Hobbits*.
28. The relationship between Frodo and Gandalf, who could be a capricious mentor, is the subject of another article.
29. Tolkien, *Fellowship of the Ring*, 94.
30. Tolkien, *Fellowship of the Ring*, 118.
31. See John von Heyking and Richard Avramenko, eds., *Friendship & Politics: Essays in Political Thought*; Jacques Derrida, *The Politics of Friendship*; P. E. Digeser, *Friendship Reconsidered: What It Means and How It Matters to Politics*; and Heather Devere, "Amity Update: The Academic Debate on Friendship and Politics." In ancient and medieval political thought, the links between friendship and politics were recognized as central, only to be largely ignored during the modern period. Recently, however, there is a resurgence of interest in friendship and politics.
32. Tolkien, *Fellowship of the Ring*, 132.
33. Tolkien himself was vexingly ambiguous in his comments on the function of Tom Bombadil in the story. See Kenneth Craven, "A Catholic Poem in Time of War," 251.
34. Tom Shippey, *The Road to Middle Earth*, 105–10; Steuard Jensen, "What Is Tom Bombadil?"
35. Tolkien, *Fellowship of the Ring*, 266.
36. There is no Orc song in Tolkien's Legendarium. However, before the action in *The Lord of the Rings*, Melkor, Sauron, and Goblins had been known to sing. See J. R. R. Tolkien, *The Silmarillion*, 16, 171; and Tolkien, *Hobbit*, 149, 243. I am grateful to my Wofford College student Clyde Houk for these references.
37. Tolkien, *Fellowship of the Ring*, 142.
38. Tolkien, *The Silmarillion*, 1–10.
39. Tolkien, *Fellowship of the Ring*, 147.
40. For Sméagol, see Tolkien, *Fellowship of the Ring*, 57–59. For Saruman, see Tolkien, *Fellowship of the Ring*, 52, 290–91; and for Denethor, see J. R. R. Tolkien, *The Return of the King*, 126–34.

41. Tolkien, *Fellowship of the Ring*, 97, 389, 393 (emphasis in the original).
42. Tolkien, *Fellowship of the Ring*, 83–87, 92.
43. Tolkien, *Fellowship of the Ring*, 112, 350, 357, 378, 429–32.
44. Tolkien, *Fellowship of the Ring*, 409.
45. Tolkien, *Fellowship of the Ring*, 282.

46. In fact, the three Elven rings were being worn (invisibly to most participants) by Elrond and Gandalf in the Council meeting itself, and by Galadriel in Lothlórien, so they were playing and would play indirect roles in supporting the Fellowship through those leaders.

47. Tolkien, *Fellowship of the Ring*, 302.
48. Tolkien, *Fellowship of the Ring*, 303.
49. Tolkien, *Fellowship of the Ring*, 309.
50. Tolkien, *Fellowship of the Ring*, 310.

51. Of course, Gollum was the tenth, uninvited, member of the Fellowship, as he shadowed their every move. However, he did not actively reenter the story until the second volume of the trilogy, *The Two Towers*.

52. It is beyond the scope of this essay to explore how the portrayal of friendship and deliberation in *The Lord of the Rings* may correspond with various theories in political thought from the ancient Greeks to the present day.

53. Tolkien, *Fellowship of the Ring*, 451.
54. Tolkien, *Fellowship of the Ring*, 451.
55. Tolkien, *Fellowship of the Ring*, 456, 457.
56. Tolkien, *Fellowship of the Ring*, 451.

BIBLIOGRAPHY

Appiah, Kwame Anthony. *Cosmopolitanism: Ethics in a World of Strangers*. New York: W. W. Norton, 2006

Arendt, Hannah. *Between Past and Future*. New York: Penguin Books, 2006.

———. *The Human Condition*. Chicago: University of Chicago Press, 1958.

———. *The Origins of Totalitarianism*. New York: Schocken Books, 1951.

———. "Philosophy and Politics." *Social Research* 57 (1990).

———. *Responsibility and Judgment*. New York: Schocken Books, 2003.

Bloom, Allan. *The Closing of the American Mind: How Higher Education Has Failed Democracy and Impoverished the Souls of Today's Students*. Rev. ed. New York: Simon & Schuster, 2012.

Carpenter, Humphrey. *J. R. R. Tolkien: A Biography*. New York: Allen & Unwin, 2000.

Chance, Jane. *"The Lord of the Rings": The Mythology of Power*. Lexington: University Press of Kentucky, 2012.

———. *Tolkien and the Invention of Myth: A Reader*. Lexington: University Press of Kentucky, 2004.

Craven, Kenneth. "A Catholic Poem in Time of War." In "J. R. R. Tolkien: Mythos and Modernity in Middle-Earth," edited by Ian Boyd. Special issue, *Chesterton Review* 28 (February–May 2002). https://web.archive.org/web/20060214120336/http://academic.shu.edu/chesterton/PDF/Review_FebMay_2002.pdf.

Derrida, Jacques. *The Politics of Friendship*. Translated by George Collins. London: Verso, 2005.

Devere, Heather. "Amity Update: The Academic Debate on Friendship and Politics." *AMITY: Journal of Friendship Studies* 1 (2013): 5–33.

Dickerson, Matthew T., and Jonathan Evans. *Ents, Elves, and Eriador: The Environmental Vision of J. R. R. Tolkien*. Lexington: University Press of Kentucky, 2011.

Digeser, P. E. *Friendship Reconsidered: What It Means and How It Matters to Politics*. New York: Columbia University Press, 2016.

Enright, Nancy. "Tolkien's Females and the Defining of Power." *Renascence* 59, no. 2 (2007): 93–108.

Fimi, Dimitra. *Tolkien, Race and Cultural History: From Fairies to Hobbits*. New York: Palgrave Macmillan, 2009.

Garth, John. *Tolkien and the Great War: The Threshold of Middle-Earth*. New York: Houghton Mifflin, 2003.

Heyking, John von, and Richard Avramenko, eds. *Friendship & Politics: Essays in Political Thought*. Notre Dame, IN: University of Notre Dame Press, 2008.

Hill, Samantha Rose. *Hannah Arendt*. New York: Reaktion Books, 2021.

Hren, Joshua. *Middle-Earth and the Return of the Common Good: J. R. R. Tolkien and Political Philosophy*. Eugene, OR: Cascade Books, 2018.

Jensen, Steuard. "What Is Tom Bombadil?" *Tolkien Meta-FAQ*, October 17, 2002. http://tolkien.slimy.com/essays/Bombadil.html.

Kimball, Bruce. *Orators & Philosophers: A History of the Idea of Liberal Education*. New York: Teachers College, Columbia University, 1986.

Krimstein, Ken. *The Three Escapes of Hannah Arendt*. New York: Bloomsbury, 2018.

Lavan, Myles, Richard E. Payne, and John Weisweiler, eds. *Cosmopolitanism and Empire: Universal Rulers, Local Elites, and Cultural Integration in the Ancient Near East and Mediterranean*. New York: Oxford University Press, 2016.

Nugent, S. Georgia. *The Liberal Arts in Action: Past, Present, and Future*. Washington, DC: Council of Independent Colleges, 2015.

Nussbaum, Martha. *The Cosmopolitan Tradition: A Noble but Flawed Ideal*. Cambridge, MA: Belknap Press of Harvard University Press, 2021.

———. *Not for Profit: Why Democracy Needs the Humanities*. Rev. ed. Princeton, NJ: Princeton University Press, 2016.

Penaluna, Regan, and Samantha Rose Hill. "Hannah Arendt: 'You See the Politics on Her Face.'" *Guernica*, October 25, 2021. https://www.guernicamag.com/samantha-rose-hill-on-hannah-arendt-you-see-the-politics-on-her-face/.

Robbins, Bruce, and Paulo Lemos Horta, eds. *Cosmopolitanisms*. New York: New York University Press, 2017.

Ruane, Abigail E., and Patrick James. *The International Relations of Middle Earth*. Ann Arbor: University of Michigan Press, 2012.

Shippey, Tom. *J. R. R. Tolkien: Author of the Century*. Boston: Houghton Mifflin, 2000.

———. *The Road to Middle Earth*. Boston: Houghton Mifflin, 2003.

Tolkien, J. R. R. Foreword to *The Fellowship of the Ring*. Vol. 1 of *The Lord of the Rings*. New York: Ballantine, 1994.

———. *The Hobbit; or, There and Back Again*. London: Allen & Unwin, 1937.
———. *The Lord of the Rings*. 3 vols. New York: Ballantine Books, 1994.
———. "On Fairy-Stories." In *Tolkien on Fairy-Stories*, edited by Verlyn Flieger and Douglas A. Anderson. New York: HarperCollins, 2014.
———. *The Return of the King*. New York: Del Rey Books, 1966.
———. *The Silmarillion*. Edited by Christopher Tolkien. 2nd ed. New York: Houghton Mifflin, 2004.
Tömmel, Tatjana Noemi. "*Vita Passiva*: Love in Arendt's *Denktagebuch*." In *Artifacts of Thinking: Reading Hannah Arendt's "Denktagebuch,"* edited by Roger Berkowitz and Ian Storey. New York: Fordham University Press, 2017.
Tyler, J. E. A. *The Complete Tolkien Companion*. 3rd rev. ed. New York: St. Martin's Griffin, 2012.
Villa, Dana, *Arendt*. New York: Routledge, 2021.
———, ed. *The Cambridge Companion to Hannah Arendt*. New York: Cambridge University Press, 2000.
Xiang, Shuchen. *Chinese Cosmopolitanism: The History and Philosophy of an Idea*. Princeton, NJ: Princeton University Press, 2023.
Young-Bruehl, Elisabeth. *Hannah Arendt: For Love of the World*. New Haven, CT: Yale University Press, 1982.
Zakaria, Fareed. *In Defense of a Liberal Education*. New York: W. W. Norton, 2016.
Zimbardo, Rose A., and Neil D. Isaacs. *Understanding "The Lord of the Rings": The Best of Tolkien Criticism*. Boston: Houghton Mifflin, 2005.

PART THREE

**LIBERAL ARTS AND THE FUTURE
OF THE CLASSROOM**

14. Academic Freedom and the Future of the Liberal Arts
Lee Ward

THE INTENTION OF THIS CHAPTER is not to provide the case for liberal education in the modern world. There are already many eloquent and impassioned defenses of the intrinsic value and social utility of the liberal arts, including several in this volume.[1] My task is more specific and perhaps more mundane. I seek to identify the major challenges confronting liberal education as institutions of higher learning across the United States undergo a massive process of structural reorganization, one that endangers the continued survival of the liberal arts in their natural habitat, namely, the modern comprehensive university and liberal arts college. I wish to suggest that the idea of academic freedom must play a central role in preserving, and even renewing, the spirit of liberal education in the contemporary academic milieu. However, my approach is different from most discussions of academic freedom today that tend to focus on the issues of faculty freedom with respect to control over teaching, research, and both intramural and extramural speech.[2] Similarly, while academic freedom is clearly related to the principles of the University of Chicago statement on free speech on campus, my concern is not to highlight the moral and ethical problems produced by popular cancel culture, or the intellectually stifling effects of decisions by hyper-risk-averse university and college senior administrators or intolerant, ideological academic colleagues dreaming up speech codes and disciplinary star chambers of various sorts. As such, I do not seek to draw further attention to the celebrated, but in truth always rather rare, cases of individual faculty disciplined or dismissed for what they teach and write. These situations are no doubt eye-catching and normally demand vociferous condemnation, but they are unrepresentative of the experiences of most American academics in the third decade of the twenty-first century.

Rather the focus of this chapter is academic freedom understood in terms of the principles of collegial governance and the system of tenure. In particular, I want to highlight how the erosion of collegial governance and tenure threaten liberal education. Discussions about academic freedom today often fail to acknowledge the dangers posed to the liberal arts by the structural changes propelled by demographic forces and shifting societal expectations about the purpose of university and college. The hallmark of the reorganization of the American university and liberal arts college in the past decade or so is, of course, the plethora of administratively driven Academic Program Reviews (APR) designed to provide a rationale for the transfer of resources from humanities, social sciences, and fine arts departments to preprofessional programs.[3] In contrast to the isolated, sensational cases of the violation of academic freedom of individual faculty, these structural changes threaten to dim the prospects for liberal education across the spectrum of American higher education spanning public and private institutions, schools both religious and secular, and promise to impact seriously and negatively practically every scholar actively engaged in the liberal arts. The focus on academic freedom understood primarily in terms of collegial governance and tenure is justified because the most transformative effects of the structural changes validated by the new-model APR are the marginalization, and even, elimination of humanities, social sciences, and fine arts departments that were not so long ago widely held to be central to the raison d'être of the modern university; and the erosion of the institutional commitment to the principle of academic tenure under the withering pressure of specious claims about "student demand" and self-serving administratively defined "strategic balance."

In what follows, I will explore the grave impact that the ongoing sector-wide institutional reorganization holds for the embattled principles of collegial governance and tenure that have survived for more than a century. The diminution of the liberal arts will likely have implications for academic freedom more broadly as liberal education and academic freedom shared a common origin in the development of the modern American university. That is so say, the erosion of the tenure norm witnessed in the movement away from liberal education toward a reprioritization of preprofessional programs as the mission of the university could in time become one of the defining characteristics of higher education per se. In response to this unprecedented challenge to liberal education, I propose a new, revitalized conception of academic freedom resting on the premise that it is academics with expertise actively engaged in research and teaching in universities and colleges, and not boards, administrators, students, consumers, government agencies, or popular culture, that possess the unique capacity to define, promote, and protect the academic mission of the modern comprehensive university and liberal arts college. But what would it take, institutionally speaking, to reverse, or at least ameliorate, the effects of the current trends? And how can the more expansive and ambitious ideal of academic freedom I propose come to life in the context of our times? Before we can address these questions, we should reacquaint ourselves with the origins of the idea of academic freedom and its role in shaping contemporary American higher education.

THE ORIGINS OF ACADEMIC FREEDOM

The modern idea of academic freedom emerged in the German universities of the nineteenth century with the concepts of *Lehrfreiheit*, the freedom to teach, and *Lernfreiheit*, the freedom to learn.[4] In the German context *Lehrfreiheit* signified certain widely recognized principles of autonomy belonging to academics as members of a professional bureaucratic class within the public service. This idea of the university as a self-governing body of scholars was largely alien to the early American model of higher education. Prior to the twentieth century, most American universities and colleges were understood to be proprietary institutions owned and directed by a religious congregation, a wealthy founder, or a board of trustees. In this condition, faculty were typically viewed as employees subject entirely to the rules of employment, discipline, and termination determined by the governing authority in the school. A combination of factors in the late nineteenth and early twentieth centuries, including American graduate students returning from their studies in Europe with an appreciation for the level of autonomy enjoyed by German academics under *Lehrfreiheit*, as well as some high-profile cases of faculty dismissal and intimidation, pushed many American academics to mobilize with the goal of institutionalizing and codifying the principles of academic freedom for scholars.[5]

This process culminated in the establishment of the American Association of University Professors. Under the leadership of its first president, philosopher

John Dewey, and Columbia University economist Edwin Seligman, the AAUP issued its *1915 Declaration of Principles on Academic Freedom and Academic Tenure*, which would become the foundational document for academic freedom in America. The 1915 *Declaration* drew on both the German ideal of academic freedom, as well as the progressive era American context of its birth, to promote the idea of universities and colleges as a "public trust" serving the "great and indispensable organ of the higher life of a civilized community." Insofar as freedom of thought, speech, and inquiry for faculty members serves the public good, then the relation of university trustees to professors cannot be understood as simply that of a "private employer to his employees." The 1915 *Declaration* defined the academic mission of the university as contributing to the "sum of human knowledge," a goal served by the scholar's "independence of thought and utterance."[6] Faculty, then, are classed as professional experts in the production of knowledge acquired through highly specialized forms of inquiry.

The general principles of academic freedom articulated in the 1915 *Declaration* would become the basis for more comprehensive codification in the years that followed. The 1920 AAUP *Statement on the Government of Colleges and Universities* placed the principle of collegial governance at the very heart of academic freedom as it stressed the importance of faculty involvement in, among other things, departmental personnel decisions, appointment of administrators, establishment of budget priorities, and the setting of educational policies. The 1940 *Statement on Academic Freedom and Tenure*, the creation of which was spearheaded by negotiations between the AAUP and the Association of American Colleges representing liberal arts colleges, would eventually be endorsed by hundreds of institutions of higher education and its principles adapted into innumerable university and college rules.[7] Arguably, the deep original connection between the cause of academic freedom and the ethos of the liberal arts college was a distinguishing feature of the American experience in contrast to the German original.

Over the course of the first part of the twentieth century, a number of factors fortuitously merged to enable the principles of academic freedom to settle into well-established norms and hardened conventions. The more secure terms of employment offered by tenure became an important recruitment tool for university presidents grappling with skyrocketing enrollments and searching for faculty as allies in the contest for control with parochial and hidebound boards of trustees.[8] There were also a series of Supreme Court decisions in the Warren Court era including *Sweezy v. New Hampshire* (1957) and *Keyishian v. Board of Regents* (1967) in which the Court waxed eloquently about the "transcendent value" of academic freedom as it benefits all of society.[9] However, we must also recognize that academic freedom has always really been more a matter of convention than law. The Warren Court opinions defended academic freedom against invasions by state legislatures, not intramural administrative decisions and policies. In recent times, federal courts have typically shown little sympathy for individual professors in cases relating to "internal" institutional decisions. Arguably, in *Garcetti v. Caballos* (2006) the Supreme Court seriously undermined academic freedom by subjecting public servants to employer discipline, if their critical or dissenting speech relates to their professional duties. Indeed, courts have generally been more solicitous to recognizing "institutional academic freedom" that protects university and college administrations from state interference. Thus, the conditions that made tenure palatable, and even desirable, to university leadership in the early twentieth century are altered in our current age of declining enrollments and bureaucratic bloat, with senior administrators surrounded by ever-expanding armies of loyal nonacademic staff. It is perhaps fair to ask if many of the universities and colleges that once fully embraced the principles of academic freedom and tenure have disappeared in all but name.

THE CHALLENGE TO LIBERAL ARTS

The golden age of the American university in the postwar period was a halcyon time for collegial governance and the system of tenure as by the 1970s nearly 70 percent of all faculty in the United States were tenured; today the figure is closer to 30 percent.[10] This was also a time when liberal education flourished in the context of massive expansion of admissions; the tremendous infusion of public money through student loans, Pell Grants, and research funding; and, of course, a burgeoning affluent middle class that was willing and able to support the largest and arguably most inclusive system of higher education in the world at the time. Even as recently as the 1990s, there were robust enrollments in social sciences, humanities, and fine arts majors and minors, not to mention the proliferation of new departments, humanities institutes, research centers, and a medley of interdisciplinary liberal studies programs.

Needless to say, much has changed in a relatively short period of time. This is now the age of the new-model Academic Program Review. This APR is unlike anything previously in the history of the modern university. Unlike the core curriculum debates of the 1980s and 1990s that actually were about ideas, the APR now is not concerned with questions about the value or problem of canonical texts and thinkers. The APR of today is not even particularly ideological apart from vague and uninspiring neoliberal tropes about adapting to the "new economy." The new-model APR is almost solely designed to facilitate the radical structural reorganization of American universities and colleges. Regardless of the internal character, traditions, and distinct academic mission of the many institutions that have already, or will no doubt in time, introduce far-reaching APRs, there are two discernible general trends. First, the APR is often a tool employed by administrations and boards to restructure institutions by weakening the social science, humanities, and fine arts departments through the elimination of majors in these areas and the replacement of these traditional degree majors with ill-conceived, faddish interdisciplinary programs. Second, the barely concealed long-term aim of the APR is to provide the rationale for the steady reduction in the number of faculty, especially tenured and tenure-stream faculty, teaching and doing research in the liberal arts.

One influential model for the new APR is the Dickeson method invented by promoters of the "competency-based" higher-education sector, but has now been widely adopted by the higher-education consulting industry. Integral to this method of APR is the effective elimination of the university department as a unit of analysis and its replacement with an evaluative process entirely reduced to programs. Significantly, this prioritization of programs also typically involves practically collapsing the distinction between academic and nonacademic "programs" inasmuch as in a truly holistic review process a BA program in philosophy is assessed by the same generic evaluative measure as "University Parking" or "Food Services." A final distinctive feature of this method of program review is its remarkably open disregard for the norms of tenure and collegial governance. As one guidebook for evaluating "academic programs and services" puts it: "Governing boards, more focused on institutional realities, are recognizing that the granting of tenure constitutes a long-term commitment with a permanence not always warranted by enrollment shifts, curricular needs, and affirmative action imperatives."[11] Under the new APR regime, senior administrators and boards are advised to consult with legal counsel about the best practices for dismissing tenured faculty.

In many ways the new APR is a symptom of the deeper malaise pervading higher education. One aspect of this problem is, of course, the well-documented rise of the "All-Administrative University."[12] It is by now a familiar tale as the research-driven professoriate ceded increasingly greater power to administrations happy to set aside the norms of meaningful collegial governance. The effects of this renunciation of responsibility are predictable, as university and college governance systems succumbed to what Robert Michels famously termed "the iron law of oligarchy," as even the most putatively consultative processes became a facade to provide a patina of democratic legitimacy for decisions already predetermined in a hierarchical structure of concentrated power.[13] In many universities and colleges today, it is not uncommon to discover (in the unlikely event that actual budget data are somehow made publicly available) that for every dollar spent on academics, another dollar is spent on administration. While the dramatic growth in administration in the last decades does not solely impact the liberal arts, it does directly contribute to the crisis in liberal education both by reducing resources available to academics in general and by giving an air of plausibility to the self-serving claims of urgency by administrations seeking to shift the remaining "scarce" resources from liberal arts to preprofessional programs demonstrating greater "student demand."[14] Another aspect of the malaise in higher education is the increasingly invasive and unacademic audit culture. Once again, while this sad development is by no means unique to the liberal arts, the ethos of the audit culture, with its penchant for quantifiable measures of market outcomes and economic models of efficiency, seems to be particularly hostile to the spirit of liberal education directed, more idealistically, toward the development of the whole person.

The massive transfer of resources to the preprofessional programs presents something of a conundrum for proponents of the new APR. In most universities and colleges, the liberal arts and sciences still remain the single largest blocs in the faculty complement, even as their proportion continues to shrink dramatically from what it was just a few decades ago. As such, what remains of the institutions of collegial governance still matter insofar as the major structural changes that the APR is meant to initiate such as eliminating departments will typically still, at least formally, require the concurrence of a considerable share of faculty in the liberal arts who have no rational or professional motivation to increase the pace of their own marginalization and redundancy. In terms of collegial governance, one of the structural pillars of academic freedom was historically the clear separation of academic matters from the financial and budgetary aspects of the institution. Program approvals, curricular changes, and structural reorganization typically require the participation and authorization of a senate, forum, or council dominated numerically by faculty. The financial side invariably follows a separate track controlled almost exclusively by senior administrators and ultimately the board. The logic of the new APR is effectively to collapse the distinction between the academic and the financial, and in the process render collegial governance largely nugatory. APRs are no longer ever genuinely academic. They are primarily an administrative tool to introduce radically new budget priorities into the preexisting institutional circuitry of the university or college. Faculty are typically excluded from the opaque, even secretive, process of budget making. Just a few decades ago, comprehensive "Budget Books" were published annually, but now budget data is usually guarded like a state secret behind the flimsy excuse that today's university and college budgets are too complex to reduce to a single publicly available document.

The departmentalized liberal arts faculty are the single most important structural force that is left in a position to frustrate, and even thwart, the major structural changes intended by the new APRs. The diminution of the departmentalized liberal arts faculty will mean the gradual reduction of the number of faculty teaching and performing research in the liberal arts, as well as the relegation of those who remain on campus to the role of service teaching for preprofessional programs. I recall one senior administrator informing a campus "town hall" meeting called to discuss that institution's APR, that "while there may no longer be an English degree, or English Department after the APR, I can assure you that English will still be taught at this university." Needless to say, this was less than reassuring to proponents of the liberal arts on campus.

The long-term effects of a sector-wide loss of liberal arts departments are potentially enormous. It would strangle the formation of new scholars and scholarship in the liberal arts, as only a handful of überelite institutions largely free from market pressures would dominate and define the meaning of liberal education. Even top-tier liberal arts colleges would feel the effect, as a paucity of graduate programs in liberal arts disciplines would produce a professional dead end for students interested in continuing their studies after graduation. This, of course, is not to mention that even elite colleges are not immune from the cultural degradation of the prestige of the liberal arts, and very few of them may prove capable of resisting the intense pressure to conform to the new practical preprofessional dispensation.

Frequently, the proponents of the new-model APR present it as an exciting opportunity to reinvent the liberal arts. While it is certainly a useful and healthy exercise genuinely to reassess the quality of liberal arts teaching and research on campus, most faculty quickly realize that the process is all about downsizing the liberal arts' footprint on campus, not about renewal. Interdisciplinary programs are sometimes advanced as a way to husband resources of liberal arts faculty and rebrand traditional subjects and disciplines in new and interesting ways. Doubtless there is something attractive about the idea of interdisciplinarity, and there are certainly iconic institutions and programs that are not organized by departments, which many supporters of liberal education cherish. However, the structural reality remains that programs are more vulnerable to cutbacks and administrative depredations than fully fledged departments. Shutting down entire departments is still capable of setting off alarm bells among donors, alumni, students, local media, and state legislatures.

Another possible future path for liberal education could be the replacement of specific subject degrees with a general liberal arts BA. Often the idea of a two- or three-year degree program is put forward as a selling point for liberal arts: students will pay less and graduate (that is, get out into the workforce) sooner than students in preprofessional programs.[15] While this may or may not be a good marketing strategy, the likely effect would be a dramatic reduction in the number of faculty required to support a two- or three-year program. It would also require rethinking appropriate undergraduate prerequisite courses for graduate programs in specific disciplines, assuming there even is a future for graduate studies in the liberal arts. One thing that does seem certain is that as the resources devoted to social sciences, humanities, and fine arts continue to decline, unseemly battles among these departments over dubious carve outs and cynical sinecures will only intensify, especially as preprofessional programs push to have ever more of their students' required courses taught in-house (for example, the School of Kinesiology offering its own sections of the required intro English course).

It is foolish to resist change tout court, and, as we have seen, higher education in the United States has experienced dramatic and positive change in the past, such as during the passage from the "age of the college" to the "age of the university" in the early twentieth century.[16] But how is the current drive for change different? To start, the transformations of the past produced salutary diversity and symbiosis between liberal arts colleges and the humanities, social sciences and fine arts departments in research universities, as both reflected different, but largely complementary, approaches to liberal education. Nowadays, the impulse is toward greater homogeneity as the value of an academic degree or program is determined increasingly by the logic of consumer demand and employment outcomes. Moreover, the academic mission of the universities and colleges was expanded and refined by past transformations that tended to strengthen the commitment to knowledge acquisition already immanent in the traditional idea of liberal education. The spirit of the new-model APR reveals a decayed sense of academic mission eroded by social, economic, and cultural forces that display little or no self-conscious commitment to the acquisition and discovery of knowledge independent of vocational or technical training.

REVIVING ACADEMIC FREEDOM

Existing organizations dedicated to protecting academic freedom such as the AAUP will be profoundly impacted by the structural changes taking place in higher education. Frankly, in coming years there will likely be fewer and fewer professors actively engaged in teaching and research in the liberal arts. While there will remain academic freedom issues in the future, the structural changes that disproportionately harm the liberal arts will naturally be of less concern to organizations like the AAUP as a whole. Indeed, many faculty colleagues in the preprofessional programs welcome the transfer of resources away from the liberal arts. Tenure, on the other hand, still retains a strong hold in the imagination of faculty, and even a continuing residual attachment among this generation of senior administrators. The self-interested motivation to defend one's own job security is understandable. However, the norms underlying the commitment to tenure may be more fragile than is often supposed. The process for terminating tenured faculty for financial exigency, once thought a veritable doomsday by administrators fearful of the potential damage done to their institution's reputation, enrollment, and credit rating, has become more routinized just in the past few years. As the idea of financial exigency continues to evolve from executive action in extremis to simply another instrument in a board and administration's managerial tool kit, the system of tenure will become increasingly unsustainable. It is even conceivable that in the future there may arise a cynical inversion of the tenure norm as more and more faculty in the liberal arts with no discernible parallel opportunities for employment in the market are employed in nontenure lecturer positions, even as tenure will become a bonus or reward incentive to recruit and retain senior administrators.

What, then, is to be done? First, there must be a major effort by organizations such as the AAUP to educate the professoriate about the importance of collegial governance as a bulwark of academic freedom. In particular, scholars engaged in liberal education should have a more realistic understanding of the value and limitations of the concept of academic freedom, and not continue to view it as a shibboleth to ennoble every panicked response to an unexpected APR outrage. More fundamentally, though, academics must reassert their ownership of the academic mission of their institutions. The idea of academic mission presupposes that there is still some, albeit perhaps vague, notion beyond the perimeter of campus that the educational purpose of universities and colleges is more meaningful than enrollment numbers and branding exercises. In other words, academic mission is inseparable from the ideals of liberal education. Academic mission also serves as a powerful rhetorical counterpoint to the hackneyed and largely contentless business term "strategic priorities." Academic mission both unites all institutions of higher education and simultaneously respects their diversity. The academic mission may take a different form and cadence in public universities established as an element of the social compact than in religious schools directed toward promotion of a particular faith tradition. Other institutions can trace their distinctive academic mission back to noble causes such as abolitionism, racial equality, and early champions of women's rights.

The concept of academic freedom is central to the idea of academic mission because faculty are uniquely equipped and motivated to define and articulate the academic mission of their institution. As such, one element of the process to renew collegial governance could be the establishment of a Committee on Academic Mission in every university and college in the land. The CAM should be composed of a solid majority of full-time faculty elected proportionately by their peers in their academic units. In most institutions this would give scholars engaged in liberal arts a powerful voice, especially if ex officio membership is kept to a minimum. The CAM should be distinct from existing academic approval processes. The CAM's role in collegial governance would be threefold. First, it would provide oversight of any university- or college-wide APR and report regularly back to existing bodies such as the faculty senate or faculty council. In order to play this role, the CAM would require access to reliable and accurate budget information, allowing it to monitor the shift of resources to the administrative from the academic and from among academic units. Second, the CAM would ensure the regular scheduling of external academic unit reviews, ideally including a member of the CAM in the review process working with the provost's office. Admittedly, this will not be a popular proposal among many of my faculty colleagues who instinctively loathe unit reviews, seeing them as yet another administration driven make-work, keep-busy project. But one of the hallmarks of the new-model APR is the suspension of all external academic unit reviews, precisely because they typically recommend that more resources be devoted to departments to ensure they can effectively deliver their degree programs. Thus, these reviews can be a useful tool for liberal arts departments facing continual calls for retrenchment by their administration. Finally, the representatives from the CAM should have ex officio membership on the board of governors. The prevailing philosophy that disapproves of any interaction between boards and independent (that is, more than token) representation from faculty is, in the context of the new-model APR, simply a technical justification for dismissing faculties' concerns. A direct connection between the CAM and the board would allow representatives of the faculty to make regular presentations and updates to the board in a manner unfiltered by layers of cumbersome bureaucracy.

Another area worthy of further consideration is broader reform of the idea of the higher-education board model. The new APR is the product of a culture of imperious managerialism encouraged by a corporate model of governance. Increasing faculty representation on boards is compatible with a more democratic citizen governance principle better suited to institutions serving the public good. The concept of academic freedom has possessed a civic duty/public good dimension tracing all the way back to its German roots in *Lehrfreiheit*. Moreover, the principle of academic freedom has already, at least formally, been recognized in the United States by the Association of Governing Boards of Universities and Colleges in their 2010 *Statement on Board Responsibility for Institutional Governance*, and as such increasing faculty representation on boards can be justified as a means to institutionalize this aspirational support for academic freedom.

A final possible object for reform could be the system of higher-education accreditation. This is admittedly a byzantine arrangement of dozens of overlapping regional, national, and specialized organizations, but the basic principle of accreditation is relatively simple. Historically institutional accreditation was required for students to receive federal (and sometimes state) grants and loans. In its modern form, conceived during the rapid expansion of higher education produced by the GI Bills of the 1940s and 1950s, accreditation was designed to protect students and the student loan system from exploitation by institutions of dubious quality. Today, in addition to its traditional quality-control role, accreditation could also serve as a support for liberal education, and indirectly academic freedom. The accreditation process could reaffirm the centrality of liberal education to the academic mission of the modern university. Should any university or four-year college of a respectable size that does not have a viable English or Philosophy Department receive accreditation as a genuine institution of higher learning? While the specific criteria for satisfying a liberal arts requirement for accreditation would likely need to be flexible, it would be reasonable to expect that every comprehensive university and four-year college demonstrate substantial commitment of budgetary resources and administrative support to teaching and research in the liberal arts. In addition, the AAUP could lobby the federal and state governments to produce legislation requiring that a certain number of faculty and resources must be devoted to liberal education in order to receive government funding.

An obvious objection to this proposed revived conception of academic freedom is that "empowered" faculty are as dangerous to academic freedom and genuine free thought and free speech as the new-model APRs. Sadly, there is some truth to this complaint. Renewed emphasis on the role of faculty in defining and preserving the academic mission may well exacerbate the moralistic intolerance and ideological fetishism already so pervasive among American academe. But mobilized faculty with institutional bases of power is arguably the structural sine qua non in any realistic effort to save liberal education. Besides, academic freedom is a robust and capacious concept that is potent enough to allow us to continue to defend scholarly speech and writings from discipline and intimidation (but not open and rational criticism) by other faculty. The great danger to liberal education in our times is not the passionate intensity of the overzealous few, but rather the cold, almost elemental logic behind grand narratives about sweeping socioeconomic and technological change. It is this adversary, the one possessing "a gaze blank and pitiless as the sun," with which we have most to contend.[17]

BRIEF REFLECTIONS ON A DECADE OR SO OF APRS

This chapter is a clarion call that among many American academics will be lost in the deafening noise of structural change already enveloping their institutions. The pace of change in universities and colleges in recent times has been uneven across the sector, but there are a few distinguishing characteristics. The first wave of change arose in the context of the austerity measures introduced in the wake of the 2008 financial crisis. At that stage, many institutions experienced steep budget cuts, hiring freezes, and the first tentative moves to terminate selected programs. These measures had a temporary "feel" and tended to target the low-hanging fruit of boutique programs with struggling enrollments. The second wave from 2010 to 2016 saw the first introduction of the new-model APRs as university and college administrations hired pricey consulting firms to manage massive data-collection processes. These APRs were enormously time consuming for faculty, department chairs, and program directors who were tasked with inputting data in self-studies and then were typically left absolutely mystified by the quantitative measures and values the process produced. While these first-generation APRs were usually billed optimistically (or euphemistically) as opportunities for institutional renewal and for inspiring corporate culture team building, they were often directed by ad hoc committees with extraordinary powers and responsibilities designed to obviate the normal academic approval processes. Fortunately, in many institutions the most radical structural changes were halted by faculty resistance expressed either through the regular channels of shared collegial governance or by emergency measures such as votes of nonconfidence against senior administrators, and in the case of some unionized faculty even strike action.

Senior administrations and boards were often surprised at the intensity of the opposition to the APR, not to mention the organizational skill and spiritedness of faculty, especially among the liberal arts and sciences. At many schools, liberal arts departments found strong allies among the departmentalized natural scientists who face similar challenges of student demand and administrations seemingly bent on reducing them to service teaching for preprofessional programs. In the second wave of change we also saw the significant role that alumni support for liberal education can play in countering administration claims about student demand. Similarly, we learned that the idea of the academic mission still retains much greater symbolic and rhetorical power than the banal platitudes of managerial consumerism. But since 2017 we seem to have entered a third and more dangerous phase of APRs. The lengthy extended periods of data collection that characterized the second wave are now replaced by secretive processes often compressed into a few short weeks, the results of which are announced in the summer when campus is quiet. The APR is now less likely to be the subject of debate and criticism as it is designed to disarm opponents by its speed and the small number of handpicked faculty and administrators who participate in the process of supplying recommendations to the senior administration and board. In 2020 the pace of radical change is sometimes presented by administrations as the product of a new uncertain pandemic reality, when one would think that a pandemic is the very worst time to make hurried decisions that will produce permanent changes to institutions as complex as the modern university and college.

Declarations, or at least thinly veiled threats, of financial exigency—once seen as taboo—are now becoming a standard feature of academic program reviews in many small and midsize colleges and universities. Faculty are sometimes intimidated by ultimatums to resign with negotiated compensation or face unceremonious dismissal as lawyered-up administrations flex their muscle. The fabled nondisclosure agreement, once the exclusive purview of disgraced senior administrators, is now an occupational hazard of the humble tenured professor facing an unwelcome career change. Needless to say, the deepest cuts and most dramatic changes disproportionately impact liberal arts departments and programs. Unless conditions are reversed soon, the process of hollowing out the liberal arts core of the modern university and college will intensify even more rapidly. Herein lies both a great problem and perhaps a new ennobling task.

NOTES

1. Some recent books that make the case for liberal education from inside and beyond the academy include Peter Augustine Lawler, *American Heresies and Higher Education*; Martha C. Nussbaum, *Not for Profit: Why Democracy Needs the Humanities*; Fareed Zakaria, *In Defense of a Liberal Education*; Mark William Roche, *Why Choose the Liberal Arts?*; and Michael S. Roth, *Beyond the University: Why Liberal Education Matters*.

2. Arguably the classic study of the development of the concept of academic freedom in the United States is Richard Hofstadter and Walter Metzger, *The Development of Academic Freedom in the United States*. Recent works on academic freedom such as Joanna Williams, *Academic Freedom in an Age of Conformity*; Matthew W. Finkin and Robert C. Post, *For the Common Good: Principles of American Academic Freedom*; and Joan Wallach Scott, *Knowledge, Power, and Academic Freedom*, tend to focus primarily on freedom of speech, teaching, and publication, rather than the structural aspects of academic freedom relating to collegial governance and tenure.

3. I define liberal arts in terms of the humanities, social sciences, and fine arts. This is not to diminish the important role that biology, physics, astronomy, and mathematics have traditionally played in liberal education, but rather to acknowledge that the natural sciences face specific challenges derived from research pressures and funding expectations different from the liberal arts. Later I will argue that natural scientists are often valuable allies of liberal arts departments in the goal to protect the academic mission of the university and college.

4. Williams, *Academic Freedom in an Age of Conformity*, 34.

5. By contrast, the principle of *Lernfreiheit* (academic freedom for students) has never really been widely accepted in America.

6. Finkin and Post, *For the Common Good*, 160, 165, 161, 35.

7. Finkin and Post, *For the Common Good*, 47.

8. Benjamin Ginsburg, *The Fall of the Faculty: The Rise of the All-Administrative University and Why It Matters*, 151–52.

9. Finkin and Post, *For the Common Good*, 186–87.

10. Ginsburg, *Fall of the Faculty*, 136.

11. Robert Dickeson, *Prioritizing Academic Programs and Services: Reallocating Resources to Achieve Strategic Balance*, 56–57, 60–61, 128.

12. Ginsburg, *Fall of the Faculty*.

13. Robert Michels, *Political Parties: A Sociological Study of the Oligarchical Tendencies of Modern Democracy*.

14. It is no small irony that liberal arts courses and degrees are actually less expensive to deliver than preprofessional courses that require greater technical support and typically include "market supplements" for faculty salary.

15. A figure no less than Allan Bloom confided that one of the great trade secrets of modern higher education is that there is no need for an undergraduate degree to be as long as four years except in the case of a few select natural sciences. For reference, see Allan Bloom, *The Closing of the American Mind: How Higher Education Has Failed Democracy and Impoverished the Souls of Today's Students*, 340.

16. Hofstadter and Metzger, *Development of Academic Freedom in the United States*.

17. William Yeats, "The Second Coming."

BIBLIOGRAPHY

Bloom, Allan. *The Closing of the American Mind: How Higher Education Has Failed Democracy and Impoverished the Souls of Today's Students*. New York: Simon & Schuster, 1987.

Dickeson, Robert. *Prioritizing Academic Programs and Services: Reallocating Resources to Achieve Strategic Balance*. San Francisco: Jossey-Bass, 2010.

Finkin, Matthew W., and Robert C. Post. *For the Common Good: Principles of American Academic Freedom*. New Haven, CT: Yale University Press, 2009.

Ginsburg, Benjamin. *The Fall of the Faculty: The Rise of the All-Administrative University and Why It Matters*. Oxford: Oxford University Press, 2011.

Hofstadter, Richard, and Walter P. Metzger. *The Development of Academic Freedom in the United States*. New York: Columbia University Press, 1955.

Lawler, Peter Augustine. *American Heresies and Higher Education*. South Bend, IN: St. Augustine's Press, 2016.

Michels, Robert. *Political Parties: A Sociological Study of the Oligarchical Tendencies of Modern Democracy*. 1911. Reprint, New York: Free Press, 1962.

Nussbaum, Martha C. *Not for Profit: Why Democracy Needs the Humanities*. Princeton, NJ: Princeton University Press, 2010.

Roche, Mark William. *Why Choose the Liberal Arts?* Notre Dame, IN: University of Notre Dame Press, 2010.

Roth, Michael S. *Beyond the University: Why Liberal Education Matters*. New Haven, CT: Yale University Press, 2014.

Scott, Joan Wallach. *Knowledge, Power, and Academic Freedom*. New York: Columbia University Press, 2019.

Williams, Joanna. *Academic Freedom in an Age of Conformity*. New York: Palgrave Macmillan, 2016.

Yeats, William Butler. "The Second Coming." In *Michael Robertes and the Dancer*. 1921. Reprint, Whitefish, MT: Kessinger, 2003.

Zakaria, Fareed. *In Defense of a Liberal Education*. New York: W. W. Norton, 2015.

15. Leo Strauss and the Humanity of Liberal Education
José Daniel Parra

LEO STRAUSS IS RECOGNIZED BY students and critics alike as one of the rediscoverers of classical political rationalism in contemporary academia. The return to classical thought, in Strauss's understanding, is a "necessary and tentative or experimental" attempt to put again to the fore some of the key Socratic questions at the origins of the examined life. Such questions, in his view, are not theorems of abstract reason, but are reflected in an ongoing relation between "the city and man." It is in this philosophical context that Strauss brings together the history of political philosophy and liberal education.

This chapter offers a detailed reading of Strauss's remarks on the rationale for liberal education in late modernity. Although the focus will be on the opening two chapters of *Liberalism Ancient and Modern*,[1] the essay draws from a variety of sources in Strauss's oeuvre. What does it mean to be liberally educated? Is it possible to somehow find accord or at least mediation between the contemplative notion of logographic necessity essential to classical thought and the sense of open contingency and spontaneity inherent to the liberal worldview? Is the study of the great books "the one thing needful" in the modern research university? These may be some of the key questions and issues that concern Strauss regarding contemporary liberal education. Strauss's remarks on the topic might be a way to begin an exploration of the meaning and purpose of the study of old books in a time of profound transformation.

WHAT IS LIBERAL EDUCATION?

Strauss begins his remarks signaling the relationship between education and culture. The aim of liberal education is to foster the intellectual, spiritual, and ethical dispositions of a "cultured human being." Strauss proposes an organic analogy between education and cultivation that is reminiscent of Aristotelian teleology.[2] Education is akin to the "cultivation of the soil and its products, taking care of the soil, improving the soil in accordance with its nature." Human culture is grounded in accordance with the cultivation of understanding. As farmers cultivate the land, teachers nurture the human understanding. The counterimage to the natural analogy would be a kind of massive industrial education of efficient mechanical production. Strauss urges a return to the organic analogy to counterbalance the predominant view of fast-paced serial production and specialization prevalent in the modern research university.

Strauss wonders though how the educators themselves are to be educated. Naturally, teachers would need to undergo a process of learning. They may also have been pupils at some point, but Strauss sees that there must be teachers who are "not in turn pupils." Such teachers are the "greatest minds." Such teachers, we are told, are extremely rare: Strauss acknowledges that it is unlikely to meet any of them in a classroom. Further, it would be a "piece of good luck if there is a single one of them alive in one's time" (3). For the most part, access to the great thinkers occurs through the study of their books. Liberal education begins studying, with proper care,[3] the great books left behind by the greatest teachers. Such care and attentiveness for Strauss implies reading the great texts with an open mind: realizing that we may find through them insights of the greatest importance.[4] Strauss is deeply skeptical of the historicist premise that we may understand a great thinker better than he understood himself. There seems to be an attitude of receptive humility, sustained wonder, reverence even, in Strauss's approach to the great texts. Liberal education is the careful study of the great books in which the "more experienced pupils assist the less experienced pupils, including the beginners."[5]

Strauss himself critically reflects on this last passage: What does it mean that the great books should be read with "proper care"? One difficulty is that the greatest minds do not say the same things regarding the most important issues. It is striking but very stimulating that the greatest minds may not agree about the most important things. One of the ways in which Strauss seeks to make sense of such disagreement involves his rediscovery of the craft of esoteric writing.[6] Strauss contends that there is "discord" in the community of the greatest minds about the most important issues. Although Strauss doesn't specify what such issues may be, a possible list may include: eros, justice, friendship, citizenship, and the meaning of the divine.

Since the greatest minds disagree in their writings, Strauss points to an opportunity for authentic philosophical reflection and exploration. Given that the texts are not monolithic, liberal education, the careful study of such authors and their writings "cannot be simply indoctrination" (4). Liberal education is not neoscholasticism in its various shapes and historical renditions.

Another difficulty lies in the meaning of the proposition "education in culture." Strauss emphasizes that his focus lies on Western culture. But why only Western culture? Isn't this a signal of unenlightened parochialism, going against the grain of "the generosity, the open-mindedness, of liberal education"? Apparently, in our age we have come to the awareness that culture is not absolute but "has become relative" (4). Strauss implies that our contemporary cultural pluralism may not be unrelated to the problem of relativism or the disastrous concept of "post-truth." Still, can there be an education that is neither absolutist nor relative? The problem is how to offer an open-minded yet healthy or wholesome liberal education.

Strauss acknowledges that it is "not easy" to understand what culture (like nature) used in the plural might mean. Not easy does not mean impossible: it may be possible to combine a plurality of perspectives with a wholesome or unitary notion of nature or of culture. Although this could possibly mean a sort of *pluralist ontology*, Strauss nevertheless associates the plural view of culture with a type of "obscurity." He relates it sociologically to the link between plural cultures and random patterns of conduct of different human groups. But merely shared patterns of behavior are not what Strauss means by culture. The meaning of "culture" for Strauss in this text is related to the Epicurean as well as biblical images of the cultivation of a garden.

Strauss's more pressing concern, however, is about the meaning of liberal education "here and now." In the context of late-modern liberal democracies, liberal education is literate education or education "in letters and through letters" (4). By way of universal literacy, modern democracy has made universal education an ideal perhaps not contemplated in the classical world. To develop this point Strauss brings Rousseau to the discussion (although without mentioning him by name): "If there were a people consisting of gods, it would rule itself democratically. A government of such perfection is not suitable for human beings" (4–5).[7] Strauss interprets this passage by way of a distinction between "the ideal of democracy" and "democracy as it is." Strauss calls the dominant view in the profession of modern political science, the realist or Machiavellian or behaviorist approach, the "extreme view" in which the ideal of democracy is taken to be a "sheer delusion."[8]

Democracy as currently conceptualized by modern political scientists seems to assume an underlying "mass culture" as its basis. Strauss wants to signal a critique of such a grasp of political science and wonders whether political science can be distinct from a discipline conditioned by an atmosphere of mass or popular culture. For Strauss, liberal education is a *pharmakon*:[9] "the counterpoison to mass culture" and its corroding tendency to produce, in the words of Max Weber, "specialists without spirit or vision, voluptuaries without heart." Strauss also depicts liberal education as a "ladder" through which our democratic disposition may be uplifted. What Strauss probably has in mind is the prospect of consciously founding, or at any rate fostering, a philosophical school within the democratic regime.[10] In Strauss's words, this may be necessary to encourage the shaping of a philosophical "aristocracy within democratic mass society." We may wonder, however, what is the political purpose and aim of such a school. Is it to be dedicated to uplift the *demos*, or is it to be necessarily devoted to the cultivation of a few ambitious and gifted students? Can somehow these two educational aims be balanced out to some extent? Beyond intimations about constitutional design, Strauss does not say much about the relation between philosophical education and a genuine uplifting of the *demos*.

Strauss does mention that liberal education will offer those who "have ears to hear" a renewed awareness of the perennial possibility of "human greatness." Notice the auditive image, which may be related to opinion and belief: we "hear" by way of extrinsic reception (oral or written), not primarily by inner self-understanding. Liberal education in Strauss's view is necessarily literate education. He expresses skepticism toward the ways of learning of what he calls "preliterate tribes." Why? Because Strauss asserts that illiterate culture is "at its best" ruled by ancestral custom. Such custom tends to trace its origins to the "gods, the sons of gods, or pupils of gods" (6). Without books or letters, later generations cannot be in direct contact with the original intent of the founders. Letters seem to make possible such contact between the founders and the "latest heirs." It is unclear, though, whether this proposition still holds in a world full of new and rediscovered resources of communication. We may need to reconsider the distinct significance of writing over other channels of communication (cf. Plato, *Phaedrus*, 274e–276a7, 276e5–277c6).

However this may be, Strauss emphasizes that we are "compelled to live with books." Since life is so brief, such compulsion leads to search for the "greatest books." The model to approach the greatest books, the *mediator* in such endeavor is the philosopher Socrates.[11] Socrates, however, did not write books, but Strauss contends that he was a careful reader of books. Socrates went over the texts of "the wise men of old" with his students and friends. Strauss references Xenophon to tell us that Socrates through the shared reading of such old books[12] led those who were listening toward "perfect gentlemanship." Strauss seems to be saying that the shared reading of the old books of the wise was how Socrates communicated with the "gentlemen," the *kaloi kagathoi*, of classical Athens.[13]

Strauss, however, immediately adds that this account is "defective." It does not tell us whether the texts Socrates studied, besides being wise, also partook in salutary goodness. We learn that the gentleman is chiefly concerned with the pursuit of honor and the preservation of the body. Strauss contrasts this concern with Plato's suggestion that education in the highest sense is philosophy: the search for wisdom or the comprehensive knowledge of the most important things. Such wholesome knowledge would be "virtue and happiness." Strauss gathers that wisdom is inaccessible to man as man, and from this concludes that, humanly speaking, virtue and happiness will "always be imperfect" (7). Although the Platonic philosopher as such is not a wise man, he nevertheless is apparently declared "the only true king." The freedom-friendly democratic regime, however, is not constitutively amenable to the logic of philosophical kingship and wisdom.[14] It seems that for the liberal democratic regime it may be hard to re-create an open disposition toward that "highest form" of humanistic education that in the classical and Renaissance literature is known as the education of princes.

Strauss explains that in the context of the modern research university people who call themselves philosophers do so mostly for "administrative convenience." In some way, philosophers are to philosophy departments what artists are to art departments: it would be "absurd," Strauss acknowledges, to find authentic philosophers and artists under such regimented conditions. Strauss modestly concludes that although we "cannot be philosophers," we can still "love philosophy" or "try to philosophize."[15] By "trying to philosophize," Strauss means "listen[ing] to the conversation" among the great minds through the comparative study of their books. The study of the great minds is not necessarily limited to reading Western thinkers: Strauss mentions the philosophical traditions of India and China, which would be worthwhile studying if we understood their languages. Liberal education is an exercise of "listening" that takes place through our dialogical study of the divergent writings of the greatest authors. If we understood their languages, there could well be a philosophical and spiritual conversation between the great authors of East and West.

The encounter between philosophical authors may come to life through our hermeneutic participation: the greatest thinkers are not dialogical and tend to "utter monologues." The greatest minds are monological even when they write dialogues. To explain this assertion, Strauss notes that there is no Platonic dialogue between two mature philosophers. The difficulty lies in doing something that, apparently, the greatest minds felt they could not authentically do: to be in conversation with one another, and hence to be authentically open to being persuaded. Strauss reiterates that the greatest minds appear to contradict one another regarding the "most important matters" (7). Such contradictions, according to Strauss, would "compel us to judge" their monologues. Strauss also acknowledges that the greatest minds are not our peers, and therefore we may not be competent judges for the task at hand.

There is a further difficulty: historicism, the belief that thought is a product of its times or of its material conditions, has made us believe that we can understand a first-rate author better or at any rate differently than he understood himself. We assume that our perspective is "somehow superior, higher than those of the greatest minds" (8). We seem to believe that the thought of the greatest minds may be completely contextual and dependent on the zeitgeist of their times. This induces us to believe that there may not be "*the* simply true substantive view," but a set of different contextual formal views. Such formally constructed views are, in turn, based on the relativity of thought taken to be dependent on its time and place. Hence, comprehensive views would seem to be pluralistically exclusive or fragmented, and "none can be simply true" (9). Our main delusion, Strauss reiterates, is that we believe we are wiser than the "wisest men of the past." So, our interest in studying their books tends to be halfhearted and conditional.

Strauss wonders about what would be needed to approach the books of the wise with a truly receptive disposition. The lack of receptivity may not be unrelated to the experience that "all simply authoritative traditions in which we could trust" seem to have been lost to we moderns. In Strauss's reckoning, at least two generations of teachers before his time have worked toward the establishment of the "simply rational society" and that increasingly removed a trustworthy *nomos* that could have provided students with reliable guidance. Philosophically speaking, this has left many students with a sense of anomie, moved to find their bearings in a tentative and experimental manner.

The loss of a stable *nomos* or overarching tradition has also renewed the possibility for philosophy. The problem is that we seem to have forgotten how to philosophize. Philosophy for Strauss does not explicitly aim at being constructive: it can only be "intrinsically edifying."[16] The exercise of philosophy, Strauss reminds us, from time to time brings us to the realization or the awareness of the understanding of understanding: the *noesis noeseos*, which for Aristotle is akin to the contemplation of the divine. This *noetic* self-examination is somehow beyond pleasure and pain or the mere judgments of sense perception. It suggests an essential awareness that leads us to "realize that all evils are in a sense necessary if there is to be understanding" (8). The intellectual realization of "logographic necessity" in Strauss's experience might be distinct from the experience of *amor fati*. In Strauss's mind, intellectual necessity may be at odds with the *logique du Coeur*. Strauss mentions the Augustinian *City of God* to convey his intellectual experience in which the apparent necessity of the intellect may also "break our hearts." In this disjuncture between "heart" and "intellect," the saturnine Strauss sides with thought: the dignity of man, in his view, is anchored in the dignity of the mind. Still, Strauss remarks that the goodness of the world, "whether we understand it as created or uncreated," is attested by being the home of the human mind.

A definitive feature of liberal education is the permanent exploration of the greatest minds. Strauss calls it "a training in the highest form of modesty" (8). It entails taking critical distance from the tendentious noise of popular culture and the vainglorious polemics of intellectuals and their enemies. It implies the humility and boldness to regard our own given views as mere opinions, and to begin examining them as such. Liberal education is reflective liberation from unexamined opinion. Strauss ends the essay proposing that liberal education can be liberation from *apeirokalia*, or the boundless "lack of experience of things beautiful" (8). In our secular world, liberal education may well be a starting point and pathway toward "experience in things beautiful."

LIBERAL EDUCATION AND RESPONSIBILITY

Strauss acknowledges that education is "in a sense" the subject matter of his courses and research. He is mostly concerned with the final cause or goal of education "at its best or its highest." In the division of labor of the modern research university, Strauss is mostly concerned with its ultimate telos, together with a peripheral and discreetly respectful relation to its administration. The key components of the telos of education are the qualities of the educator and of the pupils. In the "highest form of education," such talents are in a sense given, and the main pedagogical task is to avoid interfering with their interplay. A rule of thumb that Strauss offers to university teachers is a reminder of intellectual wonder and humility: "Always assume that there is one silent student in your class who is far superior to you in head and in heart" (9). A teacher should not have too high an opinion of his importance, while having "the highest opinion" of his duty or responsibility.

Strauss signals a distinction between the expressions "liberal education" and "responsibility." What is the difference between being liberally educated and being "responsible"? (10). Although these dispositions may not be "separable from one another," they are also not identical. Strauss reminds us that the word "responsibility" is a neologism. It is a substitute for the words "duty," "conscience," or "virtue." To be responsible means to be able to *respond*, to offer an account for actions that may be intentional or self-standing, with relative independence of consequences. We moderns seem to believe that by being responsible, or by responding for our actions, or by being sincere, we have redefined virtue. Virtue seems to become indistinguishable from decency. In our contemporary version of the human situation, we seem to prefer somewhat low-key words that tend to be not so grandiloquent and are rather pragmatic or businesslike. Strauss wonders about our substitution of the notions of virtue and conscience for the more concrete sense of responsibility.[17]

Classical liberal education in the sense of *paideia* is a form of learning that is indistinguishable from child's play.[18] At some level, however, liberal education is also addressed to the politically keen and businesslike gentlemen. The gentlemen Strauss seems to have in mind in this portion of the text are the Glaucon types, sociologically speaking "serious men" eager about their future in public affairs and concerned with the most "weighty matters." Strauss also describes them as "the earnest ones" publicly concerned with "the good order of the soul and of the city" (11). Their education needs to be based on the cultivation of "character and taste." The unacknowledged sources of this sort of education are the poets. The gentlemen are also in need of skills, especially household management, or *oikonomia*, the economy of means, as well as the skill of managing the affairs of the city. This acculturation, Strauss notes, takes place for the most part through becoming acquainted with "older or more experienced gentlemen," learning rhetoric, reading historians, studying what might be called today "comparative politics," as well as dwelling on the works of the poets and engaging directly in political life. Strauss reports that the pursuit of these activities requires leisure and some independent wealth.

The gentlemen also need to demonstrate a certain noblesse oblige to legitimize their especial education as well as their eventual exercise of political power. Strauss mentions the Aristotelian view that justice presupposes equality for equals. We may wonder whether the gentlemen are truly superior to the people at large. If access to education were a matter of chance, then the chance of becoming a gentleman would seem to be incompatible with equitable justice. A kind of democratic political compromise the gentlemen seem to have found to is to rule not by their own right, but by popular election. Strauss suggests now that for the gentlemen moral virtue is an end-in-itself, while for the nongentlemen virtue is a mere means: a means for wealth and honor. Since the gentlemen aim at moral virtue and the nongentlemen aim at wealth and honor, there may not be a common purpose between these two kinds of human character types. If they are not in agreement about "first principles," they cannot engage in genuine common deliberation.

Strauss notes that this sort of reasoning, depicting the democratic regime in terms of the fundamental and essential disagreements of the gentlemen and nongentlemen, might lead to a disheartened rejection of democracy. In a democratic regime the majority rules, but perhaps only a minority is truly educated. The democratic solution is that the majority rules on the principle, not of virtue, but of *freedom*. In this interpretative approach, Strauss mentions by name the sophist Protagoras, who came to Athens to teach the "political art." In a democracy everybody is supposed to have access to this art "somehow" (13). The majority seems to be habituated into that art by means of an effective inculcation of rewards and punishments, or by obeying the law. The "political art," however, goes beyond mere obedience, and is more directly related to the architectonic framing of the laws.[19]

In a political sense the gentlemen may "set the tone" of society, particularly by how they are perceived ruling in broad daylight. The pursuits of the gentlemen are said by Strauss to be politics and philosophy. Loosely understood, philosophy seems akin to the pursuit of "intellectual interests." But "strictly speaking," Strauss adds, philosophy means the quest for truth about the "most weighty matters." Philosophically understood liberal education changes its meaning and becomes cultivation for the love of wisdom. In this sense, Strauss helpfully clarifies that liberal education "transcends gentlemanship." The gentleman operates within the sphere of *doxa*: he accepts "on trust certain most weighty things" that the philosopher as such questions and investigates. There is a distinction therefore between the gentleman's virtue and philosophical virtue. One sign of such distinction is that the gentleman needs wealth to exercise his liberality, but the Socratic philosopher may well live with modest means. Philosophical "soul care" can occur with relative detachment regarding material possessions. In Strauss's view, the Socratic philosopher would have no need to acquire the arts for making and protecting his wealth, or to develop the "habit of self-assertion" that of necessity is part of the gentleman's character. Strauss nevertheless adds that the two kinds of virtue might not be completely independent: the gentleman's virtue may be a reflection of philosophical virtue. The rule of the gentlemen may be justified if it is a reflection or representation of philosophical virtue.

Philosophical education, education toward the love of wisdom, never ceases as long as the philosopher lives. Hence, it is "adult education par excellence" (14). This sort of cultivation is to be acquired constantly "from the start." There is a distinction between the playful education of the young gentleman and his serious future work. This distinction doesn't apply to the philosopher: Strauss highlights that the philosopher does not wish to exercise political rule, for he is concerned with the contemplation and understanding of natural necessities.

Now, if philosophers don't engage in political power tout court, then the gentlemen will appear to rule over them. This doesn't make sense to Strauss. In order to address this difficulty, Strauss introduces the question of priestcraft. Both philosophers and priests are teachers. Philosophers, however, unlike priests, may not be "constitutive parts" of the city.[20] For Strauss, philosophy and the "city of man" have different ends. There is a "fundamental disproportion" between such city and the way of life of the philosopher. Strauss stresses here that "the philosopher and the non-philosophers cannot have genuinely common deliberations" (14). Strauss's provocative suggestion may therefore be that the priests at some level act as mediators between the philosophers, the *thumotic* gentlemen, and the people at large. Strauss opts in political matters for evenhanded moderation as an alternative to overt radical speculation. Although politics generally requires stability, philosophy must be "intransigent" in its pursuit of wisdom. Philosophical radical questioning can only live "side by side" with a healthy sense of moderation and even-keeled reform in the political community. Practically speaking, the philosopher who doesn't owe his education to the city is not obliged to engage in political rule. The philosopher, however, is indebted to the city for the satisfaction of his basic needs, and that will be an incentive for him to be a lawful citizen. What is the political role of the philosopher? The philosopher by living the examined life benefits the city: the dialogical pursuit of self-knowledge has "necessarily a humanizing or civilizing effect" (15).[21] It appears that the liberal city would need philosophy indirectly or only in "diluted form." Plato uses the image of the "cave" to depict the city. The cave as such is seemingly closed, in contrast to the philosophical way of life. Strauss acknowledges that the classics were clear about the distinction between aristocracy in theory and its unlikely political actualization. The historical solution to the problem of legitimate political authority appears to have been satisfied by a mechanism of power sharing: the "mixed regime" that eventually took the shape of modern republicanism.

Ancient and modern republicanism are nevertheless distinct. Modern republicanism is based on social equality and popular sovereignty to guarantee the people's "natural rights." This is achieved mainly by way of a separation of powers meant to protect individual rights. The predominance of an emerging commercial and industrial elite based on the desire of each to improve their material conditions takes over the role of the landed gentry as the predominant social group. Politically speaking, social equality was incrementally actualized through popular secret voting in liaison with open and scrutable government activity. Government becomes representative of the people and is therefore "responsible" to them. Such responsibility, according to Strauss, is to a large extent tacit or cannot be legally defined and thus tends to also become a gray area of modern republicanism.

In the premodern world, civic responsibility used to be supported by religious education. Religiously based education used to set the tone for presecular society at large. In terms of the education of political elites, Strauss mentions John Locke to the effect that liberal education—especially the study of the ancient Greeks and Romans—used to prepare the gentlemen for political rule. The *Federalist Papers*, an eminently "sober work," points out that the "natural arbiter" between the landed and the commercial classes is the man of the "learned professions" who is likely to think in the general interests of society. Under favorable conditions, the people of the learned professions will hold the balance of power between the landed and the commercial interests. Strauss does not mention the interests or the education of the working classes. For Strauss, the question here is whether the men of the learned professions will be liberally educated. He finds probable that in our time a large number of them will be lawyers.

It is in his reflection on the question of priestcraft in modernity that Strauss references "the law profession." He quotes Edmund Burke's claim that lawyers constitute "another priesthood, administering the rites of sacred justice."[22] Strauss is suggesting that conventionally speaking both priests and lawyers perform their duties within the realm of *nomos*. Since philosophy is an ascent from *nomos* to *phusis*, there would be a key distinction between priests and lawyers, on the one hand, and philosophers, on the other.[23] One of the thought-provoking implications of this line of reasoning would be the link between historicism or the predominance of *nomos* over philosophical thought, and its corollary of the political preeminence of priests and lawyers over philosophers.

Strauss continues, again citing Burke: although the legal training strengthens the mind, "it is not apt, except in persons very happily born, to open and to liberalize the mind in exactly the same proportion" (17). There is a tendency in the craft of lawyers and priests toward a certain type of dogmatic or bounded reasoning, that is, a tendency to remain reasoning within a pregiven body of canons or doctrines.

Besides Burke, Strauss also references John Stuart Mill: for Mill, liberal education is classical education that transmits to us the "wisdom of life." Liberal education provides the foundation for ethics and philosophy in textual form and substance: the classics "used the right words in the right places" (17). Politically speaking, Mill favored proportional representation for representative government, as it offers "transcendent advantages" for helping elect people of high qualification for office. Mill also favored a liberally educated civil service. Liberal education can affect the civil service "decisively in the performance of its duties" (18).

In Strauss's estimation, the restoration of religious education to its "pristine power" is beyond the scope of his essay. He mentions or rather questions rhetorically whether the concern with liberal education for adults is not unrelated to the decay in religious education. Can or should liberal education perform the role that used to be offered by religious teachings? Instead of dwelling on this potentially thorny concern, Strauss chooses to focus on possible reforms in university departments of political science and in schools of government and law, which are the places where civil servants are mostly educated. Such changes may have less to do with the subjects taught and more with the "emphasis in the approach." In the context of these programs within the modern research university, "whatever broadens and deepens the understanding should be more encouraged than what in the best case cannot as such produce more than narrow and unprincipled efficiency" (19). Political science departments, programs of government, and law schools would benefit from studies that open the mind[24] instead of their current focus on statistical measurements to demonstrate commonplaces and their disproportionate spread of technical specialization.

Strauss accepts that university education is a "public or political power." While liberal education in the "original sense" was based on classical philosophy, the new learning of our research universities is mostly based on modern philosophy. Strauss claims that ancient philosophers and nonphilosophers pursued radically different ends: for the ancients, the fulfillment of philosophers "essentially transcends society."[25] The conception of modern philosophy, in turn, is "fundamentally democratic." From the modern perspective, the distinction between philosophers and nonphilosophers ceases to be stark: "The end of philosophy is now no longer what one may call disinterested contemplation of the eternal, but the relief of man's estate" (19). In the modern era philosophy apparently ceases to be a contemplative way of life and becomes to a large extent a practical and experimental social activity.[26]

While modern philosophy has been "inspired by biblical charity," classical philosophy was based on a pagan sense of pride. Paradoxically, Strauss also sees a contrast between the "realistic," concrete-minded moderns and the "idealistic," "heavenly," or "visionary" ancients (20). For the moderns, philosophy ceases to be an end-in-itself and eventually becomes associated with power-knowledge: knowledge becomes power for the sake of self-preservation and the fostering of economic abundance. While in the classical sense there was a separation between manual labor and science, in the modern conception philosophy-science tends to become an instrumental sort of social engineering. Modern science is therefore performed for the improvement of the people's material conditions. To assuage the people's potential disbelief about the modern project, they had to be enlightened on the advantages of applied science. An increasingly universal enlightenment, the diffusion of the new science, became therefore the "new education." Strauss finds that the universal enlightenment was the great equalizer by means of the popularization of the scientific method. Although scientific discoveries were still the purview of a few philosopher-scientists, scientific results could in principle be communicated to and used by everybody. Also, the change from deeply held religious cultures to a progressive sense of secular civilization has been made possible by means of commerce and trade, which expanded the application of the scientific method in the direction of new discoveries and inventions that are the engine of modern political economy. Now, Strauss is concerned that a problematic consequence of the modern project has been the instrumentalization of virtue. This has produced the contraction of education into different sorts of specialized practical training. The narrowing of virtue, Strauss notes, has increasingly led to its falling into disuse in our moral language. It also seems as if the old transformative experience of *metanoia* were no longer applicable to our human situation. Institutionalized rights discourses and specialized practical training seem to take the place of classical soul care as the new aim and focus of education. What the times seem to require is a process of transition from "unenlightened to enlightened self-interest" (21). The problem, therefore, is that a massive project of social engineering based on sophisticated methods of institutional design and the application of procedural legal and social norms has increasingly and overwhelmingly supplanted classical *paideia* and liberal education.

The modern world is characterized by economic plenty and equality of opportunity made possible by applied science. Strauss explains that this has led to the launching of "the age of tolerance." Hence, the modern project has produced a significant shift in the meaning of the word "humanity." While in the ancient view it used to refer to the virtue appropriate in one's dealings with the "underdog," in our age it has become the crucial virtue. Humanity becomes associated with the new virtue of compassion.

The modern project was sometimes guided by modern philosophers as advisers of princes, who as such could become "enlightened princes." As the enlightenment progressed, however, the philosophical tutelage of princes ceased to be a priority. Although the people didn't always listen to the philosopher-scientists, power became entrusted to the people, who have progressively realized that it is in their own interests to listen to the philosopher-scientists. Modern society has acquired the shape it has taken via historical rapprochement between "enlightenment from above" and the "freedom of the people."

In the contemporary separation between science and philosophy, science has now taken the upper hand, gradually gaining universal recognition. A major problem is that modern science, according to Strauss, "has no longer any essential connection with wisdom" (22). Strauss claims that the fruitful tension between liberal education and religious education has been replaced by a tension between the democratic ethos and the ethos of technocracy or specialization. Modern science is driven by utilitarian instrumentality, and this is expressed in its practical concern with medicine, human longevity, and health-related matters. Modern science increasingly legitimizes its ends by the demands of such market needs with efficiency as a key criterion.

In the modern tendency to associate learning with technical specialization, the broadening and deepening of understanding increasingly seems to lose ground vis-à-vis the disciplines of analytical logic and methodology

(23). Research universities try to counterbalance the effects of narrow specialization by means of general civilization courses, which Strauss compares to a sort "gigantic spectacle" or an "unending cinema," exciting and entertaining but perhaps lacking in genuine educational depth. The modern university, in other words, has to a tremendous extent lost sight of the key psychological and therapeutic insight that virtue is the aim of eros. The Platonic-Socratic erotic love of wisdom seems to be replaced by conventional social conditioning and the global construction of norms driven by predictable and safe social adjustment.

It is for these motives that Strauss wonders deeply about the prospects for liberal education in our late-modern condition. Still, despite these developments, Strauss feels the need to emphasize that he is no antidemocrat: he is a "friend and ally of liberal democracy" (24). Such disposition, however, prevents him from being a mere flatterer of the democratic regime. A decisive incentive to support liberal democracy is that democratic freedom makes possible the life dedicated to the love of wisdom. Strauss acknowledges that liberal democracy allows for the "cultivation of our garden."

It may be in this philosophical context that Strauss wonders whether the modern drive for specialization could be redirected toward the questions concerning "the one thing needful." For Strauss, "as matters stand," this may begin to happen in the humanities rather than in the applied sciences. The humanities are closer to "the spirit of perceptivity and delicacy" than to "the spirit of geometry" (24). The humanities and liberal education in concert can foster the study of the great books in late modernity with a transformative intent. The question is whether this can be done with a sense of generosity, playfulness, and love of learning free from the careerist vanity and revisionist vindications prevalent in large segments of today's research universities worldwide.

Strauss closes his remarks on liberal education and responsibility with a word of caution. He notes that the political earthquakes experienced in the first half of the twentieth century were to a large extent derived from misguided appropriations of the writings of Karl Marx and of Friedrich Nietzsche. This profound historical experience led him to ponder on the relationship between wisdom and political moderation. In Strauss's view of the contemporary situation, political moderation may offer a sense of steadfastness and equilibrium in contrast to "visionary expectations from politics and unmanly contempt for politics" (24). A renewed sense of clear-eyed moderation and classical *sophrosyne* might be a way to understand hubris and begin giving a hearing in the modern polity to the liberally educated.[27] Because liberal education is "concerned with the souls of men" (25), it cannot be merely automated or massive specialized training. Liberal education consists in listening to "still and small voices" as it seeks the light of understanding.

NOTES

1. Unless otherwise noted, references in the text are from Leo Strauss, *Liberalism Ancient and Modern*, 3–25. I would like to thank Peter Minowitz, Ann Ward, Constantine Vassiliou, and the two anonymous reviewers of the chapter for their stimulating comments and suggestions.

2. Aristotle, *Physics*, 192b32–33, 194a28–29, 199b15–18; Aristotle, *Politics*, 1333a29–30; Aristotle, *De Caelo*, 292b17–19.

3. Martin Heidegger, *Being and Time*, 225ff, also puts forth a "structure of care," an ontological attunement that appears to not be necessarily mediated by texts as such. For Strauss's critique of Heidegger, see "An Introduction to Heideggerian Existentialism," 27–46.

4. Leo Strauss, *Persecution and the Art of Writing*, 34–35.

5. Contrast with Plato, *Phaedrus*, 230d–e.

6. Strauss, *Persecution and the Art of Writing*, 7–21.

7. Jean Jacques Rousseau, *On the Social Contract*, 84–85.

8. Niccolò Machiavelli, *The Prince*, 61.

9. Plato, *Phaedrus*, 274d–277c6. See also Jacques Derrida, *Dissemination*, 95ff; Stanley Rosen, *Hermeneutics as Politics*, 50–86.

10. Leo Strauss, *On Tyranny*, 195.

11. Leo Strauss, *The Rebirth of Classical Political Rationalism: An Introduction to the Thought of Leo Strauss*, 103–83.

12. Xenophon, *Memorabilia*, 1:6, 14.

13. Leo Strauss, *Xenophon's Socratic Discourse*, 46–49. Consider Laurence Lampert, "Strauss' Recovery of Esotericism," 69–70. What does Strauss mean by the *kalos kagathos* type? Lampert provocatively points out that in a letter to his friend Jacob Klein (February 16, 1939), Strauss intimates that in the "Socratic circle" the notion of the *kalos kagathos* or gentleman was a "swear word, something like '*philistine*' or '*bourgeois*' in the 19th century." Strauss also critically associates Aristotle's "perfect gentleman" with the "true 'pharisee' in the Christian sense . . . who is not ashamed of anything or does not regret or repent anything he has done because he always does what is right or proper." Strauss, *Liberalism Ancient and Modern*, 268. In *On Tyranny*, Strauss offers a perhaps more evenhanded description, saying that there are two possible meanings of "gentleman" that would correspond to the "Platonic distinction between common or political virtue and genuine virtue" (109n27).

14. See Strauss, *On Tyranny*, 71, where Strauss's Xenophon holds the paradoxical view that "the wise are not concerned with freedom."

15. Compare with Nietzsche, *Beyond Good and Evil*, § 211, 268, 295. See also Martine Béland, "Vocation as Therapy: Nietzsche and the Conflict between Profession and Calling in Academia," 13–30.

16. See Pierre Hadot, *Philosophy as a Way of Life*.

17. See Nasser Behnegar, *Leo Strauss, Max Weber and the Scientific Study of Politics*, 80ff.

18. Leo Strauss, *The Argument and the Action of Plato's Laws*, 17.

19. Contrast with Plato, *Gorgias*, 521d7–9.

20. Aristotle, *Politics*, 1328b4–21.

21. Leo Strauss, *What Is Political Philosophy?*, 87; Strauss, *Persecution and the Art of Writing*, 16, 21; Leo Strauss, *The City and Man*, 19–21.

22. See Strauss, *Rebirth of Classical Political Rationalism*, 249–50.

23. Leo Strauss and Joseph Cropsey, eds., *History of Political Philosophy* (Chicago: University of Chicago Press, 1987), 1–6.

24. Contrast with George Grant, "Faith and the Multiversity," 35–77; and George Grant, "The University Curriculum," 111–33.

25. Strauss, *What Is Political Philosophy?* 38–40.

26. See Nicolas Lobkowicz, *Theory and Praxis*.

27. See also Strauss, *What Is Political Philosophy?*, 32; Strauss, *On Tyranny*, 184–86; and Rosen, *Hermeneutics as Politics*, 119.

BIBLIOGRAPHY

Aristotle. *De Caelo*. Translated by C. D. C. Reeve. Indianapolis: Hackett, 2020.

———. *Physics*. Translated by Robin Waterfield. Oxford: Oxford University Press, 2008.

———. *Politics*. Translated by Carnes Lord. Chicago: University of Chicago Press, 1984.

Behnegar, Nasser. *Leo Strauss, Max Weber and the Scientific Study of Politics*. Chicago: University of Chicago Press, 2003.

Béland, Martine. "Vocation as Therapy: Nietzsche and the Conflict between Profession and Calling in Academia." In *Nietzsche's Therapeutic Teaching*, edited by Horst Hutter and Eli Friedland. London: Bloomsbury, 2013.

Derrida, Jacques. *Dissemination*. Translated by Barbara Johnson. Chicago: University of Chicago Press, 1981.

Grant, George. "Faith and the Multiversity." In *Technology and Justice*. Toronto: Anansi, 1986.

———. "The University Curriculum." In *Technology and Empire*. Toronto: Anansi, 1969.

Hadot, Pierre. *Philosophy as a Way of Life*. Oxford: Blackwell, 1995.

Heidegger, Martin. *Being and Time*. New York: Harper Perennial Modern Classics, 2008.

Lampert, Laurence. "Strauss' Recovery of Esotericism." In *The Cambridge Companion to Leo Strauss*, edited by Steven B. Smith. Cambridge: Cambridge University Press, 2009.

Lobkowicz, Nicolas. *Theory and Praxis*. South Bend, IN: Notre Dame University Press, 1968.

Machiavelli, Niccolò. *The Prince*. 2nd ed. Translated by Harvey C. Mansfield. Chicago: University of Chicago Press, 1998.

Nietzsche, Friedrich. *Beyond Good and Evil*. Translated by Helen Zimmern. N.p.: SDE Classics, 2019.

Plato. *Gorgias*. Translated by James H. Nichols. Ithaca, NY: Cornell University Press, 1998.

———. *Phaedrus*. Translated by James H. Nichols. Ithaca, NY: Cornell University Press, 1998.

Rosen, Stanley. *Hermeneutics as Politics*. New Haven, CT: Yale University Press, 1987.

Rousseau, Jean Jacques. *On the Social Contract*. Boston: Bedford, 1978.

Strauss, Leo. *The Argument and the Action of Plato's Laws*. Chicago: University of Chicago Press, 1977.

———. *The City and Man*. Chicago: University of Chicago Press, 1978.

———. "An Introduction to Heideggerian Existentialism." In *The Rebirth of Classical Political Rationalism*. Chicago: University of Chicago Press, 1989.

———. *Liberalism Ancient and Modern*. Chicago: University of Chicago Press, 1995.

———. *On Tyranny*. Chicago: University of Chicago Press, 2000.

———. *Persecution and the Art of Writing*. Chicago: University of Chicago Press, 1988.

———. *The Rebirth of Classical Political Rationalism: An Introduction to the Thought of Leo Strauss*. Selected and introduced by Thomas L. Pangle. Chicago: University of Chicago Press, 1989.

———. *What Is Political Philosophy?* Chicago: University of Chicago Press, 1988.

———. *Xenophon's Socratic Discourse*. South Bend, IN: St. Augustine's Press, 1998.

Strauss, Leo, and Joseph Cropsey, eds. *History of Political Philosophy*. Chicago: University of Chicago Press, 1987.

Xenophon. *Memorabilia*. Translated by Amy Bonnette. Ithaca, NY: Cornell University Press, 1994.

16. Liberal Education and American Democracy
George Thomas

POET, EDITOR, AND DIPLOMAT JAMES RUSSELL LOWELL famously described the American Constitution as "a machine that would go of itself."[1] It is less often recalled that Lowell said this in an address preoccupied with the possibility of constitutional degeneration. Americans, Lowell worried, mistook their good fortune for merit and destiny, acting as if the Constitution would simply run itself, which "made us neglectful of our political duties." Our luck, Lowell impressed upon us, would eventually run out. How, then, would we maintain America's "experiment in democracy" under less auspicious circumstances?[2]

The first decades of the twenty-first century have brought home Lowell's point. American democracy is vulnerable, and we have learned that our political institutions depend on civic understandings and a modicum of civic virtue, that civic leadership plays a role in fostering the norms and habits that our constitutional institutions depend on. But how to cultivate this sort of leadership? How to cultivate a civic spirit that puts a sense of the public good ahead of personal and partisan interests? While the Constitution depends on some level of civic virtue, it does not provide for it. This problem has been with us from the beginning. As James Madison put it in *Federalist*, no. 57, "The aim of every political constitution is, or ought to be, first to obtain for rulers men who possess most wisdom to discern, and most virtue to pursue, the common good of society; and in the next place, to take the most effectual precautions for keeping them virtuous whilst they continue to hold their public trust."[3] We tend to focus on this second part: how to contain power and keep it virtuous. And the answer is usually understood to be checks and balances. Yet notice that Madison places this second. We must first attempt to secure good leaders even if, as he famously puts it, we cannot trust that they will always be at the helm. While the large republic and system of separated power was supposed to provide the space where better leaders would rise to the top, this was only a partial solution. Madison hoped that education would complement the Constitution.

Not only would education foster certain kinds of political leadership, but it was the primary way to pass on constitutional knowledge and values from one generation to the next. Madison advocated establishing a national university to this end. Along with Thomas Jefferson, he was also instrumental in establishing the University of Virginia as a "learned institution" that would help perpetuate civic and political education. Cultivating civic attitudes and understandings is essential to maintaining American constitutional democracy. But increasingly, we do not do much of it. Rather than focusing on history and civics, as Danielle Allen and Paul Carrese note as part of the Educating for American Democracy Initiative, we tend to focus on economic competitiveness and national security, which has led to a preoccupation with STEM.[4] Similar preoccupations creep into higher education, even while most of these institutions take cultivating civic-minded leadership as part of their educational mission.

The modern elite college and university have only an indirect sense of their public obligations, particularly compared to their past incarnations. Increasingly, the careerist and commercial ends of education threaten to eclipse the broader mission of college education and obscure its link to democracy, which has been most evident at leading public universities.[5] Yet alongside these careerist tendencies, there has been a resurgence of interest in civic education with a focus on American history. The 1619 Project, taking its name from the first date enslaved humans arrived in America, has sought to draw attention to the history of slavery and race that have been central (and underappreciated) features of American history.[6] The 1776 Commission, taking its name from the year the Declaration of Independence was put forward, pushed back against 1619 as politicized history; it then proceeded to offer, if anything, an even more politicized form of "patriotic" education that offered a thin and whitewashed take on American history.[7]

Still, the turn to history is a welcome development. This chapter examines the teaching of history as a powerful way to bring out American political principles.[8] The first section of this chapter looks to the history around the founding generation who saw education as an essential complement to republican government, with leading founders advocating for the development of educational institutions to complement and complete the newly established constitutional order—including the establishment of a national university. It then considers how our contemporary institutions of higher education seek to pass on and engage civic knowledge and understandings. Finally, it seeks to illustrate how American history can be taught in a manner that embraces the conflicts and controversies at the center of the American experiment in self-government. In doing so, I consider how constitutional law, which is inevitably built around constitutional disputes, might offer a particularly promising way to both teach American history and the civic attitudes necessary to sustain American democracy. Taking the tragic alongside the uplifting, we can place debates about ideas at the center of American history, helping us come to a better understanding of our history, including the civic ideas that we both share in common and disagree about.

PRESERVING THE REPUBLIC

The creators of America's government were acutely aware of the link between education and preserving the republic. So much so, they argued for the establishment of a national university to nurture and sustain the republic they created. The idea of a national university was widespread during the founding era. Compiling a list of advocates of a national university is to name the seminal political and educational figures of the day: George Washington, Benjamin Rush, Noah Webster, Benjamin Franklin, Thomas Jefferson, James Madison, and both John Adams and John Quincy Adams. And the idea of a national university was justified in civic terms: it would cultivate the habits and mindset in citizens and public officers—Madison referred to "national feelings," "liberal sentiments," and "congenial manners"—necessary to America's republican experiment.[9] As George Washington asked in proposing a national university: "A primary object of such a National Institution should be, the education of our Youth in the science of *Government*. In a Republic, what species of knowledge can be equally important? And what duty, more pressing on its Legislature, than to patronize a plan for communicating it to those, who are to be the future guardians of the liberties of the Country?"[10]

Yet this was not a public policy school, a Kennedy or Wilson School for the founding generation. On the contrary, knowledge itself, particularly detached from theological orthodoxy, was believed to be essential to the republic. University education of a wide-ranging sort was necessary to sustain a broader way of life that included things we do not usually associate with government: science, commerce, literature, and the arts, for example. In his first formal call to establish a national university, Washington insisted that nothing deserved Congress's patronage more than "the promotion of science and literature," as knowledge itself contributed to a "free constitution."[11] The Congress agreed, with both the Senate and the House passing resolutions of support echoing Washington's thought: "Literature and science are essential to the preservation of a free constitution." In the founders' eyes, successful political institutions depended on culture and ideas, which depended on education.

Those who favored a national university saw it as cultivating the understanding presupposed by the Constitution: it would foster ideas that framed how Americans understood the world. While I won't rehash the sketches of the curriculum and the subtle and insightful debates around it, the essential point is that educational institutions should be in line with more liberal-democratic understandings, particularly by removing the central features of theology that were at the heart of America's "church-state" colleges prior to the Revolution. The ideas behind the development and reformulation of the curriculum of America's "church-state" colleges would help constitute the American mind, passing down understandings by which citizens would apprehend political life.[12]

Yet even while working to cultivate liberal democratic political principles, the most visible defenders of a national university also happened to be defenders of open and free inquiry that is so central to the modern university. Indeed, for figures like Madison, the commitment to liberal principles in politics had a corollary in liberal education and its commitment to open inquiry. The constitutional order and a reconstituted university could complement one another. In this way, the language of neutrality that is so often invoked in defending both liberal democracy and liberal education is at odds with this understanding. Liberalism is not coercive and allows for a wide-ranging pluralism, but such commitments stem from liberal principles themselves and not a commitment to neutrality. The same is true for the sort of liberal education imagined by the advocates of a national university: liberal education was not neutral as to regime type, but sought to cultivate liberal-democratic understandings and commitments.

For instance, when Madison weighed what should be taught in government and law at the University of Virginia, he was clear that the aim of teaching should be "framing a political creed." As he wrote to his good friend Jefferson, "It is certainly very material that the true doctrines of liberty, as exemplified in our Political System, should be inculcated on those who are to sustain and may administer it." This posed, Madison noted, a particularly delicate problem. If the principles taught were put in very general terms, "they do not answer the purpose" in "Guarding our Republican Charters against constructive violations." But put in too particular terms, and such principles were prone to "divide & exclude" when they were meant to "unite & fortify."[13] In contrast to how we often think about both liberal democracy and liberal education, Madison offers a vision of liberal democracy and liberal education that is committed to certain substantive understandings even while being intellectually open and noncoercive. While we often invoke the language of neutrality in thinking about both liberal democracy and liberal education, this does not in fact capture how we actually think of both. I will return to this point more fully below in thinking about teaching history as part of teaching civics.

The crucial point here is the link between what Madison called learning and liberty: contrary to what we are so often taught, the leading minds from the founding generation, who also happened to be the advocates of a national university, did not think the Constitution was a "machine that would go of itself." Acute students of history, they were deeply aware that political institutions degenerate and decay. The national university would supplement America's political institutions by fostering a healthy civil society. As Jefferson put it, education will "form the statesmen, legislators and judges, on whom public prosperity and individual happiness are so much to depend."[14] Education of the sort offered at the national university would shape the public mind and forge a publicly spirited leadership class to carry the American experiment forward.

A report by the American Academy of Arts and Sciences commissioned by Congress, *The Heart of the Matter*, similarly insists that education is "the "keeper of the republic."[15] But how do American colleges and universities contribute to maintaining American democracy in the early years of the twenty-first century? At its best, liberal arts education is defended as training for democratic citizenship. The virtues of liberal education mirror the characteristics required of democratic citizens: the ability to grasp and evaluate arguments and evidence and to articulate and defend ideas in a reasoned manner. And so it may be. Yet is teaching reasoning and critical thinking enough? Does it foster civic understandings and commitments? Do we need more specific knowledge of American liberal democracy: its institutions, history, and culture? An understanding of the past may be crucial to the present and future of American democracy.

America's history is bound up with its civic identity. As *The Heart of the Matter* report observes, American democracy depends on a "shared knowledge of history, civics, and social studies," and "the humanities remind us where we have been and help us envision where we are going." This thinking runs back to the idea for a national university. Even prior to the establishment of the Constitution, Noah Webster was berating his fellow citizens for not knowing their history: insofar as we don't know our history, we lack knowledge of ourselves. Complaints of civic ignorance are as old as the Republic. Yet it was in our history, Webster insisted, that we would discover our political principles and forge a common identity. Neglecting our history, we lacked knowledge of ourselves as Americans.[16]

This thinking was also behind the creation of the core curriculum in the twentieth century at places such as Harvard and Columbia. In the middle years of the twentieth century, the famous Harvard report *General Education in a Free Society* insisted, "It is impossible to escape the realization that our society, like any society, rests on common beliefs and that a major task of education is to perpetuate them."[17] The curriculum, accordingly, aimed to nourish the "general art of the free man and the citizen" by teaching the habits of mind and character that were necessary to civic life.[18] The core, still taught at Columbia, grew out of a desire to foster a shared history and civic consciousness against the division of world war. Such courses, with an eye on fostering unity, often began as thinly veiled propaganda. But they also forced educators to think more fully about the place of American democracy within the curriculum (and within history more generally). Courses in history, philosophy, literature, and politics—which transcended all of these as modern "disciplines"—would provide a common basis of knowledge. One could have many complaints about the parochial nature of these institutions in their earlier years, and about the core in particular, but they did impart a sense of public duty.

The Harvard report distinguished between "liberal education" and an "education in liberalism." The latter was linked to a free society that sought to promote a "liberal outlook" and "the truths concerning the structure of the good life and concerning the factual conditions by which it may be achieved, truths comprising the goals of the free society."[19] Perpetuating the aptitudes and attitudes necessary for liberal democracy was part of the general education articulated and defended by the Harvard report—even if it also recognized the tension between liberal education and civic education. Following the report, even if we are skeptical that American democracy stands on some shared civic identity, there is a compelling argument that knowledge of American history, politics, and culture is essential to students being educated as America's future leaders. Francis Fukuyama argued that we don't clearly see America's current institutional decay, because we lack a historical perspective: "The historical context of American political development is all too often given short shrift."[20] Americans are notoriously ignorant of their history and their Constitution. Indeed, if polls are to be believed, such ignorance is one of the things we share in common. Even if we take an entirely pragmatic approach to the current issues that beset America, a sense of the past is essential to grappling with the present. How should we think of the persistence of racial discrimination? Should illegal immigrants be given a path to citizenship? Does increasing inequality threaten American democracy? Is the American separation of powers dysfunctional? Come up with nearly any question you want. Can we have a meaningful public debate about such vexing issues—never mind coming up with plausible solutions to them—without a fairly robust understanding American history, institutions, and culture?

CIVIC UNDERSTANDINGS AND CONTEMPORARY LIBERAL EDUCATION

For all the talk of leadership at elite colleges and universities these days, do they provide the sort of knowledge and mind-set essential to the tasks of public leadership? Most leading institutions of higher education have in common the aim of developing a set of critical skills—critical thinking and writing in particular. Looking at the top ten universities and liberal arts colleges, as ranked by *U.S. News* (and, yes, such rankings are a problem in their own right), many do this by way of breadth and distribution requirements: students must take a range of courses outside their particular area of study. Others have core requirements, where students must take interdisciplinary courses that are meant to introduce them to Western civilization, literature, philosophy, and the like, with some requiring the study of another civilization or culture or global studies. And an increasing number requiring a course in race or ethnic diversity.

Now it may well be, as Princeton University president Christopher Eisgruber argues, the civic traits we depend on in a liberal democracy—critical thought, deliberation, and toleration, for instance—will in fact be cultivated by way of general liberal education. There is a happy convergence between liberal values and liberal education. As Eisgruber puts it, "Liberal democratic government is in many respects an effort to constitute the political order on the same terms that govern rational speech."[21] Cultivating the critical rationality we depend on in a liberal democracy will naturally occur across the liberal arts curriculum—in nearly all the courses on offer from such institutions. Specific courses in *American* history, politics, or literature are unnecessary, as general courses in philosophy, science, economics, history, politics, writing, and the like will do. This may reflect the infusion of liberal-democratic understandings that frame the curriculum and mind-set of the modern college and university.

Most leading universities and liberal arts colleges implicitly seem to share President Eisgruber's sense that a range of liberal arts taught in a critical manner will map the skills and traits necessary to sustain democracy. Most of these institutions speak of cultivating leadership and citizenship. Some specifically mention, as part of their general education requirements, civic engagement. Duke University lists civic engagement as an essential part of its curriculum, while Harvard seeks to prepare students for civic life, and Bowdoin College mentions reflective citizenship as part of its overall educational mission. The University of Pennsylvania has even begun a new program, the President's Engagement Prizes, which will fully fund a local, national, or global engagement project in the year after graduation. The goal is specifically to put student's knowledge to "work for the betterment of humankind."

Yet none of the top-ranked universities or colleges has a specifically required course in American government, thought, history, literature, or culture. To be sure, such courses are taught at all these colleges and universities, but they are not a required part of the curriculum. It is also an open question whether *requiring* courses is the best way to achieve the sort of knowledge and attitudes we want to cultivate in students and citizens. Jefferson, for instance, defended an elective system at the University of Virginia as reflecting the genuine habits of self-government.[22] It may well be that an elective system is a better way to bring about the habits and knowledge we desire in citizens. When it comes to required courses that reflect on citizenship, a handful of these colleges and universities require a course in "global citizenship" or a course in preparation for "global life." Carleton College has a global citizenship requirement, Stanford University notes the importance of preparing students for global citizenship, and Haverford College has a Center for Peace and Global Citizenship. Such global requirements, along with the diversity requirement at Williams College and the requirement for courses across cultures and civilizations at Middlebury College, may well be in keeping with a broad liberal education that naturally has a cosmopolitan element. Understanding different cultures and modes of thinking, alternatives to the world we inhabit, is a crucial part of liberal education. In considering the nations of the "Globe" and the "characters and customs which distinguish them," Madison insisted on the educational benefits of such knowledge in the early nineteenth century: "An acquaintance with foreign Countries in this mode, has a kindred effect with that of seeing them as travellers, which never fails, in uncorrupted minds, to weaken local prejudices, and enlarge the sphere of benevolent feelings."[23]

AMERICAN HISTORY AND LIBERAL EDUCATION

In the same way that global concerns have been integrated into the curriculum, colleges and universities might reintegrate, so to speak, courses in American history, American government and politics, and American literature and culture that speak to American civic life. In light of America's long-overdue reckoning with racial injustice, many colleges and universities are considering adding requirements that speak to race in America or simply making certain that more such courses are offered to their students. There is a legitimate question whether civic education belongs in primary and secondary education and not in an undergraduate setting, as well as a concern that it smacks too much of patriotic attachment at odds with the aims of higher education. Yet most institutions of higher education think of themselves as contributing to democratic life and citizenship. And civic education can be integrated into liberal education in ways that are good for both education and democracy. Courses preoccupied by features of American liberal democracy can be done in what William Galston dubs an "investigative" rather than "inculcative" manner. Such a mode of teaching would "adopt the American regime as its point of departure while problematizing it as an object of inquiry."[24] Courses that focused on American history and civic institutions would introduce students to essential concepts—liberalism, democracy, rights, representation, equality, separation of powers, federalism, the rule of law—and how they have played out over the course of American history. But it would also invite students to think critically about these different issues.

One of the first great civic education projects in America—Noah Webster's *Little Reader's Assistant*—shows the promise of such an approach. Webster's *Little Reader* was aimed, as the title indicates, at young readers; it included stories that aimed to cultivate knowledge of and attachment to American history and principles, even concluding with a "short and easy" explanation of the Constitution. Yet one of the stories Webster included spoke to the treatment of enslaved Africans.

Recording the brutality of the capture, shipping, and selling of enslaved persons, Webster pushed his youthful reader to reflect on and consider the justice of the practice. "Shall this barbarous and unlawful practice always prevail? Are the negroes brutes? Or are they men like ourselves? What right hath one man to enslave another? Have not the negroes the same right to steal us, our wives and children, transport us to Africa, and reduce us to bondage, as we have to enslave them?" Webster wrote this in the second edition of the reader, after the Constitution's compromises with slavery, and even as he was writing in support of the new Constitution. In his pointed inquiries about slavery, Webster was encouraging young Americans to reflect on the justice of the practice according to the nation's own putative political principles. Webster's aim, to be sure, was to foster citizenship and attachment to the American project: he would often note that the Revolution did not end with the war, but was an ongoing part of maintaining the American experiment. Yet Webster embraced a critical and reflective form of citizenship. His other work on civic education included criticism of state establishments and religious tests for office, which he called "badges of bigotry." Webster's idea of education did not shy away from controversy, as he insisted that "a perfect freedom of debate is essential to a free government."[25]

Teaching America's real history—including the terrible injustices of the past and present—and placing contested ideas and concepts at the center of that history, is a much more powerful way to forge a sense of civic identity and prepare students for self-government than ducking "divisive concepts" and offering a sanitized version of history that takes refuge in a mythological version of the past. And the story of redeeming the promise of America is a more complete, honest, and accurate story only when it includes the ugly and brutal denial of rights and equal citizenship because of race. Disharmony is an essential part of the American story. Yet America has too often denied this struggle—particularly in how it taught history.[26]

Consider that "The 1776 Report" mentions the Civil War Amendments—the Thirteenth, Fourteenth, and Fifteenth Amendments—only in passing, despite the fact that those amendments amounted to a second founding, making the Union "worthy of the saving."[27] And it offers only a few short paragraphs on the failures of Reconstruction and the rise of Jim Crow.[28] Yet it is crucial that Americans understand that these constitutional amendments were necessary to end slavery and make Blacks equal citizens: they arose to the "dignity of a new Magna Charta."[29] It is equally important that Americans understand that the initial triumph in the years immediately after the Civil War, when Black Americans enjoyed the initial benefits of citizenship and elected members to both houses of Congress, was followed by tragic retreat.

Southern states evaded the terms of the Civil War amendments, weaving into state law a system of racial apartheid that denied Blacks the right to vote and instituted segregation between the races. The details are too numerous to list, but ponder a few highlights. Public schools and facilities were segregated on the basis of race, and private schools were prohibited from integrating. Blacks were denied the right to vote, and state-sponsored violence was routinely used against them.[30] Pause to think that the Senate filibuster, too often cavalierly defended as a procedure that forces democratic reflection, was used in the first half to the twentieth century to prevent an antilynching law. What Rogers Smith calls "ascriptive" understandings of citizenship, which hold that civic identity is grounded in ascriptive understandings of race and ethnicity, that America is fundamentally a white man's republic—have long endured, indeed persist in some quarters.[31]

All of this is ignored in the sanitized version of history on offer in the shallow "1776 Report." It spends more time on the putative challenges to liberal democracy, progressivism, and identity politics than it does on struggles for racial equality. This isn't history, but an erasure of history. It also offers a perverse view of human agency, as if ideas set in motion do all of the actual work, neglecting the hard labor and struggle by Americans that have been necessary to redeem America's promise. Such thinking prefers the abstraction of a country committed to equality, rather than the reality of a country that has struggled to make that promise real.[32] It's too bad, because the struggle is a compelling story that has shaped how we understand equality and liberty even as we continue to debate their meaning and how we ought to order them. These ideals have become more meaningful, and more fully understood, because of the struggle to realize them. This may make for a less "glorious and less teleological tell," but it is one that is more likely to be compelling. Being honest about America's history should bring the struggle over American ideas vividly to life. A self-governing people must be able to understand its history—the sublime alongside the tragic—as it carries forward the American experiment.

CONSTITUTIONAL LAW AS CIVIC EDUCATION?

An approach that situates the American regime at the center of an investigative inquiry might orient itself around constitutional law. American constitutional law is nothing less than an extended commentary on the meaning of America taught as part of a liberal and civic education. As Yale Law professor Bruce Ackerman puts it, "To discover the Constitution is to discover an important part of oneself—insofar as one recognizes oneself as an American."[33] Americans share a common history more than anything else. Understanding our history requires not just knowledge of the past, but an understanding of the political principles that underlie that history and the Constitution itself.

Canvassing our history by way of constitutional struggles, beginning with the debates over ratification that helped bring us the Bill of Rights, we can come to understand the very real struggles over the meaning of America. And we can see, too, the importance of ordinary citizens in shaping the idea of America. It is ultimately American citizens—and those who attach themselves to America by becoming citizens—who carry the American constitutional project forward. Recounting these constitutional struggles helps us understand how the struggle over civic identity and racial and ethnic discrimination has been a very real part of American history. Knowing this history helps us become more fully American. Becoming an American means embracing the exalted dimensions of our national character as articulated by a Lincoln or a Douglass (not to mention the many less well-known figures who helped America think about and live up to what its principles entailed); it also means not just acknowledging but understanding the awful incidents of racial, ethnic, and religious discrimination permitted and at times committed by our formal institutions.[34]

Yet however much we know about the Constitution, we are going to disagree with one another, often profoundly. That's the nature of constitutional government. It may even be that the more we know about the Constitution, the more likely we are to disagree. Yet the Constitution can help set the boundaries of such disagreement. And constitutional law helps provide a model of disagreement. The opinions of the Court offer reasons for its decisions, while concurring and dissenting opinions challenge the decisions of the Court. Read together, they offer a powerful and extended dialogue on the Constitution—often on the very idea of America. At one point or another, it is almost always the case that students find themselves persuaded by justices they may not generally agree with. Working through the different constitutional cases reveals that they rarely track neat ideological divisions, and often tend to break them down. We are also likely to find that, even when we agree with the result in a particular case, we frequently disagree with the Court's reasoning and logic.

It's an exercise in citizenship to think through constitutional questions on our own. Indeed, it forces us to think about how we should order and weigh different, and often competing, constitutional values and principles. And as we think about how to apply the Constitution to contemporary issues, it is striking just how much gray area there is.[35] Thinking through such issues requires us to exercise our reason and judgment, but also to acknowledge that the answers we find are not so easily or neatly arrived at. Judgments other than are own are certain to be reasonable, as there is obvious room for disagreement. Constitutional law can help tutor us where we disagree, teaching us to think and reason about the most important matters that both unite and divide us. What sort of political community did the Constitution seek to promote? What sort of world do we want to inhabit? As Madison put it, "A people who mean to be their own Governors, must arm themselves with the power which knowledge gives."[36]

Knowing the history and principles of the American polity is a first step in thinking about and applying political principles to contemporary issues. Grasping the historical antecedents of many contemporary issues may well elevate contemporary democratic discourse. This also includes criticizing pieces (or the whole) of American democracy. Studying things American, we will find that its great champions have often been its most stringent critics, pointing out how it has failed to live up to its promise. Think of Fredrick Douglass.[37] And even as "investigative" civic education by way of history or constitutional law seeks to instill civic understandings, it is a reasoned project that can be situated within a broad liberal education. Indeed, a course in comparative constitutionalism may be the most illuminating way to study America insofar as it brings to light what is unique and what is universal within American democracy. As Seymour Martin Lipset has argued, "It is impossible to understand a country without seeing how it varies from others. Those who know only one country know no country."[38] Thinking of things American can be done in ways that complement and deepen liberal education, including the global perspective many colleges view as essential to education in the twenty-first century.

LEADERSHIP AND LIBERAL EDUCATION

Elite students—at both public and private colleges and universities—who will shape American institutions and culture ought to have a rudimentary education in the American polity, to make them culturally literate individuals able to contribute to civic life in meaningful ways. (There may be a stronger case that students at less well-regarded institutions should have such an education so they can meaningfully participate in civic life.) Interestingly, the schools most serving this politically educative function today may be elite law schools and public policy schools. These institutions often combine a high level of theory and ideas as applied to current constitutional questions and questions of civic and public policy. These institutions educate an elite that goes into public office, governmental service, and civic and public life more generally. Yet aspects of this education focus on professional development, which sits uneasily alongside a more robust sense of civic life. This is particularly so with law schools, which tend to create a professional legalistic understanding of public affairs that can be profoundly at odds with wider civic understandings.

Indeed, as I noted at the outset, preprofessionalism has begun to creep into undergraduate education in ways that threaten to overshadow civic and liberal education. This development is a key reason that leadership as understood and practiced at elite educational institutions risks being engulfed by careerism and the market—by material success, which is not quite the same as leadership. And this narrow view of career and the market is one of the threats to the sort of education essential to democracy. It may be that elite institutions are best at nurturing ambition rather than civic duty. With some irony, this may well be due to the success of the commercial aspects of American democracy. Yet it is cause for concern over our civic health. Parents and students ought to be concerned about career prospects, particularly given the high cost of college. Assurances that students will thrive materially are not all bad. Colleges and universities should take it on themselves to educate parents and students along these lines: the evidence overwhelmingly suggests that students who graduate from elite institutions with a liberal arts focus thrive in career and material terms.[39] More important, though, educational institutions need to insist that the market is not the most important measure of education.

American democracy depends on generally knowledgeable citizens, but it does not count on them to be professional historians, constitutional scholars, or experts in public affairs. This says something important about the nature of American democracy: most people will be busy in private life. What Edmund Burke called "the less inquiring," with regard to public affairs, are likely to take cues on civic questions from the ideas generated by political and intellectual leaders.[40] Yet this is just why we depend on educational institutions to provide the virtues of such leadership: the people, preoccupied by private life, are unlikely to do the heavy intellectual lifting on civic questions. Preserving American democracy depends anew on each generation: it requires, in Burke's words, "much thought, deep reflection, a sagacious, powerful, and combing mind."[41] Liberal education at its best cultivates this frame of mind.

Today we are confronted with partisan divisions and the possibility of institutional decay that bring the health of American democracy into doubt. And our educational institutions, driven more and more by careerist concerns and the market, may compound the troublesome effects of self-interested institutions rather than softening them. The idea of a national university was a means of cultivating political and civic leaders, almost a hedge against self-interest. In a similar fashion, contemporary students might be lulled away from excessively careerist and commercial concerns by way of civic education. Our educational institutions could turn to the American past to help teach today's students what Alexis de Tocqueville famously called "self-interest rightly understood."[42] In just this way, the American heritage may be used to save Americans from themselves.

NOTES

1. James Russell Lowell, "The Independent in Politics," April 13, 1888, quoted in George Thomas, *The Founders and the Idea of a National University: Constituting the American Mind*, 1.

2. Thomas, *Founders and the Idea of a National University*, 1.

3. Alexander Hamilton, James Madison, and John Jay, *The Federalist Papers*, 290.

4. Danielle Allen and Paul Carrese, "Our Democracy Is Ailing: Civics Education Has to Be Part of the Cure," *Washington Post*, March 2, 2021, https://www.washingtonpost.com/opinions/2021/03/02/our-democracy-is-ailing-civics-education-has-be-part-cure/.

5. In the last decade, the Board of Overseers at the University of Virginia tried to force the president out for not speaking enough to the practical aims of university education, most notably with regard to online education and the fashionable call for MOOCs (Massive Open Online Courses). The rector of the board, a political appointee, thought it was high time to rethink the mission of Mr. Jefferson's university in the twenty-first century. The Board of Governors at the University of North Carolina (with a claim to be the oldest public university in America), urged on by the governor of the state who has been dismissive of liberal arts education, is looking to eliminate departments and areas of learning to suit market "demand." According to several members of the board, education is about jobs. Politicians, too, speak as if getting a job was the sole aim of college education. Former governor Scott Walker of Wisconsin tried to amend the University of Wisconsin's mission statement to drop language about citizenship and the pursuit of knowledge and replace it with "meeting the state's workforce needs." Senator Marco Rubio dismissed the study of Greek philosophy given one's unlikely job prospects. See George Thomas, "Liberal Education and American Democracy."

6. Nikole Hannah-Jones, "The 1619 Project," *New York Times*, August 14, 2019, https://www.nytimes.com/interactive/2019/08/14/magazine/1619-america-slavery.html.

7. The President's Advisory 1776 Commission, "The 1776 Report," January 2021, https://trumpwhitehouse.archives.gov/wp-content/uploads/2021/01/The-Presidents-Advisory-1776-Commission-Final-Report.pdf.

8. The challenge of identity politics and what could broadly be labeled political correctness, including cancel culture, raises serious questions about liberal education on the modern college and university campus. Questions around these issues are taken up in a number of other chapters and are not the focus of this chapter.

9. Reproduced in *The Speeches, Addresses and Messages of the Several Presidents of the United States at the Openings of Congress and at their Respective Inaugurations*, 333.

10. Thomas, *National University*, 30–31.

11. George Washington, "First Annual Address," January 8, 1790, https://avalon.law.yale.edu/18th_century/washs01.asp.

12. Thomas, *National University*, 127–28.

13. Thomas, *National University*, 193.

14. Thomas Jefferson, "Report of the Board of Commissioners for the University of Virginia to the Virginia General Assembly."

15. American Academy of Arts and Sciences, *The Heart of the Matter*.

16. Thomas, *National University*, 51.

17. *General Education in a Free Society: Report of the Harvard Committee*, 42–43.

18. Thomas, *National University*, 192.

19. Thomas, *National University*, 193.

20. Francis Fukuyama, "The Decay of American Political Institutions."

21. Thomas, *National University*, 219.

22. Thomas, *National University*, 232.

23. James Madison to William T. Barry, August 4, 1822, https://founders.archives.gov/documents/Madison/04-02-02-0480.

24. Thomas, *National University*, 208.

25. Thomas, *National University*, 51.

26. Thomas, *National University*, 209.

27. Abraham Lincoln, speech on the Kansas-Nebraska Act at Peoria, Illinois, 1854, 86.

28. President's Advisory 1776 Commission, "The 1776 Report," January 18, 2021, 15.

29. *The Slaughter-House Cases*, 83 US 125, 119 (1872).

30. Michael Klarman, *Unfinished Business*, 77, 79.

31. Rogers Smith, *Civic Ideals: Conflicting Visions of Citizenship in U.S. History*, 6.

32. President's Advisory 1776 Commission, "The 1776 Report," 15.

33. Thomas, *National University*, 220.

34. See, for instance, Martha Jones, *Vanguard: How Black Women Broke Barriers, Won the Vote, and Insisted on Equality for All*.

35. George Thomas, *The (Un)Written Constitution*, 136–37.

36. George Thomas, "Constitutional Law as Civic Education," 190.

37. Fredrick Douglass, "What to the Slave Is the Fourth of July?," 116.

38. Thomas, *National University*, 231.

39. Susan Svrluga, "Liberal Arts Education: Waste of Money or Practical Investment?," *Washington Post*, January 14, 2020; and "Can a Liberal Arts Degree Led to Financial Success?"

40. Thomas, *National University*, 227.

41. Edmund Burke, *Reflections on the Revolution in France*, 208.

42. Alexis de Tocqueville, *Democracy in America*, 500–504.

BIBLIOGRAPHY

American Academy of Arts and Sciences. *The Heart of the Matter*. Cambridge, MA: American Academy of Arts and Sciences, 2013.

Burke, Edmund. *Reflections on the Revolution in France*. New Haven: Yale University Press, 2008.

Douglass, Frederick. "What to the Slave Is the Fourth of July?" In *Narrative of the Life of Frederick Douglass, an American Slave, Written by Himself*, edited by John W. Blassingame, John R. McKivigan, and Peter P. Hinks. New York: W. W. Norton, 1997.

Fukuyama, Francis. "The Decay of American Political Institutions." *American Interest* 9, no. 13 (2013). https://www.the-american-interest.com/2013/12/08/the-decay-of-american-political-institutions/.

General Education in a Free Society: Report of the Harvard Committee. Cambridge, MA: Harvard University Press, 1945.

Hamilton, Alexander, James Madison, and John Jay. *The Federalist Papers*. Edited by Ian Shapiro. New Haven, CT: Yale University Press, 2009.

Jefferson, Thomas. "Report of the Board of Commissioners for the University of Virginia to the Virginia General Assembly." August 4, 1818. https://founders.archives.gov/documents/Madison/04-01-02-0289.

Jones, Martha S. *Vanguard: How Black Women Broke Barriers, Won the Vote, and Insisted on Equality for All*. New York: Basic Books, 2020.

Klarman, Michael. *Unfinished Business*. New York: Oxford University Press, 2007.

Lincoln, Abraham. Speech on the Kansas-Nebraska Act at Peoria, Illinois, 1854. In *The Writings of Abraham Lincoln*, edited by S. B. Smith. New Haven, CT: Yale University Press, 2012.

Smith, Rogers M. *Civic Ideals: Conflicting Visions of Citizenship in U.S. History*. New Haven, CT: Yale University Press, 1997.

The Speeches, Address and Messages of the Several Presidents of the United States at the Openings of Congress and at Their Respective Inaugurations. Philadelphia: Robert Desilver, 1825.

Svrluga, Susan. "Can a Liberal Arts Degree Lead to Financial Success?" *Forbes*, December 11, 2019.

Thomas, George. "Constitutional Law as Civic Education." *National Affairs* 43 (Spring 2020).

———. *The Founders and the Idea of a National University: Constituting the American Mind*. New York: Cambridge University Press, 2015.

———. "Liberal Education and American Democracy." *American Interest* (August 24, 2015).

———. *The (Un)Written Constitution*. New York: Oxford University Press, 2021.

Tocqueville, Alexis de. *Democracy in America*. Edited and translated by Harvey Mansfield and Delba Winthrop. Chicago: University of Chicago Press, 2000.

Washington, George. *First Annual Address*. January 8, 1790. Retrieved from the Avalon Project.

17. How Business Schools Can Prepare Students for Twenty-First-Century Success by Renewing Their Liberal Arts Roots

Donald Drakeman and Kendall Hack

MASTER'S OF BUSINESS ADMINISTRATION (MBA) programs promise to provide students with the tools and methods "critical to success" in their business careers.[1] For the past fifty years, that success has primarily been measured by corporate profitability, which was business's only "social responsibility," according to a highly influential essay by economist Milton Friedman in 1970.[2] But times have changed. Management guru Tom Peters now cites the "moral responsibility of enterprises,"[3] and the chief executive officers (CEOs) of many of America's largest companies declared in 2019 that "each of our stakeholders is essential."[4] Today, large numbers of students, customers, and business leaders see businesses as just one part of a broader community, and they believe that those businesses have important civic and moral responsibilities. To prepare their graduates for twenty-first-century careers, business schools need to provide the tools and methods critical to achieving this broader definition of success. How can they do so? By returning to their nineteenth-century roots.

Joseph Wharton, the nineteenth-century industrialist who endowed the first business school in America, had limited schooling, but he understood the value of a liberal arts education.[5] Because Wharton and the other founders of university-level business programs believed that students needed to learn more than just the nuts and bolts of business, one of their primary goals was to foster character formation, corporate morality, and good citizenship by providing future business leaders with a liberal arts education. Courses in government, history, and moral and political philosophy dominated the original business curriculum, accompanied by only a handful of offerings in finance, economics, and accounting. Throughout the twentieth century, however, business schools gradually, but almost completely, replaced the liberal arts with an ever-expanding list of management-related courses. Today, Wharton's MBA program neither requires students to enroll in any liberal arts courses during their two years of study nor expects them to have studied the liberal arts as undergraduates. As is common among leading business schools, the majority of students enter with degrees in business or a STEM field, and those who have "backgrounds and knowledge areas . . . [in] government . . . and the arts" are deemed "nontraditional students."[6]

This curricular drift away from the liberal arts has been accompanied by a corresponding shift away from the goal of preparing business leaders for good corporate citizenship. Instead, it has offered students courses designed to give them a set of management methods and technical skills. Yet there is plenty of room in MBA programs to reinstate their original commitment to the study of the liberal arts without diminishing the importance of the core business curriculum.[7] Adding greater attention to the liberal arts will help MBAs better understand the nature of their employers' place within the broader community, and how to fulfill what Peters calls its "moral responsibilities." It will also provide valuable insights into the political and social environment in which their businesses will operate, and it can even contribute to their own career success. In this chapter, we make a series of specific recommendations for reviving the original ideals of business education, enhancing the MBA curriculum, and revising the influential ranking systems.

THE EMERGENCE OF BUSINESS EDUCATION

Devout Quaker and metals magnate Joseph Wharton made the founding gift to the University of Pennsylvania that launched university-level business education in 1881. His aim was to educate students to manage businesses and property in a manner that would "benefit the community" and "maintain sound financial morality."[8] The new Wharton School was committed to providing "a liberal education in all matters concerning Finance and Economy."[9] The same liberal arts theme echoed throughout the plans for the many new business schools that appeared over the next few decades, with educational leaders arguing "that higher education could reform—indeed, redeem—the otherwise avaricious and amoral behavior of U.S. business."[10] The first business school to offer a graduate degree, Dartmouth's Tuck School, announced that it would "so broaden the minds and raise the ideals of its graduates that . . . the business community [will be elevated] above the plane of mere money-getting."[11] Those founding deans and philanthropists were not concerned about whether American businesses needed academic help to be financially successful, and the business schools were not principally focused on training students to make commercial enterprises more efficient or profitable. Instead, their goal was to make businesses and their managers better citizens. These "wise businessmen" would then be in a position to "solve [the] fundamental economic and social questions" confronting America, said the dean of New York University's School of Commerce in 1914.[12]

The necessary wisdom and character formation would come from studying the liberal arts, which constituted an essential accompaniment to the fairly modest number of practical elements contained in the new degree requirements. Wharton's two-year business program was layered onto two prior years of Penn's regular undergraduate course of study.[13] Tuck required three years of undergraduate studies in the liberal arts, and Harvard's graduate-only business program required a bachelor's degree for admission so "that the strictly professional work of the School may rest on a foundation of liberal studies . . . having a general value for education and culture."[14] With such a "broadening" and character-building liberal arts education serving as the essential foundation for business-related courses in accounting, finance, and related topics, the new degree programs would turn business managers into professionals on a par with their college classmates entering the learned professions of academia, law, and the ministry.[15]

Merely an initial two years of undergraduate education in the liberal arts would not necessarily be sufficient training for business. The inaugural curriculum for Wharton's degree in "finance and economy" was impressively light on business subjects (especially by twenty-first-century standards) compared to its liberal arts offerings. History, government, philosophy, and economics constituted most of the twenty-seven required courses. Eleven courses were in politics and government (American politics, civil government, comparative politics, and political theory), five courses were in history (constitutional, economic, industrial, and religious), five courses were in political economy and social science, and two courses were in philosophy (logic and moral philosophy). These liberal arts courses at Wharton followed Penn's regular first two years in which all students studied rhetoric,

English literature, history, physics, chemistry, mathematics, and languages. The remainder of the Wharton curriculum—a total of only nine courses—covered much of what is now the MBA core curriculum: accounting and finance (two courses each), currency and banking, statistics, business law, and "mercantile practice." Altogether, the Wharton courses were designed by the university first to provide "an adequate education in the principles underlying successful civil government," and second to constitute a "training suitable for those who intend to engage in business."[16]

The early curriculum at Dartmouth's pioneering graduate program was much the same. After three years of undergraduate studies—including the "prerequisites for admission [of] mathematics, literature, philosophy, at least two sciences, economics, political science, sociology, history, and two modern languages"—the first-year curriculum required "courses in economics, history, constitutional and international law, statistics, comparative politics, commercial geography, and language (English and one modern language). Only in the second year did the . . . student enroll in courses such as accounting, finance, banking, and business organization and procedure."[17] The educational philosophy behind the design of the curriculum at the first business schools is summarized in the University of Pennsylvania 1888–89 catalog, which announced that "nearly all the courses . . . may fairly lay claim to be called liberal branches *par excellence*, and such as every American citizen should pursue in outline at least as a preparation for the duties of citizenship."[18]

THE DECLINE OF THE LIBERAL ARTS IN BUSINESS SCHOOLS

Over the past 140 years, the liberal arts have moved from the core of the business curriculum to its periphery, and, more recently, to near oblivion. Meanwhile, numerous critiques of management education have appeared, even (perhaps especially) from within the business schools themselves. Harvard Business School professor Rakesh Khurana titled his 2008 history of management education "From Higher Aims to Hired Hands," and historian Steven Conn has written "The Sad History of American Business Schools."[19] Two prominent management professors, Warren Bennis and James O'Toole, penned "How Business Schools Lost Their Way" for the *Harvard Business Review*, arguing that if "business schools are to regain their relevance, they must come to grips with the reality that business management is not a scientific discipline but a profession." Decrying the overwhelming focus on "technical training," they cited Aristotle's teaching "that genuine leadership consisted in the ability to identify and serve the common good." Doing so, they argued, "requires an education in moral reasoning, which must include history, philosophy, literature, theology, and logic."[20]

Today the liberal arts are largely absent from the MBA core curriculum, apart from a business ethics class. At Wharton, for example, the core curriculum consists of two credits each of management/operations, economics, and finance/accounting; one credit each of marketing and statistics; three-quarters credit of communications; plus just a half credit of a class that combines legal studies and business ethics. Many of the leading MBA programs follow a similar model of compartmentalizing the liberal arts into a single business ethics or ethics-related class.[21] (Because Wharton is the oldest and one of the largest, and is invariably ranked in the top few business schools, we will focus primarily on its curriculum, which we have found generally to be typical of other leading MBA programs.)

The transition away from traditional liberal arts subjects (other than economics, which has been a mainstay of the business curriculum) took quite some time and proceeded at different paces depending on the institution. Some business schools founded in the first half of the twentieth century generally followed the Wharton/Tuck liberal arts model, while others focused more intently on offering classes that would train students to take hands-on roles at local businesses. Nevertheless, at least up to 1930, the liberal arts ideal remained dominant. In that year, fifty years after Joseph Wharton's pioneering investment in a liberal arts–based business education, two Penn professors surveyed the venture's educational returns.[22] Nearly a third of college graduates going into private-sector jobs were business school alumni, enrollments in American business schools had grown by more than 500 percent in the past decade, and "academic training for business" had become "an integral part of modern educational plans."[23] At the same time, Wharton's vision of a liberal arts education for business remained largely intact, and the report's authors sought to reinforce it by emphasizing that the "curriculum should recognize the educational necessity of a broad background of general and cultural knowledge," as well as "appreciation of the social and ethical aspects of the material studied."[24]

The value of that liberal arts education was clear to the Wharton alumni surveyed for the fifty-year retrospective. Of the eight components of the curriculum, only two were cited by a majority of the graduates as being of "primary" importance: English and "descriptive analysis of business activities."[25] While the alumni were less sure of the value of mandatory classes in foreign languages and the physical sciences, which received low scores, the average ratings of remaining components can be found in Table 1.[26]

Table 1. Wharton Alumni Weighted Average Ratings of the Importance of Courses, 1889–1928

Liberal Arts Courses		Business Courses	
English	92%	Descriptive analysis of business	87%
Social setting of business	73%	Administration of business	71%
History, philosophy, and culture	63%	Methods of measurement	67%

Source: James H. S. Bossard and J. Frederick Dewhurst, *University Education for Business: A Study of Existing Needs and Practices*, 229.

The graduates thus valued the social science classes on the nature and history of political and economic institutions (that is, the "social setting of business") and the humanities courses in English, history, philosophy, and the arts essentially as highly as those in business administration and statistics.[27]

The liberal arts core of the business curriculum would not endure for much longer, despite its apparent value to the business schools' founders and alumni. Several factors combined to push the liberal arts out of the business curriculum. One was the fact that twentieth-century business leaders were not necessarily as enlightened as Joseph Wharton had been when he devoted several years to studying the history of higher education before proposing his plan to the Penn trustees.[28] Investment banker Henry Clews, for example, would not hire university graduates because he wanted employees with their "natural sharpness and originality" not "dulled by ideas and theories of life entirely out of harmony" with a banking job.[29] Along the same lines, a report from the University of Wisconsin noted that some business executives "went so far as to claim that the College of Letters and Science not only did not train for business, but actually spoiled good business material."[30]

A second factor was the growth of graduate-only degrees, such as Harvard's MBA. At the outset, those programs could rely on the undergraduate curriculum to provide the foundation of a liberal arts education. That would free the MBA programs to offer classes that would provide very practical, job-oriented instruction to meet "the increasing demand of the business world for trained service," as the Tuck School put it.[31] In the first part of the twentieth century, Harvard had a signalman from the Boston and Maine Railroad help teach the course in industrial organization, and Dartmouth hired the head of a nearby life insurance company to teach the insurance classes.[32]

Another critical factor was a growing enthusiasm for applying scientific methods to the study of business. Beginning around the turn of the twentieth century, these approaches ranged from Frederick Winslow Taylor's "scientific management" of the production process to more recent fields, such as econometrics, management science, operations research, and management information systems.[33] Over time, scientific and social scientific approaches to analyzing business would come to dominate the training and research programs of business school professors and would form the basis of substantial parts of the twenty-first-century core curriculum.[34]

Then, a half century ago, University of Chicago professor and soon-to-be Nobel laureate Milton Friedman added an explicit rationale for the otherwise largely tacit demise of business schools' focus on promoting good corporate citizenship, along with the liberal arts curriculum that had been linked to it. The only "social responsibility of business," wrote Friedman, "is to increase its profits." His blunt and highly influential assessment was that those who believe "that business has a 'social conscience' . . . [are] preaching pure and unadulterated socialism."[35] An executive is "an employee of the owners of the business," responsible for "mak[ing] as much money as possible while conforming to the basic rules of society, both those embodied in law and . . . in ethical custom." Accordingly, executives interested in social and political causes should spend their "own money or time or energy, not the money of [their] employers or the time or energy [they have] contracted to devote to their purposes."[36]

Among other influences, Friedman's arguments helped push the CEO-focused Business Roundtable in the 1990s to abandon its prior view that "corporations are chartered to serve both their shareholders and society as a whole" in favor of a statement that "the paramount duty of management and of boards . . . is to the corporation's stockholders."[37] As one recent history of business schools relates, Friedman's approach had an educational consequence as well as a corporate one: "The triumph of the shareholder-value view . . . represents . . . a perfect synergy between economists, the corporate world, and business schools. It has served as the Big Idea that connects [all three] . . . and gives the business school curriculum a coherence it had not had before."[38]

Along with the elimination of the liberal arts as subjects of study, their overall presence in business school classrooms has diminished because of a dramatic shift in the educational backgrounds of the students. Liberal arts graduates made up a majority of the Harvard Business School student body in 1928, and most of the other students had science and engineering degrees from liberal arts universities that required STEM graduates to take numerous humanities courses.[39] At Penn in the 1920s, for example, engineers had to take four years of English literature, two years of English composition, two years of a modern language, and a philosophy class.[40] Even though Harvard Business School was filled with liberal arts majors and engineers who entered with humanities-rich backgrounds, the school nevertheless noted in 1928 that the "ability to write clearly and concisely is of such importance to business . . . that the school gives opportunity for all students to receive individual instruction [in] written English."[41]

Today, liberal arts graduates are a relative rarity in the top-ranked business programs. Most MBA students at schools such as Harvard and Wharton studied engineering, science, or business as undergraduates, and the liberal arts requirements in those undergraduate STEM programs have diminished considerably. A Penn undergraduate engineer today needs to take only two humanities courses (which can be design courses), two social science courses (which can be in finance), and one writing seminar (which can be pass-fail).[42] Meanwhile, as the social and political context classes have been dropped by MBA programs, and liberal arts majors have been replaced in business schools by those with STEM and business degrees, junior and senior high schools (at least in the United States) have steadily diminished their prior commitment to civics education.[43] Today's typical MBA graduate, therefore, has had little or no exposure—ever—to the kinds of humanities and social science courses that the business school founders and early graduates considered to be at least as important as the business-related curriculum.

HAS BUSINESS CHANGED ALONG WITH THE BUSINESS CURRICULUM?

The current condition of the MBA curriculum raises the question of whether business education, or business itself, has changed to such an extent that subjects that were considered by business executives to be of primary importance in the first half of the twentieth century are no longer important, or that others have become so essential that there is simply no room in two years of graduate study to include additional classes in the humanities and in the social and political setting of business. We set out to address these questions first by exploring what employers and prospective students say about what management education should entail and then by examining the curricular requirements at a number of leading MBA programs.

One recent survey, "See the Future 2020," asked employers what should be taught in business schools. Asked what topics "would be valuable . . . *in the next five years*," the most popular responses primarily focused on technical skills, although none received the endorsement of more than half of the executives: data analytics and data-driven decision making received the most positive responses, with the endorsement of 50 percent of the respondents. That response was followed by digital transformation (43 percent), artificial intelligence (35 percent), and decision making in uncertain and complex times (35 percent).[44]

The employers' answers were very different when they were asked about what potential employees should do "*to grow successful careers.*" With that longer-term perspective in mind, a very substantial majority (71 percent) of the employers said that the students "should not only learn about business, but consider adding arts, humanities and sciences to their studies." An even larger number (88 percent) "believe these studies should be used by students to develop stronger social and emotional skills and more advanced cognitive capabilities, such as logical reasoning and creativity."[45] Perhaps the best interpretation of these data is that many employers want to hire MBAs who can immediately contribute the technical skills taught in the MBA core curriculum, but they believe that, in the long run, those business graduates will be much more successful if they also study the liberal arts.

In 2019, with Friedman's views in decline, the Business Roundtable decided that executives should consider their businesses' impact on society as well as profitability, and its CEO members rotated back to the view that "each of our stakeholders is essential." They committed, among other things, to "foster . . . dignity and respect" and "protect the environment by embracing sustainable practices."[46] Potential MBA students and customers express similar views. A recent survey indicates that 70 percent of prospective business school students "named ethical leadership as important to business education," with the "next most important factor [being] diversity and equality."[47] Similarly, a 2019 survey found that "seventy percent of consumers want to know what the brands they support are doing to address social and environmental issues."[48]

The next question is whether there is any room in the curriculum for the liberal arts other than in the one vestige of business schools' original focus on cultivating morality and civic responsibility: business ethics. After Friedman's essay appeared, interest in ethics courses dropped, and by 1985 ethics could be found at only a minority of business schools.[49] Then widely published instances of corporate malfeasance in the 1980s and 1990s prompted business schools to reconsider the merits of ethics courses. In 1988 Harvard became the first elite business school in the United States to require an ethics course, which was a three-week class for entering students.[50] Soon more than 90 percent of business schools offered at least one course that includes some material relating to ethics.[51]

As of this writing, it is not unusual for MBA curricula at the leading schools to include ethics, but often only as part of a broader course in legal studies (Wharton), business and society (INSEAD), or business environment (Chicago).[52] This type of course, which is not just focused on ethics, can perhaps be seen as the modern version of the "social setting of business" courses that the 1930s Wharton alumni had prized in the 1920s, although they are generally only one class. In a number of cases, they last only half a semester, as at Tuck, where MBA students are required to enroll in "one minicourse" dealing with "the complex ethical and social challenges of business."[53] In other words, the liberal arts classes that used to fill half the curriculum now often represent just a half course.

Since leading MBA programs have often allocated so little space in their core curricula to the social, political, legal, and ethical environments affecting businesses, it would seem that essential business courses fill all of the remaining space. That is not the case. At Wharton, Harvard, Tuck, and other leading business schools, the classes that make up the core business curriculum fulfill only about 50 percent of the credits required for graduation. Students earn the remaining credits by taking electives, some of which can be chosen from virtually anywhere in the university catalog, irrespective of field of study.[54] Such cross-disciplinary flexibility indicates that the business schools do not consider every element of today's full MBA curriculum to be essential for business education, thus providing space for a return of the liberal arts.

LIBERAL ARTS COURSES FOR MBA PROGRAMS

We propose that the liberal arts should reclaim a portion of the MBA curricula. There are at least three overlapping areas where doing so will contribute meaningfully to the education of the students and to the organizations to which they will devote their careers: providing a foundation for understanding the political and social context in which businesses operate, and for evaluating how organizations can be responsible corporate citizens; enhancing the critical reasoning skills necessary for addressing business, ethical, political, and social issues; and providing the exposure to history, literature, and the arts that executives believe will be useful for MBAs' long-term career growth.

These liberal arts courses can also provide opportunities for students to become better writers. As the *Wall Street Journal* has noted, "While M.B.A. students' quantitative skills are prized by employers, their writing . . . skills have been a perennial complaint." Even at firms such as Morgan Stanley and Booz Allen Hamilton, which recruit from the most prestigious MBA programs, newly hired employees need to have their written work reviewed before it can be sent to clients, and General Mills requires that its MBA hires pass a writing training program.[55] Even if one marketing professor's judgment that business students can be "functionally illiterate"[56] is unduly harsh, it is worth bearing in mind that Wharton alumni in the 1930s ranked the importance of their English courses higher than *any* business class.[57]

Fitting an entire liberal arts education into the MBA curriculum would be impossible, but, in one semester, perhaps divided into eight half courses, business schools could provide enough material to serve as an introduction to a range of liberal arts subjects, to improve the students' writing skills, and to launch what we hope would be a lifelong engagement with the humanities. Moreover, as universities increasingly seek to offer their alumni and other members of the community postgraduation learning opportunities, they may find that these kinds of courses will be popular offerings, especially to the extent that they touch on business education's original focus on purpose, character, and the common good.[58]

How the liberal arts can best be integrated into the curriculum will undoubtedly vary from one university to another. The place to start is to focus on the liberal arts topics that were addressed by the pioneering programs at Wharton and Tuck and that, at one point, represented more than half of the business curriculum: government and politics, philosophy (moral and political philosophy, theory of knowledge, and logic), history, psychology, and sociology.[59] In the original programs at Penn and Dartmouth, these topics could often be covered by existing courses for liberal arts students because the business degree was entirely or partly an undergraduate program. For today's master's programs, it may be difficult to mix twenty-eight-year-old MBA students with eighteen-year-old undergraduates in a basic American politics or philosophy class.[60] But, at the same time, the majority of MBA students with STEM and business undergraduate degrees will be ill-prepared to enroll in the far more advanced graduate classes offered to doctoral students in those disciplines. Therefore, MBA programs may find that it would be more appropriate to offer business school classes in the liberal arts that have been designed by business school faculty in conjunction with professors from the relevant departments or to hire new faculty with training in the appropriate fields. Wharton, for example, has recently added faculty members with PhDs in liberal arts fields such as philosophy, history, government, anthropology, and psychology.[61]

There are also a number of MBA courses currently on the books that could serve as models. In some cases, faculty trained primarily in the humanities teach management classes, while in others business professors offer liberal arts courses. At Oxford's Saïd Business School, literature scholar and musician (and senior fellow in entrepreneurship) Pegram Harrison reminds MBA students that "humanities scholars have been thinking about leadership for 3000 years." His class provides lessons in leadership from musical conductors and the chance to reflect on "the art of being human" with

Shakespeare.⁶² Meanwhile, at Cambridge, economists Jochen Runde and Michael Pollitt teach Philosophy of Business, noting that although "business is sometimes presented as the antithesis of philosophy, as being about practical action . . . rather than the contemplation of abstract ideas, . . . the ideas, tools, and techniques business people use . . . all involve implicit philosophical presuppositions."⁶³ One of the Indian Institutes of Management has even launched an MBA in liberal studies, with courses in "philosophy, literature, economics and sociology" to help graduates "decode culture and technology."⁶⁴ Jennifer Kohn, an economist at Drew University, makes the case for assigning James Madison's classic *Federalist*, no. 10, on political theory in business classes, not only for its lessons in dealing with competing political interests, but also because Madison "thinks like an economist and reasons like a game theorist."⁶⁵

INCENTIVES FOR STRENGTHENING THE LIBERAL ARTS IN BUSINESS EDUCATION

Embracing curricular change does not always come easily to higher education, but business schools are likely to appreciate the power of incentives to do so better than most university endeavors. One potentially valuable one in this context would be for the most influential international rankings—the *Financial Times*, *US News and World Report*, *Forbes*, and so on—to reward MBA programs for giving the liberal arts a more prominent position in the core curriculum.

At present, the leading rankings do not focus much attention on curricular content. The *Financial Times* allocates 3 percent of its total points to the number of hours in the core curriculum devoted to ethics or corporate social responsibility.⁶⁶ Currently, however, only one of the programs with an overall ranking in the top ten also ranks in the top ten for CSR, so it would be helpful to allocate enough weight to this factor to make it meaningful in the overall rankings. It would also be beneficial to broaden its scope beyond CSR to include the full range of liberal arts classes that will provide the context and foundation for responsible business and ethical decision making.

At the same time, the *Financial Times*' more important analysis of faculty research productivity (10 percent) will need to expand beyond the current list of twenty-five designated journals, which are almost exclusively oriented toward scholarship in the fields dominating today's core curriculum. Not only should the list of journals be expanded, but, since liberal arts scholars frequently publish books rather than articles, it will be important to include the leading peer-reviewed presses, including, among others, the university presses of Cambridge, Oxford, Harvard, Princeton, and Chicago.[67] The other rankings would do well to include similar metrics. Finally, all of the ratings should find a way to include the long-term career satisfaction and success on which business students and executives are increasingly focused, rather than just the amount of compensation received in the first few years of employment, which is the factor that tends to dominate today's rankings.

THE LIBERAL ARTS AT WORK

Studying the liberal arts will also help MBAs be more successful in business, even businesses based on the newest and most exciting STEM discoveries. Take, for example, the tech sector, which is a prime destination for new MBA graduates. Today, many MBAs would jump at the chance to join the self-driving vehicle team at Tesla, GM, or many other companies. For graduates heading in that direction, it might seem that the higher the tech, the lower the need to understand anything other than business, or perhaps engineering, but that is not the case. Some serious philosophical analysis needs to occur before the car's much-anticipated commercial launch. The carmakers will have to solve one of the classic problems of modern philosophy: the trolley dilemma.[68]

One version of the trolley problem is the following: You are standing next to a very large person on a bridge, and a trolley below is about to plow into a group of people. You can push the large person off the bridge in front of the trolley to stop it, saving several lives at the expense of just one. Should you? That is what the driverless car needs to know. It must be programmed in advance for cases where an unavoidable fatal accident will either protect the person in the car at all costs or sacrifice a passenger to save the lives of multiple pedestrians.

Additionally, a range of humanities issues can be found at the core of challenging questions confronting Google, Facebook, and Apple (to name just a few) relating to personal data usage by third parties, misinformation on social media, the security of smart home electronics, and the like.[69] It turns out that the higher the tech, the greater the need for a humanities education. In fact, as early adopters of new technological opportunities, businesses will often be pioneering society's thinking about the deeper questions arising from their use. Whether they realize they are doing so requires managers with the kind of academic preparation that will help them identify and address the key issues.

MBAs headed into biotech, pharmaceuticals, or health-care management also face a life-or-death issue, one that has been debated within the humanities for ages. When there are not enough life-saving resources to help everyone, who should get them? As we write this, hospital chief executives and public health leaders are confronting this difficult question as they deal with capacity shortages caused by the COVID-19 pandemic.[70]

Around the world, much of the global health-care market is committed to a process in which a single government entity decides whether a new medicine is affordable for the whole country. That decision is based not only on complex calculations of the value of the "life-years" that could be saved across the population, but also on whether the medicines can be allocated in a just and fair manner.[71] To operate successfully in these global markets, life-sciences executives need to understand the complex pharmacoeconomic analyses involved in the relevant life-year calculations, which is something for which the existing business curriculum can prepare them. However, they also must comprehend how the various countries decide what just and fair means when it comes to accessing medicines, and that topic may be missing from the current course offerings.

This distributive justice issue has historically been the stock in trade of political theorists, theologians, and philosophers, and, in the modern world, it has become a critical question for life-sciences managers as well. A curriculum that includes discussions of Aristotle, Kant, and Mill will give business students a framework for understanding these complex decisions and a head start in assessing how theories of justice influence commercial health-care markets.

Finally, if there is any one common task shared by virtually all business graduates, it is making models: short- or long-term projections of future financial performance. Retail or wholesale, product or service, high-tech or low-, both for-profit and not-for-profit firms make their plans based on the results of these financial models. Widely available software packages enable models to consider thousands of different scenarios. In our experience, however, these powerful modeling tools often go astray long before the very first scenario is discussed. That is because the input assumptions make or break the model's logic, and the assumptions are—or should be—rooted in things you are confident that you know. Model builders often fail to think about how reliable such knowledge is, but a branch of philosophy is dedicated to just these questions. The theory of knowledge, or epistemology, asks us to consider what it means to know something.[72] Understanding these issues should be a vital part of business decision making.

CONCLUSION

The longtime admissions director at Harvard Business School has said that candidates with humanities backgrounds are uniquely valuable, as she believes that they are the ones able "to think broadly" when "taking a stand." She said: "You can learn how to do accounting. But it takes judgment to do what we do here."[73] To develop that reasoned judgment, business students will need a deeper understanding of the humanities than is likely to rub off on them from the 19 percent of their classmates who majored in the liberal arts.

As MBA programs consider how to incorporate the liberal arts into the curriculum, they should start by examining the historical dedication to the liberal arts in business education. Then they should reach out to executives who have seen how the liberal arts connect with business management in practice. Here universities can tap into the impressive number of executives—C-suite managers, entrepreneurs, consultants, bankers, and others—who have taken their liberal arts degrees into the business world and found more points of contact than professors of either management or the humanities might suspect.

By renewing their historical focus on the liberal arts, MBA programs will help MBAs, and their employers, be more thoughtful and responsible citizens. That is certainly the best reason for studying them, a goal that has become increasingly crucial in the view of corporate leaders, potential customers, and future MBA students. At the same time, as generations of business executives have observed, it will also make them more successful in business.

NOTES

1. Wharton School, "Wharton MBA Classes, Courses & Curriculum."
2. Milton Friedman, "A Friedman Doctrine: The Social Responsibility of Business Is to Increase Its Profits."
3. Tom Peters, "McKinsey's Work on Opioid Sales Represents a New Low," *Financial Times*, February 15, 2021, https://www.ft.com/content/82e98478-f099-44ac-b014-3f9b15fe6bc6.

4. See EFMD Global, "See the Future 2020," 17 (emphasis added).

5. See W. Ross Yates, *Joseph Wharton: Quaker Industrial Pioneer*. More recently, many of the tech titans have been college dropouts, while in the highly educated biotech industry, CEOs with PhDs far outnumber those with MBAs. See Donald L. Drakeman, Lisa N. Drakeman, and Nektarios Oraiopoulos, *From Breakthrough to Blockbuster: The Business of Biotechnology*, chap. 6. According to the *Economist*, nearly two hundred thousand MBA degrees have been awarded every year in the United States since 2010. See C. S-W., "Nothing Special: MBAs Are No Longer Prized by Employers," *Economist*, June 13, 2016, https://www.economist.com/whichmba/nothing-special-mbas-are-no-longer-prized-employers. Even now, after millions of MBAs have been awarded to aspiring corporate leaders, only a little over one-third of Fortune 500 CEOs hold that degree. For Fortune 500 CEOs' education, see Abigail Johnson Hess, "Here's Where 10 of the Most Powerful Fortune 500 CEOs Went to Business School." The number drops to below one-third for global CEOs. See Marc Ethier, "Only a Third of World's CEOs Have an MBA."

6. Wharton School, "Resources for Nontraditional Students." The Wharton School says, "By definition, a nontraditional MBA student is someone whose profile is distinct from the majority." A recent class profile shows that a majority of Wharton MBA students studied either business or a STEM discipline as undergraduates. See Wharton School, "Facts & Figures: Wharton MBA Class Profile."

7. We acknowledge that "liberal arts" is a flexible term in higher education today. When we refer to reviving the liberal arts in the context of business education, we are referring to the types of classes in history, government, philosophy, English, sociology, and psychology that were previously included at Wharton and other pioneering business schools. On the relative unimportance of business education for business success, see the studies summarized in Dan Rasmussen and Haonan Li, "The MBA Myth and the Cult of the CEO."

8. Quoted in Rakesh Khurana, *From Higher Aims to Hired Hands: The Social Transformation of American Business Schools and the Unfulfilled Promise of Management as a Profession*, 107; and quoted in Steven A. Sass, *The Pragmatic Imagination: A History of the Wharton School, 1881–1981*, 21. Before the Wharton gift began a process by which many bachelor's- and master's-level business degree programs were established in the late nineteenth and twentieth centuries, there were many independent commercial schools and business colleges teaching bookkeeping, shorthand, business writing, and similar subjects. See Steven Conn, *Nothing Succeeds Like Failure: The Sad History of American Business Schools*, 1–52.

9. Quoted in Sass, *Pragmatic Imagination*, 21.

10. Conn, *Nothing Succeeds Like Failure*, 43. See also Tuck School announcement, 1901–2, quoted in Khurana, *From Higher Aims*, 110.

11. Tuck School announcement, 1901–2, quoted in Khurana, *From Higher Aims*, 109.

12. Quoted in Khurana, *From Higher Aims*, 108.

13. Conn notes that, at the outset, the Wharton School was "a two-year course of study taken by students after two years taking courses in the college." The University of California at Berkeley followed the Wharton model. Conn, *Nothing Succeeds Like Failure*, 55.

14. Harvard Library, "The Graduate School of Business Administration, 1908–09," 13. For Dartmouth's curriculum, see *Catalogue of Dartmouth College Together with the Amos Tuck School of Administration and Finance, the Thayer School of Civil Engineering,*

and the Medical School for the Years 1905–1906, 215–51. The Dartmouth catalog stated that its curriculum "permits the student to receive first the benefit of a college education—to develop the man before developing the businessman." *Catalogue of Dartmouth College*, 217. Dartmouth's business graduates received a master's of commercial science. See *Catalogue of Dartmouth College*, 249. Harvard awarded its graduates a master of business administration. See Harvard Library, "Graduate School of Business Administration," 10.

15. See Khurana, *From Higher Aims*, 108. Sass notes, "These men would be an amalgam of the professional and the man of affairs. . . . Wharton's college-educated businessmen . . . would hold [a] critical position. . . of power in society and could rely on the liberal arts education that they would receive at Penn as a source of prestige, perspective, and personal character." Sass, *Pragmatic Imagination*, 35. See also Carter A. Daniel, *MBA: The First Century*.

16. University of Pennsylvania, *Catalogue and Announcements, 1888–1889*, 58.

17. Karl A. Hill, "The Amos Tuck School of Business Administration: Its Origin and Present Program," 475.

18. University of Pennsylvania, *Catalogue and Announcements, 1888–1889*, 58.

19. See Khurana, *From Higher Aims*; and Conn, *Nothing Succeeds Like Failure*.

20. Warren Bennis and James O'Toole, "How Business Schools Lost Their Way," 104. See also business dean Johan Roos, "The Renaissance We Need in Business Education." For an endorsement of a greater role for the liberal arts in undergraduate business education, see William M. Sullivan, Thomas Ehrlich, and Anne Colby, "The Carnegie Report: Looking Back and Thinking Forward."

21. See, for example, Stanford Graduate School of Business, "First-Year Curriculum"; and London Business School, "Curriculum Overview."

22. See James H. S. Bossard and J. Frederic Dewhurst, *University Education for Business: A Study of Existing Needs and Practices*, 50, 261.

23. Bossard and Dewhurst, *University Education for Business*, 23, 115, 243.

24. Quoted in Conn, *Nothing Succeeds Like Failure*, 59.

25. Bossard and Dewhurst, *University Education for Business*, 230. The eight components were English, foreign languages, methods of measurement, physical sciences, social setting of business life, descriptive analysis of business activities, administration of business activities, and studies broadly interpretive (for example, history, philosophy, and the arts). See Bossard and Dewhurst, *University Education for Business*, 223–26.

26. Only 3.2 percent cited foreign languages and 8.1 percent named physical sciences as being of primary importance. See Bossard and Dewhurst, *University Education for Business*, 226.

27. See Bossard and Dewhurst, *University Education for Business*, 224–29.

28. See Sass, *Pragmatic Imagination*, 35.

29. Quoted in Daniel, *MBA: The First Century*, 26. For an opposing view, see the University of California's 1897 catalog: "The successful administration of the vast aggregation of capital, the buying and selling of goods in the world's markets . . . require the broadest mental training and the widest knowledge that can possibly be obtained." Quoted in Daniel, *MBA: The First Century*, 41.

30. Quoted in Conn, *Nothing Succeeds Like Failure*, 60.

31. *Catalogue of Dartmouth College*, 215.

32. See Harvard Library, "Graduate School of Business Administration," 7; and *Catalogue of Dartmouth College*, 244–45. In H. L. Mencken's *American Mercury*, Arlington Stone satirized business education by highlighting some of the course offerings, ranging from Harvard's "course in Motion Pictures," through which "the faculty was augmented by such men of learning as . . . the Hon. Cecil B. De Mille," to Cincinnati's two-course sequence in "Packing House Operations," which featured "Pork Operations" and "Beef Operations." Arlington J. Stone, "The Dawn of a New Science," 455, 448.

33. Taylor taught at Harvard and later became a professor at Tuck. See Hindy Lauer Schachter, "The Role Played by Frederick Taylor in the Rise of the Academic Management Fields."

34. For a review of how these approaches influenced scholarship and teaching at Wharton, see Sass, *Pragmatic Imagination*, 55–291.

35. Friedman, "Friedman Doctrine." See also the 1971 "Powell Memorandum," in which corporate lawyer and future Supreme Court justice Lewis Powell discussed the need to defend the free-enterprise system, especially in universities. Lewis F. Powell Jr. to Eugene B. Sydnor Jr., "Confidential Memorandum: Attack on Free Enterprise System."

36. Friedman, "Friedman Doctrine."

37. Quoted in Conn, *Nothing Succeeds Like Failure*, 197–98.

38. Conn, *Nothing Succeeds Like Failure*, 199.

39. See Harvard University, *Harvard University Catalogue, 1928–29*.

40. University of Pennsylvania, *Catalogue of the University of Pennsylvania for the Session of 1923–24*.

41. Harvard University, *Harvard University Catalogue, 1928–29*, 56–57.

42. See University of Pennsylvania, "Social Science and Humanities Courses"; University of Pennsylvania, "The Writing Requirement." Similarly, at the University of Illinois, a degree in aerospace engineering requires 128 credits, of which only 18 need to be in non-STEM liberal arts courses. See University of Illinois at Urbana–Champaign, Illinois, *Academic Catalog, 2019–2020*, 11–15.

43. See Michael A. Rebell, *Flunking Democracy: Schools, Courts, and Civic Participation*.

44. EFMD Global, "See the Future 2020," 17–20 (emphasis added).

45. "See the Future 2020," 17 (emphasis added).

46. Business Roundtable, *Statement on the Purpose of a Corporation*.

47. Jonathan Moules, "Teaching Sustainability: How MBAs Are Combining Mainstream with Green-Stream," *Financial Times*, February 23, 2020, https://www.ft.com/content/5787f180-3b96-11ea-b84f-a62c46f39bc2, citing results from Carrington-Crisp's Tomorrow's MBA.

48. Markstein and Certus Insights, "Consumers Expect the Brands They Support to Be Socially Responsible."

49. See Conn, *Nothing Succeeds Like Failure*, 202, citing W. Michael Hoffmann and Jennifer Mills Moore, "Results of a Business Ethics Curriculum Survey Conducted by the Center for Business Ethics."

50. See Eric N. Berg, "Harvard Will Require M.B.A. Ethics Course," *New York Times*, July 13, 1988.

51. See Conn, *Nothing Succeeds Like Failure*, 203, citing Lyle F. Schoenfeldt, Don M. McDonald, and Stuart A. Youngblood, "The Teaching of Business Ethics: A Survey of AACSB Member Schools."

52. See Wharton School, "Wharton MBA Classes, Courses & Curriculum"; INSEAD, "MBA Core Courses"; and Chicago Booth School of Business, "MBA Curriculum."

53. Tuck School of Business, "Ethics and Social Responsibility Requirement."

54. This is according to the MBA program websites for Wharton, Tuck, Harvard, the University of Chicago, Columbia, and MIT, as of January 16, 2021.

55. See Diana Middleton, "Students Struggle for Words: Business Schools Put More Emphasis on Writing amid Employer Complaints," *Wall Street Journal*, March 3, 2011.

56. Menachem Wecker, "B-Schools Seem to Downplay Writing Skills."

57. See Bossard and Dewhurst, *University Education for Business*, 224–29.

58. In a 2016 survey, of the 74 percent of adults described as "personal learners" (that is, people not taking a class for professional certifications or training), 87 percent found the learning experience "helped them feel more capable and well-rounded," and 69 percent said it "opened up new perspectives about their lives." Pew Research Center, "Lifelong Learning and Technology."

59. For perspectives on undergraduate business education, see the Aspen Institute, *Charting a New Course for Next-Generation Business Leaders: A Toolkit for Blending the Humanities and Business in Undergraduate Education*.

60. See John A. Byrne, "Average Age & Work Experience at Top MBA Programs."

61. See, for example, University of Pennsylvania, "Julian Jonker," "Peter Conti-Brown," "Brian D. Feinstein," "Gwendolyn Gordon," and "Nina Strohminger."

62. Pegram Harrison, "Leadership Perspectives from the Humanities." The Oxford Research Centre in the Humanities (TORCH) has also sponsored "The Arts of Leading," inaugurated by historian Stephen Tuck "comparing the leadership model of Martin Luther King with leadership in the [Civil Rights Movement's] grass roots." See University of Oxford, "'Start Where the People Are: Leadership and the Civil Rights Movement' with Professor Stephen Tuck."

63. Jochen Runde and Michael Pollitt, "Cambridge MBA, 2020."

64. Prerna Sindwani, "MBA in Liberal Studies—a New Course from a Top Indian B-School." For undergraduate business schools, see Jon Marcus, "How the Humanities Can Train Entrepreneurs"; and Matt Statler and Pierre Guillet de Monthoux, "Humanities and Arts in Management Education: The Emerging Carnegie Paradigm."

65. Quoted in Jennifer L. Kohn, "Federalist #10 in Management #101: What Madison Has to Teach Managers," 686.

66. For an analysis of how programs answered this question as of 2005, see Lisa Jones Christensen et al., "Ethics, CSR, and Sustainability Education in the *Financial Times* Top 50 Global Business Schools: Baseline Data and Future Research Directions." In addition, *Bloomberg Businessweek* includes "the quality, depth, and range of instruction," with a specific focus on "real-world business situations," as judged by students, alumni, and recruiters. Best B-School Rankings, 2019–20, "Methodology."

67. These are the top five book publishers for political science, according to James C. Garand and Michael W. Giles, "Ranking Scholarly Publishers in Political Science: An Alternative Approach." A survey of philosophers named the same list, except that Routledge replaced Chicago (ranked eighth). See Brian Leiter, "Best Philosophy Publishers in English."

68. See Philippa Foot, "The Problem of Abortion and the Doctrine of the Double Effect"; and Judith Jarvis Thomson, "The Trolley Problem."

69. See, for example, the contributions in Luciano Floridi and Mariarosaria Taddeo, eds., "The Ethical Impact of Data Science."

70. See, for example, Oliver M. Fisher et al., "Distributive Justice during the Coronavirus Disease 2019 Pandemic in Australia."

71. See, for example, Drakeman, Drakeman, and Oraiopoulos, *From Breakthrough to Blockbuster*, chap. 8.

72. See, for example, Claudius Graebner, "How to Relate Models to Reality? An Epistemological Framework for the Validation and Verification of Computational Models."

73. Quoted in Oliver Staley, "If You Majored in the Humanities, You Really Should Apply to Harvard Business School."

BIBLIOGRAPHY

Aspen Institute. *Charting a New Course for Next-Generation Business Leaders: A Toolkit for Blending the Humanities and Business in Undergraduate Education.* Spring 2018. https://www.aspeninstitute.org/wp-content/uploads/2018/06/ChartingAnewCourse_ToolkitForBlending.pdf.

Bennis, Warren, and James O'Toole. "How Business Schools Lost Their Way." *Harvard Business Review* (May 2005). https://hbr.org/2005/05/how-business-schools-lost-their-way.

Best B-School Rankings, 2019–20. "Methodology." *Bloomberg Businessweek*. Accessed January 9, 2021. https://www.bloomberg.com/business-schools/2019/methodology.

Bossard, James H. S., and J. Frederic Dewhurst. *University Education for Business: A Study of Existing Needs and Practices*. Philadelphia: University of Pennsylvania Press, 1931.

Business Roundtable. *Statement on the Purpose of a Corporation*. August 19, 2019. https://s3.amazonaws.com/brt.org/BRT-StatementonthePurposeofaCorporationOctober2020.pdf.

Byrne, John A. "Average Age & Work Experience at Top MBA Programs." *Poets&Quants*, November 27, 2019. https://poetsandquants.com/2019/11/27/average-age-work-experience-at-top-mba-programs/.

Catalogue of Dartmouth College Together with the Amos Tuck School of Administration and Finance, the Thayer School of Civil Engineering, and the Medical School for the Years 1905–1906. Hanover, NH: Printed for the College, 1905.

Chicago Booth School of Business. "MBA Curriculum." MBA Programs. Accessed January 20, 2021. https://www.chicagobooth.edu/mba/academics/curriculum.

Christensen, Lisa Jones, et al. "Ethics, CSR, and Sustainability Education in the *Financial Times* Top 50 Global Business Schools: Baseline Data and Future Research Directions." *Journal of Business Ethics* 73, no. 4 (2007): 347–68.

Conn, Steven. *Nothing Succeeds Like Failure: The Sad History of American Business Schools*. Ithaca, NY: Cornell University Press, 2019.

Daniel, Carter A. *MBA: The First Century*. Lewisburg, PA: Bucknell University Press, 1998.

Drakeman, Donald L., Lisa N. Drakeman, and Nektarios Oraiopoulos. *From Breakthrough to Blockbuster: The Business of Biotechnology*. New York: Oxford University Press, 2022.

EFMD Global. "See the Future 2020." Special supplement, *Global Focus* 14, no. 2 (2020): 17–20.

Ethier, Marc. "Only a Third of World's CEOs Have an MBA." *Poets&Quants*, December 20, 2017. https://poetsandquants.com/2017/12/20/survey-only-a-third-of-worlds-ceos-have-an-mba/.

Fisher, Oliver M. et al. "Distributive Justice during the Coronavirus Disease 2019 Pandemic in Australia." *ANZ Journal of Surgery* 90 (May 2020): 961–62.

Floridi, Luciano, and Mariarosaria Taddeo, eds. "The Ethical Impact of Data Science." Special issue, *Philosophical Transactions of the Royal Society* A 374, no. 2083 (2016).

Foot, Philippa. "The Problem of Abortion and the Doctrine of the Double Effect." *Oxford Review* 5 (1967): 5–15.

Friedman, Milton. "A Friedman Doctrine: The Social Responsibility of Business Is to Increase Its Profits." *New York Times Magazine*, September 13, 1970.

Garand, James C., and Michael W. Giles. "Ranking Scholarly Publishers in Political Science: An Alternative Approach." *PS: Political Science and Politics* 44, no. 2 (2011): 325–83.

Graebner, Claudius. "How to Relate Models to Reality? An Epistemological Framework for the Validation and Verification of Computational Models." *Journal of Artificial Societies and Social Simulation* 21, no. 3 (2018).

Harrison, Pegram. "Leadership Perspectives from the Humanities." MBA, 2019–20, Saïd Business School, University of Oxford.

Harvard Library. "The Graduate School of Business Administration, 1908–09." Official Register of Harvard University 5, no. 38 (1908). https://iiif.lib.harvard.edu/manifests/view/drs:423140325$1i.

Harvard University. *Harvard University Catalogue, 1928–29*. Cambridge, MA: Harvard University Press, 1928.

Hess, Abigail Johnson. "Here's Where 10 of the Most Powerful Fortune 500 CEOs Went to Business School." *CNBC Make It*, July 12, 2018. https://www.cnbc.com/2018/07/09/where-10-powerful-fortune-500-ceos-went-to-business-school.html.

Hill, Karl A. "The Amos Tuck School of Business Administration: Its Origin and Present Program." *Journal of Higher Education* 32, no. 9 (1961): 473–79.

Hoffmann, W. Michael, and Jennifer Mills Moore. "Results of a Business Ethics Curriculum Survey Conducted by the Center for Business Ethics." *Journal of Business Ethics* 1, no. 2 (1982): 81–83.

INSEAD. "MBA Core Courses." MBA Programme. Accessed January 20, 2021. https://www.insead.edu/master-programmes/mba/core-courses.

Khurana, Rakesh. *From Higher Aims to Hired Hands: The Social Transformation of American Business Schools and the Unfulfilled Promise of Management as a Profession*. Princeton, NJ: Princeton University Press, 2007.

Kohn, Jennifer L. "Federalist #10 in Management #101: What Madison Has to Teach Managers." *Journal of Management Education* 37, no. 5 (2015): 683–703.

Leiter, Brian. "Best Philosophy Publishers in English." *Leiter Reports: A Philosophy Blog* (February 5, 2013). https://leiterreports.typepad.com/blog/2013/02/best-philosophy-publishers-in-english.html.

London Business School. "Curriculum Overview." Accessed January 21, 2021. https://www.london.edu/masters-degrees/mba/programme-content.

Marcus, Jon. "How the Humanities Can Train Entrepreneurs." *Atlantic*, September 20, 2017. https://www.theatlantic.com/education/archive/2017/09/how-the-humanities-can-train-entrepreneurs/540390/.

Markstein and Certus Insights. "Consumers Expect the Brands They Support to Be Socially Responsible." Press release, October 2, 2019. https://www.businesswire.com/news/home/20191002005697/en/Consumers-Expect-Brands-Support-Socially-Responsible.

Pew Research Center. "Lifelong Learning and Technology." March 22, 2016. https://www.pewresearch.org/internet/2016/03/22/lifelong-learning-and-technology/.

Powell, Lewis F., Jr., to Eugene B. Sydnor Jr. "Confidential Memorandum: Attack on Free Enterprise System." August 23, 1971. https://reclaimdemocracy.org/powell_memo_lewis/.

Rasmussen, Dan, and Haonan Li. "The MBA Myth and the Cult of the CEO." *Institutional Investor* (February 27, 2019). https://www.institutionalinvestor.com/article/b1db3jy3201d38/The-MBA-Myth-and-the-Cult-of-the-CEO.

Rebell, Michael A. *Flunking Democracy: Schools, Courts, and Civic Participation*. Chicago: University of Chicago Press, 2018.

Roos, Johan. "The Renaissance We Need in Business Education." *Harvard Business Review* (July 2014). https://hbr.org/2014/07/the-renaissance-we-need-in-business-education.

Runde, Jochen, and Michael Pollitt. "Cambridge MBA, 2020." Cambridge Judge Business School, University of Cambridge.

Sass, Steven A. *The Pragmatic Imagination: A History of the Wharton School, 1881–1981*. Philadelphia: University of Pennsylvania Press, 1982.

Schachter, Hindy Lauer. "The Role Played by Frederick Taylor in the Rise of the Academic Management Fields." *Journal of Management History* 16, no. 4 (2010): 437–48.

Schoenfeldt, Lyle F., Don M. McDonald, and Stuart A. Youngblood. "The Teaching of Business Ethics: A Survey of AACSB Member Schools." *Journal of Business Ethics* 10, no. 3 (1991): 237–41.

Sindwani, Prerna. "MBA in Liberal Studies—a New Course from a Top Indian B-School." *Business Insider, India* (December 18, 2019). https://www.businessinsider

.in/education/news/iim-kozhikode-introduces-mba-in-liberal-studies/article-show/72863523.cms.

Staley, Oliver. "If You Majored in the Humanities, You Really Should Apply to Harvard Business School." *Quartz* (March 9, 2016). https://qz.com/634475/if-you-majored-in-the-humanities-you-really-should-apply-to-harvard-business-school/.

Stanford Graduate School of Business. "First-Year Curriculum." Accessed January 21, 2021. https://www.gsb.stanford.edu/programs/mba/academic-experience/curriculum/first-year.

Statler, Matt, and Pierre Guillet de Monthoux. "Humanities and Arts in Management Education: The Emerging Carnegie Paradigm." *Journal of Management Education* 39, no. 1 (2015): 3–15.

Stone, Arlington J. "The Dawn of a New Science." *American Mercury* (August 1928).

Sullivan, William M., Thomas Ehrlich, and Anne Colby. "The Carnegie Report: Looking Back and Thinking Forward." In *The Routledge Companion to Reinventing Management Education*, edited by Chris Steyaert, Timon Beyes, and Martin Parker, 23–35. New York: Routledge, 2016.

Thomson, Judith Jarvis. "The Trolley Problem." *Yale Law Journal* 94, no. 6 (1985): 1395–1415.

Tuck School of Business. "Ethics and Social Responsibility Requirement." Accessed December 31, 2020. https://www.tuck.dartmouth.edu/mba/academic-experience/required-curriculum/ethics-and-social-responsibility.

University of Illinois at Urbana–Champaign, Illinois. *Academic Catalog, 2019–2020*. http://catalog.illinois.edu/archivedacademiccatalogs/2019-20.pdf.

University of Oxford. "'Start Where the People Are: Leadership and the Civil Rights Movement' with Professor Stephen Tuck." Oxford Character Project. Accessed December 27, 2020. https://oxfordcharacter.org/events/the-art-of-leadership-lectures-start-where-the-people-are-leadership-and-the-civil-rights-movement-professor-stephen-tuck.

University of Pennsylvania. "Brian D. Feinstein." Wharton School. Accessed January 21, 2021. https://lgst.wharton.upenn.edu/profile/bdfeinst/.

———. *Catalogue and Announcements, 1888–1889*. Philadelphia, 1888. https://archives.upenn.edu/digitized-resources/docs-pubs/catalogues/catalogue-1888-89.

———. *Catalogue of the University of Pennsylvania for the Session of 1923–24*. Philadelphia: University of Pennsylvania Press, 1923.

———. "Gwendolyn Gordon." Wharton School. Accessed January 21, 2021. https://lgst.wharton.upenn.edu/profile/gwgordon/.

———. "Julian Jonker." Wharton School. Accessed January 21, 2021. https://lgst.wharton.upenn.edu/profile/jonker/.

———. "Nina Strohminger." Wharton School. Accessed January 21, 2021. https://lgst.wharton.upenn.edu/profile/humean/.

———. "Peter Conti-Brown." Wharton School. Accessed January 21, 2021. https://lgst.wharton.upenn.edu/profile/petercb/.

———. "Social Science and Humanities Courses." Penn Engineering. Accessed January 21, 2021. https://ugrad.seas.upenn.edu/student-handbook/courses-requirements/social-science-and-humanities-courses/.

———. "The Writing Requirement." Penn Engineering. Accessed January 21, 2021. https://ugrad.seas.upenn.edu/student-handbook/courses-requirements/writing-requirement/.

Wecker, Menachem. "B-Schools Seem to Downplay Writing Skills." *U.S. News and World Report*, July 11, 2012. https://www.usnews.com/education/best-graduate-schools/top-business-schools/articles/2012/07/11/b-schools-seem-to-downplay-writing-skills.

Wharton School. "Facts & Figures: Wharton MBA Class Profile." MBA Program. Accessed October 16, 2020. https://mba.wharton.upenn.edu/class-profile/.

———. "Resources for Nontraditional Students." MBA Program. Accessed October 16, 2020. https://mba.wharton.upenn.edu/nontraditional-students/.

———. "Wharton MBA Classes, Courses & Curriculum." MBA Program. Accessed October 15, 2020. https://mba.wharton.upenn.edu/mba-curriculum/.

Yates, W. Ross. *Joseph Wharton: Quaker Industrial Pioneer*. Bethlehem, PA: Lehigh University Press, 1987.

18. The Role of Liberal Education in Professional Studies
Steven Frankel

IN *Democracy in America*, TOCQUEVILLE offers one of the most insightful and penetrating accounts of the prospects of higher education in America. He exposes the sharp tension between democracy and higher education and tempers our expectations for the liberal arts. A century and a half later, Allan Bloom's best-selling account of higher education, *The Closing of the American Mind*, supports and extends Tocqueville's account of the battle between professionalism and liberal education.[1] Bloom is particularly critical of the ill effects of business schools and economics departments, highlighting their negative impact on liberal education. A cursory examination of Bloom's and Tocqueville's analyses of higher education might yield an intractable or a hostile conflict between professional and liberal education in their respective works.

But this account is incomplete. A careful reading of Tocqueville and Bloom points to a possible alliance between professional studies and liberal education. As we shall see, Tocqueville's presentation of liberal education is inseparable from the study of Greek and Roman letters aristocratic societies, which differ from democracies in important ways. However, his account tempers our expectations. Studying ancient aristocracies holds little appeal for democratic citizens and is unlikely to have much effect in checking their passionate attachment to equality. Tocqueville readily concedes that education in commercial republics will focus primarily on vocational training in the service of security and comfort. At the same time, Tocqueville points to useful lessons found in classical literature, particularly on preserving freedom and enjoying our leisure. He teaches us that philosophical education in a commercial republic like ours begins with reflection on the effects of egalitarianism on our souls.

Bloom's account follows closely on the heels of Tocqueville's and extends it to the modern university. He takes up Tocqueville's analysis of the democratic soul and its indifference to tradition and aristocracy. He also takes up Tocqueville's warning that liberal education is the preserve of the few, so that taking up liberal education is the preserve of the few, intellectual, and political. Bloom identifies a variety of trends in the university, beginning with a growing penchant for historicism among humanities professors which turned them against liberal republicanism. The view that all claims about the good are values grounded in cultures or worldviews that are themselves contingent and arbitrary renders futile the search for truth and reason itself. The result, he reports, is the surrender to illiberal political factions and the creation of legions of university administrators, who effectively took over the mantel of political advocacy to prevent future uprisings. Liberal education, already a fragile flower, lost its institutional support and was left to fend for itself against more powerful opponents.

In light of these unpromising circumstances, defenders of the liberal arts must consider alternative homes from the study of classical literature and adapt the curriculum accordingly. Bloom's and Tocqueville's accounts alert us to these issues and help provide a framework for protecting liberal education. Tocqueville indicates that professional studies will always have the upper hand in a commercial democracy. Bloom shows that the causes of decline in the humanities are profound and unlikely to be repaired by the faculty or administration at the university. Both thinkers acknowledge the increasing threat posed to liberal education by the growth of professional and technical schools. To make matters worse, in many cases humanities departments have embraced teachings that turns them against the liberal arts, while professional schools are less entrenched in these ideological battles.[2] Programs and centers within the vocational schools have an opportunity to flourish with a carefully designed curriculum focused on broader questions of happiness and the search for the good. Such programs can also introduce students to constitutionalism as part of an account of commercial republicanism, which would in effect offer a shield against ideological attacks on the humanities.

TOCQUEVILLE ON LIBERAL EDUCATION

Tocqueville identifies liberal education with the study of ancient texts, particularly from Greece and Rome. Today, the justification for such a study comes from the notion that they are useful to us, teaching "critical thinking" or making us well rounded in our exposure to other cultures. Indeed, such arguments are presented to business students by humanities departments who wish to increase their enrollment. Tocqueville could not disagree more with this approach. In a short chapter titled "Study of Greek and Latin Literature," he argues studying such literature may be useful in promoting the literary culture of the nation, but that is hardly a reason to ask young people to study it.[3] To the contrary, "a study can be useful to the literature of a people and not be appropriate for their social and political needs."

In fact, the study of ancient literature presents a variety of problems for a democratic society: "If you stubbornly persisted in teaching only literature in a society where each man was led by habit to make violent efforts to increase his fortune or maintain it, you would have very polished and very dangerous citizens; for since the social and political state gives them needs every day that education would never teach them to satisfy, they would disturb the State, in the name of the Greeks and the Romans, instead of making it fruitful by their industry."[4] Commercial society shapes and directs the needs and desires of its citizens. If their education is not closely related to fulfilling those needs, the citizens will either ignore the education or else fashion the society so that it conforms to the ideals of their education; to be more precise, they will wish to overturn their commercial society.[5] To insist obstinately that every student receive a liberal education is foolhardy and naive.

But what about the alternative: Does not liberal education set ideals that we strive to realize? The fact that liberal education does not conform to our limited commercial goals, that it points to a different, and perhaps nobler, view of justice, is the very source of its value. Tocqueville argues that ancient Greece and Rome have the appearance of democratic societies, but are, in fact, aristocracies with little in common with our own commercial republic. In Athens, for instance, he reports that "all citizens took part in public affairs; but there were only 20,000 citizens out of more than 350,000 inhabitants; all the others were slaves and fulfilled most of the functions that today belong to the people and even the middle classes." The Athenian citizens governed themselves, but in truth they were only a small minority, and they also made the rules nondemocratically for the vast majority whose labor supported the entire endeavor. Intellectually, the literature of the ancient world presents "the particular vices and special qualities that characterize literature in aristocratic centuries."[6] In other words, the ancients do not provide us a model for democracy, nor can they teach us directly how modern democracy should operate.

Tocqueville discourages the view that liberal education can provide a remedy for the strong inclination of students to learn skills that will make them more productive in keeping with the commercial republic in which they live. What then is the value of liberal education in democracy? Tocqueville does not deny the importance of cultivating a taste for aristocracy among a small group of excellent students. The greatness of the ancients is their "special qualities that can serve marvelously to counterbalance our particular defects. They support us as we lean over the edge."[7]

However, after he claims that we should educate the majority of our students in business and science, he adds that "it is important that those destined by their nature or fortune to cultivate letters, or those who are predisposed to appreciate them, find schools where they can perfectly master ancient literature and be thoroughly penetrated by its spirit."[8] Liberal education, that is, the study of the ancients, should be preserved even in democracy. But Tocqueville warns us that we should not expect nor wish it to be widespread. Rather, it should be available to the intellectually and politically ambitious persons who will not be satisfied simply by the pursuit of commerce or industry.

Tocqueville tempers, in short, our expectations for the prospects of liberal education in commercial republics. He suggests that democracy blinds us to certain types of greatness and only a few students can climb out of the cave. His teaching is meant to provoke his ambitious readers to the study of the ancients, while excusing others. The prospects of liberal education in democracy are limited because its content is the study of the human condition, including the distinction between noble and vulgar souls. Such a study includes the consideration of aristocracy, which appears irrelevant, not to say fantastic, to democratic citizens.[9]

THE PROSPECTS FOR LIBERAL EDUCATION IN AMERICAN DEMOCRACY

Tocqueville's account of the democratic soul exposes the limits of education more clearly. To begin with, no education, for Tocqueville, starts from a blank slate. Echoing Aristotle's *Politics*, he argues that we are formed by our regime, our country and its laws, its social structure and customs. These are the horizons within which we begin to contemplate our own goals and ambitions. In democracy, this formation takes an unusual turn. Consider these two observations made by Tocqueville at the beginning of book 3: America is "the one country in the world where the precepts of Descartes are least studied and best followed." And "In no country in the civilized world is there less interest in philosophy than in the United States."[10] How can we be the followers of a philosopher that we have never read, particularly if we are not inclined to take philosophy seriously in the first place?

Tocqueville means that in addition to our regime's formal founding and constitution, there is an older philosophical founding that shapes us just as profoundly. For Tocqueville, Descartes "represents the doubt and distrust of authority and the reliance on individual reason that are characteristic of the American social state. Descartes, the enemy of all authority, is himself an authority to Americans, who, however, have not read his books."[11]

Our Cartesian skepticism is grounded in the conviction that we are equal, each individual endowed with enough reason to govern himself. This belief is so deeply held that it is not questioned or challenged; to the contrary, equality is self-fulfilling in democracy, which erodes dramatic differences between citizens. "As for the action that the intelligence of one man can have on that of another, it is necessarily very limited in a country where citizens, having become more or less similar, all see each other at very close range; and, not noticing in any one of them the signs of incontestable greatness and superiority, they are constantly brought back to their own reason as the most visible and nearest source of truth. Then it is not only confidence in a particular man that is destroyed, but the taste to believe any man whatsoever on his word."[12]

Our social state homogenizes us. There is no counterweight such as existed in the past, a rigid class system or the authority of our ancestral ties to check the tendency for everyone to become alike. In addition, the scope of privacy in democracy is rather narrow, and in any case, we are similar enough to each other—equal in all respects that matter most, namely, appearances—to know what the other is up to. We live so close to each other that we lack the perspective to recognize natural differences. As we become similar to each other, real differences, for practical purposes, begin to recede.

The effects of this homogeneity reinforce our individualism: we understand ourselves as individuals first, and since we are apparently alike, we do not accept anyone else's judgment as an authoritative guide. Our Cartesian skepticism is aimed not at our fundamental beliefs, but rather at the credibility of each other; to be more precise, our skepticism is aimed at the idea of wisdom itself. As a result, "each person withdraws narrowly into himself and claims (pretend) to judge the world from there."[13]

At first glance, our Cartesianism is liberating—it frees us from the yoke of traditions, authoritative or ancient claims, firm limits on the scope of our knowledge.[14] This allows us to choose our own goals and pursue ends that have immediate and useful application to our lives. But this liberation is not as enlightening as promised. The practical result, thanks to our belief in equality, is that we tend to become alike. To make matters worse, we resemble each other in that we pursue our particular desires as our primary goal so that we quickly become isolated from one another. Finally, since our liberation is grounded in the conviction that no one individual's reason is better than my own, we do not have the means to unite around a single set of beliefs. Our dogmatic belief in equality makes us weak and isolated.

This isolation makes us receptive to a new kind of tyranny, the tyranny of public opinion.[15] Once doubt takes hold of the intellect, it is paralyzed and unable to make authoritative judgments about political, moral, and religious questions. "Each person gets accustomed to having only confused and changing notions about the matters that most interest his fellows and himself." Unable to arrive at satisfactory answers to our questions, we stop thinking about them, and this "enervates [our] soul; it slackens the motivating forces of will and prepares citizens for servitude."[16] In light of our skepticism, the only authoritative voice in a democracy is the majority, and the only source of wisdom is the opinion poll. The majority has a tendency to silence unpopular truths and present its own positions as beyond question. Tocqueville's examples, the near extermination of the Indians and the enslavement of Africans, display the perverse moral effects of this majority tyranny.

In addition to the tyranny of the majority, Tocqueville refers to another source of tyranny that he calls "soft despotism." Our tendency to pursue our private self-interest (which includes pursuing the interests of our family and friends) makes us generally indifferent to government. Or, to be precise, we care about the government only as it relates to our private interests. This means that we are pleased to be subjects of the government as long as it takes care of us.

DEMOCRATIC SOLUTIONS TO "SOFT DESPOTISM"

To repeat: liberal education, the study of ancient Greece and Rome, is generally not appropriate for most democratic citizens. These ancient societies were not democracies and have little interest for citizens in democracy, who are better served by the study of business and science. But Tocqueville does recommend that some intellectually ambitious individuals continue to study the ancients. To understand why, we looked at his account of democratic citizens who are susceptible to a new type of tyranny because of their antiphilosophical, egalitarian prejudices. Liberal education, founded on the opposite conviction of inequality, particularly inequality in wisdom and virtue, has little or no appeal for most democratic citizens.

Despite this bleak picture, Tocqueville finds in democracies several sources for real freedom and even excellence. The greatest challenge is to find some means of "draw[ing] a man out of himself . . . in order to interest him in the destiny of the state." There are various strategies for doing so, including the cultivation of social and political associations on the local level, as well as encouraging citizens to participate in the administration of small affairs.[17] The two strategies that are most immediately relevant to liberal education are religion and what Tocqueville calls self-interest rightly understood.

Religion, especially Christianity, inspires "the opposite instincts" as commercial democracy—it "elevates the soul to a good beyond the good things of the earth." And it imposes on us duties that "drag man, from time to time, out of contemplation of himself." Given our Cartesianism and the limits of individual reason, some dogmatically held beliefs are necessary for the well-being of democracy and its citizens.[18] Christianity is particularly valuable in this regard since its dogmas make citizens more public spirited.[19]

Tocqueville's emphasis on Christianity will surprise some modern readers: Does not the modern university do a better job educating citizens than Christianity, since it is more inclusive, pluralistic, and just?[20] Tocqueville is skeptical of such claims because he thinks that the tendency in democracy toward rejection of authority and toward relativism is so pronounced that most attempts to change it will succumb to it.[21] In democracies, one's status is insecure, and we are constantly restless. The humanities, he says, are considered "a temporary and necessary relaxation amid the serious work of life. . . . Having only a very short time to give to letters, they want to make it entirely profitable for themselves. They love books that can be obtained without difficulty, that are quickly read, that do not require learned research to be understood. They demand easy things of beauty that reveal themselves and that can be enjoyed at once; above all, these things must have the unexpected and the new."[22]

Many students pursue liberal education for the sake of edification.[23] They wish to have their view of justice confirmed and elevated by reference to something higher than themselves (or at least by authorities other than themselves—for example, university professors). But Tocqueville argues that Christianity is more effective as a means of edifying citizens because it turns their gaze away from their central pursuit, namely, material acquisition. Furthermore, Christianity satisfies their desire to know quickly the answers to difficult existential questions.

As for our ethical education, in democratic times, the most effective teachings appeal to our interests. Self-interest is the primary fact influencing individual life in democracy. The goal, therefore, of any ethical teaching must be to connect particular interests with the interests of the community.[24] Of course, not all interests qualify for this, especially our immediate interests, our desire to fulfill our passions or to seek passing enjoyments. The key to "self-interest rightly understood" is teaching citizens that they have longer term, broader interests. This is why religion is so essential to democracy, because it bolsters this connection, particularly Christianity, which connects self-interest to love of God.[25]

To return to our original question: What then is the role of the university? It is important to note that Tocqueville does not think ethical education is a matter of taking a course in business ethics, for example. The forces that shape our souls are firmly established long before we have entered the university. Their efficacy is the result of our regime and its abstract foundations. In general, the university reinforces our previously held convictions about justice, or it eviscerates them, leaving students with a sort of soft nihilism, without conviction. The more we deny this fact, the more we are likely to fall victim to it. In order to educate its students, the university must begin with their convictions, making them as explicit so that students see them as convictions, not dogmas. It must be guided by the motto "do no harm" lest it exacerbate the tendency toward relativism, which is fatal to democracy. And it must not attempt to supplant religion, which is the most effective cure for moderating our Cartesian spirit.[26]

The goal of liberal education in a democracy should be the cultivation of a spirited and small elite, a new form of aristocracy whose model is no less than Tocqueville himself.

Such scholars may develop a certain distance from popular trends and movements, but this distance will make them less tyrannical. In fact, they will "hate the despot, and also despotism." This is why they will be friends of democracy. The spirit of friendship will allow them to criticize the regime and its citizens but always from the point of view of supporting freedom.[27] This corrects the tendency in democracy and the university to promote equality at the expense of freedom.

It is important to keep in mind Tocqueville's ambivalence toward liberal education in a commercial democracy. It would not have surprised him to see colleges making the case for liberal education in terms of acquiring a skill set (for example, critical thinking) or to help one get a job or a higher salary. The pressure on liberal education to prove itself useful in terms of measurable outcomes is the result of pressure from the regime and the tyranny of public opinion. At the same time, Tocqueville discourages us from attempting to reverse this situation and encourage more students to study classical literature. This would lead to either the debasement of liberal education or else the creation of an elite filled with contempt for democracy.[28] Liberal education may help create an elite that helps promote the constitution and laws as friends of democracy; however, the same elite presents a serious threat to the promotion of democracy.

BLOOM ON THE CONTEMPORARY STATE OF HIGHER EDUCATION

Allan Bloom's *Closing of the American Mind* shows us the enduring relevance of Tocqueville's account in understanding democracy. Bloom's book was an unlikely candidate for the best-seller list in the late 1980s. The book presents a critical and compelling commentary on the state of higher education in America. Bloom's analysis is largely shaped by Tocqueville, as he readily admits, "Tocqueville taught me the importance of the university to democratic society. His noble book, *Democracy in America*, gave voice to my inchoate sentiments. His portrait of the 'Intellectual Life of the Americans' is the mirror in which we can see ourselves. But, because the broader perspective he brings is alien, we do not immediately recognize ourselves. . . . Tocqueville shows how a democratic regime causes a particular intellectual bent which, if not actively corrected, distorts the mind's vision."[29]

Bloom recapitulates Tocqueville's argument about the tendency in democratic societies to gravitate toward intellectual homogeneity and social conformity. Democracy liberates us from authoritative opinions and leaves each individual free to decide for himself on truth and goodness. For most people, this means not the exercise of reason and contemplation, but the calculation of self-interest, and even here people need help in determining what is beneficial for the self. Though they may appear free and equal, democratic citizens are quickly enslaved by public opinion, which remains the only authoritative source of knowledge. The majority not only represents the most powerful element in democracy, but also appears to have the strongest claim to justice among equal individuals. Even those who dissent from the majority opinion hardly escape its influence; rather, they hope to transform it to match their own views. Real diversity of opinion about the principles of justice, then, hardly exists, and the alternatives are forgotten.

Only from this analysis does the purpose of liberal education become clear: true freedom means freedom of thought, which requires the cultivation and exercise of reason. This in turn requires alternative views of justice and goodness that tend to be obscured in democracy. Those views are contained in their most coherent form in old books. "To sum up, there is one simple rule for the university's activity: it need not concern itself with providing its students with experiences that are available in democratic society. They will have them in any event. It must provide them with experiences they cannot have there. Tocqueville did not believe that the old writers were perfect, but he believed that they could best make us aware of our imperfections, which is what counts for us."[30] For Bloom, the purpose of the liberal arts and the university is to train reason to make possible a fully human life. The best way to achieve this is through the study of wisdom contained largely in old books. Although Bloom does have high hopes for the university, his account is characterized by a somber skepticism. Regarding the study of fundamental alternatives through the study of great books, for example, Bloom laments: "The universities never performed this function very well. Now they have practically ceased trying."[31] Bloom's account of higher education is meant to complement and extend Tocqueville's analysis by supplementing it with the particular details of the decline of higher education in America. The middle section of *The Closing* examines the decline of political philosophy and the dominance of modern social science.[32] Bloom highlights the unexpected source of this decline, which emerged in Germany in the nineteenth and twentieth centuries, relativism and historicism. Taken together, they have created a horizon—in the words of Leo Strauss "a cave beneath the cave"—which makes liberal education impossible.[33]

The relativism that Bloom describes emerges most powerfully in Nietzsche's account of the subjectivity of all claims about the good. These "values" have no grounding in reason or universal claims about nature, and instead are relevant only to a particular culture or worldview. Yet the cultures themselves are arbitrary and contingent. As Arthur Melzer puts it, it would seem to lead to the relativizing of all moral, scientific, and philosophical thinking. If there are an indefinite number of conflicting cultures or *Weltanschauungen* of comprehensive views of God, the universe, and man, and if no standpoint outside them is possible from which to judge one truer than the others, it is hard to see how any of our most fundamental beliefs could be said to be superior to their opposites.[34]

The discovery of the relativism of all values compels us to abandon rationality and philosophy to create new, compelling beliefs: "The opinion that one knows the truth about the most important things and the opinion that there is no truth about them. Both of these opinions are fatal to philosophy; the first asserts that the quest for the truth is unnecessary, while the second asserts that it is impossible."[35]

The third section of *The Closing* shows how these ideas came to America, found a home in the university and popular culture, and soon undermined the study of Plato and Aristotle as well as the self-evident truths of the Declaration of Independence. This process reached its nadir in the sixties, when "a new generation that had not lived off inherited value fat, that had been educated in philosophic and scientific indifference to good and evil, came on the scene representing value commitment and taught their elders a most unpleasant lesson."[36] Bloom describes the timidity, not to say cowardice, of his colleagues at Cornell who abandoned the liberal arts at gunpoint. In short, Bloom shows that the humanities have become infected by historicism and that the administrators of the university are unable or unwilling to promote the liberal arts.

To return to the criticism that Bloom expects the university and liberal education to lead the regeneration of American civil and intellectual life, this is clearly not the case. What then did Bloom expect the university could achieve? Shortly after the publication of *The Closing*, he edited another book, *Confronting the Constitution*, which provides an answer. There, he recounts his confrontation with the arguments of the founders. He writes: "It required a certain de-ideologization to meet them fresh and listen to them without condescending from the heights of the twentieth century. The Framers had a keen sense of the relation between theory and practice; and their political founding was grounded in teachings about nature and the relation of justice to it. Their Bacon, Locke, and Montesquieu are worthy interlocutors-on the level of Kant, Hegel, Marx, and Nietzsche, who inspired less impressive political achievements."[37]

The framers presented an argument and wished to be judged on the reasonableness of their claims. Under the influence of historicism, however, their views on natural rights were reduced to products of unconscious drives and material cause. They were judged as a priori inadequate and rejected. Only after overcoming the historicism and relativism rife in the university and learning to take seriously the claims of the founders did Bloom realize that the Constitution "was written by a group of wise statesmen who believed in the necessity, goodness, and power of reason in the establishment of just regimes."[38]

The founding, Bloom claims, is rooted in a set of claims about nature, grasped by reason rather than tradition, authority, or revelation. As such it shares many of the presumptions of Socratic philosophy. The founders invite us to examine their claims, about natural right, for example, and to determine for ourselves whether they are rationally persuasive. American patriotism is based on reason, not instinct, passion, blood, or unquestioning loyalty to one's own. "The genius of this country, which cannot and does not wish to treat its citizens like plants rooted in its soil, has consisted in a citizenship that permits reflection on one's own interest and a calm recognition that it is satisfied by this regime. And this reflection does not end in mere mean-spirited calculation, as is often alleged by critics from the Right and the Left but leads to the peaks of philosophy. Our regime is founded on arguments, not commands."[39] Thus, Bloom presents the study of the American founding as a possible beginning for a philosophical education. The attack on the founding and the attack on liberal education go hand in hand. The idea that the founders or any thinker can, using reason, liberate themselves from prejudice—including race, class, and gender—to produce documents that others can examine and judge as reasonable is the foundation of liberal education. In promoting historicism and relativism as the final word, the university not only undermines the founding, but also destroys the possibility of liberal education. In its place, the humanities teach "that writers determine 'values' or 'world views,' that they are unconsciously motivated by 'the will to power,' and that they are the sources of the domination of men by men.[40] There are no theoretical human beings, and there is no objectivity, only commitment and subjectivity. Writers' apparently rational interpretations of a truly meaningless world provide the foundation for systems of domination and prevent the full flowering of individuals." Critics of Bloom who argue that the American project does not begin at the university are correct. But such criticism does not go far enough. The university promulgates schools of thought that are fatal to its own mission as well as the natural rights teaching of the Declaration. In other words, the university contributes substantially to the decline of liberal education and civic spiritedness.[41] The study of constitutionalism, on the other hand, strengthens the case for enlightened patriotism without destroying the possibility of philosophy.

TRENDS AND PROSPECTS IN LIBERAL EDUCATION

The trends in liberal education continue to move in the direction that Tocqueville and Bloom identified, and new developments have only accelerated them. The rising costs of higher education, for example, have increased the pressure on students to study preprofessional subjects and seek majors that promise solid prospects of employment after college. The humanities still seek to transform students, but they too have become more practical by emphasizing social action above theoretical speculation. As Howard Zinn explained, for example: "The best kind of education you can get is when you're involved in social struggles for a cause."[42] The fashionable contemporary trends in the humanities, such as identity politics and social justice, resolve the question of justice quickly and preempt the need for further discussion or debate.[43]

As for the resources to check these tendencies, one can hardly expect the faculty or administration to demand debate or inquiry.[44] Bloom reports that during the student unrest in the sixties, the administration was caught off guard and quickly succumbed to student demands. His disgust for the faculty's response is particularly pointed: "The professors, the repositories of our best traditions and highest intellectual aspirations, were fawning over what was nothing better than a rabble; publicly confessing their guilt and apologizing for not having understood the most important moral issues, the proper response to which they were learning from the mob; expressing their willingness to change the university's goals and the content of what they taught."[45] Bloom argues that the professors caved to the demands of the mob not simply to protect their comfortable, tenured positions, but primarily because they had lost sight of the fundamental mission of the university and therefore saw nothing much worth protecting in the life of the mind. Instead, these new movements promised "a moral truth superior to any the university could provide. Commitment was understood to be profounder than science, passion than reason, history than nature, the young than the old."[46] Again, Bloom interpreted the attack on the university through the lens of Tocqueville, who feared that liberal education would not be able to withstand the pressure public opinion and simply be held captive by it.[47] The 1960s began the movement to wipe out the elements of liberal education and replace them with clichés or abstractions, which flatter the passions of the movement.

Since the 1960s, university administrations have made sure to avoid being caught off guard and held at gunpoint, not by requiring a basic standard of civility or decency, but rather by internalizing student demands.[48] Now the protests for equality and justice are led by the administration. As a result, any restoration of liberal education is unlikely to be initiated by faculty or administrators. Bloom suggests an alternative, modestly recalling the creation of a "little Greek civilization program" that he helped set up at Cornell.[49] The idea was to collect a small group of faculty committed to the study of ancient philosophy and literature for a select group of interested students. The success of the project was marvelous. Today, many of its graduates have gone on to become great scholars and leading voices in the study of philosophy and liberal education.[50]

Tocqueville indicates that professional studies will always have the upper hand in a commercial democracy. Bloom shows that the causes of decline in the humanities are profound and unlikely to be repaired by the faculty or administration at the university.[51] While both accounts recognize the threat posed to liberal education by the growth in professional and technical schools, we cannot ignore that contemporary trends in the liberal arts have effectively turned them against the humanities; in contrast, professional schools tend to be less entrenched in such ideological battles. More positively, the liberal arts can make the case, as Bloom does in *The Closing*, that professional programs need the insights of the humanities to avoid a truncated or overly abstract account of human nature.[52] Programs and centers within the vocational schools have an opportunity to flourish with a carefully designed curriculum focused on broader questions of happiness and the search for the good. Such programs can also introduce students to constitutionalism as part of an account of commercial republicanism. Not only will this help resist the ideological damage done to the humanities, but it will also help students see the relation between their professional aspirations and their citizenship in a commercial republic. The appreciation of citizenship is the beginning of the rehabilitation of the humanities.

NOTES

1. Allan Bloom, *The Closing of the American Mind*.
2. See Mark Edmundson, "Teach What You Love."
3. Alexis de Tocqueville, *Democracy in America*, 815–18.
4. Tocqueville, *Democracy in America*, 817.
5. See Tim Quinn, "Tocqueville on Education and Commerce," 65. Tim Quinn writes: "Aside from the charming prospect that, inspired by the romance of antiquity, classics majors everywhere would take up arms against their regimes, Tocqueville's point is well-taken: that what is most needed to temper the materialism that engines our society, namely, the humanities, chafes against its core values." Classical studies are inescapably for the few, while "the education of the greatest number" will be "scientific, commercial and industrial rather than literary."
6. Tocqueville, *Democracy in America*, 815, 816.
7. Tocqueville, *Democracy in America*, 817.
8. Tocqueville, *Democracy in America*, 817.
9. See Patrick Deneen, "The Ignoble Lie."
10. Tocqueville, *Democracy in America*, 699, 698.

11. Tocqueville, *Democracy in America*, 699.

12. Tocqueville, *Democracy in America*, 700–701.

13. Tocqueville, *Democracy in America*, 701. See Montesquieu's analysis of England's political culture in *The Spirit of the Laws* (19.27).

14. Tocqueville uses "Cartesianism" rather casually to reflect the abandonment of tradition in favor of utility. This is not strictly speaking Descartes's position. Cartesian rationality restricts the charmed sphere of knowledge to mathematical certitudes. Modernity begins in part in a truncation of the scope of reason.

15. Note that, although equality prevents us from uniting around a single set of beliefs, it makes us receptive to the tyranny of public opinion—thereby uniting us around a single set of beliefs. The belief in equality displaces other beliefs, especially freedom.

16. Tocqueville, *Democracy in America*, 745.

17. Tocqueville, *Democracy in America*, 891, 898, 900.

18. Tocqueville, *Democracy in America*, 714.

19. John Ray and Steven Frankel, eds., *French Studies: Literature, Culture, and Politics*, 746; Tocqueville, *Democracy in America*, 708–9. Tocqueville elaborates on the specific character of modern religion.

20. See Deneen, "The Ignoble Lie."

21. Tocqueville, *Democracy in America*, 773, 775, 781. This is even true of the sciences: "Because men who live in democratic societies are constantly in a hurry to enjoy, are discontent with their position and, aspiring to change it, are not led to value the sciences except as a means to go by the easiest and shortest routes to wealth."

22. Tocqueville, *Democracy in America*, 809.

23. See Leo Strauss, "Liberal Education and Mass Democracy," 73–96.

24. Ewa Arranassow, "Beyond Utility? Tocqueville on Liberal Education and Education for Liberty." Arranassow suggests adopting the language of utilitarianism to sell liberal education to preprofessional programs: "I suggest that Tocqueville's solution to the problem of self-interest is a resource from which one can learn to defend and promote humanistic and liberal education in the age of global democracy. To do that one would have to follow the example of the American moralists who get their message across by speaking the language of their audience, i.e., the vernacular of utility" (176).

25. Tocqueville, *Democracy in America*, 927. Of course, democracy shapes the nature of religion as well. Religion changes its character: the devout are motivated not so much by love of God as by "desire to gain heaven.

26. Tocqueville, *Democracy in America*, 724.

27. Tocqueville, *Democracy in America*, 725 (quote), 780, 975.

28. The dangers presented by liberal education remind one of Lincoln's Lyceum Address, where he argues that the desire for greatness will destroy democracy: "What! think you these places would satisfy an Alexander, a Caesar, or a Napoleon? —Never! Towering genius distains a beaten path. . . . It thirsts and burns for distinction; and, if possible, it will have it, whether at the expense of emancipating slaves, or enslaving freemen." Lincoln adds that resisting such men "will require the people to be united with each other, attached to the government and laws, and generally intelligent, to successfully frustrate his designs."

29. Bloom, *Closing of the American Mind*, 246.
30. Bloom, *Closing of the American Mind*, 256.
31. See Allan Bloom, *Giants and Dwarfs: Essays, 1960–1990*, 374. Compare Bloom's essay "The Crisis of the University" (1966) with "The Democratization of the University" written just a few years later: "I wrote an article in 1966 assessing the condition of universities with respect to liberal education. At that time the picture was bleak, but there was some basis for hope. . . . That hope has all but disappeared."
32. Bloom, *Giants and Dwarfs*, 363. Bloom argues that political science is the heir "to Greek antiquity" and the "parentage of Socrates, Plato and Aristotle." But political science has all but abandoned this heritage to conform to modern social science. Instead of examining claims about justice and goodness, and categorizing regimes accordingly, modern political science assumes that such inquiry is nothing more than an exercise in subjective value judgements, and as such not part of a scientific account of politics.
33. Leo Strauss, *Persecution and the Art of Writing*, 155.
34. Arthur M. Melzer, "Esotericism and the Critique of Historicism," 282. Melzer argues: "The historicist imperative is just too powerful, too deeply woven into the pattern of our thinking, simply to be ignored. It must be confronted head on before any stable return to a non-historicist view is possible." I cite Melzer because he is an excellent guide to the thought of Leo Strauss, on whose analysis Bloom's argument rests. See especially Melzer's *Philosophy between the Lines: The Lost History of Esoteric Writing*.
35. See Bloom, "Western Civ," in *Giants and Dwarfs*, 18.
36. Bloom, *Closing of the American Mind*, 151.
37. Allan Bloom, *Confronting the Constitution*, 1.
38. Bloom, *Confronting the Constitution*, 1.
39. Bloom, *Confronting the Constitution*, 1–2.
40. Constantine Vassiliou observes that this tendency is strengthened and accelerated by technology, which compresses history and gives us the illusion of living in the eternal present.
41. See Bloom, "The Democratization of the University," in *Giants and Dwarfs*, 373–74. "In the theory and practice of our universities we have come to the stage of democratic sentiment at which Tocqueville warned that men prefer equality to freedom, where they are willing to overturn the institutions and laws necessary to freedom in order to gain the sense of equality, where they level rather than raise, indifferent to the depravations they impose on the superior and on the community at large."
42. Mary Grabar, *Debunking Howard Zinn: Exposing the Fake History That Turned a Generation against America*, 59.
43. See Greg Lukianoff and Jonathan Haidt, *The Coddling of the American Mind*.
44. For more, see Lee Ward's contribution in this volume.
45. Bloom, *Confronting the Constitution*, 313.
46. Lukianoff and Haidt, *Coddling of the American Mind*.
47. Bloom, *Confronting the Constitution*, 320. "The university was incorporated much more firmly into the system of democratic public opinion, and the condition of cave-like darkness amidst prosperity feared by Tocqueville was brought painfully near."

48. See Bloom, "The Democratization of the University," in *Giants and Dwarfs*, 375. "What I did not foresee was, on the one hand, the speed of the collapse of the administrators, and, on the other, the lack of conviction of the professors about the importance of what they were doing."

49. Bloom, *Giants and Dwarfs*, 333, 361. "One program which attempts to overcome the obstacles to utilize the resources of the contemporary university to overcome the obstacles to a liberal education is being planned by Cornell University. . . . The program will take the place of the universally criticized 'distribution requirements' and . . . the student will have free courses with which they can fulfill the technical requirements for an intended major or follow up any other interests they may have."

50. "Many of the most noted Cornell graduates between 1965 and 1970 had been [Bloom's] devoted students, including Tarcov (now a professor of political science at the University of Chicago), Paul Wolfowitz (former deputy secretary of defense and president of the World Bank), Alan Keyes (former presidential candidate and assistant secretary of state), Clifford Orwin (professor of political philosophy at the University of Toronto), Edith Jones (chief judge of the United States Court of Appeals for the Fifth Circuit), Francis Fukuyama (professor of international relations at Johns Hopkins University), William Galston (senior fellow at the Brookings Institution and former policy advisor to President Clinton)," Terence Marshall (professor at Paris X, Nanterre), and others. Tevi Troy, "Cornell's Straight Flush."

51. For more, see Lee Ward's chapter in this volume.

52. See Bloom, *Closing of the American Mind*, 359–69; and Gary Saul Morson and Morton Schapiro, *Cents and Sensibility: What Economics Can Learn from the Humanities*.

BIBLIOGRAPHY

Aristotle. *Politics*. Translated by Carnes Lord. Chicago: University of Chicago Press, 1984.
Arranassow, Ewa. "Beyond Utility? Tocqueville on Liberal Education, and Education for Liberty." *Tocqueville Review/La revue Tocqueville* 34, no. 2 (2013): 169–77.
Bloom, Allan. *The Closing of the American Mind*. New York: Simon and Schuster, 1987.
———. *Confronting the Constitution*. Washington, DC: AEI Press, 1990.
———. *Giants and Dwarfs: Essays, 1960–1990*. New York: Simon and Schuster, 1990.
Ceaser, James. "Alexis de Tocqueville on Political Science, Political Culture, and the Role of the Intellectual." *American Political Science Review* 79, no. 3 (1985): 656–72.
Deneen, Patrick J. "The Ignoble Lie." *First Things* (April 2018).
Edmonson, Mark. "Teach What You Love." *American Scholar* (Autumn 2020).
Grabar, Mary. *Debunking Howard Zinn: Exposing the Fake History That Turned a Generation against America*. Washington, DC: Regnery History, 2019.
Hancock, Ralph. "Liberal Education and Moral Liberty: Tocqueville as Critic of Bloom." In *Tocqueville's Defense of Human Liberty: Current Essays*, edited by Peter Augustine Lawler and Joseph Alulis. New York: Garland, 1993.
Lukianoff, Greg, and Jonathan Haidt. *The Coddling of the American Mind*. New York: Penguin Books, 2018.
Melzer, Arthur M. "Esotericism and the Critique of Historicism." *American Political Science Review* 100, no. 2 (2006): 279–95.

———. *Philosophy between the Lines*. Chicago: University of Chicago Press, 2014.
Morson, Gary Saul, and Morton Schapiro. *Cents and Sensibility: What Economics Can Learn from the Humanities*. Princeton, NJ: Princeton University Press, 2017.
Quinn, Tim. "Tocqueville on Education and Commerce." In *French Studies: Literature, Culture, and Politics*, edited by John Ray and Steven Frankel. Paris: Honoré Champion, 2014.
Ray, John, and Steven Frankel, eds. *French Studies: Literature, Culture, and Politics*. Paris: Honoré Champion, 2014.
Strauss, Leo. "Liberal Education and Mass Democracy." In *Higher Education and Modern Democracy: The Crisis of the Few and Many*, edited by Robert Goldwin. Chicago: Rand McNally, 1967.
———. *Persecution and the Art of Writing*. Chicago: University of Chicago Press, 1988.
Tocqueville, Alexis de. *Democracy in America*. Edited by Eduardo Nolla. Translated by James T. Schleifer. Indianapolis: Liberty Fund, 2010.
Troy, Tevi. "Cornell's Straight Flush." *City Journal* (December 13, 2009).

19. The Paradox of Liberal Education and Modernity

Gregory A. McBrayer

NEW CHALLENGES TO LIBERAL EDUCATION

FOR A VARIETY OF REASONS, liberal education has been on the decline. Soaring tuition rates have intensified the demand for degrees that yield an immediate payoff after graduation, and that demand has been met with increasing diffidence on the part of administrators and even some faculty members in the importance of a liberal arts education. Not entirely without reason, universities increasingly invest in degrees with a connection to a clearly identifiable career, something difficult to say with confidence about a liberal arts education. At countless liberal arts colleges around the United States, one increasingly sees liberal arts programs being cut, programs like classics, philosophy, religion, language, literature, music, art, and theater—even physics and chemistry, in some cases.[1] In their stead, universities retool STEM programs (science, technology, engineering, and math), create new degrees in growing sectors of the economy (like data analysis and Cybersecurity), and continue to pour money into business schools (the nicest buildings on just about every college I've worked at are the business schools). Out with the old, in with the new.

Other factors are surely at play. Universities hold they must adapt or die in a competitive market with fewer consumers, as demographers continue to prophesy a coming cliff when the number of students enrolled in colleges will drop dramatically.[2] Accordingly, apart from a handful of elite universities that appear immune from financial struggles, many colleges chase what they believe to be an ever-shrinking pool of students by rushing toward widespread conformity and maddening mediocrity. Increasingly, universities are run by administrators disconnected from the liberal arts; they have degrees in subjects like college student personnel, leadership, or higher education. They, in turn, answer to accrediting bodies with an even higher concentration of such academics. In the past couple of years, with the ubiquity of Zoom and WebEx "classrooms," skepticism regarding the liberal arts has only intensified. Parents and students see more clearly than before that a lot of the cost of a university education comes from auxiliary services—very expensive but entertaining accommodations. It has become increasingly difficult to defend liberal education in the modern world, despite the fact that such an education is now available in ways unimaginable even just a century ago.

Rather than seeking to defend liberal education, this chapter seeks to understand the technological, moral, religious, and intellectual preconditions for liberal education in the modern world. I will also offer suggestions for ways to take advantage of the opportunities modernity affords us. And while modernity offers opportunities for liberal education unknown to the premodern world, it also poses unique challenges to it. Accordingly, a guiding thesis of this chapter is that the preconditions for and requirements of liberal education in the modern world differ from what they were in the premodern world. On the one hand, modernity appears to make liberal education available to a much broader audience. But, on the other hand, modernity seems to have closed off routes to liberal education that were previously available in premodern times. Further, modernity disinclines individuals to pursue liberal education. Let me be more precise regarding the paradox of liberal education in modernity: while modernity makes liberal education possible in ways unimaginable in premodern times—by, for example, making books widely available and providing us with far-greater leisure—it simultaneously actively inhibits the longings that would lead one to pursue liberal education.

In the first part of this chapter, I will investigate the preconditions for liberal education, with particular attention to our contemporary situation, a situation marked as it is by an increasingly ubiquitous fascination with and reliance upon technology in matters related to pedagogy. Further, in this context I will also discuss the moral, religious, and intellectual education one receives prior to pursuing a liberal education, and how they affect its attainment.

In the second part of the chapter, I will examine the content of a liberal education itself, paying particular attention to how the character of modernity demands the study of some disciplines more than it does others.

In particular, I will outline a dispute between Leo Strauss and Jacob Klein regarding the appropriate place within a liberal education for the study of science, religion, and the great books. The clearest disagreement between the two thinkers regards science; Klein includes the study of science within a liberal education while Strauss appears to leave it out altogether. Next, both Klein and Strauss include reading of scriptures within a liberal education, but Klein places them on equal footing with a host of other books while Strauss emphasizes their primacy. Finally, while Klein includes the study of great books within liberal education, liberal education consists principally, if not solely, in the study of great books according to Strauss. The nature of the disagreement between these two thinkers regarding the content of a liberal education, as far as I can tell, derives from Strauss's understanding of the distinctive character of modernity.

In modernity, most education serves a practical goal, and some courses of study that once had a formidable liberating effect on students no longer do. Further, studies that perhaps had become stagnant prior to modernity may offer new paths to liberal education. Science and mathematics, for example, may no longer serve as ready paths to intellectual freedom. And the study of religious texts may now liberate students' minds in a renewed way. In our current situation, the best path for pursuing a liberal education is the continuous reading of great books, including religious books, with a teacher steeped in the liberal arts, in a setting that approximates as closely as possible the setting of an informal reading group. All other paths have become practical to the point of servility and promise little by way of intellectual nourishment.

Finally, I will address the question of educational setting, explaining why the environment within which education takes place matters, and, in particular, I will evaluate the virtual setting. I hope to show how technology can help us to pursue a liberal education in concrete ways, insofar as it provides us with new tools and avenues for its pursuit, but that it ought to be used with discernment and not as a remedy for all pedagogical issues. Here, I hope to offer suggestions for someone who would be open to a discussion of how one could pursue a great books education virtually.

THE PRECONDITIONS

In order to pursue a liberal education, the student must have access, as I mentioned above, to things like books, maps, computers, laboratories, and classrooms or even schools. But the student also must have access to good teachers, the student must have some sufficient combination of wealth and leisure, and the student must be prepared academically as well as morally. The need for good teachers is often overlooked, but crucial: "Just as the soil needs cultivators of the soil," says Leo Strauss, "the mind needs teachers."[3] In fact, he claims the most important conditions "are the qualities of the educator and the human being who is to be educated."[4] Here one runs into the unavoidable problem of picking a good teacher. Young people who have not been liberally educated are not particularly well equipped to find good teachers. In countless conversations with other students of liberal education, it is bewildering how many of us happened upon a good teacher entirely by accident, myself included. Organizations such as the American Council of Trustees and Alumni try to identify quality professors and quality programs with their "Oases of Excellence," but this only helps students who are already on the lookout for a quality liberal education.[5] For the rest, it seems to be largely up to chance. The fact that finding a good teacher relies largely on serendipity may explain why this most important feature of a liberal education is seldom discussed.

In any event, in addition to the need for a quality educator, Strauss points to the importance of wealth for liberating potential students from having to care for the necessities of life. And historically, this seems undeniable, although I would add indifference to wealth can serve the same purpose. Regardless, wealth seems to be a necessary condition to a lesser extent than ever before, or perhaps higher levels of societal wealth enable those who are not individually wealthy to pursue liberal education. One of the beautiful things about living when we do in history is that a liberal education is no longer the preserve of the prosperous, the powerful, and the privileged. In previous times, the liberal arts were the preserve of the few unburdened by the need to provide a living for themselves. No more. While people still undoubtedly face barriers, people from all walks of life—all races, genders, ethnicities, and economic classes—have open to them the possibility of pursuing a world-class education like never before. I have taught at a small regional comprehensive university, a selective liberal arts college, a small Christian liberal arts college, two flagship state universities, and an elite research university. At each, I encountered students hungry for liberal education, eager to find guides that will help them to understand their own deepest longings, and ready to brave books and authors who challenge them. Admittedly, at some schools there were only pockets of professors and students, and at others the commitment to liberal education was more widespread, but it was possible to pursue a liberal arts education at each of them.

I would venture to say citizens of every state in this union have at least one school, even a public school, where it is possible to pursue liberal education. The difference, of course, is that at some schools one need not search for it. At others, the professors are diamonds in the rough—the senior professor who still teaches Shakespeare, Jane Austen, and Dostoevsky; the young, newly minted PhD trying to revive the study of ethics at a regional state school; an instructor in a liberal arts program at an engineering school trying to expose students to the limits of technology and modernity; an art professor who finds donors and discovers a restored monastery in Italy to host students and tour the museums of Florence; clusters of students who form reading groups with the support of various nonprofits on college campuses. We live in remarkable times. That is not to say that every institution of higher education in our country is devoted to the liberal arts—far from it. And of course, the decreased commitment to liberal arts at American institutions of higher learning may even be a product of increased accessibility. But at many institutions, one can still find liberal education. Education may be the valet of activism at many an elite school—measuring "student learning outcomes," the idol of accrediting bodies, and "twenty-first-century skills," the bailiwick of small colleges and universities struggling to survive—but the heart of liberal education is still beating. Everywhere there are books, teachers who love teaching, and students hungry to learn, the heart of liberal education is still beating. Now, the old boy may be barely breathing, but the heart of liberal education is still beating. It is, after all, always available in principle.

Students must not merely be freed of the need to work in order to pursue liberal learning; they must be prepared academically. Both the character of the student and the quality of the education the student has received prior to undertaking the study of the liberal arts greatly affect the student's prospects for liberal education. In the United States, at least, liberal education happens mostly at institutions of higher learning, so students must have received a solid primary and secondary education in order to be able fully to take advantage of the benefits offered by a liberal education. One frequently reads reports that standards of primary education have declined, and these reports are no doubt worrisome, but the content of primary education remains largely uncontroversial. Students ought to be able to count, read, and write well, and they ought to have become acquainted with other subjects as well, like science, history, art, and music.

More interesting for our purposes, because of its relation to liberal education, is what Klein calls an *elemental* education. Elemental education might, he says, be the most important education we receive, although "most of the time we are not even aware of it."[6] According to Klein, an elemental education is the education one receives, for the most part passively, from our friends, families, communities, and innumerable other relations. At the point we become aware of our elemental education, we call it tradition. Insofar as Klein suggests we are always members of a community of some sort, an elemental education seems to be a hallmark of the human condition. Klein says precious little regarding the content of an elemental education, but from the sounds of it, it provides us, above all, with our moral opinions. Thus, Klein implicitly raises the question regarding the relationship between moral character and liberal education.

Elemental education is traditional; it is anything that binds us as a group. Strauss makes clear that religious education is central to what Klein calls elemental education. For Klein, traditional education takes place within a political community, but, according to Strauss, "The only teachers who are as such a constituent part of the city are the priests." Not only does elemental education include religious education, but religious education would be at its very heart. If liberal education presupposes religious education of a certain kind, then liberal education would now be in jeopardy to the degree that religious education has decayed in our time. Hear Strauss: "In the light of the original conception of modern republicanism, our present predicament appears to be caused by the decay of religious education of the people and by the decay of liberal education of the representatives of the people. By the decay of religious education I mean more than the fact that a very large part of the people no longer receive any religious education."[7] To be sure, Strauss draws a distinction between the people and the people's representatives, saying the former receive only a religious education, while the latter receive a liberal education. However, insofar as religious education is the only education sanctioned by the political community, all citizens receive a religious education, at least preliminarily. Thus, even the people's representatives would likely have received a religious education as part of their elemental education.

Patrick Deneen has argued persuasively that it is folly to separate liberal education from its moral and religious roots. As he presents it, religious individuals, and Christians in particular, are best prepared to undertake liberal education, because religious and cultural practices are central to a liberal education. He points out that liberal education is most at home in a religious setting—American universities, he reminds us, especially those connected to the liberal arts, were by and large founded as religious institutions. Accordingly, Deneen connects the decline in liberal education to the abandonment of the religious character of the American university. Only the relics of the religious character of universities remain, the gothic buildings, the titles, the robes. The institutions have become secular, so they can no longer provide students the nourishment for which they came, to "steep them in the traditions whence they came," to deepen "their knowledge of the sources of their beliefs," in order better to prepare them to contribute to the well-being of their community. Deneen's liberal education is traditional and civic, moral and religious. It depends upon and deepens traditional roots.

As Deneen sees it, a restoration of liberal education should be based upon a classical or Christian understanding of liberty, a restoration that would potentially include "compulsory attendance at chapel or Mass, parietal rules, adult-supervised extracurricular activities, and required courses in moral philosophy." Such a restored liberal education "would not be a liberation from 'the ancestral' or from nature, but rather an education in the limits that culture and nature impose upon us."[8]

If religious education is good preparation for liberal education, and if religious education has decayed in modernity, then modernity would indeed be an inhospitable environment for liberal education. There would be a certain irony here: even as modernity provides us with tools that greatly facilitate the acquisition of liberal education, as it makes its acquisition available to an ever-growing number of human beings, it robs us of the spiritual character that can prepare us to seek it. Of course, there are still religious persons in the West, and, pace Deneen, I confess many of my good students have often been deeply pious. Religious students are often attuned to questions of fundamental human importance in ways that their irreligious peers can sometimes fail to be.

But surely religious students are not the only ones predisposed to taking questions of fundamental importance seriously, even if they are the most common type. Strauss says potential students of liberal education are marked not by piety, necessarily, but by seriousness, of which piety may be a kind.[9] Strauss calls these potential students "emphatically earnest."[10] They are serious, principally, about moral matters, and their moral seriousness orients them toward the topics that are the subject of liberal education. Morally serious human beings are concerned with questions not only of piety, but of fundamental human questions generally, questions such as justice, love, courage, friendship, and wisdom.

While moral seriousness may orient one toward the right questions, the questions that animate a liberal education, Strauss shows us that a posture of moral seriousness may, at the same time, erect psychological barriers to liberal education. The tension between moral seriousness and education is more obvious in Greek, as Strauss points out, because the Greek word for "education" is etymologically linked both to "child" and to "play"—neither of which strikes one as particularly serious. Education seems to require a childlike playfulness regarding questions of fundamental human concern; one has to be able to entertain ideas that the serious person might find distasteful or ignoble. So it turns out moral seriousness has a sort of ambivalent relationship with liberal education. On the one hand, it seems to be a necessary preliminary, but, on the other hand, it can also be an impediment. Seriousness is the stuff of adults—real men, even—surely not of children, and play is beneath the dignity of the emphatically earnest.[11]

Perhaps this is why liberal education aims at the young, or, perhaps more accurately, those who seem to be partly adults and partly children: college students. They are old enough to have become serious about the questions addressed by liberal education, but young enough that their seriousness has not yet resulted in ossified answers to those questions. Among such young people one can find a healthy mixture of or salutary tension between seriousness and frivolity that is conducive to learning.

Indeed, tension seems to be at the very heart of a liberal education; liberal education is made possible by the tension between fundamental alternatives. It is only possible because there are disagreements—because the great minds disagree.[12] There are of course disagreements regarding justice, and courage, and epistemology, and the good society, but the alternative of reason versus revelation seems to be the most important disagreement, because it is all-encompassing. As Strauss says, "No alternative is more fundamental than this: human guidance or divine guidance." Further, what makes the alternative fundamental is its permanent status: the alternative is simply a human one that will always remain with us. Neither can refute the other, and so as humans we must live with this tension.[13] Indeed, Strauss speaks of the "fruitful and ennobling tension between religious education and liberal education,"[14] and he attributes the greatness of the West, in large part, to maintaining this fruitful tension. The complete victory of one over the other would be deleterious for liberal education and, by extension, civilization. Strauss thus seeks to preserve religious education, or even to revive its serious study among those interested in pursuing liberal education. He seems to do so for two reasons: First, if reason has not refuted revelation, revelation may indeed be true. Second, a reason that simply presupposes revelation to be false is blind to its own intellectual shortcomings.

Rather than declaring liberal education to be the exclusive domain of a specific tradition, Strauss helps us to see that liberal education thrives where these tensions can be explored. But, to repeat, in order for the tension to arise, there have to be compelling alternatives. We will return to the question of the role of religion within liberal education in the next part, on the content of liberal education.

WHAT ARE THE LIBERAL ARTS?

During the Middle Ages, the liberal arts were synonymous with the Trivium and the Quadrivium. The Trivium consisted of logic, grammar, and rhetoric, and the Quadrivium of arithmetic, geometry, astronomy, and music. These have been altered to various degrees over time. Almost all present-day universities require some course work in writing, but not necessarily grammar, and surely not logic and rhetoric. Mathematics requirements have persisted, and students can usually expect to study natural science, but not necessarily astronomy. And it is a rare thing indeed to find a music requirement, although "aesthetics" requirements more generally are not uncommon.[15] But by and large, most proponents of the liberal arts, I suspect, mean learning in the humanities, especially literature, philosophy, history, and perhaps religion, the disciplines in which a student would encounter great minds in great books. In fact, there is almost an identity between liberal education and great books. As Strauss notes, "Liberal education is *now* almost synonymous with the reading in common of the Great Books," and this is a good thing: "No better beginning could have been made."[16] There is something distinctive about our contemporary situation that renders other starting points obsolete. To use Strauss's formulation, we find ourselves in a cave within the cave.[17] The study of natural science, music, and art is no longer a proper starting point, according to Strauss. In fact, he remains silent about their study within a liberal education altogether. We need, according to Strauss, an education in books.

Strauss's friend and colleague Jacob Klein, who reestablished the program at St. John's College, stresses, just like Strauss, the importance of great books for a liberal education, but, contra Strauss, does not limit it to their study. In speaking of the content of liberal education, he begins first and foremost with the great books: the Old Testament, Homer, Aeschylus, Sophocles, Euripides, Plato, Aristotle, the New Testament, Augustine, Aquinas, Dante, Bacon, Shakespeare, Galileo, Descartes, Newton, Locke, Hume, Rousseau, Kant, Hegel, Darwin, great novelists of the nineteenth century, Nietzsche, Freud, and Whitehead. But Klein also includes the study of two languages, an ancient and a modern; mathematics; music; and an inquiry into nature through the study of biology and physics.[18] Klein includes much that Strauss omits, but the most interesting difference is Klein's inclusion of, and Strauss's exclusion of, the scientific study of nature. Indeed, Klein states, "It is a rather fantastic idea to equate liberal studies with the so-called humanities; as if mathematical and scientific disciplines were less human than historical or poetic or philosophical studies."[19] Strauss's view of liberal education, according to Klein, would be fantastic, the stuff of fantasy.

While it is possible Strauss omits a discussion of natural science just out of a sort of division of labor—he was a political scientist after all—or because he thought one ought to study natural science later in one's liberal education, it is curious that Strauss nowhere, to my mind, encourages the study of natural science as a part of a liberal education. He consistently exhorts students to read the great books, but nowhere does he say, for example, one ought to study chemistry. In fact, to repeat, he declared a near identity between the study of great books and liberal education. I will try to offer an explanation for why Strauss would have excluded the study of natural science supposing, as seems to be the case, that the exclusion was intentional.

The difference between Strauss and Klein appears to arise from a disagreement regarding the liberating power of the study of natural science in modernity. Strauss excludes science from all of his many exhortations to pursue liberal education for a simple, historical reason. *In our time*, science no longer performs the liberating role it once did, and the same holds for mathematics. To be sure, science and math are liberal studies, and one can still pursue them liberally, but, by and large, modernity has rendered their study illiberal; liberation is no longer the goal of such studies in modernity. As Strauss says, "Just as liberal education in its original sense was supported by classical philosophy, so the new education derives its support, if not its being, from modern philosophy."[20] Modern philosophy has had a vulgarizing or servile effect on the character of education, an effect especially pronounced in the study of natural science. And this was not accidental, but rather the intentional product of modern philosophy and modern philosophers.

Chief among the modern philosophers on whom our new education depends is Sir Francis Bacon. As Klein says, and as Strauss would likely agree, "Our relation to Nature is Baconian."[21] Bacon puts science in the service of other goals, thereby subordinating it, binding it, to practical ends. Insofar as it is bound to these ends, it does not question them; it takes them for granted. Bacon is clear that the goal of education is "the invention not of arguments but of arts; not of things in accordance with principles, but of principles themselves; not of probable reasons, but of designations and directions for works. And as the intention is different, so accordingly is the effect; the effect of the one being to overcome an opponent in argument, of the other to command [*vincintur*, better translated as "conquer"] nature in action."[22] The goal is no longer to wonder, to behold, to understand, to be liberated from one's conventional account of things. Rather, the goal now is to conquer nature and to compel her to make human life more commodious. Study is empathically put into the service of practical goals.

In perhaps his most famous language, Bacon claims the end of science ought to be the relief of man's estate:

> But the greatest error of all the rest is the mistaking or misplacing of the last or furthest end of knowledge. For men have entered into a desire of learning and knowledge, sometimes upon a natural curiosity and inquisitive appetite; sometimes to entertain their minds with variety and delight; sometimes for ornament and reputation; and sometimes

to enable them to victory of wit and contradiction; and most times for lucre and profession; and seldom sincerely to give a true account of their gift of reason *to the benefit and use of men*. . . . But as both heaven and earth do conspire and contribute to the use and benefit of man, so the end ought to be, from both philosophies to *separate and reject vain speculations*, and whatsoever is empty and void, and to preserve and augment whatsoever is solid and fruitful; that knowledge may not be as a courtesan, for pleasure and vanity only, or as a bond-woman, to acquire and gain to her master's use; but as a spouse, for generation, fruit, and comfort.[23]

The liberal approach to studies is derided as vain, useless, and misplaced. Further, Bacon alleges the apparently liberal approach actually smacks of vanity and ornamentation—looking good. Either way, it should be clear that Bacon denigrates the pursuit of knowledge for its own sake.[24]

Most of higher education, especially in the sciences, descends from Bacon and his focus on utility and beneficence. This makes sense: the modern university is *modern*, after all. To take the most obvious cases, the contemporary fascination with STEM (science, technology, engineering, and mathematics) is manifestly practical in character. That is, the study of science and mathematics is subordinated to technological concerns, advancing the goals of society. Now, to be clear, I am not disparaging the study of STEM. Important work is being done in these disciplines, highly sophisticated work, work that improves materially the lives of citizens and human beings in clear and measurable ways. Further, while the complexity of these disciplines may in effect liberate its practitioners, such liberation is not central to why they are pursued. It is a by-product, if it happens at all. Their study cannot be said to be liberal. Now, there are of course exceptions. Every science has questions of theoretical significance that can be pursued for their own sake. And there are subdisciplines and individual mathematicians and scientists who pursue those questions. Fundamental physics and abstract mathematics come to mind. Even computer science, an eminently practical discipline, is theoretically interesting and can be studied for its own sake.[25] But the fact is that most who study biology are interested in pursuing careers in medicine or related fields, and most students who are good at math and wish to pursue its study at university become engineers.

While a practically minded education may be useful both to the student and to society at large, a liberal education would be manifestly better for one who pursues it.

From the perspective of liberal education, the problem with modern science is twofold. First, as I just mentioned, it is in the service of practical ends. More problematically, modern science tends to obscure its presuppositions about the world. Chief among them is the denial of miracles, disbelief in revelation, and the insistence on a fixed natural order. These positions are epistemologically problematic to the degree that they are presupposed or unexamined. Whereas science originally was central to a liberal education, its increasing focus on practical ends makes the kinds of epistemological questions I just raised seem like pointless distractions.[26] In its pursuit of practical ends, modern science allows or even encourages theoretical questions to recede into the background. Practice can rest content with unexamined presuppositions. Liberal education cannot.

This is why Strauss insists on the primacy of great books for a liberal education in our times. Certain problems emerge for us only through their study, and we moderns seem incapable of understanding ourselves fully without confronting the challenge of the great books of the ancients, in particular, for, "Only in the light of the quarrel between the ancients and the moderns can modernity be understood."[27] Let me make Strauss's bold claim clear: we moderns cannot understand ourselves without reading the great books, especially ancient great books. And while the ancients and moderns disagree over a variety of questions, the heart of the quarrel regards religion: "a philosophy which believes that it can refute the possibility of revelation—and a philosophy which does not believe that: this is the real meaning of *la querelle des anciens et des modernes*."[28]

Liberal education is marked by an increasing familiarity with disagreements regarding questions of fundamental human importance, like the quarrel between ancients and moderns, and the keyhole through which we mere students can enter into the courts where the great minds debate these quarrels is the great books.

While there is surely a place within liberal education for lectures, discussion sections, experiments, and other activities both inside and out of a classroom, the primary mode of studying the great books ought to be simply reading the texts aloud and trying to interpret them together, teacher and student alike. Insofar as liberal education in its original sense was supported by classical philosophy, and insofar as the model liberal educator and classical philosopher is thought to have taught principally using the so-called Socratic method of question and answering, or refuting one's interlocutor using a specific form of argument called the elenchus, this suggestion seems misleading or self-serving. Further, in the *Phaedrus*, Socrates specifically deprecates the role of books in education.[29] However, despite its widespread praise and imitation, especially in law schools but also in core curricula of liberal arts colleges around the country, the so-called Socratic method was not in fact Socrates's principal mode of teaching. Rather, what we call the Socratic method was protreptic or propaedeutic; it served as a means of attracting students, showing interlocutors they did not know what they thought they knew, and, in the right cases, this newfound state of ignorance would spur students to pursue education. But more often, the interlocutor, having been brought low, simply brushes off any refutation as the result of mere word games and tricks.[30] While we see Socrates refuting interlocutors regularly in the Platonic dialogues, we do not really see him teaching anyone.[31]

And the same holds, for the most part, in Xenophon's presentation of Socrates. In the *Memorabilia*, Xenophon presents Socrates benefiting his companions, encouraging them to be continent, reconciling them with their friends and family, and exhorting and dissuading individuals to partake in or remain out of politics. However, once, ever so briefly, Xenophon shows his readers what Socratic education looked like. Over the course of a rather long chapter, Xenophon relates a series of conversations that took place between Socrates and Antiphon, a sophist who was particularly harsh toward Socrates. After Antiphon has hurled a series of insults at Socrates, questioning how someone who lived such a pathetic, miserable existence could possibly be happy, and calling Socrates's wisdom in question, Socrates responds with the following words:

> Accordingly, Antiphon, just as another is pleased by a good horse or a dog or a bird, so I myself am even more pleased by good friends, and if I possess something good I teach it, and I introduce them to others from whom, I believe, they will receive some benefit with a view to virtue. And reading collectively with my friends, I go through

the treasures of the wise men of old which they wrote and left behind in their books; and if we see something good, we pick it out; and we hold that it is a great gain if we become friends with one another.[32]

Here, in this dispute with a sophist, Xenophon's Socrates admits to being a teacher, something he denies in Plato's dialogues, and he also makes clear his principal method of instruction: he reads books with his students, his friends, the books of the wise men of old. One might say the great books. Further, by calling Socrates blessedly happy after having heard him say this, Xenophon points to the centrality of this activity both for his teaching and for his way of life.[33]

While Socrates may have engaged in dialectical battle to test the mettle of students, if he admitted them to his school, his primary avowed mode of instruction was the collective study of great books—which would undoubtedly raise a host of questions for student and teacher to discuss in conversation. Further, we need not wonder what books Socrates would have read with his students. Undoubtedly, Socrates read the works of the natural philosophers, the so-called pre-Socratics, on the one hand, and the poets, on the other.[34] To bring an earlier point to bear, Socrates most assuredly studied and read the works of the Greek poets with his students. That is, Socrates remained alive to the claims of prophecy and revelation.[35]

In our current situation, just as in Socrates's time, the best path for pursuing a liberal education is the continuous reading of great books, including religious books, with a teacher steeped in the liberal arts, in a setting that approximates as closely as possible the setting of an informal reading group among friends and potential friends. All other paths promise far less by way of intellectual nourishment.

Students and teachers attend reading groups entirely of their own volition; no one is compelled to be there. Goodwill attends reading groups; they foster friendship among the participants. Students' profound intellectual and psychological longings are given full voice, and trust emerges in ways that are too difficult to cultivate in a classroom where one encounters anonymous peers. The intimacy of a reading group mitigates the perceived need for self-censorship, which we hear is becoming increasingly common in the classroom. Students can honestly pursue fundamental questions wherever their texts, their hearts, and their minds lead them. The pace of a reading group accelerates and slows according to the interest and understanding of the members. Texts are chosen on the basis of intellectual curiosity and genuine interest. And while such groups have to arise on their own, lest they be subject to external political pressures, colleges and universities perform an invaluable function in regards their formation: they provide the opportunity for young people with a similar awareness of their own shortcomings, and a dim suspicion that great books might help them to come to terms with some of the questions with which their souls wrestle, to meet. They also employ teachers who are blessed to be able to share the reading of great books with souls who yearn for wisdom, and who, while perhaps not wise themselves, are at least more experienced in reading. Having been a part of numerous reading groups at a host of institutions over the years, I have seen firsthand the deep longing among the young for the kind of slow, careful reading of great books that can occur only in the unconfined setting of a reading group.

PURSUING THE GREAT BOOKS VIRTUALLY

Technology can facilitate the pursuit of a great books education. Proponents of liberal education have a tendency to be old fogeys, preferring the tried and true to the shiny and new. Insofar as the study of great books seems to be central to a liberal education, it is backward looking, and it therefore runs the risk of becoming traditional and parochial, stale and out-of-date. Accordingly, there is a tendency among proponents of liberal education to look askance at technology. At the other extreme, faculty can become overly reliant on technology—we have all seen a PowerPoint presentation carry more weight than it can bear. The temptation to see innovation, especially technological innovation, as a kind of panacea is strong. If retention is a problem, a new app that tracks attendance is proposed.[36] Students' attention spans seem to be shortening thanks to the ubiquity of devices, so professors are encouraged to adapt and shorten lessons and make them more fast-paced, instead of compelling students to work to train their attention for longer periods of time.[37] Student apathy? Flip the classroom![38] No two students learn the same way we are told—some are audial learners, some visual, some experiential—so faculty should deliver material in a variety of modes.[39] Students are shy—so they should be able to tweet responses to professors anonymously during class.[40] Surely, we should never encourage students to overcome their sense of shame, reminding them, as Aristotle does, that shame is not befitting an adult.[41] Proponents of these kinds of innovation do not understand that quickness of pace and entertainment are at odds with liberal education, which "consists in learning to listen to still and small voices and therefore in becoming deaf to loud-speakers. Liberal education seeks light and therefore shuns the limelight."[42] We are trying to grow attention spans, to encourage students to learn in new ways and to take responsibility for their education, to stretch them to study books they otherwise might not in ways they otherwise might not, and to be intellectually courageous in so doing.

But even the most antiquated of old fogeys, the staunchest advocate of a great books education, must be compelled to admit technology can be a boon in some cases. One need only think of the near-universal availability of books, especially in the West. Whereas 150 years ago there was only one way to hear music—in the presence of a musician, including possibly oneself—now anyone can pull up some of the greatest music by some of the greatest musicians in history. Of course, one wonders whether the ubiquity of good music disinclines amateurs from taking up an instrument, depriving themselves of the pleasures of learning, self-amusement, and self-admiration. Why pick up a trumpet when I can summon forth Miles Davis, a cello when Yo-Yo Ma is available at a moment's notice, or even a fiddle when we have the Grand Ole Opry? Still, the widespread availability of world-class music strikes me as a blessing of modernity. And it is not just music. Many of the world's greatest museums have virtual tours, and it is marvelous that a kid from inner city Baltimore or an Appalachian holler can see the Louvre or the National Gallery, even if only virtually. Ancient manuscripts are being digitized so that classicists from a handful of elite universities no longer act as gatekeepers to editorial choices with Homer, Aristotle, or Virgil. Lectures from professors at the best universities in the world are merely a click away. Mathematical problems get crowd-sourced on Twitter. One could go on.

As with many things in life, the truth regarding technology in education probably lies somewhere in the middle. The rational or reasonable use of technology can surely improve education, but innovations, even if helpful, ought to be weighed against competing concerns. Advances in science and technology ought to be argued about; there should be a *logos* (a reasoned argument) concerning the arts (*technai*), as the very name technology implies.

Judging the benefits of technology is not always an option. Recently, COVID-19 compelled educators to make a number of technological changes without adequate time for reflection; the universal reliance on Zoom and WebEx comes first and foremost to mind. The lack of reflection ought not to condemn these platforms; their synchronous mode of instruction was a godsend during the pandemic when the alternative was not meeting at all. That is not to laud these modes as perfect, or even preferable to in-person instruction, but as a substitute for the real thing, they are better than any alternative, asynchronous classes, which are basically dressed-up correspondence courses. COVID has taken us out of physical classrooms, but technology has allowed us to develop virtual ones.

For that matter, physical classrooms themselves are far from ideal, as Jacob Klein reminds us. The first obstacle to liberal education, in fact, "is the learning situation itself." Then, Klein adumbrates the best situation for students:

> more or less continuous contact between a student and his teacher, who is another student, more advanced in many ways, but still learning, himself. This situation usually does not prevail; in fact, it is extremely rare. Since time immemorial, institutions of learning, especially higher learning, have been established, called "schools"—and the ambiguity of the term becomes immediately apparent. Institutionalization means ordering of activities into certain patterns; in the case of learning activities, into classes, schedules, courses, curriculums, examinations, degrees, and all the venerable and sometimes ridiculous paraphernalia of academic life. The point is that such institutionalization cannot be avoided. . . . [The] discipline of learning seems to require an orderly and planned procedure. And yet we all know how this schedule routine can interfere with the spontaneity of questioning and learning and the occurrence of genuine wonderment. . . . Once the institutional character of learning tends to prevail, the goal of liberal education may be completely lost sight of.[43]

Klein reminds us that education should not be limited to the classroom, that we have already made compromises by fixing its pursuit in a particular location, by institutionalizing it. We professors of liberal education may extol the Socratic method, but few of us follow Socrates's rejection of the classroom setting.[44] Xenophon uses a bridle shop as the setting for his overview of Socrates's introduction to education.[45] There are some attempts, here and there, to break out of the classroom, surely in recognition of its shortcomings. The most beautiful account of such an attempt that I have come across is an innovative program for high school students on Terceira Island, off the coast of Portugal. The program there is simply called "The Republic."[46] In this program, students live together, dine together, overcome physical obstacles together, ford rivers together, hike mountains together—and all of this is combined with the common study of great books. Students learn teamwork and toughness, which they parlay into the serious study of the classics. Granted students must learn to read, write, count, and reckon, but, as Strauss reminds us, they must also learn how to wrestle, throw spears, and ride horses.[47] The Republic in the Atlantic is aware that physical education is an integral part of one's overall education. The program rightfully recognizes that there is relation between mental and physical toughness. Let us not forget that fully half of the education of the future philosophers in Plato's *Republic* is devoted to gymnastics. Colleges and universities, who have by and large removed physical education requirements in the last two generations, would do well to consider incorporating some aspects of this marvelous program.

To return to the virtual classroom, the task is the same there as it is in even the best setting: to remain focused on the goal of liberal education, producing a liberal, free human being. Admittedly, the virtual classroom seems to work better for students who know one another beforehand, who have met in person, for example, or who have even had class together in person, and it works better for students who are motivated than for those who are not. For unmotivated students, especially if they are anonymous to one another, virtual classes are simply not conducive to education.[48] But these same students struggle with in-person classes. The difference is that, in person, a professor can add an element of compulsion that is hard to imitate in a virtual setting. All of that is to say that I fully recognize the nonideal status of online learning, but it is nevertheless a useful tool if used well. Perhaps if virtual classes are to be used in the future, steps could be taken to introduce students to one another in person ahead of class, or perhaps they should meet at some interval during the course.

Sometimes virtual education cannot be avoided or is the best available practical alternative. At Ashland University, where I teach, we have had an online, synchronous graduate program for high school and middle school teachers for many years, the master of arts in history and government (MAHG). Because it is a virtual program, teachers from anywhere in the country can enroll in it. Similarly, our faculty are drawn not only from Ashland University, where the program is housed, but from many history and political science programs at colleges and universities across the country. Given the students in this program are adults, high school and middle school teachers with busy schedules, people who could never come to live in Ashland during the school years, the online synchronous program is an excellent option. In line with my remark above, students are required to come to campus at least once during a summer while they are enrolled to take a course in person. Further, these students are typically highly motivated; they hunger for intellectual conversation with peers who have a shared interest in politics and history. Indeed, I believe the MAHG is one of the best online programs in the county for teachers of history.

The pandemic has made virtual, synchronous internet-based classes much more widespread, and also more acceptable. It has also spurred pedagogical creativity. In the summer of 2020, for example, I helped to organize a dozen reading groups for students as well as a biweekly movie series over Zoom and WebEx. Students were able to join us from their homes all over the country, without having to come back to Ashland and without risking exposure to COVID-19. We offered this to students who were part of the Ashbrook program, an honors program for students of history and political science, so the students were both motivated and previously acquainted with one another. But this confirms my earlier contention that motivated students who already know one another can exploit the benefits of online education. For what it is worth, I have joined several reading groups myself during the pandemic as well—with fellow academics but also with journalists, political analysts, and other public figures. Many of these are people I knew beforehand, but they are strewn across the country from California to New York. Undertakings like these were extremely rare prior to the widespread use of videotelephony, and they are becoming more common.

Last, with two colleagues, friends really, I started a podcast during the pandemic, *The New Thinkery*. *The New Thinkery*, named after Socrates's philosophical school in Aristophanes's *Clouds*, is a podcast devoted to political philosophy and its history, along with its many guises in literature, film, and the human experience generally. It is at once serious and playful; we try to convey to listeners that we are friends with one another and that thinking together is a pleasant activity. We have recorded episodes on Plato's *Symposium*, Jonathan Swift's *Battle of the Books*, and Charles Dickens' *A Christmas Carol*, to name a few examples. We have had experts on Islamic philosophy, Shakespeare, Bacon, Aristophanes, and James Madison appear as guests. We try to model the intellectual life, the life devoted to the serious but playful study of the liberal arts, and we try to do so in a digital medium.

Doing this podcast has been one of my greatest professional pleasures. The three of us live in Colorado, Ohio, and North Carolina, but we are able to meet, read, and learn with one another thanks entirely to technology. Making this podcast allows me to continue my own liberal education, but we are also able to provide an education to others the world over through our podcast. Collectively, we have four or five decades of experience with the liberal arts, and we offer whatever we think we might have learned through podcasting. Our mode is usually to have a conversation about a great book, essay, or film that we read or watch beforehand. That is, our podcast is a de facto reading group made public. We know, because listeners have contacted us via email and Twitter, that we have undergraduates in our audience, graduate students, academics, and people who are not in academia at all, some of whom never had any formal liberal education. Further, thanks to data provided by our platform host, Libsyn, we also know that we have listeners from all fifty states and countries on all six inhabited continents. We have regular listeners from Australia, South America, Europe, and the Middle East. It might be presumptuous to think of our audience members as our students, but we are all fellow travelers in pursuit of liberal education. None of this would be possible without the benefits offered by virtual formats. Of course, there are many such podcasts devoted to the study of liberal arts, many with audiences that dwarf ours. The point is not that we are an exception; rather, podcasts are an excellent way for anyone to continue to pursue the study of the liberal arts with some guidance from others. Undergraduates are no longer the only ones with access to professors. Our experience has confirmed to us what we expected, namely, that there is a real longing outside the academy for the continued study of the liberal arts. Technology has made this podcast possible, and it has been a manifest good for us and the larger community.

CONCLUSION

Let me conclude with a caveat. The great books are not immune from the ills associated with math and science. That is to say, the great books can also be studied illiberally. Do we not know, asks Jacob Klein, that "philosophy itself can be studied in the most illiberal way?"[49] As the pursuit of liberal education is increasingly judged by its practical effects or utility, as proponents of liberal arts themselves argue on the grounds of utility, there is the risk that the study of great books can cease to provide the liberating effects they once did. Indeed, given that democracy inclines us to judge all things by utility, this is particularly problematic for us.[50]

Furthermore, the study of great books has proponents across the political spectrum who wish to subordinate it and render it illiberal; they come from the Left as well as the Right. Again, we should recall Klein's observation that the greatest threat to liberal education is the political regime we inhabit. Of course, there are opponents of great books from the Left and the Right, and their hostility is obvious and therefore easy to recognize. From the Left, great books are blamed for being the works of men, typically, who hold offensive views on contemporary issues of social justice related to sex, race, and class. From the Right, opposition tends to come from looking at education as a business, and these critics often level claims of uselessness against liberal education or irrelevance for the increasingly competitive demands of a globalized economy. But even more problematic than the opponents of liberal education are its supposed proponents who subordinate its study to other goals. Left-leaning proponents of liberal education often subordinate liberal education to activism in the name of social justice—you study the books to go out and effect change in the world. The risk here should be obvious: Why should I waste my time studying old books if the more important task is eradicating injustice (which the student already understands), an endless task? And surely a student serious about activism should not waste the precious time needed to master an ancient language. And on the Right, some support liberal education because they believe it is good because it is ours; it is traditional. In such a case, the great books can become like sediments "in the process of perpetuating the art those insights tend to approach the status of sediments, that is, of something understood derivatively and in a matter-of-course fashion."[51] The danger to reading great books in this fashion is that they cease to be liberating—they can even tighten the bonds. It is rare to find support for the study of great books for its own sake.

Nevertheless, we ought to encourage the study of great books wherever we can, whenever we can, and in whatever modality we can. This includes novel new modes made possible by technology, like Ashland's MAHG program, podcasts, and virtual reading groups. Reading great books, the best ever written by merely human hands and those that claim to be divinely inspired, together with students and teachers, this is the heart of a liberal education. Modernity makes this undertaking available to more human beings than ever before, but it also cultivates a character of soul that is disinclined to pursue it. This is all the more reason books like the present volume, which exhort to liberal education in modernity while investigating modernity's unique challenges and opportunities, are urgently needed.

NOTES

I would like to thank David Bahr and Alex Priou for their helpful comments on this paper. I would also like to thank the anonymous reviewer who helped me to sharpen my thesis and revise the structure of the chapter for greater clarity.

1. Jacob Howland and Jeffery Hockett, "How to Resist a Corporate Takeover of Your College"; Micheal T. Nietzel, "Layoffs Mount As More Colleges Confront Huge Budget Shortfalls. Tenured Faculty Are Now Being Let Go"; Daphne Chen, "Carthage College Proposal to Lay Off Faculty Draws Protest from Students," *Milwaukee Journal Sentinel*, July 19, 2020, https://www.jsonline.com/story/news/2020/07/19/carthage-college-proposal-lay-off-faculty-draws-student-protest/5468267002/.

2. Eric Hoover, "The Demographic Cliff: 5 Findings from New Projections of High School Graduates"; Nathan D. Grawe, *Demographics and the Demand for Higher Education*.

3. Leo Strauss, "What Is Liberal Education?," 3.

4. Leo Strauss, "Liberal Education and Responsibility," 11.

5. American Council of Trustees and Alumni, "Oases of Excellence."

6. Jacob Klein, "The Idea of Liberal Education," 158.

7. Strauss, "Liberal Education and Responsibility," 14, 18–19.

8. Patrick Deneen, "Science and the Decline of the Liberal Arts." Here, I suspect Deneen has in mind Socratic (freedom from the ancestral) and Baconian (freedom from the constraints of nature) conceptions of education.

9. "One has not to be naturally pious, he has merely to have a passionate interest in genuine morality in order to long with all his heart for revelation: moral man as such is

the potential believer." Leo Strauss, "The Law of Reason in the *Kuzari*," in *Persecution and the Art of Writing*, 140.

10. Strauss, "Liberal Education and Responsibility," 11. Strauss undoubtedly has in mind the serious people (*spoudaioi*) of whom Aristotle speaks in the *Nicomachean Ethics*, I.7 1098a9 and following.

11. Xenophon, *Education of Cyrus*, 2.2.13–16. Compare the opening of Xenophon's *Symposium* with the *Hellenkia*, and see Strauss's remarks on the comparison in Leo Strauss, "Greek Historians," 662. See also Plato, *Gorgias*, 484c and ff.

12. Strauss, "What Is Liberal Education?," 3–4.

13. Leo Strauss, *Natural Right and History*, 74. "All arguments in favor of revelation seem to be valid only if belief in revelation is presupposed, and all arguments against revelation seem to be valid only if unbelief is presupposed."

14. Strauss, "Liberal Education and Responsibility," 22.

15. Leo Strauss, *On Nietzsche's "Thus Spoke Zarathustra,"* 208. The inclusion of aesthetics in liberal education is a relatively recent development. "The beautiful as beautiful was a great theme of the tradition of philosophy, for the simple reason that the beautiful in the primary sense of the tradition was much more the natural beautiful than the beautiful of human art. The enormous change, which took place around 1800, was when it was declared that the true seat of beauty is not nature but the work of art."

16. Strauss, "Liberal Education and Responsibility," 24 (emphasis added).

17. "To use the classical presentation of the natural difficulties of philosophizing, namely Plato's parable of the cave, one may say that today we find ourselves in a second, much deeper cave than the lucky ignorant persons Socrates dealt with; we need history first of all in order to *ascend* to the cave from which Socrates can lead us to light; we need a propaedeutic, which the Greeks did not need, namely, learning through reading." Leo Strauss, "Review of Julius Ebbinghaus, *On the Progress of Metaphysics*," in Leo Strauss, *The Early Writings (1921–1932)*, 215.

18. Jacob Klein, "On Liberal Education," 265–67. Of course, Klein's proposed study for mathematics is Euclid, which perhaps points to a fundamental agreement with Strauss. The ancients approached mathematics differently than we do—it was not detached from trying to understand the world as we perceive it—and Euclid could also be subsumed under the great books.

19. Klein, "The Idea of Liberal Education," 166.

20. Strauss, "Liberal Education and Responsibility," 19.

21. Klein, "On Liberal Education," 266.

22. Francis Bacon, *The Great Instauration*, 21 (emphasis added). Note the original Latin is bolder.

23. Francis Bacon, *The Advancement of Learning*, I.v.11 (emphasis added).

24. Joshua Parens, *Maimonides and Spinoza: Their Conflicting Views of Human Nature*, 60. "For now, it must suffice to observe that Bacon, Descartes, and Spinoza form a united front against premodern wonder at formal wholes." What they seem to deprecate is "wonder of a deeper kind, wonder at the wholeness of natural beings and a desire to know such beings."

25. See, for example, Chris Bernhardt, *Turing's Vision: The Birth of Computer Science*. I thank Tom Cleveland for this example.

26. Fareed Zakaria, *In Defense of a Liberal Education*, 43. "Science was central to liberal education from the start. Except in those days, the reason to study it was the precise opposite of what is argued today. In the ancient world, and for many centuries thereafter, science was seen as a path to abstract knowledge. It had no practical purpose."

27. Leo Strauss, "On the Basis of Hobbes's Political Philosophy," 172.

28. Leo Strauss, "Reason and Revelation," 177.

29. Plato, *Phaedrus*, 271c and following.

30. Plato, "Cleitophon," 111–16.

31. Plato, *Parmenides*, cf. 130e, 135c–d. No doubt, readers would object and hold up many dialogues, especially the *Protagoras and Meno*, as an example of Socratic education. The *Parmenides* also presents an interesting case, but it shows Socrates as student, not a teacher. Further, Parmenides himself actually says that Socrates, although he is close, is not yet philosophic.

32. Xenophon, *Memorabilia*, 1.6.14.

33. Thomas Pangle, *The Socratic Way of Life: Xenophon's "Memorabilia,"* 60–61. Xenophon "indicates that learning from the study together of old books, that are great because they contain treasures of wisdom, is a peak activity of Socratic life and friendship. Here, finally, we see virtuous activity that Socrates did not merely turn his companions toward, but effectively led them into."

34. Pangle, *Socratic Way of Life*, 61. "We note that the 'wise men of old' to whom Socrates refers would be the 'pre-Socratic' philosophers and poets."

35. Pangle, *Socratic Way of Life*, 71–72. "To understand the full poetic teaching that underlies this rather cryptic characterization of virtue, we would need of course to follow Xenophon's prompt and study the *Works and Days*, which was doubtless one of the books of the wise men of old in which study Socrates led his close friends." References to Homer and Hesiod abound in both Xenophon's and Plato's accounts of Socrates. Socrates has memorized and reflected on poems, including those of Simonides (Plato, *Protagoras*, 339b). He says he has loved Homer since he was a child (*Republic*, 595b). With regard to the pre-Socratics, he took great interest in Zeno and Parmenides, but he was especially interested in Anaxagoras (*Phaedo*, 97c; *Apology of Socrates*, 26d). Thomas G. West and Grace Starry West, trans., *Four Texts on Socrates*: Plato's *Euthyphro*, *Apology of Socrates*, and *Crito* and Aristophanes' *Clouds*.

36. Carl Straumsheim, "A New* System for Student Success Planning."

37. Many scholars have argued that attention span of college students is only about ten to fifteen minutes. See, for example, L.T. Benjamin, "Lecturing," 57–67. However, Karen Wilson and James H. Korn dispute this contention in their article "Attention during Lectures: Beyond Ten Minutes."

38. Dan Berrett, "How 'Flipping' the Classroom Can Improve the Traditional Lecture."

39. D. A. Kolb, "Learning Styles and Disciplinary Differences," 232–55.

40. There are myriad applications for polling or surveying students instantaneously during class, like "Kahoot!" and "Tophat"; there is even one with "Socrates" in the name "Socrative." See Michelle D. Miller, "Before Adopting Classroom Technology, Figure Out Your Goals."

41. Aristotle, *Nicomachean Ethics*, 4.9 1128b10 and following.

42. Strauss, "Liberal Education and Responsibility," 25.

43. Klein, "Idea of Liberal Education," 166–67.

44. The *Theaetetus* is perhaps an exception; it takes place in something like a school setting. Socrates goes to Theodorus to inquire as to the most impressive youth he knows. Theaetetus and some fellow students then show up. There seems to be a regular meeting place for learning, and they then meet up there again the next day.

45. Xenophon, *Memorabilia*, 4.2.1.

46. Miguel Monjardino, "A Republic in the Atlantic."

47. Strauss, "Liberal Education and Responsibility," 11.

48. See Matthew J. Mayhew et al., *How College Affects Students*, 3:44–49, 124–33, 396–403.

49. Klein, "Idea of Liberal Education," 166.

50. Alexis de Tocqueville, *Democracy in America*, vol. 2, pt. 2, chap. 8, 500–503. Perhaps this is one reason Tocqueville thought the great books of Roman and Greek literature were particularly important for maintaining liberty in modern democracies (vol. 2, pt. 1, chap. 15, 450–52).

51. Klein, "On Liberal Education," 263.

BIBLIOGRAPHY

American Council of Trustees and Alumni. "Oases of Excellence." Last modified 2021. https://www.goacta.org/initiatives/oases-of-excellence/.

Aristotle. *Nicomachaen Ethics*. Translated by Susan D. Collins and Robert C. Bartlett. Chicago: University of Chicago, 2011.

Bacon, Francis. *The Advancement of Learning*. Cassell, 1893. Last modified November 4, 2014. https://www.gutenberg.org/files/5500/5500-h/5500-h.htm.

———. *The Great Instauration*. Wheeling, IL: Harlan Davidson, 1989.

Benardete. *The Being of the Beautiful*. Chicago: University of Chicago Press, 2007.

Benjamin, L. T. "Lecturing." In *The Teaching of Psychology: Essays in Honor of Wilbert J. McKeachie and Charles L. Brewer*, edited by Stephen F. Davis and William Buskist. Mahwah, NJ: Lawrence Erlbaum Associates, 2002.

Bernhardt, Chris. *Turing's Vision: The Birth of Computer Science*. Cambridge, MA: MIT Press, 2017.

Berrett, Dan. "How 'Flipping' the Classroom Can Improve the Traditional Lecture." *Chronicle of Higher Education* (February 19, 2012). https://www.chronicle.com/article/how-flipping-the-classroom-can-improve-the-traditional-lecture/.

Deneen, Patrick J. "Science and the Decline of the Liberal Arts." *New Atlantis* (Fall 2009–Winter 2010). https://www.thenewatlantis.com/publications/science-and-the-decline-of-the-liberal-arts.

Grawe, Nathan D. *Demographics and the Demand for Higher Education*. Baltimore: Johns Hopkins University Press, 2018.

Hoover, Eric. "The Demographic Cliff: 5 Findings from New Projections of High-School Graduates." *Chronicle of Higher Education* (December 5, 2020). https://www.chronicle.com/article/the-demographic-cliff-5-findings-from-new-projections-of-high-school-graduates.

Howland, Jacob, and Jeffrey Hockett. "How to Resist a Corporate Takeover of Your College." *Chronicle of Higher Education* (July 17, 2020). https://www.chronicle.com/article/how-to-resist-a-corporate-takeover-of-your-college.

Klein, Jacob. "The Idea of Liberal Education." In *Lectures and Essays*. Annapolis, MD: St. John's College Press, 1985.

———. "On Liberal Education." In *Lectures and Essays*. Annapolis, MD: St. John's College Press, 1985.

Kolb, D. A. "Learning Styles and Disciplinary Differences." In *The Modern American College: Responding to the New Realities of Diverse Students and a Changing Society*. San Francisco: Jossey-Bass, 1981.

Mayhew, Matthew J., et al. *How College Affects Students*. Vol. 3, *21st Century Evidence That Higher Education Works*. San Francisco: Jossey-Bass, 2016.

Miller, Michelle D. "Before Adopting Classroom Technology, Figure Out Your Goals." *Chronicle of Higher Education* (October 13, 2019). https://www.chronicle.com/article/before-adopting-classroom-technology-figure-out-your-goals/.

Monjardino, Miguel. "A Republic in the Atlantic." *City Journal* (Winter 2017). https://www.city-journal.org/html/republic-atlantic-14956.html.

Nietzel, Michael T. "Layoffs Mount as More Colleges Confront Huge Budget Shortfalls. Tenured Faculty Are Now Being Let Go." *Forbes*, July 21, 2020. https://www.forbes.com/sites/michaeltnietzel/2020/07/21/layoffs-mount-as-more-colleges-confront-huge-budget-shortfalls-tenured-faculty-are-now-being-let-go/?sh=7fdbe57b32bf.

Pangle, Thomas. *The Socratic Way of Life: Xenophon's "Memorabilia."* Chicago: University of Chicago Press, 2018.

Parens, Joshua. *Maimonides and Spinoza: Their Conflicting Views of Human Nature*. Chicago: University of Chicago Press, 2012.

Plato. "Cleitophon." In *The Roots of Political Philosophy*, edited by Thomas Pangle. Ithaca, NY: Cornell University Press, 1987.

———. *Gorgias*. Translated by James H. Nichols. Ithaca, NY: Cornell University Press, 1998.

———. *Parmenides*. Translated by Albert Keith Whitaker. Indianapolis: Focus (Hackett), 1996.

———. *Phaedo*. Translated by Eva Brann, Peter Kalkavage, and Eric Salem. Newburyport, MA: Focus, 1998.

———. *Phaedrus*. Translated by James H. Nichols. Ithaca, NY: Cornell University Press, 1998.

———. *Protagoras and Meno*. Translated by Robert C. Bartlett. Ithaca, NY: Cornell University Press, 2004.

———. *Republic*. Translated by Allan Bloom. New York: Basic Books, 1987.

Straumsheim, Carl. "A New* System for Student Success Planning." *Inside Higher Ed* (July 5, 2017). https://www.insidehighered.com/news/2017/07/05/colleges-need-enterprise-level-software-tackle-student-success-issues-company-says.

Strauss, Leo. *The Early Writings (1921–1932)*. Translated and edited by Michael Zank. Albany: State University of New York Press, 2002.

———. "Greek Historians." *Review of Metaphysics* 21, no. 4 (1968): 656–66.
———. "Liberal Education and Responsibility." In *Liberalism Ancient and Modern*. Chicago: University of Chicago Press, 1995.
———. *Natural Right and History*. Chicago: University of Chicago, 1965.
———. *On Nietzsche's "Thus Spoke Zarathustra."* Chicago: University of Chicago Press, 2017.
———. "On the Basis of Hobbes's Political Philosophy." In *What Is Political Philosophy?* Chicago: University of Chicago, 1959.
———. "Reason and Revelation." In *Leo Strauss and the Theological-Political Problem*, by Heinrich Meier. Translated by Marcus Brainard. New York: Cambridge University Press, 2006.
———. "What Is Liberal Education?" In *Liberalism Ancient and Modern*. Chicago: University of Chicago Press, 1995.
Tocqueville, Alexis de. *Democracy in America*. Vol. 2. Chicago: University of Chicago Press, 2000.
West, Thomas G., and Grace Starry West, trans. *Four Texts on Socrates*: Plato's *Euthyphro, Apology of Socrates*, and *Crito* and Aristophanes' *Clouds*. Ithaca, NY: Cornell University Press, 1998.
Wilson, Karen, and James H. Korn. "Attention during Lectures: Beyond Ten Minutes." *Teaching of Psychology* 34, no. 2 (2007): 85–89.
Xenophon. *Education of Cyrus*. Translated by Wayne Anbler. Ithaca, NY: Cornell University Press, 2001.
———. *Memorabilia*. Translated by Amy Bonnette. Ithaca, NY: Cornell University Press, 1994.
Zakaria, Fareed. *In Defense of a Liberal Education*. New York: W. W. Norton, 2015.

Index

academia: Academic Program Reviews, 290, 294–98, 300–304; as conversation, 216–17; freedom of speech in, 27–28; justice role of, 11–14, 23–29; and *phronesis*, 11–29; political challenges to, 186–87, 414; political role of, 158–59; and religious affiliations, 164, 165–66, 167–68, 399; revenue pressures, 176, 187; shift to science and technology in, 164, 165–66, 167–68, 210, 220, 289–301, 321–23, 404–5; and Soviet education, 187–92; virtues for, 27–29. *See also* collegial governance; crisis of liberal education; students; teachers
academic freedom: and civility, 28; and shift to science and technology, 289–301
academic mission, 298, 299–302, 303
Academic Program Reviews, 290, 294–98, 300–304
accreditation, 301–2
Ackerman, Bruce, 338
action, discipline of, 179
Adams, John, 329
Adams, John Quincy, 329
Adeimantus, 109, 110, 112, 113
Adkins-Cartee, Mary, 225–26
administrators: challenges of, 242; increase in, 295, 374; lack of liberal arts background, 393; support for tenure by, 299
aidōs, 93. *See also* shame
aisckhunē, 93. *See also* ashamedness
Allen, Danielle, 328
alma mater concept and community, 180–81
alumni support for liberal arts, 303

ambition. *See* careerism
American Academy of Arts and Sciences, 331–32
American Association of University Professors, 28, 291–92, 299–300, 301
American Council of Trustees and Alumni, 396
amor mundi, 261–63
analogy, 113, 115, 122, 135, 138n16
Antiphon, 406–7
apologia, 107, 109
Appiah, Kwame Anthony, 259–60, 263
archetypes, 157
Archias, 104–5
Archytas, 143n57
Arendt, Hannah, 248, 252, 259, 260–65
Aristotle: on character, 241; compared to Chinese philosophy, 46; on desire for knowledge, 206; on education, 4, 106, 131, 197, 241; on essence and characteristics, 80–81; on first causes, 138n24; on friendship, 262; interest in other civilizations, 58; on leadership, 351; on moral virtue, 15, 18–19, 27; and *noesis noeseos,* 313; and *phronesis,* 12, 14–24, 26; on political animal, 207–8; on prudence, 201; on shame, 93, 96, 409; on speech, 207; on suffering, 240; on wisdom, 12, 14–24, 26, 67
arithmetic, 3, 118–22, 401
arithmos term, 120–21
art, 290, 293–98, 402
ashamedness, 91–95, 97–98

Ashland University, 413, 415
Association of American Colleges, 292
Association of Governing Boards of Universities and Colleges, 301
astronomy, 3, 122, 124, 125–27, 401
audit culture, 295. *See also* Academic Program Reviews
Saint Augustine, 261–62, 313
authority: and COVID-19 pandemic, 200; and democracy, 94, 206, 377, 378–80, 382; loss of, 313, 317
Auxiliaries, 107, 108
Averintsev, Sergei, 44

Bacon, Francis, 215, 403–4
Baker, Vicki, 176
Baldwin, James, 244, 247–48
the beautiful, 67, 132, 134, 314, 416n15
Bennis, Warren, 350–51
Berry, Wendell, 253n34
Bhati, Karni Pal, 225–26
Bloom, Allan: on democracy and education, 373, 374, 381–87; on elites, 154; on Socratic philosophy, 139n27, 139n32–33; on time for degrees, 305n15
The Book of the City of Ladies (Christine de Pizan), 73–77, 82
Bowdoin college, 334
Brabant, Margaret, 74, 82
Brint, Michael, 74, 82
Brown-Grant, Rosalind, 77, 79, 80
Brownlee, Kevin, 84n29
Buddhism: and anger, 56; Orwin on, 35, 37–41, 43
budgets, 295, 296, 299, 300, 303–4
Burger, Ariel, 242
Burke, Edmund, 4, 341–42
Business Roundtable, 354, 356
business schools: and civic education, 347–62, 380; criticism of, 350–51, 373; curricula, 349–60; and great books, 375

calculation, 120–21, 126
Callicles, 124, 137n14
Cambridge University, 359
Campus Sex, Campus Security (Doyle), 228

cancel culture, 88
canon: and Christine de Pizan, 34, 71–83; criticism of, 32–33, 51–52, 54–56, 151–52; defined, 51; deparochialization of, 31–46, 51–67, 152; and particularists, 52–55, 57; student ignorance of, 36–37; and universality, 52–53, 55–58; "Westernness" of, 42–44, 52–53, 54. *See also* great books
careerism: and civic education, 328, 341–42; and cost of education, 234, 385; and degree options and enrollments, 298, 341–42; *vs.* learning for learning's sake, 157–59; and student life, 160–61, 162–63, 169, 175–77, 241–42, 393
Carleton College, 335
Carrese, Paul, 328
Cassuto, Umberto, 44
Catalina, 137n5
causes, first, 138n24
Cave image: and limits of democracy in Tocqueville, 376; in Plato/Socrates, 106–7, 110–11, 114, 115–19, 121, 125–26, 128–29, 130–31, 134, 136, 155; in Strauss, 317, 383, 402
centrifugal/centripetal individualism, 90
Cephalus, 152, 161–62
character: and moral virtue, 315, 316; and nobility, 159, 161–62; and *phronesis*, 15, 16; as precondition for liberal education, 397–98; and role of education, 154, 160, 177, 180, 241, 332, 347, 349, 358; women's, 73–77
Chinese philosophy and culture, 45–46, 53, 57–58, 61–64
Christianity: Deneen on role of in education, 164, 167, 399; in *It's a Wonderful Life* (1946), 165, 167–68; and soft despotism in Tocqueville, 379–81
Christine de Pizan, 34, 71–83, 157
church-state colleges, 330
Cicero: and civic education, 103, 104–6, 131, 133, 134; on Plato and Pythagoreans, 143n57; on reading, 185
citizenship: and cosmopolitanism, 165, 168–69; and deliberation, 198; and general education, 3–4; and great books,

Index   423

151–53; Socrates as citizen, 95; unashamed citizenship, 88. *See also* civic education; democracy; democracy and modern education

city-in-speech *(polis-*in*-logos),* 107–10, 112–19, 124, 135, 136

civic education: and canon/great books, 36, 151–53; and constitutional studies, 163, 328–29, 338–40, 374, 387; and core curricula, 332–33, 334; in *The Fellowship of the Ring* (Tolkein), 266–80; and founding fathers, 25, 327–28, 329–31, 335, 336–37, 340; and history, 328–29, 332, 333, 335–40; and justice, 106, 107, 108, 112, 118, 124, 130, 131–36, 162, 163–69; and modern liberal education, 151–55, 160, 163, 332–36; Platonic, 103–36; in primary and secondary schools, 335–36, 355; and professional schools, 341, 347–62, 374, 380; and Roman empire, 103–6; and suffering, 239–52; and virtue, 25, 104–5; and vulnerability of democracy, 25, 327–42. *See also* democracy and modern education

civility, 28–29

civil service, 319

classroom: as artificial space, 180, 410–11. *See also* online instruction; physical environment

Clews, Henry, 352

The Closing of the American Mind (Bloom), 154, 373, 374, 381–87

The Coddling of the American Mind (Lukianoff and Haidt), 246

collegial governance, 290, 294, 295–97, 299–304

Columbia University, 332–33

common good: and business programs, 351, 364; and deliberation, 198; and founding fathers, 327; and justice, 16–17; and leadership, 351

community: and access to liberal education, 164–65; and *alma mater* concept, 180–81; and citizenship, 162–63; engagement and heroism, 166–68; great books as community, 14–23, 174, 184, 190; and

identity, 90; *vs.* individualism, 163–69; of inquiry, 11–29; and online *vs.* in-person instruction, 207–8; role in liberal education, 153–57, 162–63, 207–11, 214; and student engagement, 185–86, 189–90

comparative political theory and deparochialization, 31, 37–46

compassion: and civic education, 239–52; and humanity, 321

computer science, 404

conflict, recognizing tragic, 248–49. *See also* disagreement and debate

Confronting the Constitution (Bloom), 384

Confucius and Confucianism, 57–58, 61–64

Conn, Steven, 350

constitutional studies: and Bloom, 384–86; as civic education, 163, 328–29, 338–40, 374, 387

Contenance de fame, 85n43

conversation (association) and cosmopolitanism, 259–60

core curricula: of business schools, 351–55; and civic education, 332–33, 334

Corey, Elizabeth, 242

Cornell University, 384, 386–87

Cory, William, 182

cosmopolitanism: and *amor mundi,* 261–63; and civic education requirements, 335; and civic responsibility, 165, 168–69; described, 258–59; in *The Fellowship of the Ring* (Tolkein), 257–58, 264–80; moral challenge of, 259–63; *vs.* provincialism, 257–58; rise of, 257–58

costs: and auxiliary services, 394; and careerism, 234, 385; and tuition rates, 174–75, 214, 234, 385, 393

courage, 247–48, 280

COVID-19 pandemic: as justification for change, 303; and limits of science and technology, 197–211; and online instruction, 203–4, 205, 210–11, 213, 218, 219–20, 410, 412; and shaming, 89; and suffering, 240

Craftsmen and Auxiliaries, 107, 108

crisis of liberal education: and academic freedom, 289–301; and cosmopolitanism,

crisis of liberal education (*continued*) 257–58; costs and financial pressures, 174–75, 177, 393; and drop in humanities diplomas, 175–76; and increase in administrators, 295; and shift to science and technology, 164, 165–66, 167–68, 210, 220, 289–301, 321–23, 404–5
critical race theory, 88
critical thinking skills: and democracy, 94–95; as goal of liberal education, 51–52, 182, 332, 333–34; and great books, 152, 375; and hypocrisy, 14; and Trivium, 3
Crito (Plato), 95
culture: audit culture, 295; cancel culture, 88; cultural limits on expanding canon, 35, 38–39; and education in Strauss, 307–8, 309, 310, 314; and elemental education, 398; meritocracy in non-Western cultures, 65–66; as pathology, 156; and pluralism, 309; pop culture, 310, 314; shame/guilt cultures, 87, 89. See also Chinese philosophy and culture; Greek culture; Western culture
curriculum: of business schools, 349–60; and constitutional studies, 163; core curricula and business schools, 351–55; core curricula and civic education, 332–33, 334; philosopher's curriculum of Socrates, 106, 107, 108–9, 114, 118–31, 135; at St. John's College, 33, 55–56
custom and funeral rituals, 53, 58–64
cynicism, academic, 152
Cynics, 95–98

Dallmayr, Fred R., 38
Dartmouth Tuck School of Business, 348–49, 350, 353, 356, 358
King David, 92–93
death: denial of, 247; funeral rituals, 53, 58–64
debt, student, 159, 174, 177
Delany, Sheila, 77
democracy: and attraction to change, 206–7; and limits of science and technology, 197–98, 200–201; Lincoln on, 27; and shared *ethos*, 94, 96; Socrates on transition to, 94. See also founding fathers

democracy and modern education: and academic mission, 328; Aristotle on, 197; and civic education, 25, 327–42; and classical liberal education, 311; and courage, 247; and critical thinking, 94–95; and ethical literacy, 246; and individualism, 206, 245, 378; liberal education *vs.* democratic or universal education, 134, 309–10; and meritocracy in other cultures, 65–66; and professional schools, 373–87; and shame, 87–99; in Strauss, 310, 315–22; and suffering, 240, 244–46, 249, 252; *vs.* technology, 321–22; Tocqueville on, 373–81, 386, 387, 418n50; and vengeance, 250
Democracy in America (Tocqueville), 206, 373–82
Deneen, Patrick, 163–66, 399
Denktagebuch (Arendt), 263
De Officiis (Cicero), 105
deparochialization of canon, 31–46, 51–67, 152
Descartes, René, 179, 187–88, 377
desire, discipline of, 179
despotism, soft, 378–81
Dewey, John, 292
dialectic: of self, 89–92; and Socratic education, 111–12, 114, 125, 127–31, 133, 161, 406–7
dialogue: and cosmopolitanism, 259–60; as fundamental to liberal education, 155–57, 181; with great books, 174, 312–13; and shame, 93–94; skills, 181
Diogenes, 95–98
disabilities and suffering, 249
disagreement and debate: constitutional studies as model for, 339; reason *vs.* revelation as fundamental question, 44, 400–401, 405; and recognizing tragic conflict, 248–49
discipline: and learning, 182; and reading, 179, 190
diversity: and disagreements, 161; diversity of viewpoints, 13–14, 27–28, 161, 382; interest in, 11, 51, 54, 334, 355, 356. See also deparochialization of canon

Index

Divided Line image, 106, 110–11, 113–14, 118, 122, 123, 130–31
Dolan, Frederick, 262
Douglass, Frederick, 340
Doyle, Jennifer, 228
Duke University: civic education in, 334; Duke Kunshan University, 40, 54, 64–67

Edmundson, Mark, 151–52
Educating for American Democracy Initiative, 328
education: elemental education, 398; general education, 3–4; and love of the world *(amor mundi)*, 263; physical education, 411. *See also* academia; civic education; democracy and modern education; liberal education; students; teachers
efficiency, 217
eikōn term, 110. *See also* images
Einstein, Albert, 158, 159
Eisenberg, Avigail, 82
Eisgruber, Christopher, 334
elemental education, 398
Eliade, Mircea, 188
elites. *See* nobility and elites
embodiment: in education and learning, 208, 210; and sociality in student-teacher relationships, 225, 227
Emerson, Ralph Waldo, 187
empathy: of students, 153, 249–50; of teachers, 229, 231
enlightenment, universal, 320
environment. *See* physical environment
equality: and homogeneity, 377–78, 382; and judgment, 206; and justice, 315; in Strauss, 315, 318, 321; as study area in history, 333, 338; and suffering, 245; in Tocqueville, 98–99, 206, 247, 377–79, 381. *See also* inequality
eros: and sociality in student-teacher relationships, 223–27; and Socratic education, 129, 132, 135; and virtue, 322; and women, 234
ethics: in business schools, 351, 356, 359–62, 380; and cosmopolitanism, 259; liberal education as foundation for, 319; and suffering, 246–52. *See also* morality
ethos, shared, 94, 96
Euclid, 416n48
evil, 252, 262

faculty. *See* teachers
false piety, 139n32
fame, 96–98
Federalist Papers, 318, 327–28, 359
The Fellowship of the Ring (Tolkien), 257–58, 264–80
feminism and Christine de Pizan, 72, 73, 77
figures-in-speech, 110–19, 129–31
financial exigency, 299, 303–4
Financial Times rankings, 359–60
fine arts, 290, 293–98
The Fire Next Time (Baldwin), 247–48
Flanagan, Owen, 56
Flexner, Abraham, 187
florilegia, 83n10
foreign students and canon, 36
forgiveness, 250
Forster, E. M., 31
founding fathers: Bloom's study of, 384–85; and canon, 55; and civic education, 25, 327–28, 329–31, 335, 336–37, 340; and freedom, 24–27; and national university, 328, 329–31, 335, 342
Franklin, Benjamin, 329
freedom: academic freedom, 28, 289–301; and Cave image of enslavement of mind, 115–18, 131; and founding fathers, 24–27; liberal education as freeing of mind, 4–7, 108, 116–18, 131–32, 136, 181–84; and liberal education *vs.* general education, 3–4; of press, 24; of speech, 23–29, 289; and virtue, 19
Freud, Anna, 230
Freud, Sigmund, 230, 231–32, 233
Friedman, Milton, 347, 353–54, 356
friendship: and Arendt, 261, 262–63; Aristotle on, 262; civic friendship, 268; and conversation (association), 260; in *The Fellowship of the Ring* (Tolkien), 266–69, 278, 280; and justice, 262; and politics,

friendship (*continued*)
  282n31; student-student, 153–57, 177; student-teacher, 224–27
Fukuyama, Francis, 333, 390n50
funeral rituals, 53, 58–64

Galston, William, 335–36
Garcetti v. Caballos, 293
gender: Christine de Pizan on, 72, 73–77, 80–82; and student-teacher relationships, 226, 228; and transference, 223
general civilization courses, 322
General Education in a Free Society, 332–33
Genesis, 91–92, 97
geometry, 3, 122–25, 126, 401
Gettysburg Address (Lincoln), 27
ghosts, 63
Glaucon, 106, 110, 118–35
globalization and canon, 36–37
goals of liberal education: and critical thinking skills, 51–52, 182, 332, 333–34; and humanization, 241–42; and intellect, 182–83; and self-knowledge, 182; and soul, 91; utilitarian goals, 241–42
good: academic freedom as public good, 292, 301; and *amor mundi,* 262; in Bloom, 374, 382, 383–84; and deliberation, 198; and engaging with great books, 155–56, 182, 185; and in-person *vs.* online instruction, 203–11; and justice, 16–17, 134–36, 382; liberal education as addressing, 133, 136, 154, 182, 192, 203, 215, 241–42; liberal education as good in itself, 157–59, 186, 216–17, 219; and limits of science and technology, 201–2, 215–16; and natural right, 135; and professional schools, 351, 364, 374, 387; and relativism, 374, 383; and Socratic/Platonic curriculum, 106, 110, 112–15, 117–19, 122–24, 127–30, 133; and soul, 113–15; and work, 19–20
Gorgias (Plato), 111, 114, 124, 137n14, 210
governance, collegial, 290, 294, 295–97, 299–304
graduate schools. *See* professional schools
grammar, 3, 401
Grant, George, 214–15

great books: archetypes in, 157; and Bloom, 382; and Christine de Pizan, 72–73, 81–82; and civic engagement, 151–53; as community/sanctuary, 14–23, 174, 184, 190; and crises, 179; and critical thinking, 152, 375; and deparochialization, 31–46, 51–67, 152; dialogue with, 174, 312–13; as fundamental to liberal education, 14–23, 178–80, 183, 189–92, 308–9, 401–2, 405–8; and historicism, 312–13; and judgment, 179–80, 184, 312; and justice, 34–35, 65–66, 151–53, 414; and online instruction, 395, 408–12; pedagogical strategies for, 405–8, 411–14; political use of, 414–15; and professional schools, 375; reading groups, 407–8, 412–14, 415; reading in isolation, 153–57; Soviet access to, 189; and St. John's College, 33, 55–56; and Strauss, 307, 311–14, 401–2, 405; and synthesis, 179–80, 181. *See also* canon; reading
Greek culture: cosmopolitanism in, 45, 58; funeral rituals, 53, 58–61, 64; Greek texts as non-Western, 42–44
Guardian-Rulers, education of, 106–34
guilt cultures, 87
gymnastics, 106, 108, 118, 127–28, 134, 411

Hades and Socrates, 144n68
Hadot, Pierre, 187
Haidt, Jonathan, 246
Hamilton, Alexander, 168–69
harmonics, 127–28, 134
Harrison, Pegram, 358–59
Harvard: business school and civic education, 349, 353, 354, 356, 362; core curricula and civic education, 332–33, 334
Haverford College, 335
The Heart of the Matter (American Academy of Arts and Sciences), 331–32
Hebraic texts as non-Western, 42–44
Heidegger, Martin, 261, 323n2
Hellenic texts: cosmopolitanism in, 45; as non-Western, 42–44
helplessness and democracy, 246, 247

Index

Herodotus, 45, 58, 59–61
heroism: and civic engagement, 166–68; of Hobbits, 267
Heschel, Abraham Joshua, 239, 241, 243–45, 248, 250–51, 252
Hesiod, 417n35
historicism: Bloom on, 374, 383–84; and great books, 312–13; and philosophy, 318
history: and civic education, 328–29, 332, 333, 335–40; and constitutional law, 328–29, 338–40; in modern liberal arts, 401
History (Herodotus), 59–61
Hitz, Zena, 157–58
Hobbes, Thomas, 179
The Hobbit (Tolkien), 264, 266
Hobbits and cosmopolitan education, 257–58, 264–80
Holocaust: and love of world, 262; and pedagogy of suffering, 239, 241, 243, 244–45, 246, 248, 250–51, 252
Homer, 58–59, 64, 417n35
homogeneity: of canon, 44, 54; and degree choices, 298; and equality, 377–78, 382; and individualism and democracy, 378
horizontal reading, 179
"How Business Schools Lost Their Way" (Bennis and O'Toole), 350–51
Hudley, Anne Charity, 88
humanism and civic education, 103–4, 105, 131
humanities: as core of modern liberal arts, 401; and pedagogy of suffering, 250–52; shift away from, 175–76; transfer of resources from, 290, 293–98
humanization: as aim of liberal education, 241–42, 250–52; and role of philosophy, 317; and suffering, 245
humility: and careerism, 156–57, 162; and contemplative *vs.* active life, 159; and discipline, 182; in *The Fellowship of the Ring* (Tolkien), 277; and great books, 308; and perplexity, 209; and recognizing tragic conflict, 248–49; of teacher, 314
Huot, Sylvia, 84n29

identity and self: and Christine de Pizan, 73–83; and community, 90; and fame, 97–98; identity politics, 90; and inner and outer self, 90–93, 95–98; and multiple contexts, 82–83; national identity, 26–27; and shame, 87–99; as term, 83n11. *See also* self-knowledge
Iliad (Homer), 59
illiberal study, 414
images: and astronomy, 126; and *eikōn* term, 110; and geometry, 122–23; use of by Socrates, 109–19, 129–31. *See also* Cave image
Indian Institutes of Management, 359
indifference, evil of, 252
individualism: centripetal *vs.* centrifugal, 90; *vs.* community, 163–69; and compassion, 245; and democracy, 206, 245, 378; and deparochialization of canon, 33
inequality: and access to liberal education, 154, 160–61, 164–65; interest in, 11, 12, 173, 179, 356; and leisure, 159–60; and online instruction, 214; and shame, 88
inquiry, community of, 11–29
INSEAD, 356
intellect: and doubt, 378; as goal of liberal education, 182–83; *vs.* heart in Strauss, 313; as precondition for liberal education, 394; in Socratic education, 113, 118–31, 133–34; and status of contemplative life, 158–59; and student-teacher relationships, 225, 226
Intelligible realm, 113, 114, 115, 119, 125, 128, 130
interdisciplinary programs, 294, 297
It's a Wonderful Life (1946), 154–55, 165–69

Jaffa, Harry, 5
Jaspers, Karl, 261
Jean de Meun, 72
Jefferson, Thomas: on freedom, 25; and Hamilton debates, 168–69; and national university plans, 328, 329, 335; and role of education, 25, 331; on talent, 200–201
Jewish texts as non-Western, 42–44

judgment: and Arendt, 260–61, 262, 264; and business schools, 362; and civility, 29; and constitutional studies, 340; and democracy, 206, 378, 414; and deparochialization of canon, 61, 66; discipline of, 179; and emotion, 153; in *The Fellowship of the Ring* (Tolkien), 267, 268, 271–72, 273, 275–76, 280; and general education, 4; and great books, 179–80, 184, 312; as liberal education goal, 154; and natural right, 17–18; in philosopher's curriculum, 119; and *phronesis*, 15, 16, 17, 21–22, 23, 29. See also critical thinking skills

justice: and access to liberal education, 164–65, 214; Bloom on justice movement, 386; and business programs, 361; as central to liberal education, 103, 162, 163–69, 173, 179, 337, 375, 380, 400; and civic education, 106–8, 112, 118, 124, 130, 131–36, 162, 163–69; and founding fathers, 384; and friendship, 262; and good, 16–17, 134–36, 382; as good for soul, 106; and great books, 34–35, 65–66, 151–53, 414; and meritocracy, 162, 163–64; and noblesse oblige, 315; and *phronesis*, 16–18; and reflection, 162; and religion, 380; responding to injustice with injustice, 95; role of academy in, 11–14, 23–29; and technology, 218; in Tocqueville, 375, 380

Keyishian v. Board of Regents, 293
Khurana, Rakesh, 350
King, Martin Luther, Jr., 249–50
Klein, Jacob: on elemental education, 398; on great books, 402; on illiberal study, 414; on physical classroom, 410–11; on political threat to education, 414; on role of religion, science and great books in liberal education, 395, 398, 402, 403; on Socratic curriculum, 141n46, 141n48, 142n53; on visible realm, 139n30

knowledge: and civic education, 328–30, 332, 333, 335–40; and democracy, 332–33, 382; desire for, 109, 185, 206; in *The Fellowship of the Ring* (Tolkien), 271, 273–74, 280; and first causes, 138n24; and limits of science and technology, 197, 199, 201–3, 211, 215–17, 403–4; and philosopher's curriculum, 113, 115–17, 119, 121–31, 135; and power, 320; and shame, 91–94, 99; temptation of scientific knowledge, 139n32. See also self-knowledge; wisdom
Kohn, Jennifer, 359
Kohn, Jerome, 261–62
Kristol, Irving, 31

language restrictions on expanding canon, 39–41, 46
The Last Days (1998), 251
laughing, 142n56
law and lawyers: constitutional studies as civic education, 163, 328–29, 338–40, 374, 378; law school and civic education, 341; Strauss on education of, 318–19
lectures, 181
Lehrfreiheit, 291, 301
leisure, 153–54, 159–62, 168, 175–77, 186
Lernfreiheit, 291, 304n5
Lewis, C. S., 151, 152–53
liberal arts: and accreditation, 301–2; alumni support for, 303; in business school curricula, 349–50, 357–60; and business school enrollees, 348, 350–55, 362; enrollments in, 293–94; and general BA programs, 297–98; subjects in, 3, 401; tasks of, 12–14; transfer of resources from, 290, 294–303, 393

liberal education: access to, 154, 160–61, 164–65, 214, 394, 396–97, 399; as beyond classroom setting, 153–57, 189–90, 413–14; definitions of, 32; *vs.* democratic education, 134; as freedom of mind, 4–5, 108, 116–18, 131–32, 136, 181–84; as good in itself, 157–59, 186, 216–17, 219; guarding of, 107–8, 133–34; of Hobbits, 266–80; preconditions for, 394, 395–401; as prepolitical, 5; and required courses, 335; terms for, 3, 103, 104, 181–82; as voluntary, 117, 131–32. See also canon; civic education; crisis of liberal education; democracy and modern education; goals of liberal education; great books

Index

liberalism: and canon, 37; critique by Deneen, 165–66
Liberalism Ancient and Modern (Strauss), 307
liberty, Christian concept of, 399. *See also* freedom
life and status, contemplative *vs.* active, 157–59
Light of the Sun image, 106, 113–15, 117, 129, 130–31
Lincoln, Abraham, 4, 27, 159, 388n28
Lipset, Seymour Martin, 340
listening: and civility, 28; to music, 205; role in academia, 12, 13–14, 26–29, 180, 183, 311–12, 323, 409; role in Socratic education, 129, 138n15, 138n21, 311; to scientists, 201, 202; skills, 181; and suffering, 239, 242, 248–49, 251, 252; and wisdom, 20–21, 23
literacy, universal, 309
Little Reader's Assistant (Webster), 336–37
Livingston, Alexander, 240
Locke, Jill, 88
Locke, John, 203, 318
logic, as core liberal art, 3, 401
Lorde, Audre, 224, 234
The Lord of the Rings (Tolkien), 257–58, 264–80
Lost in Thought (Hitz), 157–58
love: as antidote to suffering, 247–48; and the beautiful, 67, 143n66; political theorists' avoidance of, 240; and sacrifice, 249; of wisdom, 322; of world *(amor mundi),* 261–63
Lowell, James Russell, 327
Lukianoff, Greg, 246
Lyceum Address (Lincoln), 388n28

Machiavelli, Niccolò, 84n35, 174, 191
Madison, James, 327–28, 329, 330, 331, 335, 340
Mansfield, Harvey, 245
Marcus Tullius Cicero. *See* Cicero
Maritain, Jacques, 239, 243
Markovits, Daniel, 161
Marx, Karl, 215, 263
mathematics, 118–22, 401, 402, 403, 404

MBA programs. *See* business schools
McClay, Wilfred, 27
McWilliams, Susan, 53
Meditations (Descartes), 179
Melzer, Arthur, 383
Memorabilia (Xenophon), 406–7
Mencius, 56
Mencken, H. L., 365n32
meritocracy, 161–66, 175, 176–77
metanoia, 320–21
Metaphysics (Aristotle), 206
Michels, Robert, 295
Middlebury College, 335
Mill, John Stuart, 319
miracles, denial of, 405
mission, academic, 298, 299–302, 303
models: and astronomy, 126; and business schools, 361–62
mode of delivery language, 204–5
modernity: and *It's a Wonderful Life* (1946), 166; and liberal education as paradox, 393–415; in Strauss, 318–22, 395
Mohism, 58, 62–63
Momigliano, Arnaldo, 44
Montaigne, 185
Montás, Roosevelt, 154, 243
Montesquieu, 24
MOOCs (Massive Open Online Courses), 342n5
Mooney Suarez, Margarita A., 242
morality: and business schools, 347–48; and cosmopolitanism, 259–63; and elemental education, 398; and modern education, 398–401; moral reason, 203; moral seriousness, 400–401; moral virtue, 15, 18–19, 27, 315, 316; and *phronesis,* 18–19; and preconditions for liberal education, 394; and religious education in Strauss, 398–99; and suffering, 239–40, 242–43, 244, 246–52; of women, 72, 73–77, 80–82. *See also* ethics
Mou Zongsan, 57
Mozi, 62–63
music: access to, 409; Aristotle on, 106; in the liberal arts, 3, 401, 402; and Socratic education, 108, 118, 127–28, 134

Nardin, Terry, 31
natality, 261–62, 263
national university, establishment of, 328, 329–31, 335, 342
natural order and science, 405
natural right, 16–18, 135, 318, 384–85
natural sciences: and Academic Program Reviews, 303, 304n3; requirements, 401
Newman, John Henry [Cardinal Newman], 180
The New Thinkery (podcast), 412–13
Nicomachean Ethics (Aristotle), 12, 15–23, 93
Nietzsche, Friedrich, 156
1915 Declaration of Principles on Academic Freedom and Academic Tenure, 292
nobility and elites: and character, 159, 161–62; and civic education at elite schools, 340–42; and leisure, 161–62; and liberal education, 4, 154, 162–63, 315–16, 318, 373–74, 375–76, 381; and noblesse oblige, 162, 169, 315; *vs.* philosophers, 316–17; Strauss on, 315–18
noblesse oblige, 162, 169, 315
noesis noeseos, 313
nondisclosure agreements, 304
numbers and calculation, 118–22, 128
Nylan, Michael, 45–46

Oakeshott, Michael, 186, 194n32, 216–17
Oases of Excellence, 396
online instruction: advantages of, 204, 205, 214, 411–12, 413, 415; and great books, 395, 408–12; incorporating, 219–20, 395; limiting, 219–20; limits of, 203–11, 411; MOOCs, 342n5; shift to and COVID-19 pandemic, 203–4, 210–11, 213, 218, 219–20, 410, 412
"On the Path of Friendship" (Adkins-Cartee and Bhati), 225–26
opioid epidemic, 240
organon, 127, 140n34
Ortega y Gasset, José, 178
Orwin, Alexander, 41, 46
O'Toole, James, 350–51
The Overspent American (Schor), 176
The Overworked American (Schor), 176

Oxford University Saïd Business School, 358–59

paideia, 104, 315–16, 326. *See also* civic education; nobility and elites
Parmenides (Plato), 417n31
Parsons, William B., 41
particularity: and canon, 52–55, 57; and custom, 60–61; and identity in Christine de Pizan, 82–83
perception of soul *(organon),* 127, 140n34
perfection of perception, 127
Pericles, 18
perplexity, 208–9
Peters, Tom, 347, 348
Petrarca, Francesco, 103, 104, 131
Phaedrus (Plato), 406
philosophy and philosophers: Chinese philosophy, 45–46, 57–58, 61–64; as core of modern liberal arts, 401; modern philosophy as vulgarizing education, 403; role in politics, 317; and Socratic education, 106–34, 311; Strauss on, 311–13, 316–23
phronesis, 12, 14–29
phusis, 140n41
physical education, 411. *See also* gymnastics
physical environment: classroom as artificial space, 180, 410–11; importance of in-person instruction, 206–11; importance of setting, 161, 180, 395, 410–11; and study beyond classroom setting, 153–57, 189–90, 413–14. *See also* online instruction
Pieper, Josef, 177, 217
piety, false, 139n32
Pindar, 253n4
Plato: challenges of writing of, 143n66; Cicero on, 143n57; and civic education, 105–36; and contemplative *vs.* active life, 159; *Crito,* 95; and Diogenes, 95, 96, 97; on education's relationship to philosophy, 311; *Gorgias,* 111, 114, 124, 137n14, 210; interest in other civilizations, 58; on love, 67; and modern students, 154, 155–57; *Parmenides,* 417n31; *Phaedrus,* 406; *Protagoras and Meno,* 417n31; *Symposium,*

Index

67, 143n66; *Theaetetus,* 418n44; and unity in plurality, 183; on writing, 219. *See also The Republic;* Socrates
podcasts, 412–14, 415
Polemarchus, 110, 152
polis-in-*logos* (city-in-speech), 107–10, 112–19, 124, 135, 136
politics: as challenge in academia, 186–87, 414; and friendship, 282n31; and great books, 37, 414–15; identity politics, 90; liberal education as prepolitical, 5; political action in *The Fellowship of the Ring* (Tolkien), 265–80; political animal, 207–8; political representation, 90, 319; and professional schools, 387; role of academia in, 158–59; role of philosophy in, 317; and soul, 90; and suffering, 244–46; and tragic conflict, 248–49; and wisdom, 322–23
Politics (Aristotle), 197, 206
Pollitt, Michael, 359
postmodernism, 45
poverty, 157–58
Powell, Lewis, 365n35
praxis, 15
precision, principle of, 121, 122
preconditions for liberal education, 394, 395–401
priests, role of in Strauss, 317, 398–99
primary and secondary schooling, 335–36, 354, 397–98
Pro Archia (Cicero), 104–5
professional schools: and civic education, 341, 341, 347–62, 374, 380; democracy and liberal education in, 373–87; and general BA programs, 297–98; and great books, 375; ideologies in, 387; rise of preprofessional programs, 295–96, 341–42, 385; undergraduates' focus on, 175
Protagoras, 316
Protagoras and Meno (Plato), 417n31
provincialism: *vs.* cosmopolitanism, 257–58; in *The Fellowship of the Ring* (Tolkien), 266, 269, 271
prudence, 132, 139n34, 201–2, 211
Psalm 69, 92–93, 97
Ptolemy, 126

public opinion, tyranny of, 378, 382, 386
Pythagoreans, 121, 126

Quadrivium, 3, 401
"Quarrel of the Rose," 72
questions: life questions of students, 242; and *phronesis,* 14; reason *vs.* revelation as fundamental question, 44, 400–401, 405; role of in liberal education, 12–14, 32, 65, 173; and social sciences, 65; and Socratic method, 406, 411; and suffering, 242, 251–52; and technology, 215
Quintilian, 104

rankings, business school, 359–60
Rathnam, Lincoln, 40–41, 46
Rathnam, Lindsay Mahon, 41
reading: and access to books, 409; close reading/reading with care, 34, 308–9; and discipline, 179, 190; horizontal/vertical reading, 179; pedagogical strategies for, 405–8, 411–14; reading groups, 407–8, 412–14, 415; and Socrates, 311, 406–7; as spiritual exercise, 185, 189–92; in Strauss, 311; and synthesis, 179–80, 181; by teachers, 184–87; and vanity, 185
reading groups, 407–8, 412–14, 415
received wisdom, 21
Reed College, 51
reflection and justice, 162
relationships, sociality and student-teacher, 223–34
relativism: Bloom on, 383–84, 385; and custom, 60–61; and democracy, 379, 381; and freedom of speech, 25–26; and pluralism, 309
religion: academic religious affiliations, 164, 165–66, 167–68, 399; and church-state colleges, 330; and civic responsibility, 318–19; in Deneen, 164, 167, 399; in *It's a Wonderful Life* (1946), 165, 167–68; in Klein, 398; in the liberal arts, 401; and national identity, 26–27; and preconditions for liberal education, 394, 398–401; role of in education, 164, 167, 317, 318–19, 395, 398–401; and soft despotism, 379–81; in

religion (*continued*)
  Strauss, 317, 318–19, 395, 398–401; in Tocqueville, 379–81
representation, political, 90, 319
The Republic (Plato): and civic education, 105–36, 411; and contemplative *vs.* active life, 159; justice in, 152; leisure and nobility, 161–62; and modern students, 154, 155–57; and need for community in liberal education, 154, 155–57; shame and knowledge, 93–94
The Republic (program), 411
republicanism: and professional schools, 374, 387; role of education in, 24–25; Strauss on, 317–18, 398; and virtue, 24
research productivity in rankings, 359–60
resilience, 29
respect and shame, 95, 96, 98
responsibility: and business schools, 347–48, 353–54, 356, 358, 359, 360–62; as goal of liberal education, 160, 162–63, 164, 263, 314–15, 318, 322; and shame, 92. *See also* compassion
revelation, 44, 400–401, 405, 407
reverence, 24, 243
rhetoric: in business programs, 349–50; as core liberal art, 3, 401; and Socratic education, 110–19, 129–30, 133, 134, 135
Rhetoric (Aristotle), 96
Roman empire and civic education, 103–6
Rousseau, Jean Jacques, 309–10
Rubenstein, Richard, 246, 248
Rubio, Marco, 342n5
Runde, Jochen, 359
Rush, Benjamin, 98, 329

sacrifice, 249
Said, Edward, 68n6
Saïd Business School, 358–59
Saint Augustine, 179
Salkever, Stephen G., 31, 32–33, 45–46
Sayers, Dorothy, 3
Schor, Juliet, 176
science: as anticontemplative, 215–16, 403–4; and COVID-19 pandemic, 197–211; and material prosperity, 320–21; in modern liberal education, 394–95, 401–5; scientific method, 320, 353; shift to science and technology in academia, 164, 165–66, 167–68, 210, 289–301, 404–5; trust in, 199–201; and wisdom, 321–22
secondary schooling, 335–36, 354, 397–98
segregation, 337
self. *See* identity and self
self-control, 21
self-expression *vs.* freedom of speech, 25
self-interest, 342, 378–79, 380, 382
self-knowledge: and Christine de Pizan, 73, 74, 78–80, 82; as goal of liberal education, 53, 182; as goal of philosophy, 45, 125, 317
Seligman, Edwin, 292
Seneca, 137n6, 173, 184, 190–91, 192
Sertillanges, A.-D., 185, 189
1776 Commission, 328, 337–38
sexual misconduct, 223–24, 226–29
Shakespeare, William, 137n4
shame: and identity, 87–99; public shaming, 88–89; shame cultures, 87, 89
shamelessness, 88, 93, 94, 95, 97, 98–99
Shen, Vincent, 41, 46
Ship of State image, 106, 109, 111
1619 Project, 328
slavery: American, 336–38; Cave imagery of enslavement, 115–18, 131; in Classical era, 108, 375
sociality and student-teacher relationships, 223–34
social media, 88, 97–98
social sciences: and questioning, 65; transfer of resources from, 290, 293–98
Socrates: and apologia, 107, 109; and books and reading, 311, 406–7; as citizen, 95; and civic education, 105–36, 155; and comparativism, 48n15; death of, 116; on democracy, 94; on goodwill of teachers, 210; and Hades, 144n68; and images, 109–19, 129–31; and inner/outer self, 95; on leisure and nobility, 161–62; on losing, 29; and rhetoric, 110–19, 129–30, 133, 134, 135; and shame, 93–95, 98; on soul, 93–95, 105, 106–34

Index

Socratic method, 406, 411
soft despotism, 378–81
song in *The Lord of the Rings* (Tolkien), 270
song of dialectic, 127–31
sophia, 15–16
Șora, Mariana, 194n42
Șora, Mihai, 188–90
soul: *vs.* body, 126; Christine de Pizan on, 76, 80, 81; Cicero on, 105; democratic soul in Tocqueville, 373–74, 376, 378, 379, 380; and good, 113–15; and justice, 106; and perception *(organon)*, 127, 140n34; and *phronesis*, 15–16, 21–22; relationship to politics, 90; and shame, 89, 90, 91, 93–94, 98–99; and Socratic education, 93–95, 105, 106–34; and work, 19
Soviet liberal education, 187–92
speech: freedom of speech, 23–29, 289; human need for, 207; and *phronesis*, 23–29
Stanford University, 335
Statement on Board Responsibility for Institutional Governance (Association of Governing Boards of Universities and Colleges), 301
Statement on the Government of Colleges and Universities (AAUP), 292
status and life of mind, 157–59
stereometry, 124–25
St. John's College, 33, 55–56
Stone, Arligton, 365n32
storytelling, 264–65, 275, 280
Strauss, Leo: and great books, 307, 311–14, 401–2, 405; on liberal education, 307–23, 403; as model for deparochialization, 44; on Plato's writings, 143n66; on practical education, 411; on religion in liberal education, 317, 318–19, 395, 398–401; on science in liberal education, 395, 402; on teacher quality, 396
students: and careerism, 160–61, 162–63, 169, 175–77, 393; as consumers, 175; debt and money worries, 159, 174, 176–77; health of, 177; ignorance of canon, 36–37; and leisure, 153–54, 159–61, 162, 168, 175; life questions of, 242; reactions to Plato, 154, 155–57; solicitude by, 210;

transference and sociality, 223–34; unrest and demonstrations, 384, 386
studia humanitatis, 104, 131, 133, 134
suffering: and civic education, 239–52; and democracy, 240, 244–46, 249, 252; and knowledge in *The Fellowship of the Ring* (Tolkien), 273–74
Sun image, 106, 113–15, 117, 129, 130–31, 155
Supreme Court, 293
Sweezy v. New Hampshire, 293
Symposium (Plato), 67, 143n66
synopsis and Socratic education, 133–34
synthesis and reading, 179–80, 181

Taking Back Philosophy (Van Norden), 56
Taming of the Shrew (Shakespeare), 137n4
teachers: and academic mission, 300–302; and Academic Program Reviews, 294–97, 303; on boards, 300–301; challenges of modern, 184–87, 242; dangers to, 116–17; engagement in classroom, 180–81, 208–11; engagement online *vs.* in-person, 208–11; engagement with students outside of classroom, 185–86, 189–90; in *The Fellowship of the Ring* (Tolkien), 278; historicism by, 374; and humility, 314; and perplexity, 208–9; and *phronesis*, 14–26, 27; as precondition for liberal education, 396–97; quality of, 308, 396–97; reading by, 184–87; and reading groups, 407–8, 412–14, 415; and sexual misconduct, 223–24, 226–29; solicitude of, 209–10, 243, 244; and tenure, 186, 290–99, 303–4; transference and sociality, 223–34. *See also* collegial governance
technology: as anticontemplative, 215–16; and civic education in business schools, 360–62; and COVID-19 pandemic, 197–211; and democracy, 197–98, 200–201, 321–22; educational uses of, 203–11, 218, 408–12; as ideology, 214–20; liberal education as antithetical to, 213–20; and material prosperity, 217–18, 320–21; in modern liberal education, 394–95; shift to in academia, 164, 165–66, 167–68, 210,

technology (*continued*)
  220, 289–301, 321–23, 404–5. *See also* online instruction
temperance, 185, 323
tenderness, 243
tenure, 186, 290–99, 303–4
terror, 246, 248
Theaetetus (Plato), 418n44
Thomas, George, 4, 162, 163
Saint Thomas Aquinas, 185
thoughtlessness, 252
Thrasymachus, 93–94, 98, 121, 155
Thucydides, 179
Title IX, 228
Tocqueville, Alexis de: on education and democracy, 373–81, 386, 387, 418n50; on equality *vs.* freedom, 98–99, 206, 247, 377–79, 381; on individualistic rationalism, 206; influence on Bloom, 381–82; on self-interest, 342; on suffering, 245
Tolkien, J. R. R.: and cosmopolitanism in *The Fellowship of the Ring,* 257–58, 264–80; *The Hobbit,* 264, 266
Tom Bombadil character in *The Fellowship of the Ring* (Tolkien), 269–71, 276, 278
Tömmel, Tatjana Noemi, 263
tragic conflict, recognizing, 248–49
transference and student-teacher relationships, 223–34
Trivium, 3, 401
trolley dilemma, 360
trust: academic freedom as public trust, 292; in *The Fellowship of the Ring* (Tolkein), 267–68; in *The Fellowship of the Ring* (Tolkien), 280; and reading groups, 407; in science, 199–201
trustees and boards: and academic freedom, 292, 293; and collegial governance, 300–301
truth: love of as virtue, 28; pursuit of as unifying, 27; and role of philosophy in Strauss, 316; scientific truth, 187–88; in Socratic civic education, 108–9, 112, 113, 115, 129
Tuck School of Business, 348–49, 350, 353, 356, 358
tuition rates, 174–75, 214, 234, 293, 385
tyranny: and custom, 60, 61; of freedom without education, 5; of public opinion, 378, 382, 386; and shame/shamelessness, 93, 94; and soft despotism, 378–81

universal education, 309–10
universal enlightenment, 320
universality: of canon, 52–53, 55–58; of funeral rituals, 58–64; of philosophy, 57–58
university: establishment of national, 328, 329–31. *See also* academia
University of Chicago, 289, 356
University of Illinois, 365n42
University of North Carolina, 342n5
University of Pennsylvania, 334. *See also* Wharton School of Business
University of Virginia, 328, 335, 342n5
urban-rural tensions, 168–69
U.S. Constitution: constitutional studies as civic education, 163, 328–29, 338–40; need for civic engagement, 327, 331, 339; as self-perpetuating, 327; and slavery, 336
Uses of the Erotic (Lorde), 234
utility and utilitarianism: and illiberal study, 414; *vs.* liberal education, 173–92, 217; and liberal education marketing, 388n24; and Mozi, 63; of science and technology, 321–22, 403–5; and utilitarian use of education, 241–42

vanity, 97, 185
Van Norden, Bryan, 56
vengeance, 250
vertical reading, 179
Vidal-Naquet, Pierre, 44
virtue: in Christine de Pizan, 73–77, 80–81; and civic education, 25, 104–5; and community of inquiry, 11–12; defined, 15, 19; and eros, 322; as good in its own sake, 18–20; instrumentalization of, 320–21; and intellectual work, 185; moral virtue, 15, 18–19, 27, 315, 316; and *phronesis,* 14–29; responsibility as replacing, 314–15; Rush on cultivation of, 98; Strauss on, 314–15, 316

Visible realm, 113, 114, 128
The Vision of Christine (Christine de Pizan), 73, 77–80, 82
Vitruvius, 137n6

Walker, Scott, 342n5
Washington, George, 329–30
wealth, 316, 396
Weber, Max, 310
Webster, Noah, 329, 332, 336–37
Weil, Simone, 157
Western culture: engagement with other cultures, 45, 53, 58–61; and immigrants, 37; and "Westernness" of canon, 42–44, 52–53, 54
Wharton, Joseph, 347, 348, 352
Wharton School of Business, 348–50, 351–52, 354, 356, 357, 358
What Is Philosophy? (Ortega y Gasset), 178
Why Liberalism Failed (Deneen), 165
Wiesel, Elie, 242, 251
Willard, Charity, 72
Williams, Melissa S., 31
Williams College, 335

Winthrop, Delba, 245
wisdom: Aristotle on, 12, 14–24, 26, 67; and listening, 20–21, 23; love of, 322; and natural right, 17; and *phronesis*, 15–16, 21–23; and politics, 322–23; received, 21; and science, 321–22; Strauss on, 311, 321–23
women: Christine de Pizan's defense of, 72, 73–77, 80–82; and student-teacher relationships and transference, 223, 226, 228; suppression of the erotic in, 234
work, 19–20
writing: in business schools, 354, 357–58; emphasis on in higher education, 334, 401; Plato on, 219; and Strauss, 310–11
Wuhan University/Duke Kunshan University, 40, 54, 64–67

Xenophon, 58, 143n63, 406–7, 411
Xunzi, 63–64

Young-Bruehl, Elisabeth, 261

Zinn, Howard, 385